CALLIMACHUS
HYMNS AND EPIGRAMS

LYCOPHRON
WITH AN ENGLISH TRANSLATION BY
A. W. MAIR, D.Litt.
PROFESSOR OF GREEK, EDINBURGH UNIVERSITY

ARATUS
WITH AN ENGLISH TRANSLATION BY
G. R. MAIR, M.A.
HEADMASTER OF SPIER'S SCHOOL, BEITH

CAMBRIDGE, MASSACHUSETTS
HARVARD UNIVERSITY PRESS
LONDON
WILLIAM HEINEMANN LTD
MCMLV

First printed 1921
Revised and reprinted 1955

Printed in Great Britain

CONTENTS

CONTENTS

PREFACE TO FIRST EDITION

THIS volume was intended to appear in 1914. The delay occasioned by the war, while it has doubtless enabled improvements to be made in detail, has at the same time made it hard to observe a meticulous consistency.

Such as it is, the hope may be permitted that the book will be found helpful as an introduction to the Alexandrine literature. The scholar will readily understand that the limitations of this series compelled us to partial statement where full discussion was desirable ; he will understand, too, that to secure even such statement as we could attempt, we had to study the severest compression. In particular, it may be explained that, to satisfy the limits required for publication, a very considerable amount of work had to be ruthlessly jettisoned. At the same time the translators most cordially and gratefully acknowledge that the Editors of the series have done their utmost, by an unusual concession in the matter of notes, to render the volume useful.

To enumerate the names of the scholars who have at one time or another given us advice on special

PREFACE TO FIRST EDITION

points might seem to exaggerate the importance of the book. But, while the translators are alone responsible for their final decisions, they gratefully remember among those who have aided them: the Astronomer Royal, Sir Frank Dyson; Mr. W. T. Vesey; Mr. E. W. Maunder; the Astronomer Royal for Scotland, Professor Sampson; Professor Cossar Ewart; Professor E. T. Whittaker; Mr. F. J. M. Stratton, D.S.O.; Dr. T. G. Smyly; Professor A. S. Hunt; Professor Burnet; Professor Arthur Platt; Professor Phillimore; and among the younger men *qui olim memorabuntur*, Mr. E. P. Dickie, M.C., and Messrs. A. and N. Porteous for help in revising the proofs.

To the firm of Messrs. R. & R. Clark we owe our cordial thanks. Mr. William Maxwell has shown a warm personal interest in the progress of the work which is in accordance with the best traditions of Scottish printing. To Messrs. Clark's accomplished Reader we desire to offer no merely formal acknowledgement of the vigilance and scholarship by which the book has been materially improved.

A. W. M.

G. R. M.

PREFACE TO SECOND EDITION

SINCE the publication of the volume containing the
extant works and fragments of Callimachus edited
and translated by the late Professor A. W. Mair in
1921, much new material has been discovered, which
is already available in the two volumes of Pfeiffer's
edition of Callimachus.

In view of the large size of the volume in the Loeb
Classical Library—a volume which contains Lycophron and Aratus also—, and the necessity of making
alterations in the *Hymns* and *Epigrams* in the light of
Pfeiffer's new edition, it has been decided, in place
of a reprint of our single volume, to prepare a new
edition in two volumes :

The first contains Callimachus, *Hymns* and *Epigrams* ;
Aratus ; Lycophron—being a rearranged reprint
of the original volume of Callimachus, Aratus
and Lycophron (translated by A. W. and G. R.
Mair), but omitting the fragments of Callimachus.

The second contains a new and independent version
of the fragments of Callimachus discovered up to
date, prepared and translated by Professor C. A.
Trypanis.

E. H. WARMINGTON
EDITOR

10th August 1954

NOTE ON NEW READINGS IN
HYMNS AND *EPIGRAMS*

THE editors of the Loeb Classical Library have decided to reprint the *Hymns* and *Epigrams* of Callimachus as they appear in the 1921 edition by the late A. W. Mair. Since that edition, however, some important material, mainly from papyri, has come to light, and for this reason I have been asked to prepare a short appendix to include the most significant new readings, as well as a few convincing conjectures of recent date, which help in establishing the text. The reader who wishes a full account of the papyri, manuscripts etc., as well as a full bibliography, should consult R. Pfeiffer, *Callimachus, vol. II, Hymni et Epigrammata, Oxonii, 1953.*

I should like to make it clearly understood that I am not re-examining here the material which Mair had at his disposal in the preparation of his edition, nor do I necessarily agree with the views he puts forward.

The left-hand column gives the readings as they appear in Mair's edition ; the right-hand column the new readings and their sources.

HYMN I

LINE 19	Ἀρκαδίη	:	Ἀζηνίς Schol. Dionys. Per. 415. Arcadia was called Ἀζηνίς, " because it was a dry country."

x

NOTE ON NEW READINGS

HYMN II

LINE			
6	ἀνακλίνεσθε	:	ἀνακλίνασθε Schol. (K) Theocr. xii. 12 (*cf.* line 8).
8	ἐντύνεσθε	:	ἐ]ντύνασθε *P. Oxy.* 2258.
35	καὶ δὲ πολυκτέανος	:	καὶ που[λυκτέ]ανος *P. Oxy.* 2258.

HYMN III

22	καλέουσι	:	κ[α]λέωσι *P. Mediolan.*
61	μοχθήσειαν	:	μυχθίσσειαν *P. Ant.*

HYMN IV

39	σοι	:	τοι *P. Oxy.* 2225.
66	εὐρειάων	:	αἱ]πειάων *P. Bodl.* Translate : " over the lofty islands."
158	πολλόν	:	δεινόν *P. Oxy.* 2225. Translate : " prevented them in menacing manner."

After line 176 there are two badly mutilated lines in *P. Oxy.* 2225. Of the second of these there is no trace in the manuscripts (or Mair's edition).

178	ἠπείροι[ο φάραγγες]	:	Ἡφαί[στο]ιο φάρ[αγγ]ες *P. Oxy.* 2225. Translate : " and Crisaean plains and glens of Hephaestus." It is interesting that *P. Oxy.* 2225 confirms φάραγγες, which Mair called " a worthless attempt, found only in the late and inferior manuscripts, to supply the lacuna."
188	φαίνω	:	Φοίβου conjectured by E. Lobel from]ου in *P. Oxy.* 2225. Translate : " These are the prophecies of Phoebus."

LINE			
192	οὐχ ἑνὶ χώρῳ	:	οὐκ ἐνὶ χ]ώρῃ P. Oxy. 2225, which confirms O. Schneider's suggestion χώρῃ.
200-202	. . .	:	ὡς δ' ἴδες, [ὡς] ἔστης [ ] ιδου[.]α
	φλέξας ἐπεὶ περικαίεο †πυρί	:	θαρσαλέη τάδ' ἔλεξας [ ] . . . . ρ[ ]
	τλῆμον'	:	δαίμον' P. Oxy. 2225 as supplemented by R. Pfeiffer. Cf. Hec. fr. 260. 20 (Pfeiffer).
212	ἀλυσθμαίνουσα	:	ἀλ[υσθ]ενέο[υσα P. Oxy. 2225.
226	ἀμύνειν . . . δούλοις	:	ἀμύνεο P. Maas. δούλους P. Maas.
227	ὑμετέροις . . . ἐφετμῇ	:	ὑμετέρους P. Maas. ἐφετμήν W. Croenert. Translate lines 226-227 : " But, dear Lady—for you can—revenge yourself on your slaves, who trample upon your orders."
287	Ἱερὸν ἄστυ	:	Ἴριον ἄστυ R. Pfeiffer. Ἰρά or Ἶρος was the name of a city of Malis (cf. Steph. Byz. ad v., and Lycoph. 905 with schol.).

HYMN VI

84	ἐν ἀλλοτρίοις	:	ἐν ἀλλοτ[ρί]ᾳ P. Oxy. 2226.

Lines 91-93 are suspect. Line 91 is metrically unsound (cf. P. Maas, Metrik, § 94). Lines 92-93, as given by R. Pfeiffer from P. Oxy. 2226, read : καὶ τούτων ἔτι μέζον ἐτάκετο, μέστ' ἐπὶ νεύροις | δειλαίῳ ῥινός τε καὶ ὀστέα μῶνον ἐλείφθη.

νεύροις is a conjecture of E. Lobel from νευρ . ς of the papyrus ; L. K. Valckenaer had already suggested ῥινός τε, and J. A. Ernesti μῶνον. Translate : " Even more than these he wasted, till the poor man had only skin and bones left clinging to his sinews."

NOTE ON NEW READINGS

LINE			
106	ἤδη	:	οὐδ[ὲν P. Oxy. 2226.
110	τὰν αἴλουρον	:	τ[ὰ]ν μάλουριν P. Oxy. 2226. Translate : " the weasel."
111	μέσφ' ὄκα . . . ἔνι	:	μέστα μὲν P. Oxy. 2226. . . . ἔτι E. Lobel.
112	μῶνοι	:	μῶνον P. Oxy. 2226.
127	πᾶσαίμεσθα	:	πασεύμεσθα A. Meineke, confirmed by Schol. P. Oxy. 2258 to this passage.
132	αὐτᾶν ἱκανὸν	:	αὐτα]ῖς ἰθαρὸν P. Oxy. 2258.

EPIGRAM XXIII

Obelize lines 5-6. They come from fr. 1. 37 f. (Pfeiffer).

EPIGRAM XXIX

4	σύντονος ἀγρυπνίη	:	σύμβολον ἀγρυπνίης Ruhnken.

EPIGRAM LX

2	Λευκαρέτα τὰν μὰν	:	Λεύκαρε, τὰν O. Schneider. λίαν P. Maas.
5	ἀπώλεσε τοῦτο ποή-σας—	:	ἀπώλεσε· τοῦτο ποήσας punctuation suggested by G. M. Young.

Translate this epigram : " Leucare, Orestes of old was happy because, though mad in all else, he was not seized by the greatest madness ; he did not try the Phocian by the one test which proves a friend. Had he produced but one drama, for certain he would soon have lost his comrade. I was one of those who did, and have no more my many Pyladae."

Pfeiffer considers *Epigram* LXIV as spurious on grounds of subject-matter, style and metre. The *Planudean Anthology* (vii. 140) attributes it to Rufinus, who may have been its author.

NOTE ON NEW READINGS

LIST OF ABBREVIATIONS

P. Oxy. 2225 = Papyrus of the 2nd century A.D. edited by E.
Lobel, *The Oxyrhynchus Papyri*, xix (1948),
pp. 68 f.

P. Oxy. 2226 = Papyrus of the 2nd century A.D. edited by E.
Lobel, *The Oxyrhynchus Papyri*, xix (1948),
pp. 77 f.

P. Oxy. 2258 = Papyrus of the 6th-7th centuries A.D. edited
by E. Lobel, *The Oxyrhynchus Papyri*, xx
(1952), pp. 69 f.

P. Mediolan. = Papyrus probably of the 1st century B.C.
edited by A. Mariotti, *Acme*, i (1948), pp.
121 f.

P. Bodl. = Papyrus of the 5th-6th centuries A.D. in the
Bodleian Library, Oxford (*P. Bodl. MS. Gr.
class.* f. 109 (P)) not yet published. (*Cf.*
Pfeiffer, *Callimachus*, vol. II, pp. lii f.)

P. Ant. = Papyrus of the 4th-5th centuries A.D., edited
by C. H. Roberts, *The Antinoe Papyri*, i
(1950), pp. 43 ff.

C. A. Trypanis

Exeter College,
Oxford, 1953

xiv

INTRODUCTION

1. THE LIFE OF CALLIMACHUS

OUR authorities for the life of Callimachus are a notice in Suidas *s.v.* Καλλίμαχος and various references in other authors.

Suidas says: " Callimachus, son of Battus and Mesatma, of Cyrene, grammarian, pupil of Hermocrates of Iasos, the grammarian [an authority upon accents, *Gr. Lat.* iv. 530 f. Keil], married the daughter of Euphrates of Syracuse. His sister's son was Callimachus the younger, who wrote an epic, On Islands. So diligent was he that he wrote poems in every metre and also wrote a great number of works in prose. The books written by him amount in all to more than eight hundred. He lived in the times of Ptolemy Philadelphus [reigned 285–247 B.C.]. Before his introduction to that king he taught grammar in Eleusis, a hamlet of Alexandria. He survived to the time of Ptolemy, surnamed Euergetes, and Olympiad 127 [an error, see below], in the second year of which Ptolemy Euergetes began to reign."

Suidas gives also a notice of his nephew: " Callimachus of Cyrene, epic poet, nephew of the preceding son of Stasenor and Megatima, sister of Callimachus." From this Hemsterhys conjectured that in the first notice also Megatima should be read for Mesatma.

1

INTRODUCTION TO CALLIMACHUS

The most probable date on the whole for the birth of Callimachus is *circ.* 310 B.C. We learn from *Vit. Arat.* i. that Callimachus, both in his epigrams and also ἐν τοῖς πρὸς Πραξιφάνην, referred to Aratus as older than himself. But as they were fellow-students at Athens the difference of age is not likely to have been considerable : we may put the birth of Aratus in 315, that of Callimachus in 310.

Callimachus claimed to be descended from Battus, the founder of Cyrene (Pind. *P.* iv., v., Hdt. iv. 155 ff.): Strabo xvii. 837 λέγεται δὲ ἡ Κυρήνη κτίσμα Βάττου· πρόγονον δὲ τοῦτον ἑαυτοῦ φάσκει Καλλίμαχος. In any case he belonged to a family of some eminence, and we learn from himself that his grandfather had distinguished himself in military affairs (Epigr. xxiii.).

While still a young man he was, along with Aratus, a pupil of Praxiphanes the Peripatetic philosopher (author of treatises On Poetry, On History, etc.), in Athens (*Vit. Arat.* i., iv., and the Latin *Vit. Arat.*) probably *circ.* 287–281.

Subsequently, as Suidas tells us, he was a teacher in Eleusis, a suburb of Alexandria; afterwards he was introduced to the court of Ptolemy Philadelphus, in whose service he continued—apart from occasional excursions—till his death *circ.* 235 B.C.

The statement in Suidas that Callimachus παρέτεινε μέχρι τοῦ Εὐεργέτου κληθέντος Πτολεμαίου [came to the throne in 247], ὀλυμπιάδος δὲ ρκζʹ, ἧς κατὰ τὸ δεύτερον ἔτος [271 B.C.] ὁ Εὐεργέτης Πτολεμαῖος ἤρξατο τῆς βασιλείας is manifestly wrong. Merkel proposed to read ρλγʹ, *i.e.* 247. Kaibel makes a more elaborate conjecture, reading <ἤκμασε δὲ ἐπὶ τῆς ὀλυμπιάδος ρκζʹ> καὶ παρέτεινε . . . ὀλυμπιάδος δὲ ρλγʹ, ἧς κτλ., *i.e.* his "floruit" was in Ol. 127 and he survived to the time of Ptolemy Euergetes, Ol. 133. No passage in his works implying a later date than Ol. 133, that was assumed as the date of his death.

But we read in Suidas *s.v.* Ἀριστοφάνης Βυζάντιος . . . μαθητὴς Καλλιμάχου καὶ Ζηνοδότου· ἀλλὰ τοῦ μὲν νέος, τοῦ δὲ παῖς ἤκουσε. The natural interpretation here (though some would take the last sentence as a chiasmus) is to understand the first τοῦ as Callimachus, the second as Zenodotus; and hence it is sought to be inferred that Callimachus survived Zenodotus, whose death is put *circ.* 245-235.

Among the more distinguished pupils of Callimachus were Eratosthenes of Cyrene, Aristophanes of Byzantium, and Apollonius, a native of Alexandria or of Naucratis, but from his sojourn in Rhodes called "the Rhodian." With the last named Callimachus had a quarrel which, purely literary in its origin, developed into a bitter personal feud, and led to Apollonius withdrawing from Alexandria to Rhodes. In the view of Callimachus the day of the Homeric type of epic was past. That spacious type of poetry must now give place to a poetry more expressive of the genius of the age, the short and highly polished poem, in which the recondite learning of the time should find expression. Apollonius, on the other hand, in his *Argonautica* sought to continue the Homeric tradition. We are not concerned here to decide the dispute, but we can appreciate the two points of view. To Callimachus it may well have seemed that the long epic, written in the traditional epic language with its set phrases and formulae, could hardly be other than a weak and artificial echo of Homer: it could be no expression

3

of the living culture of Alexandria : it could have
no originality, nothing individual (Callim. *Ep.* xxx.).
To Apollonius, on the other hand, it might seem
that for Callimachus romance was dead ; and to him,
who deserves to be called the first of the romantics,
Callimachus might appear even more truly

> The idle singer of an empty day,

lifeless and "wooden" and uninspired : *cf. A.P.*
xi. 275.

The true inwardness of the quarrel may not have
been apparent to their contemporaries or even to
themselves, and it may have seemed to be merely a
question of the Small Book *v.* the Big Book.   Athen.
ii. 72 A tells us ὅτι Καλλίμαχος ὁ γραμματικὸς τὸ μέγα
βιβλίον ἴσον ἔλεγεν εἶναι τῷ μεγάλῳ κακῷ, "that a
big book is a big evil."   Even if we accept the
modern explanation that this refers merely to a
papyrus-roll (βιβλίον) of inconvenient size we have
the evidence of Callimachus himself in *Hymn. Apoll.*
105 ff. : "Spake Envy privily in the ear of Apollo :
'I admire not the poet who singeth not songs in
number as the sea.'   Apollo spurned Envy with his
foot, and spake thus : 'Great is the stream of the
Assyrian river, but much filth of earth and much
refuse it carries on its waters.   And not of every
water do the Melissae carry to Deo, but of the
trickling stream that springs from a holy fountain,
pure and undefiled, the very crown of waters.' "   It
might be fanciful to equate the λύματα (schol. *Hymn*
i. 17 λύματα· καθάρματα) and καθαρή of this passage
with the κάθαρμα of Apollonius' epigram ; but in any
case the schol. on this passage says expressly : ἐγκαλεῖ
διὰ τούτων τοὺς σκώπτοντας αὐτὸν μὴ δύνασθαι ποιῆσαι

INTRODUCTION TO CALLIMACHUS

μέγα ποίημα, ὅθεν ἠναγκάσθη ποιῆσαι τὴν Ἑκάλην. Some have supposed that Apollon. *Argon.* iii. 932 ff. ἀκλειὴς ὅδε μάντις ὃς οὐδ᾽ ὅσα παῖδες ἴσασιν οἶδε νόῳ φράσσασθαι κτλ. was a second edition insertion intended to refer to those words of Callimachus, the crow being Callimachus, Mopsus being Apollonius himself.

Doubtless Callimachus attributed the attitude of Apollonius to envy; he says of himself: ὁ δ᾽ ἤεισεν κρέσσονα βασκανίης, Epigr. xxiii. 4, cf. *Hymn. Apoll.* 105; and he wrote a poem called *Ibis,* "of studied obscurity and abuse on one Ibis, an enemy of Callimachus: this was Apollonius, who wrote the *Argonautica*" (Suidas *s.v.* Καλλίμαχος), which served as the model for Ovid's poem of the same name: Ovid, *Ibis,* 53 ff. "Postmodo, si perges, in te mihi liber iambus Tincta Lycambeo sanguine tela dabit. Nunc, quo Battiades inimicum devovet Ibin, Hoc ego devoveo teque tuosque modo. Utque ille, historiis involvam carmina caecis: Non soleam quamvis hoc genus ipse sequi. Illius ambages imitatus in Ibide dicar Oblitus moris iudiciique mei."

To understand the allusion in applying the name Ibis to Apollonius we have only to read the description of the bird in Strabo xvii. 823, where he is speaking of the botany and zoology of Egypt: "Tamest of all is the Ibis, which is like a stork in shape and size, and is of two colours, one storklike [the white or Sacred Ibis], the other all black [the Glossy Ibis]. Every crossing (τρίοδος) in Alexandria is full of them, in some respects usefully, in others not usefully. Usefully, because they pick up all sorts of vermin and the offal (ἀποκαθάρματα) in the butchers' shops and fish-shops (ὀψοπώλια). They

5

are detrimental, because they are omnivorous and unclean (παμφάγον καὶ ἀκάθαρτον) and are with difficulty prevented from polluting in every way what is clean and what is not theirs (τῶν ἀλλοτρίων)."

Callimachus, as we have seen, abhorred the common path (*E.* xxx. 1 f.), and loved the pure spring (*H. Apoll.* 110 f.). So his professed disciple Propertius iii. 1. 1 ff. says : " Callimachi Manes . . . Primus ego ingredior puro de fonte sacerdos Itala per graios orgia ferre choros. . . . Non datur ad Musas currere lata via . . . opus hoc de monte Sororum Detulit intacta pagina nostra via." To Callimachus Apollonius was a treader in the beaten track, a feeder upon the unclean. Himself he would not have poetry to be

" Like a broad highway or a populous street
      .   .   .   .   .
Or like some roadside pool, which no nice art
      Has guarded that the cattle may not beat
      And foul it with a multitude of feet."

2. CALLIMACHUS AND THE ALEXANDRINE LIBRARY

The statement, so unreservedly made in many works on Greek literature, that Callimachus succeeded Zenodotus as librarian of the Alexandrian library, would scarcely concern us here were it not that one observes in some recent writing remarks on the position of Callimachus among his contemporaries which proceed on the assumption that the librarianship of Callimachus is an ascertained fact.

INTRODUCTION TO CALLIMACHUS

The genesis of the statement is briefly this. In 1819 F. Osann discovered in a Plautine MS. in Rome a scholium which professed to be based on a note by one Caecius on the *Plutus* of Aristophanes. Osann communicated the beginning of this scholium to Meineke, who published it in his *Quaest. Scen. Spec.* iii. p. 3.

A complete copy of the scholium was published by F. Ritschl in his *Die alexandrinischen Bibliotheken,* Breslau, 1838, pp. 3-4. The MS. in which it occurs is in the library of the Collegio Romano and is a fifteenth-century parchment codex of Plautus in 4to, designated 4.C.39, containing fifteen plays. The scholium occurs on the page where the *Poenulus* ends and the *Mostellaria* begins. It runs thus:

"Ex Caecio in commento comoediarum Aristophanis poetae in pluto quam possumus opulentiam nuncupare. Alexander aetolus et Lycophron chalcidensis et Zenodotus ephestius impulsu Regis ptolemaei philadelphi cognomento, qui mirum in modum favebat ingeniis et famae doctorum hominum, graecae artis poeticos libros in unum collegerunt et in ordinem redegerunt; Alexander tragoedias, Lycophron comoedias, Zenodotus vero Homeri poemata et reliquorum illustrium poetarum. Nam Rex ille philosophis affertissimus et caeteris omnibus autoribus claris disquisitis impensa regiae munificentiae ubique terrarum quantum valuit voluminibus opera demetrii phalerii phzxa senum duas bibliothecas fecit, alteram extra Regiam, alteram autem in Regia. In exteriore autem fuerunt milia voluminum quadraginta duo et octingenta. In Regia autem bibliotheca voluminum quidem commixtorum volumina quadringenta milia, simplicium autem et digestorum milia nonaginta,

7

sicuti refert Callimacus aulicus Regius bibliothecarius
qui etiam singulis voluminibus titulos inscripsit.
Fuit praeterea qui idem asseveret eratosthenes non
ita multo post eiusdem custos bibliothecae. hec
autem fuerunt omnium gentium ac linguarum quae
habere potuit docta volumina quae summa diligentia
Rex ille in suam linguam fecit ab optimis interpretibus converti. Ceterum pisistratus sparsam prius
homeri poesim ante ptolemaeum philadelphum annis
ducentis et eo etiam amplius sollerti cura in ea quae
nunc extant redegit volumina usus ad hoc opus
divinum industria quattuor celeberrimorum et erudi-
tissimorum hominum videlicet Concyli Onomacriti
athenieñ, Zopyri heracleotae et Orphei crotoniatae.
Nam carptim prius Homerus et non nisi difficillime
legebatur. Quum etiam post pisistrati curam et
ptolemaei diligentiam aristarchus adhuc exactius in
homeri elimandam collectionem vigilavit. Helio-
dorus multa aliter nugatur quae longo convitio
cecius reprehendit. Nam ol' LXXII duobus doctis
viris a pisistrato huic negotio praepositis dicit
homerum ita fuisse compositum. Qui quidem zeno-
doti et aristarchi industria omnibus praelatam com-
probarint, quod constat fuisse falsissimum. Quippe
cum inter pisistratum et Zenodotum fuerint anni
supra ducentos. Aristarchus autem quattuor annis
minor fuerit ipso et Zenodoto atque ptolemaeo."

The unknown Caecius or Cecius W. Dindorf
(*Rhein. Mus.*, 1830, iv. p. 232) proposed to identify
with John Tzetzes.

In 1839 J. A. Cramer published at Oxford his
*Anecdota graeca e codd. manuscriptis Bibliothecae Regiae
Parisiensis.* The first of the *Anecdota* (vol. i. p.
3 ff.) is a short anonymous treatise Περὶ κωμῳδίας

8

from cod. 2677, " written apparently in the sixteenth
century" according to the Paris catalogue: but
Cramer notes that "Catalogi autem confector
indicare neglexit, interesse quaedam vacua folia inter
caetera quae Codice insunt et opusculum nostrum,
quod diversa prorsus manu scriptum videtur et
aliquantum recentiori: ut aliunde crediderim in
unum volumen cum prioribus coaluisse." Cramer
does not quite accept the identification of Cecius =
Tzetzes.

The relative portion of this treatise is as follows:
ἰστέον ὅτι Ἀλέξανδρος ὁ Αἰτωλὸς καὶ Λυκόφρων ὁ
Χαλκιδεὺς ὑπὸ Πτολεμαίου τοῦ Φιλαδέλφου προτρα-
πέντες τὰς σκηνικὰς διώρθωσαν βίβλους. Λυκόφρων
μὲν τὰς τῆς κωμῳδίας, Ἀλέξανδρος δὲ τὰς τῆς τραγῳδίας,
ἀλλὰ δὴ καὶ τὰς σατυρικάς. ὁ γὰρ Πτολεμαῖος,
φιλολογώτατος ὤν, διὰ Δημητρίου τοῦ Φαληρέως καὶ
ἑτέρων ἐλλογίμων ἀνδρῶν, δαπάναις βασιλικαῖς ἀπαντα-
χόθεν τὰς βίβλους εἰς Ἀλεξάνδρειαν συνήθροισεν, καὶ
δυσὶ βιβλιοθήκαις ταύτας ἐπέθετο. ὧν τῆς ἐκτὸς μὲν
ἀριθμὸς τετρακισμύριαι δισχίλιαι ὀκτακόσιαι, τῆς δὲ
τῶν ἀνακτόρων ἐντὸς συμμιγῶν μὲν βίβλων ἀριθμὸς
τεσσαράκοντα μυριάδες, ἀμιγῶν δὲ καὶ ἁπλῶν μυριάδες
ἐννέα· ὧν τοὺς πίνακας ὕστερον Καλλίμαχος ἐπεγρά-
ψατο. Ἐρατοσθένει δὲ ἡλικιώτῃ Καλλιμάχου παρὰ τοῦ
βασιλέως τὸ τοιοῦτον ἐνεπιστεύθη βιβλιοφυλάκιον.
(An edition of this anonymous treatise corrected from
various MSS. was published by Studemund, *Philologus*,
xlvi. (1886).)

Next in the *Rhein. Mus.* vi. (1847) H. Keil
published from a MS. at Milan, " cod. Ambrosianus
C 222 sup. 4. mai. bombycinus, saec. xiii., qui
olim Georgii Merulae fuit" the Prolegomena to
Aristophanes of John Tzetzes. The superscription

βίβλος Ἀριστοφάνους Τζέτζην φορέουσ᾽ ὑποφήτην is
followed by two versions of the Prolegomena, the
similarity of which to the scholium Plautinum completely confirms Dindorf's conjecture. The relative
passages in the two versions are as follows :

I. "Alexander the Aetolian and Lycophron the
Chalcidian encouraged by royal bounties
revised (διωρθώσαντο) for Ptolemy Philadelphus the scenic books—I mean the books
of Comedy, Tragedy, and Satyric dramas—
there being with them and helping in the
correction such a librarian of so great a
library — Eratosthenes, ὧν βίβλων τοὺς
πίνακας Καλλίμαχος ἀπεγράψατο. Alexander
corrected the Tragics, Lycophron the
Comics. νεανίαι ἦσαν Καλλίμαχος καὶ Ἐρατο-
σθένης. These revised the scenic books, as
the Aristarchuses and Zenodotuses looked
over those of the poets."

II. The second version, after a similar reference to
the founding of the library, proceeds to
mention the number of books in the two
libraries, "whereof the number in the outside library was 42,800 ; in that within the
Court and Palace the number of 'mixed'
books was 400,000, of 'simple and unmixed'
books 90,000, ὡς ὁ Καλλίμαχος νεανίσκος ὢν
τῆς αὐλῆς ὑστέρως μετὰ τὴν ἀνόρθωσιν τοὺς
πίνακας αὐτῶν ἀπεγράψατο. Eratosthenes,
his contemporary, was entrusted by the king
with such a great library. ἀλλὰ τὰ Καλλιμάχου καὶ τοῦ Ἐρατοσθένους μετὰ βραχύν τινα
χρόνον ἐγένετο τῆς συναγωγῆς τῶν βίβλων, ὡς

ἔφην, καὶ διορθώσεως, καὶ ἐπ᾽ αὐτοῦ τοῦ
Πτολεμαίου τοῦ Φιλαδέλφου."

Thus the Plautine scholium alone names Callimachus as librarian, and even the phrase "aulicus
Regius bibliothecarius" does not necessarily imply
that he was Chief Librarian. The words, in fact
seem rather to be merely a loose translation of the
statement in the second version of Tzetzes.

The Prolegomena of Tzetzes can be consulted
conveniently in the Appendix to Nauck's edition of
the *Lexicon Vindobonense*, St. Petersburg, 1867, or in
Kaibel, *Comicorum Gr. Frag.* (Berlin 1899), p. 18 ff.

3. Works

It will be convenient to divide these into two
groups.

A. Works mentioned by Suidas *s.v.* Καλλίμαχος.

His list does not profess to be complete: "among
his books are also these." The list runs as follows:
1. The Coming of Io. 2. Semele. 3. Settlements
of Argos. 4. Arcadia. 5. Glaucus. 6. Hopes
('Ελπίδες). Nothing is known of any of these.
They may not have been independent works at all,
but merely subsections of the *Aitia* or other works
mentioned below.

Suidas then mentions 7. Satyric dramas. 8.
Tragedies. 9. Comedies. 10. Lyrics (μέλη). 11. Ibis
(see above).

Then follows a list of works presumably in prose:
12. Museum. This, of which nothing is known,

11

may have been a sub-title of the Pinaces. 13. Tables of all those who were eminent in any kind of literature and of their writings (Πίνακες τῶν ἐν πάσῃ παιδείᾳ διαλαμψάντων καὶ ὧν συνέγραψαν) in 120 books. 14. Table and register of dramatic poets chronologically, from the earliest times (Πίναξ καὶ ἀναγραφὴ τῶν κατὰ χρόνους καὶ ἀπ᾽ ἀρχῆς γενομένων διδασκάλων).

No. 14 is doubtless only a sub-title of No. 13. These tables were a catalogue of the books in the larger Alexandrian Library, *i.e.* part of the Brycheion near the Museum. Besides giving a list of an author's works, this catalogue contained a biographical sketch of each author. It would seem that the authors were distributed in at least eight classes : Epic and other non-dramatic poets ; Dramatic poets ; Legislation (this was Pinax No. 3 ; Athen. 585 B, νόμον συσσιτικόν. . . ἀνέγραψε δ᾽ αὐτὸν Καλλίμαχος ἐν τῷ τρίτῳ πίνακι τῶν Νόμων); Philosophy (Diog. Laert. viii. 86 ; Athen. 252 c); History (Athen. ii. 70 B); Oratory (Athen. 669 E Καλλίμαχος ἐν τῇ τῶν Ῥητορικῶν ἀναγραφῇ); Miscellaneous (τῶν παντοδαπῶν, Athen. 244 A). The Pinaces gave also the opening words of each book and the number of lines it contained (Athen. 244 A, 585 B ; Harpocrat. *s.v.* Ἴων).

15. Table of the Glosses and Compositions of Democritus (Πίναξ τῶν Δημοκρίτου γλωσσῶν καὶ συνταγμάτων). 16. Local Month-names (Μηνῶν προσηγορίαι κατὰ ἔθνος καὶ πόλεις). 17. Foundations of Islands and Cities and changes of name (Κτίσεις νήσων καὶ πόλεων καὶ μετονομασίαι). Known only from Suidas. 18. On the Rivers in Europe. A sub-title of No. 23. 19. On strange and marvellous things in Peloponnesus and Italy. A sub-title of

No. 24. 20. Περὶ μετονομασίας ἰχθύων. 21. Περὶ
ἀνέμων. Probably sub-titles of the Ἐθ. Ὀνομ. (see
below). 22. On Birds (Περὶ ὀρνέων). This, cited by
Athen. 388 D as Περὶ ὀρνίθων, may have been a sub-
title of the Ἐθ. Ὀνομ. (see below). 23. On the
Rivers of the World (Περὶ τῶν ἐν τῇ οἰκουμένῃ ποταμῶν). 24. Collection of marvels in all the earth
according to localities (Θαυμάτων τῶν εἰς ἅπασαν τὴν
γῆν κατὰ τόπους συναγωγή). This was used by Antigonus of Carystus.

B. Works not mentioned in Suidas' list but known
of from other sources.

25. Aetia. 26. Hecale. 27. On Games (Περὶ
ἀγώνων). 28. Galatea. 29. Iambi. 30. Γραφεῖον.
31. Epigrams. 32. The Lock of Berenice (Βερενίκης
πλόκαμος) = Catullus lxvi. 33. Six Hymns. 34.
Elegy on Sosibios. 35. Ἀρσινόης γάμος, inferred
from fr. 196. 36. Branchos. 37. Περὶ λογάδων.
38. Customs of Barbarians. 39. On the Nymphs.
40. Ἐθνικαὶ Ὀνομασίαι, or local nomenclature,
Athen. 329 A (= fr. 38). To this belonged probably
not only the Περὶ μετονομασίας (κατονομασίας ?) ἰχθύων
(No. 20), but also the Περὶ ἀνέμων (No. 21), the Περὶ
ὀρνέων, No. 22 above, and the Μηνῶν προσηγορίαι,
No. 16 above. 41. On the Rivers of Asia (schol.
Ap. Rh. i. 1165). A sub-title of No. 23 above. 42.
Πρὸς Πραξιφάνη, Vit. Arati i. 43. Ὑπομνήματα
ἱστορικά.

4. The mss. of the *Hymns*

All the extant MSS. descend from a Byzantine
sylloge which contained the *Hymns* of Homer,

Callimachus, Orpheus, and Proclus. A MS. containing this collection was brought from Constantinople to Venice in 1423 by Ioannes Aurispa (Sandys, *Hist. Class. Schol.* ii. 36). Neither this MS. nor any immediate copy of it survives, but from it are derived all existing MSS. of the *Hymns* of Callimachus.

These MSS. are now divided into three families:

E, best represented by

    m (Schneider S) = Matritensis Bibl. Nat. N 24, written by Constantine Lascaris at Milan in 1464 (1454 Schn.), containing Musaeus' *Hero and Leander*, Orpheus' *Argonautica* and *Hymns*, the *Hymns* of Homer and Callimachus, and a collection of ancient epigrams.

    q (Schneider Q) = Mutinensis Bibl. Estensis iii. E 11, written by Georgius Valla of Piacenza, who died in 1499 (Sandys ii. 133). Of this MS. Schneider had only an imperfect collation, which he regrets, " nam codex inter meliores est et proxime accedere videtur ad codicis E [*i.e.* Parisinus 2763] bonitatem."

    p = Parisinus suppl. Gr. 1095 (page lost which contained iii. 66-145) olim S. Petri Perusinus (library of S. Pierre de Pérouse (Perugia)).

    d (Schneider D) = Laurentianus 32, 45. The part of this MS. which contained Callimachus is now lost, having been torn out to be printed in the *editio princeps* of Janus Lascaris, Florence 1494, which now represents the lost MS.

Other MSS. of the E-family are Schneider's V, *i.e.* the MS. from which in 1489 Angelus Politianus published his Latin version of the Bath of Pallas (Hymn v.).

Also Schneider's E, *i.e.* Parisinus 2763, written in the fifteenth century, and containing Orpheus' *Argonautica* and *Hymns*, the *Hymns* of Callimachus with marginal scholia, *Homeric Hymns*, Moschus' *Amor Fugitivus* (Ἔρως Δραπέτης), Musaeus' *Hero and Leander*, Hesiod's *Works and Days*, *Shield*, and *Theogony*, Theocritus' *Idylls*. This is the only MS. which places the Bath of Pallas after the Hymn to Demeter.

A, best represented by

> a (Schneider A) = Vaticanus 1691, fifteenth century, containing Apollonius Rhodius' *Argonautica* with scholia, Orpheus' *Argonautica* and *Hymns*, and the *Hymns* of Callimachus;

also by Vaticanus 36 (Schneider B), fifteenth century; Venetus Marcianus 480 (Schneider C), which belonged to Cardinal Bessarion and was written by Joannes Rhosus; Urbinas 145 (Schneider K), end of fifteenth century.

F, represented by

> r = Athous Laurae 587 (in the Laura monastery on M. Athos), fourteenth century.
>
> f (Schneider F) = Ambrosianus B 98, fifteenth century, containing Apollonius' *Argonautica* with scholl., Homer's *Batrachom.*, Herodotus' *Life of Homer*, *Hom. Hymns*, and Callimachus' *Hymns*, etc.

15

BIBLIOGRAPHY

Editio princeps: Joannes Lascaris, Florence, 1494 (with scholia). Aldina, Venice, 1513. Frobeniana, Basel, 1532. Vascosiana, Paris, 1549. Robortelli (?), Venice, 1555. H. Stephanus in *Poet. Gr. principes heroïci carminis*, Paris, 1566 (with the *Epigrams*). Benenatus, Paris, 1574. H. Stephanus, Paris, 1577 (with Frischlin's translation). Bonaventura Vulcanius, Antwerp, 1584. Anna Dacier (Faber); Paris, 1675.

J. G. Graevius, Utrecht, 1697 (with Bentley's collection of fragments, and Spanheim's commentary). Thomas Bentley (?), London, 1741. Stubelius, Leipzig, 1741. Bandinius, Florence, 1763–1764 (with versions in Latin and Italian). J. A. Ernesti, Leyden, 1761 (with the fragments and Spanheim's commentary). Loesner, Leipzig, 1774. de la Porte du Theil, Paris, 1775. Petrucci, Rome, 1795, 1818. W. Bilderdijk, Amsterdam, 1808. C. J. Blomfield, London, 1815 (an abbreviated Ernesti). Volger, Leipzig, 1817. Boissonade, Paris, 1824. August Meineke, Berlin, 1861, " omnes longo post se intervallo reliquit" (Schneider). O. Schneider, Leipzig, 1870–1873.

Hymns and *Epigrams*, Wilamowitz-Moellendorff, Berlin, 1882[1], 1896[2], 1907[3], Inni di Callimaco su Diana e sui Lavacri di Pallade, Recensione, Traduzione e commento, C. Nigra, Turin, 1892.

Translations: German—Ahlwardt, Berlin, 1794; Schwenk, Bonn, 1821, Stuttgart, 1833.

Italian—Hymns iii. and v., C. Nigra (see above).

16

BIBLIOGRAPHY

The Lock of Berenice, O. Nigra, Milan, 1879, S. Scalzi, Bergamo, 1895.

English—J. Banks (verse by Tytler), London, 1879.

Trans. of the epigrams by A. Hauvette (see below). *Scholia*: G. Reinecke, *De scholiis Callimacheis*, Diss. Halenses ix. 1-65 (1888).

Other Literature: A. F. Naeke, *De Call. Hecale*, Bonn, 1829. M. Haupt, *Emendationes Callimacheae*, Berlin, 1859.

Dilthey, *Analecta Callimachea*, Bonn, 1865.

W. Weinberger, *Kallim. Studien*, Vienna, 1895.

K. Kuiper, *Studia Callimachea*, Leyden, 1896, 1898.

"Kallimachos und Kyrene," E. Maass in *Hermes* 25 (1890), Studniczka in *Hermes*, 28 (1893).

Aug. Rostagni, *Poeti Alessandrini*, Turin, 1916, pp. 253-327.

"Die Locke der Berenike," Wilamowitz-Moellendorff, *Reden u. Vorträge*, Berlin, 1901, p. 195 ff.

Ph. E. Legrand, "Pourquoi furent composés les Hymnes de Callimaque," *Rev. d. Ét. anc.* 1901. C. Caesi, "Stud. Callimachei," in *Studi ital. di Filol. class.* vii. p. 301 ff., Florence, 1902.

A. Ludwich, *Callimachea*, Königsberg, 1907.

A. Hauvette, "Les Épigrammes de Callimaque." Étude critique et littéraire accompagnée d'une traduction, *Rev. d. Ét. gr.* 1907, and Paris, 1907.

New Fragments: T. Gomperz, *Aus der Hekale d. Kallim.*, Vienna, 1893; I. Nicole, *Rev. d. Ét. gr.* 1904; A. Puech, *ibid.* 1910; K. Kuiper, *ibid.* 1912 and 1916; P. Graindor, *Musée Belge*, 1911.

INTRODUCTION TO CALLIMACHUS'S
HYMNS

I

As a literary form the Callimachean Hymn is the
descendant of the Homeric. That Callimachus wrote
his Hymns with a practical purpose, to be recited on real
occasions of public or semi-public ceremony, is a very
general assumption of modern scholarship. Thus Susemihl, *Geschichte d. griech. Litt. in d. Alexandrinerzeit*,
i. 358 : " Sie waren ohne Zweifel bestimmt bei festlichen
Gelegenheiten declamirt zu werden " ; and to the same
effect Couat, *La Poésie alexandrine*, p. 198 : " Les allusions
directes qui s'y trouvent prouvent qu'ils étaient composés
pour une récitation publique, en vue de circonstances
déterminées. Ils ont le plus souvent pour objet de
célébrer dans une fête religieuse, sous le nom d'une
divinité, la grandeur du prince et la gloire de son règne."
As to the truth of the assumption one may be permitted
to be sceptical, and our scepticism is rather increased by
the poverty of the arguments adduced in its favour, and
the diversity of the theories advanced as to the particular
festival contemplated in a given Hymn. It is, moreover,
to be remembered that a poem not intended for ceremonial
performance may be none the less alive and pertinent to
real events. It is difficult to see how Tennyson's *Ode on
the Death of the Duke of Wellington* would gain either in
poetic merit or in historical value if we knew it to have
been actually performed in the Abbey ; and it would be
a matter rather of personal curiosity than of literary

18

interest to discover that Mr. Bridges' *Elegy on a Lady* was sung by a choir of maidens at a real funeral.

II.—HYMN I. TO ZEUS

After announcing his theme—the praise of Zeus—the poet refers to the rival claims of Crete and Arcadia to be the birthplace of Zeus. The Arcadian claim is preferred —Cretans are always liars (1-9). Zeus was born in Arcadia (10-33), thence he was conveyed by Neda to the Cretan cave, where he was cradled by Adrasteia, attended by the Dictaean Meliae, suckled by the she-goat Amaltheia, and fed on honey by the Panacrian bees, while the Curetes danced round him to protect him from Cronus (33-53). The mention of the Dictaean Meliae implies that the cave is on Dicte (*cf.* Arat. 33), not on Ida. The cult of the Idaean cave seems to have superseded that of Dicte, from perhaps 800 B.C. (*cf.* A. B. Cook, *Zeus*, i. 150). Zeus speedily exhibits precocious powers, and his elder brothers ungrudgingly yield to him the sovereignty of Heaven (53-59). His supremacy is due to his own prowess, not, as the old poets fabled, to the casting of lots (60-67). Zeus has all the attributes of the supreme king. The king of birds is his messenger, the kings of men derive their power from him, ἐκ δὲ Διὸς βασιλῆες = Hesiod, *Th.* 96, they are his peculiar care, above all Ptolemy (67-91). The Hymn ends with the χαιρέτισμα, which is the Prayer proper (92-97).

As to the date and destination of the poem, the idea of Richter that it was written for the accession of Ptolemy Philadelphus in 285 B.C. is rejected on the ground that the poem in no way suggests a coronation hymn. A conjecture which finds more favour is that lines 58 f., which tell of the elevation of Zeus over his older brothers, allude to the circumstances of Ptolemy's accession. Ptolemy Soter left five sons of whom Philadelphus was the youngest (Justin. xvi. 2. 7). There is no reason to suppose that they accepted Ptolemy's elevation with equanimity, nor was their fate such as to make any reference to them a happy one. Recovery of the Egyptian throne was doubtless the ultimate objective of the stormy career of Ptolemy Ceraunus, who left Egypt for the court of Lysimachus of Thrace, where with Arsinoë II. he compassed the death of the crown prince Agathocles; went thence to Seleucus whom he accompanied to Corupedion (281 B.C.) where Lysimachus fell; next assassinated Seleucus and became king of Thrace, but shortly after (280 B.C.) fell in a battle with the Gauls (Justin. xxiv. 3. 4). His brother Meleagrus who succeeded him was almost immediately deposed. As for the remaining brothers, Pausan. i. 7. 1, after mentioning the marriage of Philadelphus to Arsinoë II., says: δεύτερα δὲ ἀδελφὸν ἀπέκτεινεν Ἀργαῖον ἐπιβουλεύοντα ὡς λέγεται ... ἀπέκτεινε δὲ καὶ ἄλλον ἀδελφὸν γεγονότα ἐξ Εὐρυδίκης, Κυπρίους ἀφιστάντα αἰσθόμενος. It is argued, then, that the Hymn belongs to a time when his brothers had not yet made any move against Philadelphus. But it is difficult to assert that there was any time after the elevation of Ptolemy when their hostility was not obvious. Clearly, too, the reference, if reference there be, may just as well be an admonition, reproving their hostile attitude by appealing to the example of Zeus and his brothers. Wilamowitz, *Textgeschichte d. griech. Bukol.* p. 55, who thinks it undeniable that lines 58 f. allude to Ptolemy's succession, considers that the poem is dated by the absence of any reference to the marriage of Ptolemy and Arsinoë II. Couat dated it 280–275. Kaibel on certain metrical grounds put it later than III., V., VI., but earlier than II. and IV.

The preference given to the Arcadian tradition regarding Zeus is made by E. Maass, *Hermes* xxv. (1890), the basis of a theory of the destination of the poem. We have to do, he says, with a contamination of an originally purely Arcadian (Peloponnesian) saga with an originally purely Cretan saga in such manner that the Arcadian (Peloponnesian) is preferred. Now in the time of Battus II., *circ.* 570, we hear of a large accession of colonists from all parts of Greece to Cyrene (Herod. iv. 159), and in the

time of Battus III. troubles, doubtless due to this immigra-
tion, caused the Cyreneans to apply to Delphi. On the
advice of the oracle they asked Mantinea in Arcadia for a
commissioner to arrange their affairs. The Mantineans
sent Demonax as καταρτιστήρ, who distributed the popula-
tion in three *phylae* : 1. Theraeans and *perioeci*. 2.
Peloponnesians and Cretans. 3. All islanders (νησιῶται)
(Herod iv. 161). Maass argues that the Peloponnesian-
Cretan contamination of the Zeus tradition arose in the
2nd Cyrenean *phyle*, and for a symposium of private
persons belonging to that *phyle* the Hymn was written.
Maass' theory is entirely unnecessary. Everything points
to the original Greek settlers of Cyrene having come
from the Peloponnesus (Arcadia-Taenarus), partly direct,
partly by way of Crete. Thus from the first the Cyrenean
settlement would have been precisely of the type which
Maass desiderates and finds in the later 2nd *phyle*.

III.—HYMN II. TO APOLLO

As to the destination of this Hymn, Couat, p. 235,
Susemihl i. p. 361, Maass, *Hermes* xxv. (1890), agree that it
was written for the Carnean festival of Apollo at Cyrene.
Maass, it is true, is somewhat troubled by the "Delian"
palm. But he gravely conjectures that a scion of the
Delian tree was grown in Cyrene and he appeals to Hehn,
Kulturpflanzen, p. 224, to show that the palm is easily
transplanted. Most readers will probably feel with
Malten (*Kyrene*, p. 52, n. 1) that the conjecture is "zu
gesucht!" We entirely agree with Malten—though not
quite on the same grounds—that "obwohl er also von
den kyrenäischen Karneen handelt, hat Kallimachos
seinen Hymnus so wenig als ein sacrales Gedicht für
Kyrene gedichtet wie Goethe die Walpurgisnacht für den
Brocken."

The speaker throughout is the poet, and the occasion
imagined is the epiphany of the God. To-day Apollo is
to visit his temple. Ere yet the God veritably comes, we
perceive the signs of his approach in the quivering of the

21

holy laurel, in the trembling of the shrine. It is time for the profane to withdraw. Apollo is at the gate—the Delian palm bows to do him homage, the cry of the swan, Apollo's sacred bird, is heard on high. Let the doors of themselves roll back! Let the young men declare his praise with voice and harp! To see Apollo is not given unto all : it is the proof and promise of the Elect. That proof and that promise shall be ours. Now Apollo is present in his temple—let the youths sing his praise : so shall their days be long in the land which Apollo gave unto their fathers (1-15). Now the youths raise their song in honour of Apollo. Be silent, all ye faithful, and hearken to that Paean which wins Thetis from her mourning and stays the tears of Niobe—whose monumental grief still proclaims the sorrow and the sin of envy, of war with Heaven. Against Heaven, against my king : against my king, against Apollo ! But they who sing the praise of Apollo shall have their reward (16-29). Rich in gold is Apollo, ever beautiful and ever young, his unshorn locks shed dews of healing wheresoever he goes. He is the pattern and patron of the Archer, the Poet, the Prophet, the Physician, nay he is the Pastoral God (Nomios) as well, ever since upon earth he did such service for Admetus. Lastly, he is the Founder of Cities, ever since as a child of four years he built the Altar of Horns in Delos (29-64). Under his guidance was Cyrene founded (65 ff.). Lines 65-96 are occupied with the story of Cyrene, 97-104 with the origin of the cry *Hië Paean*. Finally 105-113 contain the remarkable parable of Envy.

The schol. on v. 106 says : " In these words he rebukes those who jeered at him as not being able to write a big poem : which taunt drove him to write the *Hecale*." It is generally assumed that Phthonos represents Apollonius Rhodius and Apollo perhaps Ptolemy. There is a striking parallel to v. 106 in Apoll. Rh. iii. 932 f. ἀκλειὴς ὅδε μάντις, ὃς οὐδ' ὅσα παῖδες ἴσασιν | οἶδε νόῳ φράσσασθαι. But into the thorny chronology of the quarrel of Callimachus and Apollonius we cannot here enter. We can only say dogmatically that there is no real difficulty in the syntax of οὐδ' ὅσα: that the construction intended is ὅσα πόντος ἀείδει, not ἐστί or the like: that πόντος is the sea, not the Euxine, as Mr. Smiley, *Hermathena* xxxix. (1913), following Voss, conjectures: and the "Assyrian river" is, as the schol. says, the Euphrates, not a river—Halys or Iris—in Leucosyria (Smiley, *l.c.*).

For the student who is interested in the relations of Callimachus and Apollonius we append a list of passages in which he may find, as he pleases, coincidence or "versteckte Kritik": Call. *H.* i. 15=A. i. 129; *H.* ii. 79=A. i. 431; *H.* ii. 96=A. ii. 711 f.; *H.* ii. 106=A. iii. 932 f.; *H.* iii. 45=A. iii. 881; *H.* iii. 108=A. i. 997; *H.* iii. 176=A. iii. 1344; *H.* iii. 182=A. iv. 961; Call. *Hec.* i. 1. 12=A. iv. 217; *Hec.* i. 2. 11=A. i. 177; *Hec.* 4=A. i. 972; *Hec.* 5=A. i. 1116; *Hec.* 6=A. iii. 277; *Hec.* 19=A. iii. 1226; Call. *fr. incert.* 9 (a)=A. iv. 1717; 9 (b)=A. ii. 1094; 21=A. iv. 1323; 64=A. i. 738; 65= A. i. 1309; 112=A. iv. 1614.

As to the date of the poem it is agreed that it must belong to a period when Egypt and Cyrene were friendly, say 258–247 B.C. In vv. 26 and 27 Callimachus speaks of "my king" in the singular. Now we know from official documents that from 267/6 to 260/259 Ptolemy had as co-regent a son named Ptolemy. It is pretty generally agreed that this son was none other than the future Euergetes (Ptolemy III.), the reason for the disappearance of his name from 260/259 being that by his betrothal to Berenice, daughter of Magas, he became virtual king of Cyrene (see introd. and notes to the *Lock of Berenice*). If this is right, then the Hymn cannot be earlier than 258 B.C. Malten (*Kyrene*, p. 51) says that if the war between Ptolemy and Cyrene, of which Polyaen. viii. 70 speaks, is rightly placed by Niese in 250–247, then the poem cannot be later than 250. The words ἡμετέροις βασιλεῦσι v. 68 are much disputed. Who are "our kings"? It seems natural to understand the Battiadae, to whom as a matter of fact the promise was made (oracles in Herod. iv. 155, 157 and Diodor. viii. 29), and so the words are understood by Maass and Studniczka. On the other hand it is pointed out that the Battiad rule came to an end and with the fall of Arcesilas IV. somewhat between 460 ned 450 B.C. Hence it is more usually supposed that the reference is to the Ptolemies generally or more particularly to Philadelphus as king of Egypt and Euergetes as king in Cyrene.

The schol. on v. 26 has βασιλῆι] τῷ Πτολεμαίῳ τῷ Εὐεργέτῃ· διὰ δὲ τὸ φιλόλογον αὐτὸν εἶναι ὡς θεὸν τιμᾷ. This is accepted by Studniczka who, proceeding on the equation Apollo = Ptolemy, thinks the king referred to must be young, *i.e.* not Philadelphus but Euergetes. But Studniczka goes farther. He holds that the scene of Cyrene's lion-slaying was originally Thessaly and that tradition was accepted by Callimachus in the Hymn to Artemis 206-8 : between that Hymn and the Hymn to Apollo a new version arose which transferred the scene to Libya : this was an invention of Callimachus intended to represent Cyrene as Berenice, daughter of Magas : the lion is Demetrius ὁ καλός whom Berenice slew : and the date of the poem is 247 when Cyrene was united to Egypt by the marriage of Euergetes and Berenice.

IV.—CYRENE

1. The legend of the nymph Cyrene was told in the *Eoeae* of Hesiod (schol. Pind. *P.* ix. 6 = Hes. fr. 149) from whom Pindar tells the story in *P.* ix. Cyrene, daughter of Hypseus, is seen by Apollo struggling with a lion near Mount Pelion. In accordance with the prophecy of Cheiron Apollo carries her to Libya where she becomes mother of Aristaeus and eponym of the city of Cyrene. According to Acesandrus of Cyrene the king of Libya at the time was Eurypylus, whose land was being ravaged by a lion. Eurypylus offered his kingdom as a reward for slaying the lion. Cyrene, having performed the feat, received the kingdom. She bare two sons, Autuchus and Aristaeus (schol. Apoll. Rh. ii. 498). According to Phylarchus she came to Libya μετὰ πλειόνων. When her company were sent out to

hunt she went with them, slew the lion and received the kingdom. She bare to Apollo two sons, Autuchus and Aristaeus. Autuchus remained in Libya, Aristaeus went to Ceos (schol. Apoll. Rh. *l.c.*). Apollonius's account in ii. 500 ff. does not mention the slaying of the lion. To Nonnus she is essentially the lion-slayer (λεοντοφόνος) 27, 263; 25, 181; 45, 21; 46, 238, etc.

2. The story of the foundation of Cyrene is told in Pindar, *P.* iv., Herod. iv. 145 ff., Lycophron 886 ff., Apoll. Rh. iv. 1232 ff. The Argonauts on their way home were driven by the wind into the Syrtes, from which they carried their ship overland for twelve days and nights to Lake Tritonis. From this they found no outlet to the sea, till Triton appeared to them, in guise of Eurypylus, son of Poseidon, who, in return for the gift of a tripod, presented Euphemus with a clod of earth and showed them the way out. The clod, which was the earnest of the possession of Libya, fell overboard and landed at Thera. Medea declared that (1) had Euphemus taken the clod home to Taenarus in Laconia, then, in the course of the great migrations from the Peloponnesus in the fourth generation, his descendants would have colonized Libya; (2) as it is, Euphemus will go with the Argonauts to Lemnus where in wedlock with a Lemnian wife he will beget descendants who will come to Thera, whence Battus will lead a colony to Libya and so in the seventeenth generation fulfil Medea's prophecy.

The fulfilment came about in this way. The descendants of Euphemus were driven from Lemnos by the Pelasgians, and came to Laconia where they settled on Taygetus. On the ground of their ancestry they were admitted to citizenship at Sparta, but when they aspired to the kingship they were thrown into prison, from which they escaped again to Taygetus. At this time Theras (see *H.* ii. 74 *n.*) was preparing to lead a colony to Calliste (Thera), and he took with him a party of the Euphemid refugees. Finally, by order of the Delphic oracle (for details see Herod. iv. 150 ff.), Battus sets out for Libya with a party of colonists. They reach Plateia, an island off the coast of Cyrenaica, where they stay for two years. Things going badly with them, they consult Delphi and learn that they must proceed to Libya itself. They cross to the mainland and settle for six years in Aziris (Azilis), τὸν νάπαι κάλλισται συγκληίουσι (Herod. iv. 157, *cf.* Callim. *H.* ii. 89). In the seventh year the Libyans conduct them westward, passing Irasa by night, until they reach the κρήνη Ἀπόλλωνος where they settle.

Here was the "Hill of Myrtles," from which Apollo and Cyrene watched the Theraeans dancing with the Libyan women—the Myrtussa of Callimachus ii. 91, the Μυρτώσιον αἶπος of Apoll. Rh. ii. 505. Smith and Porcher, *Discoveries at Cyrene* (1864), record an inscription (No. 13) found near the temple of Apollo at Cyrene which is dedicated Ἀπόλλωνι Μυρτώῳ, and they remark (p. 27) on the abundance of myrtles in the place at the present day. Here, too, was the imagined scene of the slaying of the lion by Cyrene (*cf.* Malten, *Kyrene*, p. 56).

V.—Hymn III. To Artemis

According to Susemihl (i. 360) the one thing certain about the date of this Hymn is that it was written after 277 B.C., because lines 251-258 presuppose the invasion of Asia Minor by the Gauls in 278/7 B.C., and their raid upon the Ionian towns (Pausan. x. 32. 4), when according to the dubious story of the Rhodian Cleitophon Ephesus was betrayed to them (Plut. *Parall.* 15, Müller, *F.H.G.* iv. 367). The assumption is a common one, but without the slightest foundation. Callimachus refers to the burning of the temple of Artemis at Ephesus by the Cimmerians under Lygdamis in the seventh century (Strabo i. 61, Herod. i. 15). To see in this a covert allusion to the Celts as Couat and others do is a perfectly gratuitous extravagance.

Gercke, *Rhein. Mus.* xlii. (1887), p. 273 ff., sees in v. 130 ff. an allusion to the two Arsinoës who are the εἰνάτερες and γαλόῳ: εἰνάτερες because Philadelphus, the husband of Arsinoë I., and Ceraunus, the husband of Arsinoë II., were (half) brothers, and γαλόῳ because Arsinoë I. was the wife while Arsinoë II. was the sister of Philadelphus. This would date the Hymn previous to the repudiation of Arsinoë I. and Philadelphus's marriage to Arsinoë II. Couat, on the other hand, holding that it was written for the festival of Artemis at Ephesus, dates it between 258 and 248 B.C.

E. Maass, *Hermes* xxv. (1890), propounds a theory for which there is absolutely nothing to be said, namely, that it was written for the Artemis festival of the Third Phyle at Cyrene, which, as we have seen, was made up of the Νησιῶται. It is enough to say here that there is not an atom of evidence that the Third Phyle had anything to do with Artemis, and the " surprising fact" from which his theory starts, namely, that Artemis is attended by a choir of Ocean nymphs, is of all things the least surprising. In Homer, *Od.* vi. 105, Artemis is attended by the nymphs, and though they are there said to be daughters of Zeus, the far more fundamental doctrine is that the nymphs are daughters of Ocean. They are the female counterpart of the Rivers (Ποταμοί)—see Hesiod, *Theog.* 337 ff., whose doctrine is followed by Callimachus in *Hymn* i. 35 f. And if the choir of Artemis here needs such a desperate apology, how shall we apologize for Apollonius who (iii. 881 ff.) like Callimachus makes her attended by the nymphs of Amnisus, who are at any rate grand-daughters of Oceanus ?

Maass holds that the poem must belong to a time when Alexandria and Cyrene were friendly, thus at earliest *circ.* 260 B.C. Kaibel on metrical grounds would put it earlier than any of the Hymns except vi. The early date for which Gercke argued is accepted by Studniczka, who thinks the humble rôle assigned to Cyrene in this Hymn implies a time when Alexandria and Cyrene were on such unfriendly terms that a court poet could not well occupy himself with the latter.

The lines referring to Cyrene have been the subject of much dispute: καὶ μὴν Κυρήνην ἑταρίσσαο, τῇ ποτ᾽ ἔδωκας | αὐτὴ θηρητῆρε δύω κύνε, τοῖς ἔνι κούρη | Ὑψηὶς παρὰ τύμβον Ἰωλκιον ἔμμορ' ἀέθλου (206-8). The "Iolcian tomb," according to the schol., is the tomb of Pelias. Studniczka follows Spanheim in thinking that ἔμμορ' ἀέθλου refers to Cyrene' slaying of the lion. Meineke thought the reference was to a hunting contest at the funeral games of Pelias. Malten, *Kyrene*, p. 53, says, "Daß der τύμβος 'Ιώλκιος, wo Kyrene an Wettspielen teilnimmt (ἔμμορε, sie ist also nicht die einzige, die dort wettkämpft!), ein Hinweis auf die Grabspiele zu Ehren des Pelias sei, ist eine aus der Natur der Sache ergebende Folgerung Meinekes und Vahlens. Daß in Wettspielen, an denen mehrere beteiligt sind, kein Löwenkampf figurieren kann, ist ebenso natürlich. Also besteht Kyrenes Kunst hier in einem Wettlauf inbinnen (τοῖς ἔνι) ihrer Hunde. Darüber kann man sich wundern, aber die Worte besagen dies und nichts anderes." But, apart from the fact that the freak race suggested receives no sort of support from such expressions as Hor. *Ep.* i. 18. 50 f. *cum valeas et vel cursu superare canem*, not even Malten's authority can compel us to assign an impossible meaning (1) to τοῖς ἔνι, (2) to ἔμμορε, and (3) to ἀέθλου. ἔμμορ' ἀέθλου means "won the prize," and only on that assumption is τοῖς ἔνι, "with which," perfectly natural Greek. Whether the contest was part of the funeral games of Pelias is of course a totally different question.

VI.—HYMN IV. TO DELOS

For dating this Hymn we have the references in the prophecy of Apollo to the extent of the dominion of Ptolemy Philadelphus (165–170) and to the Gauls (171–188).

Apollo, prophesying of Philadelphus, says, "beneath whose crown shall come—not loth to be ruled by a Macedonian—both continents and the lands which are set in the sea, far as where the limit of the earth is and again whence his swift horses carry the sun." We are immediately reminded of the more detailed account of Ptolemy's dominion in the xviith Idyll of Theocritus, the 'Εγκώμιον εἰς Πτολεμαῖον, where we read, 86 ff. :

INTRODUCTION TO THE *HYMNS*

καὶ μὴν Φοινίκας ἀποτέμνεται Ἀρραβίας τε
καὶ Συρίας Λιβύας τε κελαινῶν τ' Αἰθιοπήων.
Παμφύλοισί τε πᾶσι καὶ αἰχμηταῖς Κιλίκεσσι
σαμαίνει, Λυκίοις τε φιλοπτολέμοισί τε Καρσί,
καὶ νάσοις Κυκλάδεσσιν, ἐπεί οἱ νᾶες ἄρισται
πόντον ἐπιπλώοντι, θάλασσα δὲ πᾶσα καὶ αἶα,
καὶ ποταμοὶ κελάδοντες ἀνάσσονται Πτολεμαίῳ.

Into the question of the mutual relations of Theocritus and Callimachus we cannot here enter. Theocritus in his Encomium speaks of Arsinoë II. as still alive, which dates the poem before 270 B.C. Wilamowitz puts it during the First Syrian War—" als der Krieg gegen Syrien, der 274 begonnen hat, guten Fortgang nahm, aber noch im Gange war" (*Textgeschichte d. gr. Bukol.* p. 152). If we assume the year 271 B.C., the year in which that war ended, as the date of the Hymn to Delos, the dominion of Philadelphus at that date would sufficiently justify the words of Callimachus. It included, outside Egypt, Coele Syria (recovered about 280), Lycia, Caria, Miletus, the island of Cyprus, and the Cyclades.

The reference to the Gallic invasion (see notes on the passage) would suit the supposed date very well. The schol. on v. 175 says: "Brennus, the king of the Gauls, gathered together the Celts and went against Pytho, wishing to plunder the treasures of the god. But when they approached, Apollo destroyed most of them by hail. A few survived, and one Antigonus, a friend of Ptolemy Philadelphus, procured them to serve him as mercenaries, Ptolemy wanting such an army at the moment. But they were equally eager to plunder his treasures. Knowing this he arrested them and brought them to the so-called Sebennytic mouth of the Nile where he drowned them. This is the 'common struggle' which he prophesies." Some regard the Antigonus mentioned above as the king of Macedon, others as merely a recruiting agent. The account of the incident in Paus. i. 7. 2 is: "When Ptolemy was preparing to repel the aggression of Magas he procured mercenaries, among them four thousand Gauls. Finding that these were plotting to seize Egypt, he conducted them over the river to a desert island, where they perished by each other's hands and by hunger."

It should be remembered, further, that from 308 B.C. there existed the Confederation of the Islanders — Τὸ Κοινὸν τῶν Νησιωτῶν — under the protectorate of Egypt and having its headquarters at Delos. See Dittenberger, *Orient. gr. Inscr.* Nos. 25, 40, 67, *Syll.*² Nos. 202, 209, 223, 224, 471, 588. The president of the Confederation (νησίαρχος) was nominated not by the Islands but by Egypt.

VII.—V. The Bath of Pallas

No one has detected in this poem any reference to contemporary events. It shares with Hymn vi. the peculiarity of being written in the Doric dialect, while it alone forsakes the heroic for the elegiac metre. On Kaibel's metrical theory it would come third in date, after vi. and iii. As to its destination, Susemihl holds that it was written to the order of the Argives for a festival of Pallas in that city. That is the view also of F. Spiro, " Prolog und Epilog in Lykophrons Alexandra," *Hermes* xxiii. (1888) p. 194 ff., who holds further that it belongs to a period when such commissions were necessary for Callimachus, the period which he pictures in Epigrams xxviii., xxxiv., xlvii., when he was living as a poor schoolmaster in Eleusis, before his introduction to the Alexandrian court. He regards v. 56, μῦθος δ' οὐκ ἐμὸς ἀλλ' ἑτέρων,ª as the announcement by the poet of an artistic dogma which he was afterwards to express in less simple language in the *Aitia*: βροντᾶν δ' οὐκ ἐμὸν ἀλλὰ Διός, frag. incert. 146 (490). In v. 140 ff. he detects a "versteckte Kritik" of Lycophron, *Alex.* 1474 σώζων παλαιὰν Βεβρύκων παγκληρίαν, which the Hymn therefore according to Spiro presupposes.

It was the custom, we are told by the schol. on v. 1, for the women of Argos on an appointed day to carry the image of Athena and the shield of Diomede to the river Inachus and there to wash them. The image is the Palladium carried off from Troy by Odysseus and Diomede

ª " I cannot tell how the truth may be ; I say the tale as 'twas said to me." Scott, *Lay of the Last Minstrel*, ii. 22.

and by the latter brought to Argos. The shield of
Diomede was dedicated by him in Athena's temple, *cf.*
Pausan. ii. 24. 2, who mentions a temple of Athena
Oxyderces on the Acropolis at Argos dedicated by
Diomede in memory of the day when Athena took the
mist from his eyes that he might discern God and man
(*Il.* v. 127 f.).

For the widespread custom of annually bathing the
holy image we have to compare the Athenian Plynteria
(Xen. *Hell.* i. 4. 12, Plut. *Alc.* 34), also Pausan. ii. 10. 4
where, speaking of the temple of Aphrodite at Sicyon, he
says ἐσίασι μὲν δὴ ἐς αὐτὸ γυνή τε νεωκόρος . . . καὶ παρθένος
ἱερωσύνην ἐπέτειον ἔχουσα· λουτροφόρον τὴν παρθένον ὀνομάζουσι.
See further Ovid, *Fast.* iv. 336 ff., Ammian. Marc. xxiii. 3,
Tac. *Germ.* 40, and for the significance of the practice
Mannhardt, *Baumkultus* chapter vii., *Antike Wald u.
Feldkulte*, chapter v.

VIII.—HYMN VI. TO DEMETER

Nothing can be determined as to the date of this Hymn.
On Kaibel's metrical theory it is the oldest of all. The
schol. on v. 1 says : "Ptolemy Philadelphus among other
imitations of Athenian customs which he established in
Alexandria, instituted the Procession of the Basket (τὴν
τοῦ καλάθου πρόοδον). For it was the custom in Athens that
on a fixed day a basket should be borne upon a carriage
in honour of Athena." The details of this Athenian
celebration are entirely unknown, but it may be supposed
that it followed more or less closely the model of
the Athenian Thesmophoria. In that and in similar
festivals there are three essential moments : Anodos (or
Cathodos), Nesteia, Calligeneia, as they were called in
the Thesmophoria. All that can be clearly distinguished
here is that the Basket with its mystic contents is
carried in procession to the temple of the goddess,
attended by women, some of whom being uninitiated—
these, if we may infer from the Athenian Thesmophoria,
include the unmarried women—go but part of the way,
while access to the temple is confined to the initiated

(v. 118 ff.); and, further, that the procession takes place after sunset (v. 7).

IX.—TABLE OF DATES.

B.C.

323.	Ptolemy satrap of Egypt.
323–321.	Ptolemy under Perdiccas.
322.	Cyrene conquered and attached to the satrapy of Egypt.
321.	Ptolemy marries Eurydice, daughter of Antipater.
321–319.	Ptolemy under Antipater.
320.	Ptolemy seizes Coele Syria; establishes protectorate of Cyprus.
319–311.	Ptolemy under Polyperchon.
318.	Ptolemy marries Berenice.
313.	Cyrene under Ophellas revolts from Egypt.
311–305.	Ptolemy independent satrap.
310–9.	Birth of Ptolemy Philadelphus in Cos.
308.	Establishment of Τὸ Κοινὸν τῶν Νησιωτῶν under protectorate of Egypt.
	Ptolemy recovers Cyrenaica: Magas, son of Berenice, viceroy of Cyrene.
305–285.	*Ptolemy I. Soter*, king of Egypt.
285.	*Ptolemy II. Philadelphus* associated with his father as king; marries Arsinoë I., daughter of Lysimachus.
283.	Death of Ptolemy I. Soter.
280–79.	Invasion of Gauls. Ptolemy recovers Coele Syria.
277.	Ptolemy repudiates Arsinoë I. and marries his full sister Arsinoë II.
	Revolt of Magas of Cyrene, who marries Apama, daughter of Antiochus.
273–1.	First Syrian War; Lycia, Caria, etc., fall to Egypt.
270.	Death of Arsinoë II. Philadelphus.
270–258.	Co-regency of Ptolemy III. Euergetes.
267–3.	Chremonidean War.
262.	Defeat of Egyptian fleet at Cos.

32

258.   Death of Magas of Cyrene, who had betrothed his daughter Berenice to Ptolemy, afterwards Ptolemy Euergetes.

257–6.   The affair of Demetrius the Fair at Cyrene.
        Ptolemy Euergetes king of Cyrene.
        Second Syrian War.

247.   Death of Ptolemy II. Philadelphus.

247.   *Ptolemy III. Euergetes.* Cyrene united to Egypt by marriage of Ptolemy III. to Berenice, daughter of Magas.
        Third Syrian War.

221.   Death of Ptolemy III.

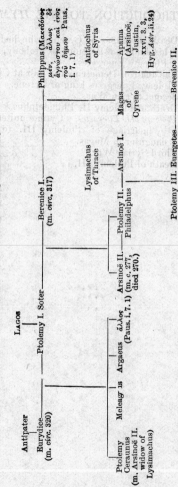

X.—STEMMA OF THE PTOLEMIES

```
                                    LAGOS
                                      |
                                Ptolemy I. Soter
```

Antipater
  |
Eurydice
(m. circ. 320)

Berenice I.
(m. circ. 317)

Philippus (Μακεδόνος
μέν, ἄλλως δὲ
ἀγνώστου καὶ ἑνὸς
τοῦ δήμου Paus.
i. 7. 1)

Antiochus
of Syria

Apama (Arsinoë,
Justin,
xxvi. 3. 3,
Hyg. Astr. ii. 24)

Magas
of
Cyrene

Berenice II.

Meleager is **Argaeus** ἄλλος
(Paus. i. 7. 1)

Arsinoë II.
(m. c. 277,
died 270.)

**Ptolemy II.
Philadelphus**

Lysimachus
of Thrace

Arsinoë I.

**Ptolemy
Ceraunus**
(m. Arsinoë II.
widow of
Lysimachus)

Ptolemy III. Energetes

CALLIMACHUS'S HYMNS

ΚΑΛΛΙΜΑΧΟΥ ΥΜΝΟΙ

I.—ΕΙΣ ΔΙΑ

Ζηνὸς ἔοι τί κεν ἄλλο παρὰ σπονδῇσιν ἀείδειν
λώιον ἢ θεὸν αὐτόν, ἀεὶ μέγαν, αἰὲν ἄνακτα,
Πηλαγόνων[1] ἐλατῆρα, δικασπόλον οὐρανίδῃσι;
  πῶς καί μιν, Δικταῖον ἀείσομεν ἠὲ Λυκαῖον;
ἐν δοιῇ μάλα θυμός, ἐπεὶ γένος ἀμφήριστον.   5
Ζεῦ, σὲ μὲν Ἰδαίοισιν ἐν οὔρεσί φασι γενέσθαι,
Ζεῦ, σὲ δ᾽ ἐν Ἀρκαδίῃ· πότεροι, πάτερ, ἐψεύσαντο;
" Κρῆτες ἀεὶ ψεῦσται·" καὶ γὰρ τάφον, ὦ ἄνα,
  σεῖο
Κρῆτες ἐτεκτήναντο· σὺ δ᾽ οὐ θάνες, ἐσσὶ γὰρ αἰεί.

---

[1] πηλαγόνων *E.M.*; πηλογόνων. The reading of the mss.
Πηλαγόνων (πηλογόνων· τῶν γιγάντων παρὰ τὸ ἐκ πηλοῦ γενέσθαι,
τουτέστι τῆς γῆς schol.) was corrected by Salmasius and
others from *E.M. s.v.* Πηλαγόνες· οἱ γίγαντες, Καλλίμαχος
" Πηλαγόνων ἐλατῆρα." Cf. Hesych. *s.v.*, Strabo vii. 331,
fr. 40.

---

[a] Mountain in Crete.
[b] Mountain in Arcadia.
[c] This proverbial saying, attributed to Epimenides, is
quoted by St. Paul, Ep. Tit. i. 12, "One of themselves, a
prophet of their own, said, The Cretans are always liars,
evil beasts, idle bellies" (κακὰ θηρία, γαστέρες ἀργαί), and
seems to be alluded to by Aratus, *Phaen.* 30 εἰ ἐτεὸν δή.

CALLIMACHUS'S HYMNS

I.—TO ZEUS

At libations to Zeus what else should rather be sung than the god himself, mighty for ever, king for ever-more, router of the Pelagonians, dealer of justice to the sons of Heaven?

How shall we sing of him—as lord of Dicte [a] or of Lycaeum [b]? My soul is all in doubt, since debated is his birth. O Zeus, some say that thou wert born on the hills of Ida [a]; others, O Zeus, say in Arcadia; did these or those, O Father, lie? "Cretans are ever liars." [c] Yea, a tomb, [d] O Lord, for thee the Cretans builded; but thou didst not die, for thou art for ever.

The explanation given by Athenodorus of Eretria *ap.* Ptolem. Hephaest. in *Photii Bibl.* p. 150 Bekk. is that Thetis and Medea, having a dispute as to which of them was the fairer, entrusted the decision to Idomeneus of Crete. He decided in favour of Thetis, whereon Medea said, "Cretans are always liars" and cursed them that they should never speak the truth. The schol. on the present passage says that Idomeneus divided the spoils of Troy unfairly.

[a] The Cretan legend was that Zeus was a prince who was slain by a wild boar and buried in Crete. His tomb was variously localized and the tradition of "the tomb of Zeus" attaches to several places even in modern times, especially to Mount Iuktas. See A. B. Cook, *Zeus*, vol. i. p. 157 ff.

CALLIMACHUS

ἐν δέ σε Παρρασίῃ [1] ‘Ρείη τέκεν, ᾗχι μάλιστα 10
ἔσκεν ὄρος θάμνοισι περισκεπές· ἔνθεν ὁ χῶρος
ἱερός, οὐδέ τί μιν κεχρημένον Εἰλειθυίης
ἑρπετὸν οὐδὲ γυνὴ ἐπιμίσγεται, ἀλλά ἑ ‘Ρείης
ὠγύγιον καλέουσι λεχώιον ’Απιδανῆες.
ἔνθα σ’ ἐπεὶ μήτηρ μεγάλων ἀπεθήκατο κόλπων
αὐτίκα δίζητο ῥόον ὕδατος, ᾧ κε τόκοιο   15
λύματα χυτλώσαιτο, τεὸν δ’ ἐνὶ χρῶτα λοέσσαι.
Λάδων ἀλλ’ οὔπω μέγας ἔρρεεν οὐδ’ ’Ερύ-
μανθος,
λευκότατος ποταμῶν, ἔτι δ’ ἄβροχος ἦεν ἅπασα
’Αρκαδίη· μέλλεν δὲ μάλ’ εὔυδρος καλέεσθαι
αὖτις· ἐπεὶ τημόσδε, ‘Ρέη ὅτ’ ἐλύσατο μίτρην,   20
ἦ πολλὰς ἐφύπερθε σαρωνίδας ὑγρὸς ’Ιάων
ἤειρεν, πολλὰς δὲ Μέλας ὤκχησεν ἁμάξας,
πολλὰ δὲ Καρνίωνος [2] ἄνω διεροῦ περ ἐόντος
ἰλυοὺς ἐβάλοντο κινώπετα, νίσσετο δ’ ἀνὴρ   25
πεζὸς ὑπὲρ Κράθίν τε πολύστιον [3] τε Μετώπην
διψαλέος· τὸ δὲ πολλὸν ὕδωρ ὑπὸ ποσσὶν ἔκειτο.
καί ῥ’ ὑπ’ ἀμηχανίης σχομένη φάτο πότνια
‘Ρείη·

---

[1] Παρρασίῃ Lascaris ; Παρνασίη.
[2] Καρνίωνος Arnaldus, cf. Paus. viii. 34, Plin. iv. 6; Καρίωνος mss.
[3] πολύστιον schol. Apoll. Rh. ii. 1172 ; πολύστειον mss. and schol. Pind. O. vi. 146 ; cf. Nicand. T. 792, 950, Δ. 466.

---

[a] Arcadia.
[b] Cf. Apoll. Rh. iv. 1240.
[c] Goddess of birth.
[d] The ancient Arcadians (schol.).
[e] River in Arcadia.
[f] Melas] Dion. Per. 415 ff. ’Αρκάδες ’Απιδανῆες ὑπὸ σκοπιὴν ’Ερυμάνθου, ἔνθα Μέλας, ὅθι Κράθις, ἵνα ῥέει ὑγρὸς ’Ιάων, ᾗχι καὶ

HYMN I

In Parrhasia [a] it was that Rheia bare thee, where was a hill sheltered with thickest brush. Thence is the place holy, and no fourfooted [b] thing that hath need of Eileithyia [c] nor any woman approacheth thereto, but the Apidanians [d] call it the primeval childbed of Rheia. There when thy mother had laid thee down from her mighty lap, straightway she sought a stream of water, wherewith she might purge her of the soilure of birth and wash thy body therein.

But mighty Ladon [e] flowed not yet, nor Erymanthus, [e] clearest of rivers; waterless was all Arcadia; yet was it anon to be called well-watered. For at that time when Rhea loosed her girdle, full many a hollow oak did watery Iaon [e] bear aloft, and many a wain did Melas [f] carry and many a serpent did Carnion, [g] wet though it now be, cast its lair; and a man would fare on foot over Crathis [h] and many-pebbled Metope, [i] athirst: while that abundant water lay beneath his feet.

And holden in distress the lady Rheia said, "Dear

ὠγύγιος μηκύνεται ὕδασι Λάδων. Herodot. i. 145 has Ὤλενος ἐν τῷ Πεῖρος ποταμὸς μέγας ἐστί. Strabo 386 has Ὤλενος, παρ' ὃν ποταμὸς μέγας Μέλας where it has been proposed to read παρ' ὃν ⟨Πεῖρος⟩ and to omit Μέλας. M. T. Smiley, in *Classical Qu.* v. (1911) p. 89 f., suggests that the Styx is meant, which supplies the waterfall near Nonacris in North Arcadia and later becomes a tributary of the Crathis (Paus. viii. 18. 4). When Leake discovered the waterfall in 1806 the natives did not know the name Styx for it but called it the Black Water (Mavro nero) or the Dragon Water. The name Πεῖρος in any case suggests a connexion with the underworld.

  [g] Carnion or Carion, river in Arcadia, Paus. viii. 34.
  [h] Crathis, river in Arcadia (and Achaea), Paus. vii. 25. 11, viii. 15. 5, viii. 18. 4.
  [i] Metope, river in Arcadia.

39

CALLIMACHUS

" Γαῖα φίλη, τέκε καὶ σύ· τεαὶ δ' ὠδῖνες ἐλαφραί."
εἶπε καὶ ἀντανύσασα θεὴ μέγαν ὑψόθι πῆχυν   30
πλῆξεν ὄρος σκήπτρῳ· τὸ δέ οἱ δίχα πουλὺ διέστη,
ἐκ δ' ἔχεεν μέγα χεῦμα· τόθι χρόα φαιδρύνασα,
ὦνα, τεὸν σπείρωσε, Νέδῃ δέ σε δῶκε κομίζειν [1]
κευθμὸν ἔσω Κρηταῖον, ἵνα κρύφα παιδεύοιο,
πρεσβυτάτῃ Νυμφέων αἵ μιν τότε μαιώσαντο,   35
πρωτίστῃ γενεῇ [2] μετά γε Στύγα τε Φιλύρην τε.
οὐδ' ἁλίην ἀπέτεισε θεὴ χάριν, ἀλλὰ τὸ χεῦμα
κεῖνο Νέδην ὀνόμηνε· τὸ μέν ποθι πουλὺ κατ' αὐτὸ
Καυκώνων πτολίεθρον, ὃ Λέπρειον [3] πεφάτισται,
συμφέρεται Νηρῆι, παλαιότατον δέ μιν ὕδωρ   40
υἱωνοί [4] πίνουσι Λυκαονίης ἄρκτοιο.

εὖτε Θενὰς ἀπέλειπεν ἐπὶ Κνωσοῖο φέρουσα,
Ζεῦ πάτερ, ἡ Νύμφη σε (Θεναὶ δ' ἔσαν ἐγγύθι
    Κνωσοῦ),
τουτάκι τοι πέσε, δαῖμον, ἄπ' ὀμφαλός· ἔνθεν
    ἐκεῖνο
Ὀμφάλιον μετέπειτα πέδον καλέουσι Κύδωνες.
Ζεῦ, σὲ δὲ Κυρβάντων ἑτάραι προσεπηχύναντο   45

[1] κομίζειν A ; κομίσσαι other MSS.
[2] πρωτίστῃ γενεῇ Schneider.
[3] Λέπριον MSS. ; corr. Wass.
[4] γυιωνοί MSS.

---

[a] Cf. Paus. iv. 33. 1, " The Messenians say that Zeus was reared among them and that his nurses were Ithome and Neda, after whom the river got its name." Cf. viii. 38 ff.

[b] Styx, daughter of Oceanus and Tethys, Hesiod, Th. 361.
[c] Philyra, daughter of Oceanus, mother of Cheiron by Cronus.

[d] Paus. iv. 20. 2. The river Neda rises in Mount Lycaeon, flows into Messenia and forms the boundary between Messenia and Elis. Cf. Strabo 348 who says it

40

Earth, give birth thou also! thy birthpangs are
light." So spake the goddess, and lifting her great
arm aloft she smote the mountain with her staff;
and it was greatly rent in twain for her and poured
forth a mighty flood. Therein, O Lord, she cleansed
thy body; and swaddled thee, and gave thee to
Neda ^a to carry within the Cretan covert, that thou
mightst be reared secretly: Neda, eldest of the
nymphs who then were about her bed, earliest birth
after Styx ^b and Philyra.^c And no idle favour did
the goddess repay her, but named that stream
Neda ^d; which, I ween, in great flood by the very city
of the Cauconians,^e which is called Lepreion,^f mingles
its stream with Nereus,^g and its primeval water do the
son's sons of the Bear,^h Lycaon's daughter, drink.

When the nymph, carrying thee, O Father Zeus,
toward Cnosus,ⁱ was leaving Thenae ⁱ—for Thenae
was nigh to Cnosus—even then, O God, thy navel
fell away: hence that plain the Cydonians^j call the
Plain of the Navel.^k But thee, O Zeus, the companions of the Cyrbantes ^l took to their arms, even

rises in Lycaeon from a spring which Rheia caused to flow
in order to wash the infant Zeus.

^e A people of Triphylia, Hom. *Od.* iii. 366.

^f Herod. iv. 148 says that Lepreon in Triphylia was
founded by the Minyae after driving out the Cauconians.

^g *i.e.* the sea.

^h Arcas, the ancestor of the Arcadians, was the son
of Zeus and Lycaon's daughter Callisto who was changed
into a bear.

ⁱ Town in Crete.

^j Cydonia, town in Crete.

^k Schol. Nicand. Alex. 7 Ὀμφαλὸς γὰρ τόπος ἐν Κρήτῃ, ὡς καὶ
Καλλίμαχος· πέσε . . . Κύδωνες. Diodor. v. 70 tells the story
(he says Zeus was carried by the Curetes) and gives the
name of the place as Omphalos and of the plain around as
Omphaleion. ^l Corybantes.

41

CALLIMACHUS

Δικταῖαι Μελίαι, σὲ δ' ἐκόμισεν Ἀδρήστεια
λίκνῳ[1] ἐνὶ χρυσέῳ, σὺ δ' ἐθήσαο πίονα μαζὸν
αἰγὸς Ἀμαλθείης, ἐπὶ δὲ γλυκὺ κηρίον ἔβρως.
γέντο γὰρ ἐξαπιναῖα Πανακρίδος ἔργα μελίσσης
Ἰδαίοις ἐν ὄρεσσι, τά τε κλείουσι Πάνακρα.   50
οὖλα δὲ Κούρητές σε περὶ πρύλιν ὠρχήσαντο
τεύχεα πεπλήγοντες,[2] ἵνα Κρόνος οὔασιν ἠχὴν
ἀσπίδος εἰσαΐοι καὶ μή σεο κουρίζοντος.

καλὰ μὲν ἠέξευ, καλὰ δ' ἔτραφες, οὐράνιε Ζεῦ,
ὀξὺ δ' ἀνήβησας, ταχινοὶ δέ τοι ἦλθον ἴουλοι.   55
ἀλλ' ἔτι παιδνὸς ἐὼν ἐφράσσαο πάντα τέλεια·
τῷ τοι καὶ γνωτοὶ προτερηγενέες περ ἐόντες
οὐρανὸν οὐκ ἐμέγηραν ἔχειν ἐπιδαίσιον οἶκον.
δηναιοὶ δ' οὐ πάμπαν ἀληθέες ἦσαν ἀοιδοί·
φάντο πάλον Κρονίδῃσι διάτριχα δώματα νεῖμαι·   60
τίς δέ κ' ἐπ' Οὐλύμπῳ τε καὶ Ἄιδι κλῆρον ἐρύσσαι,
ὃς μάλα μὴ νενίηλος; ἐπ' ἰσαίῃ γὰρ ἔοικε
πήλασθαι· τὰ δὲ τόσσον ὅσον διὰ πλεῖστον ἔχουσι.
ψευδοίμην ἀΐοντος ἅ κεν πεπίθοιεν ἀκουήν.
οὔ σε θεῶν ἐσσῆνα πάλοι θέσαν, ἔργα δὲ χειρῶν,   65

---

[1] λείκνῳ MSS.   v.l. πεπληγότες.

---

[a] The ash-tree nymphs, cf. Hesiod, Th. 187.
[b] Cf. Apoll. Rh. iii. 132 ff. Διὸς περικαλλὲς ἄθυρμα | κεῖνο, τὸ οἱ ποίησε φίλη τροφὸς Ἀδρήστεια | ἄντρῳ ἐν Ἰδαίῳ ἔτι νήπια κουρίζοντι | σφαῖραν εὐτρόχαλον; i.q. Nemesis, sister of the Curetes (schol.).
[c] The nymph or she-goat who suckled Zeus; Diodor. v. 70, Apollod. i. 5, schol. Arat. 161, Ovid, Fast. v. 115 ff.
[d] Mountains in Crete (Steph. Byz. s.v. Πάνακρα). Zeus rewarded the bees by making them of a golden bronze colour and rendering them insensible to the rigours of the mountain climate (Diodor. v. 70).
[e] Apollodor. i. 4, "The Curetes in full armour, guarding

42

the Dictaean Meliae,[a] and Adrasteia[b] laid thee to rest in a cradle of gold, and thou didst suck the rich teat of the she-goat Amaltheia,[c] and thereto eat the sweet honey-comb. For suddenly on the hills of Ida, which men call Panacra,[d] appeared the works of the Panacrian bee. And lustily round thee danced the Curetes[e] a war-dance,[f] beating their armour, that Cronus might hear with his ears the din of the shield, but not thine infant noise.

Fairly didst thou wax, O heavenly Zeus, and fairly wert thou nurtured, and swiftly thou didst grow to manhood, and speedily came the down upon thy cheek. But, while yet a child, thou didst devise all the deeds of perfect stature. Wherefore thy kindred, though an earlier generation, grudged not that thou shouldst have heaven for thine appointed habitation.[g] The ancient poets spake not altogether truly. For they said that the lot assigned to the sons of Cronus their three several abodes.[h] But who would draw lots for Olympus and for Hades—save a very fool? for equal chances should one cast lots; but these are the wide world apart. When I speak fiction, be it such fiction as persuades the listener's ear! Thou wert made sovereign of the gods not by casting of lots but by the deeds of thy

the infant in the cave, beat their shields with their spears that Cronus might not hear the child's voice."

[f] πρύλις, the Cyprian name for the πυρρίχη (Aristotle fr. 476, schol. Pind. *P.* ii. 127) or dance in armour (Pollux iv. 96 and 99); see *Classical Qu.* xxxii. p. 131.

[g] This has been supposed to refer to the fact that Ptolemy Philadelphus was the youngest of the sons of Ptolemy Soter. See Introduction.

[h] Homer, *Il.* xv. 187 ff.; *cf.* Apollodor. i. 7, Pind. *O.* vii. 54 ff.

CALLIMACHUS

σή τε βίη τό τε κάρτος, ὃ καὶ πέλας εἶσαο δίφρου.
θήκαο δ' οἰωνῶν μέγ' ὑπείροχον ἀγγελιώτην
σῶν τεράων· ἅ τ' ἐμοῖσι φίλοις ἐνδέξια φαίνοις.
εἵλεο δ' αἰζηῶν ὅ τι φέρτατον· οὐ σύ γε νηῶν
ἐμπεράμους, οὐκ ἄνδρα σακέσπαλον, οὐ μὲν ἀοιδόν· 70
ἀλλὰ τὰ μὲν μακάρεσσιν ὀλίζοσιν αὖθι παρῆκας
ἄλλα μέλειν ἑτέροισι, σὺ δ' ἐξέλεο πτολιάρχους
αὐτούς, ὧν ὑπὸ χεῖρα γεωμόρος, ὧν ἴδρις αἰχμῆς,
ὧν ἐρέτης, ὧν πάντα· τί δ' οὐ κρατέοντος ὑπ' ἰσχύν;
αὐτίκα χαλκῆας μὲν ὑδείομεν Ἡφαίστοιο, 75
τευχηστὰς δ' Ἄρηος, ἐπακτῆρας δὲ Χιτώνης
Ἀρτέμιδος, Φοίβου δὲ λύρης εὖ εἰδότας οἴμους·
ἐκ δὲ Διὸς βασιλῆες, ἐπεὶ Διὸς οὐδὲν ἀνάκτων
θειότερον· τῷ καί σφε[1] τεὴν ἐκρίναο λάξιν.
δῶκας δὲ πτολίεθρα φυλασσέμεν, ἵζεο δ' αὐτὸς 80
ἄκρησ' ἐν πολίεσσιν, ἐπόψιος οἵ τε δίκῃσι
λαὸν ὑπὸ σκολιῇσ' οἵ τ' ἔμπαλιν ἰθύνουσιν·
ἐν δὲ ῥυηφενίην ἔβαλές σφισιν, ἐν δ' ἅλις ὄλβον·
πᾶσι μέν, οὐ μάλα δ' ἶσον. ἔοικε δὲ τεκμήρασθαι
ἡμετέρῳ μεδέοντι· περιπρὸ γὰρ εὐρὺ βέβηκεν. 85
ἑσπέριος κεῖνός γε τελεῖ τά κεν ἦρι νοήσῃ·
ἑσπέριος τὰ μέγιστα, τὰ μείονα δ', εὖτε νοήσῃ.
οἱ δὲ τὰ μὲν πλειῶνι, τὰ δ' οὐχ ἑνί, τῶν δ' ἀπὸ
   πάμπαν
αὐτὸς ἄνην ἐκόλουσας, ἐνέκλασσας δὲ μενοινήν.
   χαῖρε μέγα, Κρονίδη πανυπέρτατε, δῶτορ ἑάων, 90

[1] σφε Bentley ; σφι.

---

[a] Bia and Cratos appear as personifications of the might and majesty of Zeus in Aeschylus, *P. V.*, Hesiod, *Th.* 385, etc.

[b] The eagle.

[c] Artemis Chitone (Chitonea, Athen. 629 e), so called from the tunic (chiton) in which as huntress she was represented ; not, as the schol. says, from the Attic deme Chitone.

hands, thy might and that strength [a] which thou hast
set beside thy throne. And the most excellent of
birds [b] didst thou make the messenger of thy signs;
favourable to my friends be the signs thou showest!
And thou didst choose that which is most excellent
among men—not thou the skilled in ships, nor the
wielder of the shield, nor the minstrel: these didst
thou straightway renounce to lesser gods, other cares
to others. But thou didst choose the rulers of cities
themselves, beneath whose hand is the lord of the
soil, the skilled in spearmanship, the oarsman, yea,
all things that are: what is there that is not under
the ruler's sway? Thus, smiths, we say, belong to
Hephaestus; to Ares, warriors; to Artemis of the
Tunic,[c] huntsmen; to Phoebus they that know well
the strains of the lyre. But from Zeus come kings; for
nothing is diviner than the kings of Zeus. Wherefore
thou didst choose them for thine own lot, and gavest
them cities to guard. And thou didst seat thyself
in the high places of the cities, watching who rule
their people with crooked judgements, and who rule
otherwise. And thou hast bestowed upon them
wealth and prosperity abundantly; unto all, but not
in equal measure. One may well judge by our
Ruler,[d] for he hath clean outstripped all others. At
evening he accomplisheth that whereon he thinketh
in the morning; yea, at evening the greatest things,
but the lesser soon as he thinketh on them. But the
others accomplish some things in a year, and some
things not in one; of others, again, thou thyself
dost utterly frustrate the accomplishing and thwartest
their desire.

Hail! greatly hail! most high Son of Cronus,

[d] Ptolemy II. Philadelphus, 285–247 B.C.

45

CALLIMACHUS

δῶτορ ἀπημονίης. τεὰ δ' ἔργματα τίς κεν ἀείδοι;
οὐ γένετ', οὐκ ἔσται, τίς [1] κεν [2] Διὸς ἔργματ' ἀεῖσαι. [3]
χαῖρε πάτερ, χαῖρ' αὖθι· δίδου δ' ἀρετήν τ' ἄφενός
   τε.
οὔτ' ἀρετῆς ἄτερ ὄλβος ἐπίσταται ἄνδρας ἀέξειν
οὔτ' ἀρετὴ ἀφένοιο· δίδου δ' ἀρετήν τε καὶ ὄλβον. 95

[1] ἔσται· τίς vulg.   [2] κεν MSS.; καὶ Wilamow.
[3] ἀεῖσαι Blomf. ; ἀείσοι or ἀείσει MSS.

HYMN I

giver of good things, giver of safety. Thy works who could sing? There hath not been, there shall not be, who shall sing the works of Zeus. Hail! Father, hail again! and grant us goodness and prosperity. Without goodness wealth cannot bless men, nor goodness without prosperity. Give us goodness and weal.

HYMN I

II.—ΕΙΣ ΑΠΟΛΛΩΝΑ

Οἷον ὁ τὠπόλλωνος ἐσείσατο δάφνινος ὅρπηξ,
οἷα δ' ὅλον τὸ μέλαθρον· ἑκάς, ἑκὰς ὅστις ἀλιτρός.
καὶ δή που τὰ θύρετρα καλῷ ποδὶ Φοῖβος ἀράσσει·
οὐχ ὁράᾳς; ἐπένευσεν ὁ Δήλιος ἡδύ τι φοῖνιξ
ἐξαπίνης, ὁ δὲ κύκνος ἐν ἠέρι καλὸν ἀείδει.   5
αὐτοὶ νῦν κατοχῆες ἀνακλίνεσθε πυλάων,
αὐταὶ δὲ κληῖδες· ὁ γὰρ θεὸς οὐκέτι μακρήν·
οἱ δὲ νέοι μολπήν τε καὶ ἐς χορὸν ἐντύνεσθε.

  ὡπόλλων οὐ παντὶ φαείνεται, ἀλλ' ὅ τις ἐσθλός·
ὅς μιν ἴδῃ, μέγας οὗτος, ὃς οὐκ ἴδε, λιτὸς ἐκεῖνος. 10
ὀψόμεθ', ὦ Ἑκάεργε, καὶ ἐσσόμεθ' οὔποτε λιτοί.
μήτε σιωπηλὴν κίθαριν μήτ' ἄψοφον ἴχνος
τοῦ Φοίβου τοὺς παῖδας ἔχειν ἐπιδημήσαντος,
εἰ τελέειν μέλλουσι γάμον πολιήν τε κερεῖσθαι,
ἑστήξειν δὲ τὸ τεῖχος ἐπ' ἀρχαίοισι θεμέθλοις.   15

---

  [a] The palm-tree by which Leto supported herself when
she bare Apollo. Cf. *H. Delos* 210, Hom. *H. Apoll.* 117,
Od. vi. 162 f., Theogn. 5 f. The laurel and the palm
are coupled in Euripides, *Hecuba*, 458 ff.

  [b] For the association of the swan with Apollo *cf. Hymn to
Delos* 249 ; Plato, *Phaedo*, 85 ; Manilius v. 381 "ipse Deum
cygnus condit."

  [c] The schol. on v. 12 remarks that Callimachus emphasizes
the presence of the God because "it is said in the case of
prophetic gods that the deities are sometimes present

48

II.—TO APOLLO

How the laurel branch of Apollo trembles! how trembles all the shrine! Away, away, he that is sinful! Now surely Phoebus knocketh at the door with his beautiful foot. See'st thou not? the Delian palm [a] nods pleasantly of a sudden and the swan [b] in the air sings sweetly. Of yourselves now ye bolts be pushed back, pushed back of yourselves, ye bars! The god is no longer far away. And ye, young men, prepare ye for song and for the dance.

Not unto everyone doth Apollo appear, but unto him that is good. Whoso hath seen Apollo, he is great; whoso hath not seen him, he is of low estate. We shall see thee, O Archer, and we shall never be lowly. Let not the youths keep silent lyre or noiseless step, when Apollo visits [c] his shrine, if they think to accomplish marriage and to cut the locks of age, [d] and if the wall is to stand upon its old founda-

($ἐπιδημεῖν$), sometimes absent ($ἀποδημεῖν$), and when they are present the oracles are true, when absent false." Cf. Pind. P. iv. 5 οὐκ ἀποδάμου 'Απόλλωνος τυχόντος. The Delphians celebrated the seventh day of the month Bysios—the birthday of Apollo—when he was supposed to revisit his temple, and the seventh of the holy month (Attic Anthesterion) was celebrated by the Delians when Apollo was supposed to return to Delos from the land of the Hyperboreans. (W. Schmidt, *Geburtstag im Altertum*, p. 86.) Cf. Verg. *A.* iii. 91.

[a] *i.e.* if they are to live to old age.

49

ἠγασάμην τοὺς παῖδας, ἐπεὶ χέλυς οὐκέτ᾽ ἀεργός.

εὐφημεῖτ᾽ ἀίοντες ἐπ᾽ Ἀπόλλωνος ἀοιδῇ.

εὐφημεῖ καὶ πόντος, ὅτε κλείουσιν ἀοιδοὶ

ἢ κίθαριν ἢ τόξα, Λυκωρέος ἔντεα Φοίβου.

οὐδὲ Θέτις Ἀχιλῆα κινύρεται αἴλινα μήτηρ,   20

ὁππόθ᾽ ἰὴ παιῆον ἰὴ παιῆον ἀκούσῃ.

καὶ μὲν ὁ δακρυόεις ἀναβάλλεται ἄλγεα πέτρος,

ὅστις ἐνὶ Φρυγίῃ διερὸς λίθος ἐστήρικται,

μάρμαρον ἀντὶ γυναικὸς οἰζυρόν τι χανούσης.

ἰὴ ἰὴ φθέγγεσθε· κακὸν μακάρεσσιν ἐρίζειν.   25

ὃς μάχεται μακάρεσσιν, ἐμῷ βασιλῆι μάχοιτο·

ὅστις ἐμῷ βασιλῆι, καὶ Ἀπόλλωνι μάχοιτο.

τὸν χορὸν ὡπόλλων, ὅ τι οἱ κατὰ θυμὸν ἀείδει,

τιμήσει· δύναται γάρ, ἐπεὶ Διὶ δεξιὸς ἧσται.

οὐδ᾽ ὁ χορὸς τὸν Φοῖβον ἐφ᾽ ἓν μόνον ἦμαρ ἀείσει,   30

ἔστι γὰρ εὔυμνος· τίς ἂν οὐ ῥέα Φοῖβον ἀείδοι;

χρύσεα τὠπόλλωνι τό τ᾽ ἐνδυτὸν ἥ τ᾽ ἐπιπορπὶς

ἥ τε λύρη τό τ᾽ ἄεμμα τὸ Λύκτιον ἥ τε φαρέτρη,

χρύσεα καὶ τὰ πέδιλα· πολύχρυσος γὰρ Ἀπόλλων.

καὶ δὲ πολυκτέανος· Πυθῶνί κε τεκμήραιο.   35

καὶ μὲν¹ ἀεὶ καλὸς καὶ ἀεὶ νέος· οὔποτε Φοίβου

---

¹ καὶ μὲν e; other mss. καὶ κεν.

ᵃ *i.e.* the lyre, originally made by Hermes from the shell of a tortoise. ἠγασάμην = Well done!

ᵇ Lycōreus, by-name of Apollo, from Lycoreia, town on Parnassus above Delphi : Strabo 418. 3 ὑπέρκειται δ᾽ αὐτῆς ἡ Λυκώρεια ἐφ᾽ οὗ τόπου πρότερον ἵδρυντο οἱ Δελφοὶ ὑπὲρ τοῦ ἱεροῦ. Legends of its foundation in Pausanias x. 6, 2-3. Φ. Λυκωρείοιο Apoll. Rh. iv. 1490.

ᶜ Though ἰή, not ἱή, is the usual form, it is perhaps better here to write the aspirated form to suit the suggested etymology from ἵει "shoot." See vv. 97-104 for the legend.

ᵈ Niobe, daughter of Tantalus, had, according to Hom. *Il.* xxiv. 602 ff., six sons and six daughters, who were slain by

tions. Well done the youths, for that the shell[a] is no longer idle.

Be hushed, ye that hear, at the song to Apollo; yea, hushed is even the sea when the minstrels celebrate the lyre or the bow, the weapons of Lycoreian Phoebus.[b] Neither doth Thetis his mother wail her dirge for Achilles, when she hears *Hië[c] Paeëon, Hië Paeëon*.

Yea, the tearful rock defers its pain, the wet stone that is set in Phrygia, a marble rock like a woman[d] open-mouthed in some sorrowful utterance. Say ye *Hië! Hië!* an ill thing it is to strive with the Blessed Ones. He who fights with the Blessed Ones would fight with my King[e]; he who fights with my King, would fight even with Apollo. Apollo will honour the choir, since it sings according to his heart; for Apollo hath power, for that he sitteth on the right hand of Zeus. Nor will the choir sing of Phoebus for one day only. He is a copious theme of song; who would not readily sing of Phoebus?

Golden is the tunic of Apollo and golden his mantle, his lyre and his Lyctian[f] bow and his quiver: golden too are his sandals; for rich in gold is Apollo, rich also in possessions: by Pytho mightst thou guess. And ever beautiful is he and ever

Apollo and Artemis respectively, because she boasted over their mother Leto, who had but two children. Niobe was turned into a stone, and this was identified with a rude rock figure on Mount Sipylos near Smyrna which is still to be seen. The water running down the face of the rock was supposed to be Niobe's tears—ἔνθα λίθος περ ἐοῦσα θεῶν ἐκ κήδεα πέσσει, Hom. *l.c.* 617, *cf.* "Phrygium silicem," Stat. *S.* v. 3. 87.

[e] Ptolemy III. Euergetes, according to the schol. But see Introduction.

[f] Lyctos, town in Crete.

θηλείησ᾽ οὐδ᾽ ὅσσον ἐπὶ χνόος ἦλθε παρειαῖς.
αἱ δὲ κόμαι θυόεντα πέδῳ λείβουσιν ἔλαια·
οὐ λίπος Ἀπόλλωνος ἀποστάζουσιν ἔθειραι,
ἀλλ᾽ αὐτὴν πανάκειαν· ἐν ἄστεϊ δ᾽ ᾧ κεν ἐκεῖναι   40
πρῶκες ἔραζε πέσωσιν ἀκήρια πάντ᾽ ἐγένοντο.

  τέχνῃ δ᾽ ἀμφιλαφὴς οὔ τις τόσον ὅσσον
   Ἀπόλλων·
κεῖνος ὀιστευτὴν ἔλαχ᾽ ἀνέρα, κεῖνος ἀοιδὸν
(Φοίβῳ γὰρ καὶ τόξον ἐπιτρέπεται καὶ ἀοιδή),
κείνου δὲ θριαὶ καὶ μάντιες· ἐκ δέ νυ Φοίβου   45
ἰητροὶ δεδάασιν ἀνάβλησιν θανάτοιο.

  Φοῖβον καὶ Νόμιον κικλήσκομεν ἐξέτι κείνου,
ἐξότ᾽ ἐπ᾽ Ἀμφρυσσῷ ζευγίτιδας ἔτρεφεν ἵππους
ἠιθέου ὑπ᾽ ἔρωτι κεκαυμένος Ἀδμήτοιο.
ῥεῖά κε βουβόσιον τελέθοι πλέον, οὐδέ κεν αἶγες   50
δεύοιντο βρεφέων ἐπιμηλάδες[1] ᾗσιν Ἀπόλλων
βοσκομένης᾽ ὀφθαλμὸν ἐπήγαγεν· οὐδ᾽ ἀγάλακτες
οἴιες οὐδ᾽ ἄκυθοι, πᾶσαι δέ κεν εἶεν ὕπαρνοι,
ἡ δέ κε μουνοτόκος διδυμητόκος αἶψα γένοιτο.

  Φοίβῳ δ᾽ ἑσπόμενοι πόλιας διεμετρήσαντο   55
ἄνθρωποι· Φοῖβος γὰρ ἀεὶ πολίεσσι φιληδεῖ
κτιζομένησ᾽, αὐτὸς δὲ θεμείλια Φοῖβος ὑφαίνει.
τετραέτης τὰ πρῶτα θεμείλια Φοῖβος ἔπηξε
καλῇ ἐν Ὀρτυγίῃ περιηγέος ἐγγύθι λίμνης.

  Ἄρτεμις ἀγρώσσουσα καρήατα συνεχὲς αἰγῶν   60
Κυνθιάδων φορέεσκεν, ὁ δ᾽ ἔπλεκε βωμὸν Ἀπόλλων.

---

[1] μενεμηλάδες *v.l.* in schol. ; ἐνιμηλάδες Schneider, *cf.*
Hesych. ἐμμηλάδας αἶγας.

---

 [a] As a personification Panaceia appears frequently as the
daughter of Asclepius. In the Hippocratean oath she is
named after Apollo, Asclepius, and Hygieia. Such "all-
healing" virtue was in early times ascribed to various
plants (Πάνακες Χειρώνειον, Ἀσκληπίειον, etc.).

young: never on the girl cheeks of Apollo hath
come so much as the down of manhood. His locks
distil fragrant oils upon the ground; not oil of fat
do the locks of Apollo distil but very Healing of
All.[a] And in whatsoever city those dews fall upon
the ground, in that city all things are free from harm.

None is so abundant in skill as Apollo. To him
belongs the archer, to him the minstrel; for unto
Apollo is given in keeping alike archery and song.
His are the lots of the diviner and his the seers; and
from Phoebus do leeches know the deferring of death.

Phoebus and Nomius[b] we call him, ever since the
time when by Amphrysus[c] he tended the yoke-
mares, fired with love of young Admetus.[d] Lightly
would the herd of cattle wax larger, nor would the
she-goats of the flock lack young, whereon as they feed
Apollo casts his eye; nor without milk would the ewes
be nor barren, but all would have lambs at foot; and
she that bare one would soon be the mother of twins.

And Phoebus it is that men follow when they map
out cities.[e] For Phoebus evermore delights in the
founding of cities, and Phoebus himself doth weave
their foundations. Four years of age was Phoebus
when he framed his first foundations in fair Ortygia[f]
near the round lake.[g]

Artemis hunted and brought continually the
heads of Cynthian goats and Phoebus plaited an

[b] Cf. Pind. ix. 65.
[c] River in Thessaly where Apollo tended the flocks of
Admetus. Cf. Verg. G. iii. 2 "pastor ab Amphryso."
[d] King of Pherae in Thessaly.
[e] Hence Apollo's titles Ἀρχηγέτης, Κτίστης, etc.
[f] Delos.
[g] A lake in Delos. Cf. H. iv. 261, Theognis vii, Apollo
is born ἐπὶ τροχοειδέι λίμνῃ, and Eur. I.T. 1104.

CALLIMACHUS

δείματο μὲν κεράεσσιν ἐδέθλια, πῆξε δὲ βωμὸν
ἐκ κεράων, κεραοὺς δὲ πέριξ ὑπεβάλλετο τοίχους.
ὧδ' ἔμαθεν τὰ πρῶτα θεμείλια Φοῖβος ἐγείρειν.
Φοῖβος καὶ βαθύγειον ἐμὴν πόλιν ἔφρασε Βάττῳ   65
καὶ Λιβύην ἐσιόντι κόραξ ἡγήσατο λαῷ
δεξιὸς οἰκιστῆρι¹ καὶ ὤμοσε τείχεα δώσειν
ἡμετέροις βασιλεῦσιν· ἀεὶ δ' εὔορκος Ἀπόλλων.
ὤπολλον, πολλοί σε Βοηδρόμιον καλέουσι,
πολλοὶ δὲ Κλάριον, πάντη δέ τοι οὔνομα πουλύ·   70
αὐτὰρ ἐγὼ Καρνεῖον· ἐμοὶ πατρώιον οὕτω.
Σπάρτη τοι, Καρνεῖε, τὸ δὴ πρώτιστον ἔδεθλον,
δεύτερον αὖ Θήρη, τρίτατόν γε μὲν ἄστυ Κυρήνης.
ἐκ μέν σε Σπάρτης ἕκτον γένος Οἰδιπόδαο
ἤγαγε Θηραίην ἐς ἀπόκτισιν· ἐκ δέ σε Θήρης   75
οὖλος Ἀριστοτέλης Ἀσβυστίδι πάρθετο γαίῃ,
δεῖμε δέ τοι μάλα καλὸν ἀνάκτορον, ἐν δὲ πόληι
θῆκε τελεσφορίην ἐπετήσιον, ᾗ ἐνὶ πολλοὶ
ὑστάτιον πίπτουσιν ἐπ' ἰσχίον, ὦ ἄνα, ταῦροι.
ἰὴ ἰὴ Καρνεῖε πολύλλιτε, σεῖο δὲ βωμοὶ   80
ἄνθεα μὲν φορέουσιν ἐν εἴαρι τόσσα περ Ὧραι

¹ οἰκιστῆρι Bentley ; οἰκιστήρ.

ᵃ The κερατῶν (Plut. *Thes.* 21, Dittenb. *Syll.*² No. 588,
172), βωμὸς κεράτινος (Plut. *Sollert. animal.* 35), made
entirely of horns, was one of the Seven Wonders of the
World. Cf. Anon. *De incredib.* 2 ; Ovid, *Her.* 21. 99.

ᵇ Battus (Aristoteles), founder of Cyrene, birthplace of
Callimachus.

ᶜ The raven was one of the birds sacred to Apollo.

ᵈ The Battiadae. See Introduction.

ᵉ Boëdromius : *Et. Mag. s.v.* Βοηδρομιών· ὅτι πολέμου
συστάντος Ἀθηναίοις καὶ Ἐλευσινίοις συμμαχήσαντος Ἴωνος . .
ἐνίκησαν Ἀθηναῖοι. ἀπὸ οὖν τῆς τοῦ στρατεύματος βοῆς τῆς ἐπὶ τὸ
ἄστυ δραμούσης ὅ τε Ἀπόλλων Βοηδρόμιος ἐκλήθη καὶ ἡ θυσία καὶ ὁ
μήν, καὶ τὰ Βοηδρόμια ἐτελεῖτο ἑορτή. According to schol. ἔχρησεν
αὐτοῖς ὁ θεὸς μετὰ βοῆς ἐπιθέσθαι τοῖς πολεμίοις. Doubtless the

54

altar.[a] With horns builded he the foundations, and
of horns framed he the altar, and of horns were the
walls he built around. Thus did Phoebus learn to
raise his first foundations. Phoebus, too, it was who
told Battus[b] of my own city of fertile soil, and in
guise of a raven[c]—auspicious to our founder—led his
people as they entered Libya and sware that he
would vouchsafe a walled city to our kings.[d] And
the oath of Apollo is ever sure. O Apollo! many
there be that call thee Boëdromius,[e] and many there
be that call thee Clarius[f]: everywhere is thy name
on the lips of many. But I call thee Carneius[g]; for
such is the manner of my fathers. Sparta, O
Carneius! was thy first foundation; and next
Thera; but third the city of Cyrene. From Sparta
the sixth[h] generation of the sons of Oedipus brought
thee to their colony of Thera; and from Thera lusty
Aristoteles[i] set thee by the Asbystian[j] land, and
builded thee a shrine exceeding beautiful, and in the
city established a yearly festival wherein many a
bull, O Lord, falls on his haunches for the last time.
Hië, Hië, Carneius! Lord of many prayers,—thine
altars wear flowers in spring, even all the pied
flowers which the Hours lead forth when Zephyrus

Athenians associated the name with help given them by
some superhuman champions (βοηδρόμοι = βοαθόοι, Pind. *N.*
vii. 31). Mommsen, *Feste d. Stadt Athen*, p. 171.

    [f] Clarius, by-name of Apollo, from Claros near Colophon.
    [g] Carneius, by-name of Apollo in many Dorian states, as
Sparta, Thera, Cyrene.
    [h] The genealogy is Oedipus—Polyneices—Thersander—
Tisamenus—Autesion—Theras, who led the colony to Thera
and who is sixth descendant of Oedipus according to the
Greek way of reckoning inclusively. *Cf.* Herod. iv. 147.
    [i] Battus.
    [j] The Asbystae were a people in the Cyrenaica.

CALLIMACHUS

ποικίλ' ἀγινεῦσι ζεφύρου πνείοντος ἐέρσην,
χείματι δὲ κρόκον ἡδύν· ἀεὶ δέ τοι ἀέναον πῦρ,
οὐδέ ποτε χθιζὸν περιβόσκεται ἄνθρακα τέφρη.
ἦ ῥ' ἐχάρη μέγα Φοῖβος, ὅτε ζωστῆρες Ἐνυοῦς   85
ἀνέρες ὠρχήσαντο μετὰ ξανθῇσι Λιβύσσαις,
τέθμιαι εὖτέ σφιν Καρνειάδες ἤλυθον ὧραι.
οἱ δ' οὔπω πηγῇσι[1] Κύρης ἐδύναντο πελάσσαι
Δωριέες, πυκινὴν δὲ νάπαις Ἄζιλιν ἔναιον.
τοὺς μὲν ἄναξ ἴδεν αὐτός, ἑῇ δ' ἐπεδείξατο νύμφῃ   90
στὰς ἐπὶ Μυρτούσσης κερατώδεος, ἧχι λέοντα
Ὑψηὶς κατέπεφνε βοῶν σίνιν Εὐρυπύλοιο.
οὐ κείνου χορὸν εἶδε[2] θεώτερον ἄλλον Ἀπόλλων,
οὐδὲ πόλει τόσ' ἔνειμεν ὀφέλσιμα, τόσσα Κυρήνῃ,
μνωόμενος προτέρης ἁρπακτύος. οὐδὲ μὲν αὐτοὶ   95
Βαττιάδαι Φοίβοιο πλέον θεὸν ἄλλον ἔτεισαν.

ἰὴ ἰὴ παιῆον ἀκούομεν, οὕνεκα τοῦτο
Δελφός τοι πρώτιστον ἐφύμνιον εὕρετο λαός,
ἧμος ἑκηβολίην χρυσέων ἐπεδείκνυσο τόξων.
Πυθώ τοι κατιόντι συνήντετο δαιμόνιος θήρ,   10
αἰνὸς ὄφις. τὸν μὲν σὺ κατήναρες ἄλλον ἐπ' ἄλλῳ
βάλλων ὠκὺν ὀιστόν, ἐπηύτησε δὲ λαός,
"ἰὴ ἰὴ παιῆον, ἵει βέλος." εὐθύ σε μήτηρ
γείνατ' ἀοσσητῆρα, τὸ δ' ἐξέτι κεῖθεν ἀείδῃ.
ὁ Φθόνος Ἀπόλλωνος ἐπ' οὔατα λάθριος εἶπεν   10

---

[1] πηγαῖσι schol. Pind. *P.* iv. 523 ; πηγῆς.
[2] ἔνειμε A ; ἔδειμε EF.

---

[a] Cyre: stream at Cyrene which after running some distance under ground reappears at the Temple of Apollo as the fountain of Apollo (Herod. iv. 158, Pind. *P.* iv. 294).

[b] Azilis or Aziris where the Theraeans with Battus dwelt for six years before they went to Cyrene (Herod. iv. 157 ff.).

[c] Cyrene.

[d] *i.e.* "Myrtle-hill" in Cyrene. See Introduction, p. 26.

[e] Eurypylus: prehistoric king of Libya, who offered his

56

breathes dew, and in winter the sweet crocus.
Undying evermore is thy fire, nor ever doth the
ash feed about the coals of yester-even. Greatly,
indeed, did Phoebus rejoice as the belted warriors of
Enyo danced with the yellow-haired Libyan women,
when the appointed season of the Carnean feast came
round. But not yet could the Dorians approach
the fountains of Cyre,[a] but dwelt in Azilis[b] thick with
wooded dells. These did the Lord himself behold and
showed them to his bride[c] as he stood on horned
Myrtussa[d] where the daughter of Hypseus slew the
lion that harried the kine of Eurypylus.[e] No other
dance more divine hath Apollo beheld, nor to any city
hath he given so many blessings as he hath given to
Cyrene, remembering his rape of old. Nor, again, is
there any other god whom the sons of Battus have
honoured above Phoebus.

Hië, Hië, Paeëon, we hear—since this refrain did
the Delphian folk first invent, what time thou didst
display the archery of thy golden bow. As thou
wert going down to Pytho, there met thee a beast
unearthly, a dread snake.[f] And him thou didst slay,
shooting swift arrows one upon the other; and the
folk cried "Hië, Hië, Paeëon, shoot an arrow!" A
helper[g] from the first thy mother bare thee, and ever
since that is thy praise.

Spake Envy[h] privily in the ear of Apollo: "I

kingdom to anyone who should slay the lion which was
ravaging his land. Cyrene slew the lion and so won the
kingdom (Acesandros of Cyrene in schol. Apoll. Rh. ii. 498).
   [f] In Strabo 422 Python is a man, surnamed Draco.
Pytho was popularly derived from the fact that the slain
snake rotted (πύθω) there.
   [g] Callimachus seems to adopt the old derivation of
ἀοσσητήρ from ὄσσα (voice). Thus ἀοσσητήρ=βοηθόος. For
ἐξέτι cf. H. iv. 275.   [h] See Introduction, p. 22.

CALLIMACHUS

"οὐκ ἄγαμαι τὸν ἀοιδὸν ὃς οὐδ᾽ ὅσα πόντος ἀείδει."
τὸν Φθόνον ὡπόλλων ποδί τ᾽ ἤλασεν ὧδέ τ᾽ ἔειπεν·
"'Ασσυρίου ποταμοῖο μέγας ῥόος, ἀλλὰ τὰ πολλὰ
λύματα γῆς καὶ πολλὸν ἐφ᾽ ὕδατι συρφετὸν ἕλκει.
Δηοῖ δ᾽ οὐκ ἀπὸ παντὸς ὕδωρ φορέουσι Μέλισσαι, 11
ἀλλ᾽ ἥτις καθαρή τε καὶ ἀχράαντος ἀνέρπει
πίδακος ἐξ ἱερῆς ὀλίγη λιβὰς ἄκρον ἄωτον."
  χαῖρε ἄναξ· ὁ δὲ Μῶμος, ἵν᾽ ὁ Φθόνος,[1] ἔνθα
νέοιτο.

[1] φθόνος I (Vat. 1379), L (Mosquensis), schol. Gregor.
Naz. *Catal. MSS. Clark.* p. 35 ; φθόρος.

HYMN II

admire not the poet who singeth not things for
number as the sea." [a]   Apollo spurned Envy with his
foot and spake thus : " Great is the stream of the
Assyrian river,[b] but much filth of earth and much
refuse it carries on its waters. And not of every
water do the Melissae carry to Deo,[c] but of the
trickling stream that springs from a holy fountain,
pure and undefiled, the very crown of waters."

Hail, O Lord, but Blame—let him go where Envy
dwells !

[a] *Cf.* Apoll. Rhod. iii. 932.　　　　　[b] Euphrates.
[c] Deo = Demeter, whose priestesses were called Melissae
(Bees) : Porphyr. *De antro nympharum* 18 καὶ τὰς Δήμητρος
ἱερείας ὡς τῆς χθονίας θεᾶς μύστιδας Μελίσσας οἱ παλαιοὶ ἐκάλουν
αὐτήν τε τὴν Κόρην Μελιτώδη (Theocr. xv. 94).

III.—ΕΙΣ ΑΡΤΕΜΙΝ

Ἄρτεμιν (οὐ γὰρ ἐλαφρὸν ἀειδόντεσσι λαθέσθαι)
ὑμνέομεν, τῇ τόξα λαγωβολίαι τε μέλονται
καὶ χορὸς ἀμφιλαφὴς καὶ ἐν οὔρεσιν ἑψιάασθαι,
ἀρχμενοι,[1] ὡς ὅτε πατρὸς ἐφεζομένη γονάτεσσι
παῖς ἔτι κουρίζουσα τάδε προσέειπε γονῆα   5
" δός μοι παρθενίην αἰώνιον, ἄππα, φυλάσσειν,
καὶ πολυωνυμίην, ἵνα μή μοι Φοῖβος ἐρίζῃ.
δὸς δ' ἰοὺς καὶ τόξα—ἔα, πάτερ, οὔ σε φαρέτρην
οὐδ' αἰτέω μέγα τόξον· ἐμοὶ Κύκλωπες ὀιστοὺς
αὐτίκα τεχνήσονται, ἐμοὶ δ' εὐκαμπὲς ἄεμμα·   10
ἀλλὰ φαεσφορίην τε καὶ ἐς γόνυ μέχρι χιτῶνα
ζώννυσθαι λεγνωτόν, ἵν' ἄγρια θηρία καίνω.
δὸς δέ μοι ἑξήκοντα χορίτιδας Ὠκεανίνας,
πάσας εἰνέτεας, πάσας ἔτι παῖδας ἀμίτρους·
δὸς δέ μοι ἀμφιπόλους Ἀμνισίδας εἴκοσι νύμφας,   15
αἵ τέ μοι ἐνδρομίδας τε καὶ ὁππότε μηκέτι
      λύγκας
μήτ' ἐλάφους βάλλοιμι, θοοὺς κύνας εὖ κομέοιεν,
δὸς δέ μοι οὔρεα πάντα· πόλιν δέ μοι ἥντινα νεῖμον
ἥντινα λῇς· σπαρνὸν γὰρ ὅτ' Ἄρτεμις ἄστυ κάτ-
      εισιν·

---

[1] ἀρχμενοι Blomfield; cf. fr. 9[b] and now *Aitia* iii. 1. 56,
Herodian i. p. 471, ii. p. 190 and p. 252 Lentz ; ἀρχόμενοι
or ἀρχόμενος mss.

III.—TO ARTEMIS

ARTEMIS we hymn—no light thing is it for singers
to forget her—whose study is the bow and the
shooting of hares and the spacious dance and sport
upon the mountains; beginning with the time when
sitting on her father's knees—still a little maid—
she spake these words to her sire: "Give me to
keep my maidenhood, Father, for ever: and give
me to be of many names, that Phoebus may not vie
with me. And give me arrows and a bow—stay,
Father, I ask thee not for quiver or for mighty
bow: for me the Cyclopes will straightway fashion
arrows and fashion for me a well-bent bow. But
give me to be the Bringer of Light [a] and give me to
gird me in a tunic [b] with embroidered border reaching
to the knee, that I may slay wild beasts. And
give me sixty daughters of Oceanus for my choir—
all nine years old, all maidens yet ungirdled; and
give me for handmaidens twenty nymphs of Amnisus [c]
who shall tend well my buskins, and, when I shoot
no more at lynx or stag, shall tend my swift hounds.
And give to me all mountains; and for city, assign
me any, even whatsoever thou wilt: for seldom is
it that Artemis goes down to the town. On the

[a] φωσφόρος is one of the titles of Artemis; cf. v. 204,
Eur. *Iph. in T.* 21.

[b] See note on v. 225.

[c] Amnisus, river in Crete. *Cf.* Apoll. Rhod. iii. 877 ff.

61

οὔρεσιν οἰκήσω, πόλεσιν δ' ἐπιμείξομαι ἀνδρῶν   20
μοῦνον ὅτ' ὀξείῃσιν ὑπ' ὠδίνεσσι γυναῖκες
τειρόμεναι καλέουσι βοηθόον, ᾗσί με Μοῖραι
γεινομένην τὸ πρῶτον ἐπεκλήρωσαν ἀρήγειν,
ὅττι με καὶ τίκτουσα καὶ οὐκ ἤλγησε φέρουσα
μήτηρ, ἀλλ' ἀμογητὶ φίλων ἀπεθήκατο γυίων."   25
ὣς ἡ παῖς εἰποῦσα γενειάδος ἤθελε πατρὸς
ἅψασθαι, πολλὰς δὲ μάτην ἐτανύσσατο χεῖρας,
μέχρις ἵνα ψαύσειε. πατὴρ δ' ἐπένευσε γελάσσας,
φῆ δὲ καταρρέζων "ὅτε μοι τοιαῦτα θέαιναι
τίκτοιεν, τυτθόν κεν ἐγὼ ζηλήμονος Ἥρης   30
χωομένης ἀλέγοιμι. φέρευ, τέκος, ὅσσ' ἐθελημὸς
αἰτίζεις, καὶ δ' ἄλλα πατὴρ ἔτι μείζονα δώσει.
τρὶς δέκα τοι πτολίεθρα καὶ οὐχ ἕνα πύργον ὀπάσσω,
τρὶς δέκα τοι πτολίεθρα, τὰ μὴ θεὸν ἄλλον ἀέξειν
εἴσεται, ἀλλὰ μόνην σὲ καὶ Ἀρτέμιδος καλέεσθαι·   35
πολλὰς δὲ ξυνῇ πόλιας διαμετρήσασθαι
μεσσόγεως νήσους τε· καὶ ἐν πάσῃσιν ἔσονται
Ἀρτέμιδος βωμοί τε καὶ ἄλσεα. καὶ μὲν ἀγυιαῖς
ἔσῃ καὶ λιμένεσσιν ἐπίσκοπος." ὣς ὁ μὲν εἰπὼν
μῦθον ἐπεκρήηνε καρήατι. βαῖνε δὲ κούρη   40
λευκὸν ἐπὶ Κρηταῖον ὄρος κεκομημένον ὕλῃ·
ἔνθεν ἐπ' Ὠκεανόν· πολέας δ' ἐπελέξατο νύμφας,
πάσας εἰνέτεας, πάσας ἔτι παῖδας ἀμίτρους.
χαῖρε δὲ Καίρατος ποταμὸς μέγα, χαῖρε δὲ Τηθύς,
οὕνεκα θυγατέρας Λητωΐδι πέμπον[1] ἀμορβούς.   45

---

[1] πέμπον schol. Nicand. *Th.* 349 ; πέμπειν or πέμπειν.

[a] Artemis in one aspect is Eileithyia=Lucina. She is said to have been born before Apollo and to have assisted at his birth. Hence her birthday was put on the 6th of Thargelion (Diog. L. ii. 44), while Apollo was born on the 7th. (W. Schmidt, *Geburtstag im Altertum*, p. 94.)

[b] Hence her title ἐνοδία, *A. P.* vi. 199.

mountains will I dwell and the cities of men I will
visit only when women vexed by the sharp pangs
of childbirth call me to their aid [a]—even in the
hour when I was born the Fates ordained that I
should be their helper, forasmuch as my mother
suffered no pain either when she gave me birth or
when she carried me in her womb, but without
travail put me from her body." So spake the child
and would have touched her father's beard, but
many a hand did she reach forth in vain, that
she might touch it. And her father smiled and
bowed assent. And as he caressed her, he said:
"When goddesses bear me children like this, little
need I heed the wrath of jealous Hera. Take,
child, all that thou askest, heartily. Yea, and other
things therewith yet greater will thy father give
thee. Three times ten cities and towers more than
one will I vouchsafe thee—three times ten cities
that shall not know to glorify any other god but
to glorify thee only and be called of Artemis;
and many cities will I give thee to share with
others, both inland cities and islands; and in them
all shall be altars and groves of Artemis. And thou
shalt be Watcher over Streets [b] and Harbours.[c]"
So he spake and bent his head to confirm his words.
And the maiden fared unto the white mountain of
Crete leafy with woods; thence unto Oceanus; and
she chose many nymphs all nine years old, all
maidens yet ungirdled. And the river Caeratus [d]
was glad exceedingly, and glad was Tethys that
they were sending their daughters to be handmaidens to the daughter of Leto.

[c] As goddess of mariners she is called Euporia, Limenitis
etc. So Νηοσσόος, Apoll. Rh. i. 570.
[d] River near Cnossus in Crete, Strabo 476.

CALLIMACHUS

αὖθι δὲ Κύκλωπας μετεκίαθε· τοὺς μὲν ἔτετμε
νήσῳ ἐνὶ Λιπάρῃ (Λιπάρη νέον, ἀλλὰ τότ' ἔσκεν
οὔνομά οἱ Μελιγουνίς) ἐπ' ἄκμοσιν Ἡφαίστοιο
ἑσταότας περὶ μύδρον· ἐπείγετο γὰρ μέγα ἔργον·
ἱππείην τετύκοντο Ποσειδάωνι ποτίστρην.   50
αἱ νύμφαι δ' ἔδδεισαν, ὅπως ἴδον αἰνὰ πέλωρα
πρηόσιν Ὀσσαίοισιν[1] ἐοικότα, πᾶσι δ' ὑπ' ὀφρὺν
φάεα μουνόγληνα σάκει ἴσα τετραβοείῳ
δεινὸν ὑπογλαύσσοντα, καὶ ὁππότε δοῦπον ἄκουσαν
ἄκμονος ἠχήσαντος ἐπὶ[2] μέγα πουλύ τ' ἄημα   55
φυσάων αὐτῶν τε βαρὺν στόνον· αὖε γὰρ Αἴτνη,
αὖε δὲ Τρινακίη, Σικανῶν ἕδος, αὖε δὲ γείτων
Ἰταλίη, μεγάλην δὲ βοὴν ἐπὶ Κύρνος ἀΰτει,
εὖθ' οἵ γε ῥαιστῆρας ἀειράμενοι ὑπὲρ ὤμων
ἢ χαλκὸν ζείοντα καμινόθεν ἠὲ σίδηρον   60
ἀμβολαδὶς τετυπόντες ἐπὶ[3] μέγα μοχθήσειαν.
τῶ σφεας οὐκ ἐτάλασσαν ἀκηδέες Ὠκεανῖναι
οὔτ' ἄντην ἰδέειν οὔτε κτύπον οὔασι δέχθαι.
οὐ νέμεσις· κείνους γε[4] καὶ αἱ μάλα μηκέτι τυτθαὶ
οὐδέποτ' ἀφρικτὶ μακάρων ὁρόωσι θύγατρες.   65
ἀλλ' ὅτε κουράων τις ἀπειθέα μητέρι τεύχοι,
μήτηρ μὲν Κύκλωπας ἑῇ ἐπὶ παιδὶ καλιστρεῖ,
Ἄργην ἢ Στερόπην· ὁ δὲ δώματος ἐκ μυχάτοιο
ἔρχεται Ἑρμείης σποδιῇ κεχρημένος[5] αἰθῇ·

---

[1] ὀσσείοισιν (-ησιν); corr. Meineke.   [2] ἐπὶ Bentley; ἐπεί.
[3] ἐπὶ Stephanus, Bentley; ἐπεί.
[4] κείνους δὲ; corr. Meineke.
[5] κεχριμένος in marg. e; κεχρειμένος in marg. T(aurinensis).

---

[a] Sicily.   [b] Corsica.
[c] It is hard to determine the sense of ἀμβολαδίς. The
schol. says ἐκ διαδοχῆς, *i.e.* in succession or alternately.
The same difficulty attaches to ἀμβλήδην and ἀμβολάδην,

And straightway she went to visit the Cyclopes.
Them she found in the isle of Lipara—Lipara in
later days, but at that time its name was Meligunis
—at the anvils of Hephaestus, standing round a
molten mass of iron. For a great work was being
hastened on: they fashioned a horse-trough for
Poseidon. And the nymphs were affrighted when
they saw the terrible monsters like unto the crags
of Ossa: all had single eyes beneath their brows,
like a shield of fourfold hide for size, glaring
terribly from under; and when they heard the din
of the anvil echoing loudly, and the great blast of
the bellows and the heavy groaning of the Cyclopes
themselves. For Aetna cried aloud, and Trinacia[a]
cried, the seat of the Sicanians, cried too their
neighbour Italy, and Cyrnos[b] therewithal uttered
a mighty noise, when they lifted their hammers
above their shoulders and smote with rhythmic
swing[c] the bronze glowing from the furnace or
iron, labouring greatly. Wherefore the daughters
of Oceanus could not untroubled look upon them
face to face nor endure the din in their ears. No
shame to them! on those not even the daughters
of the Blessed look without shuddering, though
long past childhood's years. But when any of the
maidens doth disobedience to her mother, the
mother calls the Cyclopes to her child—Arges or
Steropes; and from within the house comes Hermes,

which the scholiasts interpret usually as either $= ἀπὸ προοιμίου$
or as = " by spurts " (e.g. Pind. N. x. 62, where among other
explanations in the scholia one is $οὐκ ἐφεξῆς$, i.e. not
continuously). The combination of $ἀμβολάδην$ with $ζείω$
in Hom. Il. xxi. 364. Herod. iv. 181 might suggest that
here too $ἀμβολαδίς$ should be taken with $ζείοντα$ in the sense
of " sputtering," but the order of words is against that.

65

CALLIMACHUS

αὐτίκα τὴν κούρην μορμύσσεται, ἡ δὲ τεκούσης   70
δύνει ἔσω κόλπους θεμένη ἐπὶ φάεσι χεῖρας.
κοῦρα, σὺ δὲ προτέρω περ, ἔτι τριέτηρος ἐοῦσα,
εὖτ' ἔμολεν Λητώ σε μετ' ἀγκαλίδεσσι φέρουσα,
Ἡφαίστου καλέοντος ὅπως ὀπτήρια δοίη,
Βρόντεώ σε στιβαροῖσιν ἐφεσσαμένου γονάτεσσι,   75
στήθεος ἐκ μεγάλου λασίης ἐδράξαο χαίτης,
ὤλοψας δὲ βίηφι· τὸ δ' ἄτριχον εἰσέτι καὶ νῦν
μεσσάτιον στέρνοιο μένει μέρος, ὡς ὅτε κόρσην[1]
φωτὸς ἐνιδρυθεῖσα κόμην ἐπενείματ' ἀλώπηξ.

τῶ μάλα θαρσαλέη σφε τάδε προσελέξαο τῆμος   80
"Κύκλωπες, κἠμοί[2] τι Κυδώνιον εἰ δ' ἄγε τόξον
ἠδ' ἰοὺς κοίλην τε κατακληῖδα βελέμνων
τεύξατε· καὶ γὰρ ἐγὼ Λητωιὰς ὥσπερ Ἀπόλλων.
αἰ δέ κ' ἐγὼ τόξοις μονιὸν δάκος ἤ τι πέλωρον
θηρίον ἀγρεύσω, τὸ δέ κεν Κύκλωπες ἔδοιεν."   85
ἔννεπες· οἱ δ' ἐτέλεσσαν· ἄφαρ δ' ὡπλίσσαο, δαῖ-
     μον,
αἶψα δ' ἐπὶ σκύλακας πάλιν ᾔες· ἵκεο δ' αὖλιν
Ἀρκαδικὴν ἔπι Πανός. ὁ δὲ κρέα λυγκὸς ἔταμνε
Μαιναλίης, ἵνα οἱ τοκάδες κύνες εἶδαρ ἔδοιεν.
τὶν δ' ὁ γενειήτης δύο μὲν κύνας ἥμισυ πηγοὺς   90

[1] κόρσῃ Vindob. 318, Vossian. 59.
[2] κἠμοί Meineke ; ἢ ἤ μοι.

---

[a] κεχρημένος of mss. is probably correct. This participle
in late poetry is used in the vaguest way to indicate any
sort of condition.

[b] ὀπτήρια, τὰ ὑπὲρ τοῦ ἰδεῖν δῶρα (schol.), were gifts given
on seeing for the first time a new-born child (schol. Aesch.
Eum. 7 ; Nonn. v. 139). Very similar is the birthday-gift
proper, the δόσις γενέθλιος or γενέθλια· τὰ ἐπὶ τῇ πρώτῃ ἡμέρᾳ
δῶρα (Hesych.). Phoebe gave the oracle at Delphi as a
birthday gift to Phoebus. More usually ὀπτήρια = ἀνακαλυπτήρια, gifts given to the bride by the bridegroom on

66

stained[a] with burnt ashes. And straightway he plays bogey to the child and she runs into her mother's lap, with her hands upon her eyes. But thou, Maiden, even earlier, while yet but three years old, when Leto came bearing thee in her arms at the bidding of Hephaestus that he might give thee handsel[b] and Brontes[c] set thee on his stout knees— thou didst pluck the shaggy hair of his great breast and tear it out by force. And even unto this day the mid part of his breast remains hairless, even as when mange settles on a man's temples and eats away the hair.

Therefore right boldly didst thou address them then: "Cyclopes, for me too fashion ye a Cydonian[d] bow and arrows and a hollow casket for my shafts; for I also am a child of Leto, even as Apollo. And if I with my bow shall slay some wild creature or monstrous beast, that shall the Cyclopes eat." So didst thou speak and they fulfilled thy words. Straightway didst thou array thee, O Goddess, and speedily again thou didst go to get thee hounds; and thou camest to the Arcadian fold of Pan. And he was cutting up the flesh of a lynx of Maenalus[e] that his bitches might eat it for food. And to thee the Bearded[f] God gave two dogs black-and-

---

seeing her for the first time; Pollux ii. 59 ὀπτήρια τὰ δῶρα τὰ παρὰ τοῦ πρῶτον ἰδόντος τὴν νύμφην νυμφίου διδόμενα. Cf. iii. 36 τὰ δὲ παρὰ τοῦ ἀνδρὸς διδόμενα ἕδνα καὶ ὀπτήρια καὶ ἀνα-καλυπτήρια . . . καὶ προσφθεγκτήρια ἐκάλουν. Moeris 205. 24 ὀπτήρια Ἀττικῶς, ἀνακαλυπτήρια Ἑλληνικῶς.

[c] The three Cyclopes, sons of Gaia, were Brontes, Steropes, Arges (Hesiod, Th. 140).

[d] i.e. Cretan, cf. Stat. Th. iv. 269 "Cydonea harundine," vii. 339 "Cydoneas sagittas."

[e] Mountain in Arcadia.

[f] Cf. Hom. H. Pan 39.

CALLIMACHUS

τρεῖς δὲ παρουαίους [1] ἕνα δ' αἰόλον, οἵ ῥα λέοντας
αὐτοὺς αὖ ἐρύοντες, ὅτε δράξαιντο δεράων,
εἷλκον [2] ἔτι ζώοντας ἐπ' αὐλίον, ἑπτὰ δ' ἔδωκε
θάσσονας αὐράων Κυνοσουρίδας, αἵ ῥα διῶξαι
ὤκισται νεβρούς τε καὶ οὐ μύοντα λαγωόν,   95
καὶ κοίτην ἐλάφοιο καὶ ὕστριχος ἔνθα καλιαὶ
σημῆναι, καὶ ζορκὸς ἐπ' ἴχνιον ἡγήσασθαι.

ἔνθεν ἀπερχομένη (μετὰ καὶ κύνες ἐσσεύοντο)
εὖρες ἐπὶ προμολῆς' ὄρεος τοῦ Παρρασίοιο
σκαιρούσας ἐλάφους, μέγα τι χρέος· αἱ μὲν ἐπ' ὄχθης   100
αἰὲν ἐβουκολέοντο μελαμψήφιδος Ἀναύρου,
μάσσονες ἢ ταῦροι, κεράων δ' ἀπελάμπετο χρυσός·
ἐξαπίνης δ' ἔταφές τε καὶ ὃν ποτὶ θυμὸν ἔειπες
"τοῦτό κεν Ἀρτέμιδος πρωτάγριον ἄξιον εἴη."
πέντ' ἔσαν αἱ πᾶσαι· πίσυρας δ' ἔλες ὦκα θέουσα   105
νόσφι κυνοδρομίης, ἵνα τοι θοὸν ἅρμα φέρωσι.
τὴν δὲ μίαν Κελάδοντος ὑπὲρ ποταμοῖο φυγοῦσαν
Ἥρης ἐννεσίῃσιν, ἀέθλιον Ἡρακλῆι
ὕστερον [3] ὄφρα γένοιτο, πάγος Κερύνειος ἔδεκτο.

Ἄρτεμι Παρθενίη Τιτυοκτόνε, χρύσεα μέν τοι   110
ἔντεα καὶ ζώνη, χρύσεον δ' ἐζεύξαο δίφρον,

---

[1] παρουαίους Schneider after M. Haupt who conjectured παρωαίους, cf. Hesych. s.vv. παρωάς and πάρωος, Arist. H.A. ix. 45, etc. ; παρουατίους.

[2] εἷλκον e, cf. Nonn. 25. 188 ; εἷλον A.

[3] ὕστερον schol. Apoll. Rh. i. 996 ; ὕστατον.

---

[a] The ancients differed as to whether πηγός meant black or white (Hesych. s.vv. πηγός and πηγεσιμάλλῳ).

[b] It is by no means certain that the mss. παρουατίους is wrong, "with hanging ears." παρουαίους is based upon Hesych. s.vv. παρωάς, πάρωος, Aelian, H.A. viii. 12, cf. Arist. H.A. ix. 45, Dem. De cor. 260. Should we read Παραυαίους, i.e. Molossian?

white,[a] three reddish,[b] and one spotted, which pulled
down[c] very lions when they clutched their throats
and haled them still living to the fold. And he gave
thee seven Cynosurian[d] bitches swifter than the winds
—that breed which is swiftest to pursue fawns and
the hare which closes not his eyes[e]; swiftest too
to mark the lair of the stag and where the porcupine[f]
hath his burrow, and to lead upon the track of the
gazelle.

Thence departing (and thy hounds sped with
thee) thou didst find by the base of the Parrhasian
hill deer gambolling—a mighty herd. They always
herded by the banks of the black-pebbled Anaurus—
larger than bulls, and from their horns shone gold.
And thou wert suddenly amazed and saidst to thine
own heart: "This would be a first capture worthy of
Artemis." Five were they in all; and four thou
didst take by speed of foot—without chase of dogs—
to draw thy swift car. But one escaped over the
river Celadon, by devising of Hera, that it might be
in the after days a labour for Heracles,[g] and the
Ceryneian hill received her.

Artemis, Lady of Maidenhood, Slayer of Tityus,
golden were thine arms and golden thy belt, and a
golden car didst thou yoke, and golden bridles,

---

[c] αὖ ἐρύοντες, common in Oppian and Nonnus, is apparently a misunderstanding of the Homeric αὐερύοντες (=ἀνα-
Ϝερύοντες).

[d] Arcadian, cf. Stat. Th. iv. 295 "dives Cynosura ferarum."

[e] Oppian, Cyneg. iii. 511 f.

[f] Oppian, ibid. 391 ff.

[g] Apollodor. ii. 5. 3 "The third labour which he
(Eurystheus) imposed on him (Heracles) was to bring the
Cerynean hind (Κερυνῖτιν ἔλαφον) to Mycenae alive. This
was a hind . . . with golden horns, sacred to Artemis."
Cf. Pind. O. iii. 29.

CALLIMACHUS

ἐν δ' ἐβάλευ χρύσεια, θεή, κεμάδεσσι χαλινά.
ποῦ δέ σε τὸ πρῶτον κερόεις ὄχος ἦρξατ' ἀείρειν;
Αἵμῳ ἐπὶ Θρήικι, τόθεν βορέαο κατᾶιξ
ἔρχεται ἀχλαίνοισι δυσαέα κρυμὸν ἄγουσα.   115
ποῦ δ' ἔταμες πεύκην, ἀπὸ δὲ φλογὸς ἥψαο ποίης;
Μυσῷ ἐν Οὐλύμπῳ, φάεος δ' ἐνέηκας αὐτμὴν
ἀσβέστου, τό ῥα πατρὸς ἀποστάζουσι κεραυνοί.
ποσσάκι δ' ἀργυρέοιο, θεή, πειρήσαο τόξου;
πρῶτον ἐπὶ πτελέην, τὸ δὲ δεύτερον ἧκας ἐπὶ δρῦν, 120
τὸ τρίτον αὖτ' ἐπὶ θῆρα. τὸ τέτρατον οὐκέτ' ἐπὶ
      δὴν [1]
ἀλλά μιν εἰς ἀδίκων ἔβαλες πόλιν, οἵ τε περὶ σφέας
οἵ τε περὶ ξείνους ἀλιτήμονα πολλὰ τέλεσκον,
σχέτλιοι· οἷς τύνη χαλεπὴν ἐμμάξεαι ὀργήν·
κτήνεά φιν λοιμὸς [2] καταβόσκεται, ἔργα δὲ πάχνη, 125
κείρονται δὲ γέροντες ἐφ' υἱάσιν, αἱ δὲ γυναῖκες
ἢ βληταὶ θνήσκουσι λεχωίδες ἠὲ φυγοῦσαι
τίκτουσιν τῶν [3] οὐδὲν ἐπὶ σφυρὸν ὀρθὸν ἀνέστη.
οἷς [4] δέ κεν εὐμειδής τε καὶ ἵλαος αὐγάσσηαι,
κείνοις εὖ μὲν ἄρουρα φέρει στάχυν, εὖ δὲ γενέθλη 130
τετραπόδων, εὖ δ' ὄλβος ἀέξεται· οὐδ' ἐπὶ σῆμα
ἔρχονται πλὴν εὖτε πολυχρόνιόν τι φέρωσιν·
οὐδὲ διχοστασίη τρώει γένος, ἥ τε καὶ εὖ περ
οἴκους ἑστηῶτας ἐσίνατο· ταὶ δὲ θυωρὸν
εἰνάτερες γαλόῳ τε μίαν περὶ δίφρα τίθενται.   135
πότνια, τῶν εἴη μὲν ἐμοὶ φίλος ὅστις ἀληθής,
εἴην δ' αὐτός, ἄνασσα, μέλοι δέ μοι αἰὲν ἀοιδή·

---

[1] δὴν Editor ; δρῦν.   [2] λιμὸς A.
[3] τῶν δ' mss.; corr. Cobet.   [4] οὓς d and Paris. 456.

---

[a] εἰνάτερες = wives whose husbands are brothers ; γαλόῳ =
wife and sister(s) of one man. (Hom. *Il.* vi. 378.) Gercke,
Rh. Mus.

70

goddess, didst thou put on thy deer. And where first did thy horned team begin to carry thee? To Thracian Haemus, whence comes the hurricane of Boreas bringing evil breath of frost to cloakless men. And where didst thou cut the pine and from what flame didst thou kindle it? It was on Mysian Olympus, and thou didst put in it the breath of flame unquenchable, which thy Father's bolts distil. And how often goddess, didst thou make trial of thy silver bow? First at an elm, and next at an oak didst thou shoot, and third again at a wild beast. But the fourth time—not long was it ere thou didst shoot at the city of unjust men, those who to one another and those who towards strangers wrought many deeds of sin, froward men, on whom thou wilt impress thy grievous wrath. On their cattle plague feeds, on their tilth feeds frost, and the old men cut their hair in mourning over their sons, and their wives either are smitten and die in childbirth, or, if they escape, bear births whereof none stands on upright ankle. But on whomsoever thou lookest smiling and gracious, for them the tilth bears the corn-ear abundantly, and abundantly prospers the fourfooted breed, and abundant waxes their prosperity: neither do they go to the tomb, save when they carry thither the aged. Nor does faction wound their race—faction which ravages even well-established houses: but brother's wife and husband's sister set their chairs around one board.[a] Lady, of that number be whosoever is a true friend of mine, and of that number may I be myself, O Queen, and may song be my study for ever. In that song shall be the

xlii. (1887), p. 273 ff., sees an allusion to Arsinoë I. and Arsinoë II.

τῇ ἔνι μὲν Λητοῦς γάμος ἔσσεται, ἐν δὲ σὺ πολλή,
ἐν δὲ καὶ Ἀπόλλων, ἐν δ' οἵ σεο πάντες ἄεθλοι,
ἐν δὲ κύνες καὶ τόξα καὶ ἄντυγες, αἵ τέ σε ῥεῖα 14(
θηητὴν φορέουσιν, ὅτ' ἐς Διὸς οἶκον ἐλαύνεις.
ἔνθα τοι ἀντιόωντες ἐνὶ προμολῇσι δέχονται
ὅπλα μὲν Ἑρμείης Ἀκακήσιος, αὐτὰρ Ἀπόλλων
θηρίον ὅττι φέρῃσθα· πάροιθέ γέ,[1] πρίν περ ἱκέσθαι
καρτερὸν Ἀλκεΐδην· νῦν δ' οὐκέτι τοῦτον ἄεθλον 14!
Φοῖβος ἔχει, τοῖος γὰρ ἀεὶ Τιρύνθιος ἄκμων
ἕστηκε πρὸ πυλέων ποτιδέγμενος, εἴ τι φέρουσα
νεῖαι πῖον ἔδεσμα· θεοὶ δ' ἐπὶ πάντες ἐκείνῳ
ἄλληκτον γελόωσι, μάλιστα δὲ πενθερὴ αὐτή,
ταῦρον ὅτ' ἐκ δίφροιο μάλα μέγαν ἢ ὅ γε[2] χλούνην 15(
κάπρον ὀπισθιδίοιο φέροι ποδὸς ἀσπαίροντα·
κερδαλέῳ μύθῳ σε, θεή, μάλα τῷδε πινύσκει
"βάλλε κακοὺς ἐπὶ θῆρας, ἵνα θνητοί σε βοηθὸν
ὡς ἐμὲ κικλήσκωσιν.[3] ἔα πρόκας ἠδὲ λαγωοὺς
οὔρεα βόσκεσθαι· τί δέ κεν[4] πρόκες ἠδὲ λαγωοὶ 155
ῥέξειαν; σύες ἔργα, σύες φυτὰ λυμαίνονται.
καὶ βόες ἀνθρώποισι κακὸν μέγα· βάλλ' ἐπὶ καὶ
       τούς."
ὣς ἔνεπεν, ταχινὸς δὲ μέγαν περὶ θῆρα πονεῖτο.
οὐ γὰρ ὅ γε Φρυγίη περ ὑπὸ δρυῒ γυῖα θεωθεὶς

---

[1] γε Blomf. ; δέ.
[2] ὅ γε d ; ὅτε.
[3] κικλήσκωσιν F and Voss. 59 ; -ουσιν AE.
[4] τί κεν.

---

[a] Cf. the Homeric epithet of Hermes, Ἀκάκητα, Il. xvi.
185, etc.
[b] Heracles, as son of Amphitryon son of Alcaeus.
According to Apollodor. ii. 4. 12, Alcides was the original
name of Heracles, the latter name having been bestowed
upon him by the Pythian priestess when he consulted the
72

Marriage of Leto; therein thy name shall often-times be sung; therein shall Apollo be and therein all thy labours, and therein thy hounds and thy bow and thy chariots, which lightly carry thee in thy splendour, when thou drivest to the house of Zeus. There in the entrance meet thee Hermes and Apollo: Hermes, the Lord of Blessing,[a] takes thy weapons, Apollo takes whatsoever wild beast thou bringest. Yea, so Apollo did before strong Alcides[b] came, but now Phoebus hath this task no longer; in such wise the Anvil of Tiryns[c] stands ever before the gates, waiting to see if thou wilt come home with some fat morsel. And all the gods laugh at him with laughter unceasing and most of all his own wife's mother[d] when he brings from the car a great bull or a wild boar, carrying it by the hind foot struggling. With this cunning speech, goddess, doth he admonish thee: "Shoot at the evil wild beasts that mortals may call thee their helper even as they call me. Leave deer and hares to feed upon the hills. What harm could deer or hares do? It is boars which ravage the tilth of men and boars which ravage the plants; and oxen are a great bane to men: shoot also at those." So he spake and swiftly busied him about the mighty beast. For though beneath a Phrygian[e] oak his

oracle after he had gone into exile for the murder of his children. Heracles asked the oracle where he should dwell and he was told to settle in Tiryns and serve Eurystheus for twelve years.

[c] There is no reason whatever to suppose that ἄκμων here has any other than its ordinary sense of anvil, used metaphorically, as in Aesch. *Pers.* 52. It has been sometimes supposed to mean unwearied = ἀκάματος.

[d] Hera, mother of Hebe.

[e] "Phrygia, a hill in Trachis where Heracles was burnt" (schol.).

παῦσατ' ἀδηφαγίης· ἔτι οἱ πάρα νηδὺς ἐκείνη,   160
τῇ ποτ' ἀροτριόωντι συνήντετο Θειοδάμαντι.

σοὶ δ' Ἀμνισιάδες μὲν ὑπὸ ζεύγληφι λυθείσας
ψήχουσιν κεμάδας, παρὰ δέ σφισι πουλὺ νέμεσθαι
Ἥρης ἐκ λειμῶνος ἀμησάμεναι φορέουσιν
ὠκύθοον¹ τριπέτηλον, ὃ καὶ Διὸς ἵπποι ἔδουσιν·   165
ἐν καὶ χρυσείας ὑποληνίδας ἐπλήσαντο
ὕδατος, ὄφρ' ἐλάφοισι ποτὸν θυμάρμενον εἴη.
αὐτὴ δ' ἐς πατρὸς δόμον ἔρχεαι· οἱ δέ σ' ἐφ' ἕδρην
πάντες ὁμῶς καλέουσι· σὺ δ' Ἀπόλλωνι παρίζεις.

ἡνίκα δ' αἱ νύμφαι σε χορῷ ἔνι κυκλώσονται   170
ἀγχόθι πηγάων Αἰγυπτίου Ἰνωποῖο
ἢ Πιτάνης (καὶ γὰρ Πιτάνη σέθεν) ἢ ἐνὶ Λίμναις,
ἢ ἵνα, δαῖμον, Ἀλὰς Ἀραφηνίδας οἰκήσουσα
ἦλθες ἀπὸ Σκυθίης, ἀπὸ δ' εἴπαο τέθμια Ταύρων,
μὴ νειὸν τημοῦτος ἐμαὶ βόες εἵνεκα μισθοῦ   175
τετράγυον τέμνοιεν ὑπ' ἀλλοτρίῳ ἀροτῆρι·
ἦ γάρ κεν γυιαί τε καὶ αὐχένα κεκμηυῖαι

---

¹ ὠκύθοον e, cf. Hesych. s.v. ; ὠκύθεον.

ᵃ When Heracles was passing through the land of the
Dryopes, being in want of food for his young son Hyllus,
he unyoked and slaughtered one of the oxen of Theiodamas,
king of the Dryopes, whom he found at the plough. War
ensued between the Dryopes and Heracles, and the Dryopes
were defeated, and Hylas, son of Theiodamas, was taken as
a hostage by Heracles (Apollodor. ii. 7. 7, Apoll. Rh. i.
1211 ff., Ovid, *Ib.* 488). Hence Heracles got the epithet
Bouthoinas, schol. Apoll. Rh. *l.c.*, Gregor. Naz. *Or.* iv. 123.
The Lindian peasant who was similarly treated by Heracles,
and who, while Heracles feasted, stood apart and cursed
(hence curious rite at Lindos in Rhodes, where, when they

flesh was deified, yet hath he not ceased from gluttony. Still hath he that belly wherewith he met Theiodamas[a] at the plough.

For thee the nymphs of Amnisus rub down the hinds loosed from the yoke, and from the mead of Hera they gather and carry for them to feed on much swift-springing clover, which also the horses of Zeus eat ; and golden troughs they fill with water to be for the deer a pleasant draught. And thyself thou enterest thy Father's house, and all alike bid thee to a seat ; but thou sittest beside Apollo.

But when the nymphs encircle thee in the dance, near the springs of Egyptian Inopus[b] or Pitane[c]— for Pitane too is thine—or in Limnae[d] or where, goddess, thou camest from Scythia to dwell, in Alae Araphenides,[e] renouncing the rites of the Tauri,[f] then may not my kine cleave a four-acred[g] fallow field for a wage at the hand of an alien ploughman ; else surely lame and weary of neck would they come

sacrifice to Heracles, they do it with curses, Conon 11, Apollod. ii. 5. 11. 8, Lactant. *Inst. Div.* i. 21) is identified with Theiodamas by Philostr. *Imag.* ii. 24. Cf. G. Knaack, *Hermes* xxiii. (1888), p. 131 ff.

[b] Inopus in Delos was supposed to have a subterranean connexion with the Nile.

[c] On the Eurotas with temple of Artemis.

[d] This may be the Athenian Limnae (so schol.) ; but there was a Limnaeon also in Laconia with temple of Artemis and an image supposed to be that carried off by Orestes and Iphigeneia (Paus. iii. 7) from Taurica.

[e] Attic deme between Marathon and Brauron with temple of Artemis (Eurip. *Iphig. in T.* 1446 ff.).

[f] In the Crimea, where Artemis was worshipped with human sacrifice (Eurip. *l.c.*, Ovid, *Trist.* iv. 4, *Ex Ponto* iii. 2, Herod. iv. 103).

[g] The typical heroic field (Hom. *Od.* xviii. 374, Apoll. Rh. iii. 1344) ; cf. *Od.* vii. 113.

κόπρον ἔπι προγένοιντο, καὶ εἰ Στυμφαιίδες εἶεν
εἰναετιζόμεναι κεραελκέες, αἳ μέγ' ἄρισται
τέμνειν ὦλκα βαθεῖαν· ἐπεὶ θεὸς οὔποτ' ἐκεῖνον 18
ἦλθε παρ' Ἥλιος καλὸν χορόν, ἀλλὰ θεῆται
δίφρον ἐπιστήσας, τὰ δὲ φάεα μηκύνονται.

τίς δέ νύ τοι νήσων, ποῖον δ' ὄρος εὔαδε πλεῖστον,
τίς δὲ λιμήν, ποίη δὲ πόλις; τίνα δ' ἔξοχα νυμφέων
φίλαο, καὶ ποίας ἡρωίδας ἔσχες ἑταίρας; 18
εἰπέ, θεή, σὺ μὲν ἄμμιν, ἐγὼ δ' ἑτέροισιν ἀείσω.
νήσων μὲν Δολίχη, πολίων δέ τοι εὔαδε Πέργη,
Τηΰγετον δ' ὀρέων, λιμένες γε μὲν Εὐρίποιο.
ἔξοχα δ' ἀλλάων Γορτυνίδα φίλαο νύμφην,
ἐλλοφόνον Βριτόμαρτιν εὔσκοπον· ἧς ποτε Μίνως 19
πτοιηθεὶς ὑπ' ἔρωτι κατέδραμεν οὔρεα Κρήτης.
ἡ δ' ὀτὲ μὲν λασίῃσιν ὑπὸ δρυσὶ κρύπτετο νύμφη,
ἄλλοτε δ' εἰαμενῇσιν· ὁ δ' ἐννέα μῆνας ἐφοίτα
παίπαλά τε κρημνούς τε καὶ οὐκ ἀνέπαυσε διωκτύν,
μέσφ' ὅτε μαρπτομένη καὶ δὴ σχεδὸν ἧλατο πόντον 19
πρηόνος ἐξ ὑπάτοιο καὶ ἔνθορεν εἰς ἁλιήων
δίκτυα, τά σφ' ἐσάωσαν· ὅθεν μετέπειτα Κύδωνες
νύμφην μὲν Δίκτυναν, ὄρος δ' ὅθεν ἧλατο νύμφη
Δικταῖον καλέουσιν, ἀνεστήσαντο δὲ βωμοὺς
ἱερά τε ῥέζουσι· τὸ δὲ στέφος ἤματι κείνῳ 20
ἢ πίτυς ἢ σχῖνος, μύρτοιο δὲ χεῖρες ἄθικτοι·

ᵃ i.e. from Epirus. For the great size of the Ἠπειρωτικαὶ
βόες see Aristotle, H.A. iii. 21, who says that when milking
them the milker had to stand upright in order to reach the
udder. Both Stymphaea and Tymphaea seem to be attested,
though the latter seems to have the better authority (Steph.
Byz. s.v. Τύμφη).

ᵇ Hesiod, W. 436.

ᶜ Doliche : either Euboea (E.M. s.v. Εὔβοια), E. Maass,
Hermes xxv. (1890), p. 404, or Icaros (Steph. Byz. s.v. Ἴκαρος),

to the byre, yea even were they of Stymphaean [a] breed, nine [b] years of age, drawing by the horns; which kine are far the best for cleaving a deep furrow; for the god Helios never passes by that beauteous dance, but stays his car to gaze upon the sight, and the lights of day are lengthened.

Which now of islands, what hill finds most favour with thee? What haven? What city? Which of the nymphs dost thou love above the rest, and what heroines hast thou taken for thy companions? Say, goddess, thou to me, and I will sing thy saying to others   Of islands Doliche [c] hath found favour with thee, of cities Perge, [d] of hills Taygeton, [e] the havens of Euripus.   And beyond others thou lovest the nymph of Gortyn, Britomartis, [f] slayer of stags, the goodly archer; for love of whom was Minos of old distraught and roamed the hills of Crete.   And the nymph would hide herself now under the shaggy oaks and anon in the low meadows.   And for nine months he roamed over crag and cliff and made not an end of pursuing, until, all but caught, she leapt into the sea from the top of a cliff and fell into the nets of fishermen which saved her.   Whence in after days the Cydonians call the nymph the Lady of the Nets (Dictyna) and the hill whence the nymph leaped they call the hill of Nets (Dictaeon), and there they set up altars and do sacrifice.   And the garland on that day is pine or mastich, but the hands

or an island off Lycia (Steph. Byz. *s.v.* Δολιχή · νῆσος πρὸς τῇ Λυκίᾳ, ὡς Καλλίμαχος).

[d] In Pamphylia, with temple of Artemis, Strabo 667.

[e] In Laconia.

[f] Britomartis or Dictyna, a Cretan goddess sometimes represented as an attendant of Artemis, sometimes regarded as identical with her.

CALLIMACHUS

δὴ τότε γὰρ πέπλοισιν ἐνέσχετο μύρσινος ὄζος
τῆς κούρης, ὅτ' ἔφευγεν· ὅθεν μέγα χώσατο μύρτῳ.
Οὖπι ἄνασσ' εὐῶπι φαεσφόρε, καὶ δὲ σὲ κείνης
Κρηταέες καλέουσιν ἐπωνυμίην ἀπὸ νύμφης.   20

καὶ μὴν Κυρήνην ἑταρίσσαο, τῇ ποτ' ἔδωκας
αὐτὴ θηρητῆρε δύω κύνε, τοῖς ἔνι κούρη
Ὑψηὶς παρὰ τύμβον Ἰώλκιον ἔμμορ' ἀέθλου.
καὶ Κεφάλου ξανθὴν ἄλοχον Δηιονίδαο,
πότνια, σὴν ὁμόθηρον ἐθήκαο· καὶ δὲ σὲ φασὶ   21
καλὴν Ἀντίκλειαν ἴσον φαέεσσι φιλῆσαι,
αἳ πρῶται θοὰ τόξα καὶ ἀμφ' ὤμοισι φαρέτρας
ἰοδόκους ἐφόρησαν· ἀσίλλωτοι δέ φιν ὦμοι
δεξιτεροὶ καὶ γυμνὸς ἀεὶ παρεφαίνετο μαζός.
ᾔνησας δ' ἔτι πάγχυ ποδορρώρην Ἀταλάντην,   21
κούρην Ἰασίοιο συοκτόνον Ἀρκασίδαο,
καί ἑ κυνηλασίην τε καὶ εὐστοχίην ἐδίδαξας.
οὔ μιν ἐπίκλητοι Καλυδωνίου ἀγρευτῆρες
μέμφονται κάπροιο· τὰ γὰρ σημήια νίκης   220
Ἀρκαδίην εἰσῆλθεν, ἔχει δ' ἔτι θηρὸς ὀδόντας·
οὐδὲ μὲν Ὑλαῖόν τε καὶ ἄφρονα Ῥοῖκον ἔολπα
οὐδέ περ ἐχθαίροντας ἐν Ἅιδι μωμήσασθαι
τοξότιν· οὐ γάρ σφιν λαγόνες συνεπιψεύσονται,
τάων Μαιναλίη ναῖεν φόνῳ ἀκρώρεια.

       πότνια πουλυμέλαθρε, πολύπτολι, χαῖρε Χιτώνη 22
Μιλήτῳ ἐπίδημε· σὲ γὰρ ποιήσατο Νηλεὺς

---

[a] Artemis in Ephesus, Sparta, etc.   [b] Cyrene.
[c] "The tomb of Pelias" (schol.).   See Introduction.
[d] Procris.   [e] Mother of Odysseus.
[f] The ms. ἀσύλ(λ)ωτοι is quite unknown.   The translation assumes a connexion with ἀσίλλα.

78

touch not the myrtle. For when she was in flight,
a myrtle branch became entangled in the maiden's
robes; wherefore she was greatly angered against
the myrtle. Upis,[a] O Queen, fairfaced Bringer of
Light, thee too the Cretans name after that nymph.
Yea and Cyrene thou madest thy comrade, to whom
on a time thyself didst give two hunting dogs, with
whom the maiden daughter of Hypseus [b] beside the
Iolcian tomb [c] won the prize. And the fair-haired
wife [d] of Cephalus, son of Deioneus, O Lady, thou
madest thy fellow in the chase; and fair Anticleia,[e]
they say, thou didst love even as thine own eyes.
These were the first who wore gallant bow and
arrow - holding quivers on their shoulders; their
right shoulders bore the quiver strap,[f] and always
the right breast showed bare. Further thou didst
greatly commend swift-footed Atalanta,[g] the slayer
of boars, daughter of Arcadian Iasius, and taught her
hunting with dogs and good archery. They that
were called to hunt the boar of Calydon find no
fault with her; for the tokens of victory came into
Arcadia which still holds the tusks of the beast.
Nor do I deem that Hylaeus [h] and foolish Rhoecus,
for all their hate, in Hades slight her archery. For
the loins, with whose blood the height of Maenalus
flowed, will not abet the falsehood.

Lady of many shrines, of many cities, hail! Goddess of the Tunic,[i] sojourner in Miletus; for thee

[g] Atalanta took a prominent part in the hunt of the Calydonian boar, and received from Meleager the hide and head
of the boar as her prize (Paus. viii. 45).

[h] Hylaeus and Rhoecus were two centaurs who insulted
Atalanta and were shot by her (Apollod. iii. 9. 2).

[i] Chitone, by-name of Artemis as huntress, wearing a
sleeveless tunic ($\chi\iota\tau\acute{\omega}\nu$) reaching to the knees.

ἡγεμόνην, ὅτε νηυσὶν ἀνήγετο Κεκροπίηθεν.
Χησιὰς Ἰμβρασίη πρωτόθρονε, σοὶ δ' Ἀγαμέμνων
πηδάλιον νηὸς σφετέρης ἐγκάτθετο νηῷ
μείλιον ἀπλοΐης, ὅτε οἱ κατέδησας ἀήτας,   230
Τευκρῶν ἡνίκα νῆες Ἀχαιΐδες ἄστεα κήδειν
ἔπλεον ἀμφ' Ἑλένῃ Ῥαμνουσίδι θυμωθεῖσαι.

    ἢ μέν τοι Προῖτός γε δύω ἐκαθίσσατο νηούς,
ἄλλον μὲν Κορίης, ὅτι οἱ συνελέξαο κούρας
οὔρεα πλαζομένας Ἀζήνια,¹ τὸν δ' ἐνὶ Λούσοις   235
Ἡμέρῃ, οὕνεκα θυμὸν ἀπ' ἄγριον εἵλεο παίδων.
σοὶ καὶ Ἀμαζονίδες πολέμου ἐπιθυμήτειραι
ἔν ποτε παρραλίη Ἐφέσῳ βρέτας ἱδρύσαντο
φηγῷ ὑπὸ πρέμνῳ, τέλεσεν δέ τοι ἱερὸν Ἱππώ·
αὐταὶ δ', Οὖπι ἄνασσα, περὶ πρύλιν ὠρχήσαντο   240
πρῶτα μὲν ἐν σακέεσσιν ἐνόπλιον, αὖθι δὲ κύκλῳ
στησάμεναι χορὸν εὐρύν· ὑπήεισαν δὲ λίγειαι
λεπταλέον σύριγγες, ἵνα ῥήσσωσιν ² ὁμαρτῇ·
οὐ γάρ πω νέβρεια δι' ὀστέα τετρήνατο,
ἔργον Ἀθηναίης ἐλάφῳ κακόν· ἔδραμε δ' ἠχὼ   245
Σάρδιας ἔς τε νομὸν Βερεκύνθιον. αἱ δὲ πόδεσσιν
οὖλα κατεκροτάλιζον, ἐπεψόφεον δὲ φαρέτραι.

---

¹ ἀξείνια mss. ; corr. Spanheim.
² πλήσ(σ)ωσιν mss. ; πλίσσωσιν Arnaldus ; ῥήσσωσιν de Jan.

ᵃ Neleus, son of Codrus, founder of Miletus (Strabo, 633).
ᵇ Artemis Hegemone as leader of colonists (Paus. viii. 37).
ᶜ i.e. Athens.   ᵈ Cape in Samos.   ᵉ River in Samos.
ᶠ Artemis was worshipped in Ephesus with the title
Πρωτοθρονίη (Paus. x. 38. 6). For rock-cut throne on Mount
Coressus at Ephesus cf. A. B. Cook, Zeus, i. p. 140 f.
ᵍ The ἄπλοια is sometimes described as a storm, sometimes
as a dead calm.
ʰ Epithet of Helen as daughter of Nemesis, who was
worshipped at Rhamnus in Attica.
ⁱ King of Argos.

did Neleus [a] make his Guide,[b] when he put off with
his ships from the land of Cecrops.[c] Lady of
Chesion [d] and of Imbrasus,[e] throned [f] in the highest,
to thee in thy shrine did Agamemnon dedicate the
rudder of his ship, a charm against ill weather,[g]
when thou didst bind the winds for him, what time
the Achaean ships sailed to vex the cities of the
Teucri, wroth for Rhamnusian [h] Helen.

For thee surely Proetus [i] established two shrines,
one of Artemis of Maidenhood for that thou didst
gather for him his maiden daughters,[j] when they
were wandering over the Azanian [k] hills ; the other
he founded in Lusa [l] to Artemis the Gentle,[m] because
thou tookest from his daughters the spirit of wildness.
For thee, too, the Amazons, whose mind is set on
war, in Ephesus beside the sea established an image
beneath an oak trunk, and Hippo [n] performed a holy
rite for thee, and they themselves, O Upis Queen,
around the image danced a war-dance — first in
shields and in armour, and again in a circle arraying
a spacious choir. And the loud pipes thereto piped
shrill accompaniment, that they might foot the dance
together (for not yet did they pierce the bones of
the fawn, Athene's handiwork,[o] a bane to the deer).
And the echo reached unto Sardis and to the Berecynthian [p] range. And they with their feet beat
loudly and therewith their quivers rattled.

[j] For their madness and cure cf. Paus. ii. 7. 8, viii. 18. 7 f.
[k] Azania in Arcadia.   [l] In Arcadia.
[m] For the temple of Artemis Hemera or Hemerasia at
Lusa cf. Paus. viii. 18. 8.
[n] Queen of the Amazons, no doubt identical with
Hippolyte.
[o] The flute (αὐλός) invented by Athena (Pind. P. xii. 22)
was often made from fawn bones, Poll. iv. 71, Athen. 182 E,
Plut. Mor. 150 E.   [p] In Phrygia.

κεῖνο δέ τοι μετέπειτα περὶ βρέτας εὐρὺ θέμειλον
δωμήθη, τοῦ δ' οὔτε θεώτερον ὄψεται ἠὼς
οὐδ' ἀφνειότερον· ῥέα κεν Πυθῶνα παρέλθοι.   250
τῷ ῥα καὶ ἠλαίνων ἀλαπαξέμεν ἠπείλησε
Λύγδαμις ὑβριστής· ἐπὶ δὲ στρατὸν ἱππημολγῶν
ἤγαγε[1] Κιμμερίων ψαμάθῳ ἴσον, οἵ ῥα παρ' αὐτὸν
κεκλιμένοι ναίουσι βοὸς πόρον Ἰναχιώνης.
ἆ δειλὸς βασιλέων, ὅσον ἤλιτεν· οὐ γὰρ ἔμελλεν   255
οὔτ' αὐτὸς Σκυθίηνδε παλιμπετὲς οὔτε τις ἄλλος
ὅσσων ἐν λειμῶνι Καϋστρίῳ ἔσταν ἄμαξαι
νοστήσειν· Ἐφέσου γὰρ ἀεὶ τεὰ τόξα πρόκειται.

πότνια Μουνιχίη λιμενοσκόπε, χαῖρε Φεραίη.
μή τις ἀτιμήσῃ τὴν Ἄρτεμιν· οὐδὲ γὰρ Οἰνεῖ   260
βωμὸν ἀτιμήσαντι[2] καλοὶ πόλιν ἦλθον ἀγῶνες·
μηδ' ἐλαφηβολίην μηδ' εὐστοχίην ἐριδαίνειν·
οὐδὲ γὰρ Ἀτρεΐδης ὀλίγῳ ἔπι κόμπασε μισθῷ·
μηδέ τινα μνᾶσθαι τὴν παρθένον· οὐδὲ γὰρ Ὦτος,
οὐδὲ μὲν Ὠαρίων ἀγαθὸν γάμον ἐμνήστευσαν·   265
μηδὲ χορὸν φεύγειν ἐνιαύσιον· οὐδὲ γὰρ Ἱππὼ
ἀκλαυτεὶ περὶ βωμὸν ἀπείπατο κυκλώσασθαι·
χαῖρε μέγα κρείουσα καὶ εὐάντησον ἀοιδῇ.

[1] ἤλασε *Et. Gud. Et. M. s.v. ἴσος.*
[2] ἀτιμήσαντι e and Vindobon. 318; ἀτιμάσαντι Af; ἀτιμάσσαντι Schneider.

[a] A people living on the north of the Black Sea.
[b] The Cimmerian Bosporus, which was named after the Cow (βοῦς), *i.e.* Io, daughter of Inachus, king of Argos.
[c] The Cayster is a river in Lydia.
[d] Harbour of Athens, where Artemis had a temple (Paus. i. 1. 4).
[e] Artemis Pheraia is Artemis as Hecate from Pherae in Thessaly (Paus. ii. 23. 5).

And afterwards around that image was raised a shrine of broad foundations. Than it shall Dawn behold nothing more divine, naught richer. Easily would it outdo Pytho. Wherefore in his madness insolent Lygdamis threatened that he would lay it waste, and brought against it a host of Cimmerians [a] which milk mares, in number as the sand; who have their homes hard by the Straits [b] of the Cow, daughter of Inachus. Ah! foolish among kings, how greatly he sinned! For not destined to return again to Scythia was either he or any other of those whose wagons stood in the Caystrian [c] plain; for thy shafts are ever more set as a defence before Ephesus.

O Lady of Munychia,[d] Watcher of Harbours, hail, Lady of Pherae [e]! Let none disparage Artemis. For Oeneus [f] dishonoured her altar and no pleasant struggles came upon his city. Nor let any contend with her in shooting of stags or in archery. For the son [g] of Atreus vaunted him not that he suffered small requital. Neither let any woo the Maiden; for not Otus, nor Orion wooed her to their own good. Nor let any shun the yearly dance; for not tearless to Hippo [h] was her refusal to dance around the altar. Hail, great Queen, and graciously greet my song.

[f] King of Calydon in Aetolia, who neglected to sacrifice to Artemis. In anger she sent the Calydonian boar to ravage his land.

[g] Agamemnon, who shot a stag which was sacred to Artemis and boasted of the deed (Soph. *Electr.* 566 f., Hygin. *Fab.* 98). This led to the ἀπλοια at Aulis and the sacrifice of Iphigeneia.

[h] Queen of the Amazons, who founded the temple of Artemis at Ephesus.

IV.—ΕΙΣ ΔΗΛΟΝ

Τὴν ἱερήν, ὦ θυμέ, τίνα χρόνον ἢ πότ᾽[1] ἀείσεις
Δῆλον, Ἀπόλλωνος κουροτρόφον; ἢ μὲν ἅπασαι
Κυκλάδες, αἳ νήσων ἱερώταται εἰν ἁλὶ κεῖνται,
εὔυμνοι· Δῆλος δ᾽ ἐθέλει τὰ πρῶτα φέρεσθαι
ἐκ Μουσέων, ὅτι Φοῖβον ἀοιδάων μεδέοντα   5
λοῦσέ τε καὶ σπείρωσε καὶ ὡς θεὸν ᾔνεσε πρώτη.
ὡς Μοῦσαι τὸν ἀοιδὸν ὃ μὴ Πίμπλειαν ἀείσῃ[2]
ἔχθουσιν, τὼς Φοῖβος ὅτις Δήλοιο λάθηται.
Δήλῳ νῦν οἴμης ἀποδάσσομαι, ὡς ἂν Ἀπόλλων
Κύνθιος αἰνήσῃ με φίλης ἀλέγοντα τιθήνης.   10
     κείνη δ᾽ ἠνεμόεσσα καὶ ἄτροπος οἷά θ᾽ ἁλιπλὴξ
αἰθυίης καὶ μᾶλλον ἐπίδρομος ἠέπερ ἵπποις
πόντῳ ἐνεστήρικται· ὁ δ᾽ ἀμφί ἑ πουλὺς ἑλίσσων
Ἰκαρίου πολλὴν ἀπομάσσεται ὕδατος ἄχνην·
τῶ σφε καὶ ἰχθυβολῆες ἁλίπλοοι ἐννάσσαντο.   15
ἀλλά οἱ οὐ νεμεσητὸν ἐνὶ πρώτῃσι λέγεσθαι,
ὁππότ᾽ ἐς Ὠκεανόν τε καὶ ἐς Τιτηνίδα Τηθὺν
νῆσοι ἀολλίζονται, ἀεὶ δ᾽ ἔξαρχος ὁδεύει.
ἡ δ᾽ ὄπιθεν Φοίνισσα μετ᾽ ἴχνια Κύρνος ὁπηδεῖ

---

[1] εἴ ποτ᾽ Reiske.   But the text is quite right.
[2] ἀείσῃ schol. Lycophr. 275 ; ἀείσει.

---

[a] Fountain in Pieria near Mt. Olympus, sacred to the
Muses.   [b] Cynthos, mountain in Delos.
   [c] The Icarian sea, so called from Icarus, son of Daedalus,

IV.—TO DELOS

WHAT time or when, O my soul, wilt thou sing of
holy Delos, nurse of Apollo ?   Surely all the Cyclades,
most holy of the isles that lie in the sea, are goodly
theme of song.   But Delos would win the foremost
guerdon from the Muses, since she it was that bathed
Apollo, the lord of minstrels, and swaddled him, and
was the first to accept him for a god.   Even as the
Muses abhor him who sings not of Pimpleia[a] so
Phoebus abhors him who forgets Delos.   To Delos
now will I give her share of song, so that Cynthian[b]
Apollo may praise me for taking thought of his dear
nurse.

Wind-swept and stern is she set in the sea, and,
wave-beaten as she is, is fitter haunt for gulls than
course for horses.   The sea, rolling greatly round
her, casts off on her much spindrift of the Icarian[c]
water.   Wherefore also sea-roaming fishermen have
made her their home.   But none need grudge that
she be named among the first, whensoever unto
Oceanus and unto Titan Tethys the islands gather
and she ever leads the way.[d]   Behind her footsteps
follow Phoenician Cyrnus,[e] no mean isle, and

who fell into it when his father and he attempted to fly from
Crete with artificial wings to escape the wrath of Minos.
(Strabo 639, Diodor. iv. 77.)

[d] See Introduction.

[e] Corsica, colonized by the Phoenicians.

85

οὐκ ὀνοτὴ καὶ Μάκρις Ἀβαντιὰς Ἑλλοπιήων   20
Σαρδώ θ' ἱμερόεσσα καὶ ἣν ἐπενήξατο Κύπρις
ἐξ ὕδατος τὰ πρῶτα, σαοῖ δέ μιν ἀντ' ἐπιβάθρων.
κεῖναι μὲν πύργοισι περισκεπέεσσιν ἐρυμναί,
Δῆλος δ' Ἀπόλλωνι· τί δὲ στιβαρώτερον ἔρκος;
τείχεα μὲν καὶ λᾶες ὑπαὶ ῥιπῆς κε πέσοιεν   25
Στρυμονίου βορέαο· θεὸς δ' ἀεὶ ἀστυφέλικτος·
Δῆλε φίλη, τοῖός σε βοηθόος ἀμφιβέβηκεν.

εἰ δὲ λίην πολέες σε περιτροχόωσιν ἀοιδαί,
ποίῃ[1] ἐνιπλέξω σε; τί τοι θυμῆρες ἀκοῦσαι;
ἦ ὡς[2] τὰ πρώτιστα μέγας θεὸς οὔρεα θείνων   30
ἄορι τριγλώχινι, τό οἱ Τελχῖνες ἔτευξαν,
νήσους εἰναλίας εἰργάζετο, νέρθε δὲ πάσας[3]
ἐκ νεάτων ὤχλισσε καὶ εἰσεκύλισε θαλάσσῃ·
καὶ τὰς μὲν κατὰ βυσσόν, ἵν' ἠπείροιο λάθωνται,
πρυμνόθεν ἐρρίζωσε· σὲ δ' οὐκ ἔθλιψεν ἀνάγκη,   35
ἀλλ' ἄφετος πελάγεσσιν ἐπέπλεες, οὔνομα δ' ἦν σοι
Ἀστερίη τὸ παλαιόν, ἐπεὶ βαθὺν ἥλαο τάφρον
οὐρανόθεν φεύγουσα Διὸς γάμον ἀστέρι ἴση.
τόφρα μὲν οὔπω σοι χρυσέη ἐπεμίσγετο Λητώ,
τόφρα δ' ἔτ' Ἀστερίη σὺ καὶ οὐδέπω ἔκλεο Δῆλος·   40
πολλάκι σε[4] Τροιζῆνος ἀπὸ ξανθοῖο πολίχνης

---

[1] τοίη MSS.   [2] χ' ὡς MSS.
[3] δὲ πάσας MSS.; δ' ἐλάσσας Meineke; δ' ἐπάρας Schneider.
[4] πολλάκι σ' ἐκ marg. Taur., corr. Meineke; πολλάκις ἐκ.

---

[a] Euboea, which was also called Ellopia from Ellops, son of Ion (Strabo 445, Steph. B. *s.v.* Ἑλλοπία.)

[b] Sardinia.   [c] Cyprus (schol.).

[d] ἐπίβαθρον (Hom. *Od.* xiv. 449, Callim. *Hec.* 31, Apoll. Rh. i. 421) is properly the fee for entering a ship; *cf.* Eustath. on Hom. *l.c.*, Hesych. *s.v.* = ναῦλον. Here = fee for setting foot in Cyprus. *Cf.* Nonnus xiii. 457 Πάφον . . . ἐξ ὑδάτων ἐπίβαθρον ἀνερχομένης Ἀφροδίτης.

[e] Strymon, river in Thrace. (ἀφ' οὗ ὁ βορᾶς· Στρυμονίου βορέαο, Steph. B. *s.v.*)

HYMN IV

Abantian Macris[a] of the Ellopians, and delectable
Sardo,[b] and the isle[c] whereto Cypris first swam from
the water and which for fee[d] of her landing she
keeps safe. They are strong by reason of sheltering
towers, but Delos is strong by aid of Apollo. What
defence is there more steadfast? Walls and stones
may fall before the blast of Strymonian[e] Boreas;
but a god is unshaken for ever. Delos beloved, such
is the champion that encompasses thee about!

Now if songs full many circle about thee, with
what song shall I entwine thee? What is that
which is pleasing unto thee to hear? Is it the tale
how at the very first the mighty god[f] smote the
mountains with the three-forked sword which the
Telchines[g] fashioned for him, and wrought the
islands in the sea, and from their lowest foundations
lifted them all as with a lever and rolled them into
the sea? And them in the depths he rooted from
their foundations that they might forget the mainland. But no constraint afflicted thee, but free upon
the open sea thou didst float; and thy name of old
was Asteria,[h] since like a star thou didst leap from
heaven into the deep moat, fleeing wedlock with
Zeus. Until then golden Leto consorted not with
thee: then thou wert still Asteria and wert not yet
called Delos. Oft-times did sailors coming from the
town of fair-haired Troezen[i] unto Ephyra[j] within

[f] Poseidon.
[g] Mythical artificers, "notique operum Telchines," Stat. *T.*
ii. 274; *S.* iv. 6. 47.
[h] As if from *aster* = star. Stat. *A.* i. 388 "instabili Delo."
[i] Troezen, son of Pelops, founder of Troezen in Argolis
(Strabo 374, Paus. ii. 30. 8, Steph. B. *s.v.*)
[j] Ephyra, old name of Corinth (Paus. ii. 1. 1, Strabo 338,
Steph. Byz. *s.v.*)

ἐρχόμενοι Ἐφύρηνδε Σαρωνικοῦ ἔνδοθι κόλπου
ναῦται ἐπεσκέψαντο, καὶ ἐξ Ἐφύρης ἀνιόντες
οἱ μὲν ἔτ' οὐκ ἴδον αὖθι, σὺ δὲ στεινοῖο παρ' ὀξὺν
ἔδραμες Εὐρίποιο πόρον καναχηδὰ ῥέοντος,   45
Χαλκιδικῆς δ' αὐτῆμαρ ἀνηναμένη ἁλὸς ὕδωρ
μέσφ' ἐς Ἀθηναίων προσενήξαο Σούνιον ἄκρον
ἢ Χίον ἢ νήσοιο διάβροχον ὕδατι μαστὸν
Παρθενίης (οὔπω γὰρ ἔην Σάμος), ἧχι σε νύμφαι
γείτονες Ἀγκαίου Μυκαλησσίδες [1] ἐξείνισσαν.   50

ἡνίκα δ' Ἀπόλλωνι γενέθλιον οὖδας ὑπέσχες,
τοῦτό τοι ἀντημοιβὸν ἁλίπλοοι οὔνομ' ἔθεντο,
οὔνεκεν οὐκέτ' ἄδηλος ἐπέπλεες, ἀλλ' ἐνὶ πόντου
κύμασιν Αἰγαίοιο ποδῶν ἐνεθήκαο ῥίζας.

οὐδ' Ἥρην κοτέουσαν ὑπέτρεσας· ἡ μὲν ἁπάσαις   55
δεινὸν ἐπεβρωμᾶτο λεχωίσιν αἳ Διὶ παῖδας
ἐξέφερον, Λητοῖ δὲ διακριδόν, οὕνεκα μούνη
Ζηνὶ τεκεῖν ἤμελλε φιλαίτερον Ἄρεος υἷα.
τῶ ῥα καὶ αὐτὴ μὲν σκοπιὴν ἔχεν αἰθέρος εἴσω
σπερχομένη μέγα δή τι καὶ οὐ φατόν, εἶργε δὲ
Λητὼ   60
τειρομένην ὠδῖσι· δύω δέ οἱ εἴατο φρουροὶ
γαῖαν ἐποπτεύοντες, ὁ μὲν πέδον ἠπείροιο
ἥμενος ὑψηλῆς κορυφῆς ἔπι Θρήικος Αἵμου
θοῦρος Ἄρης ἐφύλασσε σὺν ἔντεσι, τὼ δέ οἱ ἵππω
ἑπτάμυχον βορέαο παρὰ σπέος ηὐλίζοντο·   65

[1] Μυκαλησσίδες Blomf., cf. Steph. Byz. s.v.; Μυκαλησίδες.

a Parthenia, old name for Samos (Steph. Byz. s.v.).
b Mycale lies on the mainland, opposite Samos, of which Ancaeus, son of Zeus or Poseidon and Astypalaia, was the mythical king. Steph. Byz., s.v. Μυκαλησσός, says ἔστι καὶ ὄρος Μυκαλησσὸς ἐναντίον Σάμου· καὶ Μυκαλησσὶς τὸ θηλυκόν.
c Stat. T. viii. 197 "partuque ligatam Delon."
d Apollo.

the Saronic gulf descry thee, and on their way back
from Ephyra saw thee no more there, but thou hadst
run to the swift straits of the narrow Euripus with
its sounding stream. And the same day, turning
thy back on the waters of the sea of Chalcis, thou
didst swim to the Sunian headland of the Athenians
or to Chios or to the wave-washed breast of the
Maiden's Isle,[a] not yet called Samos—where the
nymphs of Mycalessos,[b] neighbours of Ancaeus, entertained thee.

But when thou gavest thy soil to be the birth-
place of Apollo, seafaring men gave thee this
name in exchange, since no more didst thou float[c]
obscure (ἄδηλος) upon the water, but amid the
waves of the Aegean sea didst plant the roots of thy
feet.

And thou didst not tremble before the anger of
Hera, who murmured terribly against all child-
bearing women that bare children to Zeus, but
especially against Leto, for that she only was to bear
to Zeus a son[d] dearer even than Ares. Wherefore
also she herself kept watch within the sky, angered
in her heart greatly and beyond telling, and she
prevented Leto who was holden in the pangs of
child-birth. And she had two look-outs set to keep
watch upon the earth. The space of the continent
did bold Ares watch, sitting armed on the high top
of Thracian Haemus, and his horses were stalled by
the seven-chambered cave[e] of Boreas. And the

[e] *Cf. Stat. Th.* vi. 100 "Dat gemitum tellus : non sic
eversa feruntur Ismara, cum fracto Boreas caput extulit
antro." The cave of Boreas lay in the far North-east (Plin.
N.H. vii. 10 ; Soph. *Ant.* 983, schol. ; Apoll. Rh. i. 826 ; Sil.
It. *Prin.* viii. 513 ; Serv. Verg. *A.* x. 350, xii. 366 ; [Plutarch],
De fluv. 14. 5).

CALLIMACHUS

ἡ δ' ἐπὶ νησάων ἑτέρη σκοπὸς εὐρειάων
ἧστο κόρη Θαύμαντος ἐπαΐξασα Μίμαντι.
ἔνθ' οἱ μὲν πολίεσσιν ὅσαις ἐπεβάλλετο Λητὼ
μίμνον ἀπειλητῆρες, ἀπετρώπων δὲ δέχεσθαι.
φεῦγε μὲν Ἀρκαδίη, φεῦγεν δ' ὄρος ἱερὸν Αὔγης   70
Παρθένιον, φεῦγεν δ' ὁ γέρων μετόπισθε Φενειός.[1]
φεῦγε δ' ὅλη Πελοπηὶς ὅση παρακέκλιται Ἰσθμῷ,
ἔμπλην Αἰγιαλοῦ τε καὶ Ἄργεος· οὐ γὰρ ἐκείνας
ἀτραπιτοὺς ἐπάτησεν, ἐπεὶ λάχεν Ἴναχον Ἥρη.
φεῦγε καὶ Ἀονίη τὸν ἕνα δρόμον, αἱ δ' ἐφέποντο   75
Δίρκη τε Στροφίη τε μελαμψήφιδος ἔχουσαι
Ἰσμηνοῦ χέρα πατρός, ὁ δ' εἵπετο πολλὸν ὄπισθεν
Ἀσωπὸς βαρύγουνος, ἐπεὶ πεπάλακτο κεραυνῷ.
ἡ δ' ὑποδινηθεῖσα χοροῦ ἀπεπαύσατο νύμφη
αὐτόχθων Μελίη καὶ ὑπόχλοον ἔσχε παρειὴν   80
ἥλικος ἀσθμαίνουσα περὶ δρυός, ὡς ἴδε χαίτην
σειομένην Ἑλικῶνος. ἐμαὶ θεαί, εἴπατε Μοῦσαι,
ἦ ῥ' ἐτεὸν ἐγένοντο τότε δρύες ἡνίκα Νύμφαι;
Νύμφαι μὲν χαίρουσιν, ὅτε δρύας ὄμβρος ἀέξει,
Νύμφαι δ' αὖ κλαίουσιν, ὅτε δρυσὶν οὐκέτι φύλλα.   85
ταῖς μὲν ἔτ' Ἀπόλλων ὑποκόλπιος αἰνὰ χολώθη,

[1] Φενειός Arnaldus ; Φεναιός.

[a] Iris (Stat. *Th.* x. 123).
[b] Mimas, mountain in Ionia opposite to Chios.
[c] Auge, daughter of Aleos, king of Tegea. Her father, warned by an oracle that his sons would perish by a descendant of his daughter, made her a priestess to Athena. She became, however, mother of Telephus by Heracles and gave birth to her son on the hill Parthenium in Arcadia (Diodor. iv. 33. 7 ff.). *Cf.* Paus. viii. 48. 7, who says at Tegea Eileithyia was worshipped as Αὔγη ἐν γόνασι because Auge bare her son there. But he mentions another story which said Telephus was exposed on Parthenium.
[d] The autochthonous founder of Pheneos, town in Arcadia (Paus. viii. 14. 4).

90

other kept watch over the far-flung islands, even
the daughter *a* of Thaumas seated on Mimas,*b* whither
she had sped. There they sat and threatened all
the cities which Leto approached and prevented
them from receiving her. Fled Arcadia, fled Auge's *c*
holy hill Parthenium, fled after her aged Pheneius,*d*
fled all the land of Pelops that lies beside the
Isthmus, save only Aegialos *e* and Argos. For on
those ways she set not her feet, since Inachus *f*
belonged unto Hera. Fled, too, Aonia *g* on the
same course, and Dirce *h* and Strophia,*i* holding the
hands of their sire, dark-pebbled Ismenus*j*; far behind
followed Asopus,*k* heavy-kneed, for he was marred
by a thunderbolt. And the earth-born nymph
Melia *l* wheeled about thereat and ceased from the
dance and her cheek paled as she panted for her
coeval oak, when she saw the locks of Helicon
tremble. Goddesses mine, ye Muses, say did the
oaks come into being at the same time as the
Nymphs? The nymphs rejoice when the rain
makes the oaks to grow; and again the Nymphs
weep when there are no longer leaves upon the
oaks. And Apollo, yet in his mother's womb, was

e Aegialos sometimes denoted the whole district from
Sicyon to Buprasium (Steph. Byz. *s.v.*), *i.e.* Achaia (Paus.
v. 1. 1, vii. 1. 1, Strabo 333), here more strictly the district of
Sicyon (which was also called Aegiale, Paus. ii. 6. 5).

f Inachus, river in Argolis.

g Aonia = Boeotia.

h Dirce, river at Thebes.

i Strophia, unknown river of Boeotia.

j Ismenos, river of Boeotia.

k River in Boeotia.

l The Meliae or Ash-nymphs were of the same class as
the Dryads or Hamadryads. The Melia referred to here
was the sister of Ismenus. For the general idea *cf.* Stat.
Silv. i. 3. 59 ff.

φθέγξατο δ' οὐκ ἀτέλεστον ἀπειλήσας ἐπὶ Θήβῃ·
" Θήβη, τίπτε τάλαινα τὸν αὐτίκα πότμον ἐλέγχεις;
μήπω μή μ' ἀέκοντα βιάζεο μαντεύεσθαι.
οὔπω μοι Πυθῶνι μέλει τριποδήϊος ἕδρη,   90
οὐδέ τί πω τέθνηκεν ὄφις μέγας, ἀλλ' ἔτι κεῖνο
θηρίον αἰνογένειον ἀπὸ Πλειστοῖο καθέρπον
Παρνησὸν νιφόεντα περιστέφει ἐννέα κύκλοις·
ἀλλ' ἔμπης ἐρέω τι τομώτερον ἢ ἀπὸ δάφνης.
φεῦγε πρόσω· ταχινός σε κιχήσομαι αἵματι λούσων 95
τόξον ἐμόν· σὺ δὲ τέκνα κακογλώσσοιο γυναικὸς
ἔλλαχες. οὐ σύ γ' ἐμεῖο φίλη τροφὸς οὐδὲ Κιθαι-
                                                    ρὼν
ἔσσεται· εὐαγέων δὲ καὶ εὐαγέεσσι μελοίμην."
ὣς ἄρ' ἔφη. Λητὼ δὲ μετάτροπος αὖτις ἐχώρει.
ἀλλ' ὅτ' Ἀχαιάδες μιν ἀπηρνήσαντο πόληες   100
ἐρχομένην, Ἑλίκη τε Ποσειδάωνος ἑταίρη
Βούρά τε Δεξαμενοῖο βοόστασις Οἰκιάδαο,
ἂψ δ' ἐπὶ Θεσσαλίην πόδας ἔτρεπε, φεῦγε δ'
                                              Ἄναυρος
καὶ μεγάλη Λάρισα καὶ αἱ Χειρωνίδες ἄκραι,
φεῦγε δὲ καὶ Πηνειὸς ἑλισσόμενος διὰ Τεμπέων.   105
      Ἥρη, σοὶ δ' ἔτι τῆμος ἀνηλεὲς ἦτορ ἔκειτο
οὐδὲ κατεκλάσθης τε καὶ ᾤκτισας, ἡνίκα πήχεις
ἀμφοτέρους ὀρέγουσα μάτην ἐφθέγξατο τοῖα

---

[a] The dragon which occupied or watched Delphi and
which Apollo slew; cf. *Hymn Apoll.* 100 ff., Hom. *Hymn
Apoll.* 282 ff.
[b] River at Delphi.
[c] The laurel of the Pythian priestess at Delphi.
[d] Niobe, daughter of Tantalus and wife of Amphion of
Thebes, had twelve children—six sons and six daughters—
who were slain by Apollo and Artemis because Niobe

sore angered against them and he uttered against
Thebe no ineffectual threat: "Thebe, wherefore,
wretched one, dost thou ask the doom that shall be
thine anon? Force me not yet to prophesy against
my will. Not yet is the tripod seat at Pytho my
care; not yet is the great serpent[a] dead, but still that
beast of awful jaws, creeping down from Pleistus,[b]
wreathes snowy Parnassus with his nine coils. Nevertheless I will speak unto thee a word more clear than
shall be spoken from the laurel[c] branch. Flee on!
swiftly shall I overtake thee and wash my bow in blood.
Thou hast in thy keeping the children of a slanderous
woman.[d] Not thou shalt be my dear nurse, nor
Cithaeron.[e] Pure am I and may I be the care of them
that are pure." So he spake. And Leto turned
and went back. But when the Achaean cities refused
her as she came—Helice,[f] the companion of Poseidon,
and Bura,[g] the steading of Dexamenus, the son of
Oeceus—she turned her feet back to Thessaly.
And Anaurus fled and great Larisa and the cliffs
of Cheiron[h]; fled, too, Peneius, coiling through
Tempe.

But thy heart, Hera, was even then still pitiless
and thou wert not broken down nor didst have
compassion, when she stretched forth both her arms

boasted of the number of her children as compared with
Leto, who had but two.

[e] Cithaeron, mountain in Boeotia.

[f] Helice, town in Achaia with temple of Poseidon
Heliconios (Paus. vii. 24. 5, Strabo 384, cf. Hom. Il. xx. 404).
Helice was daughter of Selinus and by Ion mother of Bura
(Paus. vii. 1. 2, vii. 25. 5).

[g] Bura, town in Achaia, where Dexamenos a Centaur had
great cattle-stalls (schol.). In E.M. s.v. Βοῦσα he is called
Εξάδιος.

[h] Pelion in Thessaly, home of the Centaur Cheiron.

" Νύμφαι Θεσσαλίδες, ποταμοῦ γένος, εἴπατε πατρὶ
κοιμῆσαι μέγα χεῦμα· περιπλέξασθε γενείῳ   110
λισσόμεναι τὰ Ζηνὸς ἐν ὕδατι τέκνα τεκέσθαι.
Πηνειὲ Φθιῶτα, τί νῦν ἀνέμοισιν ἐρίζεις;
ὦ πάτερ, οὐ μὴν ἵππον ἀέθλιον ἀμφιβέβηκας.
ἢ ῥά τοι ὧδ' αἰεὶ ταχινοὶ πόδες, ἢ 'π' ἐμεῖο
μοῦνοι ἐλαφρίζουσι, πεποίησαι δὲ πέτεσθαι   115
σήμερον ἐξαπίνης;" ὁ δ' ἀνήκοος. " ὦ ἐμὸν ἄχθος,
ποῖ σε φέρω; μέλεοι γὰρ ἀπειρήκασι τένοντες.
Πήλιον ὦ Φιλύρης νυμφήιον, ἀλλὰ σὺ μεῖνον,
μεῖνον, ἐπεὶ καὶ θῆρες ἐν οὔρεσι πολλάκι σεῖο
ὠμοτόκους ὠδῖνας ἀπηρείσαντο λέαιναι."   120
τὴν δ' ἄρα καὶ Πηνειὸς ἀμείβετο δάκρυα λείβων
" Λητοῖ, Ἀναγκαίη μεγάλη θεός. οὐ γὰρ ἔγωγε
πότνια σὰς ὠδῖνας ἀναίνομαι· οἶδα καὶ ἄλλας
λουσαμένας ἀπ' ἐμεῖο λεχωίδας· ἀλλά μοι Ἥρη
δαψιλὲς ἠπείλησεν. ἀπαύγασαι, οἷος ἔφεδρος   125
οὔρεος ἐξ ὑπάτου σκοπιὴν ἔχει, ὅς κέ με ῥεῖα
βυσσόθεν ἐξερύσειε. τί μήσομαι; ἦ ἀπολέσθαι
ἡδύ τί τοι Πηνειόν; ἴτω πεπρωμένον ἦμαρ·
τλήσομαι εἵνεκα σεῖο καὶ εἰ μέλλοιμι ῥοάων
διψαλέην ἄμπωτιν ἔχων αἰώνιον ἔρρειν   130
καὶ μόνος ἐν ποταμοῖσιν ἀτιμότατος καλέεσθαι.
ἠνίδ' ἐγώ· τί περισσά; κάλει μόνον Εἰλήθυιαν."
εἶπε καὶ ἠρώησε μέγαν ῥόον. ἀλλά οἱ Ἄρης
Παγγαίου προθέλυμνα καρήατα μέλλεν ἀείρας
ἐμβαλέειν δίνησιν, ἀποκρύψαι δὲ ῥέεθρα·   13.

---

[a] Among the daughters of Peneios are Iphis, Atrax,
Tricca, Menippe, Daphne, and, according to some, Cyrene.

[b] Cheiron was the son of the union of Cronus and Philyra
on Mt. Pelion (Pind. *P.* iii. 1 f., ix. 30, etc.).

[c] The reference is to the helplessness and shapelessness
of the lion cub at birth. *Cf.* Aristotle, *De gen. animal.* iv. 6

and spake in vain: "Ye nymphs of Thessaly, off-spring of a river,[a] tell your sire to hush his great stream. Entwine your hands about his beard and entreat him that the children of Zeus be born in his waters. Phthiotian Peneius, why dost thou now vie with the winds? O sire, thou dost not bestride a racing horse. Are thy feet always thus swift, or are they swift only for me, and hast thou to-day been suddenly made to fly?" But he heard her not. "O burden mine, whither shall I carry thee? The hapless sinews of my feet are outworn. O Pelion, bridal chamber of Philyra,[b] do thou stay, O stay, since on thy hills even the wild lionesses oftentimes lay down their travail of untimely birth."[c] Then shedding tears, Peneius answered her: "Leto, Necessity is a great goddess. It is not I who refuse, O Lady, thy travail; for I know of others who have washed the soilure of birth in me—but Hera hath largely threatened me. Behold what manner of watcher keeps vigil on the mountain top, who would lightly drag me forth from the depths. What shall I devise? Or is it a pleasant thing to thee that Peneius should perish? Let my destined day take its course. I will endure for thy sake, even if I must wander evermore with ebbing flood and thirsty, and alone be called of least honour among rivers. Here am I! What needeth more? Do thou but call upon Eileithyia." He spake and stayed his great stream. But Ares was about to lift the peaks of Pangaeum[d] from their base and hurl them in his eddying waters and hide his streams. And from on

τὰ μὲν ἀδιάρθρωτα σχεδὸν γεννᾷ, καθάπερ ἀλώπηξ ἄρκτος λέων. The sense of ὠμός is precisely that of *crudus* in Stat. Th. iv. 280 "quercus laurique ferebant Cruda puerperia."

[a] Mountain in Thrace.

ὑψόθε δ' ἐσμαράγησε καὶ ἀσπίδα τύψεν ἀκωκῇ
δούρατος· ἡ δ' ἐλέλιξεν ἐνόπλιον· ἔτρεμε δ' Ὄσσης
οὔρεα καὶ πεδίον Κραννώνιον αἵ τε δυσαεῖς
ἐσχατιαὶ Πίνδοιο, φόβῳ δ' ὠρχήσατο πᾶσα
Θεσσαλίη· τοῖος γὰρ ἀπ' ἀσπίδος ἔβρεμεν[1] ἦχος. 140
ὡς δ' ὁπότ' Αἰτναίου ὄρεος πυρὶ τυφομένοιο
σείονται μυχὰ πάντα κατουδαίοιο γίγαντος
εἰς ἑτέρην Βριαρῆος ἐπωμίδα κινυμένοιο,
θερμάστραι[2] τε βρέμουσιν ὑφ' Ἡφαίστοιο πυράγρης
ἔργα θ' ὁμοῦ, δεινὸν δὲ πυρίκμητοί τε λέβητες 145
καὶ τρίποδες πίπτοντες ἐπ' ἀλλήλοις ἰαχεῦσι·
τῆμος ἔγεντ' ἄραβος σάκεος τόσος εὐκύκλοιο.
Πηνειὸς δ' οὐκ αὖτις ἐχάζετο, μίμνε δ' ὁμοίως
καρτερὸς ὡς τὰ πρῶτα, θοὰς δ' ἐστήσατο δίνας,
εἰσόκε οἱ Κοιῆις ἐκέκλετο "σῴζεο χαίρων, 150
σῴζεο· μὴ σύ γ' ἐμεῖο πάθῃς κακὸν εἵνεκα τῆσδε
ἀντ' ἐλεημοσύνης, χάριτος δέ τοι ἔσσετ' ἀμοιβή."

ἦ καὶ πολλὰ πάροιθεν ἐπεὶ κάμεν ἔστιχε νήσους
εἰναλίας· αἱ δ' οὔ μιν ἐπερχομένην ἐδέχοντο,
οὐ λιπαρὸν νήεσσιν Ἐχινάδες ὅρμον ἔχουσαι, 155
οὐδ' ἥτις Κέρκυρα φιλοξεινωτάτη ἄλλων,
Ἶρις ἐπεὶ πάσῃσιν ἐφ' ὑψηλοῖο Μίμαντος
σπερχομένη μάλα πολλὸν ἀπέτραπεν· αἱ δ' ὑπ'
      ὁμοκλῆς
πανσυδίῃ φοβέοντο κατὰ ῥόον ἥντινα τέτμοι.

---

[1] ἔβρεμεν e ; ἔβραμεν A ; ἔβραχεν other mss.
[2] θερμάστραι Hesychius ; θερμαύστραι.

---

[a] Cf. Frazer, G.B.³, Adonis, Attis, Osiris, i. p. 197 : "The
people of Timor, in the East Indies, think that the earth
rests on the shoulder of a mighty giant, and that when he is
weary of bearing it on one shoulder he shifts it to the other
and so causes the ground to quake." Ibid. p. 200 : "The

high he made a din as of thunder and smote his
shield with the point of his spear, and it rang with a
warlike noise. And the hills of Ossa trembled and
the plain of Crannon, and the windswept skirts of
Pindus, and all Thessaly danced for fear: such
echoing din rang from his shield. And even as
when the mount of Aetna smoulders with fire and all
its secret depths are shaken as the giant under earth,
even Briares, shifts to his other shoulder,[a] and with
the tongs of Hephaestus roar furnaces and handiwork withal; and firewrought basins and tripods ring
terribly as they fall one upon the other: such in
that hour was the rattle of the fair-rounded shield.
But Peneius retired not back, but abode his ground,
steadfast even as before, and stayed his swift eddying
streams, until the daughter[b] of Coeüs called to him:
"Save thyself, farewell! save thyself; do not for my
sake suffer evil for this thy compassion; thy favour
shall be rewarded."

So she spake and after much toil came unto the
isles of the sea. But they received her not when
she came—not the Echinades[c] with their smooth
anchorage for ships, nor Cercyra which is of all other
islands most hospitable; since Iris on lofty Mimas[d] was
wroth with them all and utterly prevented them.
And at her rebuke they fled all together, every one
that she came to, along the waters. Then she came

Tongans think that the earth is supported on the prostrate
form of the god Móooi. When he is tired of lying in one
posture, he tries to turn himself about, and that causes an
earthquake."

[b] Leto, daughter of Coeüs and Phoebe.

[c] At the mouth of the Achelous.

[d] "Windy Mimas," *Od.* iii. 172. Mountain in Erythraea
opposite Chios.

ὠγυγίην δήπειτα Κόων, Μεροπηίδα νῆσον,   160
ἵκετο, Χαλκιόπης ἱερὸν μυχὸν ἡρωίνης.
ἀλλά ἑ παιδὸς ἔρυκεν ἔπος τόδε " μὴ σύ γε, μῆτερ,
τῇ με τέκοις. οὔτ' οὖν ἐπιμέμφομαι οὐδὲ μεγαίρω
νῆσον, ἐπεὶ λιπαρή τε καὶ εὔβοτος, εἴ νύ τις ἄλλη·
ἀλλὰ οἱ ἐκ Μοιρέων τις ὀφειλόμενος θεὸς ἄλλος   165
ἐστί, Σαωτήρων ὕπατον γένος· ᾧ ὑπὸ μίτρην
ἵξεται οὐκ ἀέκουσα Μακηδόνι κοιρανέεσθαι
ἀμφοτέρη μεσόγεια καὶ αἳ πελάγεσσι κάθηνται,
μέχρις ὅπου περάτη τε καὶ ὁππόθεν ὠκέες ἵπποι
Ἠέλιον φορέουσιν· ὁ δ' εἴσεται ἤθεα πατρός.   170

καί νύ ποτε ξυνός τις ἐλεύσεται ἄμμιν ἄεθλος
ὕστερον, ὁππότ' ἂν οἱ μὲν ἐφ' Ἑλλήνεσσι μάχαι-
        ραν
βαρβαρικὴν καὶ Κελτὸν ἀναστήσαντες Ἄρηα
ὀψίγονοι Τιτῆνες ἀφ' ἑσπέρου ἐσχατόωντος
ῥώσωνται νιφάδεσσιν ἐοικότες ἢ ἰσάριθμοι   175
τείρεσιν, ἡνίκα πλεῖστα κατ' ἠέρα βουκολέονται,
φρούρια καὶ [κῶμαι Λοκρῶν καὶ Δελφίδες ἄκραι]
καὶ πεδία Κρισσαῖα καὶ ἤπειροι[ο φάραγγες]¹
ἀμφιπεριστείνωνται, ἴδωσι δὲ πίονα καπνὸν²
γείτονος αἰθομένοιο, καὶ οὐκέτι μοῦνον ἀκουῇ,   180

---

¹ The best MSS. and the Aldine (1513) have only φρούρια
καὶ (177) and καὶ πεδία Κρισσαῖα καὶ ἤπειροι (178). The words
in brackets are a worthless attempt to supply the lacunae
and are found only in the late and inferior MSS. (Schneider's
LMNO).

² καρπὸν MSS. ; corr. Reiske.

ᵃ King of Cos (Steph. Byz. s.vv. Κῶς and Μέροψ).

ᵇ Daughter of Euryplos, king of Cos, mother of Thessalos
by Heracles (Apollod. ii. 7. 8).

ᶜ Ptolemy II. Philadelphus, son of Ptolemy I. Soter and
Berenice, was born in Cos in 310/9 B.C.   The date of the

HYMN IV

unto primeval Cos, the isle of Merops,[a] the holy
retreat of the heroine Chalciope,[b] but the word of
her son restrained her : " Bear me not, mother, here.
I blame not the island nor have any grudge, since a
bright isle it is and rich in pasture as any other.
But there is due to her from the Fates another god,[c]
the most high lineage of the Saviours[d]; beneath
whose crown shall come—not loth to be ruled by a
Macedonian—both continents and the lands which
are set in the sea, far as where the end of the earth
is and again whence his swift horses carry the sun.
And he shall know the ways of his sire.

Yea and one day hereafter there shall come upon
us a common struggle, when the Titans of a later day
shall rouse up against the Hellenes barbarian sword
and Celtic war,[e] and from the furthest West rush on
like snowflakes and in number as the stars when
they flock most thickly in the sky ; forts too [and
villages of the Locrians and Delphian heights][f] and
Crisaean plains and [glens of the mainland] be
thronged about and around, and shall behold the
rich smoke of their burning neighbour, and no longer

birth of Philadelphus is now settled by the discovery of a
new fragment of the Marmor Parium (*Athen. Mitth.* xxii.
[1897]) which has : ἄρχοντος Ἀθήνησι Ἱερομνήμονος (310/9 B.C.)
Πτολεμαίου ὁ υἱὸς ἐν Κῶι ἐγένετο. *Cf.* Theocrit. xvii. 58 ff.

[d] Soter, or Saviour, a title of the Ptolemies.

[e] From 300 B.C. there was a great southward movement
of the Celts from the Balkan peninsula. In 280/279 they
invaded Greece, where they attacked Delphi, but were
miraculously routed by Apollo. It was shortly after this
that a body of them settled in the district of Asia afterwards known as Galatia (*circ.* 240 B.C.).

[f] The readings here translated are an attempt in the
inferior MSS. to supply the lacunae. They have no intrinsic
value.

CALLIMACHUS

ἀλλ' ἤδη παρὰ νηὸν ἀπαυγάζοιντο φάλαγγας[1]
δυσμενέων, ἤδη δὲ παρὰ τριπόδεσσιν ἐμεῖο
φάσγανα καὶ ζωστῆρας ἀναιδέας ἐχθομένας τε
ἀσπίδας, αἳ Γαλάτῃσι κακὴν ὁδὸν ἄφρονι φύλῳ
στήσονται· τέων αἱ μὲν ἐμοὶ γέρας, αἱ δ' ἐπὶ Νείλῳ   185
ἐν πυρὶ τοὺς φορέοντας ἀποπνεύσαντας ἰδοῦσαι
κείσονται βασιλῆος ἀέθλια πολλὰ καμόντος.
ἐσσόμενε Πτολεμαῖε, τά τοι μαντήια φαίνω.
αἰνήσεις μέγα δή τι τὸν εἰσέτι γαστέρι μάντιν
ὕστερον ἤματα πάντα. σὺ δὲ ξυμβάλλεο, μῆτερ·   190
ἔστι διειδομένη τις ἐν ὕδατι νῆσος ἀραιή,
πλαζομένη πελάγεσσι· πόδες δέ οἱ οὐχ ἑνὶ χώρῳ,
ἀλλὰ παλιρροίῃ ἐπινήχεται ἀνθέρικος ὥς,
ἔνθα νότος, ἔνθ' εὖρος, ὅπῃ φορέῃσι θάλασσα.
τῇ με φέροις· κείνην γὰρ ἐλεύσεαι εἰς ἐθέλουσαν."   195
αἱ μὲν τόσσα λέγοντος ἀπέτρεχον εἰν ἁλὶ νῆσοι·
Ἀστερίη φιλόμολπε, σὺ δ' Εὐβοίηθε κατῄεις,
Κυκλάδας ὀψομένη περιηγέας, οὔ τι παλαιόν,
ἀλλ' ἔτι τοι μετόπισθε Γεραίστιον εἵπετο φῦκος·

. . . .   200

. . . . φλέξας ἐπεὶ περικαίεο †πυρί,[2]
τλῆμον' ὑπ' ὠδίνεσσι βαρυνομένην ὁρόωσα·
"Ἥρη, τοῦτό με ῥέξον ὅ τοι φίλον· οὐ γὰρ ἀπειλὰς
ὑμετέρας ἐφύλαξα· πέρα, πέρα εἰς ἐμὲ Λητοῖ."

---

[1] φάλαγγες mss. ; corr. Bentley.
[2] The better mss. leave a vacant space for line 200 and of
line 201 have only φλέξας ἐπεὶ περικαίεο πυρί (κῆρι emend.
Bentley).   Only the late and inferior mss. (Schneider's
LMNO) supply ἔστης δ' ἐν μέσσῃσι κατοικτείρασα δὲ Λητώ | φῦκος
ἅπαν κατέφλεξας, or similar words ; a very bad attempt to fill
the lacuna.   Some verb of speaking seems necessary.

---

[a] In the course of the revolt of Magas of Cyrene Ptolemy
Philadelphus had enrolled a body of Gallic mercenaries.

by hearsay only; but already beside the temple
behold the ranks of the foemen, and already beside
my tripods the swords and cruel belts and hateful
shields, which shall cause an evil journey to the
foolish tribe of the Galatians.   Of these shields
some shall be my guerdon; others, when they have
seen the wearers perish amid fire, shall be set by
the banks of Nile *a* to be the prizes of a king who
laboured much.   O Ptolemy who art to be, these
prophecies I declare for thee.   Greatly shalt thou
praise in all the days to be him that prophesied
while yet in his mother's womb.   But mark thou,
mother : there is to be seen in the water a tiny
island, wandering over the seas.   Her feet abide not
in one place, but on the tide she swims even as a stalk
of asphodel, where the South wind or the East wind
blows, whithersoever the sea carries her.   Thither do
thou carry me.   For she shall welcome thy coming."

When he had spoken thus much, the other islands
in the sea ran away.   But thou, Asteria, lover of
song, didst come down from Euboea to visit the
round Cyclades—not long ago, but still behind thee
trailed the sea-weed of Geraestus . . . since thy
heart *b* was kindled, seeing the unhappy lady in the
grievous pangs of birth : " Hera, do to me what thou
wilt.   For I heed not thy threats.   Cross, cross
over, Leto, unto me."

They became rebellious and attempted to make themselves
masters of Egypt.   Ptolemy enticed them into a desert
island formed by the branches of the Nile, where he left
them to die by famine and mutual slaughter (Paus. i. 7. 2).
See Bouché-Leclercq, *Histoire des Lagides*, i. p. 167 ;
Mahaffy, *The Empire of the Ptolemies*, p. 124 ff.   The date
of the revolt of Magas is round about 278 B.C., and thus
about the same date as the Gallic attack on Delphi.

   b Translating κῆρι.

CALLIMACHUS

ἔννεπες· ἡ δ' ἀρητὸν¹ ἅλης ἀπεπαύσατο λυγρῆς, 205
ἕζετο δ' Ἰνωποῖο παρὰ ῥόον, ὅντε βάθιστον
γαῖα τότ' ἐξανίησιν, ὅτε πλήθοντι ῥεέθρῳ
Νεῖλος ἀπὸ κρημνοῖο κατέρχεται Αἰθιοπῆος·
λύσατο δὲ ζώνην, ἀπὸ δ' ἐκλίθη ἔμπαλιν ὤμοις
φοίνικος ποτὶ πρέμνον ἀμηχανίης ὑπὸ λυγρῆς 210
τειρομένη· νότιος δὲ διὰ χροὸς ἔρρεεν ἱδρώς.
εἶπε δ' ἀλυσθμαίνουσα "τί μητέρα, κοῦρε, βαρύνεις;
αὕτη τοι, φίλε, νῆσος ἐπιπλώουσα θαλάσσῃ.
γείνεο, γείνεο, κοῦρε, καὶ ἤπιος ἔξιθι κόλπου."
νύμφα Διὸς βαρύθυμε, σὺ δ' οὐκ ἄρ' ἔμελλες ἄπυστος 215
δὴν ἔμεναι· τοίη σε προσέδραμεν ἀγγελιῶτις,
εἶπε δ' ἔτ' ἀσθμαίνουσα, φόβῳ δ' ἀνεμίσγετο μῦθος,
"Ἥρη τιμήεσσα, πολὺ προὔχουσα θεάων
σὴ μὲν ἐγώ, σὰ δὲ πάντα, σὺ δὲ κρείουσα κάθησαι
γνησίη Οὐλύμποιο, καὶ οὐ χέρα δείδιμεν ἄλλην 220
θηλυτέρην, σὺ δ', ἄνασσα, τὸν αἴτιον εἴσεαι ὀργῆς.
Λητώ τοι μίτρην ἀναλύεται ἔνδοθι νήσου.
ἄλλαι μὲν πᾶσαί μιν ἀπέστυγον οὐδ' ἐδέχοντο·
Ἀστερίη δ' ὀνομαστὶ παρερχομένην ἐκάλεσσεν,
Ἀστερίη, πόντοιο κακὸν σάρον· οἶσθα καὶ αὐτή. 225
ἀλλά, φίλη, δύνασαι γάρ, ἀμύνειν, πότνια, δούλοις
ὑμετέροις, οἳ σεῖο πέδον πατέουσιν ἐφετμῇ."
    ἦ καὶ ὑπὸ χρύσειον ἐδέθλιον ἷζε κύων ὥς,
Ἀρτέμιδος ἥτις τε, θοῆς ὅτε παύσεται ἄγρης,
ἵζει θηρήτειρα παρ' ἴχνεσιν, οὔατα δ' αὐτῆς 230
ὀρθὰ μάλ', αἰὲν ἑτοῖμα θεῆς ὑποδέχθαι ὁμοκλήν·
τῇ ἱκέλη Θαύμαντος ὑπὸ θρόνον ἷζετο κούρη.
κείνη δ' οὐδέποτε σφετέρης ἐπιλήθεται ἕδρης,
οὐδ' ὅτε οἱ ληθαῖον ἐπὶ πτερὸν ὕπνος ἐρείσῃ,

¹ ἀρητὸν Dilthey ; ἄρητον.

─────────────────────────────
ᵃ See note on Hymn iii. 171.   ᵇ See note on Hymn ii. 4.

So didst thou speak, and she gladly ceased from her grievous wandering and sat by the stream of Inopus,[a] which the earth sends forth in deepest flood at the season when the Nile comes down in full torrent from the Aethiopian steep. And she loosed her girdle and leaned back her shoulders against the trunk of a palm-tree,[b] oppressed by grievous distress, and the sweat poured over her flesh like rain. And she spake in her weakness: "Why, child, dost thou weigh down thy mother? There, dear child, is thine island floating on the sea. Be born, be born, my child, and gently issue from the womb." O Spouse of Zeus, Lady of heavy anger, thou wert not to be for long without tidings thereof: so swift a messenger hastened to thee. And, still breathing heavily, she spake—and her speech was mingled with fear: "Honoured Hera, of goddesses most excellent far, thine am I, all things are thine, and thou sittest authentic queen of Olympus, and we fear no other female hand; and thou, O Queen, wilt know who is the cause of thine anger. Leto is undoing her girdle within an island. All the others spurned her and received her not; but Asteria called her by name as she was passing by—Asteria, that evil scum of the sea: thou knowest it thyself. But, dear Lady,—for thou canst—defend thy servants, who tread the earth at thy behest."

So she spake and seated her beside the golden throne, even as a hunting hound of Artemis, which, when it hath ceased from the swift chase, sitteth by her feet, and its ears are erect, ever ready to receive the call of the goddess. Like thereto the daughter of Thaumas sat beside the throne. And she never forgetteth her seat, not even when sleep lays upon her his forgetful wing, but there by the edge of the

103

ἀλλ' αὐτοῦ μεγάλοιο ποτὶ γλωχῖνα θρόνοιο   235
τυτθὸν ἀποκλίνασα καρήατα λέχριος εὕδει.
οὐδέ ποτε ζώνην ἀναλύεται οὐδὲ ταχείας
ἐνδρομίδας, μὴ οἵ τι καὶ αἰφνίδιον ἔπος εἴπῃ
δεσπότις. ἡ δ' ἀλεγεινὸν ἀλαστήσασα προσηύδα
"οὕτω νῦν, ὦ Ζηνὸς ὀνείδεα, καὶ γαμέοισθε   240
λάθρια καὶ τίκτοιτε κεκρυμμένα, μηδ' ὅθι δειλαὶ
δυστοκέες μογέουσιν ἀλετρίδες, ἀλλ' ὅθι φῶκαι
εἰνάλιαι τίκτουσιν, ἐνὶ σπιλάδεσσιν ἐρήμοις.
Ἀστερίη δ' οὐδέν τι βαρύνομαι εἵνεκα τῆσδε
ἀμπλακίης, οὐδ' ἔστιν ὅπως ἀποθύμια ῥέξω,   245
τόσσα δέοι [1]· μάλα γάρ τε κακῶς ἐχαρίσσατο Λητοῖ·
ἀλλά μιν ἔκπαγλόν τι σεβίζομαι, οὕνεκ' ἐμεῖο
δέμνιον οὐκ ἐπάτησε, Διὸς δ' ἀνθείλετο πόντον."
      ἡ μὲν ἔφη· κύκνοι δὲ θεοῦ μέλποντες ἀοιδοὶ
Μηόνιον Πακτωλὸν ἐκυκλώσαντο λιπόντες   250
ἑβδομάκις περὶ Δῆλον, ἐπήεισαν δὲ λοχείῃ
Μουσάων ὄρνιθες, ἀοιδότατοι πετεηνῶν·
ἔνθεν ὁ παῖς τοσσάσδε λύρῃ ἐνεδήσατο χορδὰς
ὕστερον, ὁσσάκι κύκνοι ἐπ' ὠδίνεσσιν ἄεισαν.
ὄγδοον οὐκέτ' ἄεισαν, ὁ δ' ἔκθορεν, αἱ δ' ἐπὶ μα-
            κρὸν   255
νύμφαι Δηλιάδες, ποταμοῦ γένος ἀρχαίοιο,
εἶπαν Ἐλειθυίης ἱερὸν μέλος, αὐτίκα δ' αἰθὴρ
χάλκεος ἀντήχησε διαπρυσίην ὀλολυγήν,
οὐδ' Ἥρη νεμέσησεν, ἐπεὶ χόλον ἐξέλετο Ζεύς.
χρύσεά τοι τότε πάντα θεμείλια γείνετο, Δῆλε,   260
χρυσῷ δὲ τροχόεσσα πανήμερος ἔρρεε λίμνη,
χρύσειον δ' ἐκόμησε γενέθλιον ἔρνος ἐλαίης,
χρυσῷ δὲ πλήμυρε βαθὺς Ἰνωπὸς ἑλιχθείς.

---

[1] δέ οἱ mss. ; δέω Reiske.

great throne with head a little bent aslant she sleeps.
Never does she unloose her girdle or her swift
hunting-boots lest her mistress give her some sudden
command. And Hera was grievously angered and
spake to her : " So now, O shameful creatures of
Zeus, may ye all wed in secret and bring forth in
darkness, not even where the poor mill-women bring
forth in difficult labour, but where the seals of the
sea bring forth, amid the desolate rocks. But against
Asteria am I no wise angered for this sin, nor can I
do to her so unkindly as I should—for very wrongly
has she done a favour to Leto. Howbeit I honour
her exceedingly for that she did not desecrate my
bed, but instead of Zeus preferred the sea."

She spake : and with music the swans,[a] the gods'
own minstrels, left Maeonian Pactolus and circled
seven times round Delos, and sang over the bed of
child-birth, the Muses' birds, most musical of all birds
that fly.   Hence that child in after days strung the
lyre with just so many strings—seven strings, since
seven times the swans sang over the pangs of birth.
No eighth time sang they : ere that the child leapt
forth and the nymphs of Delos, offspring of an
ancient river, sang with far-sounding voice the holy
chant of Eileithyia. And straightway the brazen
sky echoed back the far-reaching chant and Hera
grudged it not, because Zeus had taken away her
anger.   In that hour, O Delos, all thy foundations
became of gold : with gold thy round lake [b] flowed all
day, and golden foliage thy natal olive-tree put forth
and with gold flowed coiled Inopus in deep flood.

---

[a] Apoll. Rhod. iv. 1300 f. ὅτε καλὰ νάοντος ἐπ᾽ ὀφρύσι
Πακτωλοῖο κύκνοι κινήσωσιν ἐὸν μέλος.

[b] See note on Hymn ii. 59.

CALLIMACHUS

αὐτὴ δὲ χρυσέοιο ἀπ᾿ οὔδεος εἵλεο παῖδα,
ἐν δ᾿ ἐβάλευ κόλποισιν, ἔπος δ᾿ ἐφθέγξαο τοῖον· 265
" ὦ μεγάλη πολύβωμε πολύπτολι πολλὰ φέρουσα,
πίονες ἤπειροί τε καὶ αἳ περιναίετε νῆσοι·
αὐτὴ[1] ἐγὼ τοιήδε, δυσήροτος, ἀλλ᾿ ἀπ᾿ ἐμεῖο
Δήλιος Ἀπόλλων κεκλήσεται, οὐδέ τις ἄλλη
γαιάων τοσσόνδε θεῷ πεφιλήσεται ἄλλῳ, 270
οὐ Κερχνὶς κρείοντι Ποσειδάωνι Λεχαίῳ,[2]
οὐ πάγος Ἑρμείῃ Κυλλήνιος, οὐ Διὶ Κρήτη,
ὡς ἐγὼ Ἀπόλλωνι· καὶ ἔσσομαι οὐκέτι πλαγκτή."
ὧδε σὺ μὲν κατέλεξας· ὁ δὲ γλυκὺν ἔσπασε μαζόν.

τῶ καὶ νησάων ἁγιωτάτη ἐξέτι κείνου 275
κλήζῃ, Ἀπόλλωνος κουροτρόφος· οὐδέ σ᾿ Ἐννὼ
οὐδ᾿ Ἀίδης οὐδ᾿ ἵπποι ἐπιστείβουσιν Ἄρηος·
ἀλλά τοι ἀμφιετεῖς δεκατηφόροι αἰὲν ἀπαρχαὶ
πέμπονται, πᾶσαι δὲ χοροὺς ἀνάγουσι πόληες,
αἵ τε πρὸς ἠοίην αἵ θ᾿ ἕσπερον αἵ τ᾿ ἀνὰ μέσσην 280
κλήρους ἐστήσαντο, καὶ οἳ καθύπερθε βορείης
οἰκία θινὸς ἔχουσι, πολυχρονιώτατον αἷμα.
οἱ μέν τοι καλάμην τε καὶ ἱερὰ δράγματα πρῶτοι
ἀσταχύων φορέουσιν· ἃ Δωδώνηθι[3] Πελασγοὶ

---

[1] αὕτη Reiske.   [2] Λεχαίου Hemsterhuis.

[3] Δωδώνηθι marg. Taur.; Δωδώνηθε.

---

^a *i.e.* Cenchreae, one of the harbours of Corinth ("bimaris
Corinthi"), the other being Lechaeum.
^b In Arcadia.
^c The Hyperboreans, who suffered neither disease nor
age (Pind. *P.* x. 41, *O.* iii. 16 ; Hesiod fr. 209 ; Herod. iv.
32 ; Diodor. ii. 47 ; Strabo 341 ; Plin. *N.H.* iv. 89, vi. 34
and 55 ; Mela i. 12 f., iii. 36). There is a useful recent
discussion by Otto Schroeder in *Archiv f. Religionswissen-
schaft*, viii. (1904–5) p. 69 ff. The meaning of the name is
much disputed. Pindar, *O.* iii. 55, takes it to mean "the
people behind Boreas," the north wind. Modern sugges-

And thou thyself didst take up the child from
the golden earth and lay him in thy lap and thou
spakest saying: "O mighty and of many altars and
many cities, bounteous Earth! rich continents and ye
islands set around lo! I am as thou see'st—hard of
tillage; yet from me shall Apollo be called 'of
Delos,' and none other among all lands shall be so
beloved by any other god: not Cerchnis*a* so loved
by Poseidon, Lord of Lechaeum, not Cyllene's hill*b*
by Hermes, not Crete by Zeus, as I by Apollo; and
I shall no more be a wandering isle." Thus didst
thou speak and the child drew the sweet breast.

Wherefore from that day thou art famed as the
most holy of islands, nurse of Apollo's youth. On
thee treads not Enyo nor Hades nor the horses of
Ares; but every year tithes of first-fruits are sent to
thee: to thee all cities lead up choirs, both those
cities which have cast their lots toward the East and
those toward the West and those in the South, and
the peoples which have their homes above the
Northern shore, a very long-lived race.*c* These*d*
first bring thee cornstalks and holy sheaves of
corn-ears, which the Pelasgians of Dodona, who

tions are ὑπέρ + βόρα, hill, "the people over the hills,"
or *i.q.* Περφερέες, Herod. iv. 33, *cf.* Hesych. περφερέες·
θεωροί.
d The version of Callimachus is that the offerings come
from the Hyperboreans to Dodona, thence to Malis, then to
Euboea, then to Delos. Herodotus says the offerings came
from the Hyperboreans to Scythia, then from tribe to tribe
till they reached the head of the Adriatic, thence to Dodona,
then to Malis, to Carystus in Euboea, then to Andros, then
to Tenos, and thence to Delos. Pausanias, i. 31. 2, says the
Hyperboreans gave them to the Arimaspi, they to the
Issedones, then the Scythians carried them to Sinope, then
they passed through Greece to Prasiae in Attica, and were
then carried by the Athenians to Delos.

τηλόθεν ἐκβαίνοντα[1] πολὺ πρώτιστα δέχονται,   285
γηλεχέες θεράποντες ἀσιγήτοιο λέβητος·
δεύτερον Ἱερὸν ἄστυ καὶ οὔρεα Μηλίδος αἴης
ἔρχονται· κεῖθεν δὲ διαπλώουσιν Ἀβάντων
εἰς ἀγαθὸν πεδίον Ληλάντιον· οὐδ' ἔτι μακρὸς
ὁ πλόος Εὐβοίηθεν, ἐπεὶ σέο γείτονες ὅρμοι.   290
πρῶταί τοι τάδ' ἔνεικαν ἀπὸ ξανθῶν Ἀριμασπῶν
Οὖπίς τε Λοξώ τε καὶ εὐαίων Ἑκαέργη,
θυγατέρες Βορέαο, καὶ ἄρσενες οἱ τότ' ἄριστοι
ἠιθέων· οὐδ' οἵ γε παλιμπετὲς οἴκαδ' ἵκοντο,
εὔμοιροι δ' ἐγένοντο, καὶ ἀκλέες οὔποτ' ἐκεῖνοι.   295
ἦ τοι Δηλιάδες μέν, ὅτ' εὐήχης ὑμέναιος
ἤθεα κουράων μορμύσσεται, ἥλικα χαίτην
παρθενικαῖς,[2] παῖδες δὲ θέρος τὸ πρῶτον ἰούλων
ἄρσενες ἠιθέοισιν ἀπαρχόμενοι φορέουσιν.

Ἀστερίη θυόεσσα, σὲ μὲν περί τ' ἀμφί τε νῆσοι   300
κύκλον ἐποιήσαντο καὶ ὡς χορὸν ἀμφεβάλοντο·
οὔτε σιωπηλὴν οὔτ' ἄψοφον οὖλος ἐθείραις
Ἕσπερος, ἀλλ' αἰεί σε καταβλέπει ἀμφιβόητον.
οἱ μὲν ὑπαείδουσι νόμον Λυκίοιο γέροντος,
ὅν τοι ἀπὸ Ξάνθοιο θεοπρόπος ἤγαγεν Ὠλήν·   305
αἱ δὲ ποδὶ πλήσσουσι χορίτιδες ἀσφαλὲς οὖδας.
δὴ τότε καὶ στεφάνοισι βαρύνεται ἱρὸν ἄγαλμα

---

[1] εἰσβαίνοντα Meineke.
[2] παρθενικαῖς marg. e; παρθενικαί.

---

[a] The famous Δωδωναῖον χαλκεῖον (Suid. s.v., Steph. Byz. s.v. Δωδώνη, cf. Strabo, vii. fr. 3) is discussed by A. B. Cook, "The Gong at Dodona" in J.H.S. xxii. (1902) p. 5 ff., who thinks the various allusions may be harmonized if we assume that the original "gong" was the row of resonant tripods round the sacred enclosure, and that later (say 4th century B.C.) these were replaced by a more elaborate gong consisting of two pillars, on one of which was mounted the figure of a boy holding a whip formed of three chains tipped

couch upon the ground, servants of the caldron [a] which is never silent—far first receive, as these offerings enter their country from afar. Next they come to the Holy town and mountains of the Malian land; and thence they sail across to the goodly Lelantian plain [b] of the Abantes; and then not long is the voyage from Euboea, since thy havens are nigh thereto. The first to bring thee these offerings from the fair-haired Arimaspi [c] were Upis and Loxo and happy Hecaerge, daughters of Boreas, and those who then were the best of the young men. And they returned not home again, but a happy fate was theirs, and they shall never be without their glory. Verily the girls of Delos, when the sweet-sounding marriage hymn affrights the maidens' quarters, bring offerings of their maiden hair to the maidens, while the boys offer to the young men the first harvest of the down upon their cheeks.

Asteria, island of incense, around and about thee the isles have made a circle and set themselves about thee as a choir. Not silent art thou nor noiseless when Hesperus of the curling locks looks down on thee, but ringing evermore with sound. The men sing the song of the old man of Lycia—the very song which the seer Olen [d] brought thee from Xanthos: the maidens of the choir beat with their feet the steadfast ground. Then, too, is the holy image laden

with buttons which, when moved by the wind, beat upon a bronze λέβης mounted upon the other pillar. *Cf.* Callim. fr. 111.   [b] In Boeotia.

   [c] For the Arimaspi see Herod. iv. 13 ff.

   [d] Prehistoric poet from Lycia (Xanthos is a river in Lycia); Herod. iv. 35 says he wrote the hymn sung at Delphi in honour of the Hyperborean maidens. *Cf.* Paus. ix. 27. 2, Suid. *s.v.* Ὠλήν.

CALLIMACHUS

Κύπριδος ἀρχαίης ἀριήκοον, ἥν ποτε Θησεὺς
εἵσατο σὺν παίδεσσιν, ὅτε Κρήτηθεν ἀνέπλει.
οἳ χαλεπὸν μύκημα καὶ ἄγριον υἶα φυγόντες   310
Πασιφάης καὶ γναμπτὸν ἕδος σκολιοῦ λαβυρίνθου,
πότνια, σὸν περὶ βωμὸν ἐγειρομένου κιθαρισμοῦ
κύκλιον ὠρχήσαντο, χοροῦ δ' ἡγήσατο Θησεύς.
ἔνθεν ἀειζώοντα θεωρίδος ἱερὰ Φοίβῳ
Κεκροπίδαι πέμπουσι, τοπήια νηὸς ἐκείνης.   315

    'Αστερίη πολύβωμε πολύλλιτε, τίς δέ σε ναύ-
       της
ἔμπορος Αἰγαίοιο παρήλυθε νηὶ θεούσῃ;
οὐχ οὕτω μεγάλοι μιν ἐπιπνείουσιν ἀῆται,
χρειὼ δ' ὅττι τάχιστον ἄγει πλόον, ἀλλὰ τὰ λαίφη
ὠκέες ἐστείλαντο καὶ οὐ πάλιν αὖτις ἔβησαν,   320
πρὶν μέγαν ἢ¹ σέο βωμὸν ὑπὸ πληγῇσιν ἐλίξαι
ῥησσόμενον καὶ πρέμνον ὀδακτάσαι ἁγνὸν ἐλαίης
χεῖρας ἀποστρέψαντας· ἃ Δηλιὰς εὕρετο νύμφη
παίγνια κουρίζοντι κἀ Ἀπόλλωνι γελαστύν.

    ἱστίη ὦ νήσων εὐέστιε, χαῖρε μὲν αὐτή,   325
χαίροι δ' Ἀπόλλων τε καὶ ἣν ἐλοχεύσατο² Λητώ.

---

¹ μέγαν ἢ (ἦ) mss.; μεγάλη Wilamowitz.
² ἣν ἐλοχεύσατο mss.; ἢ ἐλ. Stephanus; ἤ σφ' ἐλ. Meineke;
ἢ 'νελ. Schneider; ἣν ἐλοχεύσαο Wilamow.

   ᵃ The Minotaur.
   ᵇ Pasiphaë, daughter of Helios, wife of Minos, king of Crete.
   ᶜ The ship in which Theseus carried to Crete the seven maidens and seven boys as an offering to the Minotaur.

with garlands, the famous image of ancient Cypris, whom of old Theseus with the youths established when he was sailing back from Crete. Having escaped the cruel bellowing and the wild son [a] of Pasiphaë [b] and the coiled habitation of the crooked labyrinth, about thine altar, O lady, they raised the music of the lute and danced the round dance, and Theseus led the choir. Hence the ever-living offerings of the Pilgrim Ship [c] do the sons [d] of Cecrops send to Phoebus, the gear of that vessel.

Asteria of many altars and many prayers, what merchant mariner of the Aegean passes by thee with speeding ship? Never do such mighty winds as that blow upon him, but though need urges the swiftest voyage that may be, yet they speedily furl their sails and go not on board again, ere they have circled thy great altar buffeted with blows and bitten the sacred trunk of the olive, their hands tied behind their backs. [e] These things did the nymph of Delos devise for sport and laughter to young Apollo.

O happy hearth of islands, hail to thyself! Hail also to Apollo and to her [f] whom Leto bare!

With the help of Ariadne, Theseus slew the monster (Plato, *Phaedo*, 58 b).

[d] The Athenians, who vowed that if Theseus came safely home they would send a θεωρία every year to Delos (Plato, *l.c.*).

[e] " In Delos it was the custom to run round the altar of Apollo and to beat the altar and, their hands tied behind their backs, to take a bite from the olive-tree " (schol.).

[f] Artemis.

V.—ΕΙΣ ΛΟΥΤΡΑ ΤΗΣ ΠΑΛΛΑΔΟΣ

Ὅσσαι λωτροχόοι τᾶς Παλλάδος ἔξιτε πᾶσαι,
    ἔξιτε· τᾶν ἵππων ἄρτι φρυασσομενᾶν
τᾶν ἱερᾶν ἐσάκουσα, καὶ ἁ θεὸς εὔτυκος ἕρπειν [1].
    σοῦσθέ νυν, ὦ ξανθαί, σοῦσθε Πελασγιάδες.
οὔποκ' Ἀθαναία μεγάλως ἀπενίψατο πάχεις   5
    πρὶν κόνιν ἱππειᾶν ἐξελάσαι λαγόνων,
οὐδ' ὅκα δὴ λύθρῳ πεπαλαγμένα πάντα φέροισα
    τεύχεα τῶν ἀδίκων ἦνθ' ἀπὸ γηγενέων,
ἀλλὰ πολὺ πράτιστον ὑφ' ἅρματος αὐχένας ἵππων
    λυσαμένα παγαῖς ἔκλυσεν Ὠκεανῶ   10
ἱδρῶ καὶ ῥαθάμιγγας, ἐφοίβασεν δὲ παγέντα
    πάντα χαλινοφάγων ἀφρὸν ἀπὸ στομάτων.

ὦ ἴτ' Ἀχαιιάδες, καὶ μὴ μύρα μηδ' ἀλαβάστρως
    (συρίγγων ἀίω φθόγγον ὑπαξονίων [2]),
μὴ μύρα λωτροχόοι τᾷ Παλλάδι μηδ' ἀλαβάστρως   15
    (οὐ γὰρ Ἀθαναία χρίματα μεικτὰ φιλεῖ)
οἴσετε μηδὲ κάτοπτρον· ἀεὶ καλὸν ὄμμα τὸ τήνας
    οὐδ' ὅκα τὰν Ἴδᾳ [3] Φρὺξ ἐδίκαζεν ἔριν,
οὔτ' ἐς ὀρείχαλκον μεγάλα θεὸς οὔτε [4] Σιμοῦντος
    ἔβλεψεν δίναν ἐς διαφαινομέναν·   20

---

[1] ἕρπει mss.   [2] ὑπαξόνιον e; ὑπ' ἀξονίων Schneider.
[3] Ἴδαν mss.; corr. Bentley.
[4] οὐδ'... οὐδὲ mss.; corr. Meineke.

112

V.—ON THE BATH OF PALLAS

ALL ye that are companions of the Bath of Pallas,
come forth, come forth! I heard but now the
snorting of the sacred steeds, and the goddess is
ready to go. Haste ye now, O fair-haired daughters
of Pelasgus, haste! Never did Athena wash her
mighty arms before she drave the dust from the flanks
of her horses—not even when, her armour all defiled
with filth, she returned from the battle of the
lawless Giants; but far first she loosed from the car
her horses' necks, and in the springs of Oceanus
washed the flecks of sweat and from their mouths
that champed the bit cleansed the clotted foam.

O come, daughters of Achaea, and bring not
perfume nor alabasters (I hear the voice of the axle-
naves!); bring not, ye companions of the Bath, for
Pallas perfume nor alabasters [a] (for Athena loves not
mixed unguents), neither bring ye a mirror. Always
her face is fair, and, even when the Phrygian [b] judged
the strife on Ida, the great goddess looked not into
orichalc [c] nor into the transparent eddy of Simois, nor

[a] i.e. vessels made of alabaster, used especially to hold
perfumes, cf. N.T. Matt. xxvi. 7, Mark xiv. 3, Luke
vii. 37; Theophrast. De odor. 41. [b] Paris.
[c] First mentioned Hesiod, Shield 122, Hom. H. Aphr. 9.
Already to Plato it is only a name (τὸ νῦν ὀνομαζόμενον μόνον
Critias 114 E, cf. schol. Apoll. Rh. iv. 973). Later it was
identified with the mixture of copper and zinc which the
Romans called aurichalcum, i.e. brass.

οὐδ' Ἥρα· Κύπρις δὲ διαυγέα χαλκὸν ἑλοῖσα
   πολλάκι τὰν αὐτὰν δὶς μετέθηκε κόμαν·
ἁ δέ, δὶς ἑξήκοντα διαθρέξασα διαύλως,
   οἷα παρ' Εὐρώτᾳ τοὶ Λακεδαιμόνιοι
ἀστέρες, ἐμπεράμως ἐνετρίψατο [1] λιτὰ λαβοῖσα [2]   25
   χρίματα, τᾶς ἰδίας ἔκγονα φυταλιᾶς·
ὦ κῶραι, τὸ δ' ἔρευθος ἀνέδραμε, πρώιον οἵαν
   ἢ ῥόδον ἢ σίβδας κόκκος ἔχει χροΐαν.
τῶ καὶ νῦν ἄρσεν τι [3] κομίξατε μῶνον [4] ἔλαιον,
   ᾧ Κάστωρ, ᾧ καὶ χρίεται Ἡρακλέης·   30
οἴσετε καὶ κτένα οἱ παγχρύσεον, ὡς ἀπὸ χαίταν
   πέξηται, λιπαρὸν σμασαμένα πλόκαμον.
ἔξιθ' Ἀθαναία· πάρα τοι καταθύμιος ἴλα,
   παρθενικαὶ μεγάλων παῖδες Ἀκεστοριδᾶν [5]·
ὠθάνα, φέρεται δὲ καὶ ἁ Διομήδεος ἀσπίς,   35
   ὡς ἔθος Ἀργείων τοῦτο παλαιότερον
Εὐμήδης ἐδίδαξε, τεὶν κεχαρισμένος ἱρεύς·
   ὅς ποκα βωλευτὸν [6] γνοὺς ἐπί οἱ θάνατον
δᾶμον ἑτοιμάζοντα φυγᾷ τεὸν ἱρὸν ἄγαλμα
   ᾤχετ' ἔχων, Κρεῖον δ' εἰς ὄρος ᾠκίσατο·   40
Κρεῖον ὄρος· σὲ δέ, δαῖμον, ἀπορρώγεσσιν ἔθηκεν
   ἐν πέτραις, αἷς νῦν οὔνομα Παλλατίδες.

ἔξιθ' Ἀθαναία περσέπτολι, χρυσεοπήληξ,
   ἵππων καὶ σακέων ἁδομένα πατάγῳ.

---

[1] ἐτρίψατο MSS. ; corr. Meineke.
[2] βαλοῖσα EF.   [3] τι Bergk ; τε.
[4] κομίξατε Schneider, μῶνον Ernesti ; κομίσσατε μοῦνον.
[5] Ἀρεστοριδᾶν Valckenaer.   [6] ποτε βουλευτὸν MSS.

---

[a] Tibull. i. 8. 22 " saepeque mutatas disposuisse comas."
[b] Castor and Pollux, known as stars to Eurip. *Hel.* 138 ff.,

did Hera. But Cypris took the shining bronze and often altered and again altered the same lock.[a] But Pallas, after running twice sixty double courses, even as beside the Eurotas the Lacedaemonian Stars,[b] took and skilfully anointed her with simple unguents, the birth of her own tree. And, O maidens, the red blush arose on her, as the colour of the morning rose or seed of pomegranate. Wherefore now also bring ye only the manly olive oil, wherewith Castor and wherewith Heracles anoint themselves. And bring her a comb all of gold, that she may comb her hair, when she hath anointed her glossy tresses.

Come forth, Athena! A company pleasing to thy heart awaits thee, the maiden daughters of Acestor's mighty sons.[c] And therewithal, O Athena, is borne the shield of Diomedes, since this is the Argive custom which in olden days Eumedes [d] taught them : a priest who found favour with thee : who on a time, when he knew that the people were plotting and planning death for him, fled with thy holy image and dwelt on the Creion hill—dwelt on the hill of Creion and established thee, O goddess, on the rugged rocks, whose name is now the Pallatid rocks.

Come forth, Athena, Sacker of Cities, golden-helmeted, who rejoicest in the din of horse and

etc. ; their identification with the constellation Gemini was comparatively late.

[c] Ἀκεστοριδᾶν has been unjustly suspected. It is quite correct and is a mere etymological variant for Ἀρεστοριδᾶν, since ἀκέσασθαι = ἀρέσασθαι. See Hesych. *s.vv.*

[d] "Once when the Heracleidae came against the Orestiadae, Eumedes, priest of Athena, was suspected by the Argives of wishing to betray the Palladium to the Heracleidae. Eumedes, being afraid, took the Palladium and came to the hill called Creion " (schol.).

σάμερον ὑδροφόροι μὴ βάπτετε—σάμερον "Αργος 45
 πίνετ' ἀπὸ κρανᾶν μηδ' ἀπὸ τῶ ποταμῶ,[1]
σάμερον αἱ δῶλαι τὰς κάλπιδας ἢ 's Φυσάδειαν
 ἢ ἐς 'Αμυμώναν οἴσετε τὰν Δαναῶ.
καὶ γὰρ δὴ χρυσῷ τε καὶ ἄνθεσιν ὕδατα μίξας
 ἡξεῖ φορβαίων "Ιναχος ἐξ ὀρέων 50
τἀθάνᾳ τὸ λοετρὸν ἄγων καλόν. ἀλλά, Πελασγέ,
 φράζεο μὴ οὐκ ἐθέλων τὰν βασίλειαν ἴδῃς.
ὅς κεν ἴδῃ γυμνὰν τὰν Παλλάδα τὰν πολιοῦχον,
 τὦργος ἐσοψεῖται τοῦτο πανυστάτιον.
πότνι' 'Αθαναία τὺ[2] μὲν ἔξιθι· μέσφα δ' ἐγώ τι 55
 ταῖσδ' ἐρέω. μῦθος δ' οὐκ ἐμός, ἀλλ' ἑτέρων.

παῖδες, 'Αθαναία νύμφαν μίαν ἔν ποκα Θήβαις
 πουλύ τι καὶ περὶ δὴ φίλατο τᾶν ἑταρᾶν,
ματέρα Τειρεσίαο, καὶ οὔποκα χωρὶς ἔγεντο·
 ἀλλὰ καὶ ἀρχαίων εὖτ' ἐπὶ Θεσπιέων 60
ἢ 'πὶ Κορωνείας ἢ εἰς 'Αλίαρτον ἐλαύνοι
 ἵππως, Βοιωτῶν ἔργα διερχομένα,
ἢ 'πὶ Κορωνείας,[3] ἵνα οἱ τεθυωμένον ἄλσος
 καὶ βωμοὶ ποταμῷ κεῖντ' ἐπὶ Κωραλίῳ·
πολλάκις ἁ δαίμων νιν ἑῶ ἐπεβάσατο δίφρῳ, 65
 οὐδ' ὄαροι νυμφᾶν οὐδὲ χοροστασίαι
ἁδεῖαι τελέθεσκον, ὅκ' οὐχ ἁγεῖτο Χαρικλώ·
 ἀλλ' ἔτι καὶ τήναν δάκρυα πόλλ' ἔμενεν,
καίπερ 'Αθαναίᾳ καταθύμιον ἔσσαν ἑταίραν.
 δή ποκα[4] γὰρ πέπλων λυσαμένα περόνας 70
ἵππω ἐπὶ κράνᾳ Ἑλικωνίδι καλὰ ῥεοίσᾳ
 λῶντο· μεσαμβρινὰ δ' εἶχ' ὄρος ἀσυχία.

---

[1] τῶν ποταμῶν MSS.　　　　[2] σὺ MSS.
[3] There is much uncertainty about the text here. We
assume a very bold epanaphora.　　　　[4] ποτε MSS.

shield. To-day, ye water-carriers, dip not your pitchers—to-day, O Argos, drink ye from the fountains and not from the river; to-day, ye handmaidens, carry your pitchers to Physadeia,[a] or Amymone,[b] daughter of Danaus. For, mingling his waters with gold and with flowers, Inachus will come from his pastoral hills, bringing fair water for the Bath of Athena. But beware, O Pelasgian, lest even unwittingly thou behold the Queen. Whoso shall behold Pallas, Keeper of Cities, naked, shall look on Argos for this the last time. Lady Athena, do thou come forth, and meanwhile I shall say somewhat unto these. The story is not mine but told by others.

Maidens, one nymph of old in Thebes did Athena love much, yea beyond all her companions, even the mother of Teiresias, and was never apart from her. But when she drave her steeds towards ancient Thespiae or towards Coroneia or to Haliartus, passing through the tilled fields of the Boeotians—or toward Coroneia where her fragrant grove and altars are set by the river Curalius—often did the goddess set the nymph upon her car and there was no dalliance of nymphs nor sweet ordering of dance, where Chariclo[c] did not lead.

Yet even her did many tears await in the after days, albeit she was a comrade pleasing to the heart of Athena. One day those twain undid the buckles of their robes beside the fair-flowing Fountain of the Horse on Helicon and bathed; and noontide quiet

---

[a] Spring at Argos. *Cf.* Steph. Byz. *s.v.* Ἀσβωτις.
[b] Spring at Argos. *Cf.* Apollod. ii. 1. 5, Strabo 368, Paus. ii. 37, etc.
[c] Chariclo, wife of Eueres and mother of Teiresias.

CALLIMACHUS

ἀμφότεραι λώοντο, μεσαμβριναὶ δ' ἔσαν ὧραι,
    πολλὰ δ' ἀσυχία τῆνο κατεῖχεν ὄρος.
Τειρεσίας δ' ἔτι μῶνος[1] ἅμα κυσὶν ἄρτι γένεια   75
    περκάζων ἱερὸν χῶρον ἀνεστρέφετο·
διψάσας δ' ἄφατόν τι ποτὶ ῥόον ἦλυθε κράνας,
    σχέτλιος· οὐκ ἐθέλων δ' εἶδε τὰ μὴ θεμιτά·
τὸν δὲ χολωσαμένα περ ὅμως προσέφασεν Ἀθάνα
    "τίς σε, τὸν ὀφθαλμὼς οὐκέτ' ἀποισόμενον,   80
ὦ Εὐηρείδα, χαλεπὰν ὁδὸν ἄγαγε δαίμων;"
    ἁ μὲν ἔφα, παιδὸς δ' ὄμματα νὺξ ἔλαβεν.[2]
ἑστάκη[3] δ' ἄφθογγος, ἐκόλλασαν γὰρ ἀνῖαι
    γώνατα καὶ φωνὰν ἔσχεν ἀμηχανία.
ἁ νύμφα δ' ἐβόασε "τί μοι τὸν κῶρον ἔρεξας,   85
    πότνια; τοιαῦται δαίμονες ἐστὲ φίλαι;
ὄμματά μοι τῶ παιδὸς ἀφείλεο. τέκνον ἄλαστε,
    εἶδες Ἀθαναίας στήθεα καὶ λαγόνας,
ἀλλ' οὐκ ἀέλιον πάλιν ὄψεαι. ὦ ἐμὲ δειλάν,
    ὦ ὄρος, ὦ Ἑλικὼν οὐκέτι μοι παριτέ,   90
ἦ μεγάλ' ἀντ' ὀλίγων ἐπράξαο· δόρκας ὀλέσσας
    – καὶ πρόκας οὐ πολλὰς φάεα παιδὸς ἔχεις."
ἁ καὶ ἅμ'[4] ἀμφοτέραισι φίλον περὶ παῖδα λαβοῖσα
    μάτηρ μὲν γοερᾶν οἶτον[5] ἀηδονίδων
ἆγε βαρὺ κλαίοισα, θεὰ δ' ἐλέησεν ἑταίραν·   95
    καί νιν Ἀθαναία πρὸς τόδ' ἔλεξεν ἔπος·
"δῖα γύναι, μετὰ πάντα βαλεῦ πάλιν ὅσσα δι' ὀργὰν
    εἶπας· ἐγὼ δ' οὔ τοι τέκνον ἔθηκ' ἀλαόν.
οὐ γὰρ Ἀθαναίᾳ γλυκερὸν πέλει ὄμματα παίδων
    ἁρπάζειν· Κρόνιοι δ' ὧδε λέγοντι νόμοι·   100

---

[1] μοῦνος MSS.
[2] ἔλαβεν Vindob. 318; ἔβαλεν other MSS.
[3] ἑστάκη Buttmann; ἐστάθη (ἑστάθη).

118

held all the hill. Those two were bathing and it was the noontide hour and a great quiet held that hill. Only Teiresias, on whose cheek the down was just darkening, still ranged with his hounds the holy place. And, athirst beyond telling, he came unto the flowing fountain, wretched man! and unwillingly saw that which is not lawful to be seen. And Athena was angered, yet said to him: "What god, O son of Everes, led thee on this grievous way? hence shalt thou never more take back thine eyes!"

She spake and night seized the eyes of the youth. And he stood speechless; for pain glued his knees and helplessness stayed his voice. But the nymph cried: "What hast thou done to my boy, lady? Is such the friendship of you goddesses? Thou hast taken away the eyes of my son. Foolish child! thou hast seen the breast and body of Athena, but the sun thou shalt not see again. O me unhappy! O hill, O Helicon, where I may no more come, surely a great price for little hast thou exacted. Losing a few gazelles and deer, thou hast taken the eyes of my child."

Therewith the mother clasped her beloved child in both her arms and, wailing the heavy plaint of the mournful nightingale, led him away. And the goddess Athena pitied her comrade and spake to her and said: "Noble lady, take back all the words that thou hast spoken in anger. It is not I that made thy child blind. For no sweet thing is it for Athena to snatch away the eyes of children. But the laws of Cronus order thus: Whosoever shall behold any

---

4 ἁ καὶ ἅμ' Editor; ἁ (ἡ) μὲν.
5 οἶκτον Stephanus.

CALLIMACHUS

ὅς κε τιν' ἀθανάτων, ὅκα μὴ θεὸς αὐτὸς ἕληται,
    ἀθρήσῃ, μισθῷ τοῦτον ἰδεῖν μεγάλω.
δῖα γύναι, τὸ μὲν οὐ παλινάγρετον αὖθι γένοιτο
    ἔργον· ἐπεὶ μοιρᾶν ὧδ' ἐπένησε[1] λίνα,
ἀνίκα τὸ πρᾶτόν νιν ἐγείναο· νῦν δὲ κομίζευ,   105
    ὦ Εὐηρείδα, τέλθος ὀφειλόμενον.
πόσσα μὲν ἁ Καδμηὶς ἐς ὕστερον ἔμπυρα καυσεῖ,
    πόσσα δ' Ἀρισταῖος, τὸν μόνον εὐχόμενοι
παῖδα, τὸν ἁβατὰν Ἀκταίονα, τυφλὸν ἰδέσθαι.
καὶ τῆνος μεγάλας σύνδρομος Ἀρτέμιδος   110
    ἐσσεῖτ'· ἀλλ' οὐκ αὐτὸν ὅ τε δρόμος αἵ τ' ἐν ὄρεσσι
ῥυσεῦνται ξυναὶ τᾶμος ἐκαβολίαι,
ὁππόκ'[2] ἂν οὐκ ἐθέλων περ ἴδῃ χαρίεντα λοετρὰ
    δαίμονος· ἀλλ' αὐταὶ τὸν πρὶν ἄνακτα κύνες
τουτάκι δειπνησεῦντι· τὰ δ' υἱέος ὀστέα μάτηρ   115
    λεξεῖται δρυμὼς πάντας ἐπερχομένα·
ὀλβίσταν ἐρέει σε καὶ εὐαίωνα γενέσθαι,
    ἐξ ὀρέων ἀλαὸν παῖδ' ὑποδεξαμέναν.[3]
ὦ ἑτάρα, τῷ μή τι μινύρεο· τῷδε γὰρ ἄλλα
    τεῦ χάριν ἐξ ἐμέθεν πολλὰ μενεῦντι γέρα.   120
μάντιν ἐπεὶ θησῶ νιν ἀοίδιμον ἐσσομένοισιν,
    ἢ μέγα τῶν ἄλλων δή τι περισσότερον.
γνωσεῖται δ' ὄρνιχας, ὃς αἴσιος οἵ τε πέτονται
    ἤλιθα καὶ ποίων οὐκ ἀγαθαὶ πτέρυγες.
πολλὰ δὲ Βοιωτοῖσι θεοπρόπα, πολλὰ δὲ Κάδμῳ   125
    χρησεῖ, καὶ μεγάλοις ὕστερα Λαβδακίδαις.
δωσῶ καὶ μέγα βάκτρον, ὅ οἱ πόδας ἐς δέον ἀξεῖ,
    δωσῶ καὶ βιότω τέρμα πολυχρόνιον.

[1] ἐπένησε Spanheim, Bentley; ἐπένευσε.   [2] ὁππόταν mss.
[3] ἀποδεξαμέναν Meineke; an absolute solecism, but accepted by Wilamowitz and others.

---

[a] Autonoë.
[b] Actaeon, son of Aristaeus and Autonoë, was torn to

120

of the immortals, when the god himself chooses not, at a heavy price shall he behold. Noble lady, the thing that is done can no more be taken back; since thus the thread of the Fates span when thou didst bear him at the first; but now, O son of Everes, take thou the issue which is due to thee. How many burnt offerings shall the daughter of Cadmus[a] burn in the days to come? how many Aristaeus?— praying that they might see their only son, the young Actaeon,[b] blind. And yet he shall be companion of the chase to great Artemis. But him neither the chase nor comradeship in archery on the hills shall save in that hour, when, albeit unwillingly, he shall behold the beauteous bath of the goddess. Nay, his own dogs shall then devour their former lord. And his mother shall gather the bones of her son, ranging over all the thickets. Happiest of women shall she call thee and of happy fate, for that thou didst receive thy son home from the hills—blind. Therefore, O comrade, lament not; for to this thy son— for thy sake—shall remain many other honours from me. For I will make him a seer to be sung of men hereafter, yea, more excellent far than any other. He shall know the birds — which is of good omen among all the countless birds that fly and what birds are of ill-omened flight. Many oracles shall he utter to the Boeotians and many unto Cadmus, and to the mighty sons of Labdacus in later days. Also will I give him a great staff which shall guide his feet as he hath need, and I will give him a long term of life. And he only,[c] when he dies,

pieces by his own dogs because he had seen Artemis bathing in Parthenius in the Gargaphian valley. Apollod. iii. 4. 4, Nonn. v. 287 ff., Ovid, *Met.* iii. 131 ff.

[c] Hom. *Od.* x. 494 f.

καὶ μόνος, εὖτε θάνῃ, πεπνυμένος ἐν νεκύεσσι
  φοιτασεῖ, μεγάλωι τίμιος 'Αγεσίλα.''   130
ὣς φαμένα κατένευσε· τὸ δ' ἐντελὲς ᾧ κ' ἔπι νεύσῃ[1]
  Παλλάς, ἐπεὶ μώνᾳ Ζεὺς τό γε θυγατέρων
δῶκεν 'Αθαναίᾳ, πατρώϊα πάντα φέρεσθαι,
  λωτροχόοι, μάτηρ δ' οὔτις ἔτικτε θεάν,
ἀλλὰ Διὸς κορυφά. κορυφὰ Διὸς οὐκ ἐπινεύει   135
  ψεύδεα <κοὐδὲ Διὸς ψεύδετ[2]>αι <ἁ> θυγάτηρ.

ἔρχετ' 'Αθαναία νῦν ἀτρεκές· ἀλλὰ δέχεσθε
  τὰν θεόν, ὦ κῶραι τὦργον[3] ὅσαις μέλεται,
σύν τ' εὐαγορίᾳ σύν τ' εὔγμασι σύν τ' ὀλολυγαῖς.
  χαῖρε θεά, κάδευ δ' "Αργεος 'Ιναχίω.   140
χαῖρε καὶ ἐξελάοισα, καὶ ἐς πάλιν αὖτις ἐλάσσαις
  ἵππως, καὶ Δαναῶν κλᾶρον ἅπαντα σάω.

---

[1] ἔπι νεύσῃ Wilamowitz; ἐπινεύσῃ.
[2] lacuna supplied by the Editor.
[3] τὦργον Boissonade; τῶργος.

shall walk among the dead having understanding, honoured of the great Leader of the Peoples.[a] ''

So she spake and bowed her head; and that word is fulfilled over which Pallas bows; since to Athena only among his daughters hath Zeus granted that she should win all things that belong to her sire, O companions of the Bath, and no mother bare that goddess, but the head of Zeus. The head of Zeus bows not in falsehood, and in falsehood his daughter hath no part.

Now comes Athena in very deed. O maidens, whose task it is, receive ye the goddess with pious greeting and with prayer, and with the voice of thanksgiving. Hail, goddess, and have thou Inachian Argos in thy keeping! Hail when thou drivest forth thy steeds, and home again mayst thou drive them with joy, and do thou preserve all the estate of the Danaans.

---

[a] Hades. The title Ἀγεσίλαος, which was used of Hades by Aeschylus also (Athen. iii. 99 в), refers to his character as host of the dead (οἱ πολλοί, οἱ πλείονες) and is to be compared with his titles Πολυδέγμων (Hom. *H. Dem.* 17, 31, 430), Πολυδέκτης (*ib.* 9), Πολυσημάντωρ (*ib.* 31), Πανδοκεύς (Lycophr. 655).

VI.—ΕΙΣ ΔΗΜΗΤΡΑ

Τῶ καλάθω κατιόντος ἐπιφθέγξασθε, γυναῖκες,
"Δάματερ μέγα χαῖρε πολυτρόφε πουλυμέδιμνε."
τὸν κάλαθον κατιόντα χαμαὶ θασεῖσθε βέβαλοι,[1]
μηδ' ἀπὸ τῶ τέγεος μηδ' ὑψόθεν αὐγάσσησθε
μὴ παῖς μηδὲ γυνὰ μηδ' ἃ κατεχεύατο χαίταν,   5
μηδ' ὅκ' ἀφ' αὐαλέων στομάτων πτύωμες ἄπαστοι.
Ἕσπερος ἐκ νεφέων ἐσκέψατο πανίκα νεῖται,
Ἕσπερος, ὅστε πιεῖν Δαμάτερα μῶνος ἔπεισεν,
ἁρπαγίμας ὅκ' ἄπυστα μετέστιχεν ἴχνια κώρας.
  πότνια, πῶς σε δύναντο πόδες φέρεν ἔστ' ἐπὶ
    δυθμάς,   10
ἔστ' ἐπὶ τὼς μέλανας καὶ ὅπα τὰ χρύσεα μᾶλα;
οὐ πίες οὔτ' ἄρ' ἔδες τῆνον χρόνον οὐδὲ λοέσσα.
τρὶς μὲν δὴ διέβας Ἀχελώιον ἀργυροδίναν,
τοσσάκι δ' ἀενάων ποταμῶν ἐπέρασας ἕκαστον,

---

[1] Schol. Plato, *Symp.* 218 B καὶ εἴ τις ἄλλος ἐστὶ βέβηλός
τε καὶ ἄγροικος, πύλας παμμεγάλας τοῖς ὠσὶν ἐπίθεσθε] ἐντεῦθεν
παρῴδησε Καλλίμαχος ἐν ὕμνῳ Δήμητρος καλάθου τὸ θύρας δ'
ἐπίθεσθε βέβηλοι.

---

[a] κατιόντος might mean "comes home" but probably it is
safer to take it as "comes in procession." *Cf.* κάθοδος
Herondas i. 56.

[b] *i.e.* dedicated on arriving at puberty. Or "hath her
hair unbound," *i.e.* a maiden unwed. *Cf.* schol. μηδ' ἥτις
ἄγαμός ἐστι. Scott, *Heart of Midlothian* chap. 22, says of
Effie Deans on her trial : "Her . . . tresses . . . which,

VI.—TO DEMETER

As the Basket comes,[a] greet it, ye women, saying "Demeter, greatly hail! Lady of much bounty, of many measures of corn." As the Basket comes, from the ground shall ye behold it, ye uninitiated, and gaze not from the roof or from aloft—child nor wife nor maid that hath shed her hair[b]—neither then nor when we spit from parched mouths fasting.[c] Hesperus from the clouds marks the time of its coming: Hesperus, who alone persuaded Demeter to drink, what time she pursued the unknown tracks of her stolen daughter.[d]

Lady, how were thy feet able to carry thee unto the West, unto the black[e] men and where the golden apples[f] are? Thou didst not drink nor didst thou eat during that time nor didst thou wash. Thrice didst thou cross Achelous with his silver eddies, and as often didst thou pass over each of the ever-flowing rivers, and thrice didst thou seat thee on

according to the custom of the country, unmarried women were not allowed to cover with any sort of cap, and which, alas! Effie dared no longer confine with the snood or riband which implied purity of maiden fame, now hung unbound."

[c] The second day of the Thesmophoria was a day of fasting, Nesteia.

[d] Persephone.   [e] The Aethiopians (schol.).

[f] The garden of the Hesperides.

τρὶς δ' ἐπὶ Καλλιχόρῳ ¹ χαμάδις ἐκαθίσσαο φρητί   15
αὐσταλέα ἄποτός τε καὶ οὐ φάγες οὐδὲ λοέσσα.

μὴ μὴ ταῦτα λέγωμες ἃ δάκρυον ἄγαγε Δηοῖ·
κάλλιον, ὡς πολίεσσιν ἑαδότα ² τέθμια δῶκε·
κάλλιον, ὡς καλάμαν τε καὶ ἱερὰ δράγματα πράτα
ἀσταχύων ἀπέκοψε καὶ ἐν βόας ἧκε πατῆσαι,   20
ἁνίκα Τριπτόλεμος ἀγαθὰν ἐδιδάσκετο τέχναν·
κάλλιον, ὡς, ἵνα καί τις ὑπερβασίας ³ ἀλέηται,
π . . . . ἰδέσθαι ⁴

οὔπω τὰν Κνιδίαν, ἔτι Δώτιον ἱρὸν ἔναιον,
τὶν δ' ⁵ αὐτᾷ καλὸν ἄλσος ἐποιήσαντο Πελασγοὶ   25
δένδρεσιν ἀμφιλαφές· διά κεν μόλις ἦνθεν ὀιστός·
ἐν πίτυς, ἐν μεγάλαι πτελέαι ἔσαν, ἐν δὲ καὶ ὄχναι,
ἐν δὲ καλὰ γλυκύμαλα· τὸ δ' ὥστ' ἀλέκτρινον ὕδωρ
ἐξ ἀμαρᾶν ἀνέθυε. θεὰ δ' ἐπεμαίνετο χώρῳ
ὅσσον Ἐλευσῖνι, Τριόπῳ θ' ⁶ ὅσον, ὁκκόσον Ἔννᾳ. 30
ἀλλ' ὅκα Τριοπίδαισιν ὁ δεξιὸς ἄχθετο δαίμων,
τουτάκις ἁ χείρων Ἐρυσίχθονος ἅψατο βωλά·
σεύατ' ἔχων θεράποντας ἐείκοσι, πάντας ἐν ἀκμᾷ,
πάντας δ' ἀνδρογίγαντας ὅλαν πόλιν ἀρκίος ἆραι,
ἀμφότερον πελέκεσσι καὶ ἀξίναισιν ὁπλίσσας,   35
ἐς δὲ τὸ τᾶς Δάματρος ἀναιδέες ἔδραμον ἄλσος.
ἧς ⁷ δέ τις αἴγειρος, μέγα δένδρεον αἰθέρι κῦρον,
τῷ δ' ἔπι ταὶ νύμφαι ποτὶ τῶνδιον ἐψιόωντο,

---

¹ τρὶς δ ἐπὶ καλλι . . . only is preserved in A ; the lacuna is supplied in F and late mss.
² πτολίεσσιν έα . . . A ; lacuna supplied in F.
³ ὑπερβα . . . A ; lacuna supplied in F etc.
⁴ π . . . A ; . . . ἰδέσθαι pd.
⁵ τὶν δ' mss. ; τεῖδ' Schneider.
⁶ τριόπῳ θ' LM ; Τριοπᾷδ' Schneider ; τριόπαιδ' AF ; τριόπᾳ θ' d.
⁷ ἧς d ; ἦν.

126

the ground beside the fountain Callichorus,[a] parched and without drinking, and didst not eat nor wash.

Nay, nay, let us not speak of that which brought the tear to Deo[b]! Better to tell how she gave to cities pleasing ordinances; better to tell how she was the first to cut straw and holy sheaves of corn-ears and put in oxen to tread them, what time Triptolemus[c] was taught the good craft; better to tell—a warning to men that they avoid transgression—how [she made the son of Triopas hateful and pitiful][d] to see.

Not yet in the land of Cnidus,[e] but still in holy Dotium[f] dwelt the Pelasgians and unto thyself they made a fair grove abounding in trees; hardly would an arrow have passed through them. Therein was pine, and therein were mighty elms, and therein were pear-trees, and therein were fair sweet-apples; and from the ditches gushed up water as it were of amber. And the goddess loved the place to madness, even as Eleusis, as Triopum,[g] as Enna.[h]

But when their favouring fortune became wroth with the Triopidae, then the worse counsel took hold of Erysichthon.[i] He hastened with twenty attendants, all in their prime, all men-giants able to lift a whole city, arming them both with double axes and with hatchets, and they rushed shameless into the grove of Demeter. Now there was a poplar, a great tree reaching to the sky, and thereby the nymphs were wont to sport at noontide. This poplar

[a] Callichorus, well (φρέαρ) at Eleusis, Paus. i. 38. 6.
[b] Demeter.
[c] Son of Celeus, was taught agriculture by Demeter.
[d] The lacuna is supplied in LM : ⟨θῆκατο Τριοπίδην ἐχθρὸν καὶ οἰκτρὸν⟩.   [e] In Caria.   [f] In Thessaly.
[g] i.e. Triopium in Caria.   [h] In Sicily.   [i] Son of Triopas.

ἃ πράτα πλαγεῖσα κακὸν μέλος ἴαχεν ἄλλαις.
ᾄσθετο Δαμάτηρ, ὅτι οἱ ξύλον ἱερὸν ἄλγει,   40
εἶπε δὲ χωσαμένα "τίς μοι καλὰ δένδρεα κόπτει;"
αὐτίκα Νικίππᾳ, τάν οἱ πόλις ἀράτειραν
δαμοσίαν ἔστασαν, ἐείσατο, γέντο δὲ χειρὶ
στέμματα καὶ μάκωνα, κατωμαδίαν δ' ἔχε κλᾷδα.
φᾶ δὲ παραψύχοισα κακὸν καὶ ἀναιδέα φῶτα   45
"τέκνον, ὅτις τὰ θεοῖσιν ἀνειμένα δένδρεα κόπτεις,
τέκνον ἐλίνυσον, τέκνον πολύθεστε τοκεῦσι,
παύεο καὶ θεράποντας ἀπότρεπε, μή τι χαλεφθῇ
πότνια Δαμάτηρ, τᾶς ἱερὸν ἐκκεραΐζεις."
τὰν δ' ἄρ' ὑποβλέψας χαλεπώτερον ἠὲ κυναγὸν   50
ὤρεσιν ἐν Τμαρίοισιν ὑποβλέπει ἄνδρα λέαινα
ὠμοτόκος, τᾶς φαντὶ πέλειν βλοσυρώτατον ὄμμα,
"χάζευ," ἔφα, "μή τοι πέλεκυν μέγαν ἐν χροῒ πάξω.
ταῦτα δ' ἐμὸν θησεῖ στεγανὸν δόμον, ᾧ ἔνι δαῖτας
αἰὲν ἐμοῖς ἑτάροισιν ἄδην θυμαρέας ἀξῶ."   55
εἶπεν ὁ παῖς, Νέμεσις δὲ κακὰν ἐγράψατο φωνάν.
Δαμάτηρ δ' ἄφατόν τι κοτέσσατο, γείνατο[1] δ' ἁ[2] θεύς·
ἴθματα μὲν χέρσω, κεφαλὰ δέ οἱ ἅψατ' Ὀλύμπω.
οἱ μὲν ἄρ' ἡμιθνῆτες, ἐπεὶ τὰν πότνιαν εἶδον,
ἐξαπίνας ἀπόρουσαν ἐνὶ δρυσὶ χαλκὸν ἀφέντες·   60
ἁ δ' ἄλλως μὲν ἔασεν, ἀναγκαίᾳ γὰρ ἕποντο
δεσποτικὰν ὑπὸ χεῖρα, βαρὺν δ' ἀπαμείψατ' ἄνακτα
"ναὶ ναί, τεύχεο δῶμα, κύον, κύον, ᾧ ἔνι δαῖτας

---

[1] γείνατο mss. ; γείνετο Schneider.   [2] ἁ mss. ; αὖ Bergk.

---

[a] "As priestess" (schol.).

[b] Tmarus, mountain near Dodona in Epirus.

[c] For strict sense of ὠμοτόκος see note on *Hymn* iv. 120.
Here it is no more than τοκάς "with cubs" as in Eur. *Med.*
187 τοκάδος δέργμα λέοντος.

[d] Nemesis takes note of presumptuous acts and words,
Plato, *Laws* 717 D. Nonn. *Dion.* i. 481 imitates Callimachus.

was smitten first and cried a woeful cry to the others.
Demeter marked that her holy tree was in pain, and
she was angered and said : " Who cuts down my fair
trees?" Straightway she likened her to Nicippe,
whom the city had appointed to be her public
priestess, and in her hand she grasped her fillets and
her poppy, and from her shoulder hung her key.[a]
And she spake to soothe the wicked and shameless
man and said : " My child, who cuttest down the
trees which are dedicated to the gods, stay, my child,
child of thy parents' many prayers, cease and turn
back thine attendants, lest the lady Demeter be
angered, whose holy place thou makest desolate."
But with a look more fierce than that wherewith a
lioness looks on the hunter on the hills of Tmarus[b]
—a lioness with new-born cubs,[c] whose eye they say
is of all most terrible—he said : " Give back, lest I
fix my great axe in thy flesh ! These trees shall
make my tight dwelling wherein evermore I shall
hold pleasing banquets enough for my companions."
So spake the youth and Nemesis[d] recorded his evil
speech. And Demeter was angered beyond telling
and put on her goddess shape. Her steps touched
the earth, but her head reached unto Olympus.[e]
And they, half-dead when they beheld the lady
goddess, rushed suddenly away, leaving the bronze
axes in the trees. And she left the others alone—
for they followed by constraint beneath their master's
hand—but she answered their angry king : " Yea,
yea, build thy house, dog, dog,[f] that thou art, wherein

---

[e] From Hom. *Il.* iv. 443 Ἔρις οὐρανῷ ἐστήριξε κάρη καὶ
ἐπὶ χθονὶ βαίνει. *Cf.* Verg. *A.* iv. 177, x. 767, Nonn. xxix.
320.
[f] *Cf. Aitia* iii. 1. 4.

ποιησεῖς· θαμιναὶ γὰρ ἐς ὕστερον εἰλαπίναι τοι."
ἃ μὲν τόσσ᾽ εἰποῖσ᾽ Ἐρυσίχθονι τεῦχε πονηρά.
αὐτίκα οἱ χαλεπόν τε καὶ ἄγριον ἔμβαλε λιμὸν
αἴθωνα κρατερόν, μεγάλᾳ δ᾽ ἐστρεύγετο νούσῳ.
σχέτλιος, ὅσσα πάσαιτο τόσων ἔχεν ἵμερος αὖτις.
εἴκατι δαῖτα πένοντο, δυώδεκα δ᾽ οἶνον ἄφυσσον·
τόσσα Διώνυσον γὰρ ἃ καὶ Δάματρα χαλέπτει·
καὶ γὰρ τᾷ Δάματρι συνωργίσθη Διόνυσος.
οὔτε νιν εἰς ἐράνως οὔτε ξυνδείπνια πέμπον
αἰδόμενοι γονέες, προχανὰ δ᾽ εὑρίσκετο πᾶσα.
ἦνθον Ἰτωνιάδος νιν Ἀθαναίας ἐπ᾽ ἄεθλα
Ὀρμενίδαι καλέοντες· ἀπ᾽ ὧν ἀρνήσατο μάτηρ
"οὐκ ἔνδοι, χθιζὸς γὰρ ἐπὶ Κραννῶνα βέβακε
τέλθος ἀπαιτησῶν ἑκατὸν βόας." ἦνθε Πολυξώ,
μάτηρ Ἀκτορίωνος, ἐπεὶ γάμον ἄρτυε παιδί,
ἀμφότερον Τριόπαν τε καὶ υἱέα κικλήσκοισα.
τὰν δὲ γυνὰ βαρύθυμος ἀμείβετο δάκρυ χέοισα
"νεῖταί τοι Τριόπας, Ἐρυσίχθονα δ᾽ ἤλασε κάπρος
Πίνδον ἀν᾽ εὐάγκειαν, ὁ δ᾽ ἐννέα φάεα κεῖται."
δειλαία φιλότεκνε, τί δ᾽ οὐκ ἐψεύσαο, μᾶτερ;
δαίνυεν εἰλαπίναν τις· "ἐν ἀλλοτρίοις Ἐρυσίχθων."
ἄγετό τις νύμφαν· "Ἐρυσίχθονα δίσκος ἔτυψεν,"
ἢ "ἔπεσ᾽ ἐξ ἵππων," ἢ "ἐν Ὄθρυϊ ποίμνι᾽ ἀμιθρεῖ.¹"
ἐνδόμυχος δῇπειτα πανάμερος εἰλαπιναστὰς
ἤσθιε μυρία πάντα· κακὰ δ᾽ ἐξάλλετο γαστὴρ
αἰεὶ μᾶλλον ἔδοντι, τὰ δ᾽ ἐς βυθὸν οἷα θαλάσσας
ἀλεμάτως ἀχάριστα κατέρρεεν εἴδατα πάντα.
ὡς δὲ Μίμαντι χιών, ὡς ἀελίῳ ἔνι πλαγγών,

---

¹ ἀμιθρεῖ Ruhnken, Valckenaer; ἀμι- A, ἀμ᾽ E, ἀριθμεῖ d;
ἀμέλγει F.

ᵃ Eponymous king of Ormenion in Thessaly.
ᵇ So called from her cult at Itone in Thessaly.

thou shalt hold festival; for frequent banquets shall
be thine hereafter." So much she said and devised
evil things for Erysichthon. Straightway she sent
on him a cruel and evil hunger—a burning hunger
and a strong—and he was tormented by a grievous
disease. Wretched man, as much as he ate, so much
did he desire again. Twenty prepared the banquet
for him, and twelve drew wine. For whatsoever
things vex Demeter, vex also Dionysus; for Dionysus
shares the anger of Demeter. His parents for shame
sent him not to common feast or banquet, and all
manner of excuse was devised. The sons of
Ormenus [a] came to bid him to the games of Itonian
Athene.[b] Then his mother refused the bidding:
"He is not at home; for yesterday he is gone unto
Crannon to demand a debt of a hundred oxen."
Polyxo [c] came, mother of Actorion—for she was
preparing a marriage for her child—inviting both
Triopas and his son. But the lady, heavy-hearted,
answered with tears: "Triopas will come, but
Erysichthon a boar wounded on Pindus of fair glens
and he hath lain abed for nine days." Poor child-
loving mother, what falsehood didst thou not tell?
One was giving a feast: "Erysichthon is abroad."
One was bringing home a bride: "A quoit hath
struck Erysichthon," or "he hath had a fall from his
car," or "he is counting his flocks on Othrys.[d]"
Then he within the house, an all-day banqueter, ate
all things beyond reckoning. But his evil belly
leaped all the more as he ate, and all the eatables
poured, in vain and thanklessly, as it were into the
depths of the sea. And even as the snow upon
Mimas, as a wax doll in the sun, yea, even more

^c Unknown.   ^d Mountain in Thessaly.

Hymn iv. 67 *n*.

CALLIMACHUS

καὶ τούτων ἔτι μεῖζον ἐτάκετο μέσφ' ἐπὶ νευράς·
δειλαίῳ ἶνές τε καὶ ὀστέα μῶνον ἔλειφθεν.
κλαῖε μὲν ἁ μάτηρ, βαρὺ δ' ἔστενον αἱ δύ' ἀδελφαὶ
χὠ μαστὸς τὸν ἔπωνε καὶ αἱ δέκα πολλάκι δῶλαι. 95
καὶ δ' αὐτὸς Τριόπας πολιαῖς ἐπὶ χεῖρας ἔβαλλε,
τοῖα τὸν οὐκ ἀίοντα Ποσειδάωνα καλιστρέων·
" ψευδοπάτωρ ἰδὲ τόνδε τεοῦ τρίτον, εἴπερ ἐγὼ μὲν
σεῦ τε καὶ Αἰολίδος Κανάκας γένος, αὐτὰρ ἐμεῖο
τοῦτο τὸ δείλαιον γένετο βρέφος· αἴθε γὰρ αὐτὸν 100
βλητὸν ὑπ' Ἀπόλλωνος ἐμαὶ χέρες ἐκτερέιξαν·
νῦν δὲ κακὰ βούβρωστις ἐν ὀφθαλμοῖσι κάθηται.
ἢ οἱ ἀπόστασον χαλεπὰν νόσον ἠέ νιν αὐτὸς
βόσκε λαβών· ἁμαὶ γὰρ ἀπειρήκαντι τράπεζαι.
χῆραι μὲν μάνδραι, κεναὶ δέ μοι αὔλιες ἤδη 105
τετραπόδων, ἤδη γὰρ ἀπαρνήσαντο μάγειροι."
    ἀλλὰ καὶ οὔρῃς μεγαλᾶν ὑπέλυσαν ἀμαξᾶν,
καὶ τὰν βῶν ἔφαγεν, τὰν Ἑστίᾳ ἔτρεφε μάτηρ,
καὶ τὸν ἀεθλοφόρον καὶ τὸν πολεμήιον ἵππον,
καὶ τὰν αἴλουρον, τὰν ἔτρεμε θηρία μικκά. 110
    μέσφ' ὅκα μὲν Τριόπαο δόμοις ἔνι χρήματα κεῖτο,
μῶνοι ἄρ' οἰκεῖοι θάλαμοι κακὸν ἠπίσταντο.
ἀλλ' ὅκα τὸν βαθὺν οἶκον ἀνεξήραναν[1] ὀδόντες,
καὶ τόχ' ὁ τῶ βασιλῆος ἐνὶ τριόδοισι καθῆστο
αἰτίζων ἀκόλως τε καὶ ἔκβολα λύματα δαιτός. 115

[1] ἀνεξήραναν Ernesti; ἀνεξήραινον mss.

[a] Canace, daughter of Aeolus and Enarete, mother by
Poseidon of Triopas (Diod. v. 61, Apollod. i. 7, iii. 4).
[b] This rendering, which takes βούβρωστις as abstract for
concrete, seems better than "gluttony sits in his eyes."
[c] The Greek μάγειρος is butcher as well as cook.
[d] At libations and sacrifices the first and last offerings
were made to Hestia, the goddess of the family hearth.
132

than these he wasted to the very sinews: only
sinews and bones had the poor man left. His mother
wept, and greatly groaned his two sisters, and the
breast that suckled him and the ten handmaidens
over and over. And Triopas himself laid hands on
his grey hairs, calling on Poseidon, who heeded not,
with such words as these : " False father, behold this
the third generation of thy sons—if I am son of thee
and of Canace,[a] daughter of Aeolus, and this hapless
child is mine. Would that he had been smitten by
Apollo and that my hands had buried him ! But
now he sits an accursed glutton before mine eyes.[b]
Either do thou remove from him his cruel disease or
take and feed him thyself; for my tables are already
exhausted. Desolate are my folds and empty my
byres of four-footed beasts ; for already the cooks[c]
have said me "no."

But even the mules they loosed from the great
wains and he ate the heifer that his mother was
feeding for Hestia [d] and the racing horse and the war
charger, and the cat at which the little vermin
trembled.

So long as there were stores in the house of
Triopas, only the chambers of the house were aware
of the evil thing ; but when his teeth dried up the
rich house, then the king's son sat at the crossways,[e]
begging for crusts and the cast out refuse of the

Hence the proverb ἀφ' Ἑστίας ἄρχεσθαι, which sometimes
approaches the sense of τὴν ἀφ' ἱερᾶς κινεῖν, indicating a last
desperate move, or something thorough-going (cf. Germ.
"von Hause aus." Plato, Euthyphr. 3 A, etc.).

[e] There seems to be a reference to the disposal of rubbish
at the crossways, Aesch. Cho. 97 with schol., and offerings
made to Hecate there, Aristoph. Plut. 594 with schol.
Harpocr. s.v. ὀξυθύμια. It seems possible that Hecate's name
Eucoline is a euphemism for Acoline (ἄκολος).

CALLIMACHUS

Δάματερ, μὴ τῆνος ἐμὶν φίλος, ὅς τοι ἀπεχθής,
εἴη μηδ' ὁμότοιχος· ἐμοὶ κακογείτονες ἐχθροί.
    ἄσατε[1] παρθενικαί, καὶ ἐπιφθέγξασθε τεκοῖσαι
"Δάματερ μέγα χαῖρε πολυτρόφε πουλυμέδιμνε."
χὠς αἱ[2] τὸν κάλαθον λευκότριχες ἵπποι ἄγοντι   120
τέσσαρες, ὣς ἁμῖν μεγάλα θεὸς εὐρυάνασσα
λευκὸν ἔαρ, λευκὸν δὲ θέρος καὶ χεῖμα φέροισα
ἡξεῖ καὶ φθινόπωρον, ἔτος δ' εἰς ἄλλο φυλαξεῖ.
ὡς δ' ἀπεδίλωτοι καὶ ἀνάμπυκες ἄστυ πατεῦμες,
ὣς πόδας, ὣς κεφαλὰς παναπηρέας ἔξομες αἰεί.   125
ὡς δ' αἱ[3] λικνοφόροι χρυσῶ πλέα λίκνα φέροντι,
ὣς ἁμὲς τὸν χρυσὸν ἀφειδέα πασαίμεσθα.
μέσφα τὰ τᾶς πόλιος πρυτανήια τὰς ἀτελέστως,
τὰς δὲ τελεσφορέας[4] ποτὶ τὰν θεὸν ἄχρις ὁμαρτεῖν,
αἵτινες ἑξήκοντα κατώτεραι· αἱ δὲ[5] βαρεῖαι   130
χἄτις Ἐλειθυίᾳ τείνει χέρα χἄτις ἐν ἄλγει,
ὣς ἅλις, ὡς αὐτᾶν ἱκανὸν γόνυ· ταῖσι δὲ Δηὼ
δωσεῖ πάντ' ἐπίμεστα καὶ ὡς ποτὶ ναὸν ἵκωνται.
    χαῖρε θεὰ καὶ τάνδε σάω πόλιν ἔν θ' ὁμονοίᾳ
ἔν τ' εὐηπελίᾳ, φέρε δ' ἀγρόθι νόστιμα πάντα·   135
φέρβε βόας, φέρε μᾶλα, φέρε στάχυν, οἶσε θερισμόν,
φέρβε καὶ εἰράναν, ἵν' ὃς ἄροσε τῆνος ἀμάσῃ.[6]
ἵλαθί μοι τρίλλιστε μέγα κρείοισα θεάων.

---

[1] ἄσατε F; om. AE.
[2] χὠς αἱ Stephanus; χῶσαι.
[3] ὡς αἱ mss. ; corr. Meineke.
[4] τελεσφορίας mss. ; corr. T. Bentley.
[5] αἵ τε mss. ; corr. Ernesti.
[6] ἀμάσῃ Stephanus; ἀμάσ(σ)ει mss., which may be right,
cf. fr. incert. 16.

feast. O Demeter, never may that man be my friend who is hateful to thee, nor ever may he share party-wall with me; ill neighbours I abhor.

Sing, ye maidens, and ye mothers, say with them: "Demeter, greatly hail! Lady of much bounty, of many measures of corn." And as the four white-haired horses convey the Basket, so unto us will the great goddess of wide dominion come bringing white spring and white harvest and winter and autumn, and keep us to another year. And as unsandalled and with hair unbound we walk the city, so shall we have foot and head unharmed for ever. And as the van-bearers bear vans [a] full of gold, so may we get gold unstinted. Far as the City Chambers let the uninitiated follow, but the initiated even unto the very shrine of the goddess—as many as are under sixty years. But those that are heavy [b] and she that stretches her hand to Eileithyia and she that is in pain—sufficient it is that they go so far as their knees are able. And to them Deo shall give all things to overflowing, even as if they came unto her temple.

Hail, goddess, and save this people in harmony and in prosperity, and in the fields bring us all pleasant things! Feed our kine, bring us flocks, bring us the corn-ear, bring us harvest! and nurse peace, that he who sows may also reap. Be gracious, O thrice-prayed for, great Queen of goddesses!

[a] λίκνα, skull-shaped baskets, used for offering first-fruits to the gods (cf. Hesych. s.v. λεῖκνα), also for winnowing corn and for cradles. Equivalent to Latin vannus, whence our "van" and "fan."

[b] βαρεῖα has the ambiguous sense of heavy with age (Soph. O.T. 17) or heavy with child—Lat. gravida.

ΕΠΙΓΡΑΜΜΑΤΑ

I.

Ξεῖνος Ἀταρνείτης τις ἀνείρετο Πιττακὸν οὕτω
 τὸν Μυτιληναῖον, παῖδα τὸν Ὑρράδιον [1].
"ἄττα γέρον, δοιός με καλεῖ γάμος· ἡ μία μὲν δὴ
 νύμφη καὶ πλούτῳ καὶ γενεῇ κατ' ἐμέ,
ἡ δ' ἑτέρη προβέβηκε· τί λώιον; εἰ δ' ἄγε σύμ μοι 5
 βούλευσον, ποτέρην εἰς ὑμέναιον ἄγω."
εἶπεν· ὁ δὲ σκίπωνα, γεροντικὸν ὅπλον, ἀείρας,
 "ἠνίδε, κεῖνοί σοι πᾶν ἐρέουσιν ἔπος."
οἱ δ' ἄρ' ὑπὸ πληγῇσι θοὰς βέμβικας ἔχοντες
 ἔστρεφον εὐρείῃ παῖδες ἐνὶ τριόδῳ. 10
"κείνων ἔρχεο," φησί, "μετ' ἴχνια." χὡ μὲν ἐπέστη
 πλησίον· οἱ δ' ἔλεγον· "τὴν κατὰ σαυτὸν ἔλα."
ταῦτ' ἀίων ὁ ξεῖνος ἐφείσατο μείζονος οἴκου
 δράξασθαι, παίδων κληδόνα [2] συνθέμενος,

[1] Ὑρράδιον Schneider; Ὑρραδίον.
[2] κληδόνι Diog.

---

[a] In Mysia.
[b] One of the Seven Wise Men.
[c] The peculiar Aeolic form of patronymic in -άδιος is
attested by the Greek grammarians (Bekker, *Anecd.* ii. 634,
Cramer, *Anecd. Ox.* iv. 326, etc.), who mention that Pittacus

EPIGRAMS

I.

A stranger from Atarneus [a] thus asked Pittacus [b] of Mytilene, the son of Hyrrhas [c] : "Reverend Father, two marriages invite me. One lady is my equal in wealth and blood : the other is above my station. Which is better? Come advise me whether of those I should lead to the altar."

So he spake : and Pittacus lifted up his staff, the old man's weapon, and said : "Lo! these yonder shall tell thee all." Now these were boys who at a wide crossing were spinning their swift tops with blows of the lash. "Follow their tracks," saith he. And the stranger stood by them : and they were saying : "Keep your own rank! [d]" When the stranger heard the words, he laid to heart the saying of the boys and spared to grasp at the greater estate. Now,

was called Hyrrhadius as son of Hyrrhas. But it is very likely that Ὑρραδίον is right here.

[d] The phrase τὴν κατὰ σαυτὸν ἔλα = "drive your own line," or "path" was a proverb. Suidas s.v., who gives not quite a correct rendering ("Seem to be what you are"), says some attributed it to the Pythian oracle, some to Solon, some to Chilon. It is hinted at by Aesch. *Prom.* v. 887 ff., where schol. A attributes it to Pittacus. It is imitated Aristoph. *Clouds* 25 ἔλαυνε τὸν σαυτοῦ δρόμον. A. Hauvette—"c'est-à-dire pousse la toupie qui est à ta portée, à ta hauteur"—quite misunderstands the phrase.

τὴν δ' ὀλίγην ὡς κεῖνος ἐς οἰκίον ἤγετο νύμφην.   15
οὕτω καὶ σύ γ' ἰὼν[1] τὴν κατὰ σαυτὸν ἔλα.

A.P. vii. 89, Diog. Laert. i. 79 f.

II.

Εἶπέ τις, Ἡράκλειτε, τεὸν μόρον, ἐς δέ με δάκρυ
ἤγαγεν, ἐμνήσθην δ' ὀσσάκις ἀμφότεροι
ἥλιον ἐν λέσχῃ κατεδύσαμεν· ἀλλὰ σὺ μέν που,
ξεῖν' Ἁλικαρνησεῦ, τετράπαλαι σποδιή·   5
αἱ δὲ τεαὶ ζώουσιν ἀηδόνες, ᾗσιν ὁ πάντων
ἁρπακτὴς Ἀίδης οὐκ ἐπὶ χεῖρα βαλεῖ.

A.P. vii. 80, Diog. Laert. ix. 17.

III.[2]

[Ὀξεῖαι πάντη περὶ τὸν τάφον εἰσὶν ἄκανθαι
καὶ σκόλοπες· βλάψεις τοὺς πόδας, ἢν προσίῃς·]
Τίμων μισάνθρωπος ἐνοικέω. ἀλλὰ πάρελθε
οἰμώζειν εἴπας πολλά, πάρελθε μόνον.

A.P. vii. 320, where it is attributed to Hegesippus.   Plut.
Ant. 70 quotes the last distich as τὸ περιφερόμενον Καλλι-
μάχειον.

IV.[2]

Μὴ χαίρειν εἴπῃς με, κακὸν κέαρ, ἀλλὰ πάρελθε·
ἶσον ἐμοὶ χαίρειν ἐστὶ τὸ μὴ σὲ γελᾶν.[3]

A.P. vii. 318.

---

[1] γ' ἰὼν A.P. ; Δίων Diog.
[2] Rejected by Wilamowitz.   Other epigrams on Timon
A.P. vii. 313 ff.   [3] γελᾶν mss. ; πελᾶν Jacobs.

EPIGRAMS

even as he led home the humble bride, so go thou
and keep thine own rank.

II.[a]

One told me, Heracleitus, of thy death and
brought me to tears, and I remembered how often
we two in talking put the sun to rest.[b] Thou,
methinks, Halicarnasian friend, art ashes long and
long ago ; but thy nightingales live still, whereon
Hades, snatcher of all things, shall not lay his hand.

III.

[All about my grave are sharp thorns and stakes :
thou wilt hurt thy feet if thou comest nigh :]
I, Timon,[c] hater of men, inhabit here ; but go
thou by ; curse me as thou wilt, but go.

IV.

Bid me not "farewell," evil heart, but go by.   It
is well with me if thou refrain from laughter.

[a] Quoted Diog. Laert. ix. 17, where he gives a list of
persons called Heracleitus : τρίτος ἐλεγείας ποιητὴς Ἁλικαρ-
νασσεύς, εἰς ὃν Καλλίμαχος πεποίηκεν οὕτως, Εἶπέ τις . . . βαλεῖ.
Strabo, xiv. 656, mentions among notable men of Halicarnassus Ἡράκλειτος ὁ ποιητὴς ὁ Καλλιμάχου ἑταῖρος.   An
epitaph by him is *A.P.* vii. 465 (imitated by Antip. Sid.
A.P. vii. 464).   The epigram of Callimachus is translated in
Ionica (1858, rep. 1891) by Wm. Cory (Johnson).
[b] Verg. *E*. ix. 51 f. " saepe ego longos Cantando puerum
memini me condere soles."
[c] On Timon, the Athenian misanthrope, *cf*. Aristoph.
Birds 1549, *Lys.* 809 ff. ; Lucian, *Timon* ; Diog. Laert. ix.
112 ; Plut. *Anton.* 70.   Schneider assigns the first distich to
Hegesippus, the second to Callimachus.

139

CALLIMACHUS

V.

Τίμων, οὐ γὰρ ἔτ᾽ ἐσσί, τί τοι, σκότος ἢ φάος
    ἐχθρόν;
"τὸ σκότος· ὑμέων γὰρ πλείονες εἰν Ἀίδη."

A.P. vii. 317.

VI.

Κόγχος ἐγώ, Ζεφυρῖτι, παλαίτερος [1]· ἀλλὰ σὺ νῦν με,
    Κύπρι, Σεληναίης ἄνθεμα πρῶτον ἔχεις,
ναυτίλος [2] ὃς πελάγεσσιν ἐπέπλεον, εἰ μὲν ἆηται,
    τείνας οἰκείων λαῖφος ἀπὸ προτόνων,
εἰ δὲ Γαληναίη, λιπαρὴ θεός, οὖλος ἐρέσσων   5
    ποσσί νιν [3], ὥστ᾽ ἔργῳ τοὔνομα συμφέρεται,
ἔστ᾽ ἔπεσον παρὰ θῖνας Ἰουλίδας, ὄφρα γένωμαι
    σοὶ τὸ περίσκεπτον παίγνιον, Ἀρσινόη,

---

[1] πάλαι τέρας Schneider.   [2] ναυτίλον; corr. Kaibel.
        [3] ποσσὶν ἵν᾽; corr. Hermann.

---

[a] οἱ πλείονες, as we say The Great Majority = the Dead:
Aristoph. *Eccl.* 1073; *A.P.* vii. 731, xi. 42; Suid. πλειόνων·
τῶν νεκρῶν.

[b] On a nautilus shell dedicated to Arsinoë Aphrodite of
Zephyrium (*cf.* epigr. of Poseidippus in Athen. vii. 318) by
Selenaea, daughter of Cleinias, who, we may suppose, on the
way from Smyrna to Egypt had obtained the shell at Iulis in
Ceos.   For Zephyrium *cf.* Steph. Byz. *s.v.* ἔστι καὶ ἄκρα
τῆς Αἰγύπτου ἀφ᾽ ἧς ἡ Ἀφροδίτη καὶ Ἀρσινόη Ζεφυρῖτις ὡς
Καλλίμαχος.   See W. Deonna, *Rev. Arch.* 1917, *Rev. de
l'histoire d. relig.* 80 (1919).

The epigram is quoted by Athenaeus apropos of Aristotle's
description (fr. 316) of the nautilus: "The so-called nautilus
(*i.e.* sailor) is not a polypus but resembles the polypus in the
matter of tentacles.   It has a testaceous back.   In emerging
from the water it keeps the shell atop so as not to carry

EPIGRAMS

V.

Timon (for thou art no more), which is hateful to
thee—Darkness or Light ? "The Darkness, for there
are more [a] of you in Hades."

VI.[b]

An old shell am I, O Lady of Zephyrium,[c] but now,
Cypris, I am thine, a first offering from Selenaea : I the
nautilus that used to sail upon the sea, if there were
wind, stretching my sail on my own forestays, if Calm,[d]
that bright goddess, prevailed, rowing strongly with
my feet—so that my name befits my deed !—till I
fell on the shores of Iulis, that I might become thy
admired toy, Arsinoë, and that in my chambers may

water. Then it turns over and floats on the surface, holding erect two tentacles which have a membrane between
them, similar to the skinny web seen between the toes of
fowls. Other two tentacles it lets down into the sea to
serve as rudders. When frightened by the approach of
anything it draws in its feet, fills itself with sea water and
submerges quickly." This is the Argonaut or Paper
nautilus.
   [c] Arsinoë II. Philadelphus, who died, as we now know
from a new fragment of the Mendes stele, in July 270 B.C.,
received divine honours and had, among others, a temple
at Zephyrium, a promontory between Alexandria and
the Canopic mouth of the Nile, dedicated by Callicrates
(Poseidippus *ap*. Athen. vii. 318) ὁ ναύαρχος, where she was
worshipped as Arsinoë Aphrodite (Strabo 800), *i.e.* Aphrodite
as patroness of sea-faring (Εὔπλοια, Πελαγία).
   [d] Galenaia, or Galene, a Nereid (Hes. *Th.* 244), was
the goddess of Calm, *cf.* Eurip. *Hel.* 1457 ; Paus. ii. 1. 8.
But the word is frequently used in the sense of the "calm
sea," *e.g.* Hom. *Od.* vii. 319 ἐλόωσι γαλήνην ; which justifies
us in taking νιν here to be the sea ; *cf.* νήεσσιν ἐρέσσεται
. . ὕδωρ *A.P.* iv. 3[b], 30.

141

CALLIMACHUS

μηδέ μοι ἐν θαλάμῃσιν ἔθ᾽ ὡς πάρος, εἰμὶ γὰρ
    ἄπνους,
τίκτηται νοτερῆς[1] ὤεον ἀλκυόνης.
Κλεινίου ἀλλὰ θυγατρὶ δίδου χάριν. οἶδε γὰρ ἐσθλὰ
ῥέζειν καὶ Σμύρνης ἐστὶν ἀπ᾽ Αἰολίδος.

Athen. vii. 318.

VII.

Τοῦ Σαμίου[2] πόνος εἰμὶ δόμῳ ποτὲ θεῖον ἀοιδὸν[3]
    δεξαμένου, κλείω[4] δ᾽ Εὔρυτον, ὅσσ᾽ ἔπαθεν,
καὶ ξανθὴν Ἰόλειαν, Ὁμήρειον δὲ καλεῦμαι
    γράμμα· Κρεωφύλῳ, Ζεῦ φίλε, τοῦτο μέγα.

Strabo xiv. 638, Sext. Emp. *Adv. math.* p. 609, schol.
Dion. Thrac. p. 163 (except the last four words).

VIII.

Στήλην μητρυιῆς, μικρὰν[5] λίθον, ἔστεφε κοῦρος,
    ὡς βίον ἠλλάχθαι καὶ τρόπον οἰόμενος·
ἡ δὲ τάφῳ κλινθέντα κατέκτανε παῖδα πεσοῦσα·
    φεύγετε μητρυιῆς καὶ τάφον οἱ πρόγονοι.

A.P. ix. 67 anonym. but attributed to Callim. by Planud.

[1] νοτερῆσ᾽ . . . ἀλκυονίς Kaibel.
[2] Τοῦ Σαμίου Strabo; Κρεωφύλου schol. Dion. Thrac. and
Sext. Emp.
[3] ἀοιδὸν Sext. Emp.; Ὅμηρον Strabo.
[4] κλείω Sext. Emp.; κλαίω Strabo.
[5] μιαρὰν Bentley, but *cf.* Suid. *s.v.* Κυνήγιον· . . . εἶδεν
ἐκεῖσε στήλην μικρὰν τῷ μήκει καὶ πλατείαν καὶ παχεῖαν πάνυ . . .
παρευθὺ πεσεῖν τὴν στήλην ἐκ τοῦ ἐκεῖσε ὕψους καὶ κροῦσαι τὸν
Ἱμέριον καὶ θανατῶσαι.

EPIGRAMS

no more be laid, as erstwhile—for I am dead—the eggs of the water-haunting kingfisher. But give thou grace to the Daughter of Cleinias; for she knows to do good deeds and she is from Aeolian Smyrna.

VII.

I am the work of the Samian,[a] who once received the divine singer in his house; and I celebrate the sufferings of Eurytus[b] and of fair-haired Ioleia; but I am called the writing of Homer. Dear Zeus, for Creophylus this is a great thing.

VIII.[c]

A youth was garlanding the grave-pillar of his step-mother, a short stone, thinking that with change of life her nature too was changed. But as he bent over the grave, the stone fell and killed the boy. Ye step-sons, shun even the grave of a step-mother.

[a] Strabo xiv. 638 "To Samos belonged also Creophylus who is said to have entertained Homer and received from him as a gift the inscription of the poem called 'The Taking of Oichalia' (Οἰχαλίας Ἅλωσις). But Callimachus in an epigram asserts the contrary and implies that Creophylus wrote the poem while Homer was reputed to be the author on account of the alleged entertaining." Then he quotes the epigram.

[b] Eurytus, king of Oechalia, variously localized in Thessaly (Il. ii. 730), Messenia, and Euboea. He offered to wed his daughter Iole, or Ioleia (Hesiod ap. schol. Soph. Tr. 263), to him who should defeat him in archery. Heracles defeated him, but he refused to give Iole to Heracles, who thereupon destroyed Oechalia, killed Eurytus, and carried off Iole.

[c] The unkindness of the step-mother to the first family (πρόγονοι, so A.P. ix. 68) is proverbial in the Greek and Latin poets, A.P. ix. 68 and 69.

CALLIMACHUS

IX.

Ἦλθε Θεαίτητος καθαρὴν ὁδόν. εἰ δ' ἐπὶ κισσὸν
   τὸν τεὸν οὐχ αὕτη, Βάκχε, κέλευθος ἄγει,
ἄλλων μὲν κήρυκες ἐπὶ βραχὺν οὔνομα καιρὸν
   φθέγξονται, κείνου δ' Ἑλλὰς ἀεὶ σοφίην.

A.P. ix. 565.

X.

Μικρή τις, Διόνυσε, καλὰ πρήσσοντι ποιητῇ
   ῥῆσις· ὁ μὲν "νικῶ" φησὶ τὸ μακρότατον,
ᾧ δὲ σὺ μὴ πνεύσῃς ἐνδέξιος,[1] ἤν τις ἔρηται
   "πῶς ἔβαλες"; φησί "σκληρὰ τὰ γιγνόμενα."
τῷ μερμηρίξαντι τὰ μὴ ᾿νδικα τοῦτο γένοιτο
   τοὖπος· ἐμοὶ δ', ὦναξ, ἡ βραχυσυλλαβίη.   5

A.P. ix. 566.

XI.

Τῇδε Σάων ὁ Δίκωνος Ἀκάνθιος ἱερὸν ὕπνον
   κοιμᾶται. θνήσκειν μὴ λέγε τοὺς ἀγαθούς.

A.P. vii. 451.

XII.

Ἢν δίζῃ Τίμαρχον ἐν Ἅιδος, ὄφρα πύθηαι
   ἤ τι περὶ ψυχῆς ἢ πάλι πῶς ἔσεαι,
δίζεσθαι φυλῆς Πτολεμαΐδος υἱέα πατρὸς
   Παυσανίου· δήεις δ' αὐτὸν ἐν εὐσεβέων.

A.P. vii. 520.

[1] ἐπιδέξιος Kaibel.

---

[a] Theaetetus was the author of several extant epigrams,
Diog. Laert. iv. 25, viii. 48; A.P. vii. 444, 499, 727. We

EPIGRAMS

IX.

Theaetetus [a] travelled a splendid path. If that path, Bacchus, leads not to thine ivy wreath—other men's names the heralds will voice a little while, but his skill Hellas will voice for ever.

X.

Short is the speech, Dionysus, of the successful poet : " Won," says he, at most. But if thou breathe not favourably and one ask, " What luck ? " " 'Tis a hard business," he says. Be these the words of him who broods injustice ; but mine, O Lord, the monosyllable !

XI.

Here Saon of Acanthus, son of Dicon, sleeps the holy sleep. Say not that the good die.[b]

XII.

If thou seekest Timarchus [c] in the house of Hades to learn aught of the soul, or how it shall be with thee hereafter, seek the son of Pausanias of the Ptolemaic tribe,[d] and thou shalt find him in the abode of the righteous.

may perhaps infer from *A.P.* vii. 49, which is on Ariston of Cyrene, that he belonged to that town. The reference of καθαρὴν ὁδόν is obscure : *cf.* Pind. *Isth.* iv. (v.) 23, *Ol.* vi. 23 and 73. Hauvette has " T. est entré dans une voie nouvelle."

[b] J. Montgomery : When the good man yields his breath —for the good man never dies (*Wanderer of Switz.* v.).

[c] Diog. Laert. vi. 95 mentions a philosopher Timarchus of Alexandria.

[d] This Athenian tribe was so named in honour of Ptolemy Philadelphus, Paus. i. 6. 8.

145

XIII.

Σύντομος ἦν ὁ ξεῖνος· ὁ καὶ στίχος οὐ μακρὰ λέξων
"Θῆρις Ἀρισταίου Κρής" ἐπ' ἐμοὶ δολιχός.

A.P. vii. 447.

XIV.

Κύζικον ἢν ἔλθῃς, ὀλίγος πόνος Ἱππακὸν εὑρεῖν
καὶ Διδύμην· ἀφανὴς οὔ τι γὰρ ἡ γενεή.
καί σφιν ἀνιηρὸν μὲν ἐρεῖς ἔπος, ἔμπα δὲ λέξαι
τοῦθ', ὅτι τὸν κείνων ὧδ' ἐπέχω Κριτίην.

A.P. vii. 521.

XV.

Ἦ ῥ' ὑπὸ σοὶ Χαρίδας ἀναπαύεται; "εἰ τὸν Ἀρίμμα
τοῦ Κυρηναίου παῖδα λέγεις, ὑπ' ἐμοί."
ὦ Χαρίδα, τί τὰ νέρθε; "πολὺ σκότος." αἱ δ'
ἄνοδοι τί;
"ψεῦδος." ὁ δὲ Πλούτων; "μῦθος." ἀπωλό-
μεθα.

ᵃ It seems best to take σύντομος as short of stature, *cf.*
Ovid, *Amor.* ii. 7. 59 f. "Ossa tegit tumulus, tumulus pro
corpore magnus, Quo lapis exiguus par sibi carmen habet";
but some understand it as short of speech or swift of foot.
The interpretations are various :

1. The deceased was small of stature, the monument was
small, so that the inscription, though of the shortest, was
yet too long to be written in one line (Wilamowitz).

2. The Planudean gives the epigram as one of several εἰς
ἀγωνιστάς. Hence Meineke reads ὑπ' ἐμοί, δόλιχον (*i.e.* the
long race) in the sense "Theris lies under me (the tombstone), ⟨victor⟩ in the long race." Stadtmüller reads ἐπόνει
δόλιχον.

EPIGRAMS

XIII.

Short[a] was the stranger: wherefore the line, though brief its tale: "Theris, son of Aristaeus, Cretan," is long for [upon] me.

XIV.

If thou goest to Cyzicus, it will be small trouble to find Hippacus[b] and Didyme: for not obscure is their family. And a painful message thou wilt tell them, yet tell them this, that I here cover Critias, their son.

XV.[c]

Doth Charidas rest under thee? "If thou meanest the son of Arimmas of Cyrene, under me." O Charidas, what of the world below? "Much darkness." And what of the upward way? "A lie." And Pluto? "A fable." We are undone. "This

3. Others, taking σύντομος as concise in speech, read λέξω and ὑπ' ἐμοί, δολιχός. "Th. was brief of speech: so shall the verse be: I shall not say much: Th., etc., rests under me:" too long still!

[b] For the name Hippacus cf. Pittacus, Astacus, Buttacus, Pyrrhacus. Ajax in his last words (Soph. Aj. 845 ff.) appeals to the Sun to carry the news of his death to his father and mother. Epigrams in which this last appeal is made by the epitaph on the tomb to the passenger are numerous in the Anthology: A.P. vii. 499, 500, 502, 540, 544, 569, 589, 631. Hauvette refers to C.I.A. i. 463; iv. 477[e], 477[h].

[c] On Charidas, son of Arimmas of Cyrene. Arimmas is a short form of 'Αρίμαχος and is found in Arr. Anab. iii. 6. 8 (Hoffmann, Die Makedonen, p. 193).

" οὗτος ἐμὸς λόγος ὕμμιν ἀληθινός· εἰ δὲ τὸν ἡδὺν 5
βούλει, Πελλαίου βοῦς μέγας εἰν ᾿Αίδῃ."

A.P. vii. 524.

XVI.

Δαίμονα τίς δ᾿ εὖ οἶδε τὸν αὔριον; ἀνίκα καὶ σέ
Χάρμι, τὸν ὀφθαλμοῖς χθιζὸν ἐν ἀμετέροις
τᾷ ἑτέρᾳ κλαύσαντες ἐθάπτομεν· οὐδὲν ἐκείνου
εἶδε πατὴρ Διοφῶν χρῆμ᾿ ἀνιαρότερον.

A.P. vii. 519.

XVII.

"Τιμονόη." τίς δ᾿ ἐσσί; μὰ δαίμονας, οὔ σ᾿ ἂν
ἐπέγνων,
εἰ μὴ Τιμοθέου πατρὸς ἐπῆν ὄνομα
στήλῃ καὶ Μήθυμνα, τεῇ πόλις. ἦ μέγα φημὶ
χῆρον ἀνιᾶσθαι σὸν πόσιν Εὐθυμένη.

A.P. vii. 522.

XVIII.

Κρηθίδα τὴν πολύμυθον, ἐπισταμένην καλὰ παίζειν
δίζηνται Σαμίων πολλάκι θυγατέρες,
ἡδίστην συνέριθον ἀεὶ λάλον· ἡ δ᾿ ἀποβρίζει
ἐνθάδε τὸν πάσαις ὕπνον ὀφειλόμενον.

A.P. vii. 459.

---

a The cheapness of things in Hades seems to have
been proverbial. *Cf.* Callim. *Iamb.* i. 2 ἐκ τῶν ὅκου βοῦν
κολλύβου πιπρήσκουσιν and Phot. ὀβολοῦ χίμαιρα· ἐν Ἀίδου.
Coins of Pella had ox as type (Head, *Hist. Numm.* p. 212,
cf. schol. Ambros. Theocr. i. 26) and hence may have been

that I say to you is the true tale, but if thou wouldst have the pleasant tale, a great ox costs but a copper in Hades." [a]

XVI.

Who knows aright to-morrow's [b] fortune? When even thee, Charmis, whom we saw with our own eyes yesterday, next day we laid in the grave with tears. Than that thy father Diophon hath seen nothing more painful.

XVII. [c]

"Timonoë." Who art thou? By the gods I had not known thee, were not the name of thy father Timotheus on thy tombstone, and Methymna, thy city. Great, methinks, is the sorrow of thy widowed husband Euthymenes!

XVIII.

Crathis, of many tales, skilled in pretty jest, do the daughters of the Samians oft-times seek—their sweetest companion, always talking; but she sleeps here the sleep that is due to all.

known as βόες Πελλαῖοι, as Attic drachmas were called γλαῦκες Λαυρεωτικαί (Aristoph. *Av.* 1106) or Παλλάδες (Eubulus *ap.* Poll. ix. 76), and the Corinthian coins with figure of Pegasus were called πῶλοι (Eurip. fr. 675 = Poll. ix. 75). The meaning will then be that in Hades a real βοῦς μέγας costs only a βοῦς Πελλαῖος. *Cf.* Kaibel, *Hermes* xxxi. (1896).

[b] Wilamowitz' τὸν Αὔριον is incredible. There is no such deity.

[c] Kaibel (*Hermes* xxxi. (1896)) suggests that the epigram implies an epitaph in the form Τιμονόα Τιμοθέου Μηθυμναίου, γυνὰ δὲ Εὐθυμένεος.

149

XIX.

Ὤφελε μηδ' ἐγένοντο θοαὶ νέες· οὐ γὰρ ἂν ἡμεῖς
  παῖδα Διοκλείδου Σώπολιν ἐστένομεν.
νῦν δ' ὁ μὲν εἰν ἁλί που φέρεται νέκυς, ἀντὶ δ'
    ἐκείνου
  οὔνομα καὶ κενεὸν σῆμα παρερχόμεθα.

A.P. vii. 271.

XX.

Νάξιος οὐκ ἐπὶ γῆς ἔθανεν Λύκος, ἀλλ' ἐνὶ πόντῳ
  ναῦν ἅμα καὶ ψυχὴν εἶδεν ἀπολλυμένην,
ἔμπορος Αἰγίνηθεν ὅτ' ἔπλεε. χὠ μὲν ἐν ὑγρῇ
  νεκρός, ἐγὼ δ' ἄλλως οὔνομα τύμβος ἔχων
κηρύσσω πανάληθες ἔπος τόδε " φεῦγε θαλάσσῃ   5
  συμμίσγειν ἐρίφων, ναυτίλε, δυομένων."

A.P. vii. 272.

XXI.

Δωδεκέτη τὸν παῖδα πατὴρ ἀπέθηκε Φίλιππος
  ἐνθάδε, τὴν πολλὴν ἐλπίδα, Νικοτέλην.

A.P. vii. 453.

XXII.

Ἠῶι Μελάνιππον ἐθάπτομεν, ἠελίου δὲ
  δυομένου Βασιλὼ κάτθανε παρθενικὴ
αὐτοχερί· ζώειν γὰρ ἀδελφεὸν ἐν πυρὶ θεῖσα
  οὐκ ἔτλη. δίδυμον δ' οἶκος ἐσεῖδε κακὸν

EPIGRAMS

XIX.[a]

Would that swift ships had never even been!
So should we not be mourning Sopolis, son of
Diocleides. But now he floats somewhere in the sea,
a corpse, and, in his stead, his name and empty tomb
we pass by.

XX.[b]

Not on land died Lycus of Naxos, but at sea
he saw ship and life perish together, when sailing as
a merchant from Aegina. And he in the wet sea is
a corpse, while I, the tomb that holds only his name,
proclaim this message of utter truth: Flee the
company of the sea, O mariner, when the Kids are
setting !

XXI.

Here the father laid his twelve-year son: here
Philippus laid his great hope—Nicoteles.

XXII.

At morn we buried Melanippus: as the sun set
the maiden Basilo died by her own hand; for she
could not endure to lay her brother on the pyre and
live; and the house of their father Aristippus

---

[a] Cp. A.P. vii. 496.

[b] For the cosmical setting of the Kids in December
bringing storm, as also their heliacal rising in May, cf. Plin.
N.H. xviii. 69 "haec (tempestates) ab horridis sideribus
exeunt veluti Arcturo, Orione, haedis." Hor. C. iii. 1. 28 ;
Verg. A. ix. 668. Similarly Capella, Ovid, Fast. v. 113,
M. iii. 594 ; Arat. Ph. 158 f. ; Theocr. vii. 53.

CALLIMACHUS

πατρὸς Ἀριστίπποιο, κατήφησεν δὲ Κυρήνη
πᾶσα τὸν εὔτεκνον χῆρον ἰδοῦσα δόμον.

A.P. vii. 517.

XXIII.

Ὅστις ἐμὸν παρὰ σῆμα φέρεις πόδα, Καλλιμάχου με
ἴσθι Κυρηναίου παῖδά τε καὶ γενέτην.
εἰδείης δ᾽ ἄμφω κεν· ὁ μέν κοτε πατρίδος ὅπλων
ἦρξεν, ὁ δ᾽ ἤεισεν κρέσσονα βασκανίης·
οὐ νέμεσις· Μοῦσαι γὰρ ὅσους ἴδον ὄμματι παῖδας   5
μὴ λοξῷ, πολιοὺς οὐκ ἀπέθεντο φίλους.

A.P. vii. 525.

XXIV.

Ἀστακίδην τὸν Κρῆτα τὸν αἰπόλον ἥρπασε Νύμφη
ἐξ ὄρεος, καὶ νῦν ἱερὸς Ἀστακίδης.
οὐκέτι Δικταίῃσιν ὑπὸ δρυσίν, οὐκέτι Δάφνιν
ποιμένες, Ἀστακίδην δ᾽ αἰὲν ἀεισόμεθα.

A.P. vii. 518.

XXV.

Εἶπας "Ἥλιε χαῖρε" Κλεόμβροτος Ὠμβρακιώτης
ἥλατ᾽ ἀφ᾽ ὑψηλοῦ τείχεος εἰς Ἀίδην,

On Battus, son of Callimachus the General and father of Callimachus the Poet.

Cf. Hes. *Th.* 81 f. ; Hor. *Od.* iv. 3. 1.

i.e. is become a hero. *Cf.* Wilamowitz, *Die Textgeschichte der griechischen Bukoliker*, p. 176.

152

beheld a twofold woe; and all Cyrene bowed her
head to see the home of happy children made
desolate.

XXIII.[a]

Whosoever thou art who walkest past my tomb,
know that I am son and sire of Callimachus of Cyrene.
Thou wilt know them both. For the one once led
the arms of his fatherland, the other sang songs
beyond the reach of envy. Naught in this is there
to surprise; for on whom as children the Muses
look [b] with no sidelong glance, those they do not
reject as friends when their heads are grey.

XXIV.

Astacides, the Cretan, the goat-herd, a nymph
carried off from the hill, and now Astacides is made
holy.[c] No more beneath the oaks of Dicte, no more
of Daphnis shall we shepherds sing, but always of
Astacides.

XXV.[d]

Farewell, O Sun, said Cleombrotus of Ambracia
and leapt from a lofty wall into Hades. No evil

---

[d] *A.P.* vii. 471, *cf.* xi. 354. Cleombrotus of Ambracia was
a pupil of Plato. He was in Aegina at the time of Socrates'
death, Plato, *Phaedo* 59 c. For his suicide *cf.* Lucian,
Philopatr. i. ἀλλὰ κατὰ κρημνῶν ὠθούμην ἂν ἐπὶ κεφαλῆς
σκοτοδινήσας, εἰ μὴ ἐπέκραξάς μοι, ὦ τάν, καὶ τὸ τοῦ Κλεομβρότου
πήδημα τοῦ ᾽Αμβρακιώτου ἐμυθεύθη ἐπ᾽ ἐμοί. The work of
Plato is the *Phaedo*, or *On the Soul*. *Cf.* Th. Sinko in *Eos*
xi. (1905), pp. 1 f.

CALLIMACHUS

ἄξιον οὐδὲν ἰδὼν θανάτου κακόν, ἀλλὰ Πλάτωνος
ἓν τὸ περὶ ψυχῆς γράμμ᾽ ἀναλεξάμενος.

A.P. vii. 471 ; Sext. Emp. *Adv. math.* p. 690 ; schol.
Dion. Thrac. p. 160.

XXVI.

Ἥρως Ἠετίωνος ἐπίσταθμος Ἀμφιπολίτεω
ἵδρυμαι μικρῷ μικρὸς ἐπὶ προθύρῳ
λοξὸν ὄφιν καὶ μοῦνον ἔχων ξίφος· ἀνδρὶ δ᾽ Ἐπειῷ
θυμωθεὶς πεζὸν κἀμὲ παρῳκίσατο.

A.P. ix. 336.

XXVII.

Ὤμοσε Καλλίγνωτος Ἰωνίδι μήποτ᾽ ἐκείνης
ἕξειν μήτε φίλον κρέσσονα μήτε φίλην.
ὤμοσεν· ἀλλὰ λέγουσιν ἀληθέα τοὺς ἐν ἔρωτι
ὅρκους μὴ δύνειν οὔατ᾽ ἐς ἀθανάτων.
νῦν δ᾽ ὁ μὲν ἀρσενικῷ θέρεται πυρί· τῆς δὲ ταλαίνης   5
νύμφης ὡς Μεγαρέων οὐ λόγος οὐδ᾽ ἀριθμός.

A.P. v. 6.

---

[a] Heroes were characteristically represented armed and
on horseback and attended by a snake (indicating their
chthonian nature). Eëtion is a typical Trojan (*cf.* Eëtion father
of Andromache) who hates the idea of a horse in consequence
of the wooden horse made by Epeius (*Od.* viii. 493), and
so has a hero at his door who is represented on foot.
ἀνδρί)(ἥρως is a mortal. *Cf.* Pind. *O.* ii. 2 τίν᾽ ἥρωα, τίνα
δ᾽ ἄνδρα ;

[b] Instability of lovers' vows ; *cf.* Ovid, *Ars am.* i. 633
"Iuppiter ex alto periuria ridet amantum."

[c] The Megarians : the concluding words τῆς . . . ἀριθμός are

154

had he seen worthy of death, but he had read one
writing of Plato's, *On the Soul.*

XXVI.[a]

I, a Hero, am set by the doors of Eëtion of
Amphipolis—a small statue by a small vestibule,
with coiling snake and a sword—no more: Wroth
with the man Epeius he has set me also by his
house on foot.

XXVII.[b]

Callignotus swore to Ionis that he would never
hold man or woman dearer than her. He sware:
but what they say is true—that lovers' oaths enter
not the ears of the immortals. And now his flame
is a man, while of poor Ionis there is, as of the
Megarians,[c] "nor count nor reckoning."

quoted from "Callimachus in his Epigrams" by Suidas *s.v.*
ὑμεῖς ὦ Μεγαρεῖς, where the explanation of the proverb is
given: "Mnaseas relates that the Aegians in Achaea,
having defeated the Aetolians at sea and captured from
them a penteconter, dedicated a tithe at Pytho and inquired
who were the best of the Greeks. The Pythian priestess
gave them the oracle quoted above. A Thessalian mare, a
Lacedaemonian woman, the men who drink the water of
fair Arethusa . . . ὑμεῖς δ', Αἰγιέες οὔτε τρίτοι οὔτε τέταρτοι,
οὔτε δυωδέκατοι, οὔτ' ἐν λόγῳ οὔτ' ἐν ἀριθμῷ. Ion also says
the oracle was given to the Aegians. But some think it
was spoken to the Megarians, and quote ὑμεῖς δ' ὦ Μεγαρεῖς
κτλ., as Callimachus in his Epigrams, etc." *Cf.* Suid. *s.vv.*
Αἰγιεῖς and Μεγαρέων, Steph. Byz. *s.v.* Αἴγιον, etc.

CALLIMACHUS

XXVIII.

Εἶχον ἀπὸ σμικρῶν ὀλίγον βίον οὔτε τι δεινὸν
  ῥέζων οὔτ᾿ ἀδικῶν οὐδένα. Γαῖα φίλη,
Μικύλος εἴ τι πονηρὸν ἐπήνεσα, μήτε σὺ κούφη
  γίνεο μήτ᾿ ἄλλοι δαίμονες οἵ μ᾿ ἔχετε.

A.P. vii. 460.

XXIX.

Ἡσιόδου τό τ᾿ ἄεισμα καὶ ὁ τρόπος· οὐ τὸν ἀοιδὸν
  ἔσχατον, ἀλλ᾿ ὀκνέω μὴ τὸ μελιχρότατον
τῶν ἐπέων ὁ Σολεὺς ἀπεμάξατο· χαίρετε λεπταὶ
  ῥήσιες, Ἀρήτου σύντονος ἀγρυπνίη.

A.P. ix. 507.   Arati Vit. iii. (West. p. 54).

XXX.

Ἐχθαίρω τὸ ποίημα τὸ κυκλικόν, οὐδὲ κελεύθῳ
  χαίρω τίς πολλοὺς ὧδε καὶ ὧδε φέρει,
μισῶ καὶ περίφοιτον ἐρώμενον, οὐδ᾿ ἀπὸ κρήνης
  πίνω· σικχαίνω πάντα τὰ δημόσια.
Λυσανίη, σὺ δὲ ναιχὶ καλός καλός—ἀλλὰ πρὶν εἰπεῖν 5
  τοῦτο σαφῶς Ἠχώ, φησί τις "ἄλλος ἔχει."

A.P. xii. 43.

---

[a] The name Micylus occurs as the name of a Macedonian
general in Diodor. xix. 88. 5. It is chosen here probably as
suiting the context (Micylus = small).

[b] On the *Phaenomena* of Aratus. If ἀοιδόν of all MSS.
is right, the interpretation adopted (Kaibel, *Hermes* xxix.
(1894), p. 120) seems best. It would be hazardous to take
τ. ἀ. ἔσχ. as = τ. ἔσχ. ἀ., and in that sense it would be better
to read ἀοιδῶν.

[c] "Odi profanum vulgus et arceo," Hor. *Od.* iii. 1. 1.

156

EPIGRAMS

XXVIII.

With little means I led a humble life, doing no
dreadful deed nor injuring any. Dear Earth, if I,
Micylus,[a] have praised any evil thing, be not thou
light to me, nor light ye other Spirits which have
me in your keeping.

XXIX.[b]

Hesiod's is the theme and Hesiod's the manner.
I misdoubt that not to the utter end but only the
most honeysweet of his verses has the poet of Soli
copied. Hail subtle discourses, the earnest vigil
of Aratus.

XXX.[c]

I hate the cyclic poem, nor do I take pleasure in
the road which carries many to and fro. I abhor,
too, the roaming lover, and I drink not from every
well[d]; I loathe all common things. Lysanias, thou
art, yea, fair, fair : but ere Echo has quite said the
word, says someone, " He is another's."

Echo is the companion of Pan, Eros, etc. (Plut. *Qu.
Symp.* viii. 711 E) and mother of Iynx, the Love Charmer
(Callim. *ap.* schol. Theocrit. ii. 17). Her function is
to repeat the last word or words of a sentence—here
καλός. *Cf.* Ovid, *Metam.* iii. 368 "tamen haec in fine
loquendi Ingeminat voces auditaque verba reportat," and *ib.*
380 "dixerat, Ecquis adest, et Adest responderat Echo."
The repeated καλός as part of the lover's language occurs as
early as Pind. *P.* ii. 72 καλός τοι πίθων (pet name for πίθηκος)
παρὰ παισὶν ἀεὶ καλός, and Attic vases frequently exhibit
such forms as ὁ παῖς ναιχὶ καλός, καλὸς νεανίας, ὁ παῖς καλός,
ναιχὶ καλός, Δωρόθεος καλός, ναιχὶ καλός.
   The punctuation after Ἠχώ was first proposed by E.
Petersen in 1875. The old punctuation, after σαφῶς, gave
the words ἄλλος ἔχει to Echo.   [d] *Cf.* Theogn. 959 ff.

157

XXXI.

Ἔγχει καὶ πάλιν εἰπὲ "Διοκλέος." οὐδ' Ἀχελῷος
  κείνου τῶν ἱερῶν αἰσθάνεται κυάθων.
καλὸς ὁ παῖς, Ἀχελῷε, λίην καλός, εἰ δέ τις οὐχὶ
  φησίν—ἐπισταίμην μοῦνος ἐγὼ τὰ καλά.

A.P. xii. 51.

XXXII.

Θεσσαλικὲ Κλεόνικε, τάλαν, τάλαν, οὐ μὰ τὸν ὀξὺν
  ἤλιον, οὐκ ἔγνων· σχέτλιε, ποῦ γέγονας;
ὀστέα σοι καὶ μοῦνον ἔτι τρίχες· ἦ ῥά σε δαίμων
  οὑμὸς ἔχει, χαλεπῇ δ' ἤντεο θευμορίῃ;
ἔγνων· Εὐξίθεός σε συνήρπασε, καὶ σὺ γὰρ ἐλθὼν   5
  τὸν καλόν, ὦ μοχθήρ', ἔβλεπες ἀμφοτέροις.

A.P. xii. 71.

XXXIII.

Ὠγρευτής, Ἐπίκυδες, ἐν οὔρεσι πάντα λαγωὸν
  διφᾷ καὶ πάσης ἴχνια δορκαλίδος
στείβῃ καὶ νιφετῷ κεχρημένος,[1] ἢν δέ τις εἴπῃ
  "τῇ, τόδε βέβληται θηρίον," οὐκ ἔλαβεν.
χοὐμὸς ἔρως τοιόσδε· τὰ γὰρ φεύγοντα διώκειν   5
  οἶδε, τὰ δ' ἐν μέσσῳ κείμενα παρπέταται.

A.P. xii. 102.

[1] κεχαρημένος Bentley.

ª For the custom of drinking to a person in unmixed
wine *cf. A.P.* v. 136, 137. For Achelous = water *cf.* Verg.
Georg. i. 9 "Poculaque inventis Acheloia miscuit uvis."

EPIGRAMS

XXXI.

Fill the cup and say again "To Diocles!" And Achelous[a] knows not of his sacred cups. Fair is the boy, O Achelous, and very fair : and if any denies it, may I alone know how fair he is!

XXXII.

Cleonicus of Thessaly, poor youth! poor youth! nay, by the scorching sun I knew thee not. Where, poor wretch, hast thou been? Thou hast but bones and hair.[b] Hath then the same doom overtaken thee as me, and hast thou met a hard dispensation of the gods? I know—Euxitheus hath caught thee too : for thou, too, didst come and gaze upon the fair one, poor youth, with both thine eyes.

XXXIII.[c]

The hunter on the hills, O Epicydes, searches out every hare and the tracks of every roe, beset by frost and snow. But if one say, "Lo! here is a beast shot" he takes it not. Even such is my love : it can pursue what flees from it, but what lies ready it passes by.

[b] Cf. Theocr. ii. 89.
[c] This epigram is paraphrased by Horace, *Sat.* i. 2. 105 ff. "'Leporem venator ut alta In nive sectatur, positum sic tangere nolit,' Cantat et apponit : 'meus est amor huic similis, nam Transvolat in medio posita et fugientia captat.'" The sentiment is a common one, *cf.* Ovid, *Amor.* ii. 9. 9 "Venator sequitur fugientia, capta relinquit Semper et inventis ulteriora petit"; *cf.* ii. 19. 35 ; Sappho, frag. 1. 21 καὶ γὰρ αἰ φεύγει ταχέως διώξει.

CALLIMACHUS

XXXIV.

Οἶδ᾽ ὅτι μοι πλούτου κεναὶ χέρες, ἀλλά, Μένιππε,
μὴ λέγε πρὸς Χαρίτων τοὐμὸν ὄνειρον ἐμοί.
ἀλγέω τὴν διὰ παντὸς ἔπος τόδε πικρὸν ἀκούων·
ναὶ φίλε, τῶν παρὰ σοῦ τοῦτ᾽ ἀνεραστότατον.

A.P. xii. 148.

XXXV.

Ἄρτεμι, τὶν τόδ᾽ ἄγαλμα Φιληρατὶς εἵσατο τῇδε·
ἀλλὰ σὺ μὲν δέξαι, πότνια, τὴν δὲ σάω.

A.P. vi. 347.

XXXVI.

Τίν με, λεοντάγχ᾽ ὦνα συοκτόνε, φήγινον ὄζον
θῆκε "τίς ;" Ἀρχῖνος. "ποῖος ;" ὁ Κρής.
"δέχομαι."

A.P. vi. 351.

XXXVII.

Βαττιάδεω παρὰ σῆμα φέρεις πόδας εὖ μὲν ἀοιδὴν
εἰδότος, εὖ δ᾽ οἴνῳ καίρια συγγελάσαι.

A.P. vii. 415.

XXXVIII.

Ὁ Λύκτιος Μενίτας
τὰ τόξα ταῦτ᾽ ἐπειπών

XXXIV.

Empty of wealth, I know, are my hands. But, for the Graces' sake, Menippus, tell not "my own dream to me." [a] Pained through and through am I, when I hear this bitter saying. Yes, my friend, of all I have had from thee this is the most unloverlike.

XXXV

Artemis, to thee Phileratis set up this image here Do thou accept it, Lady, and keep her safe.

XXXVI.

To thee, O Lord, Strangler of the Lion,[b] Slayer of the Boar, I, a branch of oak, am dedicated—"By whom?" Archinus. "Which?" The Cretan. "I accept."

XXXVII.

'Tis the tomb of Battus' son that thou art passing —one who was well skilled in poesy and well skilled in season to laugh over the wine.

XXXVIII.

Menitas of Lyctus dedicated this bow with these

---

[a] Proverbial of what one knows well; cf. xlix. 6.
[b] The Strangler of the Lion (λεοντάγχης; cf. κυνάγχης of Hermes, Hippon. fr. 1) is Heracles strangling the Nemean lion, a frequent type in art. e.g. on the throne at Amyclae ἀγχων Ἡρακλῆς τὸν λέοντα (Paus. iii. 18. 15). He is Slayer of the Boar, i.e. the Erymanthian Boar (Paus. viii. 24. 5).

ἔθηκε " τῇ, κέρας τοι
δίδωμι καὶ φαρέτρην
Σάραπι· τοὺς δ᾽ ὀιστοὺς
ἔχουσιν Ἑσπερῖται."

A.P. xiii. 7.

XXXIX.

Τὰ δῶρα τἀφροδίτῃ
Σῖμον ἡ περίφοιτος, εἰκόν᾽ αὐτῆς,
ἔθηκε τήν τε μίτρην
ἢ μαστοὺς ἐφίλησε τόν τε πανόν,
αὐτοὺς θ᾽ οὓς ἐφόρει τάλαινα θύρσους.[1]   5

A.P. xiii. 24.

XL.

Δήμητρι τῇ Πυλαίῃ,
τῇ τοῦτον οὐκ Πελασγῶν
Ἀκρίσιος τὸν νηὸν ἐδείματο, ταῦθ᾽ ὁ Ναυκρατίτης
καὶ τῇ κάτω θυγατρὶ
τὰ δῶρα Τιμόδημος   5
εἴσατο τῶν κερδέων δεκατεύματα· καὶ γὰρ εὔξαθ᾽
οὕτως.

A.P. xiii. 25.

XLI.

Ἱερέη Δήμητρος ἐγώ ποτε καὶ πάλιν Καβείρων,
ὦνερ, καὶ μετέπειτα Διδυμήνης

[1] θύρσους Bentley ; αὐτοὺς . . . ἐφόρει Editor ; καὶ τοὺς
αὐτοὺς ὀρῇ τάλαινα θάρσους *A.P.*

---

[a] Steph. Byz. *s.v.* Ἑσπερίς· πόλις Λιβύης, ἡ νῦν Βερονίκη.
ὁ πολίτης Ἑσπερίτης.   Καλλίμαχος ἐν τοῖς Ἐπιγράμμασιν.
[b] *Cf.* Hephaest.
[c] Acrisius, son of Abas of Argos (οὐκ Πελασγῶν). The
shrine referred to seems to be implied to be at Ther-
mopylae, *cf.* Strabo ix. 420 Ἀκρίσιος δὲ τῶν μνημονευομένων

words: "Lo! I give to thee horn and quiver,
Sarapis; but the arrows the men of Hesperis *a* have."

XXXIX.

These gifts to Aphrodite did Simon, the light o'
love, dedicate: a portrait of herself and the girdle
that kissed her breasts, and her torch, yea, and the
wands which she, poor woman, used to carry.

XL.*b*

To Demeter of the Gates, to whom Pelasgian
Acrisius *c* builded this shrine, and to her daughter
under earth, Timodemus of Naucratis *d* dedicated
these gifts as a tithe of his gains. For so he vowed.

XLI.

Priestess, Sir, of old was I of Demeter and again
of the Cabeiri and afterward of Dindymene *e*—I the

πρῶτος διατάξαι δοκεῖ τὰ περὶ τοὺς Ἀμφικτύονας (the Delphic
Amphictyony) . . . . τὴν δὲ σύνοδον Πυλαίαν ἐκάλουν . . .
ἐπειδὴ ἐν Πύλαις συνήγοντο, ἃς καὶ Θερμοπύλας καλοῦσιν· ἔθυον
δὲ τῇ Δήμητρι οἱ πυλαγόροι. As Πυλαῖος was an epithet of
Hermes as warder of the gates of Hades (schol. Hom. *Il.*
ii. 842, *cf.* πυληδόκον Hom. *H. Merc.* 15) and the leader of
the Pelasgians from Larissa was called Pylaeus (Hom. *Il.
l.c.*), the exact significance of the epithet is somewhat
difficult.

   d Naucratis, town in Egypt, founded by the Milesians,
Strabo xvi. 801.

   e Dindymene = Cybele, from Mt. Dindymus in Phrygia, at
the foot of which lay Pessinus, the early centre of her
worship, *cf.* Steph. Byz. *s.v.* Δίνδυμα . . . ἀφ' ὧν Δινδυμήνη ἡ
'Ρέα, and Catull. lxiii. 13 "Dindymenae dominae."

ἡ γρῆυς γενόμην, ἡ νῦν κόνις, ἡ 'ν [ὄτλοις
    Ἐλευθοῦς]¹
πολλῶν προστασίη νέων γυναικῶν.
καί μοι τέκν' ἐγένοντο δύ' ἄρσενα, κἠπέμυσ'
    ἐκείνων   5
εὐγήρως ἐνὶ χερσίν· ἔρπε χαίρων.

A.P. vii. 728.

XLII.

Ἥμισύ μευ ψυχῆς ἔτι τὸ πνέον, ἥμισυ δ' οὐκ οἶδ'
    εἴτ' Ἔρος εἴτ' Ἀΐδης ἥρπασε, πλὴν ἀφανές.
ἦ ῥά τιν' ἐς παίδων πάλιν ᾤχετο; καὶ μὲν ἀπεῖπον
    πολλάκι "τὴν δρῆστιν μὴ ὑποδέχεσθε νέοι."
οὗ τις συνδιφήσον· ἐκεῖσε γὰρ ἡ λιθόλευστος   5
    κείνη καὶ δύσερως οἶδ' ὅτι που στρέφεται.

A.P. xii. 73.

XLIII.²

Εἰ μὲν ἑκών, Ἀρχῖν', ἐπεκώμασα, μυρία μέμφου,
    εἰ δ' ἄκων ἥκω, τὴν προπέτειαν ἔα.

¹ Supplement by Editor.
² This epigram was found on a wall in a house on the
Esquiline in Rome (Kaibel, *Herm.* x. 1 ff.); *cf.* Kaibel, *Ep.
Gr. e lap. conlect.* p. 502.

ᵃ Aulus Gellius, *N.A.* xix. 9, has preserved an imitation
of this by Q. Catulus : "Aufugit mi animus. credo, ut solet,
ad Theotimum Devenit. sic est : perfugium illud habet.
Qui, si non interdixem, ne illunc fugitivum Mitteret ad se
intro, sed magis eiceret? Ibimus quaesitum. verum, ne
ipsi teneamur, Formido. quid ago? da, Venus, consilium."
ᵇ *Cf. A.P.* xii. 166.
ᶜ The language of this epigram is that of the Stoic logic.
προπέτεια, "rashness," is opposed to ἀπροπτωσία, *cf.* Diog. L.
vii. 46 τήν τε ἀπροπτωσίαν ἐπιστήμην τοῦ πότε δεῖ συγκατατίθεσθαι

old woman who am now dust, I who in the travail
of Eleutho was the friend of many young wives.
And two male children were born to me and in a
ripe old age I closed my eyes in their arms. Go thy
way and farewell!

XLII.[a]

Half of my soul still lives, but half I know not
whether Love or Death hath stolen: only it is
vanished.[b] Has it gone again to where the boys
are? and yet I forbade them often: "O youths,
receive not the runaway!" There help me, some
one, to search; for there somewhere of a surety flits
that lovesick one, worthy to die by stoning.

XLIII.[c]

If of my free will, Archinus, I serenaded thee,
blame me ten thousand times; but if I came unwillingly, away with rashness! Wine and Love con-

καὶ μή; ibid. 48 διατείνειν δὲ τὴν ἐν ταῖς ἀποφάσεσι προπέτειαν
καὶ ἐπὶ τὰ γινόμενα, ὥστε εἰς ἀκοσμίαν καὶ εἰκαιότητα τρέπεσθαι
τοὺς ἀγυμνάστους ἔχοντας τὰς φαντασίας. See von Arnim,
Hermes, xxv. p. 475 ἡ μὲν ἀπροπτωσία . . . ἄνελκτον (*cf.*
εἷλκεν l. 4) παρεχομένη ταῖς μὴ καταληπτικαῖς (φαντασίαις).
For v. 6 *cf.* Propert. ii. 30. 24 "Hoc si crimen erit, crimen
Amoris erit"; and in general *cf.* Propert. i. 3. 13 "et quamvis
duplici correptum ardore iuberent Hac Amor, hac Liber,
durus uterque deus"; Ovid, *Amor.* i. 6. 33 "Ergo Amor et
modicum circum mea tempora vinum," and *ibid.* v. 59 "Nox
et Amor vinumque nihil moderabile suadent: Illa pudore
vacat, Liber Amorque metu." *Cf.* Kaibel, *Hermes* xxxi.
(1896). The last two lines of the epigram are quoted by
Plutarch, *De cohib. ira*, 5.

CALLIMACHUS

Ἄκρητος καὶ Ἔρως μ' ἠνάγκασαν, ὧν ὁ μὲν αὐτῶν
εἷλκεν, ὁ δ' οὐκ εἴα τὴν προπέτειαν ἐᾶν.[1]
ἐλθὼν δ' οὐκ ἐβόησα, τίς ἢ τίνος, ἀλλ' ἐφίλησα   5
τὴν φλιήν· εἰ τοῦτ' ἔστ' ἀδίκημ', ἀδικέω.

A.P. xii. 118; Cramer, Anec. Par. iv. 384.

XLIV.

Ἕλκος ἔχων ὁ ξεῖνος ἐλάνθανεν· ὡς ἀνιηρὸν
πνεῦμα διὰ στηθέων (εἶδες;) ἀνηγάγετο,
τὸ τρίτον ἡνίκ' ἔπινε, τὰ δὲ ῥόδα φυλλοβολεῦντα
τὠνδρὸς ἀπὸ στεφάνων[2] πάντ' ἐγένοντο χαμαί·
ὤπτηται μέγα δή τι· μὰ δαίμονας οὐκ ἀπὸ ῥυσμοῦ   5
εἰκάζω, φωρὸς δ' ἴχνια φὼρ ἔμαθον.

A.P. xii. 134.

XLV.

Ἔστι τι ναὶ τὸν Πᾶνα κεκρυμμένον, ἔστι τι ταύτῃ
ναὶ μὰ Διώνυσον πῦρ ὑπὸ τῇ σποδιῇ·
οὐ θαρσέω· μὴ δή με περίπλεκε. πολλάκι λήθει
τοῖχον ὑποτρώγων ἡσύχιος ποταμός·
τῷ καὶ νῦν δείδοικα, Μενέξενε, μή με παρεισδὺς   5
οὗτος ὁ σιγέρπης[3] εἰς τὸν ἔρωτα βάλῃ.

A.P. xii. 139.

[1] σώφρονα θυμὸν ἔχειν A.P.
[2] ἀπὸ στεφάνων Athen. xv. 669 who quotes τὰ δὲ ῥόδα . . .
χαμαί; ἀπὸ στομάτων A.P.
[3] ὁ σιγέρπης Bentley ; ὀσειγαρνης.

---

[a] With this epigram cf. Asclepiades, A.P. xii. 135.
[b] Cf. A.P. 135. 4 χὠ σφιγχθεὶς οὐκ ἔμενε στέφανος.
[c] The sense seems to be that the poet, for whom the fire

166

strained me; whereof the one dragged me, the other allowed me not to away with rashness. And when I came, I did not shout thine or thy father's name, but kissed the doorpost. If this be wrong, then I have done wrong.

XLIV.[a]

The stranger had a wound and we knew it not. How painful a sigh, marked you? he heaved when he drank his third cup, and the roses, shedding their petals, fell from his garlands all upon the ground.[b] He is badly burnt, by the gods, my guess is not amiss—a thief myself I know the tracks of a thief.

XLV.[c]

There is something hidden, by Pan, there is, yes, by Dionysus, some hidden fire beneath these ashes.[d] No confidence have I: embrace me not. Oft-times the quiet river undermines the wall unmarked. So now I fear, Menexenus, lest this fawning gypsy[e] slip in and whelm me in love.

of love has burnt out, misdoubts that "still in the ashes live the wonted fires," and so rejects the advances of a flatterer. The language of v. 3 is curiously like Pind. *P.* ii. 82 διαπλέκει. οὔ οἱ μετέχω θράσεος.

[d] Hor. *Od.* ii. 1. 7 "ignes suppositos cineri doloso."

[e] σιγέρπης Bentley from Hesych. σιγέρπης· λαθροδάκτης, used of a dog which fawns only to bite. "Gypsy" may render the word, *cf.* Theocr. xv. 48.

167

XLVI.

"Ληφθήσει, περίφευγε, Μενέκρατες" εἶπα Πανήμου
εἰκάδι, καὶ Λώιου τῇ τίνι; τῇ δεκάτῃ
ἦλθεν ὁ βοῦς ὑπ' ἄροτρον ἑκούσιος. εὖ γ' ἐμὸς
Ἑρμῆς,
εὖ γ' ἐμός· οὐ παρὰ τὰς εἴκοσι μεμφόμεθα.

A.P. xii. 149.

XLVII.

Ὡς ἀγαθὰν Πολύφαμος ἀνεύρετο τὰν ἐπαοιδὰν
τὠραμένῳ· ναὶ Γᾶν, οὐκ ἀμαθὴς ὁ Κύκλωψ·
αἱ Μοῦσαι τὸν ἔρωτα κατισχναίνοντι, Φίλιππε·
ἦ πανακὲς πάντων φάρμακον ἁ σοφία.
τοῦτο, δοκέω, χἀ λιμὸς ἔχει μόνον ἐς τὰ πονηρὰ   5
τὠγαθόν· ἐκκόπτει τὰν φιλόπαιδα νόσον.
ἔσθ' ἀμὶν χἀκαστά σ'[1] ἀφειδέα ποττὸν Ἔρωτα·
"τουτί, παῖ,[2] κείρευ τὰ πτερὰ παιδάριον,
οὐδ' ὅσον ἀτταραγόν τυ δεδοίκαμες· αἱ γὰρ ἐπῳδαὶ
οἴκοι τῶ χαλεπῶ τραύματος ἀμφότεραι."   10

A.P. xii. 150.

[1] χἀκαστά σ' Editor : χἀκαστὰς.
[2] τοῦτ' εἶπαι Kaibel.

---

[a] Πάνημος = Macedonian Πάναμος (Hoffmann, *Die Make-donen*, p. 103) was originally the 9th month of the Macedonian year which began with the autumnal equinox and in which the months were: 1. Δῖος ; 2. Ἀπελλαῖος ; 3. Αὐδναῖος ; 4. Περίτιος ; 5. Δύστρος ; 6. Ξανδικός ; 7. Ἀρτεμίσιος ; 8. Δαίσιος ; 9. Πάναμος ; 10. Λώιος ; 11. Γορπιαῖος ; 12. Ὑπερβερεταῖος.

XLVI

"Thou wilt be caught! flee and save thyself, Menecrates!" said I on the 20th of Panemos,[a] and on Loios the—what?—the 10th, the ox came to the plough unbidden. Well done, my Hermes,[b] well done! with the twenty days' interval I find no fault.

XLVII.[c]

How excellent was the charm[d] that Polyphemus discovered for the lover. By Earth, the Cyclops was no fool! The Muses, O Philippus, reduce[e] the swollen wound of love. Surely the poet's skill is sovereign remedy for all ill. Methinks hunger, too, hath this good and this alone in regard to evil: it drives away the disease of love. We have both remedies against thee, remorseless Love: "There, boy; have thy wings cut, little boy! We fear thee not a jot; for we have in store both charms for thy cruel hurt."

Panemos occurs in the calendar of Boeotia, Corinth, Ephesus, etc., and Loios (Homoloios in Thessaly) is also widely found. In the Alexandrian calendar in the time of the Ptolemies Panemos = June, Loios = July, approximately.

[b] God of luck.

[c] For the love of Polyphemus see Theocr. xi. The MS. reading in v. 7 seems merely to need right punctuation, σ(ε) and Ἔρωτα being in apposition and ἕκαστα being loosely used for ἑκάτερα.

[d] The Muse.

[e] Cf. Aesch. P. V. 380.

XLVIII.

Τὴν ἁλίην Εὔδημος, ἐφ' ἧς ¹ ἅλα λιτὸν ἐπέσθων
   χειμῶνας μεγάλους ἐξέφυγεν δανέων,
θῆκε θεοῖς Σαμόθρᾳξι λέγων ὅτι τήνδε κατ' εὐχήν,
   ὦ λαοί, σωθεὶς ἐξ ἁλὸς ὧδ' ἔθετο.

A.P. vi. 301.

XLIX.

Εὐμαθίην ᾐτεῖτο διδοὺς ἐμὲ Σῖμος ὁ Μίκκου

¹ ὑφ' ἧς Bentley ; ἀφ' ἧς Blomfield.

ᵃ With this epigram should be compared the inscription found at Kuft in 1883, now in the Cairo museum (Dittenberger, *Orient. Graec. Inscr. Select.* No. 69) : Θεοῖς μεγάλοις Σαμοθρᾳξι Ἀπολλώνιος Σωσιβίου Θηραῖος ἡγεμὼν τῶν ἔξω τάξεων σωθεὶς ἐγ μεγάλων κινδύνων ἐκπλεύσας ἐκ τῆς Ἐρυθρᾶς θαλάσσης εὐχήν.

The epigram is a series of puns, based on the ambiguous sense of ἅλς as meaning either "sea" or "salt." As the sailor saved from the sea and its storms would dedicate an offering—a model perhaps of his ship—to the gods of Samothrace, so Eudemos, having escaped the storms of debt by frugal living, dedicates his salt-cellar because he is saved from salt.

ᵇ The Cabeiri, Herodot. ii. 51. Their worship reached its highest point under the Diadochi, when Samothrace became an asylum, *e.g.* for Arsinoë Philadelphos, for Perseus of Macedon (Gnaeus Octavius προσορμισάμενος τῇ Σαμοθράκῃ τὴν μὲν ἀσυλίαν παρεῖχε τῷ Περσεῖ διὰ τοὺς θεούς, Plut. *Aemil.* 26). Juv. iii. 144 "iures licet et Samothracum Et nostrorum aras." Hence "pii Samothraces," Statius, *A.* i. 832. As gods who protected sailors, Apoll. Rh. i. 915 ff., Theophr. *Char.* 25, Diodor. iv. 43. 1.

ᶜ (1) Bentley's idea that v. 4 referred to the letter Υ, which Pythagoras of Samos is said to have used to denote the divergence of the paths of virtue and vice (Persius, *Sat.* iii. 56), and that the mask of Dionysus was set up beside a representation of that letter in a boys' school, has long been exploded.

EPIGRAMS

XLVIII.[a]

The salt-cellar, whereon, by eating frugal salt
for relish, he escaped the mighty storms of debt,
Eudemus dedicated to the gods of Samothrace,[b]
saying, According to my vow, O people, saved from
salt, I dedicated this here.

XLIX.[c]

Simus, son of Miccus, offered me to the Muses,

(2) Since Bernhardy (1822) compared Aelian, *N.A.* vii. 48
and Plin. *N.H.* viii. 58, it has been seen that the reference is
to the Samian Διόνυσος κεχηνώς or Gaping Dionysus. Pliny,
who gives the fuller account, says that one Elpis of Samos
landed in Africa and near the shore he saw a lion gaping
threateningly (*hiatu minaci*). Elpis got up a tree, meanwhile invoking father Liber (*i.e.* Dionysus). The lion made
no attempt to pursue, but lay down before the tree and
seemed to solicit pity. Elpis then discovered that the
threatening gape was due to a bone which had got stuck in
the beast's jaws and that the poor animal was perishing of
hunger. At last he ventured to descend from the tree
and remove the bone. The lion showed its gratitude by
supplying him with game during his stay on the shore. For
which cause Elpis consecrated a temple in Samos to father
Liber, which from that circumstance the Greeks called the
temple of κεχηνὼς Διόνυσος. The epigram is now interpreted
to mean that a schoolboy, in fulfilment of a vow, set up in
the school a mask or bust of Διόνυσος κεχηνώς, in which his
gape was so exaggerated, either intentionally (Bergk) or
through lack of skill on the part of the artist—"the best
he could make or pay for" (Kaibel)—as to be "twice that
of the Samian Δ. κ." Here Dionysus listens to the boys
repeating *ad nauseam* ἱερὸς ὁ πλόκαμος—*i.e.* reading the
Bacchae of Euripides, the quotation (*Bacch.* 494) being used
to denote the play as we might use "Arma virumque" to
indicate the *Aeneid.*

(3) G. Kaibel in *Hermes* xxxi. (1896) disputes the use of
ὄνειαρ for ὄνειρον. Comparing (with Benndorf) the similar

171

ταῖς Μούσαις· αἱ δὲ Γλαῦκος ὅκως ἔδοσαν
ἀντ᾽ ὀλίγου μέγα δῶρον. ἐγὼ δ᾽ ἀνὰ τῇδε [1] κεχηνὼς
κεῖμαι τοῦ Σαμίου διπλόον ὁ τραγικὸς
παιδαρίων Διόνυσος ἐπήκοος· οἱ δὲ λέγουσιν   5
" ἱερὸς ὁ πλόκαμος " τοὐμὸν ὄνειαρ ἐμοί.

A.P. vi. 310.

L.

Τῆς Ἀγοράνακτός με λέγε, ξένε, κωμικὸν ὄντως
ἀγκεῖσθαι νίκης μάρτυρα τοῦ Ῥοδίου
Πάμφιλον, οὐχ ἕν᾽ [2] ἔρωτι δεδαγμένον, ἥμισυ δ᾽ ὀπτῇ
ἰσχάδι καὶ λύχνοις Ἴσιδος εἰδόμενον.

A.P. vi. 311.

LI.

Τὴν Φρυγίην Αἴσχρην, ἀγαθὸν γάλα, πᾶσιν ἐν
ἐσθλοῖς

---

[1] τήνδε ; corr. Bergk.   [2] οὐκ ἐν ; corr. Editor.

---

epigram of Asclepiades in *A.P.* vi. 308, of which the last
distich is κἀμὲ χάριν Μούσαις τὸν κωμικὸν ὧδε Χάρητα | πρεσβύτην
θορύβῳ θήκατο παιδαρίων, he emends Χάρητα to χαρέντα and
thus makes the "comic old man" enjoy the din of the
school. He thus reaches the conclusion that ὄνειαρ has
here its ordinary epic sense. Dionysus says he finds his
"pleasure" in the recitation of the line, whether it be in
the *Bacchae* as a whole or the particular scene from which
the line is taken or in the fact that the boys have still to
read the play.

(4) But in answer to Kaibel it has to be said : (1) The use
of ὄνειαρ=dream is sufficiently attested by *A.P.* vii. 42. 1
where it is probably intended to be a quotation of Suid. *s.v.*
ὄνειαρ, Eustath. Hom. *Od.* 1877. 64, etc. (2) If ὄνειαρ means
"pleasure" there is no point in τοὐμὸν . . . ἐμοί. The poet
must have written ἐμόν (or τοὐμόν) or ἐμοί but not both. On
the other hand the combination τοὐμὸν . . . ἐμοί is an essential
thing in the proverb ; thus Plato, *Rep.* 563 D, Callim. *Ep.*

172

praying for ease of learning. And they, like Glaucus[a] gave him a great gift for a small. And here I am set, gaping twice as widely as the Samian (Dionysus), the tragic Dionysus, hearkening to children as they say "Sacred is the lock of hair," [b] repeating "my own dream to me."

L.

Say, Stranger, that I am set up as a witness of the victory of Agoranax of Rhodes, a comic witness[c] indeed—Pamphilus, not a single love-worn face but half of it like roasted figs and the lamps of Isis.

LI.[d]

Phrygian Aeschra, his good nurse, so long as she

34. 2, Suid. *s.v.* ὕπαρ, Cic. *Ad Attic.* vi. 9. 3. (3) But the last objection is decisive. It is universally assumed that the mask is a mask of a Διόνυσος κεχηνώς. But that would be utterly out of place, and we are expressly told it was ὁ τραγικὸς Διόνυσος. The mask was an ordinary mask of Dionysus. What is meant is that he is so weary of the "damnable iteration" (Shakespeare) of the schoolroom that he yawns more widely than the Gaping Dionysus himself. It is needless to illustrate this use of κέχηνα (Latin *oscito*) to express boredom, *e.g.* Aristoph. *Ach.* 30.

[a] Hom. *Il.* vi. 234 ff. where Glaucus "exchanged armour with Diomedes, golden armour for armour of bronze, the price of a hundred oxen for the price of nine."

[b] Eurip. *Bacch.*

[c] For the proverbial "comic witness" *cf.* Cic. *Ad famil.* ii. 13 "mea vero officia ei non defuisse tu es testis, cui iam κωμικὸς μάρτυς, ut opinor, accedit Phania."

Pamphilus appears as a character in the *Andria* and *Hecyra* of Terence; Pamphila in Menander, *Epitrep.* 508 f. and in Terence, *Eunuchus* and *Adelphi.*

For the mask with double face *cf.* Pollux iv. 141, Quintilian xi. 3. 74.

[d] Very similar to this is *A.P.* vii. 663.

173

CALLIMACHUS

Μίκκος καὶ ζωὴν οὖσαν ἐγηροκόμει
καὶ φθιμένην ἀνέθηκεν ἐπεσσομένοισιν ὁρᾶσθαι,
ἡ γρῆυς μαστῶν ὡς ἀπέχει χάριτας.

A.P. vii. 458.

LII.

Τέσσαρες αἱ Χάριτες· ποτὶ γὰρ μία ταῖς τρισὶ τήναις
ἄρτι ποτεπλάσθη κῆτι μύροισι νοτεῖ.
εὐαίων ἐν πᾶσιν ἀρίζαλος Βερενίκα,
ἇς ἄτερ οὐδ' αὐταὶ ταὶ Χάριτες Χάριτες.

A.P. v. 145.

LIII.

Τὸν τὸ καλὸν μελανεῦντα Θεόκριτον, εἰ μὲν ἔμ' ἔχθει,
   τετράκι μισοίης, εἰ δὲ φιλεῖ, φιλέοις·
ναιχὶ πρὸς εὐχαίτεω Γανυμήδεος, οὐράνιε Ζεῦ,
   καὶ σύ ποτ' ἠράσθης—οὐκέτι μακρὰ λέγω.

A.P. xii. 230.

LIV.

Καὶ πάλιν, Εἰλήθυια, Λυκαινίδος ἐλθὲ καλεύσης
   εὔλοχος ὠδίνων ὧδε οὖν εὐτοκίῃ,
ὡς τόδε νῦν μέν, ἄνασσα, κόρης ὕπερ, ἀντὶ δὲ παιδὸς
   ὕστερον εὐώδης ἄλλο τι νηὸς ἔχοι.

A.P. vi. 146.

---

   [a] Berenice, daughter of Magas of Cyrene, and Apame ; she is the wife of Ptolemy III. Euergetes and the heroine of the *Rape of the Lock* (Βερενίκης πλόκαμος). *Cf.* Wil.-Moell. *Die Textgeschichte d. gr. Bukoliker*, p. 52 f.
   [b] Theocr. xvii. 57.
   [c] That the Theocritus of this epigram is the poet of the

174

EPIGRAMS

lived, Miccus cared for in her old age with all good things, and when she died, he set up her statue for future generations to see, so that the old woman has received thanks for her nursing breasts.

LII.

Four are the Graces; for beside those three another has been fashioned lately and is yet wet with perfume. Happy Berenice [a] and resplendent [b] among all—without whom even the Graces themselves are not Graces.

LIII.

If Theocritus [c] with finely darkening cheek hates me, four times as much mayst thou hate him, or if he loves me, love. Yea, by Ganymede of the fair locks, O Zeus in heaven, thou too hast loved.[d] I say no more.

LIV.

Even so again, Eilethyia, come thou when Lycaenis calls, to bless her pains with easy birth; so may thy fragrant shrine have, as now this offering for a girl, some other offering hereafter for a boy.

Idylls is supported by what seem to be echoes of his poetry. (1) The adverbial use of τὸ καλόν is rare in pre-Christian times, but occurs in Theocritus iii. 3 and 18, *cf.* Herod. i. 54, *A.P.* vii. 219, ps.-Lucian, *Amor.* iii. 26. (2) v. 4 is an echo of Theocr. *Idyl.* viii. 59 f. ὦ πάτερ ὦ Ζεῦ, | οὐ μόνος ἠράσθην· καὶ τὺ γυναικοφίλας. Further μελανεῦντα would imply that Theocritus was still young when he wrote Idylls iii. and viii. and made the acquaintance of Callimachus.
[d] *Cf. A.P.* v. 166.

LV.

Τὸ χρέος ὡς ἀπέχεις, Ἀσκληπιέ, τὸ πρὸ γυναικὸς
  Δημοδίκης Ἀκέσων ὤφελεν εὐξάμενος,
γινώσκειν· ἢν δ' ἄρα λάθῃ, <πάλι> καί μιν ἀπαιτῇς,
  φησὶ παρέξεσθαι μαρτυρίην ὁ πίναξ.

A.P. vi. 147.

LVI.

Τῷ με Κανωπίτᾳ Καλλίστιον εἴκοσι μύξαις
  πλούσιον ἁ Κριτίου λύχνον ἔθηκε θεῷ
εὐξαμένα περὶ παιδὸς Ἀπελλίδος· ἐς δ' ἐμὰ φέγγη
  ἀθρήσας φάσεις " Ἕσπερε πῶς ἔπεσες ; "

A.P. vi. 148.

LVII.

Φησὶν ὅ με στήσας Εὐαίνετος (οὐ γὰρ ἔγωγε
  γινώσκω) νίκης ἀντί με τῆς ἰδίης
ἀγκεῖσθαι χάλκειον ἀλέκτορα Τυνδαρίδῃσι·
  πιστεύω Φαίδρου παιδὶ Φιλοξενίδεω.

A.P. vi. 149.

LVIII.

Ἰναχίης ἔστηκεν ἐν Ἴσιδος ἡ Θάλεω παῖς
  Αἰσχυλὶς Εἰρήνης μητρὸς ὑποσχεσίῃ.

A.P. vi. 150.

LIX.

Τίς, ξένος ὦ ναυηγέ; Λεόντιχος ἐνθάδε νεκρὸν

ᵃ *i.e.* Sarapis, *cf.* Paus. ii. 4. 6 δύο (τεμένη) Σαράπιδος, ἐν
Κανώβῳ καλουμένου τὸ ἕτερον.
  ᵇ Identified here, as often, with Io, daughter of Inachus.

EPIGRAMS

LV.

Know, Asclepius, that thou hast received the debt which Aceson owed thee by his vow for his wife Demodice. But if thou dost forget and demand payment again, the tablet says it will bear witness.

LVI.

To the god [a] of Canopus did Callistion, daughter of Critias, dedicate me—a lamp enriched with twenty nozzles: a vow for her child Apellis. Looking on my light thou wilt say, "Hesperus, how art thou fallen?"

LVII.

Evaenetus, who set me up, says—for I know not —that in return for a victory of his I am offered—a bronze cock—to the Tyndaridae: I believe the son of Phaedrus, son of Philoxenides.

LVIII.

In the temple of Isis,[b] daughter of Inachus, is set the statue of Aeschylis, daughter of Thales, in fulfilment of the vow of her mother, Eirene.

LIX.

Who art thou, O shipwrecked stranger?[c] Leontichus found thee here a corpse upon the

So she is called Inachis, Ovid, *M.* ix. 686, Propert. ii. 24. 4, etc.

[c] For the order of words *cf.* Hes. *Sh.* 78; *A.P.* vi. 267. 1.

177

εὗρεν ἐπ' αἰγιαλοῦ, χῶσε δὲ τῷδε τάφῳ
δακρύσας ἐπίκηρον ἐὸν βίον· οὐδὲ γὰρ αὐτὸς
ἥσυχον, αἰθυίῃ δ' ἶσα θαλασσοπορεῖ.

A.P. vii. 277.

LX.

Εὐδαίμων ὅτι τἄλλα μανεὶς ὠρχαῖος Ὀρέστας
Λευκαρέτα τὰν μὰν οὐκ ἐμάνη μανίαν
οὐδ' ἔλαβ' ἐξέτασιν τῶ Φωκέος ἅτις ἐλέγχει
τὸν φίλον· ἀλλ' αἱ χῆν δρᾶμ' ἐδίδαξε μόνον,
ἢ τάχα κα τὸν ἑταῖρον ἀπώλεσε τοῦτο ποήσας—   5
κἠγὼ τὼς πολλὼς οὐκέτ' ἔχω Πυλάδας.

A.P. xi. 362.

LXI.

Οὗτινες Ἀλείοιο παρέρπετε σῆμα Κίμωνος,
ἴστε τὸν Ἱππαίου παῖδα παρερχόμενοι.

A.P. vii. 523.

LXII.

Αἴνιε καὶ σὺ γὰρ ὧδε Μενέκρατες οὐκ ἐπὶ πουλὺ
ἦσθα· τί σε, ξείνων λῶστε, κατειργάσατο;
ἦ ῥα τὸ καὶ Κένταυρον; "ὅ μοι πεπρωμένος ὕπνος
ἦλθεν, ὁ δὲ τλήμων οἶνος ἔχει πρόφασιν."

A.P. vii. 725.

LXIII.

Κυνθιάδες θαρσεῖτε, τὰ γὰρ τοῦ Κρητὸς Ἐχέμμα
κεῖται ἐν Ὀρτυγίῃ τόξα παρ' Ἀρτέμιδι,

---

[a] For the gull as typical of the seafarer *cf.* Callim. *Aitia*
i. 1. 34 ; *A.P.* vii. 295. 2 ; Arat. *Ph.* 296.
[b] The reading and interpretation here given were proposed
to Dr. Rouse and others (Prof. Henry Jackson, Wilamowitz,
etc.) by the Editor in March 1913. Almost the same inter-
178

beach, and covered thee in this tomb, with tears for his own hazardous life. For no quiet life is his either, but restless as the gull [a] he roams the sea.

LX.[b]

Happy was Orestes of old who, mad in all else, yet was not mad with the madness of Leucaretas, nor tried the Phocian by the one test which proves the friend; nay, had he produced but one drama, soon would he by so doing have lost his comrade— even as I have no more my many Pyladae.

LXI.

Whosoever ye be who pass the tomb of Cimon of Elis, know that ye pass the son of Hippaeus.

LXII.[c]

Menecrates of Aenus—for thou, it seems, wert not to be here for long—what, best of friends, made an end of thee? Was it that which was the undoing of the Centaur? [d] " 'Twas the destined sleep that came to me, but wretched wine has the blame."

LXIII.

Ye goats of Cynthus, be of good cheer! for now the bow of Cretan Echemmas is laid up in Ortygia in the temple of Artemis,—that bow wherewith he

pretation was given by Prof. G. A. Davies in *Classical Rev.*, May 1913, p. 91.   [c] Similar is Athen. 436 D.
    [d] Hom. *Od.* xxi. 295 οἶνος καὶ Κένταυρον ἀγακλυτὸν Εὐρυτίωνα ἄασεν.

CALLIMACHUS

οἷϛ ὑμέων ἐκένωσεν ὄροϛ μέγα· νῦν δὲ πέπαυται,
αἶγεϛ, ἐπεὶ σπονδὰϛ ἡ θεὸϛ εἰργάσατο.

A.P. vi. 121; vv. 1-2 Suidas *s.v.* Κυνθιάδεϛ.

LXIV.

Οὕτωϛ ὑπνώσαιϛ, Κωνώπιον, ὡϛ ἐμὲ ποιεῖϛ
    κοιμᾶσθαι ψυχροῖϛ τοῖσδε παρὰ προθύροιϛ.
οὕτωϛ ὑπνώσαιϛ, ἀδικωτάτη, ὡϛ τὸν ἐραστὴν
    κοιμίζειϛ, ἐλέου δ᾽ οὐδ᾽ ὄναρ ἠντίασαϛ.
γείτονεϛ οἰκτείρουσι, σὺ δ᾽ οὐδ᾽ ὄναρ. ἡ πολιὴ δὲ 5
    αὐτίκ᾽ ἀναμνήσει ταῦτά σε πάντα κόμη.

A.P. v. 23.

made the great hill empty of you. But now he hath ceased, ye goats, since the goddess hath wrought a truce.

LXIV.[a]

So mayst thou sleep, Conopion, as thou makest thy lover lie by this cold porch ; so mayst thou sleep, O most unkind, as thou makest thy lover lie ; but pity thou hast not met even in a dream. The neighbours pity, but thou not even in a dream. But the grey hair will presently remind thee of all these things.[b]

[a] This is a παρακλαυσίθυρον or Lament at the door of the beloved, *cf.* Plut. *Mor.* 753 B τίς οὖν ὁ κωλύων ἐστὶ κωμάζειν ἐπὶ θύρας, ᾄδειν τὸ παρακλαυσίθυρον, ἀναδεῖν τὰ εἰκόνια παγκρατιάζειν πρὸς τοὺς ἀντεραστάς ; ταῦτα γὰρ ἐρωτικά.
[b] *Cf. A.P.* v. 20 ; Hor. *Od.* iv. 10.

THE PHAENOMENA
OF ARATUS

THE PHENOMENA
OF ARATUS

INTRODUCTION

1. THE LIFE OF ARATUS

Authorities.—Suidas *s.v.* Ἄρατος and four ancient *Vitae.*
(A. Westermann, *Biographoi*, Brunswick, 1845, p. 52 ff.)

Vita I., first published by Petrus Victorius with other
Greek commentaries on Aratus, Florence, 1567 ; then by
Dionysius Petavius in *Uranologium*, Lutet. Paris. 1630,
p. 268 ff.

This life, once supposed to be by Achilles Tatius,
author of the romance of *Leucippe and Cleitophon* (*circ.*
fourth cent. A.D.), is shown by E. Maass, *Aratea*, Berlin,
1892, p. 16, to be by one Achilles, a grammarian, who
lived towards the end of the second or beginning of the
third cent. A.D. It is printed in Buhle ii. p. 429 ff. ;
Maass, *Comment. in Arati Reliquias* p. 76 ff.

Vita II., first published by Iriarte in *Catal. bibl. Matrit.*
i. p. 201 from cod. Matritensis lxi. written by Con-
stantinus Lascaris in A.D. 1465. This MS., which has
also *Vita IV.*, divides Aratus into four books (1) 1–450, (2)
451–732, (3) 733–818, (4) 819-end. Maass suspects that
this *Life* is the work of Sporos of Nicaea (*circ.* A.D. 200),
who commented on Aratus (Leont. Περὶ κατασκευῆς Ἀρατείας
σφαίρας ὥς φησι Σπόρος ὁ ὑπομνηματιστής ; *cf.* schol. Arat.
541, 1091). It is printed in Buhle ii. p. 442 ff. ; Maass,
Comment. in Arat. Reliq. p. 323 f.

Vita III., first ed. by Ruhnken from cod. Baroccianus
in Ernesti's edition of Callimachus i. p. 590 ; then by
Iriarte from cod. Matritensis lxvii. in *Catal. bibl. Matrit.*
p. 239. This life is also given in cod. Vindobonensis.

ARATUS

This, which is the best Life, is expressly attributed in cod. Mediolan. C 263 to Theon (Θέωνος Ἀλεξανδρέως γένος Ἀράτου) and Maass has shown that this ascription is correct (*Analecta Eratosth.* Berlin, 1883, in Kiessling u. Wilamowitz, *Philol. Untersuch.* vi.). There exists a translation of this in bad Latin (ed. Breysig, Erfurt, 1870) which occasionally fills up gaps in the Greek text. Buhle ii. 444 ff.

Vita IV., first published by Aldus Manutius, and thenceforth the *Vita* usually prefixed to editions of Aratus (*e.g.* Buhle, Bekker). It is the most worthless of the *Vitae.* Maass, *Comment. in Arat. Reliq.* p. 324 ff.

There is so much similarity between the *Vitae* that they may be assumed to be all derived ultimately from the same original Life, possibly that of the Stoic Boëthus of Sidon (*circ.* 150 B.C.) who wrote upon Aratus (*Vita II.*) in at least four books (Geminus Isag. 14 ὅθεν καὶ Βόηθος ὁ φιλόσοφος ἐν τῷ τετάρτῳ βιβλίῳ τῆς Ἀράτου ἐξηγήσεως κτλ., Cicero, *De divin.* i. 8. 13 " Atque his rerum praesensionibus Prognostica tua referta sunt. Quis igitur elicere causas praesensionum potest? Etsi video Boëthum Stoicum esse conatum, qui hactenus aliquid egit, ut earum rationem rerum explicaret, quae in mari caelove fierent." *Cf.* schol. Arat. 1091).

Aratus of Soli in Cilicia—as distinct from Soli in Cyprus—was the son of Athenodorus and Letophila (Lenodora, *Vita IV.*). His family was one of some distinction in war and in other fields (*Vita II.*). He was an older contemporary of Callimachus (*Vita I.* μέμνηται γοῦν αὐτοῦ καὶ Καλλίμαχος ὡς πρεσβυτέρου οὐ μόνον ἐν τοῖς ἐπιγράμμασιν ἀλλὰ καὶ ἐν τοῖς πρὸς Πραξιφάνην, πάνυ ἐπαινῶν αὐτὸν ὡς πολυμαθῆ καὶ ἄριστον ποιητήν; the relation is reversed in *Vita IV.* γηραιῷ δὲ τῷ Κυρηναίῳ ἐπεβάλετο, παρ' οὗ καὶ ἐπιγράμματος ἠξιώθη), and his birth may be put about 315 B.C.

He was a pupil (ἀκουστής), Suidas says, of the grammarian Menecrates of Ephesus and of the philosophers Timon and Menedemus.

Menecrates was author of an Ἔργα or poem on agri-

culture, apparently in the manner of Hesiod (*E.M. s.v.
ἠθμός. Cf.* Varro, *R.R.* i. 1. 9 "easdem res etiam quidam
versibus, ut Hesiodus Ascraeus, Menecrates Ephesius,"
and iii. 16. 18; Pliny *N.H.* Ind. viii. and xi. ; and xi. § 17).
From Varro, *R.R.* iii. 16. 18 and the last two references
in Pliny it appears that he was an authority upon bees
and the flowers on which they fed (schol. Nicand. Alex.
172). It appears from schol. Eurip. *Rhes.* 529 that he
also wrote on astronomy (Diels, *Poet. Philos. Fr.* p. 171).
We may fairly assume that it was at Ephesus and in his
earliest years that Aratus was his pupil.

Timon of Phlius (Life by Diog. Laert. ix. 12), sceptic,
philosopher, and sillographist, lived *circ.* 320–*circ.* 230
B.C. Accidentally making the acquaintance of Pyrrho,
he went to Elis and became his disciple. Afterwards he
made his living as a peripatetic teacher in the towns
about the Hellespont and Propontis, and finally settled
in Athens—some time after 276—where he spent the rest
of his life, with the exception of a short sojourn in
Thebes.

Two statements in Diog. Laert. *l.c.* are of interest for
Aratus : (*a*) § 110 ἐγνώσθη (sc. Τίμων) δὲ καὶ Ἀντιγόνῳ τῷ
βασιλεῖ καὶ Πτολεμαίῳ τῷ Φιλαδέλφῳ, ὡς αὐτὸς ἐν τοῖς ἰάμβοις
αὐτοῦ μαρτυρεῖ. (*b*) § 113 φασὶ δὲ καὶ Ἄρατον πυθέσθαι αὐτοῦ πῶς
τὴν Ὁμήρου ποίησιν ἀσφαλῶς κτήσαιτο ; τὸν δὲ εἰπεῖν, Εἰ τοῖς
ἀρχαίοις ἀντιγράφοις ἐντυγχάνοι καὶ μὴ τοῖς ἤδη διωρθωμένοις.

It would not be relevant to discuss here the question
whether Timon personally visited the court of Philadelphus, though some colour is given to that view by
the jesting reference by Timon to the Museum which
is preserved in Athen. i. 22 D. That Timon visited the
Macedonian Court is more generally accepted, in which
case the conversation between Timon and Aratus will
have taken place there *circ.* 276 B.C., the rash emenda-
tion, against which Aratus is warned, referring to the
recent edition of Zenodotus.

The third teacher of Aratus mentioned by Suidas is
Menedemus of Eretria (Life by Diog. Laert. ii. 18),
founder of the Eretrian School of philosophy, who died

ARATUS

some time not long after 278, at the age of seventy-four (Diog. Laert. *l.c.* 18). Diog. Laert. *l.c.* 10 says : ἠσπάζετο (sc. Μενέδημος) δὲ καὶ Ἄρατον καὶ Λυκόφρονα τὸν τῆς τραγῳδίας ποιητὴν καὶ τὸν Ῥόδιον Ἀνταγόραν. This would seem clearly to belong to the time when Aratus was studying in Athens, to which period also would belong his acquaintance with Callimachus, with the stoic philosopher Persaeus (*Vita IV.* probably wrongly says Persaeus was his teacher), with Praxiphanes the Peripatetic (Susemihl i. 144 ff. who puts his association with Aratus and Callimachus *circ.* 291–287).

The VIIth Idyll of Theocritus, the scene of which is laid in Cos, introduces an Aratus (98 ff.) as one apparently of the group of poets whose central figure was Philetas of Cos. It has been very generally assumed that this Aratus to whom Theocritus also addresses Idyll VI. is the author of the *Phaenomena* (so too the schol.). Against the identification it is pointed out (1) that the name Aratus was a common one in Cos, occurring on coins[a] and in inscriptions[b] of this period.   (2) That in Theocritus Ἄρατος has the first syllable short, whereas Ἄρατος of the *Phaenomena* has always in Greek the first syllable long.

Of those who accept the identification some put the Coan sojourn of Aratus before his residence in Athens (Susemihl i. 286), others put it after (Croiset v. 225).

At some date, probably *circ.* 291, Aratus came to Athens where he made the acquaintance of his somewhat younger contemporary Callimachus, and with him apparently attended the lectures of the peripatetic philosopher Praxiphanes, but afterwards attached himself to Zeno of Citium, founder of the Stoic School of philosophy.

At this time too he made the acquaintance, as we have seen, of Menedemus. Zeno was on friendly terms with Antigonus Gonatas who may have become acquainted with Aratus in Athens. It is likely then that it was at the request of Antigonus himself that Aratus went to the Macedonian court along with his fellow students Persaeus

[a] Paton and Hicks, *Inscriptions of Cos*, pp. 309, 313, 318.
[b] Paton and Hicks, Nos. 10 c 58 and 81.

and Philonides soon after Antigonus became king of all Macedonia in 276 B.C. It has been suggested that the occasion was the marriage of Antigonus with Phila, daughter of Seleucus and Stratonice, and it was then probably that Aratus produced his Hymn to Pan in honour of Antigonus' victory over the Celts at Lysimacheia in 277 B.C., allusion being made to the panic fear which had seized the enemy in that battle.

The Macedonian court was then the home of an active literary circle.

Here Aratus wrote at the instigation of Antigonus his *Phaenomena*, following the prose work of Eudoxus which bore the same name (*Vita III.* τῶν Εὐδόξου Φαινομένων) or was (*Vita I.*) entitled Κάτοπτρον.[a] This must have been between 276–274, because in the latter year this literary circle was broken up by the invasion of Pyrrhus, and it was not till 272 that Antigonus was restored.

The legend that Aratus and Nicander of Colophon were contemporaries and that at the request of Antigonus Aratus wrote the *Phaenomena*, though he had no astronomical attainments while he knew about medicine : that Nicander, on the other hand, who knew astronomy, wrote by request of Antigonus the *Theriaca* and *Alexipharmaca*, is ridiculed on chronological grounds by *Vita I.* and *Vita IV.* It is alluded to by Cicero, *De oratore* i. 69, *cf.* G. Knaack in *Hermes* xxiii. (1888), p. 313.

Upon the invasion of Pyrrhus, Aratus went to the Court of Antiochus I. (Soter), son of Seleucus, where he lived for some time and where he completed an edition of the *Odyssey* of Homer. It appears that Antiochus wished him to edit the *Iliad* as well, but this apparently he did not do. Subsequently Aratus returned to the court of Antigonus at Pella, where he died at some date previous to the death of Antigonus (who died 240–239 B.C.).

A monument was erected to him at Soli and his portrait appears on coins of that town.[b]

---

[a] Ἔνοπτρον, Hipparch. i. 2. 2.
[b] Head, *Hist. Num.* p. 729.

ARATUS

2. The Mss.

1. The two oldest mss. of the *Phaenomena* are:

M = Marcianus 476, containing Aratus (no life or title) with scholia and prefaces, and Lycophron with scholia. This ms. was written for his own use by Nicetas *diaconus* whom Maass identifies with the distinguished Bishop of Serrhai (Seres) in the eleventh century. It belonged to the library of Cardinal Bessarion and contains some annotations by him. Maass distinguishes a second hand (about thirteenth cent.) and a third, and lastly Bessarion himself (fifteenth cent.). This is both the oldest and best ms. of Aratus and represents, in all probability, the recension of Theon of Alexandria (fourth cent. A.D.) father of Hypatia and the last known member of the Alexandrian Museum, a distinguished philosopher and mathematician, author of commentaries on Aratus, Euclid, and Ptolemy. Theon's choice of readings was influenced by his apologetic tendency in favour of Aratus which led him to adopt the conjectures of Attalus of Rhodes and possibly to make conjectures of his own with a similar purpose. Some variants noted by Nicetas from another ms. may, as Maass thinks, represent the text of Sporus.

V = Vaticanus 1307 (no life, title 'Αράτου Φαινόμενα supplied by a later hand), containing Lycophron with scholl. and Aratus with scholl. The similarity of writing shows that this ms. was written about the same date as M. The two mss. agree closely even in minutiae. Bekker believed V to be the older of the two, but Maass, from a comparison of the scholia and on the ground that V is in general more corrupt than M, decides in favour of M and holds that V is derived either from M or from the archetype of M.

2. Later mss. These, dating from the thirteenth to the fifteenth century, are of two classes.

(*a*) *Interpolated mss.*, *i.e.* containing the interpolated lines of Maximus Planudes, a monk of Constantinople (fourteenth cent.). His interpolations, intended to bring Aratus into conformity with the Almagest or Megale

190

INTRODUCTION

Syntaxis of Claudius Ptolemaeus (2nd cent. A.D.), consist of 16 lines to follow *Phaen.* v. 480, 10 lines to follow v. 501, 14 lines to follow v. 514 (printed in Bekker's edition Berlin 1828).

These are: Barberinus i. 43, saec. xv. ; Bodleianus inter Baroccianos 78, saec. xv. ; Bodleianus inter Baroccianos 109, saec. xv. ; Laurentianus xxviii. 37, written at Florence in 1464 by Joannes Scutariotes and once belonging to Angelo Poliziano, the famous humanist (1454–1494) ; Vindobonensis 127 (Lambecius) 341 (Nessel). v. Buhle ii. p. 377, Groddeck, *Epist. Crit. in Arati Phaen.*, etc. The Planudean recension is of no independent value.

(*b*) *Non-interpolated* MSS.—Maass mentions (1) with scholia : Casanatensis G V 5, saec. xiv.; Vaticanus, 1910, s. xiii. vel xiv. ; Vaticanus, 1692, s. xiii. vel xiv. ; Vaticanus 121, s. xv. ; Vaticanus 199, s. xv. ; Marcianus 480, s. xv. ; Ambrosianus C 32, sup. s. xv. ; Ambrosianus H 42, sup. s. xv. ; Parisinus 2841, s. xiii. ; Parisinus 2726, s. xv. ; Parisinus 2403, s. xiii. vel xiv. ; Parisinus 2842 ; written 1475 ; Butlerianus Brit. Mus. Add. MSS. 11886, s. xv. vel xvi. ; Burneianus Brit. Mus. 63, s. xv. ; Mosquensis (scholia printed in Buhle i. p. 269 ff.).

(2) Without scholia : Laurentianus xxxi. 32, s. xv. ; Palatinus (inter Vaticanos) 137, s. xv. ; Neapolitanus bibl. nat. ii. F 37, s. xv. ; Marcianus 465, s. xv. ; Marcianus 317, s. xv. ; Parisinus 2728, s. xv. ; Parisinus 2860, s. xv. ; Parisinus 2843, s. xv. ; Palatinus 40, s. xiv. ; Rhedigeranus 35, s. xv.

Some of these have an independent value. Maass selects for his *apparatus criticus* two which he holds are not derived from M or V, though, like these, they derive from the recension of Theon ; Parisinus 2403 (A) and Parisinus 2728 (C).

It is to be added that vv. 1-9, 10-12, 778-817, 822-891 of the *Phaenomena* are preserved in the *Eclogae* of Joannes Stobaeus (sixth century).

ARATUS

3. THE SCHOLIA

The Scholia imply in general the same text as the Marcianus. Mainly, no doubt, they are founded on the commentary of Theon, but they contain also notes from the commentary of Sporos (schol. Arat. 541, 1091) and others.

4. BIBLIOGRAPHY

Editio princeps. — Aldine, Venice, October 1499 (in *Astronomi veteres*, with scholl. and Latin version, along with the *Aratea* of Cicero, Germanicus, and Avienus; the *Astronomica* of Firmicus and Manilius; *Procli diadochi Sphaera* with version by T. Linacre).

This was followed by a close succession of editions of Aratus either separately or along with kindred works (detailed account in edn. of J. T. Buhle i. xv. ff.); Gr. and Lat. with preface by Phil. Melanchthon, Wittenberg, 1521; another (?) Basel, 1523; Ceporinus, Basel, 1534; I. Mycillus, Basel, 1535; in *Sphaera atque astrorum coelestium ratio, natura et motus,* Basel, 1536; with Cicero's *Aratea* supplemented from Vergil, Germanicus, and Avienus, Joachim Perionius, Paris, 1540 (rep. Basel, 1540); c. scholl., Ceporini, Cologne, 1543; ap. Henr. Petri, Basel, 1547; ap. Guil. Morelium, Paris, 1559, 1595; *Arati Phaen. Latinis versibus reddita a Nicolao Aleno, Essextiano Anglo,* Paris, 1561; H. Stephanus (in *Poet. Graec. principes heroici carminis*), Paris, 1566 (a new recension of the text, which became the vulgate).

In 1567 appeared the *editio princeps* of the Greek commentators on Aratus (Hipparchus and Achilles [Tatius] with the scholl. and Life of Aratus), by Petrus Victorius, Florentiae, In offic. Juntarum, Bernardi filiorum.

In 1600 Hugeianus Grotius (Huig van Groot, 1583–1645) published his *Syntagma Arateorum, Opus Antiquitatis et Astronomiae studiosis utilissimum,* Ex Offic. Plantiniana, ap. Christoph. Raphelengium, Acad. Lugd. Batav. Typogr. In the epist. dedicatory, dated from The Hague VII. Cal. August. M.D., he refers with pardonable pride to his youth. The *Syntagma* contains Aratus, Cicero's

INTRODUCTION

Aratea with the lacunae supplied in the same metre by Grotius, the *Aratea* of Germanicus, for which he used a MS. from the library of Jacobus Susius (Suys) of Grysenoordt; plates of the constellations from that MS.; notes on Aratus, Cicero, and Germanicus; and Avienus with short marginal notes. Grotius' references to MSS. are very vague—"manuscriptus," "alii codices," etc.; Buhle says he used codex Palatinus — presumably Palatinus 40.

Aratus was included in the *Poet. Gr. veteres carminis her. scriptores* of Jacob. Lectius, Aureliae Allobrogum 1606; also in a collection of (mainly) astronomical works, Lyons, 1608. Other edd. are E. Schedius, Gustrou, 1631; John Fell, afterwards Bishop of Oxford, Oxford, 1672 (text mainly founded on Morel); A. M. Bandini, Florence, 1765 (with Italian verse trans. by A. M. Salvini). Buhle's judgement of Bandini is worth quoting: "In Arati editione textum Grotianum cum omnibus vitiis et mendis repetiit, ut adeo labores, de quibus conqueritur, non nisi mendaciis fingendis, quibus Florentinae ecclesiae Subdecano imponeret, contineantur. . . . Qui tandem factum est, ut putidissimus homo celeberrimae Italiae bibliothecae praeficeretur?"

The first volume of the edition of Io. Theophilus Buhle appeared at Leipzig (Weidmann) in 1793 (the preface is dated Göttingen, 21st Feb. 1793). The MSS. on which he relies are Barberinus, Rhedigeranus, Mosquensis, and the Augustanus Eclogarum Stobaei for the lines quoted by the latter from Aratus. Vol. i. contains Life of Aratus (iv.); Hypothesis; the *Phaen.* and *Diosem.* with Latin prose version facing the text and the *scholia vulgata* at the foot of the page; Leontius *De Sphaer. Aratea*; "scholia Theonis" from cod. Mosquensis; and lastly critical animadversions. Vol. ii. (same place and publisher) appeared in 1801 and contains the *Aratea* of Cicero, Germanicus (with scholl.), Avienus; notes on these; ep. crit. of G. E. Groddeck. Lives of Aratus I., II., III. and the notice in Suidas; with an essay on the life and writings of Aratus and his Latin interpreters.

Editions subsequent to Buhle are : F. C. Matthiä, Frankfort-on-Main, 1817 ; J. H. Voss (with German verse trans.), Heidelberg, 1824 ; Phil. Buttmann (critical notes), Berlin 1826 (founded on codd. Mosq., Vratislav. Barberin. Vindob, Palatin. and Bekker's collations of MSS. in France and Italy) ; I. Bekker, Berlin, 1828 (with scholl.). Bekker's text is founded on Paris. Reg. 2403, Paris. Reg. 2726, Paris. Reg. 2728, Paris. Reg. 2841, Paris. Reg. 2842, Paris. Reg. 2843, Paris. Reg. 2860, Vaticanus 1307, Vaticanus 1910, Casanatensis O. Praedicatorum Minervitanorum J. 11. 6, Laurentianus Plut. 28 cod. 37, Marcianus 476, Marcianus 480, and Palatinus (in Vaticano) 137 as far only as v. 67. Didot (in *Poet. Didact.*), Paris, 1851. Finally E. Maass, Berlin, 1893 : the standard critical edition.

Translations.—Besides those mentioned above, there are translations in French by Halma, Paris, 1823 ; in English by John Lamb, D.D., Master of Corp. Christ. Coll. Camb., London, 1848 (rhymed verse) ; by E. Poste, London, 1880.

Recent literature on Aratus includes : E. Maass, *Aratea*, Berlin, 1892, and *Commentariorum in Aratum Reliquiae*, Berlin, 1898 ; E. Bethe, *Aratillustrationen*, 1893[a] ; G. Kaibel, *Aratea* 1894[b] ; Wilamowitz-Moellendorf, *Aratos von Kos*, 1894 ; G. Dittmann, *De Hygino Arati interprete* 1900 ; J. Hoepken, *Über d. Entstehung d. Phaenomena d. Eudoxus—Aratus*, 1905 ; G. Sieg, *De Cicerone, Germanico, Avieno Arati interpretibus*, Halis Sax. 1886 ; J. Maybaum, *De Cicerone et Germanico Arati interpretibus*, Rostock, 1889 ; G. Knaack, Wil.-Moell., *Untersuch.* viii., 1886.

[a] *Rhein. Mus.* xlviii. (1893).
[b] *Hermes* xxix. (1894).

INTRODUCTION TO THE *PHAENOMENA*

I.

EUDOXUS of Cnidus, on whose prose work Aratus based his poem, lived *circa* 390–337 B.C. He was a pupil of Plato and a very distinguished mathematician. Proclus attributes to him the Fifth Book of Euclid's Elements, and among other achievements he is said to have solved the so-called " Delian problem " [a] and to have determined the volume of the pyramid and the cone by the method of exhaustion. According to Hipparchus i. 2. 2, "two books on the phenomena [*i.e.* the starry sphere] are attributed to Eudoxus, which, with very few exceptions, are in almost all points concordant. One of his books is entitled *Enoptron*, the other *Phaenomena*; it is on the latter that Aratus bases his poem."

Hipparchus, whose three books of commentary " on the *Phaenomena* of Aratus and Eudoxus" we possess, belonged to Nicaea in Bithynia and lived *circa* 190–120 B.C. His most famous achievement is his discovery of the Precession of the Equinoxes.

The poem of Aratus found many commentators, the most careful of whom, in the opinion of Hipparchus, was Attalus of Rhodes : ἐξήγησιν μὲν οὖν τῶν Ἀράτου Φαινομένων καὶ ἄλλοι πλείονες συντετάχασιν · ἐπιμελέστατα δὲ δοκεῖ πάντων Ἄτταλος ὁ καθ' ἡμᾶς μαθηματικὸς τὸν περὶ αὐτῶν πεποιῆσθαι λόγον (Hipp. i. 1. 3). Besides the commentary of Hipparchus we possess the Introduction of Geminus of Rhodes (first century B.C.), that of Achilles (*circa* A.D. 200), and lastly, the work of Leontius (*circa* A.D. 600 (?)) περὶ κατασκευῆς Ἀρατείου σφαίρας.

[a] *i.e.* the duplication of the cube (διπλασιασμὸς κύβου).

195

ARATUS

II.

Out of many the following *testimonia* may be quoted.
Hipparchus i. 1. 7 ἡ γὰρ τῶν ποιημάτων χάρις ἀξιοπιστίαν
τινα τοῖς λεγομένοις περιτίθησιν [*cf.* Pind. *O.* i. 30]. καὶ πάντες
σχεδὸν οἱ τὸν ποιητὴν τοῦτον ἐξηγούμενοι προστίθενται τοῖς ὑπ'
αὐτοῦ λεγομένοις.

Dionysius Thrax (*Vita III.* p. 59 W.): συναγορεύει δὲ αὐτῷ
[*i.e.* Hipparchus] καὶ Διονύσιος ἐν τῷ "περὶ συγκρίσεως Ἀράτου
καὶ Ὁμήρου" περὶ τῶν μαθηματικῶν, ὅσπερ γέ φησιν· "οὐ
τίθεμεν αὐτὸν ἰατρὸν εἶναι γράψαντα τὰς ἰατρικὰς δυνάμεις, οὐδὲ
μαθηματικὸν θήσομεν οὐδὲν ξένον εἰπόντα τῶν Εὐδόξου."

Leontius (Buhle i. 257 f.): ἰστέον δὲ ὅτι τὰ περὶ τῶν
ἄστρων τῷ Ἀράτῳ εἰρημένα οὐ πάνυ καλῶς εἴρηται, ὡς ἔστιν ἔκ
τε τῶν Ἱππάρχῳ καὶ Πτολεμαίῳ συντεταγμένων περὶ τούτων
μαθεῖν. αἴτιον δὲ πρῶτον μέν, ἐπεὶ καὶ τὰ Εὐδόξου, οἷς μάλιστα
ἠκολούθησεν ὁ Ἄρατος, οὐ λίαν ὀρθῶς εἴληπται, ἔπειτα δὲ ὅτι καὶ
οὐ πρὸς τὸ ἀκριβές, ὥς φησι Σπόρος ὁ ὑπομνηματιστής [com-
mentator], ἀλλὰ τὸ χρήσιμον τοῖς ναυτιλλομένοις ταῦτα οὕτω
διαγέγραπται.

Cicero, *De re publ.* 14 : "Dicebat enim Gallus sphaerae
illius alterius solidae atque plenae vetus esse inventum, et
eam a Thalete Milesio primum esse tornatam, post autem
ab Eudoxo Cnidio . . . eandem illam astris stellisque
quae caelo inhaererent esse descriptam; cuius omnem
ornatum et descriptionem sumptam ab Eudoxo multis
annis post non astrologiae [*i.e.* astronomy], sed poetica
quadam facultate versibus Aratum extulisse."

Cicero, *De orat.* i. 15 : "si constat inter doctos hominem
ignarum astrologiae ornatissimis atque optimis versibus
Aratum de caelo stellisque dixisse."

Theon, *i.e. Vita III.* p. 59 W. : ὅθεν τινὲς . . . ἔδοξαν μὴ
μαθηματικὸν εἶναι τὸν Ἄρατον· ὑπέλαβον γὰρ μηδὲν ἕτερον
τῶν Εὐδόξου Φαινομένων ποιήσαντα αὐτὸν εἰς τὸ σύγγραμμα
θεῖναι . . . βιάζονται δ' οὐ μετρίως· ἦν γὰρ καὶ τὸ εἰδέναι
μεταφράσαι ἐμπειρίας μαθηματικῆς· εὑρήσομεν δὲ αὐτὸν καὶ
ἐπιμελέστερον τὰ πλεῖστα τοῦ Εὐδόξου ἐπιστάμενον.

Achilles, *i.e. Vita I.* p. 55 W.: ἐπιτετευγμένως δ' αὐτῷ
ἐγράφη τὰ Φαινόμενα, ὡς παρευδοκιμηθῆναι πάντας ὑπ' Ἀράτου.

Vita II. p. 57 W.: ἀλλ' ὅμως πάντων λαμπρότερον ὁ Ἄρατος
ἔγραψε.

196

Callimachus, *E.* xxix.

Leonidas of Tarentum (contemporary of Aratus), *A.P.* ix. 25 :

> Γράμμα τόδ᾽ ᾽Αρήτοιο δαήμονος, ὅς ποτε λεπτῇ
>   φροντίδι δηναιοὺς ἀστέρας ἐφράσατο,
> ἀπλανέας τ᾽ ἄμφω καὶ ἀλήμονας, οἷσιν ἐναργὴς
>   ἰλλόμενος κύκλοις οὐρανὸς ἐνδέδεται.
> αἰνείσθω δὲ καμὼν ἔργον μέγα καὶ Διὸς εἶναι
>   δεύτερος, ὅστις ἔθηκ᾽ ἄστρα φαεινότερα.

Meleager, *A.P.* iv. 49 : ἄστρων τ᾽ ἴδριν ῎Αρατον.

Epigr. by Πτολεμαῖος ὁ βασιλεύς in *Vita I.*

> Πάνθ᾽ ῾Ηγησιάναξ τε καὶ ῞Ερμιππος τὰ κατ᾽ αἴθρην
>   τείρεα καὶ πολλοὶ ταῦτα τὰ φαινόμενα
> βίβλοις ἐγκατέθεντο, ἀποσκόπιοι δ᾽ ἀφάμαρτον,
>   ἀλλὰ τὸ λεπτολόγου σκῆπτρον ῎Αρατος ἔχει.

C. Helvius Cinna (Müller p. 87, Baehrens, *Fr. Rom. Poet.* 324) :

> Haec tibi Arateis multum vigilata lucernis
>   Carmina, quis ignes novimus aetherios,
> Levis in aridulo malvae descripta libello
>   Prusiaca vexi munera navicula.

Ovid, *Amor.* i. 15. 6 :

> "Cum sole et luna semper Aratus erit."

Quintilian, *Inst.* x. 1. 55 : " Arati materia motu caret, ut in qua nulla varietas, nullus adfectus, nulla persona, nulla cuiusquam sit oratio ; sufficit tamen operi cui se parem credidit."

III.

Among Roman writers Aratus attracted much attention and his influence upon Lucretius and Vergil need only be mentioned. His poem was translated by Cicero in his early youth (" admodum adulescentulus," *De nat. d.* ii. 41 ; cf. *Ad Attic.* ii. 1. 11 (June 60 B.C.) " prognostica mea cum oratiunculis propediem expecta"; as Cicero was then forty-six years of age, this would seem to imply that at first he had translated only the *Phaenomena* so-called, *i.e.* 1–732).

ARATUS

Of his translation we possess some 670 lines. Some part at least of the poem was translated by P. Terentius Varro (82–37 B.C.), surnamed Atacinus from the river Atax in his native Gallia Narbonensis, who "nomen est adsecutus interpres operis alieni," Quintil. *Inst.* x. 1. 87 (he translated also the *Argonautica* of Apoll. Rhod.). Some fragments are preserved by Servius on Verg. *G.* i. 375, 397. We have also some 857 lines of the translation of Germanicus Caesar (15 B.C.–A.D. 19), the nephew of Tiberius. We possess further the paraphrase in 1878 lines by Rufus Festus Avienus (proconsul of Africa A.D. 366). The *Astronomica* of Manilius (under Tiberius) also owes much to Aratus.

IV.

After the *Prooemium* (1–8) Aratus mentions the Axis of the stellar sphere terminating in the North and South Poles (21–26). He now proceeds to enumerate the constellations.

A. 26–318

The Northern constellations, *i.e.* those North of the Zodiac but including the zodiacal signs themselves. His method is to start with the Bears and to work Southward to the Zodiac, then return to the Bears and again work South to the Zodiac, proceeding round the Pole from East to West. Thus 1 and 2. The Bears, Ursa Minor and Ursa Major, also known as The Wains. The modern derivation of ἅμαξα is ἅμα + ἄξων, and something of the sort seems to be alluded to by Aratus in v. 27. 3. Draco. Hipparchus i. 4. 2 ff. objects that the leading stars in Ursa Minor are nearly parallel with the tail of Draco, so that it is incorrect to say with Eudoxus and Aratus that Ursa Minor is in the coil of Draco; incorrect, too, to say with Aratus 47 that the Bears are on either side of the coil, when they are really on either side of his tail. More interesting is the remark of Hipparchus i. 4. 4 ff. that Aratus should have said not *right* temple, but *left* temple. He adds an important remark : "To say, as Attalus does,

198

that Aratus conceives the head of Draco to be turned the other way and not turned towards the inside of the sphere, is quite unplausible. For all the constellations are formed with reference to our point of view and turned towards us, except when one of them is in profile (κατάγραφον). This is made clear by Aratus repeatedly; for whenever he mentions the right or left portion of a constellation, his statement agrees with this assumption." Hipparchus seems to imply that Draco is not conceived in profile (as he usually is in star-maps) and he holds that not the right temple but the left (γ Draconis) is in a straight line with the tongue of Draco and the end of the tail of the Great Bear. It may be noted that German. 58 and Avien. 162 follow Aratus in saying right temple.

4. Engonasin, the Phantom on his knees, who, according to the later interpretation, represents Hercules at the moment when he slew the Dragon which guarded the apples of the Hesperides. Hipparchus i. 4. 9 points out that Eudoxus and Aratus are guilty of an oversight in saying that Engonasin has his right foot on the head of Draco (69 f.), whereas it should be his left. Attalus attempted to exculpate Aratus by reading μέσσου δ' ἐφύπερθε καρήνου δεξιτεροῦ, *i.e.* on the middle of the right side of Draco's head—which Attalus imagines to be turned away from us (ἔξω τοῦ κόσμου). But it is shown by Hipparchus that this assumption (see above) is contrary to the practice of Aratus. Moreover it is more an oversight (παρόραμα) than an error (ἁμάρτημα) on the part of Aratus, as is shown by his other references to Engonasin 270 ff., 612 ff., 591 ff. Hipparchus is here clearly right. Heracles has his club in his right hand : the advanced knee must therefore be the left. So he is described in [Eratosth.] *Catast.* 4 and Hyginus, *Astr. s.v.* Engonasin, German. 68 ; but Avienus 192 follows Aratus in saying right foot. It is to be said, further, that the confusion of right and left is not only extremely natural but is also as a matter of fact extremely common in ancient accounts of the constellations. Moreover, many MSS. of Germanicus actually represent Engonasin as Hercules with the lion's skin

over his right arm, his club in his left, the left leg bent to the ground, the right advanced. (Boll, *Sphaera*, p. 102.)

5. The (Northern) Crown, Corona Borealis, said to be the crown of Ariadne, daughter of Minos, set among the stars by Dionysus: "Ariadneae caelestia dona Coronae," Manil. v. 21; "Coronam Gnosida," Ovid, *F.* iii. 459.

6. Ophiuchus, Serpentarius, Anguitenens, the figure of a man holding in his hands a serpent (Anguis, Serpens). He was sometimes identified with Asclepius; [Eratosth.], *Cat.* i. 6.

7. Scorpio, the Eighth Sign of the Zodiac.

8. The Claws of Scorpio, the Seventh Sign of the Zodiac; also known as Ζυγός, Libra, the Balance, the sign which the Sun enters at the Autumnal Equinox.

9. Arctophylax or Boötes with his brightest star Arcturus.

10. Virgo, the Maiden, the Sixth Sign of the Zodiac, identified with Dikē (Justice) or Astraea. In token of rustic simplicity she carries in her hand a corn-ear—represented by the bright star Spica (α Virginis). Usually this is said to be carried in her left hand [Eratosth.] *Cat.* i. 9; German. 95. Protrygeter, Vindemitor, a star on the right wing of Virgo; [Eratosth.] *l.c.*, Hygin. *s.v.* Virgo. This line 138 is given by ACM, but it is not translated by German. 141 nor Avien. 353. The schol. on 137 mentions *protrygeter*, but it is not clear whether he read it.

11. Gemini, the Twins, Castor and Pollux, Third Sign of the Zodiac.

12. Cancer, the Crab, Fourth Sign of the Zodiac.

13. Leo, the Lion, Fifth Sign of the Zodiac.

14. Auriga, the Charioteer, including the Goat, Capella (α Aurigae) and the Kids, Haedi (η, ξ Aurigae).

15. Taurus, the Bull, the Second Sign of the Zodiac, including the Hyades.

16. Cepheus.   17. Cassiepeia.   18. Andromeda.   19. Equus, Pegasus.

20. Aries, the Ram, First Sign of the Zodiac.   21.

Deltoton (*i.e.* Δ-shaped) or Trigonon, Triangulum. 22. Pisces, the Fishes, Twelfth sign of the Zodiac. 23. Perseus. 24. Pleiades in the constellation of Taurus, here treated separately on account of their importance as seasonal signs. 25. Lyra, the Lyre.

26. The Bird, the Swan (opp. to Iovis ales = Aquila, Manil. i. 350).

27. Aquarius, the Water-Carrier, Eleventh Sign of the Zodiac.

28. Capricorn, the Goat, Tenth Sign of the Zodiac.

29. Sagittarius, the Archer, Ninth Sign of the Zodiac.

30. Sagitta, the Arrow. 31. Aquila, the Eagle. 32. Delphinus, the Dolphin.

This ends the Northern constellations: Haec sunt Aquilonia signa (Manil. i. 379).

B

CONSTELLATIONS SOUTH OF THE ECLIPTIC

1. Orion. 2. Canis Major, the Dog, including Sirius (α Canis Majoris). 3. Lepus, the Hare. 4. Argo. 5. Cetus, the Whale. 6. Eridanus, the River. 7. Piscis Australis, the Southern Fish. 8. Hydor, Water. 9. Ara, the Altar. 10. Centaurus, the Centaur, often confused with the other Centaur, Sagittarius. 11. Therium, Bestia, the Wolf. 12. Hydra. 13. Crater, the Cup. 14. Corvus, the Raven. 15. Procyon.

This ends the Fixed Stars.

C

Next Aratus refers to the Five Planets which he declines to discuss. He does not name them but he means, of course, Saturn or Cronus, Jupiter or Zeus, Mars or Ares, Venus or Aphrodite, Mercury or Hermes.

ARATUS

D

Aratus next describes the Circles of the Celestial Sphere (454-461).

1. Gala, the Galaxy or Milky Way, a Great Circle of the Celestial Sphere.

2. The Tropic of Cancer, an imaginary circle $23\frac{1}{2}°$ North of the Equator, marking the extreme Northern limit of the Sun's annual path.

3. The Tropic of Capricorn, an imaginary circle $23\frac{1}{2}°$ South of the Equator, marking the extreme Southern limit of the Sun's annual path.

4. The Equator, a Great Circle of the Celestial Sphere, its plane being perpendicular to the axis of the Celestial Sphere. It is called ἰσημερινὸς κύκλος, or the Equinoctial, because when the Ecliptic or annual path of the Sun cuts it (1) when the Sun enters Aries (circa March 21), and again (2) when the Sun enters Libra (circa September 23), day and night are equal all over the globe.

5. The Zodiac, used sometimes generally in the sense of the Ecliptic, a Great Circle of the Celestial Sphere, representing the apparent annual path of the Sun among the stars. The plane of the Ecliptic is inclined to the plane of the Equator at an angle of (roughly) $23\frac{1}{2}°$. This so-called "obliquity of the Ecliptic" is what causes variation in the length of day and night at different seasons and in different latitudes. When the Zodiac is used more strictly, it means the belt of sky extending some 6 to 12 degrees on either side of the Ecliptic and comprehending the so-called zodiacal signs or constellations. In the Ecliptic lie the apparent paths of the Sun, Moon, and chief planets, and it gets its name from the fact that the Moon must be in or near the plane of the Ecliptic when an eclipse takes place.

E. 559–732

Aratus next deals with the συνανατολαί and ἀντικαταδύσεις of the constellations, i.e. what stars rise with a given zodiacal sign or set when the zodiacal sign is rising. The order in which he enumerates the signs of the Zodiac is

202

from the Summer Solstice onward : Cancer, Leo, Virgo, Libra, Scorpio, Sagittarius, Capricorn, Aquarius, Pisces, Aries, Taurus, Gemini.

Since in modern editions of the Classics statements about the rising and setting of stars are notoriously untrustworthy, it seems desirable to explain what exactly is meant by the rising and setting of a star. The early Greek writers on the matter distinguish the real or imperceptible rising and setting from the apparent or perceptible rising and setting. We thus have : (A) Real Risings and Settings. (1) The true Cosmical Rising, *i.e.* Star and Sun rise together (the star, though above the horizon, being invisible on account of its proximity to the Sun). (2) The true Cosmical Setting, *i.e.* the Star sets as the Sun rises (the star again being invisible because before it actually reaches the W. horizon it is obscured by the light of the rising Sun). (3) The true Acronychal Rising, *i.e.* the Star rises as the Sun sets (again the star is invisible as it emerges from the E. horizon because the light of the departed Sun still illuminates the sky). (4) The true Acronychal Setting, *i.e.* Star and Sun set together (the Star being therefore invisible).

But corresponding to these we have : (B) The Perceptible Risings and Settings which are of more practical importance. And these are : (1) The Heliacal rising, *i.e.* the first visible appearance of a star on the E. horizon before sunrise. The star is just sufficiently in advance of the Sun to be visible for a moment. (2) The Heliacal Setting, *i.e.* the last visible setting of a star in the evening (next night it will have reached the West while there is still too much light for it to be seen). (3) The (apparent) Acronychal Rising, *i.e.* the last visible rising of a star in the evening (next night it will have risen while there is still too much light for its emergence above the E. horizon to be seen). (4) The (apparent) Cosmical Setting, *i.e.* the first visible setting of a star in the morning (the previous night it does not quite succeed in reaching the West before sunrise ; every morning thereafter the interval between its setting and sunrise increases).

ARATUS

The Rising of a Star normally means its Heliacal Rising ; the Setting of a Star its Cosmical Setting.

Hipparchus ii. 1. 1 ff. remarks that Aratus in treating the signs of the Zodiac is concerned with the actual constellations, not with the ideal divisions of the Zodiac, and is therefore bound to be relatively inaccurate, since those constellations are sometimes less, sometimes larger than the twelfth part (δωδεκατημόριον) which they are supposed to occupy. Some of them, moreover, do not lie wholly in the Zodiac but considerably North of it, e.g. Leo and the more northerly of the two Fishes. He notes further (ii. 1. 15) that Aratus in his division of the Zodiac begins with the solstitial and equinoctial points, and so makes those points the beginnings of the signs, while Eudoxus makes those points the middle of the signs, the solstices occurring in the middle of Cancer and Capricorn, the equinoxes in the middle of Aries and Libra.

F

The Weather Signs, it is now generally agreed, are an integral part of the poem. The separate title given by some grammarian to this part of the poem is Διοσημίαι or Διοσημεῖαι, not Διοσημεῖα. For διοσημία in the sense of some significant phenomenon of the weather cf. Aristoph. *Ach.* 170 f. λέγω δ' ὑμῖν ὅτι | διοσημία 'στὶ καὶ ῥανὶς βέβληκέ με, Plut. *Mor.* 419 ε σύγχυσιν μεγάλην περὶ τὸν ἀέρα καὶ διοσημίας πολλὰς γενέσθαι, Poll. viii. 124 ἀνίστατο δὲ τὰ δικαστήρια εἰ γένοιτο διοσημία · ἐξήγηταί δὲ ἐκαλοῦντο οἱ τὰ περὶ τῶν διοσημιῶν καὶ τὰ τῶν ἄλλων ἱερῶν διδάσκοντες. *Cf.* Suid. *s.v.* διοσημία and Diodor. v. 40, speaking of the Etruscans : γράμματα δὲ καὶ φυσιολογίαν καὶ θεολογίαν ἐξεπόνησαν ἐπὶ πλέον, καὶ τὰ περὶ τὴν κεραυνοσκοπίαν μάλιστα πάντων ἀνθρώπων ἐξειργάσαντο · διὸ καὶ μέχρι τῶν νῦν χρόνων οἱ τῆς οἰκουμένης σχεδὸν ὅλης ἡγούμενοι θαυμάζουσί τε τοὺς ἄνδρας καὶ κατὰ τὰς ἐν τοῖς κεραυνοῖς διοσημίας τούτοις ἐξηγηταῖς χρῶνται.

A vexed question is the relation of the Weather Signs to the little work Περὶ σημείων which passes under the name of Theophrastus. On the one hand Maass (Introd.

to his edition, p. xxv) thinks that both are based upon an
original written in Ionic. On the other hand Kaibel
("Aratea" in *Hermes* xxix. (1894)) is of opinion that the
Περὶ σημείων was written after the publication of the poem of
Aratus and that the work shows indications of disarrange-
ment due to subsequent additions from Aratus and other
sources. As these additions agree in style and language
with the rest of the work Kaibel holds that they were
made by the author himself.

The details of the Metonic Cycle referred to in 752 ff.
cannot be discussed here, but a few words must be said.
The problem is to find a cycle which will contain a whole
number of solar years and at the same time a whole
number of synodical months. Meton found that 235
lunations amount practically to nineteen solar years. He
therefore made a Cycle of 6940 days, made up of nineteen
years with seven intercalated months. The chief relevant
texts are Theophr. Περὶ σημ. 4, Diod. xii. 36, Geminus
37 D (Petav.). The words of Aratus 754 ff. have been the
subject of much controversy. They appear to refer to the
Metonic Calendar as distinguished from the Metonic
Cycle. In his *Parapegma*[a] or Calendar the first *phenomenon*
seems to have been the rise of Orion's Belt, then the rest
of Orion, up to his foot; then Sirius; and all the other
stars, whether governing terrestrial things mainly (the
stars of Zeus) or mainly nautical affairs (the stars of
Poseidon). But Ideler i. 327 thinks the reference is to
the first and last *phenomena* recorded in the Metonic
Calendar. E. Müller supposed the Belt of Orion to
denote the beginning, while Sirius denoted the end of the
stellar year.

---

[a] It was usual for early astronomers to "fix up," παρα-
πηγνύναι, their calendars on pillars in a public place (Aelian,
V.H. x. 7); hence παράπηγμα, *affiche*, comes to mean
"calendar." Meton's calendar appears to have begun with
13th Scirophorion (27th June), 432 B.C., his first New Moon
falling on 16th July.

ΑΡΑΤΟΥ ΦΑΙΝΟΜΕΝΑ

Ἐκ Διὸς ἀρχώμεσθα, τὸν οὐδέποτ᾽ ἄνδρες ἐῶμεν
ἄρρητον· μεσταὶ δὲ Διὸς πᾶσαι μὲν ἀγυιαί,
πᾶσαι δ᾽ ἀνθρώπων ἀγοραί, μεστὴ δὲ θάλασσα
καὶ λιμένες· πάντη δὲ Διὸς κεχρήμεθα πάντες.
τοῦ γὰρ καὶ γένος εἰμέν· ὁ δ᾽ ἤπιος ἀνθρώποισιν   5
δεξιὰ σημαίνει, λαοὺς δ᾽ ἐπὶ ἔργον ἐγείρει,
μιμνήσκων βιότοιο, λέγει δ᾽ ὅτε βῶλος ἀρίστη
βουσί τε καὶ μακέλῃσι, λέγει δ᾽ ὅτε δεξιαὶ ὧραι
καὶ φυτὰ γυρῶσαι καὶ σπέρματα πάντα βαλέσθαι.
αὐτὸς γὰρ τά γε σήματ᾽ ἐν οὐρανῷ ἐστήριξεν,   10
ἄστρα διακρίνας, ἐσκέψατο δ᾽ εἰς ἐνιαυτὸν
ἀστέρας οἵ κε μάλιστα τετυγμένα σημαίνοιεν
ἀνδράσιν ὡράων, ὄφρ᾽ ἔμπεδα πάντα φύωνται.
τῷ μιν ἀεὶ πρῶτόν τε καὶ ὕστατον ἱλάσκονται.
χαῖρε, πάτερ, μέγα θαῦμα, μέγ᾽ ἀνθρώποισιν ὄνειαρ,   15
αὐτὸς καὶ προτέρη γενεή. χαίροιτε δὲ Μοῦσαι
μειλίχιαι μάλα πᾶσαι· ἐμοί γε μὲν ἀστέρας εἰπεῖν
ᾗ θέμις εὐχομένῳ τεκμήρατε πᾶσαν ἀοιδήν.

Οἱ μὲν ὁμῶς πολέες τε καὶ ἄλλυδις ἄλλοι ἐόντες[1]

---

[1] ἰόντες codd. recc., cf. schol.

[a] Cicero, De legg. ii. 3 "Ab Iove Musarum primordia
sicut in Aratio carmine orsi sumus"; Germ. Arat. 1 f. "Ab
Iove principium magno deduxit Aratus Carminis"; Avien.
Arat. 1 "Carminis inceptor mihi Iuppiter."

[b] N.T. Acts xvii. 28.   [c] Cicero ap. Priscian. x. 11.

ARATUS : PHAENOMENA

FROM Zeus let us begin ; [a] him do we mortals never leave unnamed ; full of Zeus are all the streets and all the market-places of men ; full is the sea and the havens thereof ; always we all have need of Zeus. For we are also his offspring ; [b] and he in his kindness unto men giveth favourable signs and wakeneth the people to work, reminding them of livelihood. He tells what time the soil is best for the labour of the ox and for the mattock, and what time the seasons are favourable both for the planting of trees and for casting all manner of seeds. For himself it was who set the signs in heaven,[c] and marked out the constellations, and for the year devised what stars chiefly should give to men right signs of the seasons, to the end that all things might grow unfailingly. Wherefore him do men ever worship first and last. Hail, O Father, mighty marvel, mighty blessing unto men. Hail to thee and to the Elder Race [d] ! Hail, ye Muses, right kindly, every one ! But for me, too, in answer to my prayer direct all my lay, even as is meet, to tell the stars.

They,[e] all alike, many though they be and other

---

[d] The Elder or Earlier Race is variously interpreted in the scholia as (1) = Zeus (ἐπεὶ αὐτὸς εἶ καὶ ἡ προτέρα γενεή) ; (2) = Titans ; (3) = the brothers of Zeus ; (4) = the earlier astronomers ; (5) = the heroes.   [e] Cicero, *De nat. d.* ii. 41.

οὐρανῷ ἕλκονται πάντ' ἤματα συνεχὲς αἰεί·   20
αὐτὰρ ὅ γ' οὐδ' ὀλίγον μετανίσσεται, ἀλλὰ μάλ' αὕτως
ἄξων αἰὲν ἄρηρεν, ἔχει δ' ἀτάλαντον ἀπάντη
μεσσηγὺς γαῖαν, περὶ δ' οὐρανὸν [1] αὐτὸν ἀγινεῖ.
καί μιν πειραίνουσι δύω πόλοι ἀμφοτέρωθεν·
ἀλλ' ὁ μὲν οὐκ ἐπίοπτος, ὁ δ' ἀντίος ἐκ βορέαο   25
ὑψόθεν ὠκεανοῖο· δύω δέ μιν ἀμφὶς ἔχουσαι
ΑΡΚΤΟΙ ἅμα τροχόωσι, τὸ δὴ καλέονται ᾿ΑΜΑΞΑΙ.
αἱ δ' ἤτοι κεφαλὰς μὲν ἐπ' ἰξύας αἰὲν ἔχουσιν
ἀλλήλων, αἰεὶ δὲ κατωμάδιαι φορέονται,
ἔμπαλιν εἰς ὤμους τετραμμέναι. εἰ ἐτεὸν δή,   30
Κρήτηθεν κεῖναί γε Διὸς μεγάλου ἰότητι
οὐρανὸν εἰσανέβησαν, ὅ μιν τότε κουρίζοντα
Δίκτῳ ἐν εὐώδει, ὄρεος σχεδὸν ᾿Ιδαίοιο,
ἄντρῳ ἐγκατέθεντο καὶ ἔτρεφον εἰς ἐνιαυτόν,
Δικταῖοι Κούρητες ὅτε Κρόνον ἐψεύδοντο.   3.
καὶ τὴν μὲν ΚΥΝΟΣΟΥΡΑΝ ἐπίκλησιν καλέουσιν,
τὴν δ' ἑτέρην ᾿ΕΛΙΚΗΝ. ᾿Ελίκῃ γε μὲν ἄνδρες
   ᾿Αχαιοὶ
εἰν ἁλὶ τεκμαίρονται ἵνα χρὴ νῆας ἀγινεῖν,
τῇ δ' ἄρα Φοίνικες πίσυνοι περόωσι θάλασσαν.
ἀλλ' ἡ μὲν καθαρὴ καὶ ἐπιφράσσασθαι ἑτοίμη   *
πολλὴ φαινομένη ᾿Ελίκη πρώτης ἀπὸ νυκτός·
ἡ δ' ἑτέρη ὀλίγη μέν, ἀτὰρ ναύτῃσιν ἀρείων·
μειοτέρη γὰρ πᾶσα περιστρέφεται στροφάλιγγι·
τῇ καὶ Σιδόνιοι ἰθύντατα ναυτίλλονται.

---

[1] οὐρανὸν M; οὐρανὸς AC.

---

[a] Ocean here = horizon, as usual in Aratus.
[b] The Greater and the Lesser Bear.
[c] Cic. De nat. d. ii. 41. The translation of ἔμπαλιν κτλ.
is too disputed to be discussed here.
[d] Dicton, apparently a by-form of the usual Dicte. It is,
of course, not near Ida, as Strabo points out: καὶ γὰρ ἡ

star in other path, are drawn across the heavens always through all time continually. But the Axis shifts not a whit, but unchanging is for ever fixed, and in the midst it holds the earth in equipoise, and wheels the heaven itself around.

On either side the Axis ends in two Poles, but thereof the one is not seen, whereas the other faces us in the north high above the ocean.[a] Encompassing it two Bears[b] wheel together—wherefore they are also called the Wains. Now they ever hold their heads each toward the flank of the other, and are borne along always shoulder-wise, turned alternate on their shoulders.[c] If, indeed, the tale be true, from Crete they by the will of mighty Zeus entered up into heaven, for that when in olden days he played as a child in fragrant Dicton,[d] near the hill of Ida, they set him in a cave and nurtured him for the space of a year, what time the Dictaean Curetes were deceiving Cronus. Now the one men call by name Cynosura and the other Helice. It is by Helice that the Achaeans on the sea divine which way to steer their ships, but in the other the Phoenicians put their trust when they cross the sea.[e] But Helice,[f] appearing large at earliest night, is bright and easy to mark ; but the other is small, yet better for sailors : for in a smaller orbit wheel all her stars. By her guidance, then, the men of Sidon[g] steer the straightest course.

Δίκτη πλησίον (τῆς Πράσου), οὐχ ὡς Ἄρατος " ὄρεος σχεδὸν Ἰδαίοιο." καὶ γὰρ χιλίους ἡ Δίκτη τῆς Ἴδης ἀπέχει (Strabo 478). Zenodotus of Mallos understood δίκτον as = δίκταμνον, the plant " dittany," hence the epithet " fragrant " (schol.).

[e] Ovid, *Trist.* iv. 3. 1-2 " Magna minorque ferae, quarum regis altera Graias, Altera Sidonias, utraque sicca, rates." *Cf.* Cic. *De nat. d.* ii. 42.

[f] The Great Bear (Ursa Major).   [g] The Phoenicians.

Τὰς δὲ δι' ἀμφοτέρας οἵη ποταμοῖο ἀπορρὼξ 45
εἰλεῖται μέγα θαῦμα, ΔΡΑΚΩΝ, περί τ' ἀμφί τ'
  ἐαγὼς
μυρίος· αἱ δ' ἄρα οἱ σπείρης ἑκάτερθε φέρονται
Ἄρκτοι, κυανέου πεφυλαγμέναι ὠκεανοῖο.
αὐτὰρ ὅ γ' ἄλλην μὲν νεάτῃ ἐπιτείνεται οὐρῇ,
ἄλλην δὲ σπείρῃ περιτέμνεται. ἡ μέν οἱ ἄκρη 50
οὐρὴ πὰρ κεφαλὴν Ἑλίκης ἀποπαύεται Ἄρκτου·
σπείρῃ δ' ἐν Κυνόσουρα κάρη ἔχει· ἡ δὲ κατ' αὐτὴν
εἰλεῖται κεφαλὴν καί οἱ ποδὸς ἔρχεται ἄχρις,
ἐκ δ' αὖτις παλίνορσος ἀνατρέχει. οὐ μὲν ἐκείνη
οἰόθεν οὐδ' οἷος κεφαλῇ ἐπιλάμπεται ἀστήρ, 55
ἀλλὰ δύο κροτάφοις, δύο δ' ὄμμασιν· εἷς δ' ὑπένερθεν
ἐσχατιὴν ἐπέχει γένυος δεινοῖο πελώρου.
λοξὸν δ' ἐστὶ κάρη, νεύοντι δὲ πάμπαν ἔοικεν
ἄκρην εἰς Ἑλίκης οὐρήν· μάλα δ' ἐστὶ κατ' ἰθύ
καὶ στόμα καὶ κροτάφοιο τὰ δεξιὰ νειάτῳ οὐρῇ. 60
κείνη που κεφαλὴ τῇ νίσσεται, ᾗχί περ ἄκραι
μίσγονται δύσιές τε καὶ ἀντολαὶ ἀλλήλῃσιν.

Τῇδ' αὐτοῦ μογέοντι κυλίνδεται ἀνδρὶ ἐοικὸς
εἴδωλον. τὸ μὲν οὔτις ἐπίσταται ἀμφαδὸν εἰπεῖν,

---

[a] Draco.
[b] *i.e.* never set for Northern latitudes.
[c] Cynosura (Ursa Minor).
[d] Hipparchus says it should be *left* temple.
[e] Cic. *De nat. d.* ii. 42 "Et reliquum quidem corpus Draconis totis noctibus cernimus : ' Hoc caput hic paulum sese subito aequore condit, Ortus ubi atque obitus partem admiscetur in unam.' " At latitude x° a star x° from Pole would just touch the horizon at its lowest point. The head of Draco lies between 33° and 39° from the Pole ($34\frac{2}{3}$° - 37°, Hipparch. i. 4. 8), and hence about lat. 37° it would just touch the horizon at its lowest point, *i.e.* it lies within the

PHAENOMENA

Between them, as it were the branch of a river, circles in wondrous way the Dragon,[a] winding infinite around and about ; on either side of his coil are borne along the Bears, that shun evermore the blue sea.[b] Now towards the one he stretches the end of his tail, but with the coil he intercepts the Lesser Bear.[c] The tip of his tail ends by the head of Helice, but in the coil Cynosura has her head. For his coil circles past her very head and comes near her feet, but again, turning back, runs upward. Not one lone star shines on his head, but on his brows are two stars lit, and two in his eyes, and one beneath is set upon the chin-point of the dread monster. Aslant is his head, and he seems most like as if he were nodding to the tip of the tail of Helice ; his mouth and right[d] temple straight confront the end of her tail. That head wheels near where the limits of setting and rising blend.[e]

Right there in its orbit wheels a Phantom form,[f] like to a man that strives at a task. That sign no

circle of perpetual visibility (ὁ ἀεὶ φανερὸς κύκλος) ; cf. Hipparch. l.c., who refutes Attalus who said it lay somewhat south of this. In other words, a star so situated that it rises nearly due North will set nearly due North, and the interval between setting and rising will be very short : setting and rising blend ; cf. Scott's Last Expedition (Smith, Elder & Co., 1913), chap. ix. April 23, " The long mild twilight which like a silver clasp unites to-day with yesterday ; when morning and evening sit together hand in hand beneath the starless sky of midnight." Homer's remarks upon the Laestrygones, Od. x. 82 ff., especially ἐγγὺς γὰρ νυκτός τε καὶ ἤματός εἰσι κέλευθοι, point, as Crates rightly saw (schol. Arat. 62), to a people of the Far North.

[f] Cicero, De nat. d. ii. 42 " Id autem caput [sc. Draconis] ' Attingens defessa velut maerentis imago Vertitur ' quam quidem Graeci ' Engonasin vocitant, genibus quia nixa feratur.' " See 270 n. and Introd. p. 373.

ARATUS

οὐδ' ὅτινι κρέμαται κεῖνος πόνῳ, ἀλλά μιν αὔτως   65
ΕΓΓΟΝΑΣΙΝ καλέουσι. τὸ δ' αὖτ' ἐν γούνασι κάμνον
ὀκλάζοντι ἔοικεν· ἀπ' ἀμφοτέρων δέ οἱ ὤμων
χεῖρες ἀείρονται· τάνυταί γε μὲν ἄλλυδις ἄλλη
ὅσσον ἐς ὀργυιήν· μέσσῳ δ' ἐφύπερθε καρήνῳ
δεξιτεροῦ ποδὸς ἄκρον ἔχει σκολιοῖο Δράκοντος.   70

Αὐτοῦ κἀκεῖνος ΣΤΕΦΑΝΟΣ, τὸν ἀγαυὸς ἔθηκεν
σῆμ' ἔμεναι Διόνυσος ἀποιχομένης Ἀριάδνης,
νώτῳ ὑποστρέφεται κεκμηότος Εἰδώλοιο.

Νώτῳ μὲν Στέφανος πελάει, κεφαλῇ γε μὲν ἄκρῃ
σκέπτεο πὰρ κεφαλὴν Ὀφιούχεον, ἐκ δ' ἄρ' ἐκείνης 75
αὐτὸν ἐπιφράσσαιο φαεινόμενον ΟΦΙΟΥΧΟΝ·
τοῖοί οἱ κεφαλῇ ὑποκείμενοι ἀγλαοὶ ὦμοι
εἴδονται· κεῖνοί γε καὶ ἂν διχόμηνι σελήνῃ
εἰσωποὶ τελέθοιεν· ἀτὰρ χέρες οὐ μάλα ἶσαι·
λεπτὴ γὰρ καὶ τῇ καὶ τῇ ἐπιδέδρομεν αἴγλη.   80
ἀλλ' ἔμπης κἀκεῖναι ἐπόψιαι· οὐ γὰρ ἐλαφραί·
ἀμφότεραι δ' Ὄφιος πεπονήαται, ὅς ῥά τε μέσσον
δινεύει Ὀφιοῦχον· ὁ δ' ἐμμενὲς εὖ ἐπαρηρὼς
ποσσὶν ἐπιθλίβει μέγα θηρίον ἀμφοτέροισιν,
ΣΚΟΡΠΙΟΝ, ὀφθαλμῷ τε καὶ ἐν θώρηκι βεβηκὼς   85
ὀρθός. ἀτὰρ οἱ ΟΦΙΣ γε δύω στρέφεται μετὰ χερσίν,
δεξιτερῇ ὀλίγος, σκαιῇ γε μὲν ὑψόθι πολλός.

---

[a] Engonasin, *Ingeniculus*: later supposed to be Heracles at the moment when he slew the dragon (Draco) which guarded the apples of the Hesperides (Avien. 169 ff.); also called Gnyx, *i.e.* On his knees A. 591, 615; or *Eidolon*, here and 64. By Roman poets called Nixus, Effigies, Imago. *Cf.* Avien. 631, Germ. 271.

[b] Hipparchus in *Arat. et Eudox. Phaen.* i. 2. 6 points out that both Eudoxus and Aratus say "right foot," whereas it should be "left foot."

[c] Corona Borealis. Cic. *l.c.* "Hic illa eximio posita est fulgore Corona."

212

man knows how to read clearly, nor on what task he is bent, but men simply call him On His Knees.[a] Now that Phantom, that toils on his knees, seems to sit on bended knee, and from both his shoulders his hands are upraised and stretch, one this way, one that, a fathom's length. Over the middle of the head of the crooked Dragon, he has the tip of his right foot.[b]

Here too that Crown,[c] which glorious Dionysus set to be memorial of the dead Ariadne, wheels beneath the back of the toil-spent Phantom.

To the Phantom's back the Crown is near, but by his head mark near at hand the head of Ophiuchus,[d] and then from it you can trace the starlit Ophiuchus himself: so brightly set beneath his head appear his gleaming shoulders. They would be clear to mark even at the midmonth moon, but his hands are not at all so bright; for faint runs the gleam of stars along on this side and on that. Yet they too can be seen, for they are not feeble. Both firmly clutch the Serpent,[e] which encircles the waist of Ophiuchus, but he, stedfast with both his feet well set, tramples a huge monster, even the Scorpion,[f] standing upright on his eye and breast. Now the Serpent is wreathed about his two hands—a little above his right hand, but in many folds high above his left.

---

[a] Cic. *l.c.*, "Atque haec quidem a tergo, propter caput autem Anguitenens, 'Quem claro perhibent Ophiuchum nomine Graii. Hic pressu duplici palmarum continet Anguem, Atque eius ipse manet religatus corpore torto; Namque virum medium serpens sub pectora cingit. Ille tamen nitens graviter vestigia ponit Atque oculos urguet pedibus pectusque Nepaï [=Scorpio].'" Cic. *ap.* Priscian. xiv. 52 "Huic supera duplices humeros affixa videtur Stella micans tali specie talique nitore."

[e] Serpens.　　　　Scorpio.

Καὶ δή οἱ Στεφάνῳ παρακέκλιται ἄκρα γένεια,
νειόθι δὲ σπείρης μεγάλας ἐπιμαίεο ΧΗΛΑΣ.
ἀλλ' αἱ μὲν φαέων ἐπιδευέες, οὐδὲν ἀγαυαί.   90
    Ἐξόπιθεν δ' Ἑλίκης φέρεται ἐλάοντι ἐοικὼς
ΑΡΚΤΟΦΥΛΑΞ, τόν ῥ' ἄνδρες ἐπικλείουσι ΒΟΩΤΗΝ,
οὕνεχ' ἁμαξαίης ἐπαφώμενος εἴδεται Ἄρκτου.
καὶ μάλα πᾶς ἀρίδηλος· ὑπὸ ζώνῃ δέ οἱ αὐτὸς
ἐξ ἄλλων ΑΡΚΤΟΥΡΟΣ ἑλίσσεται ἀμφαδὸν ἀστήρ.   95
    Ἀμφοτέροισι δὲ ποσσὶν ὑπὸ σκέπτοιο Βοώτεω
ΠΑΡΘΕΝΟΝ, ἥ ῥ' ἐν χερσὶ φέρει Στάχυν αἰγλήεντα.
εἴτ' οὖν Ἀστραίου κείνη γένος, ὅν ῥά τέ φασιν
ἄστρων ἀρχαῖον πατέρ' ἔμμεναι, εἴτε τευ ἄλλου,
εὔκηλος φορέοιτο· λόγος γε μὲν ἐντρέχει ἄλλος   100
ἀνθρώποις, ὡς δῆθεν ἐπιχθονίη πάρος ἦεν,
ἤρχετο δ' ἀνθρώπων κατεναντίη, οὐδέ ποτ' ἀνδρῶν
οὐδέ ποτ' ἀρχαίων ἠνήνατο φῦλα γυναικῶν,
ἀλλ' ἀναμὶξ ἐκάθητο, καὶ ἀθανάτη περ ἐοῦσα.
καί ἑ Δίκην καλέεσκον· ἀγειρομένη δὲ γέροντας,   105
ἠέ που εἰν ἀγορῇ ἢ εὐρυχόρῳ ἐν ἀγυιῇ,
δημοτέρας ἤειδεν ἐπισπέρχουσα θέμιστας.
οὔπω λευγαλέου τότε νείκεος ἠπίσταντο
οὐδὲ διακρίσιος πολυμεμφέος οὐδὲ κυδοιμοῦ,
αὔτως δ' ἔζωον· χαλεπὴ δ' ἀπέκειτο θάλασσα,   110
καὶ βίον οὔπω νῆες ἀπόπροθεν ἠγίνεσκον,
ἀλλὰ βόες καὶ ἄροτρα καὶ αὐτή, πότνια λαῶν,
μυρία πάντα παρεῖχε Δίκη, δώτειρα δικαίων.
τόφρ' ἦν, ὄφρ' ἔτι γαῖα γένος χρύσειον ἔφερβεν.
ἀργυρέῳ δ' ὀλίγη τε καὶ οὐκέτι πάμπαν ἑτοίμη¹   11

---

¹ ὁμοίη A.

ᵃ Scorpion's Claws or Libra.
ᵇ Boötes. Cic. *l.c.* " Septentriones autem sequitur ' Arctophylax, vulgo qui dicitur esse Bootes, Quod quasi temoni
adiunctam prae se quatit Arctum.' Dein quae sequuntur.

PHAENOMENA

Toward the Crown leans the Serpent's jaw, but beneath his coiling form seek thou for the mighty Claws [a]; they are scant of light and nowise brilliant.

Behind Helice, like to one that drives, is borne along Arctophylax whom men also call Boötes,[b] since he seems to lay hand on the wain-like Bear. Very bright is he all; but beneath his belt wheels a star, bright beyond the others, Arcturus himself.

Beneath both feet of Boötes mark the Maiden,[c] who in her hands bears the gleaming Ear of Corn.[d] Whether she be daughter of Astraeus, who, men say, was of old the father of the stars, or child of other sire, untroubled be her course! But another tale is current among men, how of old she dwelt on earth and met men face to face, nor ever disdained in olden time the tribes of men and women, but mingling with them took her seat, immortal though she was. Her men called Justice; but she assembling the elders, it might be in the market-place or in the wide-wayed streets, uttered her voice, ever urging on them judgements kinder to the people. Not yet in that age had men knowledge of hateful strife, or carping contention, or din of battle, but a simple life they lived. Far from them was the cruel sea and not yet from afar did ships bring their livelihood, but the oxen and the plough and Justice herself, queen of the peoples, giver of things just, abundantly supplied their every need. Even so long as the earth still nurtured the Golden Race, she had her dwelling on earth. But with the Silver Race only

Huic enim Booti 'subter praecordia fixa videtur Stella micans radiis, Arcturus nomine claro.'"
    [c] Virgo. Cic. *l.c.* "cuius [Arcturi] pedibus subiecta fertur 'Spicum inlustre tenens splendenti corpore Virgo.'"
    [d] Spica.

215

ὡμίλει, ποθέουσα παλαιῶν ἤθεα λαῶν.
ἀλλ' ἔμπης ἔτι κεῖνο κατ' ἀργύρεον γένος ἦεν·
ἤρχετο δ' ἐξ ὀρέων ὑποδείελος ἠχηέντων
μουνάξ, οὐδέ τεω ἐπεμίσγετο μειλιχίοισιν·
ἀλλ' ὁπότ' ἀνθρώπων μεγάλας πλήσαιτο κολώνας,   120
ἠπείλει δὴ ἔπειτα καθαπτομένη κακότητος,
οὐδ' ἔτ' ἔφη εἰσωπὸς ἐλεύσεσθαι καλέουσιν·
"οἵην χρύσειοι πατέρες γενεὴν ἐλίποντο
χειροτέρην· ὑμεῖς δὲ κακώτερα τεξείεσθε.
καὶ δή που πόλεμοι, καὶ δὴ καὶ ἀνάρσιον αἷμα   125
ἔσσεται ἀνθρώποισι, κακὸν δ' ἐπικείσεται ἄλγος."
ὣς εἰποῦσ' ὀρέων ἐπεμαίετο, τοὺς δ' ἄρα λαοὺς
εἰς αὐτὴν ἔτι πάντας ἐλίμπανε παπταίνοντας.
ἀλλ' ὅτε δὴ κἀκεῖνοι ἐτέθνασαν, οἱ δ' ἐγένοντο,
χαλκείη γενεή, προτέρων ὀλοώτεροι ἄνδρες,   130
οἳ πρῶτοι κακόεργον ἐχαλκεύσαντο μάχαιραν
εἰνοδίην, πρῶτοι δὲ βοῶν ἐπάσαντ' ἀροτήρων,
καὶ τότε μισήσασα Δίκη κείνων γένος ἀνδρῶν
ἔπταθ' ὑπουρανίη· ταύτην δ' ἄρα νάσσατο χώρην,
ᾗχί περ ἐννυχίη ἔτι φαίνεται ἀνθρώποισιν   13[5]
Παρθένος, ἐγγὺς ἐοῦσα πολυσκέπτοιο Βοώτεω.

  Τῆς ὑπὲρ ἀμφοτέρων ὤμων εἰλίσσεται ἀστὴρ
[δεξιτερῇ πτέρυγι· ΠΡΟΤΡΥΓΗΤΗΡ δ' αὖτε καλεῖται·]¹
τόσσος μὲν μεγέθει, τοίῃ δ' ἐγκείμενος αἴγλῃ,
οἷος καὶ μεγάλης οὐρὴν ὑποφαίνεται Ἄρκτου.   14[0]
δεινὴ γὰρ κείνη, δεινοὶ δέ οἱ ἐγγύθεν εἰσὶν
ἀστέρες· οὐκ ἂν τούς γε ἰδὼν ἐπιτεκμήραιο

---

¹ ACM ; but not translated by Germ. or Avienus.

ᵃ Cic. *De nat. d.* ii. 63 "Quibus [bubus], cum terrae
subigerentur fissione glebarum, ab illo aureo genere, ut
poetae loquuntur, vis nulla unquam adferebatur. ' Ferrea
tum vero proles exorta repente est Ausaque funestum prima

a little and no longer with utter readiness did she
mingle, for that she yearned for the ways of the
men of old. Yet in that Silver Age was she still
upon the earth; but from the echoing hills at eventide she came alone, nor spake to any man in gentle
words. But when she had filled the great heights
with gathering crowds, then would she with threats
rebuke their evil ways, and declare that never more
at their prayer would she reveal her face to man.
" Behold what manner of race the fathers of the
Golden Age *a* left behind them! Far meaner than
themselves! but ye will breed a viler progeny *b*!
Verily wars and cruel bloodshed shall be unto men
and grievous woe shall be laid upon them." Even
so she spake and sought the hills and left the people
all gazing towards her still. But when they, too,
were dead, and when, more ruinous than they which
went before, the Race of Bronze was born, who were
the first to forge the sword of the highwayman, and
the first to eat of the flesh of the ploughing-ox, then
verily did Justice loathe that race of men and fly
heavenward and took up that abode, where even
now in the night time the Maiden is seen of men,
established near to far-seen Boötes.

Above both her shoulders at her right wing
wheels a star, whereof the name is the Vintager *c*—
of such size and with such brightness set, as the star
that shines beneath the tail of the Great Bear. For
dread is the Bear and dread stars are near her.
Seeing them thou needest not further conjecture

est fabricarier ensem Et gustare manu vinctum domitumque
iuvencum.'"
    b Cf. Hor. C. iii. 6. 46 " Aetas parentum, peior avis, tulit
Nos nequiores, mox daturos Progeniem vitiosiorem."
    c Vindemiator.

ARATUS

[οἵ μιν πᾶσαν ὄπισθεν ἑλισσόμενοι τυπόωσιν,][1]   142
οἷός οἱ πρὸ ποδῶν φέρεται καλός τε μέγας τε
εἷς μὲν ὑπωμαίων, εἷς δ' ἰξυόθεν κατιόντων,
ἄλλος δ' οὐραίοις ὑπὸ γούνασιν· ἀλλ' ἄρα πάντες   145
ἁπλόοι ἄλλοθεν ἄλλος ἀνωνυμίῃ φορέονται.

Κρατὶ δέ οἱ ΔΙΔΤΜΟΙ, μέσσῃ δ' ὕπο ΚΑΡΚΙΝΟΣ
ἐστίν·
ποσσὶ δ' ὀπισθοτέροισι ΛΕΩΝ ὕπο καλὰ φαείνει.
ἔνθα μὲν ἠελίοιο θερείταταί εἰσι κέλευθοι·
αἱ δέ που ἀσταχύων κενεαὶ φαίνονται ἄρουραι   150
ἠελίου τὰ πρῶτα συνερχομένοιο Λέοντι.
τῆμος καὶ κελάδοντες ἐτησίαι εὐρέϊ πόντῳ
ἀθρόοι ἐμπίπτουσιν, ὁ δὲ πλόος οὐκέτι κώπαις
ὥριος. εὑρεῖαί μοι ἀρέσκοιεν τότε νῆες,
εἰς ἄνεμον δὲ τὰ πηδὰ κυβερνητῆρες ἔχοιεν.   155

Εἰ δέ τοι ΗΝΙΟΧΟΝ τε καὶ ἀστέρας Ἡνιόχοιο
σκέπτεσθαι δοκέει, καί τοι φάτις ἤλυθεν ΑΙΓΟΣ
αὐτῆς ἠδ' ΕΡΙΦΩΝ, οἵ τ' εἰν ἁλὶ πορφυρούσῃ
πολλάκις ἐσκέψαντο κεδαιομένους ἀνθρώπους,
αὐτὸν μέν μιν ἅπαντα μέγαν Διδύμων ἐπὶ λαιὰ   160
κεκλιμένον δήεις· Ἑλίκης δέ οἱ ἄκρα κάρηνα
ἀντία δινεύει. σκαιῷ δ' ἐπελήλαται ὤμῳ
αἲξ ἱερή, τὴν μέν τε λόγος Διὶ μαζὸν ἐπισχεῖν,
Ὠλενίην δέ μιν Αἶγα Διὸς καλέουσ' ὑποφῆται.

---

[1] Read only in later mss. *Cf.* v. 171.

[a] Cic. *ap.* Priscian. *Gramm.* vi. "Tertia sub caudam ad genus ipsum lumina pandit."

[b] Gemini. Cic. *De nat. d.* ii. 43 "Et natos Geminos invises sub caput Arcti : Subiectus mediae est Cancer, pedibusque tenetur Magnu' Leo tremulam quatiens e corpore flammam." [c] Cancer. [d] Leo.

[e] About 23rd July the Sun enters the zodiacal sign Leo: *cf.* Hipparch. ii. 1. 18 who, after quoting Aratus 149-151, remarks: "For the greatest heat occurs about the time

what stars beyond them model all her form. Such stars are borne along, beautiful and great, one in front of her forefeet, one on her flank, and one beneath her hind knees.[a] But all singly one here, one there, are wheeled along without a name.

Beneath the head of Helice are the Twins [b]; beneath her waist is the Crab [c]; beneath her hind feet the Lion[d] brightly shines. There is the Sun's hottest summer path. Then the fields are seen bereft of corn-ears, when first the Sun comes together with the Lion.[e] Then the roaring Etesian [f] winds fall swooping on the vasty deep, and voyaging is no longer seasonable for oars. Then let broad-beamed ships be my choice, and let steersmen hold the helm into the wind.

But if it be thy wish to mark Charioteer [g] and his stars, and if the fame has come to thee of the Goat [h] herself and the Kids,[i] who often on the darkening deep have seen men storm-tossed, thou wilt find him in all his might, leaning forward at the left hand of the Twins. Over against him wheels the top of Helice's head, but on his left shoulder is set the holy Goat, that, as legend tells, gave the breast to Zeus. Her the interpreters of Zeus call the Olenian

when the Dog-Star rises, which is as nearly as possible thirty days after the summer solstice. At that date, according to Aratus, the Sun is in the beginning of Leo. The sun, therefore, at this (the summer) solstice occupies the beginning of the Crab (Cancer)."

[f] The Etesian or trade-winds which blow every year in the Mediterranean during the summer, mostly from the North, begin at the rising of the Dog-Star, being preceded by the *prodromi* which, also from the North, begin eight days before the rising of the Dog-Star. The Etesian winds blow for some fifty days.   [g] Auriga.   [h] Capella.

[i] Haedi; *cf. Verg. A.* ix. 668 " pluvialibus Haedis."

ARATUS

ἀλλ' ἡ μὲν πολλή τε καὶ ἀγλαή· οἱ δέ οἱ αὐτοῦ   165
λεπτὰ φαείνονται Ἔριφοι καρπὸν κάτα χειρός.

Πὰρ ποσὶ δ' Ἡνιόχου κεραὸν πεπτηότα ΤΑΥΡΟΝ
μαίεσθαι. τὰ δέ οἱ μάλ' ἐοικότα σήματα κεῖται·
τοίη οἱ κεφαλὴ διακέκριται· οὐδέ τις ἄλλῳ
σήματι τεκμήραιτο κάρη βοός, οἷά μιν αὐτοὶ   170
ἀστέρες ἀμφοτέρωθεν ἑλισσόμενοι τυπόωσιν.
καὶ λίην κείνων ὄνομ' εἴρεται, οὐδέ τοι αὔτως
νήκουστοι ΥΑΔΕΣ. ταὶ μέν ῥ' ἐπὶ παντὶ μετώπῳ
Ταύρου βεβλέαται· λαιοῦ δὲ κέρατος ἄκρον
καὶ πόδα δεξιτερὸν παρακειμένου Ἡνιόχοιο   175
εἷς ἀστὴρ ἐπέχει· συνεληλάμενοι δὲ φέρονται,
ἀλλ' αἰεὶ Ταῦρος προφερέστερος Ἡνιόχοιο
εἰς ἑτέρην καταβῆναι, ὁμηλυσίη περ ἀνελθών.

Οὐδ' ἄρα Κηφῆος μογερὸν γένος Ἰασίδαο
αὔτως ἄρρητον κατακείσεται· ἀλλ' ἄρα καὶ τῶν   180
οὐρανὸν εἰς ὄνομ' ἦλθεν, ἐπεὶ Διὸς ἐγγύθεν ἦσαν.
αὐτὸς μὲν κατόπισθεν ἐὼν Κυνοσουρίδος Ἄρκτου
ΚΗΦΕΥΣ ἀμφοτέρας χεῖρας τανύοντι ἐοικώς·
ἴση οἱ στάθμη νεάτης ἀποτείνεται οὐρῆς
ἐς πόδας ἀμφοτέρους, ὅσση ποδὸς ἐς πόδα τείνει.   18

---

a Amalthea : Olenian as being on the arm (ὠλένη) of
Auriga or as daughter of Olenus or from Olenus or Olene in
Achaia (Strabo 387, who quotes Aratus). Cf. "Nascitur
Oleniae signum pluviale Capellae," Ovid, F. v. 113, "Oleniae
sidus pluviale Capellae," Ovid, M. iii. 594.

b The participle πεπτηώς occurs five times in Aratus, here
of Taurus, 318 of the bright stars in the Dolphin, 324 of
Orion, 353 of Andromeda, 369 of certain nameless stars.
The mss. of Homer confuse the perfect participle active of
πίπτω with that of πτήσσω (Leaf on Il. xxi. 503). There
seems reason to think that in some cases, e.g. 324, Aratus
treated πεπτηώς as from πίτνημι, πετάννυμι, in the sense of
"extended," "spread."

220

Goat.[a] Large is she and bright, but there at the
wrist of the Charioteer faintly gleam the Kids.

At the feet of Charioteer seek for the crouching[b]
horned Bull.[c] Very lifelike are his signs; so clear
defined his head : not by other sign would one mark
the head of an ox, since in such wise those very
stars, wheeling on either side, fashion it. Oft-
spoken is their name and not all unheard-of are the
Hyades.[d] Broadcast are they on the forehead of
the Bull. One star occupies the tip of his left horn
and the right foot of the Charioteer, who is close by.
Together they are carried in their course, but ever
earlier is the Bull than the Charioteer to set beneath
the West,[e] albeit they fare together at their rising.[f]

Nor all unnamed shall rest the hapless family of
Iasid Cepheus.[g] For their name, too, has come unto
heaven, for that they were near akin to Zeus.[h]
Cepheus himself is set behind the Bear Cynosura,
like to one that stretches out both his hands. From
her tail-tip to both his feet stretches a measure
equal to that from foot to foot.[i] But a little aside

[c] Taurus.

[d] Hyades in the constellation of Taurus.

[e] ἐτέρη may refer to West, as here, and 279, 659, or to
East, 571, 617, 726, always according to the context.

[f] The Bull sets sooner because he is farther South than
Auriga (schol.). For criticism of this passage cf. Hipparch.
i. 5. 14 ff.

[g] Cepheus, King of Aethiopia, father of Andromeda by
Cassiepeia. He was descended from Io whose father, according to one version, was Jasus, son of Argos (Apollod.
ii. 5).

[h] As descended from Io.

[i] Hipparchus i. 2. 12 says that this remark, in which
Aratus agrees with Eudoxus, is not true, the distance between the feet of Cepheus being less than that from either
foot to the tip of Cynosura's tail.

αὐτὰρ ἀπὸ ζώνης ὀλίγον κε μεταβλέψειας
πρώτης ἱέμενος καμπῆς μεγάλοιο Δράκοντος.
　　Τοῦ δ' ἄρα δαιμονίη προκυλίνδεται οὐ μάλα
　　　πολλὴ
νυκτὶ φαεινομένη παμμήνιδι ΚΑΣΣΙΕΠΕΙΑ·
οὐ γάρ μιν πολλοὶ καὶ ἐπημοιβοὶ γανόωσιν　　　　　190
ἀστέρες, οἵ μιν πᾶσαν ἐπιρρήδην στιχόωσιν.
οἵη δὲ κληῖδι θύρην ἔντοσθ' ἀραρυῖαν
δικλίδ' ἐπιπλήσσοντες ἀνακρούουσιν ὀχῆας,[1]
τοῖοί οἱ μουνὰξ ὑποκείμενοι ἰνδάλλονται
ἀστέρες. ἡ δ' αὕτως ὀλίγων ἀποτείνεται ὤμων　　195
ὀργυιήν. φαίης κεν ἀνιάζειν ἐπὶ παιδί.
　　Αὐτοῦ γὰρ κἀκεῖνο κυλίνδεται αἰνὸν ἄγαλμα
ΑΝΔΡΟΜΕΔΗΣ ὑπὸ μητρὶ κεκασμένον. οὔ σε μάλ' οἴω
νύκτα περισκέψασθαι, ἵν' αὐτίκα μᾶλλον ἴδηαι·
τοίη οἱ κεφαλή, τοῖοι δέ οἱ ἀμφοτέρωθεν　　　　　200
ὦμοι καὶ πόδες ἀκρότατοι καὶ ζώματα πάντα.
ἀλλ' ἔμπης κἀκεῖθι διωλενίη τετάνυσται,
δεσμὰ δέ οἱ κεῖται καὶ ἐν οὐρανῷ· αἱ δ' ἀνέχονται
αὐτοῦ πεπταμέναι πάντ' ἤματα χεῖρες ἐκεῖναι.
　　Ἀλλ' ἄρα οἱ καὶ κρατὶ πέλωρ ἐπελήλαται ΙΠΠΟΣ　205
γαστέρι νειαίρῃ· ξυνὸς δ' ἐπιλάμπεται ἀστὴρ
τοῦ μὲν ἐπ' ὀμφαλίῳ, τῆς δ' ἐσχατόωντι καρήνῳ.
οἱ δ' ἄρ' ἔτι τρεῖς ἄλλοι ἐπὶ πλευράς τε καὶ ὤμους
ἵππου δεικανόωσι διασταδὸν ἶσα πέλεθρα,
καλοὶ καὶ μεγάλοι· κεφαλὴ δέ οἱ οὐδὲν ὁμοίη,　　　210

---

[1] οἵην . . . ὀχῆες ACM.

[a] Cassiepeia offended the Nereids by vying with them in
beauty.　Hence Poseidon sent a sea-monster (Cetus) against
Aethiopia.
[b] The W-shaped constellation of Cassiepeia is a familiar
spectacle in the sky.　It is probably unnecessary to suppose
that more is meant than that C. presents roughly the same

from his belt look to find the first coil of the mighty Dragon.

Eastward his hapless wife, Cassiepeia,[a] gleaming when by night the moon is full, wheels with her scanty stars. For few and alternate stars adorn her, which expressly mark her form with lines of light. Like the key[b] of a twofold door barred within, wherewith men striking shoot back the bolts, so singly set shine her stars. But from her shoulders so faint she stretches a fathom's length. Thou would'st say she was sorrowing over her daughter.[c]

For there, too, wheels that woeful form of Andromeda, enstarred beneath her mother. Thou hast not to wait[d] for a night, I ween, whereon to see her more distinct! So bright is her head and so clearly marked are both the shoulders, the tips of her feet and all her belt. Yet even there she is racked, with arms stretched far apart, and even in Heaven bonds are her portion. Uplifted and outspread there for all time are those hands of hers.

Beneath her head is spread the huge Horse,[e] touching her with his lower belly. One common star gleams on the Horse's navel and the crown of her head. Three other separate stars, large and bright, at equal distance set on flank and shoulders, trace a square[f] upon the Horse. His head is not so brightly

aspect as that presented by the bars of a folding-door, where one half-door acts as door-post to the other and *vice versa*. If these two bars were secured by a drop-bar passing through the two, the resemblance would be clearer still.

[c] Andromeda, who was exposed to the Sea-Monster being chained to a rock until she was rescued by Perseus.

[d] *i.e.* She can be seen any night.

[e] Pegasus, the winged horse of Bellerophon.

[f] The Great Square of Pegasus, made up of α, β, γ Pegasi with α Andromedae.

οὐδ' αὐχὴν δολιχός περ ἐών. ἀτὰρ ἔσχατος ἀστὴρ
αἰθομένης γένυος καὶ κεν προτέροις ἐρίσειεν
τέτρασιν, οἵ μιν ἔχουσι περίσκεπτοι μάλ' ἐόντες.
οὐδ' ὅ γε τετράπος ἐστίν· ἀπ' ὀμφαλίοιο γὰρ ἄκρου
μεσσόθεν ἡμιτελὴς περιτέλλεται ἱερὸς Ἵππος.   215
κεῖνον δὴ καί φασι καθ' ὑψηλοῦ Ἑλικῶνος
καλὸν ὕδωρ ἀγαγεῖν εὐαλδέος Ἱππουκρήνης.
οὐ γάρ πω Ἑλικὼν ἄκρος κατελείβετο πηγαῖς,
ἀλλ' Ἵππος μιν ἔτυψε· τὸ δ' ἀθρόον αὐτόθεν ὕδωρ
ἐξέχυτο πληγῇ προτέρου ποδός· οἱ δὲ νομῆες   220
πρῶτοι κεῖνο ποτὸν διεφήμισαν Ἱππουκρήνην.
ἀλλὰ τὸ μὲν πέτρης ἀπολείβεται, οὐδέ ποτ' αὐτὸ
Θεσπιέων ἀνδρῶν ἑκὰς ὄψεαι· αὐτὰρ ὁ Ἵππος
ἐν Διὸς εἱλεῖται καί τοι πάρα θηήσασθαι.

Αὐτοῦ καὶ κριοιο θοώταταί εἰσι κέλευθοι,   225
ὅς ῥά τε καὶ μήκιστα διωκόμενος περὶ κύκλα
οὐδὲν ἀφαυρότερον τροχάει Κυνοσουρίδος Ἄρκτου,
αὐτὸς μὲν νωθὴς καὶ ἀνάστερος οἷα σελήνη
σκέψασθαι, ζώνῃ δ' ἂν ὅμως ἐπιτεκμήραιο
Ἀνδρομέδης· ὀλίγον γὰρ ὑπ' αὐτὴν ἐστήρικται.   230
μεσσόθι δὲ τρίβει μέγαν οὐρανόν, ἧχί περ ἄκραι
χηλαὶ καὶ ζώνη περιτέλλεται Ὠρίωνος.

Ἔστι δέ τοι καὶ ἔτ' ἄλλο τετυγμένον ἐγγύθι σῆμα
νειόθεν Ἀνδρομέδης, τὸ δ' ἐπὶ τρισὶν ἐστάθμηται
ΔΕΛΤΩΤΟΝ πλευρῇσιν, ἰσαιομένῃσιν ἐοικὸς   23
ἀμφοτέρῃς· ἡ δ' οὔτι τόση, μάλα δ' ἐστὶν ἑτοίμη
εὑρέσθαι· περὶ γὰρ πολέων εὐάστερός ἐστιν.
τῶν ὀλίγον Κριοῦ νοτιώτεροι ἀστέρες εἰσίν.

ᵃ The constellation of Pegasus is only a προτομή or bust,
showing head and forefeet and half the body.
ᵇ A fountain on Helicon, near Thespiae in Boeotia, said to
have been caused by the hoof of Pegasus, the winged Horse
of Bellerophon (Paus. ix. 31. 3).

marked, nor his neck, though it be long. But the farthest star on his blazing nostril could fitly rival the former four, that invest him with such splendour. Nor is he four-footed. Parted at the navel, with only half a body, wheels in heaven the sacred Horse.[a] He it was, men say, that brought down from lofty Helicon the bright water of bounteous Hippocrene.[b] For not yet on Helicon's summit trickled the fountain's springs, but the Horse smote it and straightway the gushing water was shed abroad at the stamp of his forefoot, and herdsmen were the first to call that stream the fountain of the Horse. From the rock the water wells and never shalt thou see it far from the men of Thespiae; but the Horse himself circles in the heaven of Zeus and is there for thee to behold.

There too are the most swift courses of the Ram,[c] who, pursued through the longest circuit, runs not a whit slower than the Bear Cynosura—himself weak and starless as on a moonlit night, but yet by the belt of Andromeda thou canst trace him out. For a little below her is he set. Midway he treads the mighty heavens, where wheel the tips of the Scorpion's Claws and the Belt of Orion.

There is also another sign, fashioned near, below Andromeda, Deltoton,[d] drawn with three sides, whereof two appear equal but the third is less, yet very easy to find, for beyond many is it endowed with stars. Southward a little from Deltoton are the stars of the Ram.

[c] The Ram, Aries, situated on the Equator, which is a Great Circle of the celestial globe, completes his circuit of the heavens in the same time that Ursa Minor completes her smaller circle.

[d] Triangulum.

225

Οἱ δ' ἄρ' ἔτι προτέρω, ἔτι δ' ἐν προμολῇσι νότοιο,
ΙΧΘΥΕΣ. ἀλλ' αἰεὶ ἕτερος προφερέστερος ἄλλου,   240
καὶ μᾶλλον βορέαο νέον κατιόντος ἀκούει.
ἀμφοτέρων δέ σφεων ἀποτείνεται ἠΰτε δεσμὰ
οὐραίων ἑκάτερθεν ἐπισχερὼ εἰς ἓν ἰόντων.
καὶ τὰ μὲν εἰς ἀστὴρ ἐπέχει καλός τε μέγας τε,
ὅν ῥά τε καὶ σύνδεσμον ὑπούραιον καλέουσιν.   245
Ἀνδρομέδης δέ τοι ὦμος ἀριστερὸς Ἰχθύος ἔστω
σῆμα βορειοτέρου· μάλα γάρ νύ οἱ ἐγγύθεν ἐστίν.

    Ἀμφότεροι δὲ πόδες γαμβροῦ ἐπισημαίνοιεν
ΠΕΡΣΕΟΣ, οἵ ῥά οἱ αἰὲν ἐπωμάδιοι φορέονται.
αὐτὰρ ὅ γ' ἐν βορέω φέρεται περιμήκετος ἄλλων.   250
καί οἱ δεξιτερὴ μὲν ἐπὶ κλισμὸν τετάνυσται
πενθερίου δίφροιο· τὰ δ' ἐν ποσὶν οἷα διώκων
ἴχνια μηκύνει κεκονιμένος ἐν Διὶ πατρί.

    Ἄγχι δέ οἱ σκαιῆς ἐπιγουνίδος ἤλιθα πᾶσαι
ΠΛΗΙΑΔΕΣ φορέονται. ὁ δ' οὐ μάλα πολλὸς
            ἁπάσας   255
χῶρος ἔχει, καὶ δ' αὐταὶ ἐπισκέψασθαι ἀφαυραί.
ἑπτάποροι δὴ ταί γε μετ' ἀνθρώπους ὑδέονται,
ἐξ οἷαί περ ἐοῦσαι ἐπόψιαι ὀφθαλμοῖσιν.
οὐ μέν πως ἀπόλωλεν ἀπευθὴς ἐκ Διὸς ἀστήρ,
ἐξ οὗ καὶ γενεῆθεν ἀκούομεν, ἀλλὰ μάλ' αὔτως   260
εἴρεται. ἑπτὰ δ' ἐκεῖναι ἐπιρρήδην καλέονται
Ἀλκυόνη Μερόπη τε Κελαινώ τ' Ἠλέκτρη τε
καὶ Στερόπη καὶ Τηϋγέτη καὶ πότνια Μαῖα.
αἱ μὲν ὁμῶς ὀλίγαι καὶ ἀφεγγέες, ἀλλ' ὀνομασταὶ
ἦρι καὶ ἑσπέριαι, Ζεὺς δ' αἴτιος, εἰλίσσονται,   265

---

[a] Pisces. Hipparchus i. 6. 8 f. points out that not both
but only one of the Fishes is south of the Ram.   The schol.
takes Aratus to mean south of Triangulum.

[b] a Piscium, the knot of the band of stars joining the tails
of the two Fishes.

Still farther in front of the Ram and still in the vestibule of the South are the Fishes.[a] Ever one is higher than the other, and louder hears the fresh rush of the North wind. From both there stretch, as it were, chains, whereby their tails on either side are joined. The meeting chains are knit by a single beautiful and great star, which is called the Knot of Tails.[b] Let the left shoulder of Andromeda be thy guide to the northern Fish, for it is very near.

Her two feet will guide thee to her bridegroom, Perseus,[c] over whose shoulder they are for ever carried. But he moves in the North a taller form than the others. His right hand is stretched toward the throne of the mother[d] of his bride, and, as if pursuing that which lies before his feet, he greatly strides, dust-stained, in the heaven of Zeus.

Near[e] his left thigh move the Pleiades, all in a cluster, but small is the space that holds them and singly they dimly shine. Seven are they in the songs of men, albeit only six are visible to the eyes.[f] Yet not a star, I ween, has perished from the sky unmarked since the earliest memory of man, but even so the tale is told. Those seven are called by name Halcyone, Merope, Celaeno, Electra, Sterope, Taygete, and queenly Maia. Small and dim are they all alike, but widely famed they wheel in heaven at morn and eventide, by the will of Zeus,

[c] Perseus, son of Zeus and Danaë, who rescued Andromeda.

[d] Cassiepeia, mother of Andromeda.

[e] Hipparch. i. 6. 12 criticizes this: "The left knee of Perseus is a long way from the Pleiades."

[f] The missing Pleiad is sometimes said to be Merope, sometimes Electra. Hipparch. i. 6. 14 says that by looking carefully on a clear moonless night seven stars can be seen.

ὅ σφισι καὶ θέρεος καὶ χείματος ἀρχομένοιο
σημαίνειν ἐκέλευσεν ἐπερχομένου τ᾽ ἀρότοιο.

Καὶ ΧΕΛΥΣ, ἥτ᾽ ὀλίγη· τὴν δ᾽ ἄρ᾽ ἔτι καὶ
  παρὰ λίκνῳ
Ἑρμείης ἐτόρησε, ΛΥΡΗΝ δέ μιν εἶπε λέγεσθαι.
κὰδ δ᾽ ἔθετο προπάροιθεν ἀπευθέος Εἰδώλοιο   270
οὐρανὸν εἰσαγαγών. τὸ δ᾽ ἐπὶ σκελέεσσι πέτηλον
γούνατί οἱ σκαιῷ πελάει· κεφαλή γε μὲν ἄκρη
ἀντιπέρην Ὄρνιθος ἑλίσσεται· ἡ δὲ μεσηγὺ
ὀρνιθέης κεφαλῆς καὶ γούνατος ἐστήρικται.

  Ἤτοι γὰρ καὶ Ζηνὶ παρατρέχει αἰόλος ΟΡΝΙΣ. 275
ἀλλ᾽ ὁ μὲν ἠερόεις, τὰ δέ οἱ ἔπι τετρήχυνται
ἀστράσιν οὔτι λίην μεγάλοις, ἀτὰρ οὐ μὲν ἀφαυροῖς.
αὐτὰρ ὅ γ᾽ εὐδιόωντι ποτὴν ὄρνιθι ἐοικὼς
οὔριος εἰς ἑτέρην φέρεται, κατὰ δεξιὰ χειρὸς
Κηφείης ταρσοῖο τὰ δεξιὰ πείρατα τείνων,   280
λαιῇ δὲ πτέρυγι σκαρθμὸς παρακέκλιται Ἵππου.

  Τὸν δὲ μετασκαίροντα δύ᾽ Ἰχθύες ἀμφινέμονται
Ἵππον· πὰρ δ᾽ ἄρα οἱ κεφαλῇ χεὶρ ὙΔΡΟΧΟΟΙΟ
δεξιτερὴ τετάνυσθ᾽· ὁ δ᾽ ὀπίστερος Αἰγοκερῆος
τέλλεται. αὐτὰρ ὅ γε πρότερος καὶ νειόθι μᾶλλον   285
κέκλιται ΑΙΓΟΚΕΡΩΣ, ἵνα τε τρέπετ᾽ ἠελίου ἴς.
μὴ κείνῳ ἐνὶ μηνὶ περικλύζοιο θαλάσσῃ
πεπταμένῳ πελάγει κεχρημένος. οὔτε κεν ἠοῖ
πολλὴν πειρήνειας, ἐπεὶ ταχινώταταί εἰσιν·
οὔτ᾽ ἄν τοι νυκτὸς πεφοβημένῳ ἐγγύθεν ἠὼς   290
ἔλθοι καὶ μάλα πολλὰ βοωμένῳ. οἱ δ᾽ ἀλεγεινοὶ

ᵃ Their heliacal rising (ἑῴα ἀνατολή) in May was the sign
of harvest; their cosmical setting (ἑῴα δύσις) in November
the sign of the sowing-season; *cf.* Hesiod, *W.* 383 ff. So
Theophrast. *De sign.* i. 6 διχοτομεῖ δὲ τὸν μὲν ἐνιαυτὸν Πλειάς
τε δυομένη καὶ ἀνατέλλουσα.

who bade them tell of the beginning of Summer and of Winter and of the coming of the ploughing-time.[a]

Yonder, too, is the tiny Tortoise,[b] which, while still beside his cradle, Hermes pierced for strings and bade it be called the Lyre: and he brought it into heaven and set it in front of the unknown Phantom.[c] That Croucher on his Knees comes near the Lyre with his left knee, but the top of the Bird's head wheels on the other side, and between the Bird's head and the Phantom's knee is enstarred the Lyre.

For verily in heaven there is outspread a glittering Bird.[d] Wreathed in mist is the Bird, but yet the parts above him are rough with stars, not very large, yet not obscure. Like a bird in joyous flight, with fair weather it glides to the west, with the tip of its right wing outstretched towards the right hand of Cepheus, and by its left wing is hung in the heavens the prancing Horse.

Round the prancing Horse range the two Fishes. By the Horse's head is stretched the right hand of Hydrochous.[e] He is behind Aegoceros,[f] who is set in front and further down, where the mighty Sun turns.[g] In that month use not the open sea[h] lest thou be engulfed in the waves. Neither in the dawn canst thou accomplish a far journey, for fast to evening speed the dawns; nor at night amid thy fears will the dawn draw earlier near, though loud and instant be thy cry. Grievous then is the crash-

[b] Lyra. For the invention of the lyre by Hermes *cf.* Hom. *H. Herm.* 39 ff.

[c] Engonasin; *cf.* v. 66 n.   [d] Cygnus, the Swan.

[e] Aquarius, the Water-bearer.   [f] Capricorn.

[g] Tropic of Capricorn, so called because the Sun enters the zodiacal sign of Capricorn at the winter solstice, *i.e.* 22nd December.

[h] μὴ ... θαλάσσῃ quoted by [Longin.] *De sublim.* xxvi. 1.

τῆμος ἐπιρρήσσουσι νότοι, ὁπότ' Αἰγοκερῆϊ
συμφέρετ' ἠέλιος· τότε δὲ κρύος ἐκ Διός ἐστιν
ναύτῃ μαλκιόωντι κακώτερον. ἀλλὰ καὶ ἔμπης
ἤδη πάντ' ἐνιαυτὸν ὑπὸ στείρῃσι θάλασσα   295
πορφύρει· ἴκελοι δὲ κολυμβίσιν αἰθυίῃσιν
πολλάκις ἐκ νηῶν πέλαγος περιπαπταίνοντες
ἤμεθ' ἐπ' αἰγιαλοὺς τετραμμένοι· οἱ δ' ἔτι πόρσω
κλύζονται· ὀλίγον δὲ διὰ ξύλον "Αϊδ' ἐρύκει.

Καὶ δ' ἂν ἐπὶ[1] προτέρῳ γε, θαλάσσῃ πολλὰ
    πεπονθώς,   300
Τόξον ὅτ' ἠέλιος καίει καὶ ῥύτορα Τόξου,
ἑσπέριος κατάγαιο, πεποιθὼς οὐκέτι νυκτί.
σῆμα δέ τοι κείνης ὥρης καὶ μηνὸς ἐκείνου
Σκορπίος ἀντέλλων εἴη πυμάτης ἐπὶ νυκτός.
ἤτοι γὰρ μέγα τόξον ἀνέλκεται ἐγγύθι κέντρου   305
ΤΟΞΕΥΤΗΣ· ὀλίγον δὲ παροίτερος ἵσταται αὐτοῦ
Σκορπίος ἀντέλλων, ὁ δ' ἀνέρχεται αὐτίκα μᾶλλον.
τῆμος καὶ κεφαλὴ Κυνοσουρίδος ἀκρόθι νυκτὸς
ὕψι μάλα τροχάει, ὁ δὲ δύεται ἠῶθι πρὸ
ἀθρόος Ὠρίων, Κηφεὺς δ' ἀπὸ χειρὸς ἐπ' ἰξύν.   310

Ἔστι δέ τις προτέρω βεβλημένος ἄλλος ΟΙΣΤΟΣ
αὐτὸς ἄτερ τόξου· ὁ δέ οἱ παραπέπταται Ὄρνις
ἀσσότερον βορέω. σχεδόθεν δέ οἱ ἄλλος ἄηται
οὐ τόσσος μεγέθει, χαλεπός γε μὲν ἐξ ἁλὸς ἐλθεῖν
νυκτὸς ἀπερχομένης· καί μιν καλέουσιν ΑΗΤΟΝ.   315
ΔΕΛΦΙΣ δ', οὐ μάλα πολλός, ἐπιτρέχει Αἰγο-
    κερῆϊ

---

[1] ἔτι C; read ἔτι προτέρω?

---

[a] [Longin.] De subl. x. 5-6 contrasts this passage of Aratus,
ὀλίγον . . . ἐρύκει, with Hom. Il. xv. 624-628 (ending τυτθὸν γὰρ
ὑπὲκ θανάτοιο φέρονται), and awards the palm for sublimity to
Homer.

ing swoop of the South winds when the Sun joins Aegoceros, and then is the frost from heaven hard on the benumbed sailor. Not but that throughout the year's length the sea ever grows dark beneath the keels, and, like to diving seagulls, we often sit, spying out the deep from our ship with faces turned to the shore ; but ever farther back the shores are swept by the waves and only a thin plank staves off Death.[a]

But even in the previous month,[b] storm-tossed at sea, when the Sun scorches the Bow and the Wielder [c] of the Bow, trust no longer in the night but put to shore in the evening. Of that season and that month let the rising of Scorpion at the close of night be a sign to thee. For verily his great Bow does the Bowman draw close by the Scorpion's sting, and a little in front stands the Scorpion at his rising, but the Archer [c] rises right after him. Then, too, at the close of night Cynosura's head runs very high, but Orion just before the dawn wholly sets and Cepheus from hand to waist.[d]

Further up there is another Arrow [e] shot—alone without a bow. By it is the Bird [f] outspread nearer the North, but hard at hand another bird [g] tosses in storm, of smaller size but cruel in its rising from the sea when the night is waning, and men call it the Eagle (Storm-bird).[h]

Over Aegoceros floats the Dolphin [i] with few

[b] November, when the Sun enters Sagittarius.
[c] Sagittarius.
[d] Vv. 303 ff. are discussed by Hipparch. i. 7. 1-18.
[e] Sagitta.　　　　[f] Cygnus.　　　[g] Aquila, Eagle.
[h] Aëtos, here derived from ἄηται, "is blown."
[i] Delphinus.

231

μεσσόθεν ἠερόεις· τὰ δέ οἱ περὶ τέσσαρα κεῖται
γλήνεα, παρβολάδην δύο πὰρ δύο πεπτηῶτα.

Καὶ τὰ μὲν οὖν βορέω καὶ ἀλήσιος ἠελίοιο
μεσσηγὺς κέχυται· τὰ δὲ νειόθι τέλλεται ἄλλα   320
πολλὰ μεταξὺ νότοιο καὶ ἠελίοιο κελεύθου.

Λοξὸς μὲν Ταύροιο τομῇ ὑποκέκλιται αὐτὸς
ΩΡΙΩΝ. μὴ κεῖνον ὅτις καθαρῇ ἐνὶ νυκτὶ
ὑψοῦ πεπτηῶτα παρέρχεται ἄλλα πεποίθοι
οὐρανὸν εἰσανιδὼν προφερέστερα θηήσασθαι.   325

Τοῖός οἱ καὶ φρουρὸς ἀειρομένῳ ὑπὸ νώτῳ
φαίνεται ἀμφοτέροισι ΚΥΩΝ ὑπὸ ποσσὶ βεβηκώς,
ποικίλος, ἀλλ' οὐ πάντα πεφασμένος· ἀλλὰ κατ'
    αὐτὴν
γαστέρα κυάνεος περιτέλλεται, ἡ δέ οἱ ἄκρη
ἀστέρι βέβληται δεινῇ γένυς, ὅς ῥα μάλιστα   330
ὀξέα σειριάει· καί μιν καλέουσ' ἄνθρωποι
ΣΕΙΡΙΟΝ. οὐκέτι κεῖνον ἅμ' ἠελίῳ ἀνιόντα
φυταλιαὶ ψεύδονται ἀναλδέα φυλλιόωσαι.
ῥεῖα γὰρ οὖν ἔκρινε διὰ στίχας ὀξὺς ἀΐξας,
καὶ τὰ μὲν ἔρρωσεν, τῶν δὲ φλόον ὤλεσε πάντα.   335
κείνου καὶ κατιόντος ἀκούομεν· οἱ δὲ δὴ ἄλλοι
σῆμ' ἔμεναι μελέεσσιν ἐλαφρότεροι περίκεινται.

Ποσσὶν δ' 'Ωρίωνος ὑπ' ἀμφοτέροισι ΛΑΓΩΟΣ
ἐμμενὲς ἤματα πάντα διώκεται. αὐτὰρ ὅ γ' αἰεὶ
Σείριος ἐξόπιθεν φέρεται μετιόντι ἐοικώς,   340
καί οἱ ἐπαντέλλει, καί μιν κατιόντα δοκεύει.

'Η δὲ Κυνὸς μεγάλοιο κατ' οὐρὴν ἕλκεται ΑΡΓΩ

---

[a] The Ecliptic or apparent path of the Sun among the
stars.

[b] As the constellation of Taurus represents only the forequarters of the Bull it is natural to take τομή = προτομή,
"forequarters." The schol., however, takes it as "section,"
i.e. the section of the Zodiac represented by the Bull.

bright stars and body wreathed in mist, but four
brilliants adorn him, set side by side in pairs.

Now these constellations lie between the North
and the Sun's wandering path,[a] but others many in
number rise beneath between the South and the
Sun's course.

Aslant beneath the fore-body[b] of the Bull is set
the great Orion. Let none who pass him spread
out on high on a cloudless night imagine that, gazing
on the heavens, one shall see other stars more fair.

Such a guardian, too, beneath his towering back
is seen to stand on his hind legs, the Dog[c] star-
enwrought, yet not clearly marked in all his form,
but right by his belly he shows dark. The tip of
his terrible jaw is marked by a star that keenest of
all blazes with a searing flame and him men call
Seirius.[d] When he rises with the Sun,[e] no longer do
the trees deceive him by the feeble freshness of their
leaves. For easily with his keen glance he pierces
their ranks, and to some he gives strength but of
others he blights the bark utterly. Of him too at
his setting[f] are we aware, but the other stars of the
Dog are set round with fainter light to mark his legs.

Beneath both feet of Orion is the Hare[g] pursued
continually through all time, while Seirius behind is
for ever borne as in pursuit. Close behind he rises
and as he sets he eyes the setting Hare.

Beside the tail of the Great Dog the ship Argo[h] is

---

[c] Canis Major, the Great Dog.   [d] Sirius, α Canis Majoris.
[e] In July.   [f] In the end of November.   [g] Lepus.
[h] "At Canis ad caudam serpens prolabitur Argo | Con-
versam prae se portans cum lumine puppim," Cic. De nat.
d. ii. 44; cf. Eratosth. Catast. 35 εἰς δὲ τὰ ἄστρα ἀνετέθη τὸ
εἴδωλον οὐχ ὅλον αὐτῆς, οἱ δ' οἴακές εἰσιν ἕως τοῦ ἱστοῦ σὺν τοῖς
πηδαλίοις.

τ.ρυμνόθεν· οὐ γὰρ τῇ γε κατὰ χρέος εἰσὶ κέλευθοι,
ἀλλ' ὄπιθεν φέρεται τετραμμένη, οἷα καὶ αὐταὶ
νῆες, ὅτ' ἤδη ναῦται ἐπιστρέψωσι κορώνην   345
ὅρμον ἐσερχόμενοι· τὴν δ' αὐτίκα πᾶς ἀνακόπτει
νῆα, παλιρροθίη δὲ καθάπτεται ἠπείροιο·
ὣς ἥ γε πρύμνηθεν Ἰησονὶς ἕλκεται Ἀργώ.
καὶ τὰ μὲν ἠερίη καὶ ἀνάστερος ἄχρι παρ' αὐτὸν
ἱστὸν ἀπὸ πρώρης φέρεται, τὰ δὲ πᾶσα φαεινή.   350
καί οἱ πηδάλιον κεχαλασμένον ἐστήρικται
ποσσὶν ὑπ' οὐραίοισι Κυνὸς προπάροιθεν ἰόντος.

Τὴν δὲ καὶ οὐκ ὀλίγον περ ἀπόπροθι πεπτηυῖαν
Ἀνδρομέδην μέγα ΚΗΤΟΣ ἐπερχόμενον κατεπείγει.
ἡ μὲν γὰρ Θρήϊκος ὑπὸ πνοιῇ βορέαο   355
κεκλιμένη φέρεται, τὸ δέ οἱ νότος ἐχθρὸν ἀγινεῖ
κῆτος, ὑπὸ Κριῷ τε καὶ Ἰχθύσιν ἀμφοτέροισιν,
βαιὸν ὑπὲρ Ποταμοῦ βεβλημένον ἀστερόεντος.

Οἷον γὰρ κἀκεῖνο θεῶν ὑπὸ ποσσὶ φορεῖται
λείψανον ΗΡΙΔΑΝΟΙΟ, πολυκλαύτου ποταμοῖο.   360
καὶ τὸ μὲν Ὠρίωνος ὑπὸ σκαιὸν πόδα τείνει·
δεσμοὶ δ' οὐραῖοι, τοῖς Ἰχθύες ἄκροι ἔχονται,
ἄμφω συμφορέονται ἀπ' οὐραίων κατιόντες·
Κητείης δ' ὄπιθεν λοφίης ἐπιμὶξ φορέονται
εἰς ἓν ἐλαυνόμενοι· ἐνὶ δ' ἀστέρι πειραίνονται   365
Κήτεος, ὃς κείνου πρώτῃ ἐπίκειται ἀκάνθῃ.

Οἱ δ' ὀλίγῳ μέτρῳ ὀλίγη δ' ἐγκείμενοι αἴγλῃ

---

^a Hipparch. i. 8. 1 criticizes this: the bright stars, κ on
the deck, β on the keel, lie considerably East of the Mast.
^b See note on 167.
^c Cetus.
^d Hipparch. i. 8. 5.
^e Eridanus, Flumen, the River, sometimes called the Nile.
The Eridanus was identified with the river Po, into which
Phaëthon fell and where his sisters, the Heliades, wept for

hauled stern-foremost. For not hers is the proper course of a ship in motion, but she is borne backwards, reversed even as real ships, when already the sailors turn the stern to the land as they enter the haven, and every one back-paddles the ship, but she rushing sternward lays hold of the shore. Even so is the Argo of Jason borne along stern-foremost. Partly in mist is she borne along, and starless from her prow even to the mast,[a] but the hull is wholly wreathed in light. Loosed is her Rudder and is set beneath the hind feet of the Dog, as he runs in front.

Andromeda, though she cowers[b] a good way off, is pressed by the rush of the mighty Monster[c] of the Sea. For her path lies under the blast of Thracian Boreas, but the South wind drives against her, beneath the Ram and the Pair of Fishes, the hateful Monster, Cetus, set as he is a little above the Starry River.[d]

For alone are those poor remains of Eridanus,[e] River of many tears, also borne beneath the feet of the Gods. He winds beneath Orion's left foot, but the Shackles, wherewith the Fishes' tails are held, reach from their tails and join together, and behind the neck of Cetus they mingle their path and fare together. They end in a single star of Cetus, set where meet his spine and head.

Other stars,[f] mean in size and feeble in splendour,

him; 'poor remains,' because Eridanus was partly burnt up. Aratus is the first to call the River Eridanus.

[f] Stars lying between Argo and Cetus and the Hare, which were not grouped as a constellation and given a special name. Hipparch. i. 8. 2 f. says the "nameless stars" really lie between the River and the Helm of Argo.

μεσσόθι πηδαλίου καὶ Κήτεος εἱλίσσονται,
γλαυκοῦ πεπτηῶτες ὑπὸ πλευρῇσι Λαγωοῦ
νώνυμοι· οὐ γάρ τοί γε τετυγμένου εἰδώλοιο   370
βεβλέαται μελέεσσιν ἐοικότες, οἷά τε πολλὰ
ἑξείης στιχόωντα παρέρχεται αὐτὰ κέλευθα
ἀνομένων ἐτέων· τά τις ἀνδρῶν οὐκέτ᾽ ἐόντων
ἐφράσατ᾽ ἠδ᾽ ἐνόησεν ἅπαντ᾽ ὀνομαστὶ καλέσσαι
ἤλιθα μορφώσας. οὐ γάρ κ᾽ ἐδυνήσατο πάντων   375
οἰόθι κεκριμένων ὄνομ᾽ εἰπεῖν, οὐδὲ δαῆναι.
πολλοὶ γὰρ πάντη, πολέων δ᾽ ἐπὶ ἶσα πέλονται
μέτρα τε καὶ χροιή, πάντες γε μὲν ἀμφιέλικτοι.
τῶ καὶ ὁμηγερέας οἱ ἐείσατο ποιήσασθαι
ἀστέρας, ὄφρ᾽ ἐπιτὰξ ἄλλῳ παρακείμενος ἄλλος   380
εἴδεα σημαίνοιεν. ἄφαρ δ᾽ ὀνομαστὰ γένοντο
ἄστρα, καὶ οὐκέτι νῦν ὑπὸ θαύματι τέλλεται ἀστήρ.
ἀλλ᾽ οἱ μὲν καθαροῖς ἐναρηρότες εἰδώλοισιν
φαίνονται· τὰ δ᾽ ἔνερθε διωκομένοιο Λαγωοῦ
πάντα μάλ᾽ ἠερόεντα καὶ οὐκ ὀνομαστὰ φέρονται.   385

   Νειόθι δ᾽ Αἰγοκερῆος, ὑπὸ πνοιῇσι νότοιο,
ΙΧΘΥΣ ἐς Κῆτος τετραμμένος αἰωρεῖται
οἶος ἀπὸ προτέρων, ΝΟΤΙΟΝ δέ ἑ κικλήσκουσιν.

   Ἄλλοι δέ, σποράδην ὑποκείμενοι Ὑδροχοῆϊ,
Κήτεος αἰθερίοιο καὶ Ἰχθύος ἠερέθονται   390
μέσσοι νωχελέες καὶ ἀνώνυμοι· ἐγγύθι δέ σφεων,
δεξιτερῆς ἀπὸ χειρὸς ἀγαυοῦ Ὑδροχόοιο,
οἵη τίς τ᾽ ὀλίγη χύσις ὕδατος ἔνθα καὶ ἔνθα
σκιδναμένου, χαροποὶ καὶ ἀναλδέες εἱλίσσονται.
ἐν δέ σφιν δύο μᾶλλον ἐειδόμενοι φορέονται   395

---

   [a] Hipparch. i. 8. 8 ff. discusses 367-385. As against
Attalus who accused Aratus of redundancy and obscurity,
Hipparchus thinks Aratus has given a masterly exposition
(κεκρατημένως ἀποδεδωκέναι) of what was in his mind, namely,

236

wheel between the Rudder of Argo and Cetus, and beneath the grey Hare's sides they are set without a name. For they are not set like the limbs of a fashioned figure, such as, many in number, fare in order along their constant paths, as the years are fulfilled—stars, which someone of the men that are no more noted and marked how to group in figures and call all by a single name. For it had passed his skill to know each single star or name them one by one. Many are they on every hand and of many the magnitudes and colours are the same, while all go circling round. Wherefore he deemed fit to group the stars in companies, so that in order, set each by other, they might form figures. Hence the constellations got their names, and now no longer does any star rise a marvel from beneath the horizon. Now the other stars are grouped in clear figures and brightly shine, but those beneath the hunted Hare are all clad in mist and nameless in their course.[a]

Below Aegòceros before the blasts of the South wind swims a Fish, facing Cetus, alone and apart from the former Fishes; and him men call the Southern Fish.[b]

Other stars, sparsely set beneath Hydrochoüs,[c] hang on high between Cetus in the heavens and the Fish, dim and nameless, and near them on the right hand of bright Hydrochoüs, like some sprinkled drops of water lightly shed on this side and on that, other stars wheel bright-eyed though weak. But among them are borne two of more lustrous form,

that he who first grouped the stars in constellations decided to group and name only those stars which spatially belonged together, neglecting those which did not naturally form a group or figure.

[b] Piscis Australis.   [c] Aquarius.

237

ARATUS

ἀστέρες, οὔτε τι πολλὸν ἀπήοροι, οὔτε μάλ' ἐγγύς·
εἷς μὲν ὑπ' ἀμφοτέροισι ποσὶν καλός τε μέγας τε
Ὑδροχόου, ὁ δὲ κυανέου ὑπὸ Κήτεος οὐρῇ.
τοὺς πάντας καλέουσιν Ὕδωρ. ὀλίγοι γε μὲν ἄλλοι
νειόθι Τοξευτῆρος ὑπὸ προτέροισι πόδεσσιν
διωτοὶ κύκλῳ περιηγέες εἰλίσσονται.   400

Αὐτὰρ ὑπ' αἰθομένῳ κέντρῳ τέραος μεγάλοιο
Σκορπίου, ἄγχι νότοιο, ΘΥΤΗΡΙΟΝ αἰωρεῖται.
τοῦ δ' ἤτοι ὀλίγον περ ἐπὶ χρόνον ὑψόθ' ἐόντος
πεύσεαι· ἀντιπέρην γὰρ ἀείρεται Ἀρκτούροιο.   405
καὶ τῷ μὲν μάλα πάγχυ μετήοροί εἰσι κέλευθοι
Ἀρκτούρῳ, τὸ δὲ θᾶσσον ὑφ' ἑσπερίην ἅλα νεῖται.
ἀλλ' ἄρα καὶ περὶ κεῖνο Θυτήριον ἀρχαίη Νύξ,
ἀνθρώπων κλαίουσα πόνον, χειμῶνος ἔθηκεν
εἰναλίου μέγα σῆμα. κεδαιόμεναι γὰρ ἐκείνη   410
νῆες ἄπο φρενός εἰσι, τὰ δ' ἄλλοθεν ἄλλα πιφαύ-
        σκει
σήματ', ἐποικτείρουσα πολυρροθίους ἀνθρώπους.
τῷ μή μοι πελάγει νεφέων εἰλυμένον ἄλλων
εὔχεο μεσσόθι κεῖνο φανήμεναι οὐρανῷ ἄστρον,
αὐτὸ μὲν ἀνέφελόν τε καὶ ἀγλαόν, ὕψι δὲ μᾶλλον   415
κυμαίνοντι νέφει πεπιεσμένον, οἷά τε πολλὰ
θλίβετ' ἀναστέλλοντος ὀπωρινοῦ ἀνέμοιο.
πολλάκι γὰρ καὶ τοῦτο νότῳ ἔπι σῆμα τιτύσκει
Νὺξ αὐτή, μογεροῖσι χαριζομένη ναύτῃσιν.
οἱ δ' εἰ μέν κε πίθωνται ἐναίσιμα σημαινούσῃ,   420

---

[a] This is not Sagittarius but the Centaur, usually identified with Cheiron. Both being regarded as centaurs they are often confused. Even the name Cheiron is sometimes used of Sagittarius, e.g. Germanicus, *Arat.* 668.
[b] These form Corona Australis, the Southern Crown, Στέφανος Νότιος.

238

not far apart and yet not near: one beneath both
feet of Hydrochoüs, a goodly star and bright, the
other beneath the tail of dark-blue Cetus. This
cluster as a whole men call The Water. But others
low beneath the forefeet of the Archer (Centaur),[a]
turned in a circled ring,[b] go wheeling round the sky.

Below the fiery sting of the dread monster, Scorpion,
and near the South is hung the Altar.[c] Brief is the
space thou wilt behold it above the horizon: for it
rises over against Arcturus.[d] High runs the path of
Arcturus, but sooner passes the Altar to the western
sea. But that Altar even beyond aught else hath
ancient Night, weeping the woe of men, set to be a
mighty sign of storm at sea. For ships in trouble
pain her heart, and other signs in other quarters she
kindles in sorrow for mariners, storm-buffeted at sea.
Wherefore I bid thee pray, when in the open sea,
that that constellation wrapt in clouds appear not
amidst the others in the heavens, herself unclouded
and resplendent but banked above with billowing
clouds, as often it is beset when the autumn wind
drives them back. For often Night herself reveals
this sign, also, for the South Wind in her kindness to
toiling sailors. If they heed her favouring signs and

---

[c] Ara, fabled to be the altar on which the gods swore
when Zeus proceeded against Cronus : " Inde Nepae [i.e.
Scorpion] cernes propter fulgentis acumen | Aram quam flatu
permulcet spiritus austri," Cic. De nat. d. ii. 44. " Neve
sinisterior pressam rota ducat ad Aram," Ovid, M. ii. 139.

[d] i.e., according to the interpretation of Hipparchus and
Attalus, the Altar is as far from the South Pole (νότιος
πόλος, ἀφανὴς πόλος) as Arcturus is from the visible Pole
(ὁ ἀεὶ φανερὸς πόλος). This, says Hipparchus, is not true, as
Arcturus is 59° from the North Pole, while a, the bright star
in the middle of the Altar, is only 46° from the South Pole
(Hipparch. i. 8. 14 f.).

αἶψά τε κοῦφά τε πάντα καὶ ἄρτια ποιήσωνται,
αὐτίκ' ἐλαφρότερος πέλεται πόνος· εἰ δέ κε νηῒ
ὑψόθεν ἐμπλήξῃ δεινὴ ἀνέμοιο θύελλα
αὔτως ἀπρόφατος, τὰ δὲ λαίφεα πάντα ταράξῃ,
ἄλλοτε μὲν καὶ πάμπαν ὑπόβρυχα ναυτίλλονται,   425
ἄλλοτε δ', αἴ κε Διὸς παρανισσομένοιο τύχωσιν
εὐχόμενοι, βορέω δὲ παραστράψῃ ἀνέμου ἲς,
πολλὰ μάλ' ὀτλήσαντες ὅμως πάλιν ἐσκέψαντο
ἀλλήλους ἐπὶ νηΐ. νότον δ' ἐπὶ σήματι τούτῳ
δείδιθι,[a] μέχρι βορῆος ἀπαστράψαντος ἴδηαι.   430
εἰ δέ κεν ἑσπερίης μὲν ἁλὸς ΚΕΝΤΑΥΡΟΥ ἀπείη
ὦμος[b] ὅσον προτέρης, ὀλίγη δέ μιν εἰλύοι ἀχλὺς
αὐτόν, ἀτὰρ μετόπισθεν ἐοικότα σήματα τεύχοι
Νὺξ ἐπὶ παμφανόωντι Θυτηρίῳ, οὔ σε μάλα χρὴ
ἐς νότον ἀλλ' εὔροιο περισκοπέειν ἀνέμοιο.   435

Δήεις δ' ἄστρον ἐκεῖνο δύω ὑποκείμενον ἄλλοις·
τοῦ γάρ τοι τὰ μὲν ἀνδρὶ ἐοικότα νειόθι κεῖται
Σκορπίου, ἱππούραια δ' ὑπὸ σφίσι Χηλαὶ ἔχουσιν.
αὐτὰρ ὁ δεξιτερὴν αἰεὶ τανύοντι ἔοικεν
ἀντία δινωτοῖο Θυτηρίου, ἐν δέ οἱ ἀπρὶξ   44
ἄλλο μάλ' ἐσφήκωται ἐληλάμενον διὰ χειρὸς
ΘΗΡΙΟΝ·[c] ὣς γάρ μιν πρότεροι ἐπεφημίξαντο.[d]

---

[a] For the gen. after ἴδηαι cf. Aristoph. *Frogs* 815.

[b] *i.e.* when the shoulder of the Centaur culminates
(μεσουρανεῖ). Hipparch. i. 8. 19 ff. complains that Aratus
does not specify which shoulder, which is not a matter of in-
difference, as they would not both culminate at the same time.

[c] Centaur, *cf.* " Propterque Centaurus, ' Cedit equi partes
properans subiungere Chelis. Hic dextram porgens, Quadrupes qua vasta tenetur, Tendit et illustrem truculentus
cedit ad Aram,' " Cic. *De nat. d.* ii. 44.

[d] Hipparch. i. 8. 21 f. says Aratus is wrong here, since
nearly the whole of the Centaur lies under Virgo, only his
right hand and the forelegs of the horse stretching below
the Claws.

quickly lighten their craft and set all in order, on a
sudden lo! their task is easier : but if from on high
a dread gust of wind smite their ship, all unforeseen,
and throw in turmoil all the sails, sometimes they
make their voyage all beneath the waves, but at
other times, if they win by their prayers Zeus to
their aid, and the might of the north wind pass in
lightning, after much toil they yet again see each
other on the ship. But at this sign fear the South
Wind, until thou see'st ^a the North Wind come with
lightning. But if the shoulder of Centaur is as far
from the western as from the eastern sea,^b and a
faint mist veils it, while behind Night kindles like
signs of storm upon the gleaming Altar, thou must not
look for the South, but bethink thee of an East Wind.

The constellation of Centaur^c thou wilt find
beneath two others. For part in human form lies
beneath Scorpio, but the rest, a horse's trunk and
tail, are beneath the Claws.^d He ever seems to
stretch his right hand^e towards the round Altar, but
through his hand is drawn and firmly grasped
another sign—the Beast,^f for so men of old have
named it.

^e Hipparch. i. 8. 23 objects that between his right hand
and the Altar lies the whole of the Beast (Θηρίον) and most
parts of the Scorpion ; cf. v. 402 f.

^f Fera or the Wolf. Manilius i. 440 confuses the Beast
with the Cetus of Andromeda. The Centaur was represented
as holding in his left a *thyrsus* with a Hare hung upon it, in
his right a *Therium*, of what nature the ancients did not de-
fine; cf. Cic. *Arat.* 211 "Hic dextram porgens quadrupes qua
vasta tenetur | Quam nemo certo donavit nomine Graium."
Frequently the Beast is confused with the Hare, but in later
times it is generally known as the Wolf. Cf. [Eratosth.]
Catast. 40 ἔχει δὲ καὶ ἐν ταῖς χερσὶ τὸ λεγόμενον Θηρίον . . .
τινὲς δὲ ἀσκὸν φασιν αὐτὸ εἶναι οἴνου, ἐξ οὗ σπένδει τοῖς θεοῖς ἐπὶ τὸ
Θυτήριον. ἔχει δὲ αὐτὸ ἐν τῇ δεξιᾷ χειρί, ἐν δὲ τῇ ἀριστερᾷ θύρσον.

241

ARATUS

ἈΛΛ' ἔτι γάρ τε καὶ ἄλλο περαιόθεν ἕλκεται
ἄστρον·
ὝΔΡΗΝ μιν καλέουσι. τὸ δὲ ζώοντι ἐοικὸς
ἠνεκὲς εἰλεῖται· καί οἱ κεφαλὴ ὑπὸ μέσσον   445
Καρκίνον ἱκνεῖται, σπείρη δ' ὑπὸ σῶμα Λέοντος,
οὐρὴ δὲ κρέμαται ὑπὲρ αὐτοῦ Κενταύροιο.
μέσση δὲ σπείρη ΚΡΗΤΗΡ, πυμάτη δ' ἐπίκειται
εἴδωλον ΚΟΡΑΚΟΣ σπείρην κόπτοντι ἐοικός.
   Καὶ μὴν καὶ ΠΡΟΚΤΩΝ Διδύμοις ὕπο καλὰ
      φαείνει.   450
   Ταῦτά κε θηήσαιο παρερχομένων ἐνιαυτῶν
ἑξείης παλίνωρα· τὰ γὰρ καὶ πάντα μάλ' αὔτως
οὐρανῷ εὖ ἐνάρηρεν ἀγάλματα νυκτὸς ἰούσης.
   Οἱ δ' ἐπιμὶξ ἄλλοι πέντ' ἀστέρες, οὐδὲν ὁμοῖοι,
παντόθεν εἰδώλων δυοκαίδεκα δινεύονται.   455
οὐκ ἂν ἔτ' εἰς ἄλλους ὁρόων ἐπιτεκμήραιο
κείνους ἧχι κέονται· ἐπεὶ πάντες μετανάσται,
μακροὶ δέ σφεων εἰσὶν ἑλισσομένων ἐνιαυτοί,
μακρὰ δὲ σήματα κεῖται ἀπόπροθεν εἰς ἓν ἰόντων.
οὐδ' ἔτι θαρσαλέος κείνων ἐγώ· ἄρκιος εἴην   460
ἀπλανέων τά τε κύκλα τά τ' αἰθέρι σήματ' ἐνισπεῖν.
   Ἤτοι μὲν τά γε κεῖται ἀλίγκια δινωτοῖσιν
τέσσαρα, τῶν κε μάλιστα πόθη ὄφελός τε γένοιτο

---

^a περαιόθεν occurs four times in Aratus, here and 606, 645,
720. In the last three cases it means "from the Eastern
horizon." The schol. on the present passage says "either
from the East or from a quarter beyond and farther than the
Centaur." ^b Crater, the Cup.
   ^c Corvus, the Crow. Both these small constellations lie
on the back of Hydra.
   ^d Procyon or Canis Minor.
   ^e The Fixed Stars. ^f The Planets.
   ^g The reference, as the scholiast says, is to the "great
Platonick yeere" (Herrick), the μέγας or τέλεος ἐνιαυτός, when
242

Another constellation trails beyond,[a] which men call the Hydra. Like a living creature it winds afar its coiling form. Its head comes beneath the middle of the Crab, its coil beneath the body of the Lion, and its tail hangs above the Centaur himself. Midway on its coiling form is set the Crater,[b] and at the tip the figure of a Raven[c] that seems to peck at the coil.

There, too, by the Hydra beneath the Twins brightly shines Procyon.[d]

All these constellations thou canst mark as the seasons pass, each returning at its appointed time: for all are unchangingly and firmly fixed[e] in the heavens to be the ornaments of the passing night.

But of quite a different class are those five other orbs,[f] that intermingle with them and wheel wandering on every side of the twelve figures of the Zodiac. No longer with the others as thy guide couldst thou mark where lies the path of those, since all pursue a shifty course, and long are the periods of their revolution and far distant lies the goal of their conjunction.[g] When I come to them my daring fails, but mine be the power to tell of the orbits of the Fixed Stars and Signs in heaven.

These orbits[h] lie like rings, four in number, chief in interest and in profit, if thou wouldst mark the

there is a general reversion of nature to the position at the beginning of the period, a so-called ἀποκατάστασις. Then the planets moving in different orbits and with different speeds complete their orbits together (Plato, *Timaeus* 39).

[h] The four rings are the Great Circles of the Equator and the Ecliptic and the smaller circles of the Tropic of Cancer and the Tropic of Capricorn. Thus in size the Equator is equal to the Ecliptic, while the two Tropics are equal to one another.

μέτρα περισκοπέοντι κατανομένων ἐνιαυτῶν.
σήματα δ' εὖ μάλα πᾶσιν ἐπιρρήδην περίκειται 465
πολλά τε καὶ σχεδόθεν πάντη συνεεργμένα πάντα.
αὐτοὶ δ' ἀπλανέες καὶ ἀρηρότες ἀλλήλοισιν
πάντες· ἀτὰρ μέτρῳ γε δύω δυσὶν ἀντιφέρονται.

Εἴ ποτέ τοι νυκτὸς καθαρῆς, ὅτε πάντας
ἀγαυοὺς
ἀστέρας ἀνθρώποις ἐπιδείκνυται οὐρανίη Νύξ, 470
οὐδέ τις ἀδρανέων φέρεται διχόμηνι σελήνη,
ἀλλὰ τά γε κνέφαος διαφαίνεται ὀξέα πάντα—
εἴ ποτέ τοι τημόσδε περὶ φρένας ἵκετο θαῦμα,
σκεψαμένῳ πάντη κεκεασμένον εὐρέϊ κύκλῳ
οὐρανόν, ἢ καί τίς τοι ἐπιστὰς ἄλλος ἔδειξεν 475
κεῖνο περιγληνὲς τροχαλόν, ΓΑΛΑ μιν καλέουσιν·
τῷ δ' ἤτοι χροιὴν μὲν ἀλίγκιος οὐκέτι κύκλος
δινεῖται, τὰ δὲ μέτρα τόσοι πισύρων περ ἐόντων
οἱ δύο, τοὶ δέ σφεων μέγα μείονες εἰλίσσονται.

Τῶν ὅ μὲν ἐγγύθεν ἐστὶ κατερχομένου βορέαο. 480
ἐν δέ οἱ ἀμφότεραι κεφαλαὶ Διδύμων φορέονται,
ἐν δέ τε γούνατα κεῖται ἀρηρότος Ἡνιόχοιο,
λαιὴ δὲ κνήμη καὶ ἀριστερὸς ὦμος ἐπ' αὐτῷ
Περσέος, Ἀνδρομέδης δὲ μέσην ἀγκῶνος ὕπερθεν
δεξιτερὴν ἐπέχει· τὸ μὲν οἱ θέναρ ὑψόθι κεῖται, 485
ἀσσότερον βορέαο, νότῳ δ' ἐπικέκλιται ἀγκών·
ὁπλαὶ δ' Ἵππειοι, καὶ ὑπαύχενον Ὀρνίθειον
ἄκρη σὺν κεφαλῇ, καλοί τ' Ὀφιούχεοι ὦμοι,
αὐτὸν δινεύονται ἐληλάμενοι περὶ κύκλον·
ἡ δ' ὀλίγον φέρεται νοτιωτέρη, οὐδ' ἐπιβάλλει, 49
Παρθένος· ἀλλὰ Λέων καὶ Καρκίνος· οἱ μὲν ἄρ'
ἄμφω
ἐξείης κέαται βεβλημένοι, αὐτὰρ ὁ κύκλος

---

a Hipparch. i. 9. 1 ff. reads ἀπλατέες, *i.e.* without breadth,

measures of the waning and the waxing of the
Seasons. On all are set beacon lights, many in
number, all every way closely penned together.
The circles are immovable,[a] and fitted each to
other, but in size two are matched with two.

If ever on a clear night, when Night in the
heavens shows to men all her stars in their brightness and no star is borne faintly gleaming at the
mid-month moon, but they all sharply pierce the
darkness—if in such an hour wonder rises in thy
heart to mark on every side the heaven cleft by a
broad belt,[b] or if someone at thy side point out that
circle set with brilliants—that is what men call the
Milky Way. A match for it in colour thou wilt find
no circle wheel, but in size two of the four belts are
as large, but the other two are far inferior.

Of the lesser circles one[c] is nigh to Boreas at his
coming, and on it are borne both the heads of the
Twins and the knees of the stedfast Charioteer, and
above him are the left shoulder and shin of Perseus.[d]
It crosses Andromeda's right arm above the elbow.[e]
Above it is set her palm, nearer the north, and southward leans her elbow. The hoofs of the Horse, the
head and neck of the Bird[f] and Ophiuchus' bright
shoulders[g] wheel along this circle in their course.
The Maiden[h] is borne a little to the South and does
not touch the Belt, but on it are the Lion and the
Crab. Thereon are they both established side by

---

which he defends against δὲ πλατέες, which was preferred by
Attalus.
  [b] The Galaxy or Milky Way.   [c] Tropic of Cancer.
  [a] Hipparch. i. 10 disputes these statements ; cf. i. 2.
  [e] Hipparch. i. 10. 6.
  [f] Hipparch. i. 10. 7.   [g] Hipparch. i. 10. 9.
  [h] Virgo, cf. Hipparch. i. 10. 10.

ARATUS

τὸν μὲν ὑπὸ στῆθος καὶ γαστέρα μέχρι παρ' αἰδῶ
τέμνει, τὸν δὲ διηνεκέως ὑπένερθε χελείου
Καρκίνον, ἧχι μάλιστα διχαιόμενόν κε νοήσαις 495
ὀρθόν, ἵν' ὀφθαλμοὶ κύκλου ἑκάτερθεν ἴοιεν.
τοῦ μέν, ὅσον τε μάλιστα, δι' ὀκτὼ μετρηθέντος,
πέντε μὲν ἔνδια στρέφεται καθ' ὑπέρτερα γαίης,
τὰ τρία δ' ἐν περάτῃ· θέρεος δέ οἱ ἐν τροπαί εἰσιν.
ἀλλ' ὁ μὲν ἐν βορέω περὶ Καρκίνον ἐστήρικται. 500

    "Αλλος δ' ἀντιόωντι νότῳ μέσον Αἰγοκερῆα
τέμνει καὶ πόδας Ὑδροχόου καὶ Κήτεος οὐρήν·
ἐν δέ οἵ ἐστι Λαγωός· ἀτὰρ Κυνὸς οὐ μάλα πολλὴν
αἴνυται, ἀλλ' ὁπόσην ἐπέχει ποσίν· ἐν δέ οἱ
Ἀργώ,
καὶ μέγα Κενταύροιο μετάφρενον, ἐν δέ τε κέντρον 505
Σκορπίου, ἐν καὶ Τόξον ἀγαυοῦ Τοξευτῆρος.
τὸν πύματον καθαροῖο παρερχόμενος βορέαο
ἐς νότον ἠέλιος φέρεται· τρέπεταί γε μὲν αὐτοῦ
χειμέριος. καί οἱ τρία μὲν περιτέλλεται ὑψοῦ
τῶν ὀκτώ, τὰ δὲ πέντε κατώρυχα δινεύονται. 51

    Μεσσόθι δ' ἀμφοτέρων, ὅσσος πολιοῖο Γά-
λακτος,
γαῖαν ὑποστρέφεται κύκλος διχόωντι ἐοικώς·
ἐν δέ οἱ ἤματα νυξὶν ἰσαίεται ἀμφοτέρῃσιν,
φθίνοντος θέρεος, τοτὲ δ' εἴαρος ἱσταμένοιο.
σῆμα δέ οἱ Κριὸς Ταύροιό τε γούνατα κεῖται, 5
Κριὸς μὲν κατὰ μῆκος ἐληλάμενος διὰ κύκλου,
Ταύρου δὲ σκελέων ὅσση περιφαίνεται ὀκλάξ.
ἐν δέ τέ οἱ ζώνη εὐφεγγέος Ὠρίωνος

---

[a] Hipparch. i. 3. 5 ff., i. 9. 10.
[b] Summer Solstice, the longest day, 22nd June.
[c] Tropic of Capricorn, Hipparch. i. 2. 21, i. 10. 16.
[d] Winter Solstice, the shortest day, 22nd December.

246

side, but the circle cuts the Lion beneath breast and belly lengthwise to the loins, and the Crab it cuts clean through by the shell where thou canst see him most clearly cut, as he stands upright with his eyes on either side of the Belt. The circle is divided, as well as may be, into eight parts, whereof five in the daytime wheel on high above the earth and three beneath the horizon.[a] In it is the Turning-point of the Sun in summer.[b] This circle is set round the Crab in the North.

But there is another circle[c] to match in the South. It cuts through the middle of Aegoceros, the feet of Hydrochoüs, and the tail of the sea-monster, Cetus, and on it is the Hare. It claims no great share of the Dog, but only the space that he occupies with his feet. In it is Argo and the mighty back of the Centaur, the sting of Scorpio, and the Bow of the bright Archer. This circle the sun passes last as he is southward borne from the bright north, and here is the Turning-point of the sun in winter.[d] Three parts of eight of his course are above and five below the horizon.

Between the Tropics a Belt,[e] peer of the grey Milky Way, undergirds the earth and with imaginary line bisects the sphere. In it the days are equal to the nights[f] both at the waning of the summer and the waxing of the spring. The sign appointed for it is the Ram[g] and the knees of the Bull—the Ram being borne lengthwise through it, but of the Bull just the visible bend of the knees. In it are the Belt of the well-starred Orion and the coil of the

---

[e] The κύκλος ἰσημερινός or Equator, a Great Circle like the Milky Way.

[f] Spring and Autumn Equinoxes, Hipparch. i. 9. 9.

[g] Hipparch. i. 10. 18 ff.

καμπῇ τ' αἰθομένης Ὕδρης· ἐνί οἱ καὶ ἐλαφρὸς
Κρητήρ, ἐν δὲ Κόραξ, ἐνὶ δ' ἀστέρες οὐ μάλα
   πολλοί   520
Χηλάων· ἐν τῷ δ' Ὀφιούχεα γοῦνα φορεῖται.
οὐ μὴν Αἰητοῦ ἀπαμείρεται, ἀλλά οἱ ἐγγὺς
Ζηνὸς ἀητεῖται μέγας ἄγγελος. ἡ δὲ κατ' αὐτὸν
ἱππείη κεφαλὴ καὶ ὑπαύχενον εἰλίσσονται.

    Τοὺς μὲν παρβολάδην ὀρθοὺς περιβάλλεται
   ἄξων   525
μεσσόθι πάντας ἔχων· ὁ δὲ τέτρατος ἐσφήκωται
λοξὸς ἐν ἀμφοτέροις, οἵ μίν ῥ' ἑκάτερθεν ἔχουσιν
ἀντιπέρην τροπικοί, μέσσος δέ ἑ μεσσόθι τέμνει.
οὔ κεν Ἀθηναίης χειρῶν δεδιδαγμένος ἀνὴρ
ἄλλῃ κολλήσαιτο κυλινδόμενα τροχάλεια   530
τοῖά τε καὶ τόσα πάντα περισφαιρηδὸν ἑλίσσων,
ὣς τά γ' ἐναιθέρια πλαγίῳ συναρηρότα κύκλῳ
ἐξ ἠοῦς ἐπὶ νύκτα διώκεται ἤματα πάντα.
καὶ τὰ μὲν ἀντέλλει καὶ αὐτίκα νειόθι δύνει
πάντα παραβλήδην· μία δέ σφεων ἐστὶν ἑκάστου 535
ἑξείης ἑκάτερθε κατηλυσίη τ' ἄνοδός τε.
αὐτὰρ ὅ γ' ὠκεανοῦ τόσσον παραμείβεται ὕδωρ,
ὅσσον ἀπ' Αἰγοκερῆος ἀνερχομένοιο μάλιστα
Καρκίνον εἰς ἀνιόντα κυλίνδεται· ὅσσον ἀπάντῃ
ἀντέλλων ἐπέχει, τόσσον γε μὲν ἀλλόθι δύνων.   54•
ὅσσον δ' ὀφθαλμοῖο βολῆς ἀποτέμνεται αὐγή,
ἑξάκις ἂν τόσση μιν ὑποδράμοι. αὐτὰρ ἑκάστη
ἴσῃ μετρηθεῖσα δύω περιτέμνεται ἄστρα.
Ζῴδιον δέ ἑ κύκλον ἐπίκλησιν καλέουσιν.

---

    [a] Or " is blown "; ἀητεῖται is ἅπ. λεγ., see v. 315.
    [b] Tropic of Cancer, Tropic of Capricorn, and the Equator.
    [c] Ecliptic, κύκλος λοξός, *circulus obliquus*, the apparent path
of the Sun in the heavens.

gleaming Hydra: in it, too, the dim-lit Crater and
the Crow and the scanty-starred Claws and the
knees of Ophiuchus are borne. But it has no share
in the Eagle, but near it flies [a] the mighty messenger
of Zeus. Facing the Eagle wheel the head and
neck of the Horse.

These three Belts [b] are parallel, and at right angles
to the Axis which they surround and which is the
centre of them all, but the fourth [c] aslant is fixed
athwart the Tropics: they on opposite sides of the
Equator support it at either limit, but the Equator
bisects it. Not otherwise would a man skilled in
the handicraft of Athena join the whirling Belts,
wheeling them all around, so many and so great like
rings, just as the Belts in the heavens, clasped by
the transverse circle, hasten from dawn to night
throughout all time. The three Belts [d] rise and set
all parallel but ever single and the same is the point
where in due order each rises or sets at East or West.
But the fourth circle passes over as much water of
ocean [e] as rolls between the rising of Aegoceros, and
the rising of the Crab: as much as it occupies in
rising, so much it occupies in setting. As long as is
the ray cast to heaven from the glance of the eye, six
times as long a line would subtend this Belt. Each
ray, measured of equal length, intercepts two constellations.[f] This circle is called the Belt of the Zodiac.

[d] Hipparch. ii. 1. 17.

[e] The distance between the point of the horizon (ocean)
where the Sun rises at Mid-Winter and the point where he
rises at Mid-Summer.

[f] Each side of a regular hexagon inscribed in a circle is
equal to the radius of the circle (Euclid iv. 15). If the
earth be regarded as the centre of the celestial sphere, the
ray cast from the eye of the observer to the vault of heaven

Τῷ ἔνι Καρκίνος ἐστί, Λέων δ' ἐπὶ τῷ, καὶ ὑπ'
αὐτὸν 545
Παρθένος· αἱ δ' ἐπί οἱ Χηλαὶ καὶ Σκορπίος αὐτός,
Τοξευτής τε καὶ Αἰγόκερως, ἐπὶ δ' Αἰγοκερῆϊ
Ὑδροχόος· δύο δ' αὐτὸν ὑπ' Ἰχθύες ἀστερόωνται·
τοὺς δὲ μέτα Κριός, Ταυρός δ' ἐπὶ τῷ Δίδυμοί τε.
ἐν τοῖς ἠέλιος φέρεται δυοκαίδεκα πᾶσιν 550
πάντ' ἐνιαυτὸν ἄγων, καί οἱ περὶ τοῦτον ἰόντι
κύκλον ἀέξονται πᾶσαι ἐπικάρπιοι ὧραι.

Τοῦ δ' ὅσσον κοίλοιο κατ' ὠκεανοῖο δύηται,
τόσσον ὑπὲρ γαίης φέρεται· πάσῃ δ' ἐπὶ νυκτὶ
ἐξ αἰεὶ δύνουσι δυωδεκάδες κύκλοιο, 555
τόσσαι δ' ἀντέλλουσι. τόσον δ' ἐπὶ μῆκος ἑκάστη
νὺξ αἰεὶ τετάνυσται, ὅσον τέ περ ἥμισυ κύκλου
ἀρχομένης ἀπὸ νυκτὸς ἀείρεται ὑψόθι γαίης.

Οὔ κεν ἀπόβλητον δεδοκημένῳ ἤματος εἴη 560
μοιράων σκέπτεσθαι ὅτ' ἀντέλλησιν ἑκάστη·
αἰεὶ γὰρ τάων γε μιῇ συνανέρχεται αὐτὸς
ἠέλιος. τὰς δ' ἄν κε περισκέψαιο μάλιστα
εἰς αὐτὰς ὁρόων· ἀτὰρ εἰ νεφέεσσι μέλαιναι
γίνοιντ' ἢ ὄρεος κεκρυμμέναι ἀντέλλοιεν,
σήματ' ἐπερχομένῃσιν ἀρηρότα ποιήσασθαι. 565
αὐτὸς δ' ἄν μάλα τοι κεράων ἑκάτερθε διδοίη
Ὠκεανός, τά τε πολλὰ περιστρέφεται ἑοῖ αὐτῷ,
νειόθεν ὁππῆμος κείνων φορέῃσιν ἑκάστην.

Οὔ οἱ ἀφαυρότατοι, ὅτε ΚΑΡΚΙΝΟΣ ἀντέλλησιν,
ἀστέρες ἀμφοτέρωθεν ἑλισσόμενοι περίκεινται, 570

is the radius of the sphere, and six lines of that length will
give the inscribed regular hexagon. Each of those sides
will subtend an arc of the sphere containing two signs of the
Zodiac. Bisect each side, and each half side will correspond
to one sign. This method of describing the Zodiac is what

250

PHAENOMENA

In it is the Crab; after the Crab the Lion and beneath him the Maiden; after the Maiden the Claws and the Scorpion himself and the Archer and Aegoceros, and after Aegoceros Hydrochoüs. Beneath him are enstarred the Two Fishes and after them the Ram and next the Bull and the Twins. In them, twelve in all, has the sun his course as he leads on the whole year, and as he fares around this belt, all the fruitful seasons have their growth.

Half this Belt is set below the hollow of the horizon, and half is above the earth. Every night six constellations of this circle's twelve set and as many rise; as long is each night ever stretched as half the belt rises above the earth from the fall of night.[a]

Not useless were it for one who seeks for signs of coming day to mark when each sign of the Zodiac rises. For ever with one of them the sun himself rises. One could best search out those constellations by looking on themselves, but if they be dark with clouds or rise hidden behind a hill, get thee fixed signs for their coming. Ocean himself will give thee signs at either horn—the East or the West—in the many constellations that wheel about him, when from below he sends forth each rising sign.

Not very faint are the wheeling constellations that are set about Ocean at East or West, when the Crab

Vergil refers to in *Ecl.* iii. 40 ff. "In medio duo signa, Conon et—quis fuit alter Descripsit radio totum qui gentibus orbem, Tempora quae messor, quae curvus arator haberet?" Our "ray" is, of course, derived from *radius*.

[a] The Zodiac is a Great Circle and therefore is bisected by any other Great Circle, *e.g.* the horizon. Now day lasts while the Sun is above the horizon. When the Sun is setting a half circle of the Zodiac has risen since his rising, *i.e.* six zodiacal signs.

ARATUS

τοὶ μὲν δύνοντες, τοὶ δ' ἐξ ἑτέρης ἀνιόντες.
δύνει μὲν Στέφανος, δύνει δὲ κατὰ ῥάχιν Ἰχθύς.
ἥμισυ μέν κεν ἴδοιο μετήορον, ἥμισυ δ' ἤδη
ἐσχατιαὶ βάλλουσι κατερχομένου Στεφάνοιο.
αὐτὰρ ὅ γ' ἐξόπιθεν τετραμμένος ἄλλα μὲν οὔπω   575
γαστέρι νειαίρῃ, τὰ δ' ὑπέρτερα νυκτὶ φορεῖται.
τὸν δὲ καὶ εἰς ὤμους κατάγει μογερὸν Ὀφιοῦχον
Καρκίνος ἐκ γονάτων, κατάγει δ' Ὄφιν αὐχένος
    ἐγγύς.
οὐδ' ἂν ἔτ' Ἀρκτοφύλαξ εἴη πολὺς ἀμφοτέρωθεν,
μείων ἡμάτιος, τὸ δ' ἐπὶ πλέον ἔννυχος ἤδη.   580
τέτρασι γὰρ μοίραις ἄμυδις κατιόντα Βοώτην
Ὠκεανὸς δέχεται· ὁ δ' ἐπὴν φάεος κορέσηται,
βουλυτῷ ἐπέχει πλεῖον δίχα νυκτὸς ἰούσης,
ἦμος ὅτ' ἠελίοιο κατερχομένοιο δύηται.
κεῖναί οἱ καὶ νύκτες ἐπ' ὀψὲ δύοντι λέγονται.   585
ὡς οἱ μὲν δύνουσιν, ὁ δ' ἀντίος, οὐδὲν ἀεικής,
ἀλλ' εὖ μὲν ζώνῃ, εὖ δ' ἀμφοτέροισι φαεινὸς
ὤμοις Ὠρίων, ξίφεός γε μὲν ἶφι πεποιθώς,
πάντα φέρων Ποταμόν, κέραος παρατείνεται ἄλλου.
    Ἐρχομένῳ δὲ ΛΕΟΝΤΙ τὰ μὲν κατὰ πάντα
        φέρονται   590
Καρκίνῳ ὅσσ' ἐδύοντο, καὶ Αἰετός. αὐτὰρ ὅ γε
    Γνὺξ

---

[a] i.e. facing the East; or reversed, i.e. standing upon his
head, cf. 620 (Hipparch. ii. 16), 669.   Hence in later times
he is also θεός τις κατακέφαλα κείμενος.   The peculiarity of his
rising feet-foremost and setting head-foremost (Hygin. *Astr.*
iii. 5 "Hic occidens capite prius quam reliquo corpore devenit
ad terram; qui cum totus occidit ut pendere pedibus
ex Arctico circulo videatur, exoriens ante pedibus quam
reliquis membris ") is referred to by Manilius v. 645 ff.   He
who is born under this constellation—" Nixa genu species et

rises, some setting in the West and others rising in
the East. The Crown sets and the Southern Fish as
far as its back. Half the setting Crown is visible in
the sky but half already sinks beneath the verge.
Of Engonasin, backward turned,[a] the waist is still
visible but his upper parts are borne in night. The
rise of the Crab brings down from knee to shoulder
the wretched Ophiuchus and Ophis to the neck. No
longer great on both sides of the horizon is Arctophylax but only the lesser portion is visible, while the
greater part is wrapt in night. For with four signs [b]
of the Zodiac Boötes sets and is received in the
bosom of ocean; and when he is sated with the
light he takes till past midnight in the loosing of
his oxen,[c] in the season when he sets with the sinking sun. Those nights are named after his late
setting. So these stars are setting, but another,
facing them, no dim star, even Orion with glittering
belt and shining shoulders and trusting in the might
of his sword, and bringing all the River,[d] rises from
the other horn, the East.

At the coming of the Lion those constellations
wholly set, which were setting when the Crab rose,
and with them sets the Eagle. But the Phantom

Graio nomine dicta Engonasi (ignota facies sub origine
constat)"—will be plotter and a footpad, or—a tight-rope
walker : "Et si forte aliquas animis exsurget in artes | In
praerupta dabit studium vendetque periclo | Ingenium. Ac
tenues ausus sine limite grassus | Certa per extentos ponet
vestigia funes, At caeli meditatus iter vestigia perdet |
Paene sua et pendens populum suspendet ab ipso."

[b] Hipparch. ii. 19.
[c] Boötes takes a long time to set because he sets in a
perpendicular position, while he rises quickly (608) because
he is in a horizontal position (Hipparch. ii. 17 ff.).
[d] Eridanus.

ARATUS

ἥμενος ἄλλα μὲν ἤδη, ἀτὰρ γόνυ καὶ πόδα λαιὸν
οὔπω κυμαίνοντος ὑποστρέφει ὠκεανοῖο.
ἀντέλλει δ' Ὕδρης κεφαλὴ χαροπός τε Λαγωὸς
καὶ Προκύων πρότεροί τε πόδες Κυνὸς αἰθομένοιο. 595
    Οὐ μέν θην ὀλίγους γαίης ὑπὸ νείατα βάλλει
ΠΑΡΘΕΝΟΣ ἀντέλλουσα. Λύρη τότε Κυλληναίη
καὶ Δελφὶς δύνουσι καὶ εὐποίητος Ὀϊστός·
σὺν τοῖς Ὄρνιθος πρῶτα πτερὰ μέσφα παρ' αὐτὴν
οὐρὴν καὶ Ποταμοῖο παρηορίαι σκιόωνται· 600
δύνει δ' Ἱππείη κεφαλή, δύνει δὲ καὶ αὐχήν.
ἀντέλλει δ' Ὕδρη μὲν ἐπὶ πλέον ἄχρι παρ' αὐτὸν
Κρητῆρα, φθάμενος δὲ Κύων πόδας αἴνυται ἄλλους,
ἕλκων ἐξόπιθεν πρύμνην πολυτειρέος Ἀργοῦς.
ἡ δὲ θέει γαίης ἱστὸν διχόωσα κατ' αὐτόν, 605
Παρθένος ἦμος ἅπασα περαιόθεν ἄρτι γένηται.
    Οὐδ' ἂν ἐπερχόμεναι ΧΗΛΑΙ, καὶ λεπτὰ φάουσαι,
ἄφραστοι παρίοιεν, ἐπεὶ μέγα σῆμα Βοώτης
ἀθρόος ἀντέλλει βεβολημένος Ἀρκτούροιο.
Ἀργὼ δ' εὖ[1] μάλα πᾶσα μετήορος ἔσσεται ἤδη· 610
ἀλλ' Ὕδρη, κέχυται γὰρ ἐν οὐρανῷ ἤλιθα πολλή,
οὐρῆς ἂν δεύοιτο. μόνην δ' ἐπὶ Χηλαὶ ἄγουσιν[2]
δεξιτερὴν κνήμην αὐτῆς ἐπιγουνίδος ἄχρις
αἰεὶ Γνύξ, αἰεὶ δὲ Λύρη παραπεπτηῶτος, 615
ὄντινα τοῦτον ἄϊστον ὑπουρανίων εἰδώλων
ἀμφότερον δύνοντα καὶ ἐξ ἑτέρης ἀνιόντα
πολλάκις αὐτονυχεὶ θηεύμεθα. τοῦ μὲν ἄρ' οἴη
κνήμη σὺν Χηλῇσι φαείνεται ἀμφοτέρῃσιν·
αὐτὸς δ' ἐς κεφαλὴν ἔτι που τετραμμένος ἄλλη 620
Σκορπίον ἀντέλλοντα μένει καὶ ῥύτορα Τόξου·

[1] εὖ Hipparch. cod. L ii. 2. 42. Cf. Cic. Arat. 396
"Totaque iam supera fulgens prolabitur Argo"; German.
617 "Celsaque puppis habet"; Avien. 1133 "iam celso
Thessala puppis Aethere subvehitur"; οὐ ACM and schol.

254

PHAENOMENA

On His Knees sinks all save knee and left foot
beneath the stormy ocean. Up rises the Hydra's
head and the bright-eyed Hare and Procyon and
the forefeet of the flaming Dog.

Not few, either, are the constellations which the
Maiden at her rising sends beneath the verge of
earth. Then set the Cyllenian Lyre, the Dolphin
and the shapely Arrow. With them the wing-tips
of the Bird [a] up to her very tail and the farthest
reaches of the River are overshadowed. The head of
the Horse [b] sets, sets too his neck. The Hydra rises
higher as far as Crater, and before her the Dog brings
up his hind feet, dragging behind him the stern of
Argo of many stars. And she rises above the earth,
cleft right at the mast, just when the whole of the
Maiden has risen.

Nor can the rising Claws, though faintly shining,
pass unremarked, when at a bound [c] the mighty sign
of Boötes rises, jewelled with Arcturus.[d] Aloft is
risen all of Argo, but the Hydra, shed as she is afar
over the heavens, will lack her tail. The Claws bring
only the right leg as far as the thigh of that Phantom
that is ever On his Knees, ever crouching by the Lyre
—that Phantom, unknown among the figures of the
heavens, whom we often see both rise and set on the
selfsame night. Of him only the leg is visible at the
rising of both the Claws: he himself head-down-
ward [e] on the other side awaits the rising Scorpion
and the Drawer of the Bow.[f] For they bring him:

[a] Cygnus. [b] Pegasus. [c] See 585 n.
[d] The brightest star in Boötes (α Bootis).
[e] Cf. 575. [f] Sagittarius.

---

[2] 613 δεινὸν ἐφεστηῶτ' Ὀφιουχέα· τοῦ μὲν ἔπειτα A; om.
CM.

ARATUS

οἱ γάρ μιν φορέουσιν, ὁ μὲν μέσον ἄλλα τε πάντα,
χεῖρα δέ οἱ σκαιὴν κεφαλὴν θ' ἅμα Τόξον ἀγινεῖ.
ἀλλ' ὁ μὲν ὣς τρίχα πάντα καταμελεϊστὶ φορεῖται·
ἥμισυ δὲ Στεφάνοιο καὶ αὐτὴν ἔσχατον οὐρὴν
Κενταύρου φορέουσιν ἀνερχόμεναι ἔτι Χηλαί.   625
τῆμος ἀποιχομένην κεφαλὴν μέτα δύεται Ἵππος,
καὶ προτέρου Ὄρνιθος ἐφέλκεται ἔσχατος οὐρή.
δύνει δ' Ἀνδρομέδης κεφαλή· τὸ δέ οἱ μέγα δεῖμα
Κήτεος ἠερόεις ἐπάγει νότος· ἀντία δ' αὐτὸς
Κηφεὺς ἐκ βορέω μεγάλῃ ἀνὰ χειρὶ κελεύει.   630
καὶ τὸ μὲν ἐς λοφιὴν τετραμμένον ἄχρι παρ' αὐτὴν
δύνει, ἀτὰρ Κηφεὺς κεφαλῇ καὶ χειρὶ καὶ ὤμῳ.

    Καμπαὶ δ' ἂν Ποταμοῖο καὶ αὐτίκ' ἐπερχομένοιο
ΣΚΟΡΠΙΟΥ ἐμπίπτοιεν εὐρρόου ὠκεανοῖο·
ὃς καὶ ἐπερχόμενος φοβέει μέγαν Ὠρίωνα.   635
Ἄρτεμις ἱλήκοι· προτέρων λόγος, οἵ μιν ἔφαντο
ἑλκῆσαι πέπλοιο, Χίῳ ὅτε θηρία πάντα
καρτερὸς Ὠρίων στιβαρῇ ἐπέκοπτε κορύνῃ,
θήρης ἀρνύμενος κείνῳ χάριν Οἰνοπίωνι.
ἡ δέ οἱ ἐξαυτῆς ἐπετείλατο θηρίον ἄλλο,   640
νήσου ἀναρρήξασα μέσας ἑκάτερθε κολώνας,
Σκορπίον, ὅς ῥά μιν οὖτα καὶ ἔκτανε πολλὸν ἐόντα
πλειότερος προφανείς, ἐπεὶ Ἄρτεμιν ἤκαχεν αὐτήν.
τούνεκα δὴ καί φασι περαιόθεν ἐρχομένοιο
Σκορπίου Ὠρίωνα περὶ χθονὸς ἔσχατα φεύγειν.   645
οὐδὲ μέν, Ἀνδρομέδης καὶ Κήτεος ὅσσ' ἐλέλειπτο,
κείνου ἔτ' ἀντέλλοντος ἀπευθέες, ἀλλ' ἄρα καὶ τοὶ
πανσυδίῃ φεύγουσιν. ὁ δὲ ζώνῃ τότε Κηφεὺς
γαῖαν ἐπιξύει, τὰ μὲν ἐς κεφαλὴν μάλα πάντα
βάπτων ὠκεανοῖο, τὰ δ' οὐ θέμις, ἀλλὰ τά γ'   650
      αὐταὶ
Ἄρκτοι κωλύουσι, πόδας καὶ γοῦνα καὶ ἰξύν.

256

PHAENOMENA

Scorpion brings his waist and all aforesaid; the Bow
his left hand and head. Even so in three portions is
he all brought up piecemeal above the horizon.
Half the Crown and the tip of the Centaur's tail are
upraised with the rising Claws. Then is the Horse
setting after his vanished head, and dragged below
is the tail-tip of the Bird,[a] already set. The head of
Andromeda is setting and against her is brought by
the misty South the mighty terror, Cetus, but over
against him in the North Cepheus with mighty hand
upraised warns him back. Cetus, neck downward,
sets to his neck, and Cepheus with head and hand
and shoulder.

The winding River[b] will straightway sink in fair
flowing ocean at the coming of Scorpion, whose
rising puts to flight even the mighty Orion. Thy
pardon, Artemis, we crave! There is a tale told by
the men of old, who said that stout Orion laid hands
upon her robe, what time in Chios he was smiting
with his strong club all manner of beasts, as a service
of the hunt to that King Oenopion. But she forth-
with rent in twain the surrounding hills of the
island and roused against him another kind of beast
—even the Scorpion, who proving mightier wounded
him, mighty though he was, and slew him, for that
he had vexed Artemis. Wherefore, too, men say
that at the rising of the Scorpion in the East Orion
flees at the Western verge. Nor does what was left
of Andromeda and of Cetus fail to mark his rise but
in full career they too flee. In that hour the belt of
Cepheus grazes earth as he dips his upper parts in
the sea, but the rest he may not—his feet and knees
and loins, for the Bears themselves forbid. The

[a] Cygnus.   [b] Eridanus.

257

ἡ δὲ καὶ αὐτὴ παιδὸς ἐπείγεται εἰδώλοιο
δειλὴ Κασσιέπεια. τὰ δ' οὐκέτι οἱ κατὰ κόσμον
φαίνεται ἐκ δίφροιο, πόδες καὶ γούναθ' ὕπερθεν,   655
ἀλλ' ἥ γ' ἐς κεφαλὴν ἴση δύετ' ἀρνευτῆρι
μειρομένη γονάτων, ἐπεὶ οὐκ ἄρ' ἔμελλεν ἐκείνη
Δωρίδι καὶ Πανόπῃ μεγάλων ἄτερ ἰσώσασθαι.
ἡ μὲν ἄρ' εἰς ἑτέρην φέρεται· τὰ δὲ νειόθεν ἄλλα
οὐρανὸς ἀντιφέρει, Στεφάνοιό τε δεύτερα κύκλα   660
Ὕδρης τ' ἐσχατιήν, φορέει τ' ἔπι Κενταύροιο
σῶμά τε καὶ κεφαλὴν καὶ Θηρίον ὅ ῥ' ἐνὶ χειρὶ
δεξιτερῇ Κένταυρος ἔχει. τοὶ δ' αὖθι μένουσιν
τόξον ἐπερχόμενον πρότεροι πόδες ἱππότα Φηρός.

Τόξῳ καὶ σπείρῃ Ὄφιος καὶ σῶμ' Ὀφιούχου   665
ἀντέλλει ἐπιόντι· καρήατα δ' αὐτὸς ἀγινεῖ
Σκορπίος ἀντέλλων, ἀνάγει δ' αὐτὰς Ὀφιούχου
χεῖρας καὶ προτέρην Ὄφιος πολυτειρέος ἀγήν.[1]
τοῦ γε μὲν Ἐγγόνασιν, περὶ γὰρ τετραμμένος αἰεὶ
ἀντέλλει, τότε μὲν περάτης ἐξέρχεται ἄλλα,   670
γυῖά τε καὶ ζώνη καὶ στήθεα πάντα καὶ ὦμος
δεξιτερῇ σὺν χειρί· κάρη δ' ἑτέρης μετὰ χειρὸς
Τόξῳ ἀνέρχονται καὶ ΤΟΞΟΤΗΙ ἀντέλλοντι.
σὺν τοῖς Ἑρμαίη τε Λύρη καὶ στήθεος ἄχρις
Κηφεὺς ἠῴου παρελαύνεται ὠκεανοῖο,   675
ἦμος καὶ μεγάλοιο Κυνὸς πᾶσαι ἀμαρυγαὶ
δύνουσιν, καὶ πάντα κατέρχεται Ὠρίωνος,
πάντα γε μὴν ἀτέλεστα διωκομένοιο Λαγωοῦ.
ἀλλ' οὐχ Ἡνιόχῳ Ἔριφοι οὐδ' Ὠλενίη Αἶξ
εὐθὺς ἀπέρχονται· τὰ δέ οἱ μεγάλην ἀνὰ χεῖρα   680

---

[1] ἀγήν (with υ erased) M; αὐγήν AC.

hapless Cassiepeia herself too hastes after the figure of her child.[a] No longer in seemly wise does she shine upon her throne, feet and knees withal, but she headlong plunges like a diver, parted at the knees; for not scatheless was she to rival Doris and Panope.[b] So she is borne towards the West, but other signs in the East the vault of heaven brings from below, the remaining half of the Crown[c] and the tail of the Hydra, and uplifts the body and head of the Centaur and the Beast that the Centaur holds in his right hand. But the fore-feet of the Centaur-Knight[d] await the rising of the Bow.

At the coming of the Bow up rises the coil of the Serpent and the body of Ophiuchus. Their heads the rising of the Scorpion himself brings and raises even the hands of Ophiuchus and the foremost coil of the star-bespangled Serpent. Then emerge from below some parts of Engonasin, who ever rises feet-foremost,[e] to wit, his legs, waist, all his breast, his shoulder with his right hand; but his other hand and his head arise with the rising Bow and the Archer. With them the Lyre of Hermes and Cepheus to his breast drive up from the Eastern Ocean, what time all the rays of the mighty Dog are sinking and all of Orion setting, yea, all the Hare, which the Dog pursues in an unending race. But not yet depart the Kids of the Charioteer and the Arm-borne (Olenian) Goat[f]; by his great hand

---

[c] *i.e.* of Corona Borealis (*cf.* 625), as Hipparchus, who agrees with the statement, interprets τὸ λοιπὸν τοῦ Στεφάνου. Grotius wrongly supposed the words to mean Corona Australis—which was unknown to Aratus under that name. See 401 *n.*

[d] Φήρ of the Centaur, as in Pind. *P.* iv. 119, iii. 6, etc.

[e] *Cf.* 620 *n.*   [f] *Cf.* 164 *n.*

λάμπονται, καί οἱ μελέων διακέκριται ἄλλων
κινῆσαι χειμῶνας ὅτ' ἠελίῳ συνίωσιν.
   Ἀλλὰ τὰ μὲν, κεφαλήν τε καὶ ἄλλην χεῖρα καὶ
ἰξύν,
ΑΙΓΟΚΕΡΩΣ ἀνιὼν κατάγει· τὰ δὲ νείατα πάντα
αὐτῷ Τοξευτῆρι κατέρχεται. οὐδέ τι Περσεὺς   685
οὐδέ τι ἄκρα κόρυμβα μένει πολυτείρεος Ἀργοῦς·
ἀλλ' ἤτοι Περσεὺς μὲν ἄτερ γουνός τε ποδός τε
δεξιτεροῦ δύεται, πρύμνης δ' ὅσον ἐς περιαγήν·
αὐτὴ δ' Αἰγοκερῆι κατέρχεται ἀντέλλοντι,
ἧμος καὶ Προκύων δύεται, τὰ δ' ἀνέρχεται ἄλλα,   690
Ὄρνις τ' Αἰητός τε τά τε πτερόεντος Ὀϊστοῦ
τείρεα καὶ νοτίοιο Θυτηρίου ἱερὸς ἕδρη.
   Ἵππος δ' ὙΔΡΟΧΟΟΙΟ νέον περιτελλομένοιο
ποσσί τε καὶ κεφαλῇ ἀνελίσσεται· ἀντία δ' Ἵππου
ἐξ οὐρῆς Κένταυρον ἐφέλκεται ἀστερίη Νύξ.   695
ἀλλ' οὐ οἱ δύναται κεφαλὴν οὐδ' εὐρέας ὤμους
αὐτῷ σὺν θώρηκι χαδεῖν. ἀλλ' αἴθοπος Ὕδρης
αὐχενίην κατάγει σπείρην καὶ πάντα μέτωπα.
ἡ δὲ καὶ ἐξόπιθεν πολλὴ μένει· ἀλλ' ἄρα καὶ τὴν
αὐτῷ Κενταύρῳ, ὁπότ' ΙΧΘΥΕΣ ἀντέλλωσιν,   700
ἀθρόον ἐμφέρεται. ὁ δ' ἐπ' Ἰχθύσιν ἔρχεται Ἰχθὺς
αὐτῷ κυανέῳ ὑποκείμενος Αἰγοκερῆι,
οὐ μὲν ἄδην, ὀλίγον δὲ δυωδεκάδ' ἀμμένει ἄλλην.
οὕτω καὶ μογεραὶ χεῖρες καὶ γοῦνα καὶ ὦμοι
Ἀνδρομέδης δίχα πάντα, τὰ μὲν πάρος, ἄλλα δ'
ὀπίσσω,   70
τείνεται, ὠκεανοῖο νέον ὁπότε προγένωνται
Ἰχθύες ἀμφότεροι. τὰ μέν οἱ κατὰ δεξιὰ χειρὸς
αὐτοὶ ἐφέλκονται, τὰ δ' ἀριστερὰ νειόθεν ἕλκει
ΚΡΙΟΣ ἀνερχόμενος. τοῦ καὶ περιτελλομένοιο
ἑσπερόθεν κεν ἴδοιο Θυτήριον· αὐτὰρ ἐν ἄλλῃ   71

they shine, and are eminent beyond all his other limbs in raising storms, when they fare with the sun.

His head, hand and waist set at the rising of Aegoceros [a] : from waist to foot he sets at the rising of the Archer. Nor do Perseus and the end of the stern of jewelled Argo remain on high, but Perseus sets all save his knee and right foot and Argo is gone save her curved stern. She sinks wholly at the rising of Aegoceros, when Procyon sets too, and there rise the Bird [b] and the Eagle and the gems of the winged Arrow and the sacred Altar, that is established in the South.

When Hydrochoüs [c] is just risen, up wheel the feet and head of the Horse. But opposite the Horse starry Night draws the Centaur, tail-first, beneath the horizon, but cannot yet engulf his head and his broad shoulders, breast and all. But she sinks beneath the verge the coiling neck and all the brow of the gleaming Hydra. Yet many a coil of the Hydra remains, but Night engulfs her wholly with the Centaur, when the Fishes rise ; with the Fishes the Fish [d] which is placed beneath azure Aegoceros rises—not completely but part awaits another sign of the Zodiac. So the weary hands and knees and shoulders of Andromeda are parted —stretched some below and others above the horizon, when the Two Fishes are newly risen from the ocean. Her right side the Fishes bring, but the left the rising Ram. [e] When the latter rises, the Altar is seen setting in the West, while in the

---

[a] Capricorn.   [b] Cygnus.   [c] Aquarius.
[d] The Southern Fish, Piscis Australis.
[e] Aries.

Περσέος ἀντέλλοντος ὅσον κεφαλήν τε καὶ ὤμους.
  Αὐτὴ δὲ ζώνη καί κ' ἀμφήριστα πέλοιτο
ἢ Κριῷ λήγοντι φαείνεται ἢ ἐπὶ ΤΑΥΡΩΙ,
σὺν τῷ πανσυδίῃ ἀνελίσσεται. οὐδ' ὅ γε Ταύρου
λείπεται ἀντέλλοντος, ἐπεὶ μάλα οἱ συναρηρὼς   715
Ἡνίοχος φέρεται· μοίρῃ γε μὲν οὐκ ἐπὶ ταύτῃ
ἀθρόος ἀντέλλει, Δίδυμοι δέ μιν οὖλον ἄγουσιν.
ἀλλ' Ἔριφοι λαιοῦ τε θέναρ ποδὸς Αἰγὶ σὺν αὐτῇ
Ταύρῳ συμφορέονται, ὅτε λοφίη τε καὶ οὐρὴ
Κήτεος αἰθερίοιο περαιόθεν ἀντέλλωσιν.   720
δύνει δ' Ἀρκτοφύλαξ ἤδη πρώτῃ τότε μοίρῃ
τάων, αἳ πίσυρές μιν ἄτερ χειρὸς κατάγουσιν
λαιῆς· ἡ δ' αὐτῷ μεγάλη ὑποτέλλεται Ἄρκτῳ.
  Ἀμφότεροι δὲ πόδες καταδυομένου Ὀφιούχου,
μέσφ' αὐτῶν γονάτων, ΔΙΔΥΜΟΙΣ ἔπι σῆμα τετύχθω   725
ἐξ ἑτέρης ἀνιοῦσι. τότ' οὐκέτι Κήτεος οὐδὲν
ἕλκεται ἀμφοτέρωθεν, ὅλον δέ μιν ὄψεαι ἤδη.
ἤδη καὶ Ποταμοῦ πρώτην ἁλὸς ἐξανιοῦσαν
ἀγὴν ἐν καθαρῷ πελάγει σκέψαιτό κε ναύτης,
αὐτὸν ἐπ' Ὠρίωνα μένων, εἴ οἷ ποθι σῆμα   730
ἢ νυκτὸς μέτρων ἠὲ πλόου ἀγγείλειεν.
πάντη γὰρ τά γε πολλὰ θεοὶ ἄνδρεσσι λέγουσιν.

ΔΙΟ-   Οὐχ ὁράᾳς; ὀλίγη μὲν ὅταν κεράεσσι σελήνη
ΣΗΜΙΑΙ ἑσπερόθεν φαίνηται, ἀεξομένοιο διδάσκει
μηνός· ὅτε πρώτη ἀποκίδναται αὐτόθεν αὐγή,   735
ὅσσον ἐπισκιάειν, ἐπὶ τέτρατον ἦμαρ ἰοῦσα·
ὀκτὼ δ' ἐν διχάσει· διχόμηνα δὲ παντὶ προσώπῳ.   5

---

^a Taurus.   ^b Gemini.
^c Cf. 581.   ^d Eridanus.

East may be seen rising as much as the head and shoulders of Perseus.

As to his belt itself disputed might it be whether it rises as the Ram ceases to rise or at the rising of the Bull,*a* with whom he rises wholly. Nor lags behind the Charioteer at the rising of the Bull, for close are set their courses. But not with that sign does he rise completely, but the Twins *b* bring him wholly up. The Kids and the sole of the Charioteer's left foot and the Goat herself journey with the Bull, what time the neck and tail of Cetus, leviathan of the sky, rise from below. Now Arctophylax is beginning to set with the first of those four *c* constellations of the Zodiac that see him sink wholly, save his never setting left hand that rises by the Great Bear.

Let Ophiuchus setting from both feet even to his knees be a sign of the rising of the Twins in the East. Then no longer is aught of Cetus beneath the verge, but thou shalt see him all. Then, too, can the sailor on the open sea mark the first bend of the River *d* rising from the deep, as he watches for Orion himself to see if he might give him any hint of the measure of the night or of his voyage. For on every hand signs in multitude do the gods reveal to man.

Markest thou not ? Whenever the Moon with WEATHER SIGNS slender horns shines forth in the West, she tells of a new month beginning : when first her rays are shed abroad just enough to cast a shadow, she is going to the fourth day : with orb half complete she proclaims eight days : with full face the mid-day of the

αἰεὶ δ' ἄλλοθεν ἄλλα παρακλίνουσα μέτωπα
εὕρει ὁποσταίη μηνὸς περιτέλλεται ἠώς.

"Ακρα γε μὴν νυκτῶν κεῖναι δυοκαίδεκα μοῖραι 740
ἄρκιαι ἐξειπεῖν· τὰ δέ που μέγαν εἰς ἐνιαυτόν,
ὥρη μέν τ' ἀρόσαι νειούς, ὥρη δὲ φυτεῦσαι,   10
ἐκ Διὸς ἤδη πάντα πεφασμένα πάντοθι κεῖται.
καὶ μέν τις καὶ νηὶ πολυκλύστου χειμῶνος
ἐφράσατ' ἢ δεινοῦ μεμνημένος Ἀρκτούροιο   745
ἠέ τεων ἄλλων, οἵ τ' ὠκεανοῦ ἀρύονται
ἀστέρες ἀμφιλύκης, οἵ τε πρώτης ἔτι νυκτός.   15
ἤτοι γὰρ τοὺς πάντας ἀμείβεται εἰς ἐνιαυτὸν
ἠέλιος μέγαν ὄγμον ἐλαύνων, ἄλλοτε δ' ἄλλῳ
ἐμπλήσει, τοτὲ μέν τ' ἀνιὼν τοτὲ δ' αὐτίκα δύνων· 750
ἄλλος δ' ἀλλοίην ἀστὴρ ἐπιδέρκεται ἠῶ.

Γινώσκεις τάδε καὶ σύ, τὰ γὰρ συναείδεται ἤδη   20
ἐννεακαίδεκα κύκλα φαεινοῦ ἠελίοιο,
ὅσσα τ' ἀπὸ ζώνης εἰς ἔσχατον Ὠρίωνα
Νὺξ ἐπιδινεῖται Κύνα τε θρασὺν Ὠρίωνος   755
οἵ τε Ποσειδάωνος ὁρώμενοι ἢ Διὸς αὐτοῦ
ἀστέρες ἀνθρώποισι τετυγμένα σημαίνουσιν.   25
τῶ κείνων πεπόνησο· μέλοι δέ τοι, εἴ ποτε νηὶ
πιστεύεις, εὑρεῖν ὅσα που κεχρημένα κεῖται
σήματα χειμερίοις ἀνέμοις ἢ λαίλαπι πόντου.   760
μόχθος μέν τ' ὀλίγος, τὸ δὲ μυρίον αὐτίκ' ὄνειαρ
γίνετ' ἐπιφροσύνης αἰεὶ πεφυλαγμένῳ ἀνδρί.   30
αὐτὸς μὲν τὰ πρῶτα σαώτερος, εὖ δὲ καὶ ἄλλον
παρειπὼν ὤνησεν, ὅτ' ἐγγύθεν ὦρορε χειμών.

Πολλάκι γὰρ καί τίς τε γαληναίη ὑπὸ νυκτὶ   765

ᵃ Both the (heliacal) rising (in September) of Arcturus
and his (cosmical) setting (in March) brought stormy
weather. In the *Rudens* of Plautus the Prologue is spoken
by Arcturus who says (70 f.) "Nam signum Arcturus
omnium sum acerrimum : Vehemens sum exoriens, quom

month ; and ever with varying phase she tells the
date of the dawn that comes round.

Those twelve signs of the Zodiac are sufficient to
tell the limits of the night. But they to mark the
great year—the season to plough and sow the
fallow field and the season to plant the tree—are
already revealed of Zeus and set on every side.
Yea, and on the sea, too, many a sailor has
marked the coming of the stormy tempest, remembering either dread Arcturus[a] or other stars that
draw from ocean in the morning twilight or at the
first fall of night. For verily through them all the
Sun passes in yearly course, as he drives his mighty
furrow, and now to one, now to another he draws
near, now as he rises and anon as he sets, and ever
another star looks upon another morn.

This thou too knowest, for celebrated by all now
are the nineteen cycles[b] of the bright Sun—thou
knowest all the stars wheeled aloft by Night from
Orion's belt to the last of Orion and his bold hound,
the stars of Poseidon, the stars of Zeus, which, if
marked, display fit signs of the seasons. Wherefore
to them give careful heed and if ever thy trust is
in a ship, be it thine to watch what signs in the
heavens are labouring under stormy winds or squall
at sea. Small is the trouble and thousandfold the
reward of his heedfulness who ever takes care.
First he himself is safer, and well, too, he profits
another by his warning, when a storm is rushing
near.

For oft, too, beneath a calm night the sailor

occido vehementior"; *cf.* Hor. *C.* iii. 1. 27 f. " saevus Arcturi
cadentis Impetus."

[b] The nineteen-year cycle of Meton. For this and following lines see Introduction, p. 379.

ARATUS

νῆα περιστέλλει πεφοβημένος ἦρι θαλάσσης·
ἄλλοτε δὲ τρίτον ἦμαρ ἐπιτρέχει, ἄλλοτε πέμπτον, 35
ἄλλοτε δ' ἀπρόφατον κακὸν ἵκετο· πάντα γὰρ οὔπω
ἐκ Διὸς ἄνθρωποι γινώσκομεν, ἀλλ' ἔτι πολλὰ
κέκρυπται, τῶν αἴ κε θέλῃ καὶ ἐσαυτίκα δώσει 770
Ζεύς· ὁ γὰρ οὖν γενεὴν ἀνδρῶν ἀναφανδὸν ὀφέλλει,
πάντοθεν εἰδόμενος, πάντῃ δ' ὅ γε σήματα φαίνων. 40
ἄλλα δέ τοι ἐρέει ἤπου διχόωσα σελήνη
πληθύος ἀμφοτέρωθεν ἢ αὐτίκα πεπληθυῖα·
ἄλλα δ' ἀνερχόμενος, τοτὲ δ' ἄκρῃ νυκτὶ κελεύων 775
ἠέλιος· τὰ δέ τοι καὶ ἀπ' ἄλλων ἔσσεται ἄλλα
σήματα καὶ περὶ νυκτὶ καὶ ἤματι ποιήσασθαι. 45
  Σκέπτεο δὲ πρῶτον κεράων ἑκάτερθε σελήνην.
ἄλλοτε γάρ τ' ἄλλῃ μιν ἐπιγράφει ἕσπερος αἴγλῃ,
ἄλλοτε δ' ἀλλοῖαι μορφαὶ κερόωσι σελήνην 780
εὐθὺς ἀεξομένην, αἱ μὲν τρίτῃ, αἱ δὲ τετάρτῃ·
τάων καὶ περὶ μηνὸς ἐφεσταότος κε πύθοιο. 50
λεπτὴ μὲν καθαρή τε περὶ τρίτον ἦμαρ ἐοῦσα
εὔδιός κ' εἴη· λεπτὴ δὲ καὶ εὖ μάλ' ἐρευθὴς
πνευματίη· παχίῃσι δὲ καὶ ἀμβλείῃσι κεραίαις 785
τέτρατον ἐκ τριτάτοιο φόως ἀμενηνὸν ἔχουσα
ἢ νότῳ ἀμβλύνται ἢ ὕδατος ἐγγὺς ἐόντος. 55
εἰ δέ κ' ἀπ' ἀμφοτέρων κεράων, τρίτον ἦμαρ
   ἄγουσα,
μήτ' ἐπινευστάζῃ μήθ' ὑπτιόωσα φαείνῃ,
ἀλλ' ὀρθαὶ ἑκάτερθε περιγνάμπτωσι κεραῖαι, 790
ἑσπέριοί κ' ἄνεμοι κείνην μετὰ νύκτα φέροιντο.
εἰ δ' αὔτως ὀρθὴ καὶ τέτρατον ἦμαρ ἀγινεῖ, 60
ἥ τ' ἂν χειμῶνος συναγειρομένοιο διδάσκοι.

ᵃ Verg. *Georg.* i. 424-435, Plin. *N.H.* xviii. 347 "Proxima sint iure lunae praesagia," etc. For this part of Aratus the reader should consult the whole of Plin. *N.H.* xviii. § 218-end.

266

shortens sail for fear of the morning sea. Sometimes the storm comes on the third day, sometimes on the fifth, but sometimes the evil comes all unforeseen. For not yet do we mortals know all from Zeus, but much still remains hidden, whereof, what he will, even hereafter will he reveal; for openly he aids the race of men, manifesting himself on every side and showing signs on every hand. Some messages the Moon will convey with orb half-full as she waxes or wanes, others when full: others the Sun by warnings at dawn and again at the edge of night, and other hints from other source can be drawn for day and night.

Scan first the horns on either side the Moon.[a] For with varying hue from time to time the evening paints her and of different shape are her horns at different times as the Moon is waxing—one form on the third day and other on the fourth. From them thou canst learn touching the month that is begun. If she is slender and clear about the third day,[b] she heralds calm: if slender and very ruddy, wind[c]; but if thick and with blunted horns she show but a feeble light on the third and fourth night, her beams are blunted by the South wind or imminent rain. If on the third night neither horn nod forward or lean backward, if vertical they curve their tips on either side, winds from the West will follow that night. But if still with vertical crescent she bring the fourth day too, she gives warning of gathering storm.[d]

[b] Theophr. *De signis* 51 καὶ ὁ μεὶς ἐὰν τριταῖος ὢν λαμπρὸς ᾖ, εὐδιεινόν.

[c] Theophr. 12 ἐὰν μὲν ᾖ πυρώδης, πνευματώδη σημαίνει τὸν μῆνα, ἐὰν δὲ ζοφώδης, ὑδατώδη.

[d] Theophr. 38 χειμῶνος δὲ τάδε . . . τὸ σηλήνιον ἐὰν ὀρθὸν ᾖ μέχρι τετράδος καὶ εἰ εὔκυκλον, χειμάσει μέχρι διχοτόμου.

267

εἰ δέ κέ οἱ κεράων τὸ μετήορον εὖ ἐπινεύῃ,
δειδέχθαι βορέω· ὅτε δ' ὑπτιάῃσι, νότοιο.   795
αὐτὰρ ἐπὴν τριτόωσαν ὅλος περὶ κύκλος ἑλίσσῃ
πάντῃ ἐρευθόμενος, μάλα κεν τότε χείμερος εἴη·   65
μείζονι δ' ἂν χειμῶνι πυρώτερα φοινίσσοιτο.
      Σκέπτεο δ' ἐς πληθύν τε καὶ ἀμφότερον
      διχόωσαν,
ἠμὲν ἀεξομένην ἠδ' ἐς κέρας αὖθις ἰοῦσαν,   800
καί οἱ ἐπὶ χροιῇ τεκμαίρεο μηνὸς ἑκάστου.
πάντῃ γὰρ καθαρῇ κε μάλ' εὔδια τεκμήραιο·   70
πάντα δ' ἐρευθομένη δοκέειν ἀνέμοιο κελεύθους·
ἄλλοθι δ' ἄλλο μελαινομένη δοκέειν ὑετοῖο.
σήματα δ' οὐ μάλα πᾶσιν ἐπ' ἤμασι πάντα τέτυκται·   805
ἀλλ' ὅσα μὲν τριτάτῃ τε τεταρταίῃ τε πέλονται,
μέσφα διχαιομένης, διχάδος γε μὲν ἄχρις ἐπ'
      αὐτὴν   75
σημαίνει διχόμηνον, ἀτὰρ πάλιν ἐκ διχομήνου
ἐς διχάδα φθιμένην· ἔχεται δέ οἱ αὐτίκα τετρὰς
μηνὸς ἀποιχομένου, τῇ δὲ τριτάτῃ ἐπιόντος.   810
εἰ δέ κέ μιν περὶ πᾶσαν ἁλωαὶ κυκλώσωνται
ἢ τρεῖς ἠὲ δύο περικείμεναι ἠὲ μί' οἴη,   80
τῇ μὲν ἰῇ ἀνέμοιο γαληναίης τε δοκεύειν,
ῥηγνυμένη ἀνέμοιο, μαραινομένη δὲ γαλήνης·

---

[a] Theophr. 27 ἔστι δὲ σημεῖα ἐν ἡλίῳ καὶ σελήνῃ τὰ μὲν
μέλανα ὕδατος τὰ δ' ἐρυθρὰ πνεύματος. ἐὰν δὲ ὁ μεὶς βορείου
ὄντος ὀρθὸς εἱστήκῃ, ζέφυροι εἰώθασιν ἐπιπνεῖν καὶ ὁ μὴν χειμερινὸς
διατελεῖ. ὅταν μὲν ἡ κεραία (ἡ ἄνω) τοῦ μηνὸς ἐπικύπτῃ, βόρειος
ὁ μείς. ὅταν δὲ ἡ κάτωθεν νότιος· ἐὰν δὲ ὀρθὸς καὶ μὴ καλῶς
ἐγκεκλιμένος μέχρι τετράδος καὶ εὔκυκλος εἴωθε χειμάζειν μέχρι
διχομηνίας. σημαίνει ζοφώδης μὲν ὢν ὕδωρ, πυρώδης δὲ πνεῦμα.
[b] Theophr. 8 ὡς δ' αὔτως ἔχει καὶ περὶ τὸν μῆνα ἕκαστον·
διχοτομοῦσι γὰρ αἵ τε πανσέληνοι καὶ αἱ ὀγδόαι καὶ αἱ τετράδες, ὥστε
ἀπὸ νουμηνίας ὡς ἀπ' ἀρχῆς δεῖ σκοπεῖν, μεταβάλλει γὰρ ὡς ἐπὶ τὸ

If her upper horn nod forward,[a] expect thou the North wind, but if it lean backward, the South. But when on the third day a complete halo, blushing red, encircles her, she foretells storm and, the fiercer her blush, the fiercer the tempest.

Scan her when full and when half-formed on either side of full, as she waxes from or wanes again to crescent form, and from her hue forecast each month. When quite bright her hue, forecast fair weather; when ruddy, expect the rushing wind; when dark stained with spots, look out for rain. But not for every day is appointed a separate sign,[b] but the signs of the third and fourth day betoken the weather up to the half Moon; those of the half Moon up to full Moon; and in turn the signs of the full Moon up to the waning half Moon; the signs of the half Moon are followed by those of the fourth day from the end of the waning month, and they in their turn by those of the third day of the new month. But if halos[c] encircle all the Moon, set triple or double about her or only single—with the single ring, expect wind or calm[d]; when the ring is broken, wind[e]; when faint and fading, calm;

πολὺ ἐν τῇ τετράδι, ἐὰν δε μή, ἐν τῇ ὀγδόῃ, εἰ δὲ μή, πανσελήνῳ· ἀπὸ δὲ πανσελήνου εἰς ὀγδόην φθίνοντος, καὶ ἀπὸ ταύτης εἰς τετράδα, ἀπὸ δὲ τετράδος εἰς τὴν νουμηνίαν.

[c] ἀλωή (ἅλως), lit. "threshing-floor." Seneca, *N.Q.* i. 2 "coloris varii circulum . . . hunc Graeci halo vocant, nos dicere coronam aptissime possumus . . . tales splendores Graeci areas vocaverunt, quia fere terendis frugibus destinata loca rotunda sunt."

[d] Theophr. 51 ἅλως δὲ ἐὰν ὁμαλῶς παγῇ καὶ μαρανθῇ, εὐδίαν σημαίνει.

[e] Theophr. 31 αἱ ἅλωνες περὶ τὴν σελήνην πνευματώδεις μᾶλλον ἢ περὶ ἥλιον· σημαίνουσι δὲ πνεῦμα ῥαγεῖσαι περὶ ἄμφω, καὶ ᾗ ἂν ῥαγῇ, ταύτῃ πνεῦμα.

ταὶ δύο δ' ἂν χειμῶνι περιτροχάοιντο σελήνην· 815
μείζονα δ' ἂν χειμῶνα φέροι τριέλικτος ἀλωή,
καὶ μᾶλλον μελανεῦσα, καὶ εἰ ῥηγνύατο μᾶλλον. 85
καὶ τὰ μὲν οὖν ἐπὶ μηνὶ σεληναίης κε πύθοιο.
   Ἠελίοιο δέ τοι μελέτω ἑκάτερθεν ἰόντος.
ἠελίῳ καὶ μᾶλλον ἐοικότα σήματα κεῖται, 820
ἀμφότερον δύνοντι καὶ ἐκ περάτης ἀνιόντι.
μή οἱ ποικίλλοιτο νέον βάλλοντος ἀρούρας 90
κύκλος, ὅτ' εὐδίου κεχρημένος ἤματος εἴης,
μηδέ τι σῆμα φέροι, φαίνοιτο δὲ λιτὸς ἀπάντη.
εἰ δ' αὔτως καθαρόν μιν ἔχοι βουλύσιος ὥρη, 825
δύνοι δ' ἀνέφελος μαλακὴν ὑποδείελος αἴγλην,
καί κεν ἐπερχομένης ἠοῦς ἔθ' ὑπεύδιος εἴη. 95
ἀλλ' οὐχ ὁππότε κοῖλος ἐειδόμενος περιτέλλῃ,
οὐδ' ὁπότ' ἀκτίνων αἱ μὲν νότον αἱ δὲ βορῆα
σχιζόμεναι βάλλωσι, τὰ δ' αὖ περὶ μέσσα φαείνῃ, 830
ἀλλά που ἢ ὑετοῖο διέρχεται ἢ ἀνέμοιο.
   Σκέπτεο δ', εἴ κέ τοι αὐγαὶ ὑπείκωσ' ἠελίοιο, 100
αὐτὸν ἐς ἠέλιον· τοῦ γὰρ σκοπιαὶ καὶ ἄρισται·
εἴ τί οἱ ἤπου ἔρευθος ἐπιτρέχει, οἷά τε πολλὰ
ἑλκομένων νεφέων ἐρυθαίνεται ἄλλοθεν ἄλλα, 835
ἢ εἴ που μελανεῖ· καί τοι τὰ μὲν ὕδατος ἔστω
σήματα μέλλοντος, τὰ δ' ἐρεύθεα πάντ' ἀνέμοιο. 105
εἴ γε μὲν ἀμφοτέροις ἄμυδις κεχρημένος εἴη,

---

[a] Verg. *G.* i. 438 ff. "Sol quoque et exoriens et cum se
condet in undas, Signa dabit ; solem certissima signa sequuntur, Et quae mane refert et quae surgentibus astris. Ille
ubi nascentem maculis variaverit ortum, Conditus in nubem,
medioque refugerit orbe, Suspecti tibi sint imbres ; namque
urguet ab alto Arboribusque satisque Notus pecorique
sinister."

[b] Theophr. 50 ἥλιος μὲν ἀνιὼν λαμπρὸς καὶ μὴ καυματίας καὶ
μὴ ἔχων σημεῖον μηδὲν ἐν ἑαυτῷ εὐδίαν σημαίνει.

[c] Theophr. 50 καὶ δυόμενος ἥλιος χειμῶνος εἰς καθαρὸν εὐδιεινός,

two rings girding the Moon forebode storm; a triple
halo would bring a greater storm, and greater still,
if black, and more furious still, if the rings are
broken. Such warnings for the month thou canst
learn from the Moon.

To the Sun's [a] march at East and West give heed.
His hints give even more pertinent warning both at
setting, and when he comes from below the verge.
May not his orb, whenever thou desirest a fair day,
be variegated when first his arrows strike the earth,
and may he wear no mark at all but shine stainless
altogether.[b] If again thus all pure he be in the
hour when the oxen are loosed, and set cloudless in
the evening with gentle beam, he will still be at
the coming dawn attended with fair weather.[c]
But not so, when he rises with seemingly hollow
disk, nor when his beams part to strike or North or
South, while his centre is bright. But then in truth
he journeys either through rain or through wind.[d]

Scan closely, if his beams allow thee, the Sun
himself, for scanning him is best, to see if either
some blush run over him, as often he shows a blush or
here or there, when he fares through trailing clouds,
or if haply he is darkened. Let the dark stain be
sign to thee of coming rain, and every blush be sign
of wind. But if he is draped both black and red at

ἐὰν μὴ ταῖς προτέραις ἡμέραις εἰς μὴ καθαρὸν δεδυκὼς ᾖ ἐξ εὐδιῶν.
οὕτω δὲ ἄδηλον. καὶ ἐὰν χειμάζοντος ἡ δύσις γένηται εἰς καθαρόν,
εὐδιεινόν. Verg. G. i. 458 ff. "At si cum referetque diem
condetque relatum, Lucidus orbis erit, frustra terrebere
nimbis, Et claro silvas cernes Aquilone moveri."

[d] Theophr. 26 καὶ ἐὰν κοῖλος φαίνηται ὁ ἥλιος, ἀνέμου ἢ ὕδατος
τὸ σημεῖον . . . ἐὰν αἱ ἀκτῖνες αἱ μὲν πρὸς βορρᾶν, αἱ δὲ πρὸς
νότον σχίζωνται τούτου μέσου ὄντος κατ' ὄρθρον, κοινὸν ὕδατος καὶ
ἀνέμου σημεῖόν ἐστιν (Verg. G. i. 445 f.). Plin. N.H. xviii.
342 "Primumque a sole capimus praesagia," etc.

καί κεν ὕδωρ φορέοι καὶ ὑπηνέμιος τανύοιτο.
εἰ δέ οἱ ἢ ἀνιόντος ἢ αὐτίκα δυομένοιο   840
ἀκτῖνες συνίωσι καὶ ἀμφ' ἑνὶ πεπλήθωσιν,
ἤ ποτε καὶ νεφέων πεπιεσμένος ἢ ὅ γ' ἐς ἠῶ   110
ἔρχηται παρὰ νυκτός, ἢ ἐξ ἠοῦς ἐπὶ νύκτα,
ὕδατί κεν κατιόντι παρατρέχοι ἤματα κεῖνα.
μηδ' ὅτε οἱ ὀλίγη νεφέλη πάρος ἀντέλλησιν,   845
τὴν δὲ μέτ' ἀκτίνων κεχρημένος αὐτὸς ἀερθῇ,
ἀμνηστεῖν ὑετοῖο. πολὺς δ' ὅτε οἱ περὶ κύκλος   115
οἷον τηκομένῳ ἐναλίγκιος εὐρύνηται
πρῶτον ἀνερχομένοιο, καὶ ἂψ ἐπὶ μεῖον ἴῃσιν,
εὔδιός κε φέροιτο· καὶ εἴ ποτε χείματος ὥρῃ   850
ὠχρήσαι κατιών. ἀτὰρ ὕδατος ἠμερινοῖο
γινομένου κατόπισθε περὶ νέφεα σκοπέεσθαι   120
κὰδ δὴ δυομένου τετραμμένος ἠελίοιο.
ἢν μὲν ὑποσκιάῃσι μελαινομένη εἰκυῖα
ἠέλιον νεφέλη, ταὶ δ' ἀμφί μιν ἔνθα καὶ ἔνθα   855
ἀκτῖνες μεσσηγὺς ἑλισσόμεναι διχόωνται,
ἦ τ' ἂν ἔτ' εἰς ἠῶ σκέπαος κεχρημένος εἴης.   125
εἰ δ' ὁ μὲν ἀνέφελος βάπτοι ῥόου ἑσπερίοιο,
ταὶ δὲ κατερχομένου νεφέλαι καὶ ἔτ' οἰχομένοιο
πλησίαι ἑστήκωσιν ἐρευθέες, οὔ σε μάλα χρὴ   860
αὔριον οὐδ' ἐπὶ νυκτὶ περιτρομέειν ὑετοῖο·
ἀλλ' ὁπότ' ἠελίοιο μαραινομένῃσιν ὁμοῖαι   130
ἐξαπίνης ἀκτῖνες ἀπ' οὐρανόθεν τανύωνται,
οἷον ἀμαλδύνονται ὅτε σκιάῃσι κατ' ἰθὺ
ἱσταμένη γαίης τε καὶ ἠελίοιο σελήνη.   865

---

[a] Verg. *G.* i. 450 ff. " Hoc etiam emenso cum iam decedit Olympo, Profuerit meminisse magis ; nam saepe videmus Ipsius in vultu varios errare colores : Caeruleus pluviam denuntiat, igneus Euros ; Sin maculae incipient rutilo immiscerier igni, Omnia tum pariter vento nimbisque videbis

PHAENOMENA

once, he will bring rain and will strain beneath the
wind.[a]   But if the rays of the rising or setting Sun
converge and crowd on one spot, or if he go from
night to dawn, or from dawn to night, closely beset
with clouds, those days will run in company with
rushing rain.   Nor be thou heedless of rain, what
time before him rises a thin mist, after which the
Sun himself ascends with scanty beams.[b]   But when
a broad belt of mist seems to melt and widen before
the rising Sun and anon narrows to less, fair will be
his course, and fair too, if in the season of winter his
hue wax wan at eventide.[c]   But for to-morrow's
rain face the setting Sun and scan the clouds.   If a
darkening cloud overshadow the Sun and if around
that cloud the beams that wheel between the Sun
and it part to either side of the cloud, thou shalt
still need shelter for the dawn.[d]   But if without a
cloud he dip in the western ocean, and as he is
sinking, or still when he is gone, the clouds stand
near him blushing red, neither on the morrow
nor in the night needst thou be over-fearful of
rain.   But fear the coming rain when on a sudden
the Sun's rays seem to thin and pale [e]—just as they
often fade when the Moon overshadows them, what
time she stands straight between the earth and

Fervere.   non illa quisquam me nocte per altum Ire neque
ab terra moneat convellere funem"; *cf.* Theophr. 27.

[b] Verg. *G.* i. 446 ff. "ubi pallida surget Tithoni croceum
linquens Aurora cubile, Heu male tum mitis defendet pam-
pinus uvas."

[c] Theophr. 50 καὶ ἐὰν δύνων χειμῶνος ὠχρὸς ᾖ, εὐδίαν
σημαίνει.

[d] Theophr. 11 καὶ ἐὰν καταφερομένου τοῦ ἡλίου ὑφίστηται
νέφος ὑφ' οὗ ἐὰν σχίζωνται αἱ ἀκτῖνες, χειμερινὸν τὸ σημεῖον.

[e] Theophr. 13 καὶ ὅταν ἀνίσχοντος τοῦ ἡλίου αἱ αὐγαὶ οἷον
ἐκλείποντος χρῶμα ἴσχωσιν, ὕδατος σημεῖον.

οὐδ᾽, ὅτε οἱ ἐπέχοντι φανήμεναι ἠῶθι πρὸ
φαίνονται νεφέλαι ὑπερευθέες ἄλλοθεν ἄλλαι, **135**
ἄρραντοι γίνονται ἐπ᾽ ἤματι κείνῳ ἄρουραι.
μηδ᾽ αὔτως, ἔτ᾽ ἐόντι πέρην ὁπότε προταθεῖσαι
ἀκτῖνες φαίνονται ἐπίσκιοι ἠῶθι πρό, **870**
ὕδατος ἢ ἀνέμοιο κατοισομένου λελαθέσθαι.
ἀλλ᾽ εἰ μὲν κεῖναι μᾶλλον κνέφαος φορέοιντο **140**
ἀκτῖνες, μᾶλλόν κεν ἐφ᾽ ὕδατι σημαίνοιεν·
εἰ δ᾽ ὀλίγος τανύοιτο περὶ δνόφος ἀκτίνεσσιν,
οἷόν που μαλακαὶ νεφέλαι φορέουσι μάλιστα, **875**
ἤ τ᾽ ἂν ἐπερχομένοιο περιδνοφέοιντ᾽ ἀνέμοιο.
οὐδὲ μὲν ἠελίου σχεδόθεν μελανεῦσαι ἁλωαὶ **14**
εὔδιοι· ἀσσότεραι δὲ καὶ ἀστεμφὲς μελανεῦσαι
μᾶλλον χειμέριαι· δύο δ᾽ ἂν χαλεπώτεραι εἶεν.

Σκέπτεο δ᾽ ἢ ἀνιόντος ἢ αὐτίκα δυομένοιο, **88**
εἴ πού οἱ νεφέων τὰ παρήλια κικλήσκονται
ἢ νότου ἠὲ βορῆος ἐρεύθεται ἢ ἑκάτερθεν, **15**
μηδ᾽ οὕτω σκοπιὴν ταύτην ἀμενηνὰ φυλάσσειν.
οὐ γάρ, ὅτ᾽ ἀμφοτέρωθεν ὁμοῦ περὶ μέσσον
ἔχουσιν
ἠέλιον κεῖναι νεφέλαι σχεδὸν ὠκεανοῖο,
γίνεται ἀμβολίη διόθεν χειμῶνος ἰόντος. **88**
εἴ γε μὲν ἐκ βορέαο μί᾽ οἴη φοινίσσοιτο, **1**
ἐκ βορέω πνοιάς κε φέροι, νοτίη δὲ νότοιο,
ἢ καί που ῥαθάμιγγες ἐπιτροχόωσ᾽ ὑετοῖο.

Ἑσπερίοις καὶ μᾶλλον ἐπίτρεπε σήμασι τούτοις· **8**
ἑσπερόθεν γὰρ ὁμῶς σημαίνεται ἐμμενὲς αἰεί.

ᵃ Cicero *ap.* Priscian. x. 11 "Ut cum Luna means Hype-
rionis officit orbi, Stinguuntur radii caeca caligine tecti."

ᵇ Theophr. 10 ὕδατος μὲν οὖν σημεῖα τὰ τοιαῦτα δοκεῖ εἶναι.
ἐναργέστατον μὲν οὖν τὸ ἑωθινόν, ὅταν πρὸ ἡλίου ἀνατολῆς φαίνηται
ἐπιφοινίσσον σημεῖον· ἢ γὰρ αὐθημερινὸν ἐπισημαίνει ἢ τριῶν
ἡμερῶν ὡς ἐπὶ τὸ πολύ.

Sun[a]: nor are the fields unwetted on that day, when
before the dawn, as the Sun delays to shine, reddish
clouds appear here or there.[b] Be not heedless either
of wind or rain[c] to come, when, while the Sun is still
below the verge, his precursor beams shine shadowy
in the dawn.   The more those beams are borne in
shadow, the surer sign they give of rain, but if but
faint the dusk that veils his beams, like a soft mist
of vapour, that veil of dusk portends wind.   Nor are
dark halos[d] near the Sun signs of fair weather:
when nearer the Sun and dark without relief, they
portend greater storms: if there are two rings, they
will herald tempests fiercer still.

Mark as the Sun is rising or setting, whether the
clouds, called parhelia,[e] blush (on South or North or
both), nor make the observation in careless mood.
For when on both[f] sides at once those clouds gird
the Sun, low down upon the horizon, there is no
lingering of the storm that comes from Zeus.   But
if only one shine purple to the North, from the
North will it bring the blast; if in the South, from
the South; or down pour the pattering raindrops.[g]

With even greater care mark those signals when
in the West, for from the West the warnings are
given ever with equal and unfailing certainty.

[c] Theophr. 11 καὶ ἐὰν ἐκ νεφελῶν ἀνέχῃ, ὑδατικόν, καὶ ἐὰν
ἀκτῖνες ἀνίσχοντος ἀνατείνωσι πρὶν ἀνατεῖλαι, κοινὸν ὕδατος
σημεῖον καὶ ἀνέμου.

[d] Theophr. 22 καὶ ἅλως αἱ μέλαιναι ὑδατικόν, καὶ μᾶλλον αἱ
δείλης.

[e] So-called "mock suns," "imagines solis" (Seneca, N.Q.
i. 11).

[f] Theophr. 22 ἐὰν παρήλιοι δύο γένωνται, καὶ ὁ μὲν νοτόθεν, ὁ
δὲ βορρᾶθεν, καὶ ἅλως ἅμα, ὕδωρ διὰ ταχέων σημαίνουσι; cf.
Seneca, N.Q. i. 12.

[g] Theophr. 29 παρήλιος ὁπόθεν ἂν ᾖ, ὕδωρ ἢ ἄνεμον σημαίνει.

Σκέπτεο καὶ ΦΑΤΝΗΝ. ἡ μέν τ᾽ ὀλίγη εἰκυῖα   160
ἀχλύϊ βορραίη ὑπὸ Καρκίνῳ ἡγηλάζει·
ἀμφὶ δέ μιν δύο λεπτὰ φαεινόμενοι φορέονται
ἀστέρες, οὔτε τι πολλὸν ἀπήοροι, οὔτε μάλ᾽ ἐγγύς,   895
ἀλλ᾽ ὅσσον τε μάλιστα πυγούσιον οἴσασθαι·
εἷς μὲν πὰρ βορέαο· νότῳ δ᾽ ἐπικέκλιται ἄλλος.   165
καὶ τοὶ μὲν καλέονται ΟΝΟΙ· μέσσῃ δέ τε Φάτνη.
ἥτε καὶ ἐξαπίνης πάντα Διὸς εὐδιόωντος
γίνετ᾽ ἄφαντος ὅλη· τοὶ δ᾽ ἀμφοτέρωθεν ἰόντες   900
ἀστέρες ἀλλήλων αὐτοσχεδὸν ἰνδάλλονται·
οὐκ ὀλίγῳ χειμῶνι τότε κλύζονται ἄρουραι.   170
εἰ δὲ μελαίνηται, τοὶ δ᾽ αὐτίκ᾽ ἐοικότες ὦσιν
ἀστέρες ἀμφότεροι, περί χ᾽ ὕδατι σημαίνοιεν.
εἰ δ᾽ ὁ μὲν ἐκ βορέω Φάτνης ἀμενηνὰ φαείνοι   905
λεπτὸν ἐπαχλύων, νότιος δ᾽ Ὄνος ἀγλαὸς εἴη,
δειδέχθαι ἀνέμοιο νότου· βορέω δὲ μάλα χρὴ   175
ἔμπαλιν ἀχλυόεντι φαεινομένῳ τε δοκεύειν.

Σῆμα δέ τοι ἀνέμοιο καὶ οἰδαίνουσα θάλασσα
γινέσθω καὶ μακρὸν ἐπ᾽ αἰγιαλοὶ βοόωντες,   910
ἀκταί τ᾽ εἰνάλιοι ὁπότ᾽ εὔδιοι ἠχήεσσαι
γίνονται, κορυφαί τε βοώμεναι οὔρεος ἄκραι.   180

Καί δ᾽ ἂν ἐπὶ ξηρὴν ὅτ᾽ ἐρωδιὸς οὐ κατὰ κόσμον
ἐξ ἁλὸς ἔρχηται φωνῇ περιπολλὰ λεληκώς,
κινυμένου κε θάλασσαν ὕπερ φορέοιτ᾽ ἀνέμοιο.   915
καί ποτε καὶ κέπφοι, ὁπότ᾽ εὔδιοι ποτέονται,
ἀντία μελλόντων ἀνέμων εἰληδὰ φέρονται.   185
πολλάκι δ᾽ ἀγριάδες νῆσσαι ἢ εἰναλίδιναι

ᵃ Cicero ap. Priscian. xvi. 16 and xviii. 172 " Ast autem
tenui quae candet lumine Phatne."
ᵇ Praesepe; Theophr. 23 ἐν τῷ καρκίνῳ δύο ἀστέρες εἰσίν, οἱ
καλούμενοι ὄνοι, ὧν τὸ μεταξὺ τὸ νεφέλιον ἡ φάτνη καλουμένη.
τοῦτο ἐὰν ζοφῶδες γίνηται, ὑδατικόν. Plin. N.H. xviii. 353.
276

Watch, too, the Manger.[a]   Like a faint mist in
the North it plays the guide beneath Cancer.
Around it are borne two faintly gleaming stars, not
far apart nor very near but distant to the view a
cubit's length, one on the North, while the other
looks towards the South.   They are called the
Asses, and between them is the Manger.[b]   On a
sudden, when all the sky is clear, the Manger
wholly disappears, while the stars that go on either
side seem nearer drawn to one another: not slight
then is the storm with which the fields are deluged.
If the Manger darken[c] and both stars remain un-
altered, they herald rain.   But if the Ass to the
North of the Manger shine feebly through a faint
mist, while the Southern Ass is gleaming bright,
expect wind from the South: but if in turn the
Southern Ass is cloudy and the Northern bright,
watch for the North wind.

A sign of wind be the swelling sea,[d] the far
sounding beach, the sea-crags when in calm they
echo, and the moaning of the mountain crests.

When, too, the heron[e] in disordered flight comes
landward from the sea with many a scream, he is
precursor of the gale at sea.   Anon, too, the stormy
petrels when they flit in calm, move in companies to
face the coming winds.   Oft before a gale the wild

---

[c] Theophr. 43 ἡ τοῦ ὄνου φάτνη εἰ συνίσταται καὶ ζοφερὰ
γίνεται, χειμῶνα σημαίνει.

[d] Verg. G. i. 356 ff. ; Theophr. 29 θάλασσα οἰδοῦσα, καὶ
ἀκταὶ βοῶσαι καὶ αἰγιαλὸς ἠχῶν ἀνεμώδης ; cf. 31 ; Cic. De div.
i. 8 ; Plin. N.H. xviii. 359 f.

[e] Theophr. 28 αἴθυιαι καὶ νῆτται καὶ ἄγριαι καὶ τιθασαὶ ὕδωρ
μὲν σημαίνουσι δυόμεναι, πτερυγίζουσαι δὲ ἄνεμον. οἱ κέπφοι
εὐδίας οὔσης ὅποι ἂν πέτωνται ἄνεμον προσημαίνουσι. . . . ἐρωδιὸς
ἀπὸ θαλάττης πετόμενος καὶ βοῶν πνεύματος σημεῖόν ἐστι, καὶ ὅλως
βοῶν μέγα ἀνεμώδης.

αἴθυιαι χερσαῖα τινάσσονται πτερύγεσσιν·
ἢ νεφέλη ὄρεος μηκύνεται ἐν κορυφῇσιν.   920
ἤδη καὶ πάπποι, λευκῆς γήρειον ἀκάνθης,
σῆμ' ἐγένοντ' ἀνέμου, κωφῆς ἁλὸς ὁππότε πολλοὶ 190
ἄκρον ἐπιπλώωσι, τὰ μὲν πάρος, ἄλλα δ' ὀπίσσω.

   Καὶ θέρεος βρονταί τε καὶ ἀστραπαὶ ἔνθεν ἴωσιν,
ἔνθεν ἐπερχομένοιο περισκοπέειν ἀνέμοιο.   925
καὶ διὰ νύκτα μέλαιναν ὅτ' ἀστέρες ἀΐσσωσιν
ταρφέα, τοὶ δ' ὄπιθεν ῥυμοὶ ὑπολευκαίνωνται, 195
δειδέχθαι κείνοις αὐτὴν ὁδὸν ἐρχομένοιο
πνεύματος· ἢν δὲ καὶ ἄλλοι ἐναντίοι ἀΐσσωσιν,
ἄλλοι δ' ἐξ ἄλλων μερέων, τότε δὴ πεφύλαξο   930
παντοίων ἀνέμων, οἵ τ' ἄκριτοί εἰσι μάλιστα,
ἄκριτα δὲ πνείουσιν ἐπ' ἀνδράσι τεκμήρασθαι. 200

   Αὐτὰρ ὅτ' ἐξ εὔροιο καὶ ἐκ νότου ἀστράπτῃσιν,
ἄλλοτε δ' ἐκ ζεφύροιο, καὶ ἄλλοτε πὰρ βορέαο,
δὴ τότε τις πελάγει ἔνι δείδιε ναυτίλος ἀνήρ,   935
μή μιν τῇ μὲν ἔχῃ πέλαγος τῇ δ' ἐκ Διὸς ὕδωρ·
ὕδατι γὰρ τοσσαῖδε περὶ στεροπαὶ φορέονται, 205
πολλάκι δ' ἐρχομένων ὑετῶν νέφεα προπάροιθεν
οἷα μάλιστα πόκοισιν ἐοικότα ἰνδάλλονται,

ᵃ Theophr. 34 πρὸς κορυφῆς ὄρους ὁπόθεν ἂν νεφέλη μηκύνηται,
ταύτῃ ἄνεμος πνευσεῖται ; cf. Theophr. 45.
  ᵇ Theophr. 37 ἐὰν ἐν τῇ θαλάττῃ πάπποι φέρωνται πολλοὶ οἱ
γινόμενοι ἀπὸ τῶν ἀκανθῶν, ἄνεμον σημαίνουσιν ἔσεσθαι μέγαν.
Verg. G. i. 368 f. "Saepe levem paleam et frondes volitare
caducas, Aut summa nantes in aqua colludere plumas."
  ᶜ Theophr. 32 θέρους ὅθεν ἂν ἀστραπαὶ καὶ βρονταὶ γίνωνται,
ἐντεῦθεν πνεύματα γίνεται ἰσχυρά· ἐὰν μὲν σφόδρα καὶ ἰσχυρὸν
ἀστράπτῃ, θᾶττον καὶ σφοδρότερον πνεύσουσιν, ἐὰν δ' ἠρέμα καὶ
μανῶς, κατ' ὀλίγον.
  ᵈ Theophr. 13 ἀστέρες πολλοὶ διάττοντες ὕδατος ἢ πνεύματος,
καὶ ὅθεν ἂν διάττωσιν, ἐντεῦθεν τὸ πνεῦμα ἢ τὸ ὕδωρ; 34 οἱ
κομῆται ἀστέρες ὡς τὰ πολλὰ πνεύματα σημαίνουσιν ; 37 ὅθεν

ducks or sea-wheeling gulls beat their wings on the shore, or a cloud is lengthwise resting on the mountain peaks.[a] Marked, too, ere now as sign of wind have been the withered petals, the down of the white thistle,[b] when they abundant float, some in front and others behind, on the surface of the silent sea.

From the quarter whence come the peals of summer thunder[c] and the lightning flash, thence expect the onset of the gale. When through the dark night shooting stars[d] fly thick and their track behind is white, expect a wind coming in the same path. If other shooting stars confront them and others from other quarters dart, then be on thy guard for winds from every quarter—winds, which beyond all else are hard to judge, and blow beyond man's power to predict.

But when from East and South the lightnings flash,[e] and again from the West and anon from the North, verily then the sailor on the sea fears to be caught at once by the waves beneath and the rain from heaven. For such lightnings herald rain. Often before the coming rain fleece-like clouds[f] appear or

---

ἂν ἀστέρες διᾴττωσι πολλοί, ἄνεμον ἐντεῦθεν· ἐὰν δὲ πανταχόθεν ὁμοίως, πολλὰ πνεύματα σημαίνουσι. Verg. G. i. 365 ff. "Saepe etiam stellas, vento impendente, videbis Praecipites caelo labi, noctisque per umbram Flammarum longos a tergo albescere tractus."

[e] Theophr. 21 ἀστραπαὶ δὲ ἐάν γε πανταχόθεν γένωνται, ὕδατος ἂν ἢ ἀνέμου σημεῖον. Verg. G. i. 370 ff. "At Boreae de parte trucis cum fulminat, et cum Eurique Zephyrique tonat domus, omnia plenis Rura natant fossis, atque omnis navita ponto, Humida vela legit."

[f] Theophr. 13 ὅταν νεφέλαι πόκοις ἐρίων ὅμοιαι ὦσιν, ὕδωρ σημαίνει. Varro Atac. ap. Serv. on Verg. G. i. 397 "nubes ⟨ceu⟩ vellera lanae Stabunt"; cf. Verg. l.c.

ἢ διδύμη ἔζωσε διὰ μέγαν οὐρανὸν ἶρις,   940
ἢ καί πού τις ἅλωα μελαινομένην ἔχει ἀστήρ.

Πολλάκι λιμναῖαι ἢ εἰνάλιαι ὄρνιθες   210
ἄπληστον κλύζονται ἐνιέμεναι ὑδάτεσσιν,
ἢ λίμνην πέρι δηθὰ χελιδόνες ἀΐσσονται
γαστέρι τύπτουσαι αὔτως εἰλυμένον ὕδωρ,   945
ἢ μᾶλλον δειλαὶ γενεαί, ὕδροισιν ὄνειαρ,
αὐτόθεν ἐξ ὕδατος πατέρες βοόωσι γυρίνων,   215
ἢ τρύζει ὀρθρινὸν ἐρημαίη ὀλολυγών,
ἤ που καὶ λακέρυζα παρ' ἠϊόνι προὐχούσῃ
χείματος ἐρχομένου χέρσῳ ὑπέτυψε κορώνη,   950
ἤ που καὶ ποταμοῖο ἐβάψατο μέχρι παρ' ἄκρους
ὤμους ἐκ κεφαλῆς, ἢ καὶ μάλα πᾶσα κολυμβᾷ,   220
ἢ πολλὴ στρέφεται παρ' ὕδωρ παχέα κρώζουσα.

Καὶ βόες ἤδη τοι πάρος ὕδατος ἐνδίοιο
οὐρανὸν εἰσανιδόντες ἀπ' αἰθέρος ὠσφρήσαντο·   955
καὶ κοίλης μύρμηκες ὀχῆς ἐξ ὤεα πάντα
θᾶσσον ἀνηνέγκαντο· καὶ ἀθρόοι ὤφθεν ἴουλοι   225
τείχη ἀνέρποντες, καὶ πλαζόμενοι σκώληκες
κεῖνοι, τοὺς καλέουσι μελαίνης ἔντερα γαίης.

ᵃ Theophr. 22 ἐάν τε πολλαὶ ἴριδες γένωνται, σημαίνει ὕδωρ
ἐπὶ πολύ.   ᵇ Cf. Theophr. l.c. ἅλως αἱ μέλαιναι ὑδατικόν.
ᶜ Theophr. 15 ὄρνιθες λουόμενοι μὴ ⟨οἱ?⟩ ἐν ὕδατι βιοῦντες
ὕδωρ ἢ χειμῶνας σημαίνουσι.   Varro Atac. ap. Serv. Verg. G.
i. 375 "Tum liceat pelagi volucres tardaeque paludis Cernere
inexpleto studio certare lavandi Et velut insolitum pennis
infundere rorem"; cf. Verg. i. 383 ff.; Plin. N.H. xviii. 362.
ᵈ Varro Atac. l.c. = Verg. G. i. 377 "Aut arguta lacus
circumvolitavit hirundo."
ᵉ Theophr. 15 χελιδόνες τῇ γαστρὶ τύπτουσαι τὰς λίμνας ὕδωρ
σημαίνουσι.
ᶠ Theophr. 15 βάτραχοι μᾶλλον ᾄδοντες σημαίνουσιν ὕδωρ.
Cic. De div. i. 9 ; Verg. G. i. 378.
ᵍ Theophr. 42 ὀλολυγὼν ᾄδουσα μόνη ἀκρωρίας (early morn)

a double rainbow ᵃ girds the wide sky or some star
is ringed with darkening halo.ᵇ

Often the birds ᶜ of lake or sea insatiably dive and
plunge in the water, or around the mere for long the
swallowsᵈ dart, smiting with their breasts the rippling
water,ᵉ or more hapless tribes, a boon to watersnakes,
the fathers ᶠ of the tadpoles croak from the lake
itself, or the lonely tree-frog ᵍ drones his matin lay,
or by jutting bank the chattering crow ʰ stalks on
the dry land before the coming storm, or it may be
dips from head to shoulder in the river, or even
dives completely, or hoarsely cawing ruffles it beside
the water.

And ere now before rain from the sky, the oxen ⁱ
gazing heavenward have been seen to sniff the air,
and the ants ʲ from their hollow nests bring up in
haste all their eggs, and in swarms the centipedes ᵏ
are seen to climb the walls, and wandering forth
crawl those worms that men call dark earth's in-

χειμέριον; cf. Theophr. 15 ὁ χλωρὸς βάτραχος ἐπὶ δένδρου ᾄδων
ὕδωρ σημαίνει. According to one interpretation in the schol.
the ὀλολυγών is "a bird like a turtle-dove" (τρυγών). Cic.
De div. i. 8 translates it by acredula, apparently = owl. In
Theocr. vii. 139 ὀλολυγών is now taken to be the tree-frog
(green frog), not, as some supposed, the nightingale.

ʰ Theophr. 16, Cic. De div. i. 8 "Fuscaque non nunquam
cursans per litora cornix Demersit caput et fluctum cervice
recepit"; Verg. G. 388 f. "Tum cornix plena pluviam vocat
improba voce Et sola in sicca secum spatiatur arena."

ⁱ Varro Atac. l.c. "Et bos suspiciens caelum, mirabile
visu, Naribus aerium patulis decerpsit odorem"; cf. Cic.
De div. i. 9; Verg. G. i. 375 f.

ʲ Theophr. 22 μύρμηκες ἐν κοίλῳ χωρίῳ ἐὰν τὰ ᾠὰ ἐκφέρωσιν
ἐκ τῆς μυρμηκιᾶς ἐπὶ τὸ ὑψηλὸν χωρίον, ὕδωρ σημαίνουσιν, ἐὰν δὲ
καταφέρωσιν, εὐδίαν. Verg. G. i. 379 f. "Saepius et tectis
penetralibus extulit ova Angustum formica terens iter."

ᵏ Theophr. 19 ἴουλοι πολλοὶ πρὸς τοῖχον ἕρποντες ὑδατικόν.

καὶ τιθαὶ ὄρνιθες, ταὶ ἀλέκτορος ἐξεγένοντο,　　960
εὖ ἐφθειρίσσαντο καὶ ἔκρωξαν μάλα φωνῇ,
οἷόν τε σταλάον ψοφέει ἐπὶ ὕδατι ὕδωρ.　　230

Δή ποτε καὶ γενεαὶ κοράκων καὶ φῦλα κολοιῶν
ὕδατος ἐρχομένοιο Διὸς πάρα σῆμ᾽ ἐγένοντο,
φαινόμενοι ἀγεληδὰ καὶ ἰρήκεσσιν ὁμοῖον　　965
φθεγξάμενοι. καί που κόρακες δίους σταλαγμοὺς
φωνῇ ἐμιμήσαντο σὺν ὕδατος ἐρχομένοιο·　　235
ἤ ποτε καὶ κρώξαντε βαρείῃ δισσάκι φωνῇ
μακρὸν ἐπιρροιζεῦσι τιναξάμενοι πτερὰ πυκνά·
καὶ νῆσσαι οἰκουροὶ ὑπωρόφιοί τε κολοιοὶ　　970
ἐρχόμενοι κατὰ γεῖσα τινάσσονται πτερύγεσσιν,
ἢ ἐπὶ κῦμα διώκει ἐρωδιὸς ὀξὺ λεληκώς.　　240

Τῶν τοι μηδὲν ἀπόβλητον πεφυλαγμένῳ ὕδωρ
γινέσθω· μηδ᾽ εἴ κεν ἐπὶ πλέον ἠὲ πάροιθεν
δάκνωσιν μυῖαι καὶ ἐφ᾽ αἵματος ἱμείρωνται,　　975
ἢ λύχνοιο μύκητες ἀγείρωνται περὶ μύξαν
νύκτα κατὰ σκοτίην· μηδ᾽ ἢν ὑπὸ χείματος ὥρην　　245
λύχνων ἄλλοτε μέν τε φάος κατὰ κόσμον ὀρώρῃ,
ἄλλοτε δ᾽ ἀΐσσωσιν ἄπο φλόγες ἠΰτε κοῦφαι
πομφόλυγες, μηδ᾽ εἴ κεν ἐπ᾽ αὐτόφι μαρμαίρωσιν　　980
ἀκτῖνες, μηδ᾽ ἢν θέρεος μέγα πεπταμένοιο

---

[a] Theophr. 42 γῆς ἔντερα πολλὰ φαινόμενα χειμῶνα σημαίνει.

[b] Theophr. 17 ὅλως δὲ ὄρνιθες καὶ ἀλεκτρυόνες φθειριζόμενοι ὑδατικὸν σημεῖον καὶ ὅταν μιμῶνται ὕδωρ ὡς ὗον.

[c] Theophr. 16 κόραξ πολλὰς μεταβάλλειν εἰωθὼς φωνὰς τούτων ἐὰν ταχὺ δὶς φθέγξηται καὶ ἐπιρροιζήσῃ καὶ τινάξῃ τὰ πτερά, ὕδωρ σημαίνει. καὶ ἐὰν ὑετῶν ὄντων πολλὰς μεταβάλλῃ φωνάς . . . καὶ ἐάν τε εὐδίας ἐάν τε ὕδατος ὄντος μιμῆται τῇ φωνῇ οἷον σταλαγμούς, ὕδωρ σημαίνει. ἐάν τε κόρακες ἐάν τε κολοιοὶ ἄνω πέτωνται καὶ ἱερακίζωσιν, ὕδωρ σημαίνουσι ; cf. Verg. G. i. 381 f.

[d] Theophr. 18 καὶ ἡ νῆττα ἥμερος ἐὰν ὑπιοῦσα ὑπὸ τὰ γεῖσα ἀποπτερυγίζηται, ὕδωρ σημαίνει, ὁμοίως δὲ καὶ κολοιοὶ καὶ ἀλεκτρυόνες, ἐάν τε ἐπὶ λίμνῃ ἢ θαλάττῃ ἀποπτερυγίζωνται, ὡς νῆττα ὕδωρ σημαίνει. καὶ ἐρωδιὸς ὄρθριον φθεγγόμενος ὕδωρ ἢ

testines *a* (earthworms). Tame fowl *b* with father
Chanticleer well preen their plumes and cluck aloud
with voice like noise of water dripping upon water.

Ere now, too, the generations of crows *c* and tribes
of jackdaws have been a sign of rain to come from
Zeus, when they appear in flocks and screech like
hawks. Crows, too, imitate with their note the
heavy splash of clashing rain, or after twice croaking
deeply they raise a loud whirring with frequent
flapping of their wings, and ducks *d* of the homestead
and jackdaws which haunt the roof seek cover under
the eaves and clap their wings, or seaward flies the
heron with shrill screams.

Slight not aught of these things when on thy guard
for rain, and heed the warning, if beyond their wont
the midges *e* sting and are fain for blood, or if on a
misty night snuff gather on the nozzle of the lamp, *f*
or if in winter's season the flame of the lamp now
rise steadily and anon sparks fly fast from it, like
light bubbles, or if on the light itself there dart
quivering rays, or if in height of summer the

πνεῦμα σημαίνει. καὶ ἐὰν ἐπὶ θάλατταν πετόμενος βοᾷ μᾶλλον
ὕδατος σημεῖον ἢ πνεύματος καὶ ὅλως βοῶν ἀνεμῶδες ; cf. Verg.
G. i. 363 f. "notasque paludes Deserit atque altam supra
volat ardea nubem."

e Theophr. 23 καὶ τὸ δημόσιον τὸ περὶ τὰς μυίας λεγόμενον
ἀληθές· ὅταν γὰρ δάκνωσι σφόδρα, ὕδατος σημεῖον.

f Verg. *G.* i. 390 ff. "Ne nocturna quidem carpentes
pensa puellae Nescivere hiemem, testa cum ardente viderent
Scintillare oleum et putris concrescere fungos." Theophr. 14
οἱ μύκητες ἐὰν νότια ᾖ, ὕδωρ σημαίνουσι, σημαίνουσι δὲ καὶ
ἄνεμον κατὰ λόγον ὡς ἂν ἔχωσι πλήθους καὶ μεγέθους, σμικροὶ
δὲ καὶ κεγχρώδεις καὶ λαμπροὶ ὕδωρ καὶ ἄνεμον. καὶ ὅταν
χειμῶνος τὴν φλόγα (ὁ λύχνος) ἀπωθῇ διαλιπὼν οἷον πομφόλυγας,
ὕδατος σημεῖον, καὶ ἐὰν πηδῶσιν αἱ ἀκτῖνες ἐπ᾽ αὐτὸν καὶ ἐὰν
σπινθῆρες ἐπιγένωνται ; 34 μύκητες ἐπὶ λύχνου νότιον πνεῦμα ἢ
ὕδωρ σημαίνουσιν.

ARATUS

νησαῖοι ὄρνιθες ἐπασσύτεροι φορέωνται. 250
μηδὲ σύ γ᾽ ἢ χύτρης ἠὲ τρίποδος πυριβήτεω,
σπινθῆρες ὅτ᾽ ἔωσι πέρι πλέονες, λελαθέσθαι·
μηδὲ κατὰ σποδιὴν ὁπότ᾽ ἄνθρακος αἰθομένοιο 985
λάμπηται πέρι σήματ᾽ ἐοικότα κεγχρείοισιν,
ἀλλ᾽ ἐπὶ καὶ τὰ δόκευε περισκοπέων ὑετοῖο. 255

Εἴ γε μὲν ἠερόεσσα παρὲξ ὄρεος μεγάλοιο
πυθμένα τείνηται νεφέλη, ἄκραι δὲ κολῶναι
φαίνωνται καθαραί, μάλα κεν τόθ᾽ ὑπεύδιος εἴης. 990
εὐδιός κ᾽ εἴης καὶ ὅτε πλατέος παρὰ πόντου
φαίνηται χθαμαλὴ νεφέλη, μηδ᾽ ὑψόθι κύρῃ, 260
ἀλλ᾽ αὐτοῦ πλαταμῶνι παραθλίβηται ὁμοίη.

Σκέπτεο δ᾽ εὔδιος μὲν ἐὼν ἐπὶ χείματι μᾶλλον,
ἐς δὲ γαληναίην χειμωνόθεν.· εὖ δὲ μάλα χρὴ 995
ἐς Φάτνην ὁράᾳν, τὴν Καρκίνος ἀμφιελίσσει,
πρῶτα καθαιρομένην πάσης ὑπένερθεν ὁμίχλης· 265
κείνη γὰρ φθίνοντι καθαίρεται ἐν χειμῶνι.

Καὶ φλόγες ἡσύχιαι λύχνων καὶ νυκτερίη γλαὺξ
ἥσυχον ἀείδουσα μαραινομένου χειμῶνος 100
γινέσθω τοι σῆμα, καὶ ἥσυχα ποικίλλουσα
ὥρῃ ἐν ἑσπερίῃ κρώξῃ πολύφωνα κορώνη· 270
καὶ κόρακες μοῦνοι μὲν ἐρημαῖοι βοόωντες
δισσάκις, αὐτὰρ ἔπειτα μετ᾽ ἀθρόα κεκλήγοντες·
πλειότεροι δ᾽ ἀγεληδόν, ἐπὴν κοίτοιο μέδωνται, 100

ᵃ Theophr. 19 χύτρα σπινθηρίζουσα πᾶσα περίπλεως ὕδατος σημεῖον.
ᵇ Theophr. 25 φασὶ δέ τινες καὶ εἰ ἐν ἄνθραξι λαμπρὰ χάλαζα ἐπιφαίνηται, χάλαζαν προσημαίνειν ὡς τὰ πολλά· ἐὰν δὲ ὥσπερ κέγχροι μικροὶ λαμπροὶ πολλοί, ἀνέμου μὲν ὄντος εὐδίαν, μὴ ἀνέμου δὲ ὕδωρ ἢ ἄνεμον ; cf. 42.
ᶜ Theophr. 51 Ὄλυμπος δὲ καὶ Ἄθως καὶ ὅλως τὰ ὄρη τὰ σημαντικὰ ὅταν τὰς κορυφὰς καθαρὰς ἔχωσιν, εὐδίαν σημαίνει. καὶ

284

PHAENOMENA

island birds are borne in crowding companies. Be not heedless of the pot [a] or tripod on the fire, if many sparks encircle it, nor heedless when in the ashes of blazing coal [b] there gleam spots like millet seed, but scan those too when seeking signs of rain.

But if a misty cloud [c] be stretched along the base of a high hill, while the upper peaks shine clear, very bright will be the sky. Fair weather, too, shalt thou have, when by the sea-verge is seen a cloud low on the ground, never reaching a height, but penned there like a flat reef of rock.

Seek in calm for signs of storms, and in storm for signs of calm. Scan well the Manger,[d] whereby wheels the Crab, when first it is freed of every covering cloud. For its clearing marks the waning tempest.

Take for sign of storm abating the steady-burning flame of the lamp,[e] the gentle hooting of the owl at night,[f] and the crow [g] if with gentle varying note she caw at eventide, and the rooks,[h] when singly they utter two lonely notes followed by frequent rapid screams, and when in fuller company they

ὅταν τὰ νέφη πρὸς τὴν θάλασσαν αὐτὴν παραζωννύῃ, εὐδιεινόν; cf. Verg. G. i. 401.

[a] Theophr. 51 ἡ τοῦ ὄνου φάτνη ὅτε ἂν καθαρὰ καὶ λαμπρὰ φαίνηται, εὐδιεινόν.

[e] Theophr. 54 λύχνος χειμῶνος καιόμενος ἡσυχαῖος εὐδίαν σημαίνει.

[f] Theophr. 52 γλαῦξ ἡσυχαῖον φθεγγομένη ἐν χειμῶνι εὐδίαν προσημαίνει· καὶ νύκτωρ χειμῶνος ἡσυχαῖον ᾄδουσα. Verg. G. i. 402 f. "Solis et occasum servans de culmine summo Nequiquam seros exercet noctua cantus."

[g] Theophr. 53 κορώνη ἕωθεν εὐθὺς ἐὰν κράξῃ τρίς, εὐδίαν, καὶ ἑσπέρας χειμῶνος ἡσυχαῖον ᾄδουσα.

[h] Theophr. 52 κόραξ δὲ μόνος μὲν ἡσυχαῖον κράζων, καὶ ἐὰν τρὶς κράξῃ, μετὰ τοῦτο πολλάκις κράξῃ, εὐδιεινός.

φωνῆς ἔμπλειοι· χαίρειν κέ τις οἴσσαιτο,
οἷα τὰ μὲν βοόωσι λιγαινομένοισιν ὁμοῖα,   275
πολλὰ δὲ δενδρείοιο περὶ φλόον, ἄλλοτ' ἐπ' αὐτοῦ,
ἠχί τε κείουσιν καὶ ὑπότροποι ἀπτερύονται.
καὶ δ' ἄν που γέρανοι μαλακῆς προπάροιθε
    γαλήνης   1010
ἀσφαλέως τανύσαιεν ἕνα δρόμον ἤλιθα πᾶσαι,
οὐδὲ παλιρρόθιοί κεν ὑπεύδιοι φορέοιντο.   280
    Ἧμος δ' ἀστερόθεν καθαρὸν φάος ἀμβλύνηται,
οὐδέ ποθεν νεφέλαι πεπιεσμέναι ἀντιόωσιν,
οὐδέ ποθεν ζόφος ἄλλος ὑποτρέχῃ οὐδὲ σελήνη,   1015
ἀλλὰ τά γ' ἐξαπίνης αὕτως ἀμενηνὰ φέρωνται,
μηκέτι τοι τόδε σῆμα γαληναίης ἐπικείσθω,   285
ἀλλ' ἐπὶ χεῖμα δόκευε· καὶ ὁππότε ταὶ μὲν ἔωσιν
αὐτῇ ἐνὶ χώρῃ νεφέλαι, ταὶ δ' ἄλλαι ὑπ' αὐταῖς
ταὶ μὲν ἀμειβόμεναι, ταὶ δ' ἐξόπιθεν φορέωνται.   1020
    Καὶ χῆνες κλαγγηδὸν ἐπειγόμεναι βρωμοῖο
χειμῶνος μέγα σῆμα, καὶ ἐννεάγηρα κορώνη   290
νύκτερον ἀείδουσα, καὶ ὀψὲ βοῶντε κολοιοί,
καὶ σπίνος ἠῶα σπίζων, καὶ ὄρνεα πάντα
ἐκ πελάγους φεύγοντα, καὶ ὀρχίλος ἢ καὶ ἐριθεὺς   1025
δύνων ἐς κοίλας ὀχεάς, καὶ φῦλα κολοιῶν
ἐκ νομοῦ ἐρχόμενα τραφεροῦ ἐπὶ ὄψιον αὐλιν.   295
οὐδ' ἂν ἐπιξουθαὶ μεγάλου χειμῶνος ἰόντος

ᵃ Verg. *Georg.* i. 410 ff. "Tum liquidas corvi presso ter
gutture voces Aut quater ingeminant, et saepe cubilibus
altis, Nescio qua praeter solitum dulcedine laeti, Inter se in
foliis strepitant; iuvat imbribus actis Progeniem parvam
dulcisque revisere nidos."

ᵇ Theophr. 52 ὅταν γέρανοι πέτωνται καὶ μὴ ἀνακάμπτωσιν,
εὐδίαν σημαίνει· οὐ γὰρ πέτονται πρὶν ἢ ἂν πετόμενοι καθαρὰ
ἴδωσιν. Contrast the sign of storm, Theophr. 38 ἐὰν ὑποστραφῶσι (γέρανοι) πετόμενοι, χειμῶνα σημαίνουσι. Verg. *G.* i. 373 ff.

bethink them of the roost,[a] full of voice. One would think them glad, seeing how they caw now in shrill screams, now with frequent flight around the foliage of the tree, now on the tree, whereon they roost, and anon they wheel and clap their wings. Cranes,[b] too, before a gentle calm will wing their way steadily onward in one track, all in a company, and in fair weather will be borne in no disordered flight.

But when the clear light from the stars is dimmed, though no thronging clouds veil, nor other darkness hide nor Moon obscure, but the stars on a sudden thus causelessly wax wan, hold that no more for sign of calm but look for storm. Foul weather, too, will come, when of the clouds some are stationary,[c] but others passing by and others following after.

Sure signs of storm are geese[d] hastening with many a cackle to their food, the nine-generation crow cawing at night,[e] the jackdaw chattering late, the chaffinch[f] piping in the dawn, waterfowl all fleeing inward from the sea,[g] the wren[h] or the robin retreating into hollow clefts, and tribes of jackdaws returning late to roost from dry feeding-grounds. When the furious tempest is imminent, the tawny

"nunquam imprudentibus imber Obfuit: aut illum surgentem vallibus imis Aeriae fugere grues."

[e] Theophr. 45 ὅταν ἑστώτων νεφῶν ἕτερα ἐπιφέρηται, τὰ δ' ἠρεμῇ, χειμέρια.

[d] Theophr. 39 χῆνες βοῶντες μᾶλλον ἢ περὶ σῖτον μαχόμενοι χειμέριον.

[e] Theophr. 39 κορώνη καὶ κόραξ καὶ κολοιὸς ὀψὲ ᾄδοντες χειμέριοι.

[f] Theophr. 39 σπίνος σπίζων ἕωθεν χειμέριον.

[g] Theophr. 40 ἐὰν ἐκ πελάγους ὄρνιθες φεύγωσι, χειμῶνα σημαίνουσι; cf. Verg. G. i. 360 f.

[h] Theophr. 39 ὄρχιλος εἰσιὼν καὶ εἰσδυόμενος εἰς ὀπὰς χειμῶνα σημαίνουσι καὶ ἐριθεὺς ὡσαύτως.

πρόσσω ποιήσαιντο νομὸν κηροῖο μέλισσαι,
ἀλλ' αὐτοῦ μέλιτός τε καὶ ἔργων εἰλίσσονται·   1030
οὐδ' ὑψοῦ γεράνων μακραὶ στίχες αὐτὰ κέλευθα
τείνονται, στροφάδες δὲ παλιμπετὲς ἀπονέονται.   300
μηδ', ὅτε νηνεμίη κεν ἀράχνια λεπτὰ φέρηται,
καὶ φλόγες αἰθύσσωσι μαραινόμεναι λύχνοιο,
ἢ πῦρ αὔηται σπουδῇ καὶ ὑπεύδια λύχνα,   1035
πιστεύειν χειμῶνι. τί τοι λέγω ὅσσα πέλονται
σήματ' ἐπ' ἀνθρώπους; δὴ γὰρ καὶ ἀεικέι τέφρῃ   305
αὐτοῦ πηγνυμένη νιφετοῦ ἐπιτεκμήραιο,
καὶ λύχνῳ χιόνος, κέγχροις ὅτ' ἐοικότα πάντη
κύκλῳ σήματ' ἔχει πυριλαμπέος ἐγγύθι μύξης,   1040
ἄνθρακι δὲ ζώοντι χαλάζης, ὁππότε λαμπρὸς
αὐτὸς ἐείδηται, μέσσῳ δέ οἱ ἠῦτε λεπτὴ   310
φαίνηται νεφέλη, πυρὸς ἔνδοθεν αἰθομένοιο.

Πρῖνοι δ' αὖ καρποῖο καταχθέες οὐδὲ μέλαιναι
σχῖνοι ἀπείρητοι· πάντη δέ τε πολλὸς ἁλωεὺς   105
αἰεὶ παπταίνει, μή οἱ θέρος ἐκ χερὸς ἔρρῃ.
πρῖνοι μὲν θαμινῆς ἀκύλου κατὰ μέτρον ἔχουσαι   31.
χειμῶνός κε λέγοιεν ἐπὶ πλέον ἰσχύσοντος·
μὴ μὲν ἅδην ἔκπαγλα περιβρίθοιεν ἀπάντη,
τηλοτέρω δ' αὐχμοῖο συνασταχύοιεν ἄρουραι.   10

ᵃ Theophr. 46 ὅταν μέλιτται μὴ ἀποπέτωνται μακρὰν ἀλλ'
αὐτοῦ ἐν τῇ εὐδίᾳ πέτωνται, χειμῶνα ἐσόμενον σημαίνει ; Verg.
G. iv. 191 ff. "Nec vero a stabulis pluvia impendente
recedunt Longius aut credunt caelo adventantibus Euris, Sed
circum tutae sub moenibus urbis aquantur, Excursusque
breves tentant."

ᵇ Theophr. 38 ἐὰν ὑποστραφῶσι (γέρανοι) πετόμενοι χειμῶνα
σημαίνουσι.

ᶜ Theophr. 29 ἀράχνια πολλὰ φερόμενα πνεῦμα ἢ χειμῶνα
σημαίνει.

ᵈ Theophr. 29 ἐὰν πῦρ μὴ θέλῃ ἅπτεσθαι, χειμέριον· καὶ
ἐὰν λύχνος ἅπτεσθαι μὴ ἐθέλῃ, χειμῶνα σημαίνει.

ᵉ Theophr. 42 τέφρα πηγνυμένη νιφετόν (σημαίνει).

bees[a] go not far afield to cull wax, but wheel hard
by their honey and their stores, nor do cranes[b] on
high in long lines wing their steady onward course,
but wheel and double in their flight.   Look, too,
for foul weather, when in windless calm airy
gossamers[c] are flying, and when the rays of the
lamp are wan and flickering, or when in fair weather
fire and torches[d] are hard to kindle.   Why recount
all the warning hints that come to men?   The
unsightly clotting of the ash[e] is sign of snow: the
ring of spots like millet[f] seed around the blazing
wick of the lamp betokens snow; but sign of hail[g]
are live coals, when they outward brightly shine,
but in their centre appears, as it were, a hazy mist
within the glowing fire.

Nor are holm-oaks,[h] laden with acorns, and the
dark mastich[i] untried.   With frequent glance on
every side the miller ever peers, anxious lest the
summer slip from his hand.   Holm-oaks with
moderate crops of frequent acorns will tell of heavy
storm to come.   Pray that they may not be exceedingly heavy laden, but only that far from
drought the cornfields flourish even as they.

---

[f] Theophr. 42 ἐὰν ὥσπερ κέχροις πολλοῖς κατάπλεως (ὁ λύχνος)
ᾖ, χειμερίσει· καὶ ἐὰν κύκλῳ περὶ τὸ λαμπρὸν ὦσιν εὐδίας
οὔσης, χιονικόν.

[g] Theophr. 25 φασὶ δέ τινες καὶ εἰ ἐν ἄνθραξι λαμπρὰ χάλαζα
ἐπιφαίνηται, χάλαζαν προσημαίνειν ὡς τὰ πολλά.

[h] Theophr. 45 οἱ πρῖνοι ἐὰν εὐκαρπῶσι, χειμῶνες πολλοὶ
σφόδρα γίνονται; 49 οἱ πρῖνοι ὅταν εὐκαρπῶσι σφόδρα, ὡς μὲν τὰ
πολλὰ χειμῶνα ἰσχυρὸν σημαίνουσιν, ἐνίοτε δὲ καὶ αὐχμούς φασι
γίνεσθαι.

[i] *Pistacia Lentiscus* L. See M. de Thevenot, *Travels
into the Levant*, Eng. trans. Lond. 1687, i. chap. lxii. for
the confusion of σχῖνος, σκίλλα (*Urginea maritima*); *cf.* Plut.
Per. 3.

ARATUS

τριπλόα δὲ σχῖνος κυέει, τρισσαὶ δέ οἱ αὖξαι
γίνονται καρποῖο, φέρει δέ τε σήμαθ' ἑκάστη   320
ἐξείης ἀρότῳ. καὶ γάρ τ' ἀροτήσιον ὥρην
τριπλόα μείρονται, μέσσην καὶ ἐπ' ἀμφότερ' ἄκρα·
πρῶτος μὲν πρώτην ἄροσιν, μέσσος δέ τε μέσσην   1055
καρπὸς ἀπαγγέλλει, πυμάτην γε μὲν ἔσχατος
    ἄλλων.

ὅντινα γὰρ κάλλιστα λοχαίη σχῖνος ἄρηται,   325
κείνῳ γ' ἐξ ἄλλων ἄροσις πολυλήϊος εἴη,
τῷ δέ γ' ἀφαυροτάτῳ ὀλίγη, μέσσῳ δέ τε μέσση.
αὔτως δ' ἀνθέρικος τριχθὰ σκίλλης ὑπερανθεῖ   1060
σήματ' ἐπιφράσσασθαι ὁμοίου ἀμητοῖο.
ὅσσα δ' ἐνὶ σχίνου ἀροτὴρ ἐφράσσατο καρπῷ,   330
τόσσα δὲ καὶ σκίλλης τεκμαίρεται ἄνθεϊ λευκῷ.

    Αὐτὰρ ὅτε σφῆκες μετοπωρινὸν ἤλιθα πολλοὶ
πάντη βεβρίθωσι, καὶ ἑσπερίων προπάροιθεν   1065
Πληϊάδων εἴποι τις ἐπερχόμενον χειμῶνα,
οἷος ἐπὶ σφήκεσσιν ἑλίσσεται αὐτίκα δῖνος.   335
θήλειαι δὲ σύες, θήλεια δὲ μῆλα καὶ αἶγες
ὁππότ' ἀναστρωφῶσιν ὀχῆς, τὰ δέ γ' ἄρσενα πάντα
δεξάμεναι πάλιν αὖτις ἀναβλήδην ὀχέωνται,   107
αὔτως κε σφήκεσσι μέγαν χειμῶνα λέγοιεν.

---

[a] Theophr. 55 ὁ τῆς σχίνου καρπὸς σημαίνει τοὺς ἀρότους·
ἔχει δὲ τρία μέρη καὶ ἔστιν ὁ πρῶτος τοῦ πρώτου ἀρότου σημεῖον,
ὁ δεύτερος τοῦ δευτέρου, ὁ τρίτος τοῦ τρίτου· καὶ ὡς ἂν τούτων
κλίνῃ κάλλιστα καὶ γένηται ἁδρότατος, οὕτως ἕξει καὶ ὁ κατὰ
τοῦτον ἄροτος ; Cic. De div. i. 9 (quoted Plin. N.H. xviii. 228)
"Iam vero semper viridis semperque gravata Lentiscus
triplici solita est grandescere fetu, Ter fruges fundens tria
tempora monstrat arandi."
    [b] Theophr. H.P. vii. 13. 6 ποιεῖται δὲ (ἡ σκίλλα) τὰς ἀνθή-

PHAENOMENA

Thrice[a] the mastich buds and thrice wax ripe its
berries. Each crop in turn brings a sign for the
sowing. For men divide the sowing season into
three—early, middle, late. The first crop of mastich
heralds the first of grain; the second the middle;
the latest the last of all. The richest crop that
the teaming mastich bears will hint of the wealthiest
harvest from the plough: the meanest crop foretells scanty grain, and average mastich heralds
average corn. Likewise the stalk of the squill[b]
flowers thrice to give hint of corresponding harvest.
All the hints the farmer marked in the mastich
crop, the same he learns from the white blossom of
the squill.

But when in autumn frequent swarms of wasps[c]
crowd on every side, one can foretell the winter-
storm to come even before the Pleiads are wester-
ing,[d] swift and sudden as the eddy wherein the
wasps are wheeling. Sows and ewes and she-goats,
when after mating with the male they mate again,[e]
equally with wasps foretell heavy storm. When she-

σεις τρεῖς ὧν ἡ μὲν πρώτη δοκεῖ σημαίνειν τὸν πρῶτον ἄροτον, ἡ δὲ
δευτέρα τὸν μέσον, ἡ δὲ τρίτη τὸν ἔσχατον. ὡς γὰρ ἂν αὖται
γένωνται, καὶ οἱ ἄροτοι σχεδὸν οὕτως ἐκβαίνουσιν.
[c] Theophr. 47 ἔστι δὲ σημεῖον χειμώνων μεγάλων καὶ ὄμβρων
καὶ ὅταν γένωνται ἐν τῷ μετοπώρῳ πολλοὶ σφῆκες.
[d] The scholl. wrongly explain this of the " evening rising "
(ἑσπερία ἀνατολή) of the Pleiades. The reference is to the
time when in the morning they are near the Western
horizon, precisely as in Theocritus vii. 53 ἑσπερίοις Ἐρίφοις
means when the Kids are in the West in the morning. The
setting of the Pleiades marked the beginning of Winter;
here early Winter comes before they set. The statements
in the Calendars of late Greek and Roman writers have to
be used with the greatest caution.
[e] Theophr. 25 ὅταν (πάλιν) ὀχεύωνται πρόβατα ἢ αἶγες, χειμῶνος
μακροῦ σημεῖον.

ARATUS

ὀψὲ δὲ μισγομένων αἰγῶν μήλων τε συῶν τε   340
χαίρει ἄνολβος ἀνήρ, ὅ οἱ οὐ μάλα θαλπιόωντι
εὔδιον φαίνουσι βιβαιόμεναι ἐνιαυτόν.

Χαίρει καὶ γεράνων ἀγέλαις ὡραῖος ἀροτρεὺς   1075
ὥριον ἐρχομέναις, ὁ δ᾽ ἀώριος αὐτίκα μᾶλλον·
αὕτως γὰρ χειμῶνες ἐπέρχονται γεράνοισιν·   345
πρώϊα μὲν καὶ μᾶλλον ὁμιλαδὸν ἐρχομένῃσιν
πρώϊον· αὐτὰρ ὅτ᾽ ὀψὲ καὶ οὐκ ἀγεληδὰ φανεῖσαι
πλειότερον φορέονται ἐπὶ χρόνον οὐδ᾽ ἅμα πολλαί,   1080
ἀμβολίῃ χειμῶνος ὀφέλλεται ὕστερα ἔργα.

Εἰ δὲ βόες καὶ μῆλα μετὰ βρίθουσαν ὀπώρην   350
γαῖαν ὀρύσσωσιν, κεφαλὰς δ᾽ ἀνέμοιο βορῆος
ἀντία τείνωσιν, μάλα κεν τότε χείμερον αὐταὶ
Πληϊάδες χειμῶνα κατερχόμεναι φορέοιεν·   1085
μὴ δὲ λίην ὀρύχοιεν· ἐπεὶ μέγας οὐ κατὰ κόσμον
γίνεται οὔτε φυτοῖς χειμὼν φίλος οὔτ᾽ ἀρότοισιν.   355
ἀλλὰ χιὼν εἴη πολλὴ μεγάλαις ἐν ἀρούραις,
μήπω κεκριμένη μηδὲ βλωθρῇ ἐπὶ ποίῃ,
ὄφρα τις εὐεστοῖ χαίρῃ ποτιδέγμενος ἀνήρ.   1090

Οἱ δ᾽ εἶεν καθύπερθεν ἐοικότες ἀστέρες αἰεί·
μηδ᾽ εἷς μήτε δύω μήτε πλέονες κομόωντες·   360
πολλοὶ γὰρ κομόωσιν ἐπ᾽ αὐχμηρῷ ἐνιαυτῷ.

Οὐδὲ μὲν ὀρνίθων ἀγέλαις ἠπειρόθεν ἀνήρ,
ἐκ νήσων ὅτε πολλαὶ ἐπιπλήσσωσιν ἀρούραις,
ἐρχομένου θέρεος χαίρει· περιδείδιε δ᾽ αἰνῶς   109?
ἀμητῷ, μή οἱ κενεὸς καὶ ἀχύρμιος ἔλθῃ   365
αὐχμῷ ἀνιηθείς. χαίρει δέ που αἰπόλος ἀνὴρ

---

[a] Theophr. 54 πρόβατα ὀψὲ ὀχευόμενα εὐδιεινὸν ἀποτελοῦσι τὸ σημεῖον. Contrast 40 πρόβατα ἐὰν πρωῒ ὀχεύηται, πρωῖον χειμῶνα σημαίνουσι.

[b] Theophr. 38 γέρανοι ἐὰν πρωῒ πέτωνται καὶ ἀθρόοι, πρωῒ χειμάσει, ἐὰν δὲ ὀψὲ καὶ πολὺν χρόνον, ὀψὲ χειμάσει.

[c] Theophr. 41 μετοπώρῳ ἐὰν πρόβατα ἢ βόες ὀρύττωσι . . .

292

PHAENOMENA

goats and ewes and sows mate late *a* in the season, the poor man rejoices, because their mating reveals to him that is thinly clad the coming of an open winter.

In seasonable flight of thronging cranes *b* rejoices the seasonable farmer : in untimely flight the untimely ploughman. For ever so the winters follow the cranes : early winters, when their flight is early and in flocks : when they fly late and not in flocks, but over a longer period in small bands, the later farming benefits by the delay of winter.

If oxen and sheep *c* after the heavy-laden Autumn dig the ground and stretch their heads to face the North wind, verily the Pleiads at their setting will bring a stormy winter. Pray that their digging be not excessive, for then is the winter exceedingly severe and a foe both to tree and tilth. May deep snow clothe the mighty fields, veiling the tender shoot, not yet separate nor tall, so that the anxious husbandman may rejoice in well-being.

May the stars above shine ever with due brightness ; and may no comets,*d* one nor two nor more, appear ! for many comets herald a season of drought.

Nor on the mainland *e* does the husbandman rejoice at the coming of summer to see trooping flocks of birds, when from the islands they alight upon his fields, but exceeding dread is his for the harvest, lest vexed by drought it come with empty ears and chaff. But the goat-herd rejoices even in

τὸν χειμῶνα χειμέριον σημαίνει. ἐν δὲ τῷ Πόντῳ φασὶν ὅταν Ἀρκτοῦρος ἀνατείλῃ θᾶττον, ἐναντίους τῷ βορρᾷ νέμεσθαι.

d Theophr. 34 οἱ κομῆται ἀστέρες ὡς τὰ πολλὰ πνεύματα σημαίνουσιν, ἐὰν δὲ πολλοί, καὶ αὐχμόν.

e Theophr. 17 καὶ θέρους ὅταν πολλοὶ ἀθρόοι φανῶσιν ὄρνιθες οἱ βιοτεύουσιν ἐν νήσῳ, ὕδωρ σημαίνουσιν· ἐὰν δὲ μέτριοι, ἀγαθὸν αἰξὶ καὶ βοτοῖς, ἐὰν δὲ πολλοὶ ὑπερβολῇ, αὐχμὸν ἰσχυρόν.

αὐταῖς ὀρνίθεσσιν, ἐπὴν κατὰ μέτρον ἴωσιν,
ἐλπόμενος μετέπειτα πολυγλαγέος ἐνιαυτοῦ.   1100
οὕτω γὰρ μογεροὶ καὶ ἀλήμονες ἄλλοθεν ἄλλοι
ζώομεν ἄνθρωποι. τὰ δὲ πὰρ ποσὶ πάντες ἑτοῖμοι 370
σήματ' ἐπιγνῶναι καὶ ἐσαυτίκα ποιήσασθαι.

'Αρνάσι μὲν χειμῶνας ἐτεκμήραντο νομῆες,
ἐς νομὸν ὁππότε μᾶλλον ἐπειγόμενοι τροχόωσιν,   1105
ἄλλοι δ' ἐξ ἀγέλης κριοί, ἄλλοι δὲ καὶ ἀμνοὶ
εἰνόδιοι παίζωσιν ἐρειδόμενοι κεράεσσιν·   375
ἢ ὁπότ' ἄλλοθεν ἄλλοι ἀναπλήσσωσι πόδεσσιν
τέτρασιν οἱ κοῦφοι, κεραοί γε μὲν ἀμφοτέροισιν·
ἢ καὶ ὅτ' ἐξ ἀγέλης ἀεκούσια κινήσωσιν   1110
δείελον εἰσελάοντες ὅμως, τὰ δὲ πάντοθι ποίης
δάκνωσιν πυκινῇσι κελευόμενα λιθάκεσσιν.   380

'Εκ δὲ βοῶν ἐπύθοντ' ἀρόται καὶ βουκόλοι
ἄνδρες
κινυμένου χειμῶνος· ἐπεὶ βόες ὁππότε χηλὰς
γλώσσῃ ὑπωμαίοιο ποδὸς περιλιχμήσωνται,
ἢ κοίτῳ πλευρὰς ἐπὶ δεξιτερὰς τανύσωνται,   1115
ἀμβολίην ἀρότοιο γέρων ἐπιέλπετ' ἀροτρεύς.   385
οὐδ' ὅτε μυκηθμοῖο περίπλειοι ἀγέρωνται
ἐρχόμεναι σταθμόνδε βόες βουλύσιον ὥρην,
σκυθραὶ λειμῶνος πόριες καὶ βουβοσίοιο   1120
αὐτίκα τεκμαίρονται ἀχείμεροι ἐμπλήσεσθαι.
οὐδ' αἶγες πρίνοιο περισπεύδουσαι ἀκάνθαις   390
εὔδιοι, οὐδὲ σύες φορυτῷ ἐπιμαργαίνουσαι.

ᵃ Theophr. 15 βοῦς τὴν προσθίαν ὁπλὴν λείξας χειμῶνα ἢ
ὕδωρ σημαίνει.

ᵇ Theophr. 41 βόες . . ἐπὶ τὸ δεξιὸν κατακλινόμενοι χειμέριον ;
54 βοῦς ἐπὶ τὸ ἀριστερὸν ἰσχίον κατακλινόμενος εὐδίαν σημαίνει,
. . ἐπὶ δεξιὸν δὲ χειμῶνα.

ᶜ Theophr. 49 καὶ τὸ πανταχοῦ δὲ λεγόμενον σημεῖον δημόσιον
χειμέριον ὅταν σύες [μύες Th. ; μῦες (sic) Wimmer, Hort] περὶ

the birds, when they come in moderate flocks
with promise of a season of plenteous milk.
For thus do we poor, changeful mortals win in
divers ways our livelihood, and all are ready to
mark the warnings at their feet and adopt them
for the moment.

Sheep warn the shepherd of coming storm when
they rush to pasture in haste beyond their wont, but
some behind the flock, now rams, now lambs, sport
by the way with butting horns, when some here,
some there, they bound aloft, the sillier young with
four feet off the ground, the horned elders with two,
or when the shepherd moves an unwilling flock,
though it be evening when he drives them to their
pens, while ever and anon they pluck the grass,
though urged by many a stone.

From oxen too the ploughman and the neat-herd
learn of the stirring of the storm. When oxen lick [a]
with their tongue around the hooves of their fore-feet
or in their stalls stretch themselves on their right
side,[b] the old ploughman expects the sowing to be
delayed. When with ceaseless lowing the kine
collect as they wend at eventide to their stalls,
the heifers reluctant to leave the meadow pasture-
land give warning that anon they will not feed in
stormless weather. Not fair weather do the goats
betide when greedy for prickly holm-oak, and the
sows rage furiously over their bedding.[c]

φορυτοῦ μάχωνται καὶ φέρωσιν. Verg. G. i. 399 f. (a good
weather sign is when) " non ore solutos Immundi meminere
sues iactare maniplos." Plut. Mor. 129 A seems to attribute
this sign to Democritus : ἄτοπον γάρ ἐστι κοράκων μὲν λα-
ρυγγισμοῖς καὶ κλωσμοῖς (κλωγμοῖς) ἀλεκτορίδων καὶ " συσὶν ἐπὶ
φορυτῷ μαργαινούσαις," ὡς ἔφη Δημόκριτος, ἐπιμελῶς προσέχειν,
σημεῖα ποιουμένους πνευμάτων καὶ ὄμβρων.

Καὶ λύκος ὁππότε μακρὰ μονόλυκος ὠρύηται,
ἢ ὅγ' ἀροτρήων ὀλίγον πεφυλαγμένος ἀνδρῶν   1125
ἔργα κατέρχηται, σκέπαος χατέοντι ἐοικώς,
ἐγγύθεν ἀνθρώπων, ἵνα οἱ λέχος αὐτόθεν εἴη,   395
τρὶς περιτελλομένης ἠοῦς χειμῶνα δοκεύειν.
οὕτω καὶ προτέροις ἐπὶ σήμασι τεκμήραιο
ἐσσομένων ἀνέμων ἢ χείματος ἢ ὑετοῖο,   1130
αὐτὴν ἢ μετὰ τὴν ἢ καὶ τριτάτην ἔτ' ἐς ἠῶ.

   'Αλλὰ γὰρ οὐδὲ μύες, τετριγότες εἴ ποτε μᾶλλον 400
εὔδιοι ἐσκίρτησαν ἐοικότες ὀρχηθμοῖσιν,
ἄσκεπτοι ἐγένοντο παλαιοτέροις ἀνθρώποις·
οὐδὲ κύνες· καὶ γάρ τε κύων ὠρύξατο ποσσὶν   1135
ἀμφοτέροις χειμῶνος ἐπερχομένοιο δοκεύων,
καὶ κεῖνοι χειμῶνα μύες τότε μαντεύονται.   405
καὶ μὴν ἐξ ὕδατος καὶ καρκίνος ᾤχετο χέρσον,
χειμῶνος μέλλοντος ἐπαΐσσεσθαι ὁδοῖο.

   Καὶ μύες ἡμέριοι ποσσὶ στιβάδα στρωφῶντες 1140
κοίτης ἱμείρονται, ὅτ' ὄμβρου σήματα φαίνοι.

   Τῶν μηδὲν κατόνοσσο· καλὸν δ' ἐπὶ σήματι
     σῆμα   410
σκέπτεσθαι· μᾶλλον δὲ δυοῖν εἰς ταὐτὸν ἰόντων
ἐλπωρὴ τελέθοι, τριτάτῳ δέ κε θαρσήσειας.
αἰεὶ δ' ἂν παριόντος ἀριθμοίης ἐνιαυτοῦ   1145
σήματα, συμβάλλων εἴ που καὶ ἐπ' ἀστέρι τοίη
ἠὼς ἀντέλλοντι φαείνεται ἢ κατιόντι,   415
ὁπποίην καὶ σῆμα λέγοι. μάλα δ' ἄρκιον εἴη
φράζεσθαι φθίνοντος ἐφισταμένοιό τε μηνὸς
τετράδας ἀμφοτέρας· αἱ γάρ τ' ἄμυδις συνιόντων   1150
296

PHAENOMENA

When a solitary wolf[a] howls loud, or when, as if he sought for shelter, recking little of farmer men, he descends to the cultivated lands near to men to seek a lair there, expect a storm when the third dawn comes round. So, too, by the previous signs thou canst forecast the winds or storm or rain to come on the self-same day or on the morrow or it may be on the third morn.

Mice,[b] too, as sign of storm, whenever with louder squeaking than their wont they gambolled and seemed to dance in fair weather, were not unmarked by the weather-seers of old. Nor were dogs. The dog[c] with both his paws digs when he suspects the coming of a storm, and then too those mice turn prophets. And landward comes the crab, when the storm is about to burst.

Mice in the daytime toss straw and are fain to build a nest when Zeus shows signs of rain.

Make light of none of these warnings. Good rule it is to look for sign confirming sign. When two point the same way, forecast with hope; when three, with confidence. Thou canst always add the signs of the passing season, comparing whether at rising or at setting of a star the day dawn such as the calendar would herald. It would profit much to mark the last four days of the old and the first four of the new month.[d] They hold the terms of

[a] Theophr. 46 λύκος ὠρυόμενος χειμῶνα σημαίνει διὰ τριῶν ἡμερῶν. λύκος ὅταν πρὸς τὰ ἔργα ὁρμᾷ ἢ εἴσω χειμῶνος ὥρᾳ, χειμῶνα σημαίνει εὐθύς.

[b] Theophr. 41 μύες τρίζοντες καὶ ὀρχόμενοι χειμέριον.

[c] Theophr. 42 κύων τοῖς ποσὶν ὀρύττουσα . . . χειμέριον.

[d] Theophr. 5 μάλιστα δὲ κυριώτατα (sc. σημεῖα) ἀπὸ τοῦ ἡλίου καὶ τῆς σελήνης. ἡ γὰρ σελήνη νυκτὸς οἷον ἥλιός ἐστι· διὸ καὶ αἱ σύνοδοι τῶν μηνῶν χειμέριοί εἰσιν ὅτι ἀπολείπει τὸ φῶς τῆς σελήνης ἀπὸ τετράδος φθίνοντος μέχρι τετράδος ἱσταμένου . . .

ARATUS

μηνῶν πείρατ᾽ ἔχουσιν, ὅτε σφαλερώτερος αἰθὴρ
ὀκτὼ νυξὶ πέλει, χήτει χαροποῖο σελήνης.   420
    Τῶν ἅμυδις πάντων ἐσκεμμένος εἰς ἐνιαυτὸν
οὐδέποτε σχεδίως κεν ἐπ᾽ αἰθέρι τεκμήραιο.

the meeting months, when the sky on eight nights is deceptive beyond its wont for lack of the bright-eyed Moon.

Study all the signs together throughout the year and never shall thy forecast of the weather be a random guess.

LYCOPHRON

INTRODUCTION

1. THE LIFE OF LYCOPHRON

OUR authorities for the life of Lycophron are a notice in Suidas *s.v.* Λυκόφρων, and a Life by Tzetzes prefixed to his commentary (Westermann, *Biogr.* p. 142), and some scattered references in other authors. The information which these give us is of the scantiest kind, and in the matter of dates we have to depend on various inferences.

Lycophron was a native of Chalcis in Euboea; son of Socles (possibly the Socles of Athen. xi. 473 A) and the adoptive son of the historian Lycus of Rhegium, of whom Suidas *s.v.* Λύκος says: "Also called Butheras, of Rhegium, historian, father of Lycophron the tragedian; flourished in the time of the Diadochi and was plotted against by Demetrius of Phalerum. He wrote a history of Libya, and on Sicily."

The date of Lycophron's birth may be put about 330–325 B.C. His earlier years seem to have been spent in Chalcis and Athens, possibly also in Rhegium, and his literary activity was devoted to the writing of tragedies.

In those early years he naturally came in contact with Menedemus (died soon after 278 B.C.) of Eretria, founder of the Eretrian or Neo-Megarian School of Philosophy (Life in Diog. Laert. ii. chap. 17); *cf.* Diog. Laert. ii. 132. Menedemus was fond of entertaining and held *symposia* both of poets and musicians. Ἠσπάζετο δὲ καὶ Ἄρατον καὶ Λυκόφρονα τὸν τῆς τραγῳδίας ποιητὴν καὶ τὸν Ῥόδιον Ἀνταγόραν (epic poet: some lines of his to Eros preserved in Diog. Laert. iv. 26 f.). To this period must belong the *Menedemus* of Lycophron, which was a satyric

LYCOPHRON

drama : Diog. Laert. ii. 140 ἃ πάντα φησὶν ὁ Λυκόφρων ἐν τοῖς πεποιημένοις Σατύροις αὐτῷ, οὓς Μενέδημον ἐπέγραψεν, ἐγκώμιον τοῦ φιλοσόφου ποιήσας τὸ δρᾶμα. ὧν καί τινά ἐστι τοιαυτί·

> ὡς ἐκ βραχείας δαιτὸς ἡ βαιὰ κύλιξ
> αὐτοῖς κυκλεῖται πρὸς μέτρον, τράγημα δὲ
> ὁ σωφρονιστὴς τοῖς φιληκόοις λόγος.

(fr. 3 Nauck)

(*i.e.* " When after a scanty meal the little cup circles among them moderately and for desert the studious guests have improving conversation ").

Athen. ii. 55 D " Lycophron of Chalcis in a satyric drama which he wrote in mockery (ἐπὶ καταμωκήσει) on Menedemus the philosopher, from whom was named the sect (αἵρεσις) of the Eretrics, making fun of the banquets of the philosophers says καὶ δημόκοινος . . . συμπότης" (see below). Athen. x. 419 f., after an amusing description from the *Life of Menedemus* by Antigonus of Carystus of the banquets of Menedemus, adds : " Lycophron of Chalcis, too, bears witness with regard to these, having written a satyric play *Menedemus* (γράψας σατύρους Μενέδημον), in which Silenus says to the satyrs :

> παῖδες κρατίστου πατρὸς ἐξωλέστατοι,
> ἐγὼ μὲν ὑμῖν, ὡς ὁρᾶτε, στρηνιῶ·
> δεῖπνον γὰρ οὔτ' ἐν Καρίᾳ, μὰ τοὺς θεούς,
> οὔτ' ἐν Ῥόδῳ τοιοῦτον οὔτ' ἐν Λυδίᾳ
> κατέχω δεδειπνηκώς. Ἄπολλον ὡς καλόν.

(fr. 1 Nauck)

(*i.e.* " Cursed children of most excellent father, I, as you see, wax riotous. For not in Caria, by the gods, nor in Rhodes, nor in Lydia, do I remember to have dined so well ! Apollo ! what a feast !") ; and again :

> ἀλλὰ κυλίκιον
> ὑδαρὲς ὁ παῖς περιῆγε τοῦ πεντωβόλου,
> ἀτρέμα παρεξεστηκός. ὅ τ' ἀλιτήριος
> καὶ δημόκοινος ἐπεχόρευε δαψιλῆς
> θέρμος πενήτων καὶ τρικλίνου συμπότης.

(fr. 2 Nauck)

INTRODUCTION

(*i.e.* " But the boy carried round a watery cup of five-obol wine, slightly turned ; and the accursed hangman lupine danced on abundantly—the boon-companion of poor men and the dining-room ").

He goes on to say that discussions were carried on over their wine (ζητήσεις ἦσαν παρὰ πότον),

τράγημα γὰρ
ὁ σωφρονιστὴς πᾶσιν ἐν μέσῳ λόγος.

(fr. 3 Nauck)

(*i.e.* " For dessert improving conversation ").

It is related, too, that their meetings were often so prolonged that

ὁ τὴν ἕω καλῶν
κατέλαβεν ὄρνις, τοῖσι δ' οὐδέπω κόρος.

(fr. 4 Nauck)

(*i.e.* " Chanticleer, calling the dawn, surprised them still unsatisfied ").

It was inevitable that Lycophron should be attracted by the brilliant literary society then flourishing in Alexandria. Thither accordingly he went, at what date we do not precisely know. But we have seen that Suidas, in his notice of Lycus, mentions the enmity which existed between that historian and Demetrius of Phalerum. Demetrius apparently enjoyed great influence with Ptolemy I., whom he advised to put the crown of Egypt past the son of Berenice. That son came to the throne as Ptolemy II. Philadelphus in 285 B.C. on the abdication of his father, and, after the death of the latter in 283 B.C., he put Demetrius under ward μέχρι τι δόξει περὶ αὐτοῦ. Shortly afterwards Demetrius was bitten in his sleep by an asp and died (Diog. Laert. v. 78). The removal of his adoptive father's enemy would open the way for Lycophron to go to the court of Ptolemy, and we shall probably be sufficiently near the truth if we suppose that he went to Alexandria *circ.* 285-283 B.C.

Here Lycophron was entrusted with the arrangement of the Comic Poets in the royal library, and it was then doubtless that he wrote his treatise Περὶ κωμῳδίας : Athen.

LYCOPHRON

iv. 140 A ; vii. 278 A B Λυκόφρων ἐν τοῖς περὶ κωμῳδίας ; xi. 485 D Λυκόφρων δ' ἐν τῷ θ' περὶ κωμῳδίας ; xi. 501 D E ; xiii. 555 A Λυκόφρων ὁ Χαλκιδεὺς ἐν τοῖς περὶ κωμῳδίας.

How long Lycophron remained in Alexandria, or whether he died there, we have no knowledge. Nor do we know anything of the circumstances of his death beyond what we gather from Ovid, *Ibis* 531 f., who seems to imply that he was killed by an arrow :

> Utque cothurnatum cecidisse Lycophrona narrant,
> Haereat in fibris fixa sagitta tuis.

2. WORKS

The notice in Suidas *s.v.* Λυκόφρων after mentioning his parentage proceeds: "Grammarian and maker of tragedies. At any rate he is one of the seven who were called the Pleias. His tragedies are *Aeolus, Andromeda, Aletes* (Wanderer), *Aeolides,[a] Elephenor, Heracles, Hiketae* (Suppliants), *Hippolytus, Cassandreis, Laios, Marathonii, Nauplius, Oedipus a' β', Orphanus* (Orphan), *Pentheus, Pelopidae, Symmachi* (Allies), *Telegonus, Chrysippus.* Of these the *Nauplius* is a revised version (διασκευή). He also wrote the play called *Alexandra*, the obscure poem (τὸ σκοτεινὸν ποίημα)."

The Πλειάς was the name given by the later Alexandrine scholars to the seven most eminent tragic poets of the time of Ptolemy Philadelphus. The list is variously given. Schol. A Hephaest. p. 140 Consbr. gives Homer the younger (son of Andromachus and Myro), Sositheus, Lycophron, Alexander (Aetolus), Philicus (Philiscus), Dionysiades. Here some name is wanting. Choeroboscus, Hephaest. p. 236 Consbr., gives the last three as Aeantiades, Sosiphanes, Philicus, but mentions that for Aeantiades and Sosiphanes some give Dionysiades (Strabo xiv. 675) and Euphronius.

According to Tzetzes in *Lyc.* pp. 262 and 270 (Müller) Lycophron wrote in all either 64 or 46 tragedies. The list in Suidas, apparently extracted from a more complete

---

[a] Αἰθαλίδης O. Iahn, *Philol.* xxviii. 6.

list, is in a roughly alphabetical order. It need only be noticed further that some of the titles suggest Lycophron's tendency to use the less familiar myths, while the *Cassandreis* apparently dealt with the fortunes of the people of Cassandreia = Potidaea (Strabo vii. 330) on the isthmus of Pallene, and was thus founded on contemporary history.

Besides the fragments of the *Menedemus* quoted above we have four lines from the *Pelopidae* preserved in J. Stobaeus, *Floril.* 119. 13 Λυκόφρονος ἐκ Πελοπιδῶν·

> ἀλλ' ἡνίκ' ἂν μὲν ᾖ πρόσω τὸ κατθανεῖν,
> Ἅιδης ποθεῖται τοῖς δεδυστυχηκόσιν·
> ὅταν δ' ἐφέρπῃ κῦμα λοίσθιον βίου,
> τὸ ζῆν ποθοῦμεν· οὐ γὰρ ἔστ' αὐτοῦ κόρος.

(fr. 5 Nauck)

> While death is far away
>   Sad hearts are fain to die;
> But when the latest wave
>   Of life draws nigh,
> We fain would live, for life
>   Knows no satiety.

The date of the *Alexandra* has been the subject of much dispute.

It is argued, on the one hand, that it belongs to the early or Chalcis - Athens period of Lycophron's life because (1) it shows no trace of Attic or Sicilian comedy, while it is full of echoes of tragic, lyric, and iambic poets; (2) it shows no special knowledge of Egyptian geography nor any trace of his special relation to the Ptolemaic court. Thus *Alexandra* 576 Triton = Nile, while in 848 Asbystes = Nile. Wilamowitz held that Callim. fr. 13 (from the *Aitia* i.) *ap.* Steph. Byz. *s.v.* Ἀσβυστία· οἵη τε Τρίτωνος ἐφ' ὕδασιν Ἀσβύσταο is meant as a tacit correction of this. (But it is quite in Lycophron's manner to use either Triton or Asbystes indifferently to mean Libyan.) On these grounds it is argued that the *Alexandra* as a whole may be dated as early as 295 B.C.

As against this it is urged (1) that Lycophron would scarcely have been included in the Pleias, if on coming to Alexandria he had ceased to write tragedy. (2) The

LYCOPHRON

enormous number of tragedies ascribed to him implies a prolonged activity in that kind.

But two passages in the *Alexandra* cause special difficulty : vv. 1226-1280 and 1446-1450.

The first of these passages raised difficulties in the mind of the schol. Marc. (Theon?) v. 1226 f. ἐντεῦθεν περὶ Ῥωμαίων λέγει καὶ Λυκόφρονος ἑτέρου νομιστέον εἶναι τὸ ποίημα, οὐ τοῦ γράψαντος τὴν τραγῳδίαν· συνήθης γὰρ ὢν τῷ Φιλαδέλφῳ οὐκ ἂν περὶ Ῥωμαίων διελέγετο (cf. Tzetz. *ad loc.* περὶ Ῥωμαίων ἐντεῦθεν διαλαμβάνει. τὰ δὲ λοιπὰ τοῦ σχολίου γέλοια· φασὶ γὰρ Λυκόφρονος ἑτέρου εἶναι τὸ ποίημα . . . διελέγετο), *i.e.* Lycophron at the court of the Ptolemies would not have referred to the Romans as holding "the sceptre and monarchy of earth and sea" (1229).

But apart from the position of Lycophron as a court poet, a further difficulty was raised by C. J. Fox (1749-1806), in his correspondence with Gilbert Wakefield (1756-1801). Fox pointed out that a Greek poet of Lycophron's time, *i.e.* before the First Punic War (264-241 B.C.), could not have referred to the power of Rome in the terms of 1226 ff. and 1446 ff. which also apparently refer to Rome.

R. P. Knight to Dr. Parr, Whitehall, Jan. 22 : " Fox and I have been lately reading Lycophron, and having been both startled with the distinctness of some predictions of events which happened long after the age when he is supposed to have flourished, we have had some correspondence upon the subject, but without any other effect than increasing our perplexity. The *Testimonium Veterum,* published with Potter's edition, is strong in support of the authenticity of this poem, and of its being written by one of the Pleiades, as they are called ; yet in v. 1226 *et seq.* there is a distinct prediction of the universality of the Roman Empire ; and in v. 446, as distinct a one of the fall of the Macedonian monarchy μεθ' ἕκτην γενεάν (*sic*) from Alexander, who is clearly described. Perseus, indeed, was not the sixth king of Macedonia from Alexander, but, nevertheless, he was the sixth in the line of descent of his own family from that conqueror,

INTRODUCTION

which is more in point. Cannot you prove that Lycophron
was a Jew or Atheist who conversed with some inspired
persons of that nation? What a triumph would it be for
Revelation! for, except the prophecies of Isaiah concern-
ing Cyrus, there are none in the sacred volume half so
unequivocal; and the merely human testimony (the only
one which infidels will admit) in support of the prophecies
of Isaiah, is weak indeed when compared with that in
support of Lycophron" (Parr's Works vii. p. 304).

Niebuhr [a] assumed that the *Alexandra* was the work of
a later poet who wrote after the First Punic war. In
general scholars have inclined to one or other theory:
that the passages in question are later interpolations,
or that the *Alexandra* as a whole is the work of a later
poet.

The reference in 1435 ff. is exceedingly obscure.
According to Wilamowitz the lines refer to Alexander the
Great. The Argives who must bow themselves before
him are the Persians, who are in 1442 designated by the
word ὅμαιμοι as brothers of Alexander; ᾧ 1446 is, according to Wilamowitz, Alexander. He translates μεθ' ἕκτην
γένναν αὐθαίμων ἐμός as "mihi post sex generationes co-
gnatus," and he reckons the six generations backwards
from Cassandra thus: Cassandra—Priam—Laomedon—
Ilos—Tros—Dardanus—Zeus, whose son was Perseus,
ancestor of the Argeads and the Persians, Hdt. vii. 150.
Hence he concludes that αὐθαίμων ἐμός must be either the
Persian people generally, or a definite Persian. He himself decides for Artabazos, father of Barsine, whose son
(Heracles) by Alexander was put to death by Polyperchon
in 309 B.C. (L. 801 ff.).

Holzinger [b] takes the reference in 1435 ff. to be to
Pyrrhus (αἴθων, 1439). The wolf of Galadra is Demetrius
Poliorcetes. The sons of Cassander, who as sons of
Thessalonice are Argeads, were compelled to give up the

[a] B. G. Niebuhr, "Ueber das Zeitalter Lykophrons des
Dunkeln," *Rhin. Mus.*, 1827, pp. 108 ff.
[b] *Lykophron's Alexandra, gr. u. deutsch,* C. von
Holzinger, Leipzig, 1895.

throne of Macedonia to Demetrius. The blood-relation of Cassandra is Fabricius, who is the εἶς τις παλαιστής 1447. Holzinger takes μεθ' ἕκτην γένναν—most improbably—to mean "after six crops," in reference to the six years' duration of the campaign of Pyrrhus in Italy. Holzinger puts the date of the *Alexandra* about 274 B.C

William N. Bates in *Harvard Studies in Classical Philology* vi. (Boston, 1895) discusses "The Date of Lycophron" p. 75 f. This discussion appears to be entirely without value, but his conclusion may be quoted : Lycophron "was born between 325 and 320, wrote his *Alexandra* about 295, was appointed to arrange the comedies in the Alexandrian library in 285–284" (this is based on the assumption that the *Alexandra* was imitated in the βωμός of Dosiades written 285–270 (Wilamowitz), 292–290 (Susemihl)) ; "about 280 he was flourishing as a tragic poet, and continued as such down to the date of his death, which must have occurred before the year 250, and probably shortly before the year 265."

The problem of the *Alexandra* is discussed by P. Corssen, "Ist die Alexandra dem Tragiker Lykophron abzusprechen?" *Rhein. Mus.* lxviii., 1913, pp. 321–335.

He agrees with Sudhaus that the Lion 1439 is Alexander the Great and that the Ἀργεῖοι 1443 = Πέρσαι (*cf.* Herodot. vii. 150) ; but he does not agree with him in identifying αὐθαίμων ἐμός 1446 with T. Quinctius Flamininus, who defeated Philip V. of Macedon at Cynoscephalae in 197 B.C.

To that identification he objects that (1) σκύλων ἀπαρχάς κτλ. 1450 would in that case be meaningless, as the Romans got no immediate profit from the war with Philip; (2) the victory of Flamininus, in alliance with the Achaeans and actively supported by the Aetolians, the fruits of which fell to the Greeks, the ancient enemies of Troy, could in no sense be regarded as a revenge for the destruction of Troy.

Corssen's own view is briefly as follows : The struggle is between Asia and Europe, which have nothing in common (1283 f.). In this struggle the two great events are the destruction of Troy by Agamemnon and the expedition

INTRODUCTION

of Xerxes against Greece. According to Herodotus it was in the destruction of Troy that the Persians found the ground of their hostility to Greece. Accordingly, to the sack of Troy by Agamemnon 1369 ff. corresponds the expedition of Xerxes 1412 ff. The long struggle between Asia and Europe is ended by Alexander the Great 1439 ff., who as successor to Agamemnon leads the hosts of Europe against Asia.

The leading idea in the poet's mind is not of " reconciliation " either between Rome and Macedon or between Rome and Greece—but of the equating justice of Fate. What Troy lost in the East is balanced by the success of Troy's descendants—the Romans—in the West, and this is expressed in 1226 ff.

Here arises the difficulty of the words γῆς καὶ θαλάσσης σκῆπτρα καὶ μοναρχίαν.

Now if by μοναρχία we understand world-dominion, then that could not be predicated of the Romans even after the battle of Cynoscephalae, in view of the fact that the power of Syria and Egypt was still unshaken. World-dominion could not be predicated before the battle of Pydna in 168 B.C.

The poet of the *Alexandra* knows nothing of the extent of the Roman dominion as at the beginning of the second century B.C. The limits of the Roman kingdom known to him must be assumed to coincide with the limits of the kingdom of Aeneas as described in 1238 ff., together with the extensions made through the struggle of the Romans with the sixth successor of Alexander the Great (1450).

From the conquest of the Persians by Alexander the poet passes to Pyrrhus and the Romans.

The Lion of 1440 is clearly a definite person and, as the ancient scholia recognized, must be Alexander the Great, who is a Thesprotian, *i.e.* an Epeirote, on his mother's side, and a Chalastraean, *i.e.* a Macedonian, (Strabo vii. 330. 20) on the father's side, and is moreover a descendant of Aeacus and Dardanus (1440) through his mother : ἡ δὲ ᾿Ολυμπιὰς ἡ μήτηρ αὐτοῦ εἰς Πύρρον τὸν ᾿Αχιλλέως

311

LYCOPHRON

καὶ Ἕλενον τὸν Πριάμου τὸ γένος τὸ ἀνέκαθεν ἀνέφερεν, ὥς φησι Θεόπομπος καὶ Πύρανδρος. ἀναφέρεται δὲ ὁ Πύρρος εἰς Αἰακόν, ὁ δὲ Ἕλενος εἰς Δάρδανον (schol. Lycophr.).

Now if the Lion is Alexander, the Wolf of Galadra (a Macedonian town, according to Steph. Byz.) must be distinguished from him. The explanation of the expression is no longer apparent, but the Wolf must embody the whole nation which, finally, was conquered by the Romans.

The six generations must be represented by the kings of Macedon. Including Alexander, we get Pyrrhus in the sixth place, thus : Alexander, died 323 ; Philip Arrhidaeus, died 317 ; Cassander, died 297 ; his three sons 297–295 ; Demetrius Poliorcetes 294–288 ; Pyrrhus. The fact that Pyrrhus immediately lost the throne of Macedon does not prevent the poet from seeing in him the heir of Alexander who, turning against the descendants of the Trojans, renews the old struggle. The "wrestler" (1447) is, like the Wolf of Galadra, not an individual but the whole people.

When the poet says that the Romans came into collision with Pyrrhus by sea and by land, that is not in the strict sense true. But Pyrrhus suffered from Rome's allies, the Carthaginians, a heavy defeat at sea, which benefited Rome as well, and the Romans themselves, through the Greek towns of South Italy, won importance at sea, so that the expression γῆς καὶ θαλάσσης σκῆπτρα καὶ μοναρχίαν referring to the successes won in the Tarentine War, is not entirely without justification. But the term μοναρχία is to be understood in the light of the historical idea which underlies the whole poem ; i.e. the Persians handed over the sceptre of their old dominion, for which Asia and Europe had fought from of old, to the Wolf of Galadra. Pyrrhus loses the sceptre to the Romans, and thus the old dominion, which was taken from Priam by Agamemnon, reverts again to the Trojans.

With Pyrrhus the Romans made neither peace nor treaty. Pyrrhus gave up the struggle and went back home. But before Tarentum fell, the astute Ptolemy, rightly recognizing the importance of the Roman victory.

INTRODUCTION

hastened to conclude an alliance with them. The
Romans on their side sent an embassy in 273 B.C. to
Alexandria, which was honoured by Ptolemy with valuable
gifts, which, however, the ambassador handed over to the
state. (Dio Cassius fr. 41, Livy, Perioch. xiv.) The
personal object to be supplied with εἰς διαλλαγὰς μολών
is, accordingly, not the defeated party. After his victory
the Roman will conclude agreements and be celebrated as
the most honourable friend.

On this interpretation the prophecies of Cassandra do
not go beyond the poet's own time, and his glorification of
the Romans does not stand in contradiction to the policy
of his royal master.

Thus the statement of Suidas that the author of the
Alexandra was Lycophron the tragic poet is confirmed.
Nor is there good ground for doubting his statement that
Lycophron of Chalcis, son of Socles, was adopted by
Lycus of Rhegium. Beloch, holding that Suidas has
confused two different Lycophrons—(1) of Chalcis, son of
Socles, author of the *Alexandra*, (2) son of the historian
Lycus of Rhegium, the tragic poet at the Court of Ptolemy
Philadelphus—found support for this theory (1) in
Suidas *s.v.* Λύκος where Lycus is called the father of the
tragic Lycophron, (2) in the Tzetzes' Life where it is said :
ὁ Λυκόφρων οὑτοσὶ τῷ μὲν γένει Χαλκιδεὺς ἦν υἱὸς Σωκλέους ἢ
Λύκου τοῦ ἱστοριογραφοῦντος κατά τινας.

This, Corssen says, is merely a wilful perversion of the
tradition, induced by the surprise which the Scholiast
expressses that a court poet of Philadelphus should have
expressed himself in praise of the Romans. But just this
surprise shows what the tradition was.

To the objection that, if the author of the *Alexandra*
were the adoptive son of Lycus, he would not have passed
over the works of his adoptive father and confined himself
exclusively to Timaeus, Corssen replies by an endeavour
to show that in his account of the fortunes of Diomedes
and his companions (615 ff.) Lycophron does in fact follow
Lycus in opposition to Timaeus.

Corssen's conclusion is that external evidence and the

313

LYCOPHRON

results of an analysis of the poem agree excellently, and
thereby the abstruse poem of Lycophron obtains the
importance of a historical document which strikingly
reflects the great impression which the victory of the
Roman arms over the Hellenistic king made upon his
contemporaries.

3. MANUSCRIPTS

The critical recension of E. Scheer (Berlin, 1881) is
based on the following MSS. :

Class I.—A = Marcianus 476 (Venetus lxx. 3). This,
which is by far the best MS. of Lycophron, belongs to the
eleventh century and bears to have been written by one
Nicetas a deacon.   After the Argument there is a marginal
note : κἀνταῦθα συνήθροισα λέξικοῦ λέξεις | νικήτας οὐλάχιστος τῶν
διακόνων.   Scheer, *Rhein. Mus.* xxxiv., identified this
Nicetas with the distinguished bishop of Serrhai (Seres) in
the eleventh century.

The MS. extends to sixty-five folia, sixty-two of which
are written upon.   Foll. 2–30ᵛ contain Aratus with the
scholia ; fol. 31ʳ to the middle of fol. 62 contain
Lycophron's *Alexandra* with scholia and two paraphrases—
an older (P) and a more recent (p).

V = Vaticanus 1307.   This is a copy of a copy (X) of A
and it is occasionally useful as A has suffered alteration
by two later hands A², A³, subsequent to the time when
the copy (X) was made.   V itself has suffered similar
interpolation, but it is not often that A and V have suffered
in the same passage.

B = Coislinianus 345 belonging to the tenth century.
It is so called as belonging to the collection of Henri
Charles du Cambout de Coislin (1664–1732), Bishop of
Metz, now in the Bibl. Nat., Paris.   This MS. contains
a number of Lexica and amongst them from p. 225 to p.
253 λέξεις ἀλεξάνδρας καὶ ὑπόθεσις.

At the end is τέλος σὺν θεῷ τοῦ λεξικοῦ λυκόφρονος.

The reason of it being included among Lexica is that
the lines are broken up into sections to each of which is
appended the interpretation of paraphrase P.   Thus v. 1

314

λέξω τὰ πάντα : φράσω τὰ πάντα : νητρεκῶς : ἀληθῶς. καὶ γὰρ
ἐπιτατικῶς νοοῦμεν τὸ ἦ, ὡς τὸ νήχυτος καὶ νήδυμος : ἀρχῆς ἀπ'
ἄκρας : ἅ με πυνθάνῃ καὶ ἐρωτᾷς : ἢν δὲ μηκυνθῇ λόγος : ἐὰν δ'
ἐκταθῇ τὸ ἔπος.

"The MS.," says Scheer, "which is most elegantly
written, has in fol. 225ʳ 35 lines, of which 7 contain the
Argument μαντευομένην . . . ἄπαντα ; the other pages have 36
lines each, except the last, which has 27 lines. The lemmata
are marked off from the paraphrase by two points usually
and small spaces : rarely by a colon, very rarely by a
comma. Much more often the scribe has forgotten to
distinguish the lemmata from the paraphrase ; at other
times he has omitted the paraphrase or the lemma or
both : finally he has repeatedly confused the sequence of
the sections of lines. The MS. is so full of errors that
I have seen no MS. of Lycophron—except Par. 2840—so
corrupt."

Class II.—C = Parisinus 2723. The subscription states
that the MS. was finished in June 1282. Foll. 1-76 contain
the *Alexandra* of Lycophron with the commentary of Isaac
Tzetzes. The colour of the ink shows that the scribe
took many various readings from the MS. which he was
copying and afterwards wrote between the lines and in
the margin and even inserted in the text (C²) other
readings from a second MS., from which also he inserted
interlinear scholia, the greater part of which was not
derived from the commentary of Tzetzes. There are also
a few corrections by a third hand (C³).

D = Parisinus 2403, thirteenth century. The MS.
consists of 308 folia, of which foll. 58-99 contain the
Alexandra with the commentary of Tzetzes. There are
many interlinear scholia mostly from the commentary
of Tzetzes, also *variae lectiones* mostly inserted by the
original copyist, very few added later (D²).

E = Palatinus graecus 218, fourteenth century. Foll.
9-65 contain the *Alexandra* with the commentary of
Tzetzes and many *variae lectiones* copied by the scribe
along with the text and occasional corrections by another
hand (E²).

LYCOPHRON

4. The Paraphrases

We have two paraphrases of the *Alexandra* :

P, the older, composed by some Byzantine grammarian and based on an ancient body of scholia, is best preserved in B, on which, accordingly, Scheer bases his recension, using as subsidiary aids A and Vaticanus 117, a fourteenth century MS. containing the *Alexandra* with the commentary of Tzetzes (foll. 30-113), both of which give P in a less perfect form.

p, a later paraphrase of uncertain date based upon P. Scheer's recension is based on A with the subsidiary aid of V.

5. The Scholia

The scholia of Lycophron are very excellent and are probably ultimately based on the commentary of Theon, son of Artemidorus, a grammarian of the time of Augustus and Tiberius, who wrote commentaries on Theocritus, Apollonius, Callimachus, Nicander, and Lycophron, as well as on some of the older classical poets. *Cf.* Steph. Byz. *s.v.* Κύτινα πόλις Θεσσαλίας, ὡς Θέων ἐν ὑπομνήματι Λυκόφρονος. So *id. s.v.* Αἴνεια . . . Θέων ὑπομνηματίζων τὸν Λυκόφρονα.

The ancient scholia are best represented by Marcianus 476 ; also Vaticanus 1307—a grandchild as we have seen of Marcianus 476—and Neopolitanus, Bibl. Nat. ii. D 4, a thirteenth-century MS. wrongly inscribed Ἰσαακίου τοῦ Τζέτζου σχόλια εἰς Λυκόφρονα, the scholia being in the main the ancient scholia, only some gaps due to injury to the original MS. having been filled up with the scholia of Tzetzes in the fifteenth century.

In addition to the ancient scholia we have further the commentary of Tzetzes (twelfth century): εἰς τὸν Λυκόφρονα σχόλια Ἰσαακίου γραμματικοῦ τοῦ Τζέτζου.

This commentary is in all MSS. ascribed to Isaac Tzetzes ; so also in John Tzetzes' commentary on the *Works and Days of Hesiod* (p. 10 Gaisford). But there is extant a letter in Parisinus 2565 Bibl. Reg. (No. xx.) of

316

INTRODUCTION

John Tzetzes to one Basilius, who had apparently, after Isaac's death, inquired of John whether it were true that he and not Isaac was the real author of the commentary on Lycophron. The letter runs thus: "To the First Secretary of the Patriarch (of Constantinople), Basilius of Achrida (town on lake of same name near Monastir) who had found in the title of John Tzetzes on Lycophron the name of Isaac Tzetzes. Pheidias, the famous sculptor, doing a favour by the law of friendship to Agoracritus, a painter by profession, but an unskilful one, having with great sculptural skill made the image of Zeus and Nemesis at Rhamnus, ascribed it to him, inscribing on it ΑΓΟΡΑΚΡΙΤΟΥ ΠΑΡΙΟΥ, and by means of that inscription made up to him for his lack of skill. If, then, Pheidias by the law of friendship did not hesitate in a matter of the highest moment to do a favour to a man unskilful in his art, am I to be behind him in regard to my brother, a carpenter, in Pindar's phrase, of deft hymns and incomparably dearer to me than Agoracritus was to Pheidias, inasmuch as brotherhood is a more compelling bond of affection than friendship? In this spirit both Pheidias and I ordered our inscriptions. But neither Pheidias of old suffered, nor has Tzetzes now suffered, from mental derangement or lethargy so as to reach such a pitch of madness as to forget his own name as some have suspected." So, too, in *Chil.* ix. 298 John Tzetzes refers to the commentary as his own work : ἐν δὲ τοῖς εἰς Λυκόφρονα ἐμοὶ ἐξηγηθεῖσι καὶ περὶ τούτου ἔγραψα τότε τοῦ Ζωΐλλίου.

Scheer is of opinion that the commentary was in the first place composed by John Tzetzes, who handed it over for revision and publication to his brother Isaac, who for his trouble received the credit of authorship. This would account for the numerous inconsistencies and contradictions of the commentary. Collaboration is implied by the words : οὕτως ἡμῖν τοῖς Τζετζίοις [τ. Τζ. is lacking in *a* (Par. 2723)] δοκεῖ ἔχειν (Tzetz. *ad Lycophr.* 17). Moreover, Scheer points out that in Tzetz. *Lycophr.* 1226 occur the words Ἰωάννης δὲ ὁ φιλόπονός φησιν εἶναι † βαίου. This had been taken to mean Ἰωάννης Φιλόπονος, a proper name. But Scheer takes these words to refer to John Tzetzes, and he points out that these words occur only in Parisinus 2723 (a) which may be taken to represent the commentary as first published by Isaac, while they have disappeared in the MSS. which represent subsequent revisions by John, of which there were several.

The chief MSS. which contain the Tzetzes commentary are classified thus :

Class I. — a = Parisinus 2723, representing the commentary as originally published by Isaac Tzetzes.

Class II.—Representing revisions by John Tzetzes, and including: Parisinus 2403 ; Vaticanus 1306 ; Palatinus 18 ; Ambrosianus 222 (this last representing the final recension by John Tzetzes).

The commentary of Tzetzes is based on a *corpus* of scholia similar to that contained in the Marcianus, with additions from other sources (discussed by Scheer ii. pp. xiv. ff.).

6. BIBLIOGRAPHY

Editio princeps.—Aldus Manutius, Venice, 1513 (with Pindar, Callimachus, Dionysius Periegetes); Paul Lecisius, Basel, 1548 (with Tzetzes' commentary); Canter, Basel, 1566 ; Meursius, Leyden, 1597 ; Potter, Oxford, 1697 ; Reichard, Leipzig, 1788 ; C. G. Müller, Leipzig, 1811 ; Sebastiani, Rome, 1830 ; Bachmann, Leipzig, 1830 ; Dehèque, Paris, 1853 ; G. Kinkel, Leipzig, 1880 (with scholia Marciana); E. Scheer vol. i. (text, critical notes and the two paraphrases) Berlin, 1881 ; vol. ii. (scholia) Berlin, 1908 ; C. von Holzinger, Leipzig, 1895 (text with German blank verse translation to face the text, introduction, and commentary). E. Ciaceri, Catane, Giannotta, 1901, text, trans. and commentary. Translation by Joseph Justus Scaliger, 1584. Text and trans. F. D. Dehèque, Paris, 1853. Viscount Royston, translation and notes, Cambridge, at the University Press, 1806.

Editio princeps of Tzetzes, Oporinus, Basel, 1546. Other literature : J. Konze, *De Lycophr. dictionis pro-*

INTRODUCTION

prietate in universum ratione simul habita Homeri et tragicorum, Münster, 1870; C. H. G. Voelcker, *De Lycophronis Cassandrae vv. 13–15*, Giessen, 1820; Scheer, *Nonnulli Lycophronis loci*, Plön, 1876; W. N. Bates, *Harvard Studies in Classical Philology*, vol. vi., Boston, 1895 ("The Date of Lycophron"); Gasse, *De L. mythographo*, 1910; I. Geffcken, "Zwei Dramen [Elephenor and Nauplios] des Lykophron," *Hermes* xxvi. (1891) pp. 33–42; also the same writer on Timaeos' *Geographie d. Westens*, Philol. Unters. (Kiessling-Moellendorff) 13, Berlin, 1892.

ΛΥΚΟΦΡΟΝΟΣ

ΑΛΕΞΑΝΔΡΑ

Λέξω τὰ πάντα νητρεκῶς, ἅ μ' ἱστορεῖς,
ἀρχῆς ἀπ' ἄκρας· ἢν δὲ μηκυνθῇ λόγος,
σύγγνωθι δέσποτ'· οὐ γὰρ ἥσυχος κόρη
ἔλυσε χρησμῶν, ὡς πρίν, αἰόλον στόμα,
ἀλλ' ἄσπετον χέασα παμμιγῆ ·βοὴν   **5**
δαφνηφάγων φοίβαζεν ἐκ λαιμῶν ὄπα,
Σφιγγὸς κελαινῆς γῆρυν ἐκμιμουμένη.
τῶν ἄσσα θυμῷ καὶ διὰ μνήμης ἔχω,
κλύοις ἄν, ὦναξ, κἀναπεμπάζων φρενὶ
πυκνῇ διοίχνει δυσφάτους αἰνιγμάτων   **10**
οἴμας τυλίσσων, ᾗπερ εὐμαθὴς τρίβος
ὀρθῇ κελεύθῳ τἀν σκότῳ ποδηγετεῖ.
ἐγὼ δ' ἄκραν βαλβῖδα μηρίνθου σχάσας,
ἄνειμι λοξῶν εἰς διεξόδους ἐπῶν,
πρώτην ἀράξας νύσσαν ὡς πτηνὸς δρομεύς.   **15**

    Ἠὼς μὲν αἰπὺν ἄρτι Φηγίου πάγον
κραιπνοῖς ὑπερποτᾶτο Πηγάσου πτεροῖς,
Τιθωνὸν ἐν κοίταισι τῆς Κέρνης πέλας
λιποῦσα, τὸν σὸν ἀμφιμήτριον κάσιν.

---

        [a] Priam.   [b] Cassandra.
    [c] The runner breaks the "tape" and takes off.

LYCOPHRON

ALEXANDRA

The speaker is a slave appointed to watch Cassandra and report her prophecies. He addresses Priam.

ALL will I tell truly that thou askest from the utter beginning, and if the tale be prolonged, forgive me, master.[a] For not quietly as of old did the maiden[b] loose the varied voice of her oracles, but poured forth a weird confused cry, and uttered wild words from her bay-chewing mouth, imitating the speech of the dark Sphinx. Thereof what in heart and memory I hold, hear thou, O King; and, pondering with wise mind, wind and pursue the obscure paths of her riddles, whereso a clear track guides by a straight way through things wrapped in darkness. And I, cutting the utter bounding thread,[c] will trace her paths of devious speech, striking the starting-point like winged runner.

Dawn was just soaring over the steep crag of Phegion[d] on swift wings of Pegasus, leaving in his bed by Cerne[e] Tithonus,[f] brother of thine by

[a] Mountain in Aethiopia.
[e] Cerne, a fabled island in the remotest East (Plin. *N.H.* vi. 198 ff.) or West (Strabo i. 47).
[f] Son of Laomedon and Strymo or Rhoeo, and so half-brother of Priam.

321

οἱ δ' οὖσα γρώνης εὐγάληνα χερμάδος   20
ναῦται λίαζον κἀπὸ γῆς ἐσχάζοσαν
ὕσπληγγας. αἱ δὲ παρθενοκτόνον Θέτιν
ἰουλόπεζοι θεῖνον εὐῶπες σπάθαις
πελαργοχρῶτες, αἱ Φαλακραῖαι κόραι,
ὑπὲρ Καλυδνῶν λευκὰ φαίνουσαι πτίλα,   25
ἄφλαστα, καὶ φώσσωνας ὠργυιωμένους
ἀπαρκτίαις πρηστῆρος αἴθωνος πνοαῖς.
ἡ δ' ἔνθεον σχάσασα βακχεῖον στόμα,
Ἄτης ἀπ' ἄκρων βουπλανοκτίστων λόφων,
τοιῶνδ' ἀπ' ἀρχῆς ἦρχ' Ἀλεξάνδρα λόγων·   30

Αἰαῖ, τάλαινα θηλαμῶν, κεκαυμένη
καὶ πρόσθε μὲν πεύκαισιν οὐλαμηφόροις
τριεσπέρου λέοντος, ὅν ποτε γνάθοις
Τρίτωνος ἠμάλαψε κάρχαρος κύων·
ἔμπνους δὲ δαιτρὸς ἡπάτων φλοιδούμενος   35
τινθῷ λέβητος ἀφλόγοις ἐπ' ἐσχάραις
σμήριγγας ἐστάλαξε κωδείας πέδῳ,
ὁ τεκνοραίστης, λυμεὼν ἐμῆς πάτρας,
ὁ δευτέραν τεκοῦσαν ἄτρωτον βαρεῖ
τύψας ἀτράκτῳ στέρνον, ἔν τ' αὐλῷ μέσῳ   40
πατρὸς παλαιστοῦ χερσὶν ὀχμάσας δέμας

---

[a] Apoll. Rh. iv. 1731 ὑπεύδια πείσματ' ἔλυσαν.
[b] i.e. the ships of Paris built of wood from Phalacra in the Troad.
[c] i.e. the Sea (Hellespont in wider sense; "maiden-slaying" in reference to death of Helle).
[d] Two islands near Tenedos.   [e] Cassandra.
[f] Ate, thrown out of Olympus by Zeus (Il. xix. 126), fell on a hill in the Troad which was hence called the Hill of Doom (Ἄτης λόφος). Dardanus was warned by Apollo not to build a city there. But Ilus, his great-grandson, being told by an oracle to found a city where a certain cow should rest, did so; and this place chanced to be the Hill of Doom.

another mother, and the sailors loosed in calm
weather the cables [a] from the grooved rock and
cut the landward ropes. And the centipede fairfaced stork-hued daughters of Phalacra [b] smote
maiden-slaying Thetis [c] with their blades, over
Calydnae [d] showing their white wings, their stern-
ornaments, their sails outspread by the northern
blasts of flaming stormwind: then Alexandra [e]
opened her inspired Bacchic lips on the high Hill
of Doom [f] that was founded by the wandering cow
and thus began to speak :

Alas ! hapless nurse [g] of mine burnt even afore-
time by the warlike pineships of the lion [h] that was
begotten in three evenings, whom of old Triton's
hound of jagged teeth devoured with his jaws. But
he, a living carver of the monster's liver, seething in
steam of cauldron on a flameless hearth, shed to
ground the bristles of his head ; he the slayer of his
children, [i] the destroyer of my fatherland ; who smote
his second mother [j] invulnerable with grievous shaft
upon the breast ; who, too, in the midst of the race-
course seized in his arms the body of his wrestler

---

[g] Ilios.

[h] Heracles. For his birth *cf.* Apollod. ii. 61 Ζεὺς . . . τὴν
μίαν τριπλασιάσας νύκτα. When Laomedon refused to pay
Poseidon and Apollo for building the walls of Troy, a sea-
monster appeared to which an oracle required that Hesione,
daughter of Laomedon, should be exposed. Heracles
entered the belly of the monster (Triton's hound) and cut its
inside to pieces. Laomedon had promised to give Heracles
the horses of Tros as a reward for slaying the monster and
when he broke his word, Heracles burnt Troy.

[i] Heracles slew his children by Megara daughter of Creon.

[j] Hera: Hom. *Il.* v. 392 f. ; " second mother " because
Athena tricked her into suckling him.

LYCOPHRON

Κρόνου παρ' αἰπὺν ὄχθον, ἔνθα γηγενοῦς
ἵππων ταρακτής ἐστιν Ἰσχένου τάφος,
ὁ τὴν θαλάσσης Αὐσονίτιδος μυχοὺς
στενοὺς ὀπιπεύουσαν ἀγρίαν κύνα   45
κτανὼν ὑπὲρ σπήλυγγος ἰχθυωμένην,
ταυροσφάγον λέαιναν, ἣν αὖθις πατὴρ
σάρκας καταίθων λοφνίσιν δωμήσατο,
Λέπτυνιν οὐ τρέμουσαν, οὐδαίαν θεόν·
ἐξηνάριξεν ὅν ποτ' ἀξίφῳ δόλῳ   50
νέκυς, τὸν Ἅιδην δεξιούμενον πάλαι·
λεύσσω σε, τλῆμον, δεύτερον πυρουμένην
ταῖς τ' Αἰακείοις χερσὶ τοῖς τε Ταντάλου
Λέτριναν οἰκουροῦσι λειψάνοις πυρὸς
παιδὸς καταβρωθέντος αἰθάλῳ δέμας,   55
τοῖς Τευταρείοις βουκόλου πτερώμασι·
τὰ πάντα πρὸς φῶς ἡ βαρύζηλος δάμαρ,
στείλασα κοῦρον τὸν κατήγορον χθονός,
ἄξει, πατρὸς μομφαῖσιν ἠγριωμένη,
λέκτρων θ' ἕκατι τῶν τ' ἐπεισάκτων γάμων.   60
αὐτὴ δὲ φαρμακουργός, οὐκ ἰάσιμον
ἕλκος δρακοῦσα τοῦ ξυνευνέτου λυγρὸν
Γιγαντοραίστοις ἄρδισιν τετρωμένου

---

[a] Zeus.   [b] At Olympia.
[c] A giant : his tomb at Olympia where as Taraxippus he
causes horses to shy.
[d] Scylla, whom Heracles slew because she robbed him of
one of the oxen of Geryon. Her father, Phorkys, restored
her to life by burning her body.
[e] Persephone : τὴν λεπτύνουσαν τὰ σώματα τῶν ἀπο-
θνῃσκόντων (schol.).
[f] Nessus the Centaur, when dying by the arrow of
Heracles, gave of his blood a pretended love-charm to
Deianeira who smeared with it a mantle for Heracles which
consumed him ; cf. Soph. Tr. 555 ff.

sire ^{a} beside the steep hill of Cronus,^{b} where is the horse-affrighting tomb of earth-born Ischenus ^{c}; who also slew the fierce hound ^{d} that watched the narrow straits of the Ausonian sea, fishing over her cave, the bull-slaying lioness whom her father restored again to life, burning her flesh with brands: she who feared not Leptynis,^{e} goddess of the underworld. But one day with swordless guile a dead corse ^{f} slew him: yea, even him ^{g} who of old overcame Hades; I see thee, hapless city, fired a second time by Aeacean hands ^{h} and by such remains ^{i} as the funeral fire spared to abide in Letrina ^{j} of the son ^{k} of Tantalus when his body was devoured by the flames, with the winged shafts of the neat-herd Teutarus ^{l}; all which things the jealous spouse ^{m} shall bring to light, sending her son ^{n} to indicate the land, angered by her father's ^{o} taunts, for her bed's sake and because of the alien bride.^{p} And herself,^{q} the skilled in drugs, seeing the baleful wound incurable of her husband ^{r} wounded by the giant-slaying arrows of

^{g} Heracles, who wounded Hades at Pylus, $Il.$ v. 395.

^{h} Neoptolemus.

^{i} The bones of Pelops were brought from Letrina near Olympia to Troy, as an oracle declared that Troy could not otherwise be taken. ^{j} In Elis. ^{k} Pelops.

^{l} Teutarus, Scythian who taught Heracles archery and bequeathed his bow and arrows to him. Heracles bequeathed them to Philoctetes, who with them slew Paris and enabled the Greeks to take Troy.

^{m} Oenone, the first wife of Paris, sent her son to guide the Greeks. When Philoctetes slew Paris with the bow which Heracles had used in the battle of the gods against the giants, Oenone threw herself upon his corpse and died with him; $cf.$ Tennyson, $Oenone.$

^{n} Corythus, son of Oenone by Paris.

^{o} Cebren, father of Oenone.

^{p} Helen. ^{q} Oenone. ^{r} Paris.

LYCOPHRON

πρὸς ἀνθοπλίτου, ξυνὸν ὀγχήσει μόρον,
πύργων ἀπ' ἄκρων πρὸς νεόδμητον νέκυν 65
ῥοιζηδὸν ἐκβράσασα κύμβαχον δέμας·
πόθῳ δὲ τοῦ θανόντος ἠγκιστρωμένη,
ψυχὴν περὶ σπαίροντι φυσήσει νεκρῷ.

Στένω, στένω σε δισσὰ καὶ τριπλᾶ, δορὸς
αὖθις πρὸς ἀλκὴν καὶ διαρπαγὰς δόμων 70
καὶ πῦρ ἐναυγάζουσαν αἰστωτήριον.
στένω σε, πάτρα, καὶ τάφους Ἀτλαντίδος
δύπτου κέλωρος, ὅς ποτ' ἐν ῥαπτῷ κύτει,
ὁποῖα πορκὸς Ἰστριεὺς τετρασκελής,
ἀσκῷ μονήρης ἀμφελυτρώσας δέμας, 75
Ῥειθυμνιάτης κέπφος ὣς ἐνήξατο,
Ζήρυνθον ἄντρον τῆς κυνοσφαγοῦς θεᾶς
λιπὼν ἐρυμνὸν κτίσμα Κυρβάντων Σάον,
ὅτ' ἠμάθυνε πᾶσαν ὀμβρήσας χθόνα
Ζηνὸς καχλάζων νασμός· οἱ δὲ πρὸς πέδῳ 80
πύργοι κατηρείποντο, τοὶ δὲ λοισθίαν
νήχοντο μοῖραν προὐμμάτων δεδορκότες.
φηγὸν δὲ καὶ δρύκαρπα καὶ γλυκὺν βότρυν
φάλλαι τε καὶ δελφῖνες αἵ τ' ἐπ' ἀρσένων
φέρβοντο φῶκαι λέκτρα θουρῶσαι βροτῶν. 85

Λεύσσω θέοντα γρυνὸν ἐπτερωμένον
τρήρωνος εἰς ἅρπαγμα Πεφναίας κυνός,
ἣν τόργος ὑγρόφοιτος ἐκλοχεύεται,
κελυφάνου στρόβιλον ὠστρακωμένην.

Καὶ δή σε ναύτην Ἀχερουσία τρίβος 90

ᵃ Philoctetes. ᵇ Electra.
ᵉ Dardanus, buried in Troy, was son of Zeus and Electra,
daughter of Atlas. During the Deluge he swam from
Samothrace to the Troad.
ᵈ In North Crete. ᵉ In Samothrace.
ᶠ Hecate. ᵍ Samothrace.
326

his adversary,[a] shall endure to share his doom, from the topmost towers to the new slain corpse hurtling herself head foremost, and pierced by sorrow for the dead shall breathe forth her soul on the quivering body.

I mourn, mourn twice and three times for thee who lookest again to the battle of the spear and the harrying of thy halls and the destroying fire. I mourn for thee, my country, and for the grave of Atlas' daughter's[b] diver son,[c] who of old in a stitched vessel, like an Istrian fish-creel with four legs, sheathed his body in a leathern sack and, all alone, swam like a petrel of Rheithymnia,[d] leaving Zerynthos,[e] cave of the goddess[f] to whom dogs are slain, even Saos,[g] the strong foundation of the Cyrbantes, what time the plashing rain of Zeus laid waste with deluge all the earth.[h] And their towers were hurled to the ground, and the people set themselves to swim, seeing their final doom before their eyes. And on oat and acorn and the sweet grape browsed the whales and the dolphins and the seals that are fain of the beds of mortal men.[i]

I see the winged firebrand[j] rushing to seize the dove,[k] the hound of Pephnos,[l] whom the water-roaming vulture brought to birth, husked in a rounded shell.[m]

And thee, cuckold sailor,[n] the downward path of

[h] See H. Usener, *Die Sintflutsagen*, pp. 45 f.
[i] For the seal's affection for man *cf.* Aelian, *N.A.* iv. 56.
[j] Paris.   [k] Helen.   [l] In Laconia.
[m] Referring to Zeus and Leda, and the birth of Helen from an egg.
[n] Paris reaches Taenarum in Laconia where was a fabled entrance to Hades; passes Onugnathus and Las and through the "two thoroughfares" (entrance and exit between Cranaë and the mainland) to Gytheion.

καταιβάτις πύγαργον, οὐ πατρὸς κόπρους
στείβοντα ῥακτῶν βουστάθμων, ξενώσεται,
ὡς πρόσθε, κάλλους τὸν θυωρίτην τριπλαῖς.
ἀλλ' ὀστρίμων μὲν ἀντὶ Γαμφηλὰς ὄνου
καὶ Λᾶν περάσεις, ἀντὶ δ' εὐχίλου κάπης   95
καὶ μηλιαυθμῶν ἠδὲ χερσαίας πλάτης
τράμπις σ' ὀχήσει καὶ Φερέκλειοι πόδες
δισσὰς σαλάμβας κἀπὶ Γυθείου πλάκας,
ἐν αἷσι πρὸς κύνουρα καμπύλους σχάσας
πεύκης ὀδόντας, ἕκτορας πλημμυρίδος,   100
σκαρθμῶν ἰαύσεις εἰναφώσσωνα στόλον.

Καὶ τὴν ἄνυμφον πόρτιν ἁρπάσας λύκος,
δυοῖν πελειαῖν ὠρφανισμένην γονῆς
καὶ δευτέραν εἰς ἄρκυν ὀθνείων βρόχων
ληῖτιν ἐμπταίσασαν ἰξευτοῦ πτερῷ,   105
Θύσαισιν ἁρμοῖ μηλάτων ἀπάργματα
φλέγουσαν ἐν κρόκαισι καὶ Βύνη θεᾷ,
θρέξεις ὑπὲρ Σκάνδειαν Αἰγίλου τ' ἄκραν,
αἴθων ἐπακτὴρ καγχαλῶν ἀγρεύματι.

Νήσῳ δ' ἐνὶ δράκοντος ἐκχέας πόθον   110
Ἀκτῆς, διμόρφου γηγενοῦς σκηπτουχίας,
τὴν δευτέραν ἔωλον οὐκ ὄψει Κύπριν,
ψυχρὸν παραγκάλισμα κἀξ ὀνειράτων
κεναῖς ἀφάσσων ὠλέναισι δέμνια.

---

[a] Onugnathus, cape in Laconia.
[b] In Laconia.
[c] Builder of the ships of Paris.
[d] Haven near Sparta.
[e] Paris sailed with nine ships (schol.).
[f] Paris.
[g] Helen, who was not wedded to Paris.
[h] Iphigeneia, Helen's daughter by Theseus, and Hermione,
her daughter by Menelaus.
[i] Helen was first carried off by Theseus.

Acheron shall receive, walking no more the byres of thy father's rugged steadings, as once when thou wert arbiter of beauty for the three goddesses. But in place of stables thou shalt pass the Jaws of the Ass [a] and Las,[b] and instead of well-foddered crib and sheepfold and landsman's blade a ship and oars of Phereclus [c] shall carry thee to the two thorough-fares and the levels of Gytheion,[d] where, on the rocks dropping the bent teeth of the pine-ship's anchors to guard against the flood, thou shalt rest from gambols thy nine-sailed [e] fleet.

And when thou, the wolf,[f] shalt have seized the unwed heifer,[g] robbed of her two dove daughters [h] and fallen into a second [i] net of alien snares and caught by the decoy of the fowler, even while upon the beach she burns [j] the firstlings of the flocks to the Thysad nymphs and the goddess Byne, then shalt thou speed past Scandeia [k] and past the cape of Aegilon,[l] a fierce hunter exulting in thy capture.

And in the Dragon's Isle [m] of Acte,[n] dominion of the twyformed son [o] of earth, thou shalt put from thee thy desire; but thou [p] shalt see no morrow's aftermath of love, fondling in empty arms a chill embrace and a dreamland bed.[q] For the sullen

[j] Helen was carried off by Paris when she was sacrificing to the Thysades (Thyiades) and Byne = Ino Leucothea.

[k] Haven of Cythera (*Il.* x. 268).

[l] Island between Cythera and Crete.

[m] Cranaë (Hom. *Il.* iii. 445, *cf.* Paus. iii. 22. 1), where the bedding of Paris and Helen took place, is generally localized near Gytheion in Laconia. Here it is identified with the so-called Helen's Isle near Sunium. Tzetzes took it to mean Salamis.

[n] Attica. [o] Erechtheus. [p] Paris.

[q] Proteus replaced the real Helen by a phantom.

LYCOPHRON

ὁ γάρ σε συλλέκτροιο Φλεγραίας πόσις 115
στυγνὸς Τορώνης, ᾧ γέλως ἀπέχθεται
καὶ δάκρυ, νῆις δ' ἐστὶ καὶ τητώμενος
ἀμφοῖν, ὁ Θρήκης ἔκ ποτ' εἰς ἐπακτίαν
Τρίτωνος ἐκβολαῖσιν ἠλοκισμένην
χέρσον περάσας, οὐχὶ ναυβάτῃ στόλῳ, 120
ἀλλ' ἀστίβητον οἶμον, οἷά τις σιφνεύς,
κευθμῶνος ἐν σήραγγι τετρήνας μυχούς,
νέρθεν θαλάσσης ἀτραποὺς διήνυσε,
τέκνων ἀλύξας τὰς ξενοκτόνους πάλας
καὶ πατρὶ πέμψας τὰς ἐπηκόους λιτὰς 125
στῆσαι παλίμπουν εἰς πάτραν, ὅθεν πλάνης
Παλληνίαν ἐπῆλθε γηγενῶν τροφόν—
κεῖνός σε, Γουνεὺς ὥσπερ, ἐργάτης δίκης
τῆς θ' Ἡλίου θυγατρὸς Ἰχναίας βραβεύς,
ἐπεσβολήσας λυγρὰ νοσφιεῖ γάμων, 130
λίπτοντα κάσσης ἐκβαλὼν πελειάδος·
ὃς τοὺς Λύκου τε καὶ Χιμαιρέως τάφους
χρησμοῖσι κυδαίνοντας οὐκ αἰδούμενος
οὐδ' Ἀνθέως ἔρωτας οὐδὲ τὸν ξένοις
σύνδορπον Αἰγαίωνος ἁγνίτην πάγον 135
ἔτλης θεῶν ἀλοιτὸς ἐκβῆναι δίκην,

ᵃ Proteus came from his home in Egypt to Pallene
(=Phlegra, Herod. viii. 123 in Chalcidice), the birth-place of
the giants, where he married Torone, by whom he had two
sons who slew strangers by compelling them to wrestle with
them and were in the end themselves slain by Heracles.
Proteus, vexed by the wickedness of his sons, besought his
father Poseidon for a passage under the sea back to Egypt.
On his sons' death he could neither be sorry nor glad.
ᵇ Nile.   ᶜ Tmolus and Telegonus.

husband,[a] whose spouse is Torone of Phlegra, even
he to whom laughter and tears are alike abhorred
and who is ignorant and reft of both ; who once on a
time crossed from Thrace unto the coastland which
is furrowed by the outflow of Triton [b] ; crossed not
by sailing ship but by an untrodden path, like some
moldwarp, boring a secret passage in the cloven
earth, made his ways beneath the sea, avoiding the
stranger-slaying wrestling of his sons [c] and sending
to his sire [d] prayers which were heard, even that he
should set him with returning feet in his fatherland,[e]
whence he had come as a wanderer to Pallenia, nurse
of the earth-born—he, like Guneus,[f] a doer of
justice and arbiter of the Sun's daughter of Ichnae,[g]
shall assail thee with evil words and rob thee of thy
bridal, casting thee forth in thy desire from thy
wanton dove : thee who, regarding not the tombs of
Lycus and Chimaereus [h], glorious in oracles, nor thy
love of Antheus [i] nor the pure salt of Aigaeon [j]
eaten by host and guest together, didst dare to sin
against the gods and to overstep justice, kicking the

---

[a] Poseidon.   [e] Egypt.

[f] Guneus, an Arab famous for justice, whom Semiramis
made arbiter between the Phoenicians and Babylonians
(schol.).

[g] Themis Ichnaia, worshipped at Ichnae in Thessaly
(Strabo 435).

[h] L. and C., sons of Prometheus and Celaeno, were buried
in the Troad. The Lacedaemonians, being visited by a
plague, were bidden by an oracle to " propitiate the Cronian
daemons in Troy," and Menelaus was sent to make offerings
at their graves.

[i] Son of Antenor, was loved by Paris who killed him
unwittingly. Menelaus, being at the time in Troy, took
Paris with him to Sparta to save him from punishment.
Thus Paris, as guest of Menelaus, had " eaten his salt."

[j] Poseidon = Sea.

331

λάξας τράπεζαν κἀνακυπώσας Θέμιν,
ἄρκτου τιθήνης ἐκμεμαγμένος τρόπους.

   Τοιγὰρ ψαλάξεις εἰς κενὸν νευρᾶς κτύπον,
ἄσιτα κἀδώρητα φορμίζων μέλη·   140
κλαίων δὲ πάτραν τὴν πρὶν ἠθαλωμένην
ἴξῃ χεροῖν εἴδωλον ἠγκαλισμένος
τῆς πενταλέκτρου θυιάδος Πλευρωνίας.
γυιαὶ γὰρ εὐναστῆρας ἄμναμοι τριπλαῖς
πήναις κατεκλώσαντο δηναιᾶς Ἁλὸς   145
νυμφεῖα πεντάγαμβρα δαίσασθαι γάμων.

   Δοιὼ μὲν ἁρπακτῆρας αὐγάσει λύκους,
πτηνοὺς τριόρχας αἰετοὺς ὀφθαλμίας,
τὸν δ' ἐκ Πλυνοῦ τε κἀπὸ Καρικῶν ποτῶν
βλαστόντα ῥίζης, ἡμικρῆτα βάρβαρον,   150
Ἐπειόν, οὐκ Ἀργεῖον ἀκραιφνῆ γοναῖς,
οὗ πάππον ἐν γαμφαῖσιν Ἐνναία ποτὲ
Ἕρκυνν' Ἐρινὺς Θουρία Ξιφηφόρος
ἄσαρκα μιστύλασα τύμβευσεν φάρῳ,
τὸν ὠλενίτην χόνδρον ἐνδατουμένη.   155
ὃν δὴ δὶς ἡβήσαντα καὶ βαρὺν πόθον

---

[a] Paris, exposed when a child, was suckled by a she-bear.
[b] Helen, daughter of Leda, daughter of Thestius, son of Agenor, son of Pleuron.
[c] The Fates—Clotho, Lachesis, Atropos, daughters of Tethys.
[d] Theseus, Menelaus, Paris, Deiphobus, Achilles.
[e] Theseus and Paris.
[f] Menelaus is a descendant of Atlas (Atlas—Sterope—Oenomaus — Hippodameia — Pelops — Atreus — Menelaus) who dwells in Libya, here indicated by Plynos in Cyrenaica (Strabo 838). Carian either refers to Καρικὸν τεῖχος (Steph. B.) in Libya or to the Carians having once dwelt in Lacedaemon (schol.) or to Minos' dominion over the Carians. Menelaus is thus a "barbarian" and through his mother. Aerope, daughter of Catreus, son of Minos, he is "half-

table and overturning Themis, modelled in the ways
of the she-bear *a* that suckled thee.

Therefore in vain shalt thou twang the noisy
bowstring, making melodies that bring nor food nor
fee ; and in sorrow shalt thou come to thy fatherland that was burnt of old, embracing in thine
arms the wraith of the five-times-married frenzied
descendant *b* of Pleuron. For the lame daughters *c*
of the ancient Sea with triple thread have decreed
that her bedfellows shall share their marriage-feast
among five bridegrooms. *d*

Two *e* shall she see as ravening wolves, winged
wanton eagles of sharp eyes ; the third *f* sprung
from root of Plynos and Carian waters, a half-Cretan
barbarian, an Epeian, no genuine Argive by birth :
whose grandfather *g* of old Ennaia *h* Hercynna Erinys
Thuria, the Sword-bearer, cut fleshless with her
jaws and buried in her throat, devouring the gristle
of his shoulder : his who came to youth again and

Cretan." As grandson of Hippodameia he is an Epeian=
Elean (Pind. *O.* ix. 58, x. 35).

g Pelops was served up by his father Tantalus at a banquet
to the gods, when Demeter ate part of his shoulder unwittingly. Restored to life and carried off by Poseidon
(Pind. *O.* i. 40), he was sent by Zeus to Elis where he
overcame Oenomaus in a chariot-race and won his daughter
Hippodameia for his bride, after thirteen previous suitors
had been slain by her father (Pind. *O.* i. 81 ff.). His victory
was due to the treachery of Oenomaus' charioteer Myrtilus,
son of Hermes, who, when he asked Pelops for the price of
his treachery, was by him hurled into the sea, which was
hence called Myrtoan (Paus. viii. 14. 11), cursing with his
last breath the house of Pelops.

h Demeter : E. in reference to rape of Persephone in
Enna ; H. by-name of Demeter at Lebadeia in Boeotia ;
E. at Thelpusa in Arcadia (Callim. fr. incert. 91) ; Th. =
" Passionate " with grief for her daughter (schol.) ; Sw., cult-
name of Demeter in Boeotia (schol.).

LYCOPHRON

φυγόντα Ναυμέδοντος ἁρπακτήριον
ἔστειλ᾽ Ἐρεχθεὺς εἰς Λετριναίους γύας
λευρὰν ἀλετρεύσοντα Μόλπιδος πέτραν,
τοῦ Ζηνὶ δαιτρευθέντος Ὀμβρίῳ δέμας,   160
γαμβροκτόνον ῥαίσοντα πενθεροφθόροις
βουλαῖς ἀνάγνοις, ἃς ὁ Καδμίλου γόνος
ἤρτυσε. τὸν δὲ λοῖσθον ἐκπιὼν σκύφον
φερωνύμους ἔδυψε Νηρέως τάφους,
πανώλεθρον κηλῖδα θωύξας γένει,   165
ὁ τὴν πόδαργον Ψύλλαν ἡνιοστροφῶν
καὶ τὴν ὁπλαῖς Ἅρπινναν Ἁρπυίαις ἴσην.

Τὸν δ᾽ αὖ τέταρτον αὐθόμαιμον ὄψεται
κίρκου καταρρακτῆρος, ὅν τε συγγόνων
τὰ δευτερεῖα τῆς δαϊσφάλτου πάλης   170
λαβόντα κηρύξουσιν. ἐν δὲ δεμνίοις
τὸν ἐξ ὀνείρων πέμπτον ἐστροβημένον
εἰδωλοπλάστῳ προσκαταξανεῖ ῥέθει,
τὸν μελλόνυμφον εὐνέτην Κυταϊκῆς,
τῆς ξεινοβάκχης, ὅν ποτ᾽ Οἰνώνης φυγάς,   175
μύρμων τὸν ἑξάπεζον ἀνδρώσας στρατόν,
Πελασγικὸν Τυφῶνα γεννᾶται πατήρ,
ἀφ᾽ ἑπτὰ παίδων φειψάλῳ σποδουμένων
μοῦνον φλέγουσαν ἐξαλύξαντα σποδόν.

Χὠ μὲν παλιμπόρευτον ἵξεται τρίβον,   180
σφῆκας δαφοινοὺς χηραμῶν ἀνειρύσας,
ὁποῖα κοῦρος δῶμα κινήσας καπνῷ·

---

[a] Poseidon.   [b] Zeus.   [c] Elis or Olympia.
[d] During a drought in Elis Molpis offered himself as a victim to Zeus Ombrius.
[e] Oenomaus, father of Hippodameia.
[f] Myrtilus, son of Cadmilus = Hermes; charioteer of Oenomaus.   [g] Myrtoan Sea.
[h] Psylla and Harpinna, horses of Oenomaus.
[i] Deiphobus.   [i] Paris.

334

escaped the grievous raping desire of the Lord[a] of
Ships and was sent by Erechtheus[b] to Letrina's
fields to grind the smooth rock[c] of Molpis[d]—whose
body was served as sacrifice to Rainy Zeus—that he
might overcome the wooer-slayer[e] by the unholy
device for slaying his father-in-law which the son[f]
of Cadmilus devised; who drinking his last cup dived
into his tomb in Nereus—the tomb[g] which bears
his name—crying a blighting curse upon the race;
even he who held the reins of swift-footed Psylla
and Harpinna[h] hoofed even as the Harpies.

The fourth[i] again shall she see own brother of
the swooping falcon[j]; him whom they shall proclaim
to have won the second[k] prize among his brothers
in the wrestling of war. And the fifth[l] she shall
cause to pine upon his bed, distracted by her
phantom face in his dreams; the husband to be of
the stranger-frenzied lady[m] of Cyta; even him whom
one day the exile[n] from Oenone[o] fathered, turning
into men the six-footed host of ants,[p]—the Pelasgian
Typhon, out of seven sons[q] consumed in the flame
alone escaping the fiery ashes.

And he[r] shall come upon his homeward path,
raising the tawny wasps from their holes, even
as a child disturbs their nest with smoke. And

[k] *i.e.* next to Hector.   [l] Achilles.

[m] Medeia from Cyta in Phasis, married in Elysium to
Achilles, *cf.* 798.

[n] Peleus, exiled for slaying his half-brother Phocus (Pind.
N. v. 12 ff.).

[o] Aegina.

[p] Hesiod, fr. 76 (100), tells how Aegina was populated by
turning ants into men.

[q] Thetis to test the immortality of her sons by Peleus
put them into the fire. Six sons perished in this way. The
seventh, Achilles, was saved by his father.   [r] Paris.

οἱ δ' αὖ προγεννήτειραν οὐλαμωνύμου
βύκταισι χερνίψαντες ὠμησταὶ πόριν,
τοῦ Σκυρίου δράκοντος ἔντοκον λεχώ,   185
ἣν ὁ ξύνευνος Σαλμυδησίας ἁλὸς
ἐντὸς ματεύων, Ἑλλάδος καρατόμον,
δαρὸν φαληριῶσαν οἰκήσει σπίλον
Κελτοῦ πρὸς ἐκβολαῖσι λιμναίων ποτῶν,
ποθῶν δάμαρτα, τήν ποτ' ἐν σφαγαῖς κεμὰς   190
λαιμὸν προθεῖσα φασγάνων ἒκ ῥύσεται.
βαθὺς δ' ἔσω ῥηγμῖνος αὐδηθήσεται
ἔρημος ἐν κρόκαισι νυμφίου δρόμος,
στένοντος ἄτας καὶ κενὴν ναυκληρίαν
καὶ τὴν ἄφαντον εἶδος ἠλλοιωμένην   195
γραῖαν σφαγείων ἠδὲ χερνίβων πέλας
Ἅιδου τε παφλάζοντος ἐκ βυθῶν φλογὶ
κρατῆρος, ὃν μέλαινα ποιφύξει φθιτῶν
σάρκας λεβητίζουσα δαιταλουργία.

Χὠ μὲν πατήσει χῶρον αἰάζων Σκύθην,   200
εἰς πέντε που πλειῶνας ἱμείρων λέχους.
οἱ δ' ἀμφὶ βωμὸν τοῦ προμάντιος Κρόνου
σὺν μητρὶ τέκνων νηπίων κρεανόμου
ὅρκων τὸ δευτερούχον ἄρσαντες ζυγὸν
στερρὰν ἐνοπλίσουσιν ὠλέναις πλάτην,   205
σωτῆρα Βάκχον τῶν πάροιθε πημάτων

---

[a] Iphigeneia.
[b] Neoptolemus, here son of Achilles and Iphigeneia; called "the dragon of Scyrus" because he was reared by Deidamia, daughter of Lycomedes, king of Scyrus. In one version Deidamia is his mother.   [c] Achilles.
[d] Iphigeneia became priestess of Artemis Taurica in the Crimea, where she had to sacrifice Greeks who came there.
[e] Island of Leuce.   [f] Danube.
[g] When Iphigeneia was being sacrificed at Aulis, Artemis substituted a deer for her.

ALEXANDRA

they in their turn shall come, sacrificing cruelly
to the blustering winds the heifer[a] that bare the
war-named son,[b] the mother that was brought to
bed of the dragon of Scyrus; for whom her
husband[c] shall search within the Salmydesian Sea,
where she cuts the throats of Greeks,[d] and shall
dwell for a long space in the white-crested rock[e] by
the outflowing of the marshy waters of the Celtic
stream[f]; yearning for his wife whom at her slaying
a hind shall rescue from the knife, offering her own
throat instead.[g] And the deep waste within the
wash of the waves upon the beach shall be called
the Chase[h] of the bridegroom, mourning his ruin
and his empty seafaring and her that vanished and
was changed to an old witch,[i] beside the sacrificial
vessels and the lustral water and the bowl of Hades
bubbling from the depths with flame, whereon the
dark lady will blow, potting the flesh of the dead
as might a cook.

And he[j] lamenting shall pace the Scythian land
for some five years yearning for his bride.[k] And
they,[l] beside the altar of the primal prophet,
Cronus, who devours the callow young with their
mother,[m] binding themselves by the yoke of a second
oath,[n] shall take in their arms the strong oar, invoking him who saved them in their former woes, even

[h] Achilleius Dromus, a strip of land between the Dnieper
and the Crimea (Herod. iv. 55).   [i] Iphigeneia in Tauris.
   [j] Achilles.   [k] Iphigeneia.   [l] The Greeks at Aulis.
   [m] Hom. *Il.* ii. 308 ff.   At the altar of Zeus in Aulis a
snake devoured a sparrow with her brood of eight. Calchas
interprets the omen to mean that the war against Troy will
last nine years, and that the city will be taken in the tenth.
   [n] The earlier oath was taken by the suitors of Helen, who
swore to her father, Tyndareus, to support the successful
suitor.

337

LYCOPHRON

Σφάλτην ἀνευάζοντες, ᾧ ποτ᾽ ἐν μυχοῖς
Δελφινίου παρ᾽ ἄντρα Κερδῴου θεοῦ
Ταύρῳ κρυφαίας χέρνιβας κατάρξεται
ὁ χιλίαρχος τοῦ πολιρραίστου στρατοῦ.   210
ᾧ θυμάτων πρόσπαιον ἐκτίνων χάριν
δαίμων Ἐνόρχης Φιγαλεὺς Φαυστήριος
λέοντα θοίνης, ἴχνος ἐμπλέξας λύγοις,
σχήσει, τὸ μὴ πρόρριζον αἰστῶσαι στάχυν
κείροντ᾽ ὀδόντι καὶ λαφυστίαις γνάθοις.   215

Λεύσσω πάλαι δὴ σπεῖραν ὁλκαίων κακῶν,
σύρουσαν ἄλμῃ κἀπιροιζοῦσαν πάτρᾳ
δεινὰς ἀπειλὰς καὶ πυριφλέκτους βλάβας.

Ὡς μή σε Κάδμος ὤφελ᾽ ἐν περιρρύτῳ
Ἴσσῃ φυτεῦσαι δυσμενῶν ποδηγέτην,   220
τέταρτον ἐξ Ἄτλαντος ἀθλίου σπόρον,
τῶν αὐθομαίμων συγκατασκάπτην Πρύλιν,
τόμουρε πρὸς τὰ λῷστα νημερτέστατε·
μηδ᾽ Αἰσακείων οὑμὸς ὤφελεν πατὴρ
χρησμῶν ἀπῶσαι νυκτίφοιτα δείματα,   22.
μιᾷ δὲ κρύψαι τοὺς διπλοῦς ὑπὲρ πάτρας
μοίρᾳ, τεφρώσας γυῖα Λημναίῳ πυρί·
οὐκ ἂν τοσῶνδε κῦμ᾽ ἐπέκλυσεν κακῶν.

Καὶ δὴ Παλαίμων δέρκεται βρεφοκτόνος

---

[a] Agamemnon sacrifices in Apollo's temple at Delphi.
[b] Dionysus. For his cult at Phigaleia in Elis *cf*. Paus.
viii. 39. 4.
[c] Telephus king of Mysia who, when fighting Achilles,
was tripped up by the tendrils of a vine, Dionysus thus
requiting sacrifices made to him by Agamemnon at Delphi.
[d] Lesbos.   [e] Cadmus = Cadmilus (*cf*. 162) = Hermes.
[f] Atlas—Maia—Hermes—Prylis, son of Issa.

338

Bacchus, the Overthrower, to whom, the bull-god, one day in the shrine beside the cavern of Delphinius the Gainful god, the lord *a* of a thousand ships, a city-sacking host, shall make secret sacrifice. And in un-looked-for requital of his offerings the god of Phigaleia, the lusty Torch-god,*b* shall stay the lion *c* from his banquet, entangling his foot in withes, so that he destroy not utterly the cornfield of men, nor lay it waste with tooth and devouring jaws.

Long since I see the coil of trailing woes dragging in the brine and hissing against my father-land dread threats and fiery ruin.

Would that in sea-girt Issa *d* Cadmus *e* had never begotten thee to be the guide of the foemen, fourth *f* in descent from unhappy Atlas, even thee, Prylis, who didst help to overthrow thine own kindred,*g* prophet most sure of best fortune *h*! And would that my father *i* had not spurned the nightly terrors of the oracles of Aesacus and that for the sake of my fatherland he had made away with the two in one doom, ashing their bodies with Lemnian fire.*j* So had not such a flood of woes overwhelmed the land.

And now Palaemon,*k* to whom babes are slain,

e The Trojans, related through Electra, mother of Dar-danus and daughter of Atlas.

h Prylis prophesied the taking of Troy by the Wooden Horse. That was best fortune for the Greeks. For τόμουρος *cf.* Hesych. *s.v.*, Strabo 328.

i Priam, whom his son Aesacus advised to kill Hecuba and Paris, because before the birth of the latter Hecuba dreamed that she had borne a fire-brand.

j Proverbial. Lemnos through the "volcano" of Mosy-chlos is much associated with Hephaestus.

k Son of Ino Leucothea, worshipped in Tenedos with sacrifices of children.

LYCOPHRON

ζέουσαν αἰθυίαισι πλεκτανοστόλοις   230
γραῖαν ξύνευνον Ὠγένου Τιτηνίδα.

Καὶ δὴ διπλᾶ σὺν πατρὶ ῥαίεται τέκνα,
στερρῷ τυπέντι κλεῖδας εὐάρχῳ μύλῳ,
τὰ πρόσθεν αὐλητῆρος ἐκπεφευγότα
ψυδραῖσι φήμαις λαρνακοφθόρους ῥιφάς,   235
ᾧ δὴ πιθήσας στυγνὸς ἄρταμος τέκνων,
αἰθυιόθρεπτος πορκέων λιναγρέτης,
κρηθμοῖσι καὶ ῥαιβοῖσι νηρίταις φίλος,
χηλῷ κατεδρύφαξε διπτύχους γονάς.
σὺν τοῖς δ᾽ ὁ τλήμων, μητρὸς οὐ φράσας θεᾶς   240
μνήμων ἐφετμάς, ἀλλὰ ληθάργῳ σφαλείς,
πρηνὴς θανεῖται στέρνον οὐτασθεὶς ξίφει.

Καὶ δὴ στένει Μύρινα καὶ παράκτιοι
ἵππων φριμαγμὸν ἠόνες δεδεγμέναι,
ὅταν Πελασγὸν ἅλμα λαιψηροῦ ποδὸς   245
εἰς θῖν᾽ ἐρείσας λοισθίαν αἴθων λύκος
κρηναῖον ἐξ ἄμμοιο ῥοιβδήσῃ γάνος,
πηγὰς ἀνοίξας τὰς πάλαι κεκρυμμένας.

Καὶ δὴ καταίθει γαῖαν ὀρχηστὴς Ἄρης,
στρόμβῳ τὸν αἱματηρὸν ἐξάρχων νόμον.   250
ἅπασα δὲ χθὼν προὐμμάτων δῃουμένη

---

[a] Tethys (the sea), wife of Ogenos=Oceanus.

[b] The Greek ships reach Tenedos.

[c] Tennes and Hemithea (H. Usener, *Die Sintflutsagen*, pp. 90 ff.), children of Cycnus by his first wife, Procleia. His second wife, Philonome, abetted by the flute-player, Molpos, induced Cycnus to set them adrift upon the sea in an ark. Tennes, who was really a son of Apollo, came to land in the island of Leucophrys, which, after his name, was thence called Tenedos.

[d] Cycnus, son of Poseidon and Calyce, slain with his children, Tennes and Hemithea, by Achilles. This was an auspicious omen for the success of the Greeks at Troy.

340

ALEXANDRA

beholds the hoary Titanid bride *a* of Ogenus seething with the corded gulls.*b*

And now two children *c* are slain together with their father *d* who is smitten on the collar-bone with the hard mill-stone, an omen of good beginning; those children which before escaped when cast out to death in an ark through the lying speech of the piper,*e* to whom hearkened the sullen butcher *f* of his children—he the gull-reared, captive of the nets of fishermen, friend of winkle and bandy sea-snail —and imprisoned his two children in a chest. And therewithal the wretch,*g* who was not mindful to tell the bidding of the goddess mother but erred in forgetfulness, shall die upon his face, his breast pierced by the sword.

And now Myrina *h* groans and the sea-shores awaiting the snorting of horses, when the fierce wolf *i* shall leap the swift leap of his Pelasgian foot upon the last beach and cause the clear spring *j* to gush from the sand, opening fountains that hitherto were hidden.

And now Ares, the dancer, fires the land, with his conch leading the chant of blood. And all the land lies ravaged before my eyes and, as it were

e Molpos, who supported the false accusation made against Tennes by his step-mother, after the fashion of Phaedra.

f Cycnus, who was exposed on the sea-shore by his mother, and was fed by sea-birds until he was taken by some fishermen.

g Mnemon, who was sent by Thetis to warn Achilles not to slay Tennes. He failed to deliver his message, and Achilles in anger slew him.

h In the Troad, Hom. *Il.* ii. 811.   *i* Achilles.

j When Achilles leapt ashore at Troy, a spring arose under his footprint, *cf.* 279.

341

κεῖται, πέφρικαν δ' ὥστε ληίου γύαι
λόγχαις ἀποστίλβοντες, οἰμωγῇ δέ μοι
ἐν ὠσὶ πύργων ἐξ ἄκρων ἰνδάλλεται,
πρὸς αἰθέρος κυροῦσα νηνέμους ἕδρας,   255
γόῳ γυναικῶν καὶ καταρραγαῖς πέπλων,
ἄλλην ἐπ' ἄλλῃ συμφορὰν δεδεγμένων.

   Ἐκεῖνό σ', ὦ τάλαινα καρδία, κακὸν
ἐκεῖνο δάψει πημάτων ὑπέρτατον,
εὖτ' ἂν λαβράζων περκνὸς αἰχμητὴς χάρων, 260
πτεροῖσι χέρσον αἰετὸς διαγράφων
ῥαιβῷ τυπωτὴν τόρμαν ἀγκύλῃ βάσει,
κλάζων τ' ἄμικτον στόματι ῥιγίστην βοήν,
τὸν φίλτατόν σου τῶν ἀγαστόρων τρόφιν
Πτῴου τε πατρὸς ἁρπάσας μετάρσιον,   265
ὄνυξι γαμφηλαῖσί θ' αἱμάσσων δέμας,
ἔγχωρα τίφη καὶ πέδον χραίνῃ φόνῳ,
λευρᾶς βοώτης γατομῶν δι' αὔλακος.
λαβὼν δὲ ταύρου τοῦ πεφασμένου δάνος,
σκεθρῷ ταλάντῳ τρυτάνης ἠρτημένον,   270
αὖθις τὸν ἀντίποινον ἐγχέας ἴσον
Πακτώλιον σταθμοῖσι τηλαυγῆ μύδρον,
κρατῆρα Βάκχου δύσεται, κεκλαυσμένος
νύμφαισιν αἷ φίλαντο Βηφύρου γάνος
Λειβηθρίην θ' ὕπερθε Πιμπλείας σκοπήν, 275
ὁ νεκροπέρνας, ὃς προδειμαίνων πότμον

---

[a] Achilles. The ref. is to the dragging of the body of
Hector by Achilles, Hom. *Il.* xxii. 395 ff.   [b] Hector.
  [c] Apollo, who, in one version, was father of Hector. He
had a famous temple on Mt. Ptoön in Boeotia. Herod.
viii. 135.
  [d] Hector.   [e] Achilles.
  [f] In reference to Hom. *Il.* xxii. 351, where Achilles says
he would not give back the body of Hector for his weight in
gold; hence the legend that Priam actually ransomed his

fields of corn, bristle the fields of the gleaming
spears. And in my ears seems a voice of lamentation from the tower tops reaching to the windless
seats of air, with groaning of women and rending
of robes, awaiting sorrow upon sorrow.

That woe, O my poor heart, that woe shall wound
thee as a crowning sorrow, when the dusky, sworded,
bright-eyed eagle [a] shall rage, with his wings marking out the land—the track traced by bandied
crooked steps—and, crying with his mouth his dis-
sonant and chilly cry, shall carry aloft the dearest
nursling [b] of all thy brothers, dearest to thee and to
his sire the Lord of Ptoön,[c] and, bloodying his body
with talon and beak, shall stain with gore the land,
both swamp and plain, a ploughman cleaving a
smooth furrow in the earth. And having slain the
bull [d] he [e] takes the price thereof, weighed in the
strict balance of the scales.[f] But one day he shall
for recompense pour in the scales an equal weight of
the far-shining metal of Pactolus [g] and shall enter
the cup of Bacchus,[h] wept by the nymphs who love
the clear waters of Bephyras [i] and the high seat of
Leibethron [j] above Pimpleia [k]; even he, the trafficker
in corpses, who, fearing beforehand his doom, shall

body for its weight in gold, an idea which seems to have
been used in the lost play of Aeschylus Φρύγες or Ἕκτορος
λύτρα, and which appears in certain vase-paintings. *Cf.*
Robert, *Bild und Lied*, p. 142.

[g] When Achilles was slain, his body was redeemed for an
equal weight of gold from Pactolus (*cf.* Herod. v. 101).

[h] When Dionysus was chased by Lycurgus he gave to
Thetis a cup which in Naxos he had received from Hephaestus. In this were put the ashes of Achilles and Patroclus.

[i] River flowing from Olympus.

[j] Town on east slope of Olympus.

[k] Spring in Pieria, near Olympus.

καὶ θῆλυν ἀμφὶ σῶμα τλήσεται πέπλον
δῦναι, παρ' ἱστοῖς κερκίδος ψαύσας κρότων,
καὶ λοῖσθος εἰς γῆν δυσμενῶν ῥῖψαι πόδα,
τὸ σόν, ξύναιμε, κἂν ὕπνῳ πτήσσων δόρυ.   280

  Ὦ δαῖμον, οἷον κίον' αἰστώσεις δόμων,
ἔρεισμα πάτρας δυστυχοῦς ὑποσπάσας·
οὐ μὴν ἀνατεί γ' οὐδ' ἄνευ μόχθων πικρῶν
πένθους θ' ὁ λῃστὴς Δωριεὺς γελᾷ στρατός,
ἐπεγκαχάζων τοῦ δεδουπότος μόρῳ,   285
ἀλλ' ἀμφὶ πρύμναις τὴν πανυστάτην δραμὼν
πεύκαις βίου βαλβῖδα συμφλεχθήσεται,
καλῶν ἐπ' εὐχαῖς πλεῖστα Φύξιον Δία
πορθουμένοισι κῆρας ἀρκέσαι πικράς.
τότ' οὔτε τάφρος, οὔτε ναυλόχων σταθμῶν   290
πρόβλημα καὶ σταυροῖσι κορσωτὴ πτέρυξ,
οὐ γεῖσα χραισμήσουσιν, οὐδ' ἐπάλξιες·
ἀλλ' ὡς μέλισσαι συμπεφυρμένοι καπνῷ
καὶ λιγνύος ῥιπαῖσι καὶ γρυνῶν βολαῖς
ἄφλαστα καὶ κόρυμβα καὶ κληδὼν θρόνους   295
πυκνοὶ κυβιστητῆρες ἐξ ἑδωλίων
πηδῶντες αἱμάξουσιν ὀθνείαν κόνιν.

  Πολλοὺς δ' ἀριστεῖς πρωτόλειά θ' Ἑλλάδος
αἰχμῇ φέροντας καὶ σποραῖς ὠγκωμένους,
αἱ σαὶ καταξανοῦσιν ὄβριμοι χέρες,   300
φόνῳ βλύουσαι κἀπιμαιμῶσαι μάχης.
ἐγὼ δὲ πένθος οὐχὶ μεῖον οἴσομαι,
τὰς σὰς στένουσα καὶ δι' αἰῶνος ταφάς.
οἰκτρὸν γάρ, οἰκτρὸν κεῖν' ἐπόψομαι φάος
καὶ πημάτων ὕψιστον, ὧν κράντης χρόνος,   305
μήνης ἑλίσσων κύκλον, αὐδηθήσεται.

_____

  a When Calchas prophesied that Troy could not be taken
without Achilles, Thetis, knowing that if he went to Troy
344

endure to do upon his body a female robe,[a] handling
the noisy shuttle at the loom, and shall be the last
to set his foot in the land of the foe, cowering, O
brother,[b] even in his sleep before thy spear.

O Fate, what a pillar of our house shalt thou
destroy, withdrawing her mainstay from my unhappy
fatherland! But not with impunity, not without
bitter toil and sorrow shall the pirate Dorian host
laugh exulting in the doom of the fallen; but by
the sterns running life's last lap shall they be burnt[c]
along with the ships of pine, calling full often to
Zeus the Lord of Flight to ward off bitter fate from
them who perish. In that day nor trench nor
defence of naval station nor stake-terraced palisade
nor cornice shall avail nor battlements. But, like
bees, confused with smoke and rush of flame and
hurling of brands, many a diver shall leap from deck
to sternpeak and prowpeak and benched seats and
stain with blood the alien dust.

And many chieftains, and many that bore away
the choicest of the spoils won by Hellas and gloried
in their birth, shall thy mighty hands destroy, filled
full with blood and eager for battle. But not the
less sorrow shall I bear, bewailing, yea, all my life
long, thy burial. For pitiful, pitiful shall that day
be for mine eyes and crown of all my woes that
Time, wheeling the moon's orb, shall be said to
bring to pass.

he must perish, disguised him as a girl in female clothes and
put him in the charge of Lycomedes, king of Scyrus, with
whose daughters he was reared (Apollod. iii. 174). The
episode was the subject of a painting by Polygnotus (Paus.
i. 22. 6). [b] Hector.

[c] The reference is to the burning of the Greek ships by
the Trojans, *Il.* xv. 704 ff.

LYCOPHRON

Αἰαῖ, στενάζω καὶ σὸν εὔγλαγον θάλος,
ὦ σκύμνε, τερπνὸν ἀγκάλισμα συγγόνων,
ὅς τ' ἄγριον δράκοντα πυρφόρῳ βαλὼν
ἴυγγι τόξων, τὸν τυπέντα δ' ἐν βρόχοις   310
μάρψας ἀφύκτοις βαιὸν ἀστεργῆ χρόνον,
πρὸς τοῦ δαμέντος αὐτὸς οὐ τετρωμένος,
καρατομηθεὶς τύμβον αἱμάξεις πατρός.

Οἴμοι δυσαίων, καὶ διπλᾶς ἀηδόνας
καὶ σόν, τάλαινα, πότμον αἰάζω, σκύλαξ·   315
ὧν τὴν μὲν αὐτόπρεμνον ἡ τοκὰς κόνις
χανοῦσα κευθμῷ χείσεται διασφάγος,
λεύσσουσαν ἄτην ἀγχίπουν στεναγμάτων,
ἵν' ἄλμα πάππου καὶ χαμευνάδος μόροι
τῆς λαθρονύμφου πόρτιος μεμιγμένοι   320
σκύμνῳ κέχυνται, πρὶν λαφύξασθαι γάνος,
πρὶν ἐκ λοχείας γυῖα χυτλῶσαι δρόσῳ·
σὲ δ' ὠμὰ πρὸς νυμφεῖα καὶ γαμηλίους
ἄξει θυηλὰς στυγνὸς Ἴφιδος λέων,
μητρὸς κελαινῆς χέρνιβας μιμούμενος,   325
ἣν εἰς βαθεῖαν λαιμίσας ποιμανδρίαν
στεφηφόρον βοῦν δεινὸς ἄρταμος δράκων

ᵃ Troilus, youngest son of Priam, loved by Achilles and
by him slain at the altar of Apollo Thymbraeus (Stat. *S.* ii.
6. 32).
    ᵇ Achilles.
    ᶜ Apollo of Thymbra, whose son, in one version, Troilus
was.
    ᵈ Laodice and Polyxena, sisters of Cassandra.
    ᵉ Hecuba.

Ay! me, for thy fair-fostered flower,[a] too, I groan, O lion whelp, sweet darling of thy kindred, who didst smite with fiery charm of shafts the fierce dragon[b] and seize for a little loveless while in unescapable noose him that was smitten, thyself unwounded by thy victim: thou shalt forfeit thy head and stain thy father's[c] altar-tomb with thy blood.

O, me unhappy! the two nightingales[d] and thy fate, poor hound,[e] I weep. One,[f] root and branch, the dust that gave her birth shall, yawning, swallow in a secret cleft, when she sees the approaching feet of lamentable doom, even where her ancestor's[g] grove is, and where the groundling heifer[h] of secret bridal lies in one tomb with her whelp,[i] ere ever it drew the sweet milk and ere she cleansed her with fresh water from the soilure of childbed. And thee[j] to cruel bridal and marriage sacrifice the sullen lion,[k] child of Iphis,[l] shall lead, imitating his dark mother's lustrations; over the deep pail the dread butcherly dragon shall cut thy throat, as it were a garlanded heifer, and slay thee

[f] Laodice, on the capture of Troy, was swallowed up by the earth near the tomb of Ilos (Apollod. epit. v. 25).

[g] Ilos, *Il.* xi. 166.

[h] Cilla was sister of Hecuba and wife of Thymoetes, brother of Priam. On the same day Hecuba gave birth to Paris and Cilla to Munippus, the father being Priam. When told by an oracle to destroy "her who had just given birth and her child" Priam killed Cilla and her child.

[i] Munippus.

[j] Polyxena, sacrificed by Neoptolemus at the grave of Achilles.

[k] Neoptolemus.

[l] Iphigeneia, mother, in one version, of Neoptolemus by Achilles.

ῥαίσει τριπάτρῳ φασγάνῳ Κανδάονος,
λύκοις τὸ πρωτόσφακτον ὅρκιον σχάσας.
σὲ δ' ἀμφὶ κοίλην αἰχμάλωτον ἠόνα   330
πρέσβυν Δολόγκων δημόλευστον ὠλένῃ
ἐπεσβόλοις ἀραῖσιν ἠρεθισμένη
κρύψει κύπασσις χερμάδων ἐπομβρία,
Μαίρας ὅταν φαιουρὸν ἀλλάξῃς δομήν.

    'Ο δ' ἀμφὶ τύμβῳ τἀγαμέμνονος δαμεὶς   335
κρηπῖδα πήγῳ νέρθε καλλυνεῖ πλόκῳ,
ὁ πρὸς καλύπτρης τῆς ὁμαίμονος τάλας
ὠνητὸς αἰθαλωτὸν εἰς πάτραν μολών,
τὸ πρὶν δ' ἀμυδρὸν οὔνομ' αἰστώσας σκότῳ,
ὅταν χέλυδρος πυρσὸν ὠμόθριξ βαρὺν   340
ἀπεμπολητὴς τῆς φυταλμίας χθονὸς
φλέξας τὸν ὠδίνοντα μορμωτὸν λόχον
ἀναψαλάξῃ γαστρὸς ἑλκύσας ζυγά,
τῆς Σισυφείας δ' ἀγκύλης λαμπουρίδος
λάμψῃ κακὸν φρύκτωρον αὐτανέψιος   345
τοῖς εἰς στενὴν Λεύκοφρυν ἐκπεπλωκόσι
καὶ παιδοβρῶτος Πορκέως νήσους διπλᾶς.

    'Εγὼ δὲ τλήμων ἡ γάμους ἀρνουμένη,
ἐν παρθενῶνος λαΐνου τυκίσμασιν
ἄνις τεράμνων εἰς ἀνώροφον στέγην   350

---

[a] Candaon here = Hephaestus, who gave the sword to
Peleus, he to Neoptolemus. This seems to refer the lines
to the sacrifice of Polyxena. Otherwise it would be natural
to refer ἤν to Iphigeneia. ὅρκιον σχάσας : cf. Homer's ὅρκια
πιστὰ ταμόντες (*Il.* iii. 73 etc.). *Poimandria* is another name
for Tanagra in Boeotia, and τανάγρα is an ἀγγεῖον χαλκοῦν ἐν
ᾧ ἤρτυον τὰ κρέα (Hesych. *s.v.*) ; hence the use of ποιμανδρία
= ἀγγεῖον, in Lycophron's manner.
    [b] Hecuba.   [c] Hecuba is stoned to death.
    [d] Maira, the hound of Erigone ; here hound generally ;
Hecuba was turned into a hound ; *cf.* 315.

with the thrice-descended sword of Candaon,[a] shedding for the wolves the blood of the first oath-sacrifice. And thee,[b] again, an aged captive by the hollow strand, stoned by the public arm of the Doloncians, roused thereto by the railing curses, a robe shall cover with a rain of stones,[c] when thou shalt put on thee sable-tailed form of Maira.[d]

And he,[e] slain beside the altar tomb of Agamemnon,[f] shall deck the pedestal with his grey locks—even he who, a poor prisoner ransomed for his sister's[g] veil, came to his country devastated with fire, and shrouded in dim darkness his former name [h] —what time the fierce-crested serpent,[i] seller of the land that bred him, kindles the grievous torch and draws the belly-bands and lets slip the travailing terrible ambush,[j] and when the own cousin [k] of the crafty reynard, son [l] of Sisyphus, lights his evil beacon for them who sailed away to narrow Leucophrys [m] and the two islands [n] of child-devouring Porceus.[o]

And I, unhappy, who refused wedlock, within the building of my stony maiden chamber without ceiling, hiding my body in the unroofed tenement

---

[e] Priam was slain by Neoptolemus at the altar of Zeus Herceius.
  [f] *i.e.* Zeus-Agamemnon.   [g] Hesione.
  [h] Podarces, the earlier name of Priam. When captured by Heracles and Telamon, Hesione purchased (ἐπρίατο) his life with her veil. Hence his name Priamus.
  [i] Antenor, said to have been a traitor to Troy.
  [j] The wooden horse.   [k] Sinon.
  [l] Odysseus.   [m] Tenedos.   [n] Calydnae.
  [o] Porceus and Chariboea, the snakes which came from Calydnae and killed Laocoön and his sons. For a discussion of the story see Robert, *Bild und Lied* (Berlin 1881), Excursus I.

εἰρκτῆς ἀλιβδύσασα λυγαίας δέμας,
ἡ τὸν Θοραῖον Πτῷον Ὠρίτην θεὸν
λίπτοντ᾽ ἀλέκτρων ἐκβαλοῦσα δεμνίων,
ὡς δὴ κορείαν ἄφθιτον πεπαμένη
πρὸς γῆρας ἄκρον, Παλλάδος ζηλώμασι   355
τῆς μισονύμφου Λαφρίας Πυλάτιδος,
τῆμος βιαίως φάσσα πρὸς τόργου λέχος
γαμψαῖσιν ἅρπαις οἰνὰς ἑλκυσθήσομαι,
ἡ πολλὰ δὴ Βούδειαν Αἴθυιαν Κόρην
ἀρωγὸν αὐδάξασα τάρροθον γάμων.   360
ἡ δ᾽ εἰς τέραμνα δουρατογλύφου στέγης
γλήνας ἄνω στρέψασα χώσεται στρατῷ,
ἐξ οὐρανοῦ πεσοῦσα καὶ θρόνων Διός,
ἄνακτι πάππῳ χρῆμα τιμαλφέστατον.
ἑνὸς δὲ λώβης ἀντί, μυρίων τέκνων   365
Ἑλλὰς στενάξει πᾶσα τοὺς κενοὺς τάφους,
οὐκ ὀστοθήκαις, χοιράδων δ᾽ ἐφημένους,
οὐδ᾽ ὑστάτην κεύθοντας ἐκ πυρὸς τέφρην
κρωσσοῖσι ταρχυθεῖσαν, ἢ θέμις φθιτῶν,
ἀλλ᾽ οὔνομ᾽ οἰκτρὸν καὶ κενηρίων γραφὰς   370
θερμοῖς τεκόντων δακρύοις λελουμένας
παίδων τε καὶ θρήνοισι τοῖς ὁμευνίδων.

    Ὀφέλτα καὶ μύχουρε χοιράδων Ζάραξ
σπίλοι τε καὶ Τρυχάντα καὶ τραχὺς Νέδων
καὶ πάντα Διρφωσσοῖο καὶ Διακρίων   375
γωλειὰ καὶ Φόρκυνος οἰκητήριον,
ὅσων στεναγμῶν ἐκβεβρασμένων νεκρῶν
σὺν ἡμιθραύστοις ἰκρίοις ἀκούσετε,
ὅσων δὲ φλοίσβων ῥαχίας ἀνεκβάτου
δίναις παλιρροίοισιν ἕλκοντος σάλου,   380

---

[a] Apollo.   [b] Aias Oiliades, the Locrian Aias.
[c] Athena. Sea-gull as goddess of sea-faring (Paus. i. 5. 3).

of my dark prison: I who spurned from my maiden
bed the god Thoraios,[a] Lord of Ptoön, Ruler of the
Seasons, as one who had taken eternal maidenhood
for my portion to uttermost old age, in imitation of
her who abhors marriage, even Pallas, Driver of the
Spoil, the Wardress of the Gates—in that day, as a
dove, to the eyrie of the vulture,[b] in frenzy shall be
haled violently in crooked talons, I who often invoked
the Maiden,[c] Yoker of Oxen, the Sea-gull, to help
and defend me from marriage. And she unto the
ceiling of her shrine carven of wood shall turn up
her eyes and be angry with the host, even she that
fell[d] from heaven and the throne of Zeus, to be a
possession most precious to my great grandfather[e]
the King. And for the sin of one man[f] all Hellas
shall mourn the empty tombs of ten thousand children—not in receptacles of bones, but perched on
rocks, nor hiding in urns the embalmed last ashes
from the fire, as is the ritual of the dead, but a
piteous name and legends on empty cairns, bathed
with the burning tears of parents and of children
and mourning of wives.

O Opheltes[g] and Zarax,[g] who keepest the secret
places of the rocks, and ye cliffs, and Trychantes,[g]
and rugged Nedon,[g] and all ye pits of Dirphossus[g]
and Diacria,[g] and thou haunt of Phorcys[h]! what
groaning shall ye hear of corpses cast up with decks
broken in twain, and what tumult of the surge that
may not be escaped, when the foaming water
drags men backward in its swirling tides! And how

[a] *i.e.* the Palladium, heaven-fallen image of Athena.
[e] Ilus.   [f] Aias Oiliades.
[g] Hills in Euboea, in reference to wreck of Greeks on
coast of Euboea on way home from Troy.
[h] Coast of Euboea; Phorcys, the old man of the sea.

ὅσων δὲ θύννων ἠλοκισμένων ῥαφὰς
πρὸς τηγάνοισι κρατός, ὧν καταιβάτης
σκηπτὸς κατ' ὄρφνην γεύσεται δῃουμένων,
ὅταν καρηβαρεῦντας ἐκ μέθης ἄγων
λαμπτῆρα φαίνῃ τὸν ποδηγέτην σκότου   385
σίντης, ἀγρύπνῳ προσκαθήμενος τέχνῃ.

    Τὸν δ' οἷα δύπτην κηρύλον διὰ στενοῦ
αὐλῶνος οἴσει κῦμα γυμνήτην φάγρον,
διπλῶν μεταξὺ χοιράδων σαρούμενον.
Γυραῖσι δ' ἐν πέτραισι τερσαίνων πτερὰ   390
στάζοντα πόντου, δευτέραν ἅλμην σπάσει,
βληθεὶς ἀπ' ὄχθων τῷ τριωνύχῳ δορί,
ᾧ νιν κολαστὴς δεινὸς οὐτάσας λατρεὺς
ἀναγκάσει φάλλαισι κοινωνεῖν δρόμου
κόκκυγα κομπάζοντα μαψαύρας στόβους.   395
ψυχρὸν δ' ἐπ' ἀκταῖς ἐκβεβρασμένον νέκυν
δελφῖνος ἀκτὶς Σειρία καθαυανεῖ.
τάριχον ἐν μνίοις δὲ καὶ βρύοις σαπρὸν
κρύψει κατοικτίσασα Νησαίας κάσις,
Δίσκου μεγίστου τάρροθος Κυναιθέως.   400
τύμβος δὲ γείτων ὄρτυγος πετρουμένης
τρέμων φυλάξει ῥόχθον Αἰγαίας ἁλός.
τὴν Καστνίαν δὲ καὶ Μελιναίαν θεὸν
λυπρὸς παρ' Ἅιδην δεννάσει κακορροθῶν,
ἥ μιν παλεύσει δυσλύτοις οἴστρου βρόχοις,   405

---

    [a] Nauplius, king of Euboea, who, in revenge for the
death of his son Palamedes, whom the Greeks stoned to
death on a charge of treason, lured the Greeks on their
way from Troy upon the rocks of Euboea.
    [b] Aias Oiliades, the Locrian, wrecked by Poseidon on the
Gyrae.
    [c] Cliffs near Myconos and Tenos, where the Locrian Aias
was saved after his shipwreck.

many tunnies with the sutures of their heads split upon the frying-pan! of whom the down-rushing thunderbolt in the darkness shall eat as they perish : when the destroyer [a] shall lead them, their heads yet aching from the debauch, and light a torch to guide their feet in the darkness, sitting at his unsleeping art.

And one,[b] like a diving kingfisher, the wave shall carry through the narrow strait, a naked glutton-fish swept between the double reefs. And on the Gyrae [c] rocks drying his feathers dripping from the sea, he shall drain a second draught of the brine, hurled from the banks by the three-taloned spear, wherewith his dread punisher,[d] that once was a thrall,[e] shall smite him and compel him to run his race among the whales, blustering, like a cuckoo, his wild words of abuse. And his chilly dolphin's dead body cast upon the shore the rays of Seirius shall wither. And, rotten mummy-fish, among moss and seaweed Nesaia's sister [f] shall hide him for pity, she that was the helper [g] of the most mighty Quoit,[h] the Lord of Cynaetha. And his tomb beside the Quail [i] that was turned to stone shall trembling watch the surge of the Aegean sea. And bitter in Hades he shall abuse with evil taunts the goddess [j] of Castnion and Melina, who shall entrap him in the unescapable meshes of desire, in a love that is no

---

[a] Poseidon.
[e] Poseidon as servant of Laomedon, in building the walls of Troy.
[f] Thetis. [g] Hom. *Il.* i. 396 ff.
[h] Zeus in reference to his being swallowed by Cronus. For worship of Zeus at Cynaetha in Arcadia *cf.* Paus. v. 22. 1.
[i] Ortygia = Delos, where the Locrian Aias was buried.
[j] Aphrodite.

ἔρωτας οὐκ ἔρωτας, ἀλλ' Ἐρινύων
πικρὰν ἀποψήλασα κηρουλκὸν πάγην.

῞Απασα δ' ἄλγη δέξεται κωκυμάτων,
ὅσην ῞Αρατθος ἐντὸς ἠδὲ δύσβατοι
Λειβήθριαι σφίγγουσι Δωτίου πύλαι,   410
οἷς οὑμὸς ἔσται κἀχερουσίαν πάρα
ῥηγμῖνα δαρὸν ἐστεναγμένος γάμος.
πολλῶν γὰρ ἐν σπλάγχνοισι τυμβευθήσεται
βρωθεὶς πολυστοίχοισι καμπέων γνάθοις
νήριθμος ἐσμός· οἱ δ' ἐπὶ ξένης ξένοι,   415
παῶν ἔρημοι δεξιώσονται τάφους.

Τὸν μὲν γὰρ Ἠιὼν Στρυμόνος Βισαλτία,
Ἀψυνθίων ἄγχουρος ἠδὲ Βιστόνων,
κουροτρόφον πάγουρον Ἠδωνῶν πέλας
κρύψει, πρὶν ἢ Τυμφρηστὸν αὐγάσαι λέπας,   420
τὸν πατρὶ πλεῖστον ἐστυγημένον βροτῶν,
ὅμηρον ὅς μιν θῆκε τετρήνας λύχνους,
ὅτ' εἰς νόθον τρήρωνος ηὐνάσθη λέχος.

Τρισσοὺς δὲ ταρχύσουσι Κερκάφου νάπαι
῞Αλεντος οὐκ ἄπωθε καύηκας ποτῶν·   425
τὸν μέν, Μολοσσοῦ Κυπέως Κοίτου κύκνον,
συὸς παραπλαγχθέντα θηλείας τόκων,
ὅτ' εἰς ὀλύνθων δῆριν ἑλκύσας σοφὴν
τὸν ἀνθάμιλλον αὐτὸς ἐκ μαντευμάτων

---

[a] Greece, especially North Hellas.
[b] River of Ambracia.   [c] Near Olympus.
[d] In Thessaly.   [e] Thesprotia.
[f] Phoenix, tutor of Achilles (Hom. *Il.* ix. 432 ff.). Died
on his way home from Troy and was buried at Eion.
[g] In Thessaly.
[h] Amyntor who, from jealousy of Clytia and his son
Phoenix, put out the latter's eyes (Apollod. iii. 13. 8).
[i] Clytia.

love but springing for him the bitter death-drawing snare of the Erinyes.

And woes of lamentation shall the whole land[a] hear—all that Aratthos[b] and the impassable Leibethrian gates[c] of Dotion[d] enclose : by all these, yea, even by the shore of Acheron,[e] my bridal shall long be mourned. For in the maws of many sea-monsters shall be entombed the countless swarm devoured by their jaws with many rows of teeth ; while others, strangers in a strange land, bereft of relatives, shall receive their graves.

For one[f] Bisaltian Eion by the Strymon, close marching with the Apsynthians and Bistonians, nigh to the Edonians, shall hide, the old nurse of youth, wrinkled as a crab, ere ever he behold Tymphrestus' crag[g] : even him who of all men was most hated by his father,[h] who pierced the lamps of his eyes and made him blind, when he entered the dove's[i] bastard bed.

And three[j] sea-gulls the glades of Cercaphus shall entomb, not far from the waters of Aleis : one[k] the swan of Molossus Cypeus Coetus,[l] who failed to guess the number of the brood-sow's young, when, dragging his rival[m] into the cunning contest of the wild figs, himself, as the oracle foretold, shall err

---

[j] Calchas, Idomeneus, Sthenelus, all buried at foot of Cercaphus near Colophon.

[k] Calchas, the prophet, hence the swan of Apollo (here indicated by three obscure cult-names), was warned that he should die when he met a superior prophet. Meeting Mopsus, Calchas proposed the problem of telling how many figs there were on a certain fig-tree. Mopsus answered correctly, and in turn asked Calchas to foretell how many young a certain brood sow would throw. Unable to answer Calchas died of grief.

[i] Apollo.

[m] Mopsus.

σφαλεὶς ἰαύσει τὸν μεμορμένον πότμον· 430
τὸν δ' αὖ τέταρτον ἐγγόνων Ἐρεχθέως,
Αἴθωνος αὐτάδελφον ἐν πλασταῖς γραφαῖς·
τρίτον δέ, τοῦ μόσσυνας Ἐκτήνων ποτὲ
στερρᾷ δικέλλῃ βουσκαφήσαντος γόνον,
ὃν Γογγυλάτης εἷλε Βουλαῖος Μυλεύς, 435
ἀγηλάτῳ μάστιγι συνθραύσας κάρα,
ἦμος ξυναίμους πατρὸς αἱ Νυκτὸς κόραι
πρὸς αὐτοφόντην στρῆνον ὥπλισαν μόρου.

Δοιοὶ δὲ ῥείθρων Πυράμου πρὸς ἐκβολαῖς
αὐτοκτόνοις σφαγαῖσι Δηραίνου κύνες 440
δμηθέντες αἰχμάσουσι λοισθίαν βοὴν
πύργων ὑπὸ πτέρναισι Παμφύλου κόρης.
αἰπὺς δ' ἁλιβρὼς ὄχμος ἐν μεταιχμίῳ
Μάγαρσος ἀγνῶν ἠρίων σταθήσεται,
ὡς μὴ βλέπωσι, μηδὲ νερτέρων ἕδρας 445
δύντες, φόνῳ λουσθέντας ἀλλήλων τάφους.

Οἱ πέντε δὲ Σφήκειαν εἰς Κεραστίαν
καὶ Σάτραχον βλώξαντες Ὑλάτου τε γῆν
Μορφὼ παροικήσουσι τὴν Ζηρυνθίαν.

---

[a] Idomeneus, son of Deucalion, son of Minos, son of Zeus, came safely home to Crete but afterwards went to Italy and finally Colophon (Serv., Verg. *A.* iii. 401). In *Od. l.c.* Odysseus pretends to be Aethon, brother of Idomeneus.

[b] Zeus.   [c] Homer, *Od.* xix. 181 ff.

[d] Sthenelus, son of Capaneus. The latter was one of the Epigoni against Thebes (Ectenes=Thebans, *cf.* Paus. ix. 5.1), who boasted that he would take the town in spite of Zeus (Aesch. *Sept.* 440), and was slain by a thunderbolt.

[e] Thebans.

[f] Zeus. For Ζεὺς Βουλαῖος *cf.* Paus. i. 3. 5.   [g] Erinyes.

[h] Eteocles and Polyneices, at once sons and brothers of Oedipus.   [i] Oedipus.

[j] Amphilochus and Mopsus: as prophets they are called hounds of Apollo. When Amphilochus wished to visit Argos, the home of his father Amphiaraus, he entrusted

356

and sleep the destined sleep; the next,[a] again, fourth in descent from Erechtheus,[b] own brother of Aethon[c] in the fictitious tale; and third,[d] the son of him that with stern mattock ploughed the wooden walls of the Ectenes,[e] whom Gongylates,[f] the Counsellor, the Miller, slew and brake his head in pieces with his curse-expelling lash, what time the maiden daughters of Night[g] armed them that were the brothers[h] of their own father[i] for the lust of doom dealt by mutual hands.

And two[j] by the mouth of the streams of Pyramus,[k] hounds of Deraenus,[l] shall be slain by mutual slaughter, and fight their last battle at the foot of the towers of the daughter[m] of Pamphylus. And a steep sea-bitten fortress, even Magarsus, shall stand between their holy cairns, so that even when they have gone down to the habitations of the dead, they may not behold each other's tombs, bathed in blood.

And five[n] shall come to the Horned Isle[o] of Wasps and Satrachus[p] and the land of Hylates,[q] and dwell beside Morpho[r] the Lady of Zerynthus.

---

the town of Mallos in Cilicia, which they had jointly founded, to Mopsus for one year. As on his return Mopsus refused him his share in the town, they fought a duel in which both fell. They were buried on opposite sides of Magarsus, a hill near Mallos. [k] In Cilicia.

[i] Apollo: cult name from Deraenus near Abdera.

[m] Magarsus, foundress of Magarsus in Cilicia.

[n] Teucer, Agapenor, Acamas, Praxandrus, Cepheus.

[o] Cyprus. [p] River in Cyprus.

[q] Apollo. For Apollo Hylates cf. inscription from Egypt (probably Kuft) of third century B.C. Dittenb. *Orient. Graec. Inscrip. Select.* No. 53 Ἀπόλλωνι Ὑλάτηι Ἀρτέμιδι Φωσφόρωι Ἀρτέμιδι Ἐνοδίαι Λητοῖ Εὐτέκνωι Ἡρακλεῖ Καλλινίκωι Ἀπολλώνιος διοικητής. This specially Cyprian by-name was found also near Magnesia on the Maeander (Paus. x. 32. 6).

[r] Aphrodite: cf. Paus. iii. 15. 10.

LYCOPHRON

Ὁ μὲν πατρὸς μομφαῖσιν ἠλαστρημένος   450
Κυχρεῖος ἄντρων Βωκάρου τε ναμάτων,
οὑμὸς ξύναιμος, ὡς ὁπατρίου φονεὺς
πώλου, νόθον φίτυμα, συγγενῶν βλάβη,
τοῦ λύσσαν ἐν ποίμναισιν αἰχμητηρίαν
χέαντος, ὃν χάρωνος ὠμηστοῦ δορὰ   455
χαλκῷ τορητὸν οὐκ ἔτευξεν ἐν μάχῃ,
μίαν πρὸς Ἅιδην καὶ φθιτοὺς πεπαμένον
κέλευθον, ἣν γωρυτὸς ἔκρυψε Σκύθης,
ἦμος καταίθων θύσθλα Κωμύρῳ λέων
σφῷ πατρὶ λάσκε τὰς ἐπηκόους λιτάς,   460
σκύμνον παρ᾽ ἀγκάλαισιν αἷτα βράσας.
οὐ γάρ τι πείσει φῖτυν, ὡς ὁ Λήμνιος
πρηστὴρ Ἐννοῦς, οὔποτ᾽ εἰς φύζαν τραπεὶς
ταῦρος βαρύφρων, δυσμενεστάτου ξένων
ἔτυψε δώρῳ σπλάγχνον, ἀρνεύσας λυγρὸν   465
πήδημα πρὸς κνώδοντος αὐτουργοὺς σφαγάς.
ἐλᾷ δὲ πάτρας τῆλε Τραμβήλου κάσιν,
ὃν ἡ ξύναιμος πατρὸς ἐκλοχεύεται,
δοθεῖσα πρωταίχμεια τῷ πυργοσκάφῳ.
ἣν δή ποτ᾽, ἐν ῥήτραισι δημοτῶν σταθείς,   470
γλαυκῷ κελαινὸν δόρπον ὤτρυνεν κυνὶ
στεῖλαι τριπλᾶς θύγατρας ὁ σπείρας βάβαξ,

---

[a] Teucer, son of Telamon and Hesione, daughter of Laomedon, was banished from Salamis by his father when he returned from Troy without Aias.
[b] Telamon.   [c] Prehistoric king of Salamis.
[d] River in Salamis.
[e] Hesione was sister of Priam.   [f] Aias.
[g] Heracles' lion-skin (Pind. *I.* 5 (6)).
[h] Aias was vulnerable in one part only (Plato, *Symp.* 219 E), viz. his side. The story followed here is that when Aias was an infant Heracles wrapped him in his lion's skin,

ALEXANDRA

One [a] shall be he that shall be banished by his father's [b] taunts from the cave of Cychreus [c] and the waters of Bocarus [d]; even he my cousin, [e] as a bastard breed, the ruin of his kin, the murderer of the colt [f] begotten by the same father; of him who spent his sworded frenzy on the herds; whom the hide of the lion [g] made invulnerable by the bronze in battle and who possessed but one [h] path to Hades and the dead—that which the Scythian quiver covered, what time the lion, [i] burning sacrifice to Comyrus, [j] uttered to his sire his prayer that was heard, while he dandled in his arms his comrade's cub. For he [k] shall not persuade his father [l] that the Lemnian thunderbolt [m] of Enyo—he the sullen bull that never turned to flee—smote his own bowels with the gift of his bitterest foe, [n] diving in a sorrowful leap on the sword's edge in self-wrought slaughter. Far from his fatherland his sire shall drive Trambelus' [o] brother, whom my father's [p] sister [q] bare, when she was given to him [r] who razed the towers as firstfruits of the spear. She it was that the babbler, [s] the father of three daughters, standing up in the council of his townsmen, urged should be offered as

and prayed to Zeus that the child might be invulnerable where the lion's skin touched him. The quiver of Heracles prevented the skin from touching him at one place, where he was therefore vulnerable. For another version *cf.* Pind. *Isth.* v. (vi.).

[i] Heracles.
[j] Zeus.
[k] Teucer.
[l] Telamon.
[m] Aias, son of Telamon.
[n] Hector's sword (Soph. *Aj.* 815 ff.).
[o] Son of Telamon and Hesione, and so brother of Teucer.
[p] Priam. [q] Hesione. [r] Telamon.
[s] Phoenodamas, whom Laomedon asked to expose his three daughters to the sea-monster.

τῷ πᾶσαν ἅλμη πηλοποιοῦντι χθόνα,
ὅταν κλύδωνας ἐξερεύγηται γνάθων,
λάβρῳ σαλεύων πᾶν τρικυμίᾳ πέδον.   475
ὁ δ᾽ ἀντὶ πιποῦς σκορπίον λαιμῷ σπάσας
Φόρκῳ κακῆς ὠδῖνος ἔκλαυσεν βάρος,
χρῄζων πυθέσθαι πημάτων ξυμβουλίαν.

Ὁ δεύτερος δὲ νῆσον ἀγρότης μολών,
χερσαῖος αὐτόδαιτος ἐγγόνων δρυὸς   480
λυκαινομόρφων Νυκτίμου κρεανόμων,
τῶν πρόσθε μήνης φηγίνων πύρνων ὀχὴν
σπληδῷ κατ᾽ ἄκρον χεῖμα θαλψάντων πυρός,
χαλκωρυχήσει καὶ τὸν ἐκ βόθρου σπάσει
βῶλον, δικέλλῃ πᾶν μεταλλεύων γνύθος.   485
οὗ φῖτυν ἠνάριξεν Οἰταῖος στόνυξ,
βουβῶνος ἐν τόρμαισι θρυλίξας δέμας.
ἔγνω δ᾽ ὁ τλήμων σὺν κακῷ μαθὼν ἔπος,
ὡς πολλὰ χείλευς καὶ δεπαστραίων ποτῶν
μέσῳ κυλίνδει μοῖρα παμμήστωρ βροτῶν.   490
ὁ δ᾽ αὐτὸς ἀργῷ πᾶς φαληριῶν λύθρῳ
στόρθυγξ δεδουπὼς τὸν κτανόντ᾽ ἠμύνατο,
πλήξας ἀφύκτως ἄκρον ὀρχηστοῦ σφυρόν.

---

[a] Sea-monster sent by Poseidon when Laomedon refused
to pay him for building the walls of Troy.
[b] Hesione : "woodpecker" merely contrasts the feeble-
ness of Hesione with the scorpion, Heracles.
[c] Heracles ; cf. 34 n.
[d] A sea-god, son of Pontus and Gaia.
[e] Agapenor from Arcadia.   [f] Arcadians.
[g] Son of Lycaon, king of Arcadia, who was slain and
served as food by his father to Zeus, who was Lycaon's
guest. Zeus turned Lycaon and his sons into wolves.

dark banquet for the grey hound,[a] which with briny water was turning all the land to mud, spewing waves from his jaws and with fierce surge flooding all the ground. But, in place of the woodpecker,[b] he swallowed in his throat a scorpion [c] and bewailed to Phorcus [d] the burden of his evil travail, seeking to find counsel in his pain.

The second [e] who comes to the island is a countryman and a landsman, feeding on simple food, one of the sons [f] of the oak, the wolf-shaped devourers of the flesh of Nyctimus,[g] a people that were before the moon,[h] and who in the height of winter heated in the ashes of the fire their staple of oaken bread; he shall dig for copper [i] and from the trench drag the soil, mining with mattock every pit. His father [j] the tusk [k] of Oeta slew, crushing his body in the regions of the belly. In sorrow, wretched man, he learnt the truth of the saying that the all-devising fate of men rolls many a thing betwixt the life and the draught of the cup.[l] That same tusk, all flecked with glistening foam, when he had fallen took vengeance on his slayer, smiting with unescapable blow the dancer's ankle-bone.

[h] *i.e.* of primeval antiquity (Apoll. Rh. iv. 264).
[i] Copper mines in Cyprus.
[j] Ancaeus.
[k] The Calydonian Boar.
[l] Two Ancaei are known to mythology—Ancaeus of Arcadia and Ancaeus of Samos. Of the latter—who is often confused with the other—it is told that when planting a vine it was prophesied that he would never taste its fruit. Just when he was about to drink the wine of its grapes, there came the news of the Calydonian Boar. He went to the hunt and was killed. Hence proverb: πολλὰ μεταξὺ πέλει κύλικος καὶ χείλεος ἄκρου. He is the " dancer" (493) either as a warrior or in reference to Hom. *Il.* xvi. 745 (Holzinger).

LYCOPHRON

Τρίτος δὲ τοῦ μάρψαντος ἐκ κοίλης πέτρας
κέλωρ γίγαντος ὅπλα, τοῦ ποτ' εἰς λέχος   495
λαθραῖον αὐτόκλητος Ἰδαία πόρις
ἡ ζῶσ' ἐς Ἅιδην ἵξεται καταιβάτις,
θρήνοισιν ἐκτακεῖσα, Μουνίτου τοκάς·
ὃν δή ποτ' ἀγρώσσοντα Κρηστώνης ἔχις
κτενεῖ, πατάξας πτέρναν ἀγρίῳ βέλει,   500
ὅταν τεκόντος αἰχμάλωτος εἰς χέρας
ἡ πατρομήτωρ τὸν δνόφῳ τεθραμμένον
βάλῃ νεογνὸν σκύμνον. ᾗ μόνῃ ζυγὸν
δούλειον ἀμφήρεισαν Ἀκταίων λύκοι
τῆς ἁρπαγείσης ἀντίποινα θυιάδος,   505
ὧν ὀστράκου στρόβιλος ἐντετμημένος
κόρσην σκεπάζει ῥῦμα φοινίου δορός.
τὰ δ' ἄλλα θριπόβρωτος ἄψαυστος δόμων
σφραγὶς δοκεύει, θάμβος ἐγχώροις μέγα.
ἃ δὴ πρὸς ἄστρων κλίμακα στήσει δρόμον   510
τοῖς ἡμιθνήτοις διπτύχοις Λαπερσίοις·
οὓς μήποτ', ὦ Ζεῦ σῶτερ, εἰς πάτραν ἐμὴν
στείλαις ἀρωγοὺς τῇ δισαρπάγῳ κρεκί,
μηδὲ πτερωτὰς ὁπλίσαντες ὁλκάδας

---

[a] Acamas, son of Theseus. Theseus was son of Aegeus
(really of Poseidon) and Aethra, daughter of Pittheus of
Troezen. Aegeus hid his sword and shoes under a rock to
serve as tokens by which their son might make himself
known to his father when he grew up. Before the Trojan
war Acamas went to Troy with Diomede to demand back
Helen. Here, by Laodice, daughter of Priam, he had a son
Munitus who was reared by his grandmother Aethra, who
was then in Troy in attendance on Helen. When Troy was
taken, Aethra gave up Munitus to Acamas, while Laodice
was swallowed by the earth near the tomb of Ilus. Munitus
afterwards died by the bite of a snake in Thrace.

[b] Theseus.   [c] Aegeus.   [d] Acamas.

ALEXANDRA

And the third [a] is the son of him [b] who took from
the hollow of the rock the arms of the giant [c]; even
he [d] into whose secret bed shall come self-invited that
heifer [e] of Ida who shall go down to Hades alive, [f]
worn out with lamentation, the mother of Munitus,
whom one day, as he hunts, a viper of Crestone [g]
shall kill, striking his heel with fierce sting; what
time into his father's [h] hands that father's father's [i]
mother, [j] taken captive, shall lay the young cub [k]
reared in the dark: she on whom alone the wolves [l]
which harried the people of Acte [m] set the yoke of
slavery in vengeance for the raped Bacchant, [n] those
wolves whose head a cloven egg-shell [o] covers, to
guard them from the bloody spear; all else the
worm-eaten untouched seal [p] watches in the halls,
a great marvel to the people of the country. Which
things shall rear a ladder to the trace of the stars
for the twin half-mortal Lapersii. [q] Whom, O
Saviour Zeus, never mayst thou send against my
fatherland to succour the twice-raped corncrake, [r]
nor may they equip their winged ships and from the

---

[e] Laodice.   [f] See v. 314 *n.*   [g] In Thrace.
[h] Acamas.   [i] Theseus.
[j] Aethra, mother of Theseus; Munitus, son of Acamas.
[k] Munitus.   [l] The Dioscuri.
[m] Attica.   [n] Helen.
[o] The Dioscuri wear a conical cap resembling half an egg-
shell, half the Leda-egg from which they were born.
[p] Worm-eaten wood was used in early times as a seal.
[q] The Dioscuri, *i.e.* Castor and Pollux, who shared their
immortality day and day about, Hom. *Od.* xi. 298 ff.,
Pind. *P.* xi. 63 ff. They received divine honours in Athens
because when they invaded Attica they carried off Aethra
but touched nothing else. They are called Lapersii because
they sacked Las in Laconia.
[r] Helen as a child was carried off by Theseus, later by
Paris.

LYCOPHRON

πρύμνης ἀπ' ἄκρας γυμνὸν αἰψηρὸν πόδα
εἰς Βεβρύκων ῥίψειαν ἐκβατηρίαν,
μηδ' οἱ λεόντων τῶνδε καρτερώτεροι,
ἀλκὴν ἄμικτοι, τοὺς Ἄρης ἐφίλατο,
καὶ δῖ' Ἐννώ, καὶ τριγέννητος θεὰ
Βοαρμία Λογγᾶτις Ὁμολωὶς Βία.
οὐκ ἄν, τὰ χειρώνακτες ἐργάται διπλοῖ,
Δρύμας τε καὶ Πρόφαντος, ὁ Κρώμνης ἄναξ,
ἐλατύπησαν κοιράνῳ ψευδωμότῃ,
ἒν ἦμαρ ἀρκέσειε πορθηταῖς λύκοις
στέξαι βαρεῖαν ἐμβολὴν ῥαιστηρίαν,
καίπερ πρὸ πύργων τὸν Καναστραῖον μέγαν
ἐγχώριον γίγαντα δυσμενῶν μοχλὸν
ἔχοντα, καὶ τὸν πρῶτον εὐστόχῳ βολῇ
μαιμῶντα τύψαι ποιμνίων ἀλάστορα.
οὗ δή ποτ' αἴθων πρῶτα καινίσει δόρυ
κίρκος θρασὺς πήδημα λαιψηρὸν δικών,
Γραικῶν ἄριστος, ᾧ πάλαι τεύχει τάφους
ἀκτὴ Δολόγκων εὐτρεπὴς κεκμηκότι,
Μαζουσία προὔχουσα χερσαίου κέρως.
   Ἀλλ' ἔστι γάρ τις, ἔστι καὶ παρ' ἐλπίδα
ἡμῖν ἀρωγὸς πρευμενὴς ὁ Δρύμνιος
δαίμων Προμανθεὺς Αἰθίοψ Γυράψιος,
ὅς, τὸν πλανήτην Ὀρθάνην ὅταν δόμοις
σίνιν καταρρακτῆρα δέξωνται πικρὸν
οἱ δεινὰ κἀπόθεστα πείσεσθαί ποτε

515
520
525
530
535
540

ᵃ i.e. Troy.   ᵇ Idas and Lynceus, sons of Apharsus.
ᶜ Athena Tritogeneia, a much-disputed title. Boarmia,
etc., are said to be Boeotian cult-names of Athena.
ᵈ Apollo in Miletus.   ᵉ Poseidon in Thurii.
ᶠ In Paphlagonia.   ᵍ Laomedon.
ʰ Hector: called Canastraean because he is a "giant,"
and the home of the Giants is Pallene with its town
Canastraeum.
364

stern end set their naked swift foot in the landing-
place [a] of the Bebryces! Neither may those others [b]
who are mightier than these lions, the unapproachable in valour, whom Ares loves and divine Enyo
and the goddess that was born on the third day,[c]
Boarmia Longatis Homolois Bia. The walls which the
two working craftsmen, Drymas [d] and Prophantus,[e]
Lord of Cromna,[f] built for the king [g] that brake his
oath, would not avail for one day against the ravaging
wolves, to keep out their grievous ruinous assault,
even though they have before the towers the mighty
Canastraean,[h] the native giant, as a bar against the
foemen, eager to smite with well-aimed shaft the
first harrier of the flocks. His spear shall a bold
falcon [i] first handsel, swooping a swift leap, best of
the Greeks, for whom, when he is dead, the ready
shore of the Doloncians [j] builds of old a tomb, even
Mazusia jutting from the horn of the dry land.

But we have one,[k] yea one beyond our hope,
for gracious champion, even the god Drymnius
Promantheus Aethiops Gyrapsius, who, when they [l]
who are destined to suffer things dread and undesir-
able shall receive in their halls their fatal guest,[m]
the swooping robber, the wandering Orthanes,[n] and

[i] Protesilaus of Thessaly was first to leap ashore at Troy
and was slain by Hector.

[j] Thracian Chersonese, where Protesilaus was buried near
Mazusia, opposite Sigeum (Strabo vii. 331 fr. 52, cf. xiii.
595).

[k] Zeus: the cult-names Drym. and Pr. are Zeus in
Pamphylia and Thurii respectively; A. and G. in Chios.

[l] The Laconians. [m] Paris.

[n] A licentious deity, cf. Strabo 588 οὐδὲ γὰρ Ἡσίοδος οἶδε
Πρίαπον, ἀλλ' ἔοικε τοῖς Ἀττικοῖς Ὀρθάνῃ καὶ Κονισάλῳ καὶ
Τύχωνι καὶ τοῖς τοιούτοις. So Athen. 441 f. couples Orthanes
and Conisalus.

μέλλοντες, ἔν τε δαιτὶ καὶ θαλυσίοις
λοιβαῖσι μειλίσσωσιν ἀστεργῆ Κράγον,
θήσει βαρὺν κολῳὸν ἐν λέσχαις μέσον.
καὶ πρῶτα μὲν μύθοισιν ἀλλήλους ὀδὰξ
βρύξουσι κηκασμοῖσιν ὠκρωμένοι,
αὖθις δ' ἐναιχμάσουσιν αὐτανέψιοι,   545
ἀνεψιαῖς ὄρνισι χραισμῆσαι γάμους
βιαιοκλῶπας ἁρπαγάς τε συγγόνων
χρῄζοντες, ἀλφῆς τῆς ἀεδνώτου δίκην.
ἦ πολλὰ δὴ βέλεμνα Κνηκιὼν πόρος   550
ριφέντα τόλμαις αἰετῶν ἐπόψεται,
ἄπιστα καὶ θαμβητὰ Φηραίοις κλύειν.
ὁ μὲν κρανείᾳ κοῖλον οὐτάσας στύπος
φηγοῦ κελαινῆς διπτύχων ἕνα φθερεῖ,
λέοντα ταύρῳ συμβαλόντα φύλοπιν.   555
ὁ δ' αὖ σιγύμνῳ πλεύρ' ἀναρρήξας βοὸς
κλινεῖ πρὸς οὖδας. τῷ δὲ δευτέραν ἔπι
πληγὴν ἀθαμβὴς κριὸς ἐγκορύψεται,
ἄγαλμα πήλας τῶν Ἀμυκλαίων τάφων.
ὁμοῦ δὲ χαλκὸς καὶ κεραύνιοι βολαὶ   560
ταύρους καταξανοῦσιν, ὧν ἀλκὴν ἑνὸς
οὐδ' ὁ Σκιαστὴς Ὀρχιεὺς Τιλφούσιος
ἐμέμψατ', ἐν χάρμαισι ραιβώσας κέρας.
καὶ τοὺς μὲν Ἅιδης, τοὺς δ' Ὀλύμπιοι πλάκες
παρ' ἦμαρ αἰεὶ δεξιώσονται ξένους,   565
φιλανθομαίμους, ἀφθίτους τε καὶ φθιτούς.

---

^a Zeus, to prevent the Dioscuri going against Troy,
involves them in a quarrel with the sons of Aphareus.
  ^b Idas and Lynceus fight with Castor and Polydeuces,
Pind. *N.* x.
  ^c Phoebe and Hilaeira, daughters of Leucippus.
  ^d River near Sparta.

366

ALEXANDRA

when at banquet and festival they shall seek to
propitiate the inexorable Lord[a] of Cragos, shall put
in the midst of their talk grievous wrangling. And
first in words they shall tear each other with their
teeth, exasperate with jeers; but anon the own
cousins[b] shall ply the spear, eager to prevent the
violent rape of their cousin birds,[c] and the carrying
off of their kin, in vengeance for the traffic without
gifts of wooing. Surely many a shaft shall the
stream of Cnacion[d] behold hurled by the daring of
the eagles, incredible and marvellous for the
Pheraeans[e] to hear. One[f] with his spear of cornel-
wood shall smite the hollow trunk of the black oak
and shall slay one[g] of the pair—a lion joining battle
with a bull. The other[h] in turn with his lance
shall pierce the side of the ox[i] and bring him to
the ground. But against him[j] the undaunted ram[k]
shall butt a second blow, hurling the headstone of the
Amyclaean tomb. And bronze spear and thunder-
bolts together shall crush the bulls[l]—whereof one[m]
had such valour as even Sciastes Orchieus,[n] Lord of
Tilphossa, did not scorn, when he bent his bow in
battle. And the one pair[o] Hades shall receive: the
others[p] the meadows of Olympus shall welcome as
guests on every alternate day, brothers of mutual love,
undying and dead.

[e] In Messenia; Hom. *Il.* ix. 151.
[f] Idas.   [g] Castor.   [h] Polydeuces.
[i] Lynceus.   [j] Polydeuces.
[k] Idas hurls the tombstone of his father, Aphareus, at
Polydeuces, Pind. *N.* x. 66.
[l] I. and L.
[m] Idas who fought with Apollo for Marpessa, daughter of
Evenus.   [n] Apollo.
[o] Idas and Lynceus, Castor and Polydeuces.
[p] Hom. *Od.* xi. 303; Pind. *N.* x. 55 ff.; Apollod. iii. 137.

367

LYCOPHRON

Καὶ τῶν μὲν ἡμῖν εὐνάσει δαίμων δόρυ,
βαιόν τι μῆχαρ ἐν κακοῖς δωρούμενος.
ἄλλων δ' ἄπλατον χειρὶ κινήσει νέφος,
ὧν οὐδ' ὁ 'Ροιοῦς ἶνις εὐνάζων μένος   570
σχήσει, τὸν ἐννέωρον ἐν νήσῳ χρόνον
μίμνειν ἀνώγων, θεσφάτοις πεπεισμένους,
τροφὴν δ' ἀμεμφῆ πᾶσι τριπτύχους κόρας
ἴσκων παρέξειν, Κυνθίαν ὅσοι σκοπὴν
μίμνοντες ἠλάσκουσιν 'Ινωποῦ πέλας,   575
Αἰγύπτιον Τρίτωνος ἕλκοντες ποτόν.
ἃς δὴ Πρόβλαστος ἐξεπαίδευσε θρασὺς
μυληφάτου χιλοῖο δαιδαλευτρίας
ἕρπιν τε ῥέζειν ἠδ' ἀλοιφαῖον λίπος,
οἰνοτρόπους Ζάρηκος ἐκγόνους φάβας.   580
αἳ καὶ στρατοῦ βούπειναν ὀθνείων κυνῶν
τρύχουσαν ἀλθανοῦσιν, ἐλθοῦσαί ποτε
Σιθῶνος εἰς θυγατρὸς εὐναστήριον.

Καὶ ταῦτα μὲν μίτοισι χαλκέων πάλαι
στρόμβων ἐπιρροιζοῦσι γηραιαὶ κόραι·   585
Κηφεὺς δὲ καὶ Πράξανδρος, οὐ ναυκληρίας
λαῶν ἄνακτες, ἀλλ' ἀνώνυμοι σποραί,
πέμπτοι τέταρτοι γαῖαν ἵξονται θεᾶς
Γόλγων ἀνάσσης· ὧν ὁ μὲν Λάκων' ὄχλον
ἄγων Θεράπνης, θάτερος δ' ἀπ' 'Ωλένου   590
Δύμης τε Βουραίοισιν ἡγεμὼν στρατοῦ.

---

[a] The Greek expedition against Troy under Agamemnon.
[b] Anius, son of Apollo and Rhoeo, king of Delos and priest of Apollo, asked the Greeks to stay for nine years in Delos.
[c] Delos.
[d] Which said that Troy would not be taken till the tenth year.

So their spear shall god lull to rest for us, granting us a brief remedy in our woe. But a cloud of others [a] unapproachable in their might shall he rouse—whose rage not even the son [b] of Rhoeo shall lull nor stay, though he bid them abide for the space of nine years in his island,[c] persuaded by his oracles,[d] and though he promise that his three daughters [e] shall give blameless sustenance to all who stay and roam the Cynthian hill beside Inopus,[f] drinking the Egyptian waters of Triton. These daughters lusty Problastus[g] taught to be skilled in contriving milled food and to make wine and fatty oil—even the dove grand-daughters of Zarax,[h] skilled to turn things into wine. These shall heal the great and wasting hunger of the host of alien hounds,[i] coming one day to the grave of Sithon's daughter.[j]

These things the Ancient Maidens [k] whirl on with rushing thread of brazen spindles. But Cepheus[l] and Praxandrus,[m] not princes of a naval host but a nameless brood, fifth and fourth shall come to the land [n] of the goddess [o] queen of Golgi; whereof the one shall lead a Laconian troop from Therapna; the other from Olenos and Dyme shall lead his host of the men of Bura.

[e] Oeno, Spermo, Elais, who had the gift of producing wine, corn, and oil at will. Collectively called Oenotropi.
[f] River in Delos fabled to have a connexion with the Nile.
[g] Dionysus.
[h] First husband of Rhoeo and so step-father of Anius.
[i] The Greeks at Troy, suffering from hunger, sent Palamedes to fetch the Oenotropi buried at Rhoeteum in the Troad.
[j] Rhoeteia, daughter of Sithon, King of Thrace.
[k] The Moirai or Fates.   [l] From Achaia.
[m] From Therapnae in Laconia.
[n] Cyprus.   [o] Aphrodite.

LYCOPHRON

'Ο δ' 'Αργύριππα Δαυνίων παγκληρίαν
παρ' Αὐσονίτην Φυλαμὸν δωμήσεται,   595
πικρὰν ἑταίρων ἐπτερωμένην ἰδὼν
οἰωνόμικτον μοῖραν, οἳ θαλασσίαν
δίαιταν αἰνέσουσι, πορκέων δίκην,
κύκνοισιν ἰνδαλθέντες εὐγλήνοις δομήν.
ῥάμφεσσι δ' ἀγρώσσοντες ἐλλόπων θορούς   600
φερώνυμον νησῖδα νάσσονται πρόμου,
θεατρομόρφῳ πρὸς κλίτει γεωλόφῳ
ἀγυιοπλαστήσαντες ἐμπέδοις τομαῖς
πυκνὰς καλιάς, Ζῆθον ἐκμιμούμενοι.
ὁμοῦ δ' ἐς ἄγραν κἀπὶ κοιταίαν νάπην   605
νύκτωρ στελοῦνται, πάντα φεύγοντες βροτῶν
κάρβανον ὄχλον, ἐν δὲ γραικίταις πέπλοις
κόλπων ἰαυθμοὺς ἠθάδας διζήμενοι,
καὶ κρίμνα χειρῶν κἀπιδόρπιον τρύφος
μάζης σπάσονται, προσφιλὲς κνυζούμενοι,   610
τῆς πρὶν διαίτης τλήμονες μεμνημένοι.
Τροιζηνίας δὲ τραῦμα φοιτάδος πλάνης
ἔσται κακῶν τε πημάτων παραίτιον,
ὅταν θρασεῖα θουρὰς οἰστρήσῃ κύων
πρὸς λέκτρα. τύμβος δ' αὐτὸν ἐκσώσει μόρου   615
Ὁπλοσμίας, σφαγαῖσιν ἠὐτρεπισμένον.
κολοσσοβάμων δ' ἐν πτυχαῖσιν Αὐσόνων

---

[a] Diomedes, son of Tydeus of Aetolia. Returning to
Argos he found his wife in adultery with Cometes. He
escaped their machinations by taking refuge at the altar of
Hera. He then left Argos and came to Daunia in Italy.
Daunus, the king of the country being engaged in war,
Diomedes helped him. Winning the war, Daunus proposed
to give him either the booty or the land. Alaenus, being
made arbiter, awarded the land to Daunus, the booty to
Diomede, who in anger cursed the land that it should never
370

Another[a] shall found Argyrippa,[b] a Daunian estate beside Ausonian Phylamus,[c] seeing the bitter fate of his comrades turned to winged birds, who[d] shall accept a sea life, after the manner of fishermen, like in form to bright-eyed swans. Seizing in their bills the spawn of fishes they shall dwell in an island[e] which bears their leader's name, on a theatre-shaped rising ground, building in rows their close-set nests with firm bits of wood, after the manner of Zethus.[f] And together they shall betake them to the chase and by night to rest in the dell, avoiding all the alien crowd of men, but in folds of Grecian robes seeking their accustomed resting-place they shall eat crumbs from the hand and fragments of cake from the table, murmuring pleasantly, remembering, hapless ones, their former way of life.[g] His wounding of the Lady[h] of Troezen shall be part cause of his wild wandering and of his evil sufferings when a wild lustful bitch[i] shall be frenzied for adulterous bed. But the altar-tomb of Hoplosmia[j] shall save him from doom, when already prepared for slaughter. And in the glen of Ausonia[k] he shall

be fruitful save for one of Aetolian blood. He erected pillars throughout Daunia to signify that the land belonged to him. After his death Daunus caused them to be thrown into the sea but they miraculously returned to their place.

[b] Arpi (Strabo 283).

[c] Unknown river in Italy.

[d] For the story *cf.* Ovid, *M.* xiv. 498 ff.; Verg. *A.* xi. 271 ff.; Strabo 284.

[e] Insulae Diomedeae.

[f] With his brother Amphion he built the walls of Thebes.

[g] Antonin. Lib. 37; Aelian, *H.A.* i. 1; Plin. *N.H.* x. 127; Aristot. *M.* 80.

[h] Aphrodite, Hom. *Il.* v. 335 ff.

[i] Aegialeia, daughter of Adrastus, wife of Diomedes.

[j] Hera.   [k] Italy.

LYCOPHRON

σταθεὶς ἐρείσει κῶλα χερμάδων ἔπι
τοῦ τειχοποιοῦ γαπέδων Ἀμοιβέως,
τὸν ἑρματίτην νηὸς ἐκβαλὼν πέτρον.
κρίσει δ' Ἀλαίνου τοῦ κασιγνήτου σφαλεὶς
εὐχὰς ἀρούραις ἀμφ' ἐτητύμους βαλεῖ,   620
Δηοῦς ἀνεῖναι μήποτ' ὄμπνιον στάχυν,
γύας τιθαιβώσσοντος ἀρδηθμῷ Διός,
ἢν μή τις αὐτοῦ ῥίζαν Αἰτωλῶν σπάσας
χέρσον λαχήνῃ, βουσὶν αὔλακας τεμών.
στήλαις δ' ἀκινήτοισιν ὀχμάσει πέδον,   625
ἃς οὔτις ἀνδρῶν ἐκ βίας καυχήσεται
μετοχλίσας ὀλίζον. ἦ γὰρ ἀπτέρως
αὐταὶ παλιμπόρευτον ἵξονται βάσιν
ἄνδηρ' ἀπέζοις ἴχνεσιν δατούμεναι.
θεὸς δὲ πολλοῖς αἰπὺς αὐδηθήσεται,   630
ὅσοι παρ' Ἰοῦς γρῶνον οἰκοῦνται πέδον,
δράκοντα τὸν φθείραντα Φαίακας κτανών.

Οἱ δ' ἀμφικλύστους χοιράδας Γυμνησίας
σισυρνοδῦται καρκίνοι πεπλωκότες
ἄχλαινον ἀμπρεύσουσι νήλιποι βίον,   635
τριπλαῖς δικώλοις σφενδόναις ὡπλισμένοι.
ὧν αἱ τεκοῦσαι τὴν ἑκηβόλον τέχνην
ἄδορπα παιδεύσουσι νηπίους γονάς.
οὐ γάρ τις αὐτῶν ψίσεται πύρνον γνάθῳ,
πρὶν ἂν κρατήσῃ ναστὸν εὐστόχῳ λίθῳ   640
ὑπὲρ τράφηκος σῆμα κείμενον σκοποῦ.

---

[a] Stones from walls of Troy used by Diomedes as ballast
for his ships.
[b] Poseidon, who built the walls of Troy.
[c] Alaenus, half-brother of Diomedes.
[d] Demeter.
[e] Reference to the Dasii, according to Holzinger, cf. Sil.
Ital. Pun. xiii. 32, etc.

372

stand like a colossus resting his feet on the boulders,[a] the foundations of Amoebeus,[b] the builder of the walls, when he has cast out of his ship the ballast stones. And, disappointed by the judgement of his brother Alaenus,[c] he shall cast an effectual curse upon the fields, that they may never send up the opulent corn-ear of Deo,[d] when Zeus with his rain nurtures the soil, save only if one [e] who draws his blood from his own Aetolian stock shall till the land, cleaving the furrows with team of oxen. And with pillars not to be moved he shall hold fast the land : pillars which no man shall boast to have moved even a little by his might. For as on wings they shall come back again, traversing with trackless steps the terraces. And a high god shall he be called by many, even by those who dwell by the cavernous plain[f] of Io, when he shall have slain the dragon that harried the Phaeacians.[g]

And others [h] shall sail to the sea-washed Gymnesian [i] rocks—crab-like, clad in skins—where cloakless and unshod they shall drag out their lives, armed with three two-membered slings.[j] Their mothers shall teach the far-shooting art to their young offspring by supperless discipline. For none of them shall chew bread with his jaws, until with well-aimed stone he shall have won the cake set as

---

[f] The Ionian sea.

[g] Cercyraeans. The dragon is the Colchian dragon which followed Jason to Corcyra to recover the Golden Fleece. It was slain by Diomede.

[h] Boeotians.   [i] The Balearic Isles.

[j] Diodor. v. 18 : Strabo 168. The dwellers in the Balearic Isles (or Gymnesiae) were famous slingers (hence popular derivation from βάλλω—Βαλιαρεῖς). They carried three slings, one on head, one round neck, the third round waist.

καὶ τοὶ μὲν ἀκτὰς ἐμβατήσονται λεπρὰς
Ἰβηροβοσκοὺς ἄγχι Ταρτησοῦ πύλης,
Ἄρνης παλαιᾶς γέννα, Τεμμίκων πρόμοι,
Γραῖαν ποθοῦντες καὶ Λεοντάρνης πάγους   645
Σκῶλόν τε καὶ Τέγυραν Ὀγχηστοῦ θ᾽ ἕδος
καὶ χεῦμα Θερμώδοντος Ὑψάρνου θ᾽ ὕδωρ.

Τοὺς δ᾽ ἀμφὶ Σύρτιν καὶ Λιβυστικὰς πλάκας
στενήν τε πορθμοῦ συνδρομὴν Τυρσηνικοῦ
καὶ μιξόθηρος ναυτιλοφθόρους σκοπὰς   650
τῆς πρὶν θανούσης ἐκ χερῶν Μηκιστέως
τοῦ στερφοπέπλου Σκαπανέως Βοαγίδα
ἁρπυιογούνων κλώμακάς τ᾽ ἀηδόνων
πλαγχθέντας, ὠμόσιτα δαιταλωμένους,
πρόπαντας Ἅιδης πανδοκεὺς ἀγρεύσεται,   655
λώβαισι παντοίαισιν ἐσπαραγμένους,
ἕνα φθαρέντων ἄγγελον λιπὼν φίλων
δελφινόσημον κλῶπα Φοινίκης θεᾶς.
ὃς ὄψεται μὲν τοῦ μονογλήνου στέγας
χάρωνος, οἴνης τῷ κρεωφάγῳ σκύφον   660
χερσὶ προτείνων, τοὐπιδόρπιον ποτόν.
ἐπόψεται δὲ λείψανον τοξευμάτων
τοῦ Κηραμύντου Πευκέως Παλαίμονος,
οἳ πάντα θρανύξαντες εὔτορνα σκάφη
σχοίνῳ κακὴν τρήσουσι κεστρέων ἄγρην.   665
ἄλλος δ᾽ ἐπ᾽ ἄλλῳ μόχθος ἄθλιος μενεῖ,
τοῦ πρόσθεν αἰεὶ πλεῖον ἐξωλέστερος.

---

[a] Odysseus and his comrades.
[b] Straits of Messana.   [c] Scylla.
[d] Heracles at Macistus in Elis (Strabo 348). Spademan
in ref. to cleaning the Augean stables; cattle-driver in ref.
to the cattle of Geryon.   [e] Sirens.
[f] Odysseus, who had a dolphin for device upon his shield.
[g] Athena, the Palladium.   [h] Polyphemus.

374

a mark above the board. These shall set foot on the rough shores that feed the Iberians near the gate of Tartessus—a race sprung from ancient Arne, chieftains of the Temmices, yearning for Graea and the cliffs of Leontarne and Scolus and Tegyra and Onchestus' seat and the flood of Thermodon and the waters of Hypsarnus.

Others [a] shall wander beside Syrtis and the Libyan plains and the narrow meet of the Tyrrhenian Strait [b] and the watching-place fatal to mariners of the hybrid monster [c] that formerly died by the hand of Mecisteus,[d] the hide-clad Spademan, the Cattle-driver, and the rocks of the harpy-limbed nightingales.[e] There, devoured raw, Hades, mine host, shall seize them all, torn with all manner of evil entreatment; and he shall leave but one [f] to tell of his slaughtered friends, even the man of the dolphin device, who stole the Phoenician goddess.[g] He shall see the dwelling of the one-eyed lion,[h] offering in his hands to that flesh-eater the cup of the vine as an after-supper draught.[i] And he shall see the remnant [j] that was spared by the arrows of Ceramyntes Peuceus Palaemon.[k] That remnant shall break in pieces all the well-turned hulls and shall with rushes pierce their evil spoil, as it were of fishes.[l] Unhappy labour after labour shall await him, each more baleful than that which went before.

[i] Hom. *Od.* ix. 345 ff. [j] Laestrygones.
[k] Heracles, who, when the Laestrygones attempted to rob him of the cattle of Geryon, slew them all but a remnant. Ceramyntes = Alexicacos, Heracles as averter of evil; Peuceus, cult-name of Heracles in Iberia (schol.) or Abdera (*E.M.*); Palaemon *i.e.* Wrestler (παλαίειν = to wrestle).
[l] The Laestrygones attacked the ships and the crews of Odysseus, ἰχθῦς δ᾽ ὡς πείροντες ἀτερπέα δαῖτα φέροντο (Hom. *Od.* x. 124).

ποία Χάρυβδις οὐχὶ δαίσεται νεκρῶν;
ποία δ' Ἐρινὺς μιξοπάρθενος κύων;
τίς οὐκ ἀηδὼν στεῖρα Κενταυροκτόνος   670
Αἰτωλὶς ἢ Κουρῆτις αἰόλῳ μέλει
πείσει τακῆναι σάρκας ἀκμήνους βορᾶς;
ποίαν δὲ θηρόπλαστον οὐκ ἐσόψεται
δράκαιναν, ἐγκυκῶσαν ἀλφίτῳ θρόνα,
καὶ κῆρα κνωπόμορφον; οἱ δὲ δύσμοροι   675
στένοντες ἄτας ἐν συφοῖσι φορβάδες
γίγαρτα χιλῷ συμμεμιγμένα τρυγὸς
καὶ στέμφυλα βρύξουσιν. ἀλλά νιν βλάβης
μῶλυς σαώσει ῥίζα καὶ Κτάρος φανεὶς
Νωνακριάτης Τρικέφαλος Φαιδρὸς θεός.   680

Ἥξει δ' ἐρεμνὸν εἰς ἀλήπεδον φθιτῶν
καὶ νεκρόμαντιν πέμπελον διζήσεται
ἀνδρῶν γυναικῶν εἰδότα ξυνουσίας,
ψυχαῖσι θερμὸν αἷμα προσράνας βόθρῳ,
καὶ φασγάνου πρόβλημα, νερτέροις φόβον,   685
πήλας ἀκούσει κεῖθι πεμφίγων ὄπα
λεπτὴν ἀμαυρᾶς μάστακος προσφθέγμασιν.

Ὅθεν Γιγάντων νῆσος ἡ μετάφρενον
θλάσασα καὶ Τυφῶνος ἀγρίου δέμας
φλογμῷ ζέουσα δέξεται μονόστολον,   690
ἐν ᾗ πιθήκων πάλμυς ἀφθίτων γένος
δύσμορφον εἰς κηκασμὸν ᾤκισεν τόσων,
οἳ μῶλον ὠρόθυναν ἐκγόνοις Κρόνου.

---

^a *Od.* xii. 430 ff.   ^b Scylla.   ^c Siren.

^d The Centaurs who escaped from Heracles were so
charmed by the song of the Sirens that they forgot to eat
and so perished.

^e The Sirens were daughters of Acheloüs, a river which
divides Aetolia from Arcarnania ; Curetid = Acarnanian
(Strabo 462 f.).

376

ALEXANDRA

What Charybdis [a] shall not eat of his dead? What half-maiden Fury-hound [b]? What barren nightingale,[c] slayer of the Centaurs,[d] Aetolian or Curetid,[e] shall not with her varied melody tempt them to waste away through fasting from food? What beast-moulding dragoness [f] shall he not behold, mixing drugs with meal, and beast-shaped doom? And they, hapless ones, bewailing their fate shall feed in pigstyes, crunching grapestones mixed with grass and oilcake. But him the drowsy root shall save from harm and the coming of Ctaros,[g] the Bright Three-headed [h] god of Nonacris.[i]

And he shall come to the dark plain of the departed and shall seek the ancient seer [j] of the dead, who knows the mating of men and women.[k] He shall pour in a trench [l] warm blood for the souls, and, brandishing before him his sword to terrify the dead, he shall there hear the thin voice of the ghosts, uttered from shadowy lips.

Thereafter the island [m] that crushed the back of the Giants and the fierce form of Typhon, shall receive him journeying alone: an island boiling with flame, wherein the king of the immortals established an ugly race of apes, in mockery of all who raised war against the sons of Cronus. And passing the

[f] Circe turned the comrades of Odysseus into swine, but Odysseus was saved by the magical plant μῶλυ given him by Hermes (*Od.* x. 302 ff.).   [g] Hermes.

[h] Suid. *s.v.* τρικέφαλος, where it is explained as ὥσπερ διδάσκων τὰς ὁδούς, *i.e.* Hermes as Guide, facing three ways at the cross roads.   [i] In Arcadia.   [j] Teiresias.

[k] Apollod. iii. 71 f.; *cf.* Ovid, *M.* iii. 324 "Venus huic erat utraque nota."   [l] Hom. *Od.* xi. 23 ff.

[m] Pithecussa = Aenaria, under which the giant Typhoeus lies buried and where the Cercopes were turned into apes by Zeus to mock the giants (Ovid, *M.* xiv. 90).

LYCOPHRON

Βαίου δ' ἀμείψας τοῦ κυβερνήτου τάφον
καὶ Κιμμέρων ἔπαυλα κἀχερουσίαν   695
ῥόχθοισι κυμαίνουσαν οἴδματος χύσιν
Ὄσσαν τε καὶ λέοντος ἀτραποὺς βοῶν
χωστὰς Ὀβριμοῦς τ' ἄλσος οὐδαίας Κόρης,
Πυριφλεγές τε ῥεῖθρον, ἔνθα δύσβατος
τείνει πρὸς αἴθραν κρᾶτα Πολυδέγμων λόφος,   700
ἐξ οὗ τὰ πάντα χύτλα καὶ πᾶσαι μυχῶν
πηγαὶ κατ' Αὐσονῖτιν ἕλκονται χθόνα,
λιπὼν δὲ Ληθαιῶνος ὑψηλὸν κλέτας
λίμνην τ' Ἄορνον ἀμφιτορνωτὴν βρόχῳ
καὶ χεῦμα Κωκυτοῖο λαβρωθὲν σκότῳ,   705
Στυγὸς κελαινῆς νασμόν, ἔνθα Τερμιεὺς
ὁρκωμότους ἔτευξεν ἀφθίτοις ἕδρας,
λοιβὰς ἀφύσσων χρυσέαις πέλλαις γάνος,
μέλλων Γίγαντας κἀπὶ Τιτῆνας περᾶν·
θήσει Δαείρᾳ καὶ ξυνευνέτῃ δάνος,   710
πήληκα κόρσῃ κίονος προσαρμόσας.
κτενεῖ δὲ κούρας Τηθύος παιδὸς τριπλᾶς,
οἴμας μελῳδοῦ μητρὸς ἐκμεμαγμένας,
αὐτοκτόνοις ῥιφαῖσιν ἐξ ἄκρας σκοπῆς
Τυρσηνικὸν πρὸς κῦμα δυπτούσας πτεροῖς,   715

---

^a Baiae was named from the steersman of Odysseus who
perished during the Italian wanderings of Odysseus (Strabo
245, Steph. Byz. *s.v.*; Sil. Ital. viii. 539).
^b *Od.* xi. 14 ff. ; located near Cumae (Strabo 244).
^c The *palus Acherusia* near Cumae (Strabo 244).
^d Hill in Italy (schol.).
^e Heracles, who built a dam between the Lucrine Lake
and the sea (Strabo 245 ; Diodor. iv. 22).
^f Persephone, her grove near Avernus (Strabo 245, *cf.*
Hom. *Od.* x. 509).
^g Pyriphlegethon (Strabo 244).

tomb of Baius,[a] his steersman, and the dwellings of
the Cimmerians [b] and the Acherusian [c] waters swelling
with heaving surge and Ossa [d] and the cattle-path
built by the lion [e] and the grove of Obrimo,[f] the
Maiden who dwells beneath the earth, and the Fiery
Stream,[g] where the difficult Polydegmon [h] hill
stretches its head to the sky; from which hill's
depths draw all streams and all springs throughout
the Ausonian land; and leaving the high slope of
Lethaeon [i] and the lake Aornus [j] rounded with a
noose and the waters of Cocytus [k] wild and dark,
stream of black Styx, where Termieus [l] made the
seat of oath-swearing [m] for the immortals, drawing
the water in golden basins for libation, when he
was about to go against the Giants and Titans—he
shall offer up a gift to Daeira and her consort,[n]
fastening his helmet to the head of a pillar. And
he shall slay the triple daughters [o] of Tethys' son,
who imitated the strains of their melodious
mother [p] : self-hurled [q] from the cliff's top they dive
with their wings into the Tyrrhenian sea, where the

---

[h] A lofty mountain in Italy, from which they say flow all
the rivers in Italy (schol.) (Apennines?).

[i] Hill in Italy (schol.).

[j] Lacus Avernus near Cumae; for its circular shape cf.
Strabo 244, Aristot. M. 102.

[k] Branch of the Styx, Od. x. 514.   [l] Zeus.

[m] Hom. Il. xv. 37, etc. The gods swear by the Styx.

[n] Persephone and Pluto, to whom Odysseus dedicated his
helmet upon a pillar.

[o] Sirens, daughter of Acheloüs, son of Tethys. Here
three, while Hom. Od. xii. 52 and 167 uses the dual.

[p] Melpomene.

[q] The Sirens were doomed to die when anyone passed
their shores safely (Hygin. Fab. 125 and 141). When
Odysseus did so, they threw themselves from the Sirenes
rocks (Strabo 247) into the sea.

LYCOPHRON

ὅπου λινεργὴς κλῶσις ἑλκύσει πικρά.
τὴν μὲν Φαλήρου τύρσις ἐκβεβρασμένην
Γλάνις τε ῥείθροις δέξεται τέγγων χθόνα·
οὗ σῆμα δωμήσαντες ἔγχωροι κόρης
λοιβαῖσι καὶ θύσθλοισι Παρθενόπην βοῶν   720
ἔτεια κυδανοῦσιν οἰωνὸν θεάν.
ἀκτὴν δὲ τὴν προὔχουσαν εἰς Ἐνιπέως
Λευκωσία ῥιφεῖσα τὴν ἐπώνυμον
πέτραν ὀχήσει δαρόν, ἔνθα λάβρος Ἴς
γείτων θ' ὁ Λᾶρις ἐξερεύγονται ποτά.   725
Λίγεια δ' εἰς Τέρειναν ἐκναυσθλώσεται,
κλύδωνα χελλύσσουσα. τὴν δὲ ναυβάται
κρόκαισι ταρχύσουσιν ἐν παρακτίαις,
Ὠκινάρου δίναισιν ἀγχιτέρμονα.
λούσει δὲ σῆμα βούκερως νασμοῖς Ἄρης   730
ὀρνιθόπαιδος ἴσμα φοιβάζων ποτοῖς.
πρώτῃ δὲ καὶ ποτ' αὖθι συγγόνων θεᾷ
κραίνων ἁπάσης Μόψοπος ναυαρχίας
πλωτῆρσι λαμπαδοῦχον ἐντυνεῖ δρόμον,
χρησμοῖς πιθήσας. ὃν ποτ' αὐξήσει λεὼς   735
Νεαπολιτῶν, οἳ παρ' ἄκλυστον σκέπας
ὅρμων Μισηνοῦ στύφλα νάσσονται κλίτη.
Βύκτας δ' ἐν ἀσκῷ συγκατακλείσας βοὸς

---

[a] Parthenope, washed ashore and buried at Naples,
previously called Phalerum from its founder Phalerus (Steph.
Byz. s.v.).   [b] Clanius, river near Naples.
[c] An athletic contest was annually held in her honour
(Strabo 246).
[d] Another of the Sirens, cast ashore at Poseidonia=
Paestum.   [e] Poseidon.
[f] Leucosia, small island near Paestum (Strabo 123, etc.).
[g] Rivers of Italy (schol.).
[h] Ligeia, the third Siren, is cast ashore at Tereina in
Bruttium (Steph. Byz. s.v. Τέρεινα).

bitter thread spun by the Fates shall draw them.
One [a] of them washed ashore the tower of Phalerus
shall receive, and Glanis [b] wetting the earth with its
streams.   There the inhabitants shall build a
tomb for the maiden and with libations and sacrifice
of oxen shall yearly honour [c] the bird goddess
Parthenope.   And Leucosia [d] shall be cast on the
jutting strand of Enipeus [e] and shall long haunt the
rock [f] that bears her name, where rapid Is and
neighbouring Laris [g] pour forth their waters.   And
Ligeia [h] shall come ashore at Tereina spitting out
the wave.   And her shall sailormen bury on the
stony beach nigh to the eddies of Ocinarus ; and an
ox-horned Ares [i] shall lave her tomb with his streams,
cleansing with his waters the foundation of her whose
children were turned into birds.   And there one
day in honour of the first goddess of the sisterhood
shall the ruler [j] of all the navy of Mopsops array
for his mariners a torch-race,[k] in obedience to an
oracle, which one day the people of the Neapolitans
shall celebrate, even they who shall dwell on bluff
crags beside Misenum's [l] sheltered haven untroubled
by the waves.
     And he shall shut up the blustering winds [m] in

     [a] Unknown.
     [j] Diotimus, an Athenian admiral, who came to Naples
and there in accordance with an oracle sacrificed to
Parthenope and established a torch-race in her honour
(Timaeus *ap.* schol.).   Thuc. i. 45 mentions an Athenian
admiral Diotimus who is presumably the person meant.
Mopsops, an old king of Attica.
     [k] In honour of Parthenope in Naples.
     [l] Cape near Cumae, called after Misenus, a companion of
Odysseus (Strabo xxvi.).
     [m] Odysseus receives from Aeolus the winds tied up in an
ox-skin, *Od.* x. 19 ff.

LYCOPHRON

παλινστροβήτοις πημοναῖς ἀλώμενος
κεραυνίῃ μάστιγι συμφλεχθήσεται
καύηξ, ἐρινοῦ προσκαθήμενος κλάδῳ,   740
ὡς μὴ καταβρόξῃ νιν ἐν ῥόχθοις κλύδων,
Χάρυβδιν ἐκφυσῶσαν ἑλκύσας βυθῷ.
βαιὸν δὲ τερφθεὶς τοῖς Ἀτλαντίδος γάμοις,
ἀναυλόχητον αὐτοκάβδαλον σκάφος   745
βῆναι ταλάσσει καὶ κυβερνῆσαι τάλας
αὐτουργότευκτον βᾶριν εἰς μέσην τρόπιν
εἰκαῖα γόμφοις προστετραγανωμένην.
ἧς οἷα τυτθὸν Ἀμφίβαιος ἐκβράσας
τῆς κηρύλου δάμαρτος ἀπτῆνα σπόρον   750
αὐταῖς μεσόδμαις καὶ σὺν ἰκρίοις βαλεῖ
πρὸς κῦμα δύπτην ἐμπεπλεγμένον κάλοις.
πόντου δ' ἄυπνος ἐνσαρούμενος μυχοῖς,
ἀστῷ σύνοικος Θρηκίας Ἀνθηδόνος
ἔσται. παρ' ἄλλου δ' ἄλλος, ὡς πεύκης κλάδον,   755
βύκτης στροβήσει φελλὸν ἐνθρώσκων πνοαῖς.
μόλις δὲ Βύνης ἐκ παλιρροίας κακῆς
ἄμπυξ σαώσει στέρνα δεδρυφαγμένον
καὶ χεῖρας ἄκρας, αἷς κρεαγρεύτους πέτρας
μάρπτων ἁλιβρώτοισιν αἱμαχθήσεται   760
στόρθυγξι. νῆσον δ' εἰς Κρόνῳ στυγουμένην
Ἅρπην περάσας, μεζέων κρεανόμον,
ἄχλαινος ἵκτης, πημάτων λυγρῶν κόπις,
τὸν μυθοπλάστην ἐξυλακτήσει γόον,
ἀρὰς τετικὼς τοῦ τυφλωθέντος δάκους.   765

---

[a] Hom. *Od.* xii. 432 ff.
[b] Calypso, Hom. *Od.* vii. 245 ff.
[c] Raft of Odysseus, Hom. *Od.* v. 234 ff.   [d] Poseidon.
[e] Glaucus, son of Poseidon, was a fisherman from Anthedon in Boeotia who became a god of the sea. Once a year he visited all coasts and islands (schol. Plato, *Rep.* x. 611).

382

the hide of an ox, and wandering in woes that ebb
and flow, he, the sea-gull, shall be burnt with the
lash of the thunderbolt, clinging to the branch of
a wild fig-tree [a] so that the wave which draws
spouting Charybdis to the deep may not swallow
him in the surge. And, after brief pleasure in
wedlock with the daughter [b] of Atlas, he dares to
set foot in his offhand vessel [c] that never knew a
dockyard and to steer, poor wretch, the bark which
his own hands made, vainly fastened with dowels
to the midst of the keel. Wherefrom Amphibaeus [d]
shall toss him forth, as it were the tiny unfledged
brood of the halcyon's bride, and cast him, with mid-
beams and deck together, headlong as a diver into
the waves, entangled in the ropes, and sleepless,
swept in the secret places of the sea, he shall dwell
with the citizen [e] of Thracian Anthedon. And like a
branch of pine, blast after blast shall toss him as a
cork, leaping on him with their gusts. And hardly
shall the frontlet of Byne [f] save him from the evil
tide with torn breast and fingers wherewith he shall
clutch the flesh-hooking rocks and be stained with
blood by the sea-bitten spikes. And crossing to
the island [g] abhorred by Cronus—the isle of the
Sickle that severed his privy parts—he a cloakless
suppliant, babbling of awful sufferings, shall yelp
out his fictitious tale of woe, paying the curse of
the monster [h] whom he blinded. Ah! not yet, not

[f] Ino Leucothea, by whose veil Odysseus was saved
(*Od.* v. 334 ff.).

[g] Corcyra, under which was buried the sickle (δρεπάνη,
ἅρπη), with which Zeus mutilated Cronus, or Cronus mutilated Uranus (Hesiod, *Th.* 162, 179; Apoll. Rh. iv. 985 f.).
Hence its old name Drepane.

[h] The Cyclops Polyphemus, who cursed Odysseus (*Od.*
ix. 534).

LYCOPHRON

οὔπω μάλ', οὔπω· μὴ τοσόσδ' ὕπνος λάβοι
λήθης Μέλανθον ἐγκλιθένθ' Ἱππηγέτην.
ἥξει γάρ, ἥξει ναύλοχον Ῥείθρου σκέπας
καὶ Νηρίτου πρηῶνας. ὄψεται δὲ πᾶν
μέλαθρον ἄρδην ἐκ βάθρων ἀνάστατον   770
μύκλοις γυναικόκλωψιν. ἡ δὲ βασσάρα
σεμνῶς κασωρεύουσα κοιλανεῖ δόμους,
θοίναισιν ὄλβον ἐκχέασα τλήμονος.
αὐτὸς δὲ πλείω τῶν ἐπὶ Σκαιαῖς πόνους
ἰδὼν μολοβρός, τλήσεται μὲν οἰκετῶν   775
στυγνὰς ἀπειλὰς εὐλόφῳ νώτῳ φέρειν
δέννοις κολασθείς, τλήσεται δὲ καὶ χερῶν
πληγαῖς ὑπείκειν καὶ βολαῖσιν ὀστράκων.
οὐ γὰρ ξέναι μάστιγες, ἀλλὰ δαψιλὴς
σφραγὶς μενεῖ Θόαντος ἐν πλευραῖς ἔτι,   780
λύγοισι τετρανθεῖσα, τὰς ὁ λυμεὼν
ἐπεγκολάπτειν ἀστένακτος αἰνέσει,
ἑκουσίαν σμώδιγγα προσμάσσων δομῇ,
ὅπως παλεύσῃ δυσμενεῖς, κατασκόποις
λώβαισι καὶ κλαυθμοῖσι φηλώσας πρόμον.   785
ὃν Βομβυλείας κλιτὺς ἡ Τεμμικία
ὕψιστον ἡμῖν πῆμ' ἐτέκνωσέν ποτε,
μόνος πρὸς οἴκους ναυτίλων σωθεὶς τάλας.
λοῖσθον δὲ καύηξ ὥστε κυμάτων δρομεύς,
ὡς κόγχος ἅλμῃ πάντοθεν περιτριβείς,   790
κτῆσίν τε θοίναις Πρωνίων λαφυστίαν

ᵃ Poseidon.   ᵇ In Ithaca.
ᶜ Penelope's suitors. μύκλος = ὄνος, the ass being the type
of lust (Pind. *P*. x. 36).
ᵈ Penelope.
ᵉ *Od*. xvii. 219, xviii. 26.
ᶠ *Od*. xix. 66 ff. etc.
ᵍ In order to enter Troy as a spy Odysseus got himself

384

yet! Let not such sleep of forgetfulness find
Melanthus,[a] the Lord of Horses, bending. For
he shall come, he shall come to Rheithron's[b]
sheltering haven and the cliffs of Neriton.[b] And
he shall behold all his house utterly overthrown
from its foundations by lewd wife-stealers.[c] And
the vixen,[d] primly coquetting, will make empty
his halls, pouring forth the poor wight's wealth in
banqueting. And he himself, poor parasite,[e] shall
see trouble beyond what he endured at the Scaean
gates; he shall endure to bear with submissive back
sullen threats from his own slaves[f] and to be
punished with jeers; shall endure, too, to submit
to buffeting of fists and hurling of potsherds. For
not alien stripes but the liberal seal of Thoas[g] shall
remain upon his sides, engraved with rods: stripes
which he, our destroyer, shall consent without a
murmur to have engraved upon him, putting the
voluntary weal upon his frame, that he may ensnare
the foemen, with spying wounds and with tears
deceiving our king.[h] He whom of old the Temmi-
cian[i] hill of Bombyleia[j] bare to be our chiefest
bane—he alone of all his mariners, wretched one,
shall win safely home. And lastly, like a sea-gull
that roams the waves, worn all about by the salt
water even as a shell and finding his possessions
swallowed up in banqueting of the Pronians[k] by the

beaten and wounded by Thoas by way of disguise (*Il. Parv.*
Kinkel, p. 42). *Cf.* Homer, *Odyssey*, iv. 244 ff.

   [h] Priam.
   [i] Boeotian: according to one legend Odysseus was born
in Boeotia (Müller, *F.H.G.* i. 426).
   [j] Athena, inventor of flute (Pind. *P.* xii.), worshipped
under this name in Boeotia.
   [k] The wooers of Penelope; Pronians=Cephallenians; *cf.*
Προνναῖοι, Thuc. ii. 30.

πρὸς τῆς Λακαίνης αἰνοβακχεύτου κιχών,
σύφαρ θανεῖται πόντιον φυγὼν σκέπας
κόραξ σὺν ὅπλοις Νηρίτων δρυμῶν πέλας.
κτενεῖ δὲ τύψας πλευρὰ λοίγιος στόνυξ
κέντρῳ δυσαλθὴς ἔλλοπος Σαρδωνικῆς.   795
κέλωρ δὲ πατρὸς ἄρταμος κληθήσεται,
Ἀχιλλέως δάμαρτος αὐτανεψίος.
μάντιν δὲ νεκρὸν Εὐρυτὰν στέψει λεὼς
ὅ τ᾽ αἰπὺ ναίων Τραμπύας ἐδέθλιον,
ἐν ᾗ ποτ᾽ αὖθις Ἡρακλῆ φθίσει δράκων   800
Τυμφαῖος ἐν θοίναισιν Αἰθίκων πρόμος,
τὸν Αἰακοῦ τε κἀπὸ Περσέως σποράς
καὶ Τημενείων οὐκ ἄπωθεν αἱμάτων.

Πέργῃ δέ μιν θανόντα, Τυρσηνῶν ὄρος,   805
ἐν Γορτυναίᾳ δέξεται πεφλεγμένον,
ὅταν στενάζων κῆρας ἐκπνεύσῃ βίον
παιδός τε καὶ δάμαρτος, ἣν κτείνας πόσις
αὐτὸς πρὸς Ἅιδην δευτέραν ὁδὸν περᾷ,
σφαγαῖς ἀδελφῆς ἠλοκισμένος δέρην,   810
Γλαύκωνος Ἀψύρτοιό τ᾽ αὐτανεψίας.

Χὢ μὲν τοσούτων θῖνα πημάτων ἰδὼν
ἄστρεπτον Ἅιδην δύσεται τὸ δεύτερον,
γαληνὸν ἦμαρ οὔποτ᾽ ἐν ζωῇ δρακών.
ὦ σχέτλι᾽, ὡς σοι κρεῖσσον ἦν μίμνειν πάτρᾳ   815
βοηλατοῦντα καὶ τὸν ἐργάτην μύκλον

---

[a] Penelope, as daughter of Icarius, brother of Tyndareus.
[b] Spear of Telegonus tipped with spine of thornback.
[c] Telegonus, son of Odysseus and Circe.
[d] Achilles in Elysium (Simonid. fr. 213, Ibyc. fr. 37) has
to wife Medeia, daughter of Aeëtes, brother of Circe.
[e] Polyperchon, king of the Epeirotes, murdered in
309 B.C. Heracles, son of Alexander the Great and Barsine
(Paus. ix. 7. 2).
[f] Odysseus.   [g] Unknown hill in Etruria.

Laconian lady [a] of fatal frenzy, ancient as a crow he shall flee with his weapons the shelter of the sea and in wrinkled age die beside the woods of Neriton. The deadly spike,[b] hard to heal, of the Sardinian fish shall wound his sides with its sting and kill him; and his son [c] shall be called the butcher of his father, that son who shall be the own cousin of the bride [d] of Achilles. And in death he shall be garlanded as a seer by the Eurytanian folk and by the dweller in the steep abode of Trampya, wherein one day hereafter the Tymphaean dragon,[e] even the king of the Aethices, shall at a feast destroy Heracles sprung from the seed of Aeacus and Perseus and no stranger to the blood of Temenus.

When he [f] is dead, Perge,[g] hill of the Tyrrhenians, shall receive his ashes in the land of Gortyn [h]; when, as he breathes out his life, he shall bewail the fate of his son [i] and his wife,[j] whom her husband [k] shall slay and himself next pass to Hades, his throat cut by the hands of his sister, the own cousin of Glaucon and Apsyrtus.[l]

And having seen such a heap of woes he shall go down a second [m] time to unturning Hades, having never beheld a day of calm in all his life. O wretched one! how much better had it been for thee to remain in thy homeland driving oxen, and

[h] Cortona in Etruria, where Odysseus was said to be buried.

[i] Telemachus.   [j] Circe.

[k] Telemachus, who married Circe and killed her, and was himself killed by Cassiphone, daughter of Odysseus and Circe, and thus half-sister of Telemachus.

[l] Aeëtes, Pasiphaë, Circe, are children of Helios, and thus Apsyrtus, son of Aeëtes, Glaucon (Glaucus), son of Pasiphaë, Cassiphone, daughter of Circe, are cousins.

[m] He had gone to Hades before as a living man.

LYCOPHRON

κάνθων᾽ ὑπὸ ζεύγλαισι μεσσαβοῦν ἔτι
πλασταῖσι λύσσης μηχαναῖς οἰστρημένον
ἢ τηλικῶνδε πεῖραν ὀτλῆσαι κακῶν.

ὁ δ᾽ αἰνόλεκτρον ἁρπαγεῖσαν εὐνέτης   820
πλάτιν ματεύων, κληδόνων πεπυσμένος,
ποθῶν δὲ φάσμα πτηνὸν εἰς αἴθραν φυγόν,
ποίους θαλάσσης οὐκ ἐρευνήσει μυχούς;
ποίαν δὲ χέρσον οὐκ ἀνιχνεύσει μολών;
ἐπόψεται μὲν πρῶτα Τυφῶνος σκοπάς,   825
καὶ πέμπελον γραῦν μαρμαρουμένην δέμας,
καὶ τὰς Ἐρεμβῶν ναυβάταις ἠχθημένας
προβλῆτας ἀκτάς. ὄψεται δὲ τλήμονος
Μύρρας ἐρυμνὸν ἄστυ, τῆς μογοστόκους
ὠδῖνας ἐξέλυσε δενδρώδης κλάδος,   830
καὶ τὸν θεᾷ κλαυσθέντα Γαύαντος τάφον
Σχοινῆδι μουσόφθαρτον Ἀρέντᾳ Ξένῃ,
κραντῆρι λευκῷ τόν ποτ᾽ ἔκτανε πτέλας.
ἐπόψεται δὲ τύρσιας Κηφηίδας
καὶ Λαφρίου λάκτισμαθ᾽ Ἑρμαίου ποδὸς   835
δισσάς τε πέτρας, κέπφος αἷς προσήλατο
δαιτὸς χατίζων. ἀντὶ θηλείας δ᾽ ἔβη
τὸν χρυσόπατρον μόρφνον ἁρπάσας γνάθοις,

---

[a] Odysseus, feigning madness to avoid going to Troy (*Od.* ii. 170, xxiv. 115), yoked to his plough an ox and an ass (schol.) or a horse and an ox (Hygin. *Fab.* 95).

[b] Menelaus ; for his wanderings in search of Helen *cf. Od.* iv. 81 ff.

[c] Helen.   [d] *Cf.* 112 ff., 131.   [e] Cilicia.

[f] Cyprus. When Aphrodite hid from the gods on Mount Casion in Cyprus, her hiding-place was revealed by an old woman, whom for her treachery Aphrodite turned into stone.

[g] Aethiopians or Arabians.

[h] Byblus in Phoenicia. Myrrha, before the birth of Adonis, was turned into a tree (myrrh) by Aphrodite (Apollod. iii. 184, Anton. Lib. 34).

388

to harness still the working stallion ass to the yoke,
frenzied with feigned pretence of madness,[a] than to
suffer the experience of such woes!

And he [b] again—the husband seeking for his
fatal bride [c] snatched from him, having heard rumours,
and yearning for the winged phantom [d] that fled to
the sky,—what secret places of the sea shall he not
explore? What dry land shall he not come and
search? First he shall visit the watching-place of
Typhon,[e] and the old hag turned to stone,[f] and the
jutting shores of the Erembi,[g] abhorred by mariners.
And he shall see the strong city of unhappy Myrrha,[h]
who was delivered of the pangs of child-birth by a
branching tree; and the tomb of Gauas [i] whose
death the Muses wrought—wept by the goddess [j] of
the Rushes,[k] Arenta, the Stranger [l]: Gauas whom
the wild boar slew with white tusk. And he shall
visit the towers [m] of Cepheus and the place [n] that
was kicked by the foot of Hermes Laphrios, and
the two rocks on which the petrel leapt in quest
of food, but carried off in his jaws, instead of a
woman,[o] the eagle son [p] of the golden Sire—a male

[i] Adonis, son of Myrrha, killed by a boar (Apollod. iii.
183), to hunt which he had been incited by the Muses' praise
of hunting (schol.).   [j] Aphrodite.

[k] Name of Aphrodite in Samos.

[l] Aphrodite in Memphis (Herod. ii. 112).

[m] Aethiopia, cf. Arat. 183.

[n] In Aethiopia was a place Ἑρμοῦ πτέρνη where the foot
of Hermes, who was here watching Io, caused a spring to
burst forth.

[o] Andromeda, exposed to the sea-monster Cetus (petrel
here, in Lycophron's manner).

[p] Perseus, son of Zeus and Danaë, whom Zeus visited in
a golden shower, rescued Andromeda. He allowed himself
to be swallowed by the beast, whose inwards he then cut to
pieces with a sickle.

τὸν ἡπατουργὸν ἄρσεν' ἀρβυλόπτερον.
πεφήσεται δὲ τοῦ θεριστῆρος ξυρῷ   840
φάλαινα δυσμίσητος ἐξινωμένη,
ἱπποβρότους ὠδῖνας οἴξαντος τόκων
τῆς δειρόπαιδος μαρμαρώπιδος γαλῆς·
ὃς ζωοπλαστῶν ἄνδρας ἐξ ἄκρου ποδὸς
ἀγαλματώσας ἀμφελυτρώσει πέτρῳ,   845
λαμπτηροκλέπτης τριπλανοῦς ποδηγίας.

    Ἐπόψεται δὲ τοὺς θερειπότους γύας
καὶ ῥεῖθρον Ἀσβύσταο καὶ χαμευνάδας
εὐνάς, δυσόδμοις θηρσὶ συγκοιμώμενος.
καὶ πάντα τλήσεθ' οὕνεκ' Αἰγύας κυνὸς   850
τῆς θηλύπαιδος καὶ τριάνορος κόρης.
ἥξει δ' ἀλήτης εἰς Ἰαπύγων στρατόν,
καὶ δῶρ' ἀνάψει παρθένῳ Σκυλητρίᾳ
Ταμάσσιον κρατῆρα καὶ βοάγριον
καὶ τὰς δάμαρτος ἀσκέρας εὐμάριδας.   855
ἥξει δὲ Σῖριν καὶ Λακινίου μυχούς,
ἐν οἷσι πόρτις ὄρχατον τεύξει θεᾷ
Ὁπλοσμίᾳ φυτοῖσιν ἐξησκημένον.
γυναιξὶ δ' ἔσται τεθμὸς ἐγχώροις ἀεὶ
πενθεῖν τὸν εἰνάπηχυν Αἰακοῦ τρίτον   860

----

^a Perseus cuts off the head of Medusa; from the blood
spring the horse Pegasus and the man Chrysaor.

^b Medusa, called a weasel because weasels were supposed to
give birth through the neck (Ant. Lib. xxix.; Ovid, *M.* ix. 323).

^c Perseus with the Gorgon's head turned Polydectes, king
of Seriphos, and his people to stone (Pind. *P.* x. 48, xii. 14).

^d The daughters of Phorcys, the Graeae, had but one eye
in common (Aesch. *P. V.* 795), which Perseus stole but restored
when they consented to guide him to the Nymphs, who gave
him winged shoes, a wallet, and the cap of invisibility.

^e Egypt.   ^f The Nile.

^g *i.e.* seals; Homer, *Odyssey* iv. 351 ff.

^h Helen.   Aegyan = Laconian, *cf.* Steph. Byz. *s.v.* Αἴγυς.

with winged sandals who destroyed his liver. By
the harvester's blade shall be slain the hateful whale
dismembered : the harvester [a] who delivered of her
pains in birth of horse and man the stony-eyed
weasel [b] whose children sprang from her neck.
Fashioning men as statues from top to toe he shall
envelop them in stone [c]—he that stole the lamp of
his three wandering guides. [d]

And he shall visit the fields [e] which drink in
summer and the stream of Asbystes [f] and the couch
on the ground where he shall sleep among evil-
smelling beasts. [g] And all shall he endure for the
sake of the Aegyan bitch, [h] her of the three husbands, [i]
who bare only female children. [j] And he shall come
as a wanderer to the folk of the Iapyges [k] and offer
gifts to the Maiden of the Spoils, [l] even the mixing-
bowl from Tamassus [m] and the shield of oxhide and
the fur-lined shoes of his wife. And he shall come
to Siris [n] and the recesses of Lacinium, [o] wherein a
heifer [p] shall fashion an orchard for the goddess
Hoplosmia, [q] furnished with trees. And it shall be
for all time an ordinance for the women of the land
to mourn [r] the nine-cubit hero, [s] third in descent

[i] Menelaus, Paris, Deïphobus.
[j] Iphigeneia and Hermione.   [k] In S.E. Italy.
[l] Athena Ἀγελείη (Hom.). The reference is to *Castrum
Minervae*, south of Hydruntum ; *cf.* Strabo 281.
   [m] In Cyprus, famous for metal-work (Strabo 255 and 684).
   [n] On the Gulf of Tarentum (Strabo 264).
   [o] Cape near Croton with temple of Hera Lacinia (Steph.
Byz. *s.v.* Λακίνιον, Livy xxiv. 3).
   [p] Thetis, who dedicated Lacinium to Hera (Serv. on *Aen.*
iii. 552).   [q] Hera in Elis (schol.).
   [r] The women of Croton mourn for Achilles and wear no
gay dress.
   [s] Achilles, son of Peleus, son of Aeacus and of Thetis,
daughter of Doris ; "nine-cubit" *i.e.* of heroic stature.

καὶ Δωρίδος, πρηστῆρα δαΐου μάχης,
καὶ μήτε χρυσῷ φαιδρὰ καλλύνειν ῥέθη,
μήθ᾽ ἀβροπήνους ἀμφιβάλλεσθαι πέπλους
κάλχῃ φορυκτούς, οὕνεκεν θεᾷ θεὸς
χέρσου μέγαν στόρθυγγα δωρεῖται κτίσαι.   865
ἥξει δὲ ταύρου γυμνάδας κακοξένους
πάλης κονίστρας, ὅν τε Κωλῶτις τεκνοῖ,
Ἀλεντία κρείουσα Λογγούρου μυχῶν,
Ἄρπης Κρόνου πήδημα Κογχείας θ᾽ ὕδωρ
κάμψας, Γονοῦσάν τ᾽ ἠδὲ Σικανῶν πλάκας,   870
καὶ θηροχλαίνου σηκὸν ὠμηστοῦ λύκου,
ὃν Κρηθέως ἄμναμος ὁρμίσας σκάφος
ἔδειμε πεντήκοντα σὺν ναυηγέταις.
κρόκαι δὲ Μινυῶν εὐλιπῆ στελγίσματα
τηροῦσιν, ἅλμης οὐδὲ φοιβάζει κλύδων   875
οὐδ᾽ ὀμβρία σμήχουσα δηναιὸν νιφάς.
   Ἄλλους δὲ θῖνες οἵ τε Ταυχείρων πέλας
μύρμηκες αἰάζουσιν ἐκβεβρασμένους
ἔρημον εἰς Ἄτλαντος οἰκητήριον
θρυλιγμάτων δέρτροισι προσσεσηρότας·   880
Μόψον Τιταιρώνειον ἔνθα ναυβάται
θανόντα ταρχύσαντο, τυμβείαν δ᾽ ὑπὲρ
κρηπῖδ᾽ ἀνεστήλωσαν Ἀργῴου δορὸς
κλασθὲν πέτευρον, νερτέρων κειμήλιον,
Αὔσιγδα Κινύφειος ᾗ τέγγων ῥόος   885

---

[a] Thetis to Hera.
[b] Lacinium.
[c] Eryx, son of Butes and Aphrodite, who compelled
strangers to wrestle with him till he was slain by Heracles.
At Mount Eryx in Sicily was a temple of Aphrodite Erycinia.
[d] Aphrodite in Cyprus (schol.).
[e] Aphrodite in Colophon (schol.).
[f] Unknown.   [g] Drepanum in Sicily.

from Aeacus and Doris, the hurricane of battle
strife, and not to deck their radiant limbs with
gold, nor array them in fine-spun robes stained
with purple—because a goddess[a] to a goddess[a]
presents that great spur[b] of land to be her dwelling-
place. And he shall come to the inhospitable
wrestling-arena of the bull[c] whom Colotis[d] bare,
even Alentia,[e] Queen of the recesses of Longuros,[f]
rounding the Cronos' Sickle's leap[g] and the water
of Concheia,[f] and Gonusa[f] and the plains of the
Sicanians, and the shrine of the ravenous wolf[h] clad
in the skin of a wild beast, which the descendant
of Cretheus, when he had brought his vessel to
anchor, built with his fifty mariners. And the
beach still preserves the oily scrapings of the bodies
of the Minyans, nor does the wave of the brine cleanse
them, nor the long rubbing of the rainy shower.

And others[i] the shores and reefs near Taucheira[j]
mourn, cast upon the desolate dwelling-place[k] of
Atlas, grinning on the points of their wreckage:
where Mopsus[l] of Titaeron died and was buried
by the mariners, who set over his tomb's pedestal
a broken blade from the ship Argo, for a possession
of the dead,—where the Cinypheian stream[m] fattens

[h] Heracles, with the lion's skin, to whom Jason, son of
Aeson, son of Cretheus, built a temple in Aethalia (Elba),
where curiously coloured pebbles were supposed to get their
colour from the flesh-scrapings (ἀποστλεγγίσματα) of the
Argonauts (Minyae) (Diodor. iv. 56, Strabo 224, Apoll. Rh.
iv. 654, Arist. *Mirab.* 105).

[i] Guneus, Prothous, and Eurypylus wander to Libya.
[j] Near Cyrene (Herod. iv. 171).   [k] Libya.
[l] Mopsus from Titaron in Thessaly was the seer of the
Argonauts. He was killed by snake-bite in Libya (Apoll. Rh.
iv. 1502).
[m] Cinyps (Herod. iv. 175).

LYCOPHRON

νασμοῖς λιπαίνει, τῷ δὲ Νηρέως γόνῳ
Τρίτωνι Κολχὶς ὤπασεν δάνος γυνὴ
χρυσῷ πλατὺν κρατῆρα κεκροτημένον,
δείξαντι πλωτὴν οἶμον, ᾗ διὰ στενῶν
μύρμων ἐνήσει Τῖφυς ἄθραυστον σκάφος.   890
Γραικοὺς δὲ χώρας τουτάκις λαβεῖν κράτη
θαλασσόπαις δίμορφος αὐδάζει θεός,
ὅταν παλίμπουν δῶρον ἄγραυλος λεὼς
Ἕλλην' ὀρέξῃ νοσφίσας πάτρας Λίβυς.
εὐχὰς δὲ δειμαίνοντες Ἀσβύσται κτέαρ   895
κρύψουσ' ἄφαντον ἐν χθονὸς νειροῖς μυχοῖς,
ἐν ᾗ Κυφαίων δύσμορον στρατηλάτην
ναύταις συνεκβράσουσι Βορραῖαι πνοαί,
τόν τ' ἐκ Παλαύθρων ἔκγονον Τενθρηδόνος,
Ἀμφρυσίων σκηπτοῦχον Εὐρυαμπίων,   900
καὶ τὸν δυνάστην τοῦ πετρωθέντος λύκου
ἀποινοδόρπου καὶ πάγων Τυμφρηστίων.
ὧν οἱ μὲν Αἰγώνειαν ἄθλιοι πάτραν
ποθοῦντες, οἱ δ' Ἐχῖνον, οἱ δὲ Τίταρον
Ἱρόν τε καὶ Τρηχῖνα καὶ Περραιβικὴν   905
Γόννον Φάλανναν τ' ἠδ' Ὀλοσσόνων γύας
καὶ Κασταναίαν, ἀκτέριστον ἐν πέτραις
αἰῶνα κωκύσουσιν ἠλοκισμένοι.

---

[a] Between Taucheira and Cyrene.
[b] Son of Poseidon and Amphitrite, daughter of Nereus.
[c] Medeia.
[d] Triton guided the Argonauts out of Lake Tritonis, receiving from Jason a bronze tripod (here a mixing-bowl),
which he placed in his temple, declaring that when a
descendant of the Argonauts should recover the tripod, a
hundred Greek cities would be founded near Lake Tritonis.
When the neighbouring tribes heard this, they hid the
tripod (Herod. iv. 179 ; Apoll. Rh. iv. 529 ff., 1547 ff. ; Diodor.
iv. 56).   [e] Steersman of the Argo (Apoll. Rh. i. 105).
[f] Triton, half-man, half-fish.

Ausigda[a] with its waters, and where to Triton,[b] descendant of Nereus, the Colchian woman[c] gave as a gift the broad mixing-bowl[d] wrought of gold, for that he showed them the navigable path whereby Tiphys[e] should guide through the narrow reefs his ship undamaged. And the twy-formed god,[f] son of the sea, declares that the Greeks shall obtain the sovereignty of the land[g] when the pastoral people of Libya shall take from their fatherland and give to a Hellene the home-returning gift. And the Asbystians, fearing his vows, shall hide the treasure from sight in low depths of the earth, whereon the blasts of Boreas shall cast with his mariners the hapless leader[h] of the men of Cyphos and the son[i] of Tenthredon from Palauthra,[j] king of the Amphrysians of Euryampus,[k] and the lord[l] of the Wolf[m] that devoured the atonement and was turned to stone and of the crags of Tymphrestus.[n] Of whom some, unhappy, yearning for their fatherland of Aegoneia,[o] others for Echinos,[o] others for Titaros[n] and for Iros[n] and for Trachis[p] and Perrhaebic Gonnos[n] and Phalanna,[n] and the fields of the Olossonians,[n] and Castanaia,[q] torn on the rocks shall bewail their fate that lacks the rites of funeral.

[g] Founding of Cyrene (Pind. *P*. iv.)
[h] Guneus from Cyphos in Perrhaebia (*Il*. ii. 748).
[i] Prothoüs, *Il*. ii. 756.   [j] In (Thessalian) Magnesia.
[k] On the Amphrysus in Thessaly.
[l] Eurypylus from Ormenion in Thessaly (*Il*. ii. 734).
[m] When Peleus had collected a herd of cattle as an atonement for the murder of Actor, son of Acastus (schol.) or Eurytion (Ant. Lib. 38) or Phocus (Ovid, *M*. xi. 381), the herd was devoured by a wolf which Thetis turned into stone. This stone is variously located in Thessaly or Phocis.
[n] In Thessaly.   [o] In Malis.
[p] Near Mount Oeta.   [q] In Magnesia.

LYCOPHRON

Ἄλλην δ' ἐπ' ἄλλῃ κῆρα κινήσει θεός,
λυγρὴν πρὸ νόστου συμφορὰν δωρούμενος.   910

Τὸν δ' Αἰσάρου τε ῥεῖθρα καὶ βραχύπτολις
Οἰνωτρίας γῆς κεγχρίνῃ βεβρωμένον
Κρίμισα φιτροῦ δέξεται μιαιφόνον·
αὐτὴ γὰρ ἄκραν ἄρδιν εὐθυνεῖ χεροῖν
Σάλπιγξ ἀποψάλλουσα Μαιώτην πλόκον·   915
Δύρα παρ' ὄχθαις ὅς ποτε φλέξας θρασὺν
λέοντα ῥαιβῷ χεῖρας ὥπλισε Σκύθῃ
δράκοντ' ἀφύκτων γομφίων λυροκτύπῳ.
Κρᾶθις δὲ τύμβους ὄψεται δεδουπότος,
εὐρὰξ Ἀλαίου Παταρέως ἀνακτόρων,   920
Ναύαιθος ἔνθα πρὸς κλύδων' ἐρεύγεται.
κτενοῦσι δ' αὐτὸν Αὔσονες Πελλήνιοι
βοηδρομοῦντα Λινδίων στρατηλάταις,
οὓς τῆλε Θερμύδρου τε Καρπάθου τ' ὁρῶν
πλάνητας αἴθων Θρασκίας πέμψει κύων,   925
ξένην ἐποικήσοντας ὀθνείαν χθόνα.
ἐν δ' αὖ Μακάλλοις σηκὸν ἔγχωροι μέγαν
ὑπὲρ τάφων δείμαντες, αἰανῇ θεὸν
λοιβαῖσι κυδανοῦσι καὶ θύσθλοις βοῶν.

---

[a] Philoctetes, son of Poeas from Magnesia, returns from
Troy to his home, but owing to a sedition went to S. Italy,
where he founded Chone, Petelia, and Crimisa (Strabo 254).

[b] Near Croton (Strabo 262).

[c] Philoctetes having been bitten by a viper was left by
the Greeks in Lemnos, but as Troy could not be taken
without the bow and arrows of Heracles which he had, they
afterwards brought him to Troy, where he killed Paris.

[d] Paris, in reference to Hecuba's dream.

[e] Athena in Argos (Paus. ii. 21. 3), where was a temple of
Athena Salpinx, said to have been founded by Hegeleos,
son of Tyrsenus, the reputed inventor of the trumpet.

[f] *i.e.* Scythian.

One evil fate after another shall god arouse, presenting them with grievous calamity in place of return to their homes.

Another [a] shall the streams of Aesarus [b] and the little city of Crimisa in the Oenotrian land receive: even the snake-bitten [c] slayer of the fire-brand [d]; for the Trumpet [e] herself shall with her hand guide his arrow point, releasing the twanging Maeotian [f] bowstring. On the banks of Dyras [g] he burnt of old the bold lion,[h] and armed his hands with the crooked Scythian dragon [i] that harped with unescapable teeth. And Crathis [j] shall see his tomb when he is dead, sideways from the shrine of Alaeus [k] of Patara, where Nauaethus [l] belches seaward. The Ausonian Pellenians [m] shall slay him when he aids the leaders of the Lindians,[n] whom far from Thermydron [o] and the mountains of Carpathus [p] the fierce hound Thrascias [q] shall send wandering to dwell in a strange and alien soil. But in Macalla,[r] again, the people of the place shall build a great shrine above his grave and glorify him as an everlasting god with libations and sacrifice of oxen.

[g] River near Oeta where Heracles was cremated by Philoctetes who inherited his bow and arrows.
[h] Heracles.   [i] Heracles' bow.
[j] River near Sybaris.
[k] At Crimisa Philoctetes built a temple to Apollo Alaeus (i.e. " of wandering "). Patara in Lycia had a famous temple of Apollo (Strabo 666).
[l] River near Croton where Trojan captive women burnt the Greek ships (Strabo 262).
[m] Philoctetes died fighting for Rhodian settlers in Italy, who had been carried thither by the N.N.W. wind, against settlers from Pellene in Achaea.
[n] Lindos in Rhodes.   [o] Harbour of Lindos.
[p] Island between Rhodes and Crete.
[q] N.N.W. wind.   [r] Town in Chonia.

'Ο δ' ἱπποτέκτων Λαγαρίας ἐν ἀγκάλαις,   930
ἔγχος πεφρικὼς καὶ φάλαγγα θουρίαν,
πατρῷον ὅρκον ἐκτίνων ψευδώμοτον,
ὃν ἀμφὶ μήλων τῶν δορικτήτων τάλας
πύργων Κομαιθοῦς συμπεφυρμένων στρατῷ
στεργοξυνεύνων οὕνεκεν νυμφευμάτων   935
Ἀλοῖτιν ἔτλη τὴν Κυδωνίαν Θρασὼ
ὁρκωμοτῆσαι τόν τε Κρηστώνης θεὸν
Κανδάον' ἢ Μάμερτον ὁπλίτην λύκον,
ὁ μητρὸς ἐντὸς δελφύος στυγνὴν μάχην
στήσας ἀραγμοῖς πρὸς κασίγνητον χεροῖν,   940
οὔπω τὸ Τιτοῦς λαμπρὸν αὐγάζων φάος
οὐδ' ἐκφυγὼν ὠδῖνας ἀλγεινὰς τόκων.
τοιγὰρ πόποι φύξηλιν ἤνδρωσαν σπόρον,
πύκτην μὲν ἐσθλόν, πτῶκα δ' ἐν κλόνῳ δορός,
καὶ πλεῖστα τέχναις ὠφελήσαντα στρατόν·   945
ὃς ἀμφὶ Κῖριν καὶ Κυλιστάνου¹ γάνος
ἔπηλυς οἴκους τῆλε νάσσεται πάτρας,
τὰ δ' ἐργαλεῖα, τοῖσι τέτρηνας βρέτας
τεύξει ποτ' ἐγχώροισι μέρμερον βλάβην,
καθιερώσει Μυνδίας ἀνακτόροις.   950
"Αλλοι δ' ἐνοικήσουσι Σικανῶν χθόνα,
πλαγκτοὶ μολόντες, ἔνθα Λαυμέδων τριπλᾶς

¹ Κυλιστάνου Scheer from E.M. 544. 30 Κυλιστάρ(ν)ου.

ᵃ Near Thurii in S. Italy, founded by Epeius (Strabo 263).   ᵇ Epeius.
ᶜ In later epic Epeius is typical coward (Q. Smyrn. iv. 323 ; xii. 28, etc.).   ᵈ Panopeus.
ᵉ Panopeus went with Amphitryon against the Taphians and Teleboans. Pterelaus, king of the former, had a lock of golden hair which made him invincible. Comaetho, his daughter, fell in love with Amphitryon and cut off the lock. Amphitryon captured the city of Pterelaus and put to death Comaetho. Panopeus seized some of the spoils

398

In the sheltering arms of Lagaria [a] shall dwell
the builder [b] of the horse. Afraid [c] of the spear and
the impetuous phalanx, he pays for the false oath
of his father [d] regarding the spear-won herds, which
wretched man, when the towers of Comaetho [e] were
confounded by the army in the cause of loving
marriage, he dared to swear by Aloetis Cydonia Thraso, [f]
and by the god [g] of Crestone, [h] Candaon or Mamertus,
warrior wolf. He [i] even within his mother's womb
arrayed hateful battle against his brother with blows of
his hands, while he looked not yet on the bright light of
Tito, nor had yet escaped the grievous pains of birth.
And for his false oath the gods made his son grow
to be a coward man, a good boxer but a skulker in
the mellay of the spear. By his arts he most greatly
helped the host; and by Ciris [j] and the bright waters
of Cylistanus he shall dwell as an alien, far from his
fatherland; and the tools wherewith he shall bore
the image and fashion sad ruin for the people of my
country, he shall consecrate in the shrine of Myndia. [k]
And others shall dwell in the land [l] of the
Sicanians, wandering to the spot where Laomedon, [m]

unjustly, but denied it on oath, swearing falsely by Athena
and Ares.

[f] Athena Aloetis, as avenger of sin; Cydonia, cult-name
of Athena in Elis where she had a temple founded by
Clymenus from Cydonia in Crete; Thraso ("Bold"), as
warlike goddess.

[g] Ares. Here Candaon must be a title of Ares, but in
328 Hephaestus.   [h] In Thrace.

[i] P. fought with his brother Crisus in his mother's womb.
[j] = Aciris, river near Siris (Strabo 264), in Lucania.
[k] Athena, from her cult at Myndus in Caria.   [l] In Sicily.
[m] When Phoenodamas refused to expose his daughters to
the sea-beast, Laomedon had to expose his own daughter
Hesione. In revenge he gave the daughters of Phoenodamas to some merchants to expose in the far West.

ναύταις ἔδωκε Φοινοδάμαντος κόρας,
ταῖς κητοδόρποις συμφοραῖς δεδηγμένος,
τηλοῦ προθεῖναι θηρσὶν ὠμησταῖς βορὰν   955
μολόντας εἰς γῆν ἕσπερον Λαιστρυγόνων,
ὅπου συνοικεῖ δαψιλὴς ἐρημία.
αἱ δ' αὖ παλαιστοῦ μητέρος Ζηρυνθίας
σηκὸν μέγαν δείμαντο, δωτίνην θεᾷ,
μόρον φυγοῦσαι καὶ μονοικήτους ἔδρας,   960
ὧν δὴ μίαν Κριμισός, ἰνδαλθεὶς κυνί,
ἔζευξε λέκτροις ποταμός· ἡ δὲ δαίμονι
τῷ θηρομίκτῳ σκύλακα γενναῖον τεκνοῖ,
τρισσῶν συνοικιστῆρα καὶ κτίστην τόπων.
ὃς δὴ ποδηγῶν πτόρθον Ἀγχίσου νόθον   965
ἄξει τρίδειρον νῆσον εἰς ληκτηρίαν,
τῶν Δαρδανείων ἐκ τόπων ναυσθλούμενον.
Αἰγέστα τλῆμον, σοὶ δὲ δαιμόνων φραδαῖς
πένθος μέγιστον καὶ δι' αἰῶνος πάτρας
ἔσται πυρὸς ῥιπαῖσιν ἠθαλωμένης.   970
μόνη δὲ πύργων δυστυχεῖς κατασκαφὰς
νήπαυστον αἰάζουσα καὶ γοωμένη
δαρὸν στενάξεις. πᾶς δὲ λυγαίαν λεὼς
ἐσθῆτα προστρόπαιον ἐγχλαινούμενος
αὐχμῷ πινώδης λυπρὸν ἀμπρεύσει βίον.   975
κρατὸς δ' ἄκουρος νῶτα καλλυνεῖ φόβῃ,
μνήμην παλαιῶν τημελοῦσ' ὀδυρμάτων.
     Πολλοὶ δὲ Σῖριν ἀμφὶ καὶ Λευταρνίαν

---

[a] Aphrodite, as in 449 ; but in 1178 Hecate.
[b] Eryx ; see 866 f.
[c] Aegesta. A dog, representing Crimisus, appears on coins of (S)egesta (Sestri) (Head, *Hist. Num.* p. 164 f.).

stung by the ravages of the gluttonous sea-monster, gave to mariners to expose the three daughters of Phoenodamas that they should be devoured by ravenous wild beasts, there far off where they came to the land of the Laestrygonians in the West, where dwells always abundant desolation. And those daughters in their turn built a great shrine for the Zerynthian [a] mother of the wrestler,[b] as a gift to the goddess, for as much as they had escaped from doom and lonely dwelling. Of these one [c] the river Crimisus, in the likeness of a dog, took to be his bride : and she to the half-beast god bears a noble whelp,[d] settler and founder of three places.[e] That whelp shall guide the bastard [f] scion of Anchises and bring him to the farthest bounds of the three-necked island,[g] voyaging from Dardanian places. Hapless Aegesta ! to thee by devising of the gods there shall be most great and age-long sorrow for my country when it is consumed by the breath of fire. And thou alone shalt groan for long, bewailing and lamenting unceasingly the unhappy overthrow of her towers. And all thy people, clad in the sable garb of the suppliant, squalid and unkempt, shall drag out a sorrowful life, and the unshorn hair of their heads shall deck their backs, keeping the memory of ancient woes.[h]

And many shall dwell by Siris [i] and Leutarnia's [j]

[a] Aegestes.
[e] Aegesta, Eryx, Entella.
[f] Elymus, eponym of the Elymi.
[g] Sicily.
[h] The native garb of the people of Segesta is interpreted as mourning for Troy ; cf. 863, 1137.
[i] In Lucania.
[j] Coast of Calabria.

LYCOPHRON

ἄρουραν οἰκήσουσιν, ἔνθα δύσμορος
Κάλχας ὀλύνθων Σισυφεὺς ἀνηρίθμων   980
κεῖται, κάρα μάστιγι γογγύλῃ τυπείς,
ῥείθροισιν ὠκὺς ἔνθα μύρεται Σίνις,
ἄρδων βαθεῖαν Χωνίας παγκληρίαν.
πόλιν δ' ὁμοίαν Ἰλίῳ δυσδαίμονες
δείμαντες, ἀλγυνοῦσι Λαφρίαν κόρην   985
Σάλπιγγα, δῃώσαντες ἐν ναῷ θεᾶς
τοὺς πρόσθ' ἔδεθλον Ξουθίδας ᾠκηκότας.
γλήναις δ' ἄγαλμα ταῖς ἀναιμάτοις μύσει,
στυγνὴν Ἀχαιῶν εἰς Ἰάονας βλάβην
λεῦσσον φόνον τ' ἔμφυλον ἀγραύλων λύκων,   990
ὅταν θανὼν λήταρχος ἱρείας σκύλαξ
πρῶτος κελαινῷ βωμὸν αἱμάξῃ βροτῷ.
    Ἄλλοι δὲ πρῶνας δυσβάτους Τυλησίους
Λίνου θ' ἁλισμήκτοιο δειραίαν ἄκραν
Ἀμαζόνος σύγκληρον ἄρσονται πέδον,   995
δούλης γυναικὸς ζεύγλαν ἐνδεδεγμένοι,
ἣν χαλκομίτρου θῆσσαν ὀτρηρῆς κόρης
πλανῆτιν ἄξει κῦμα πρὸς ξένην χθόνα.
ἧς ἐκπνεούσης λοῖσθον ὀφθαλμὸς τυπεὶς
πιθηκομόρφῳ πότμον Αἰτωλῷ φθόρῳ   100[0]
τεύξει τράφηκι φοινίῳ τετμημένῳ.

---

[a] In connexion with Heracles and his carrying off of
the oxen of Geryon, legend told that Heracles, seeing a
seer (here called Calchas) sitting under a fig-tree, asked him
how many figs were on the tree. "Ten bushels and one
fig," said the seer. When Heracles vainly tried to put the
odd fig into the tenth bushel, the seer mocked him and
Heracles killed him with his fist.
[b] Sisyphus is the type of cleverness.
[c] The fist of Heracles.   [d] i.e. Siris.
[e] Achaeans come from Troy and settle near Siris on the
site of the later Heracleia. They kill the Ionians, the

402

fields, where lies the unhappy Calchas *a* who Sisyphus-
like *b* counted the unnumbered figs, and who was
smitten on the head by the rounded scourge *c*—
where Sinis' *d* swift stream flows, watering the rich
estate of Chonia. There the unhappy men shall
build a city like Ilios,*e* and shall vex the Maiden *f*
Laphria Salpinx by slaying in the temple of the
goddess the descendants *g* of Xuthus who formerly
occupied the town. And her image shall shut its
bloodless eyes, beholding the hateful destruction of
Ionians by Achaeans and the kindred slaughter of
the wild wolves, when the minister son of the
priestess dies and stains first the altar with his dark
blood.

And others shall take to them the steep Tylesian *h*
hills and sea-washed Linos' *h* hilly promontory, the
territory of the Amazon,*i* taking on them the yoke of a
slave woman, whom, as servant of the brazen-mailed
impetuous maiden,*j* the wave shall carry wandering
to an alien land: slave of that maiden whose eye,
smitten as she breathes her last, shall bring doom to
the ape-formed Aetolian pest,*k* wounded by the

previous settlers, in the temple of Ilian Athena; *cf.* Aristot.
Mirab. 106, Athen. xii. 523, Strabo 264 (who says it was
the Ionians who murdered the earlier Trojan settlers).

f Athena, *cf.* 356, 915.
g Ionians, Ion being son of Xuthus.
h Unknown, but apparently in Bruttium.
i Clete, nurse of Penthesileia.
j When Clete heard that Penthesileia had fallen at Troy,
she set out in search of her but was carried by stress of
weather to Italy where she found a town which bore her
name in Bruttium.
k Thersites (for his deformity *cf. Il.* ii. 216 ff.) from
Aetolia. When Achilles slew Penthesileia, Thersites insulted the corpse by thrusting his spear in her eye, where-
upon Achilles killed him (Q. Smyrn. i. 660 ff.).

Κροτωνιᾶται δ' ἄστυ πέρσουσίν ποτε
'Αμαζόνος, φθέρσαντες ἄτρομον κόρην
Κλήτην, ἄνασσαν τῆς ἐπωνύμου πάτρας.
πολλοὶ δὲ πρόσθεν γαῖαν ἐκ κείνης ὀδὰξ   1005
δάψουσι πρηνιχθέντες, οὐδ' ἄτερ πόνων
πύργους διαρραίσουσι Λαυρήτης γόνοι.

   Οἱ δ' αὖ Τέρειναν, ἔνθα μυδαίνει ποτοῖς
'Ωκίναρος γῆν, φοῖβον ἐκβράσσων ὕδωρ,
ἄλη κατοικήσουσι κάμνοντες πικρᾷ.   1010

   Τὸν δ' αὖ τὰ δευτερεῖα καλλιστευμάτων
λαβόντα, καὶ τὸν ἐκ Λυκορμαίων ποτῶν
στρατηλάτην σὺν, καρτερὸν Γόργης τόκον,
τῇ μὲν Λίβυσσαν ψάμμον ἄξουσι πνοαὶ
Θρῇσσαι ποδωτοῖς ἐμφορούμεναι λίνοις,   1015
τῇ δ' ἐκ Λιβύσσης αὖθις ἐμπίπτων νότος
εἰς 'Αργυρίνους καὶ Κεραυνίων νάπας
ἄξει βαρεῖ πρηστῆρι ποιμαίνων ἅλα.
ἔνθα πλανήτην λυπρὸν ὄψονται βίον
Λακμωνίου πίνοντες Αἴαντος ῥοάς.   1020
Κρᾶθις δὲ γείτων ἠδὲ Μυλάκων ὅροις
χῶρος[1] συνοίκους δέξεται Κόλχων Πόλαις,
μαστῆρας οὓς θυγατρὸς ἔστειλεν βαρὺς
Αἴας Κορίνθου τ' ἀρχός, Εἰδυίας πόσις,
τὴν νυμφαγωγὸν ἐκκυνηγετῶν τρόπιν,   1025
οἳ πρὸς βαθεῖ νάσσαντο Διζηροῦ πόρῳ.

----

[1] ὅρος (cod. B) χώρας Scheer.

----

[a] *E.M. s.v.* Κλείτη says that not only the city but also the
queens who succeeded the first Cleite (Clete) bore the same
name.   As Clete was mother of Caulon, founder of Caulonia,
the reference seems to be to the taking of Caulonia by
Croton.

[b] Daughter of Lacinius and wife of Croton (schol.).

[c] In Bruttium.   [d] Nireus (Hom. *Il.* ii. 671 ff.).

[e] Thoas.   [f] =Evenus in Aetolia (Strabo 451).

ALEXANDRA

bloody shaft. And the men of Croton shall sack the
city of the Amazon, destroying the dauntless maiden
Clete,[a] queen of the land that bears her name. But,
ere that, many shall be laid low by her hand and
bite the dust with their teeth, and not without
labour shall the sons of Laureta[b] sack the towers.

Others, again, in Tereina,[c] where Ocinarus moistens
the earth with his streams, bubbling with bright
water, shall dwell, weary with bitter wandering.

And him,[d] again, who won the second prize for
beauty, and the boar leader[e] from the streams of
Lycormas,[f] the mighty son of Gorge,[g] on the one
hand the Thracian blasts, falling on taut sails, shall
carry to the sands of Libya; on the other hand from
Libya again the blast of the South wind shall carry
them to the Argyrini[h] and the glades of Ceraunia,[i]
shepherding the sea with grievous hurricane. And
there they shall see a sorry wandering life, drinking
the waters of Aias[j] which springs from Lacmon.[k]
And neighbouring Crathis[l] and the land of the
Mylaces[m] shall receive them in their bounds to dwell
at Polae,[n] the town of the Colchians whom the angry
ruler[o] of Aea and of Corinth, the husband of Eiduia,[p]
sent to seek his daughter,[q] tracking the keel[r] that
carried off the bride; they settled by the deep
stream of Dizerus.[s]

[g] Daughter of Oeneus.
[h] In Epirus (Steph. B.).   [i] Mountain in Epirus.
[j] i.e. the Auas or Aoüs (Strabo 271, 316).
[k] = Lacmus; cf. Herod. ix. 23.
[l] Unknown river in Illyria.
[m] Illyrians (λλλός = μυλλός, i.e. " squinting ").
[n] Cf. Callim. fr. incert. 2 n.   [o] Aeëtes.
[p] Hes. Th. 958, where Aeëtes, son of Helios, is husband
of Idyia, daughter of Oceanus.
[q] Medeia.   [r] Argo.   [s] In Illyria (Steph. B.).

405

LYCOPHRON

Ἄλλοι δὲ Μελίτην νῆσον Ὀθρωνοῦ πέλας
πλαγκτοὶ κατοικήσουσιν, ἣν πέριξ κλύδων
ἔμπλην Παχύνου Σικανὸς προσμάσσεται,
τοῦ Σισυφείου παιδὸς ὀχθηρὰν ἄκραν   1030
ἐπώνυμόν ποθ' ὑστέρῳ χρόνῳ γράφων
κλεινόν θ' ἵδρυμα παρθένου Λογγάτιδος,
Ἕλωρος ἔνθα ψυχρὸν ἐκβάλλει ποτόν.

Παπποκτόνος δ' Ὀθρωνὸν οἰκήσει λύκος,
τηλοῦ πατρῷα ῥεῖθρα Κοσκύνθου ποθῶν.   1035
ὃς ἐν θαλάσσῃ χοιράδων βεβὼς ἔπι
ῥήτρας πολίταις τὰς στρατοπλώτους ἐρεῖ.
χέρσου πατρῴας οὐ γὰρ ἂν φονῇ ποσὶ
ψαῦσαι, μέγαν πλειῶνα μὴ πεφευγότα,
Δίκης ἐάσει τάρροθος Τελφουσία   1040
Λάδωνος ἀμφὶ ῥεῖθρα ναίουσα σκύλαξ.
ὅθεν, πεφευγὼς ἑρπετῶν δεινὴν μάχην
δρακοντομόρφων, εἰς Ἀμαντίαν πόλιν
πλώσει. πέλας δὲ γῆς Ἀτιντάνων μολών,
Πράκτιν παρ' αὐτὴν αἰπὺ νάσσεται λέπας,   1045
τοῦ Χαονίτου νᾶμα Πολυάνθους δρέπων.

Ὁ δ' Αὐσονείων ἄγχι Κάλχαντος τάφων,

---

  a Malta.

  b Hesych. *s.v.* Ὀθρωνός says "island off Corcyra"; so
  Pliny, *N.H.* iv. 52. Hence Scheer supposed that Lycophron
  confused Melita = Malta with the Illyrian Melita = Meleda.
  But Steph. Byz. *s.v.* Ὀθρ. says "according to some an island
  to the south of Sicily."

  c Cape in south-east Sicily, of which the western point
  was called Ὀδυσσεία ἄκρα (Ptolem. iii. 4. 7).

  d Odysseus, according to one legend son of Anticleia
  and Sisyphus.   *e* Athena ; *cf.* 520.

  f River near Pachynus.   *g* Island near Corcyra.

  h Elephenor of Euboea (*Il.* ii. 540) having unwittingly
  slain his grandfather Abas had to go into exile for a year.
  Meanwhile the Trojan war breaks out, in which as a suitor

ALEXANDRA

Other wanderers shall dwell in the isle of Melita,[a] near Othronus,[b] round which the Sicanian wave laps beside Pachynus,[c] grazing the steep promontory that in after time shall bear the name of the son[d] of Sisyphus and the famous shrine of the maiden Longatis,[e] where Helorus[f] empties his chilly stream.

And in Othronus[g] shall dwell the wolf[h] that slew his own grandfather, yearning afar for his ancestral stream of Coscynthus.[i] Standing in the sea upon the rocks he shall declare to his countrymen the compact of the sailing army. For never will the ally of Justice, the Telphusian hound[j] that dwells by the streams of Ladon, allow the murderer to touch with his feet his fatherland, if he has not spent a great year in exile. Thence, fleeing from the terrible warfare of the serpent-shaped vermin,[k] he shall sail to the city of Amantia,[l] and coming nigh to the land of the Atintanians,[m] right beside Practis[n] shall he dwell upon a steep hill, drinking the waters of Chaonian Polyanthes.

And near the Ausonian false-tomb of Calchas[o]

of Helen (Apollod. iii. 130) he has to take part. When he comes to summon the Abantes to the war he may not land, but must speak from a rock in the sea; *cf.* Arist. 'Aθ. Πολ. 57.   [i] In Euboea (schol.).

[j] Demeter - Erinys, cult at Telphusa or Thelpusa in Arcadia.   [k] Reference unknown.

[l] = 'Aβαντία in Illyricum.

[m] In Epeirus (Strabo 326).   [n] Unknown.

[o] Calchas was buried near Colophon (*cf.* 424 f.), but "there are shown in Daunia on a hill called Drion two *heroa* (hero-shrines), one of Calchas on the top of the hill, where those who consult him sacrifice to him a black ram and sleep upon the skin; the other of Podaleirius at the foot of the hill. . . . From it flows a small stream which is a sovereign remedy (πάνακες) for the diseases of cattle" (Strabo 284).

δυοῖν ἀδελφοῖν ἅτερος, ψευδηρίων
ξένην ἐπ' ὀστέοισιν ὀγχήσει κόνιν.
δοραῖς δὲ μήλων τύμβον ἐγκοιμωμένοις   1050
χρήσει καθ' ὕπνον πᾶσι νημερτῆ φάτιν,
νόσων δ' ἀκεστὴς Δαυνίοις κληθήσεται,
ὅταν κατικμαίνοντες 'Αλθαίνου ῥοαῖς
ἀρωγὸν αὐδήσωσιν 'Ηπίου γόνον
ἀστοῖσι καὶ ποίμναισι πρευμενῆ μολεῖν.   1055
ἔσται ποτὲ πρεσβεῦσιν Αἰτωλῶν φάος
ἐκεῖ γοηρὸν καὶ πανέχθιστον φανέν,
ὅταν Σαλάγγων γαῖαν 'Αγγαίσων θ' ἕδη
μολόντες αἰτίζωσι κοιράνου γύας,
ἐσθλῆς ἀρούρης πῖαρ ἔγκληρον χθονός.   1060
τοὺς δ' εἰς ἐρεμνὸν ζῶντας ὠμησταὶ τάφον
κρύψουσι κοίλης ἐν μυχοῖς διασφάγος.
τοῖς δ' ἀκτέριστον σῆμα Δαυνῖται νεκρῶν
στήσουσι χωστῷ τροχμάλῳ κατηρεφές,
χώραν διδόντες, ἥν περ ἔχρηζον λαβεῖν,   1065
τοῦ κρατοβρῶτος παιδὸς ἄτρεστον κάπρου.

Τῶν Ναυβολείων δ' εἰς Τέμεσσαν ἐγγόνων
ναῦται καταβλώξουσιν, ἔνθα Λαμπέτης
'Ιππωνίου πρηῶνος εἰς Τηθὺν κέρας

ᵃ Podaleirius.
ᵇ Podaleirius and Machaon, sons of Asclepius, from
Thessaly (Il. ii. 730 f.).
ᶜ Stream flowing from Mount Drion.   ᵈ Asclepius.
ᵉ Justin xii. 2 says Brundusium was founded by the
Aetolians under Diomede. When the Aetolians were ex-
pelled by the Apulians they consulted the oracles and got
the answer "locum quem repetissent perpetuo possessuros."
Accordingly they sent ambassadors to demand restitution of
the city. The Apulians, having learnt of the oracle, killed
the ambassadors and buried them in the city, "perpetuam
ibi sedem habituros."
ᶠ Unknown.   ᵍ Diomedes.
408

one [a] of two brothers [b] shall have an alien soil over
his bones and to men sleeping in sheepskins on his
tomb he shall declare in dreams his unerring message
for all. And healer of diseases shall he be called
by the Daunians, when they wash the sick with the
waters of Althaenus [c] and invoke the son of Epius [d]
to their aid, that he may come gracious unto men
and flocks. There some time for the ambassadors [e]
of the Aetolians shall dawn a sad and hateful day,
when, coming to the land of the Salangi [f] and the seats
of the Angaesi, [f] they shall ask the fields of their lord, [g]
the rich inheritance of goodly soil. Alive in a dark
tomb within the recesses of a hollow cleft shall the
savages hide them; and for them the Daunites shall
set up a memorial of the dead without funeral rites,
roofed with piled stones, giving them the land which
they desired to get,—the land of the son [g] of the
dauntless boar [h] who devoured the brains [i] of his enemy.

And the mariners of the descendants [j] of Naubolus
shall come to Temessa, [k] where the hard horn of the
Hipponian [l] hill inclines to the sea of Lampeta. [m]

---

[h] Tydeus fought with Polyneices in Argos. Adrastus had
received an oracle that he should marry his daughters to a
lion and a boar, and a seer now recognized in Polyneices the
lion, in Tydeus the boar (Eur. *Suppl.* 140 ff.).

[i] In the war of the Seven against Thebes Melanippos
(Aesch. *Sept.* 415) was opposed to Tydeus (*ibid.* 377).
Tydeus was wounded by Melanippos whom he then slew.
As Tydeus lay dying, Athena brought a drug which was to
make him immortal. But Amphiaraus, who hated Tydeus,
cut off the head of Melanippos and gave it to Tydeus who
opened it and supped the brains (Apollod. iii. 76).

[j] Schedius and Epistrophus, sons of Iphitus, son of
Naubolus, from Phocis (*Il.* ii. 517).

[k] Tempsa in Bruttium (Strabo 255).

[l] Vibo Valentia (Strabo 256), in Bruttium.

[m] Clampetia, in Bruttium.

σκληρὸν νένευκεν. ἀντὶ δὲ Κρίσης ὅρων   1070
Κροτωνιᾶτιν ἀντίπορθμον αὔλακα
βοῶν ἀροτρεύσουσιν ὁλκαίῳ πτερῷ,
πάτραν Λίλαιαν κἀνεμωρείας πέδον
ποθοῦντες Ἀμφισσάν τε καὶ κλεινὰς Ἄβας.
Σήταια τλῆμον, σοὶ δὲ πρὸς πέτραις μόρος   1075
μίμνει δυσαίων, ἔνθα γυιούχοις πέδαις
οἴκτιστα χαλκείῃσιν ὠργυιωμένη
θανῇ, πυρὶ φλέξασα δεσποτῶν στόλον,
ἔκβλητον αἰάζουσα Κράθιδος πέλας
τόργοισιν αἰώρημα φοινίοις δέμας.   1080
σπιλὰς δ' ἐκείνη σῆς φερώνυμος τύχης
πόντον προσαυγάζουσα φημισθήσεται.

   Οἱ δ' αὖ Πελασγῶν ἀμφὶ Μέμβλητος ῥοὰς
νῆσόν τε Κερνεᾶτιν ἐκπεπλωκότες
ὑπὲρ πόρον Τυρσηνὸν ἐν Λαμητίαις   1085
δίναισιν οἰκήσουσι Λευκανῶν πλάκας.

   Καὶ τοὺς μὲν ἄλγη ποικίλαι τε συμφοραὶ
ἄνοστον αἰάζοντας ἕξουσιν τύχην
ἐμῶν ἕκατι δυσγάμων ῥυσταγμάτων.

   Οὐδ' οἱ χρόνῳ μολόντες ἀσπαστῶς δόμους   1090
εὐκταῖον ἐκλάμψουσι θυμάτων σέλας,
χάριν τίνοντες Κερδύλᾳ Λαρυνθίῳ.
τοιαῖσδ' ἐχῖνος μηχαναῖς οἰκοφθορῶν
παραιολίξει τὰς ἀλεκτόρων πικρὰς
στεγανόμους ὄρνιθας. οὐδὲ ναυφάγοι   1095
λήξουσι πένθους δυσμενεῖς φρυκτωρίαι
πτόρθου διαρραισθέντος, ὃν νεοσκαφὲς

---

^a Phocian towns (*Il. l.c.* .
^b Setaea, a Trojan captive, set fire to the Greek ships.
Hence Setaeum, cliff near Sybaris.

And in place of the bounds of Crisa[a] they shall till with ox-drawn trailing ploughshare the Crotonian fields across the straits, longing for their native Lilaea[a] and the plain of Anemoreia[a] and Amphissa[a] and famous Abae.[a] Poor Setaea[b]! for thee waits an unhappy fate upon the rocks, where, most pitifully outstretched with brazen fetters on thy limbs, thou shalt die, because thou didst burn the fleet of thy masters: bewailing near Crathis thy body cast out and hung up for gory vultures to devour. And that cliff, looking on the sea, shall be called by thy name in memory of thy fate.

And others again beside the Pelasgian streams of Membles and the Cerneatid isle shall sail forth and beyond the Tyrrhenian strait occupy in Lametian waters Leucanian plains.

And griefs and varied sufferings shall be the lot of these—bewailing their fate which allows them not to return home, on account of my haling to unhappy marriage.

Nor shall they who after many days come gladly home kindle the flame of votive offering in gratitude to Cerdylas Larynthius.[c] With such craft shall the hedgehog[d] ruin their homes and mislead the house-keeping hens embittered against the cocks. Nor shall the ship-devouring hostile beacons abate their sorrow for his shattered scion,[e] whom a new-dug

[c] Zeus. The meaning of these cult-names is quite obscure: Cerdylas possibly = Κτήσιος, Zeus as god of property.

[d] Nauplius ("hedgehog," from proverbial craftiness of that animal, Ael. *N.A.* vi. 54), in revenge for his son Palamedes, lures the Greeks by false beacons on to the rocks and by lies induces their wives to be faithless.

[e] Palamedes, stoned to death by the Greeks, was buried by Achilles and Aias near Methymna (in Lesbos).

κρύψει ποτ' ἐν κλήροισι Μηδύμνης στέγος.
    Ὁ μὲν γὰρ ἀμφὶ χύτλα τὰς δυσεξόδους
ζητῶν κελεύθους αὐχενιστῆρος βρόχου   1100
ἐν ἀμφιβλήστρῳ συντεταργανωμένος
τυφλαῖς ματεύσει χερσὶ κροσσωτοὺς ῥαφάς.
θερμὴν δ' ὑπαὶ λουτρῶνος ἀρνεύων στέγην
τιβῆνα καὶ κύπελλον ἐγκάρῳ ῥανεῖ,
τυπεὶς σκεπάρνῳ κόγχον εὐθήκτῳ μέσον.   1105
οἰκτρὰ δὲ πέμφιξ Ταίναρον πτερύξεται,
λυπρὰν λεαίνης εἰσιδοῦσ' οἰκουρίαν.
ἐγὼ δὲ δροίτης ἄγχι κείσομαι πέδῳ,
Χαλυβδικῷ κνώδοντι συντεθραυσμένη,
ἐπεί με, πεύκης πρέμνον ἢ στύπος δρυὸς   1110
ὅπως τις ὑλοκουρὸς ἐργάτης ὀρεύς,
ῥήξει πλατὺν τένοντα καὶ μετάφρενον,
καὶ πᾶν λακίζουσ' ἐν φοναῖς ψυχρὸν δέμας
δράκαινα διψὰς κἀπιβᾶσ' ἐπ' αὐχένος
πλήσει γέμοντα θυμὸν ἀγρίας χολῆς,   1115
ὡς κλεψίνυμφον κοὐ δορίκτητον γέρας
δύσζηλος ἀστέμβακτα τιμωρουμένη.
βοῶσα δ' οὐ κλύοντα δεσπότην πόσιν
θεύσω κατ' ἴχνος ἠνεμωμένη πτεροῖς.
σκύμνος δὲ πατρὸς κῆρα μαστεύων φόνου   1120
εἰς σπλάγχν' ἐχίδνης αὐτόχειρ βάψει ξίφος,
κακὸν μίασμ' ἔμφυλον ἀλθαίνων κακῷ.
    Ἐμὸς δ' ἀκοίτης, δμωΐδος νύμφης ἄναξ,
Ζεὺς Σπαρτιάταις αἱμύλοις κληθήσεται,
τιμὰς μεγίστας Οἰβάλου τέκνοις λαχών.   1125

---

    [a] Agamemnon is killed in the bath by Clytemnestra.
    [b] In Laconia, where there was a descent to Hades.
        [c] Clytaemnestra.
    [d] The Chalybes in Pontus were famous workers in metal.

ALEXANDRA

habitation in the territory of Methymna shall hide.

One *a* at the bath while he seeks for the difficult exits of the mesh about his neck, entangled in a net, shall search with blind hands the fringed stitching. And diving under the hot covering of the bath he shall sprinkle with his brains tripod and basin, when he is smitten in the midst of the skull with the well-sharpened axe. His piteous ghost shall wing its way to Taenarus,*b* having looked on the bitter housekeeping of the lioness.*c* And I beside the bath shall lie on the ground, shattered by the Chalybdic *d* sword. For she shall cleave me—broad tendon and back—even as a woodcutter workman on the mountains cleaves trunk of pine or stem of oak—and, sand-viper as she is, will rend all my cold body in blood and set her foot on my neck and glut her laden soul of bitter bile, taking relentless vengeance on me in evil jealousy, as if I were a stolen bride and not a spear-won prize. And calling on my master and husband,*e* who hears no more, I shall follow his track on wings of the wind. But a whelp,*f* seeking vengeance for his father's blood, shall with his own hand plunge his sword in the entrails of the viper, with evil healing the evil pollution of his race.

And my husband, lord of a slave bride, shall be called Zeus *g* by the crafty Spartiates, obtaining highest honours from the children of Oebalus.*h* Nor

e Agamemnon.
f Orestes, son of Agamemnon, slays his mother Clytaemnestra.
g Zeus-Agamemnon, worshipped in Sparta.
h Father of Tyndareus.

LYCOPHRON

οὐ μὴν ἐμὸν νώνυμνον ἀνθρώποις σέβας
ἔσται, μαρανθὲν αὖθι ληθαίῳ σκότῳ.
ναὸν δέ μοι τεύξουσι Δαυνίων ἄκροι
Σάλπης παρ᾽ ὄχθαις, οἵ τε Δάρδανον πόλιν
ναίουσι, λίμνης ἀγχιτέρμονες ποτῶν.   1130
κοῦραι δὲ παρθένειον ἐκφυγεῖν ζυγὸν
ὅταν θέλωσι, νυμφίους ἀρνούμεναι
τοὺς Ἑκτορείοις ἠγλαϊσμένους κόμαις,
μορφῆς ἔχοντας σίφλον ἢ μῶμαρ γένους,
ἐμὸν περιπτύξουσιν ὠλέναις βρέτας,   1135
ἄλκαρ μέγιστον κτώμεναι νυμφευμάτων,
Ἐρινύων ἐσθῆτα καὶ ῥέθους βαφὰς
πεπαμέναι θρόνοισι φαρμακτηρίοις.
κείναις ἐγὼ δηναιὸν ἄφθιτος θεὰ
ῥαβδηφόροις γυναιξὶν αὐδηθήσομαι.   1140

Πένθος δὲ πολλαῖς παρθένων τητωμέναις
τεύξω γυναιξὶν αὖθις, αἳ στρατηλάτην
ἀθεσμόλεκτρον, Κύπριδος λῃστὴν θεᾶς,
δαρὸν στένουσαι, κλῆρον εἰς ἀνάρσιον
πέμψουσι παῖδας ἐστερημένας γάμων.   1145
Λάρυμνα, καὶ Σπερχειέ, καὶ Βοάγριε,
καὶ Κῦνε, καὶ Σκάρφεια, καὶ Φαλωριάς,
καὶ Ναρύκειον ἄστυ, καὶ Θρονίτιδες
Λοκρῶν ἀγυιαί, καὶ Πυρωναῖαι νάπαι,
καὶ πᾶς Ὀδοιδόκειος Ἰλέως δόμος,   1150

---

[a] " A lake in Italy " (schol.); possibly the reference is to
Salapia.   [b] Unknown.

[c] The schol. says this means that the hair is worn long
behind and shorn in front. *Cf.* Hesych. *s.v.* Ἑκτόρειοι·
κομῆται. Δαύνιοι καὶ Πευκέτιοι ἔχοντες τὴν ἀπ᾽ Ἰλίου τοῖς ὤμοις
περικεχυμένην τρίχα (Plut. *Thes.* 5).

[d] Aristot. *Mirab.* 109 refers to the black clothes worn by all
Daunians, male or female. The schol. quotes Timaeus for
the statement that the Daunian women wore a dark dress,

414

shall my worship be nameless among men, nor fade hereafter in the darkness of oblivion. But the chiefs of the Daunians shall build for me a shrine on the banks of Salpe,[a] and those also who inhabit the city of Dardanus,[b] beside the waters of the lake. And when girls wish to escape the yoke of maidens, refusing for bridegrooms men adorned with locks such as Hector wore,[c] but with defect of form or reproach of birth, they will embrace my image with their arms, winning a mighty shield against marriage, having clothed them in the garb of the Erinyes[d] and dyed their faces with magic simples. By those staff-carrying women I shall long be called an immortal goddess.

And to many women robbed of their maiden daughters I shall bring sorrow hereafter. Long shall they bewail the leader[e] who sinned against the laws of marriage, the pirate of the Cyprian goddess,[f] when they shall send to the unkindly shrine[g] their daughters reft of marriage. O Larymna[h] and Spercheius and Boagrius and Cynus and Scarpheia and Phalorias and city of Naryx and Locrian streets of Thronium and Pyronaean glades and all the house of Ileus son of Hodoedocus—ye

were girt with broad ribands, wore τὰ κοῖλα τῶν ὑποδημάτων, i.e. reaching to the calves of the leg (ἐς μέσην τὴν κνήμην ἀνήκοντα, Poll. v. 18, cf. vii. 84, Ael. N.A. vi. 23), carried a wand in their hands, and painted their faces with a reddish colour—suggesting the Furies of tragedy.

[e] Aias the Locrian, son of Oileus (Ileus), who assaulted Cassandra in the temple of Athena.

[f] Aphrodite.

[g] Shrine of Athena in Troy. The reference is to the Locrian maiden-tribute. See Callim. Aet. i. 8 n. and cf. Strabo 601 and Plut. De ser. vindict. 557.

[h] This and the other places named are in Locris.

LYCOPHRON

ὑμεῖς ἐμῶν ἕκατι δυσσεβῶν γάμων
ποινὰς Γυγαίᾳ τίσετ' Ἀγρίσκᾳ θεᾷ,
τὸν χιλίωρον τὰς ἀνυμφεύτους χρόνον
πάλου βραβείαις γηροβοσκοῦσαι κόρας.
αἷς ἀκτέριστος ἐν ξένῃ ξέναις τάφος   1155
ψάμμῳ κλύδωνος λυπρὸς ἐκκλυσθήσεται,
φυτοῖς ἀκάρποις γυῖα συμφλέξας ὅταν
Ἥφαιστος εἰς θάλασσαν ἐκβράσῃ σποδὸν
τῆς ἐκ λόφων Τράρωνος ἐφθιτωμένης.
ἄλλαι δὲ νύκτωρ ταῖς θανουμέναις ἴσαι   1160
Σιθῶνος εἰς θυγατρὸς ἵξονται γύας,
λαθραῖα κἀκκέλευθα παπταλώμεναι,
ἕως ἂν εἰσθρέξωσιν Ἀμφείρας δόμους
λιταῖς Σθένειαν ἴκτιδες γουνούμεναι.
θεᾶς δ' ὀφελτρεύσουσι κοσμοῦσαι πέδον,   1165
δρόσῳ τε φοιβάσουσιν, ἀστεργῆ χόλον
ἀστῶν φυγοῦσαι. πᾶς γὰρ Ἰλιεὺς ἀνὴρ
κόρας δοκεύσει, πέτρον ἐν χεροῖν ἔχων,
ἢ φάσγανον κελαινόν, ἢ ταυροκτόνον
στερρὰν κύβηλιν, ἢ Φαλακραῖον κλάδον,   1170
μαιμῶν κορέσσαι χεῖρα διψῶσαν φόνου.
δῆμος δ' ἀνατεὶ τὸν κτανόντ' ἐπαινέσει,
τεθμῷ χαράξας, τοὐπιλώβητον γένος.

Ὦ μῆτερ, ὦ δύσμητερ, οὐδὲ σὸν κλέος
ἄπυστον ἔσται, Περσέως δὲ παρθένος   1175
Βριμὼ Τρίμορφος θήσεταί σ' ἐπωπίδα

---

a Athena Gygaea either, in spite of the quantity, from the Γυγαίη λίμνη in Lydia (Strabo 626) or *cf.* Γυγᾶ· Ἀθηνᾶ ἐγχώριος (Boeotian?) Hesych. Agrisca as goddess of agriculture.

b Holzinger takes this to mean that the first Locrian maiden escaped her pursuers by jumping into the sea from Cape Traron in the Troad. It seems better to suppose it

for the sake of my impious wedlock shall pay
penance to the goddess Gygaea Agrisca,[a] for the
space of a thousand years fostering to old age your
unwed daughters by the arbitrament of the lot.
And they, aliens in an alien land, shall have without
funeral rites a tomb, a sorry tomb in wave-washed
sands, when Hephaestus burns with unfruitful plants
the limbs of her [b] that perishes from Traron's peaks,
and tosses her ashes into the sea. And, to fill the
place of those that shall die, others shall come by
night to the fields [c] of Sithon's daughter by secret
paths and glancing fearfully, until they rush into
the shrine of Ampheira [d] as suppliants beseeching
with their prayers Stheneia.[d]   And they shall sweep
and array the floor of the goddess and cleanse it
with dew, having escaped the loveless anger of the
citizens. For every man of Ilios shall keep watch
for the maidens, with a stone in his hands, or a
dark sword or hard bull-slaying axe, or shaft from
Phalacra,[e] eager to sate his hand athirst for blood.
And the people shall not harm him who slays that
race of reproach, but shall praise him and grave his
name by ordinance.

O mother,[f] O unhappy mother! thy fame, too,
shall not be unknown, but the maiden daughter [g]
of Perseus, Triform Brimo, shall make thee her

means that the ashes of every maiden who died were cast
into the sea from Cape Traron.

   [c] Rhoeteum, *cf.* 583.

   [d] Athena Ampheira as a name of Athena is unknown ;
'Αθήνη Σθενιάς was worshipped in Troezen (Paus. ii. 30. 6 ff.).

   [e] *Cf.* 24.

   [f] Hecuba, who was turned into a dog and stoned to
death.

   [g] Hecate, daughter of Asteria and Perses (Perseus) son
of Crius and Eurybia.

LYCOPHRON

κλαγγαῖσι ταρμύσσουσαν ἐννύχοις βροτούς,
ὅσοι μεδούσης Στρυμόνος Ζηρυνθίας
δείκηλα μὴ σέβουσι λαμπαδουχίαις,
θύσθλοις Φεραίαν ἐξακεύμενοι θεάν.   1180
ψευδήριον δὲ νησιωτικὸς στόνυξ
Πάχυνος ἕξει σεμνὸν ἐξ ὀνειράτων
ταῖς δεσποτείαις ὠλέναις ὠγκωμένον
ῥείθρων Ἑλώρου πρόσθεν ἐκτερισμένης·
ὃς δὴ παρ' ἀκταῖς τλήμονος ῥανεῖ χοάς,   1185
τριαύχενος μήνιμα δειμαίνων θεᾶς,
λευστῆρα πρῶτον οὕνεκεν ῥίψας πέτρον
Ἅιδῃ κελαινῶν θυμάτων ἀπάρξεται.
    Σὺ δ', ὦ ξύναιμε, πλεῖστον ἐξ ἐμῆς φρενὸς
στερχθείς, μελάθρων ἔρμα καὶ πάτρας ὅλης,   1190
οὐκ εἰς κενὸν κρηπῖδα φοινίξεις φόνῳ
ταύρων, ἄνακτι τῶν Ὀφίωνος θρόνων
πλείστας ἀπαρχὰς θυμάτων δωρούμενος.
ἀλλ' ἄξεταί σε πρὸς γενεθλίαν πλάκα
τὴν ἐξόχως Γραικοῖσιν ἐξυμνημένην,   1195
ὅπου σφε μήτηρ ἡ πάλης ἐμπείραμος
τὴν πρόσθ' ἄνασσαν ἐμβαλοῦσα Ταρτάρῳ
ὠδῖνας ἐξέλυσε λαθραίας γονῆς,
τὰς παιδοβρώτους ἐκφυγοῦσ' ὁμευνέτου
θοίνας ἀσέπτους, οὐδ' ἐπίανεν βορᾷ   1200
νηδύν, τὸν ἀντίποινον ἐγμάψας πέτρον,
ἐν γυιοκόλλοις σπαργάνοις εἰλημένον,
τύμβος γεγὼς Κένταυρος ὠμόφρων σπορᾶς.
νήσοις δὲ μακάρων ἐγκατοικήσεις μέγας

---

[a] Hecate.

[b] In Thessaly. Hecate with torch appears on coins of Pherae (Head, *H.N.* 307 f.).

[c] Cenotaph of Hecuba built in Sicily by Odysseus.

[d] Hecate.   [e] Hector.   [f] Zeus.

418

attendant, terrifying with thy baying in the night all mortals who worship not with torches the images of the Zerynthian queen of Strymon,[a] appeasing the goddess of Pherae[b] with sacrifice. And the island spur of Pachynus shall hold thine awful cenotaph,[c] piled by the hands of thy master, prompted by dreams when thou hast gotten the rites of death in front of the streams of Helorus. He shall pour on the shore offerings for thee, unhappy one, fearing the anger of the three-necked goddess,[d] for that he shall hurl the first stone at thy stoning and begin the dark sacrifice to Hades.

And thou, O brother,[e] most beloved of my heart, stay of our halls and of our whole fatherland, not in vain shalt thou redden the altar pedestal with blood of bulls, giving full many a sacrificial offering to him[f] who is lord of Ophion's[g] throne. But he shall bring thee to the plain of his nativity,[h] that land celebrated above others by the Greeks, where his mother,[i] skilled in wrestling, having cast into Tartarus the former queen, delivered her of him in travail of secret birth, escaping the child-devouring unholy feast of her spouse[j]; and he fattened not his belly with food, but swallowed instead the stone, wrapped in limb-fitting swaddling-clothes: savage Centaur, tomb of his own offspring. And in the Islands of the Blest[k] thou shalt dwell,

[g] A Titan, who preceded Zeus as king of the gods.

[h] Thebes, where was a place called Διὸς Γοναί (schol. *Il.* xiii. 1). The Thebans were told by an oracle to bring Hector's bones to Thebes (Paus. ix. 18).

[i] Rhea overcame Eurynome, wife of Ophion.

[j] Cronus, called Centaur as father of Cheiron.

[k] In Thebes was a place called Μακάρων νῆσοι. Hesych. *s.v.* M. νῆσος says it is the acropolis of Thebes.

ἥρως, ἀρωγὸς λοιμικῶν τοξευμάτων,   1205
ὅπου σε πεισθεὶς Ὠγύγου σπαρτὸς λεὼς
χρησμοῖς Ἰατροῦ Λεψίου Τερμινθέως
ἐξ Ὀφρυνείων ἠρίων ἀνειρύσας
ἄξει Καλύδνου τύρσιν Ἀόνων τε γῆν
σωτῆρ᾽, ὅταν κάμνωσιν ὁπλίτῃ στρατῷ   1210
πέρθοντι χώραν Τηνέρου τ᾽ ἀνάκτορα.
κλέος δὲ σὸν μέγιστον Ἐκτήνων πρόμοι
λοιβαῖσι κυδανοῦσιν ἀφθίτοις ἴσον.

   Ἥξει δὲ Κνωσσὸν κἀπὶ Γόρτυνος δόμους
τοὐμὸν ταλαίνης πῆμα, πᾶς δ᾽ ἀνάστατος   1215
ἔσται στρατηγῶν οἶκος. οὐ γὰρ ἥσυχος
πορκεὺς δίκωπον σέλμα ναυστολῶν ἐλᾷ,
Λεῦκον στροβήσων φύλακα τῆς μοναρχίας,
ψυδραῖσί τε ἔχθραν μηχαναῖς ἀναπλέκων.
ὃς οὔτε τέκνων φείσετ᾽ οὔτε συγγάμου   1220
Μήδας δάμαρτος, ἠγριωμένος φρένας,
οὐ Κλεισιθήρας θυγατρός, ἧς πατὴρ λέχος
θρεπτῷ δράκοντι συγκαταινέσει πικρόν.
πάντας δ᾽ ἀνάγνοις χερσὶν ἐν ναῷ κτενεῖ,
λώβαισιν αἰκισθέντας Ὀγκαίου βόθρου.   1225

   Γένους δὲ πάππων τῶν ἐμῶν αὖθις κλέος
μέγιστον αὐξήσουσιν ἄμναμοί ποτε,
αἰχμαῖς τὸ πρωτόλειον ἄραντες στέφος,
γῆς καὶ θαλάσσης σκῆπτρα καὶ μοναρχίαν
λαβόντες. οὐδ᾽ ἄμνηστον, ἀθλία πατρίς,   1230

---

   [a] The Thebans sprang from the dragon's teeth sown by
Cadmus.   [b] Early king of Thebes.
   [c] Apollo.   [d] In the Troad.
   [e] Early king of Thebes.   [f] Boeotians.
   [g] Son and priest of Ptoian Apollo in Boeotia.
   [h] Boeotians.   [i] In Crete.
   [j] Nauplius (cf. 1093) goes to Crete, where he incites

ALEXANDRA

a mighty hero, defender of the arrows of pestilence, where the sown [a] folk of Ogygus,[b] persuaded by the oracles of the Physician [c] Lepsius Termintheus, shall lift thee from thy cairn in Ophryneion [d] and bring thee to the tower of Calydnus [e] and the land of the Aonians [f] to be their saviour, when they are harassed by an armed host which seeks to sack their land and the shrine of Tenerus.[g] And the chiefs of the Ectenes [h] shall with libations celebrate thy glory in the highest, even as the immortals.

And unto Cnossus [i] and the halls of Gortyn [i] shall come the woe of me unhappy, and all the house of the rulers shall be overthrown. For not quietly shall the fisherman [j] voyage, rowing his two-oared boat, to stir up Leucus, guardian of the kingdom, and weaving hate with lying wiles. He shall spare neither the children nor Meda the wedded wife, in the rage of his mind, nor the daughter Cleisithera, whom her father shall betroth unhappily to the serpent [k] whom he himself has reared. All will he slay with impious hands in the temple, maltreated and abused in the Trench of Oncaea.[l]

And the fame of the race of my ancestors shall hereafter be exalted to the highest by their descendants,[m] who shall with their spears win the foremost crown of glory, obtaining the sceptre and monarchy of earth and sea.[n] Nor in the darkness

Leucus, to whom Idomeneus during his absence in Troy had entrusted his kingdom, to seize the throne and to murder Meda, wife of Idomeneus, and her children, Iphiclus and Lycus, as well as his own bride, Cleisithera, daughter of Idomeneus.

[k] Leucus, exposed in infancy, had been adopted by Idomeneus.

[l] Demeter Erinys.   [m] The Romans.

[n] See Introduction, pp. 482 f.

LYCOPHRON

κῦδος μαρανθὲν ἐγκατακρύψεις ζόφῳ.
τοιούσδ' ἐμός τις σύγγονος λείψει διπλοῦς
σκύμνους λέοντας, ἔξοχον ῥώμῃ γένος,
ὁ Καστνίας τε τῆς τε Χειράδος γόνος,
βουλαῖς ἄριστος, οὐδ' ὀνοστὸς ἐν μάχαις.   1235
ὃς πρῶτα μὲν Ῥαίκηλον οἰκήσει μολών,
Κισσοῦ παρ' αἰπὺν πρῶνα καὶ Λαφυστίας
κερασφόρους γυναῖκας. ἐκ δ' Ἀλμωπίας
πάλιμπλανήτην δέξεται Τυρσηνία
Λιγγεύς τε θερμῶν ῥεῖθρον ἐκβράσσων ποτῶν,   1240
καὶ Πῖσ' Ἀγύλλης θ' αἱ πολύρρηνοι νάπαι.
σὺν δέ σφι μίξει φίλιον ἐχθρὸς ὢν στρατόν,
ὅρκοις κρατήσας καὶ λιταῖς γουνασμάτων
νάνος, πλάναισι πάντ' ἐρευνήσας μυχὸν
ἁλός τε καὶ γῆς. σὺν δὲ δίπτυχοι τόκοι   1245
Μυσῶν ἄνακτος, οὗ ποτ' Οἰκουρὸς δόρυ
γνάμψει Θέοινος, γυῖα συνδήσας λύγοις,
Τάρχων τε καὶ Τυρσηνός, αἴθωνες λύκοι,
τῶν Ἡρακλείων ἐκγεγῶτες αἱμάτων.
ἔνθα τράπεζαν εἰδάτων πλήρη κιχών,   1250
τὴν ὕστερον βρωθεῖσαν ἐξ ὀπαόνων,
μνήμην παλαιῶν λήψεται θεσπισμάτων.

---

^a Romulus and Remus.   ^b Aeneas.
^c Roma : ῥώμη.   ^d Aphrodite, mother of Aeneas.
^e On the Thermaic Gulf.
^f Worshippers of Dionysus (Laphystius) in Macedonia.
^g In Macedonia (Thuc. ii. 9).   ^h Etruria.
ⁱ Unknown : Arnus?   ^j In Etruria.
^k Odysseus, who is said to have met Aeneas in Italy.
Hellanicus *ap.* Dion. Hal. *A.R.* 72.
^l Odysseus is here identified with the Nanus or Nanas of
Etruscan legend.   ^m Telephus, *cf.* 207 ff.
ⁿ Heracles, father of Telephus.
^o Verg. *A.* iii. 251 ff.   Aeneas in the Strophades south of

422

ALEXANDRA

of oblivion, my unhappy fatherland, shalt thou hide
thy glory faded.   Such a pair of lion whelps *a* shall
a certain kinsman *b* of mine leave, a breed eminent
in strength *c* : the son of Castnia *d* called also Cheiras,
—in counsel best and not to be despised in battle.
He shall first come to occupy Rhaecelus *e* beside the
steep crag of Cissus *e* and the horned women *f* of
Laphystius.   And from Almopia *g* in his wandering
Tyrsenia *h* shall receive him and Lingeus *i* bubbling
forth its stream of hot waters, and Pisa *j* and the
glades of Agylla,*j* rich in sheep.   And with him
shall an erstwhile foe *k* join a friendly army, winning
him by oaths and prayers and clasped knees : even
the Dwarf *l* who in his roaming searched out every
recess of sea and earth ; and therewithal the two
sons of the King *m* of the Mysians, whose spear one
day shall be bent by the Housekeeping God of
Wine, who shall fetter his limbs with twisted
tendrils : even Tarchon and Tyrsenus, tawny wolves,
sprung from the blood of Heracles.*n*   There he shall
find full of eatables a table *o* which is afterwards
devoured by his attendants and shall be reminded
of an ancient prophecy.   And he shall found in

Zacynthus receives from 'the harpy Celaeno an oracle of
Apollo declaring that Aeneas should not found a city in
Italy till hunger should compel the Trojan exiles to "eat
their tables."   The prophecy is fulfilled Verg. *A.* vii. 109 ff.
Aeneas and his company reach the Tiber.   They take their
meal on the banks of the river, using wheaten cakes on
which to lay their other eatables.   When these are consumed,
hunger causes them to eat the wheaten cakes as well.
Thereupon Iulus exclaims : " Heus ! etiam mensas con-
sumimus ! "   Vergil in the latter passage attributes the
prophecy to Anchises.   Varro, in Serv. on *Aen.* iii. 256, says
Aeneas got it at Dodona, Dion. Hal. *A.R.* i. 55 says from
the Erythraean Sibyl in the Troad

κτίσει δὲ χώραν ἐν τόποις Βορειγόνων
ὑπὲρ Λατίνους Δαυνίους τ' ᾠκισμένην,
πύργους τριάκοντ', ἐξαριθμήσας γονὰς   1255
συὸς κελαινῆς, ἣν ἀπ' Ἰδαίων λόφων
καὶ Δαρδανείων ἐκ τόπων ναυσθλώσεται,
ἰσηρίθμων θρέπτειραν ἐν τόκοις κάπρων·
ἧς καὶ πόλει δείκηλον ἀνθήσει μιᾷ
χαλκῷ τυπώσας καὶ τέκνων γλαγοτρόφων.   1260
δείμας δὲ σηκὸν Μυνδίᾳ Παλληνίδι,
πατρῴῳ ἀγάλματ' ἐγκατοικεῖ θεῶν.
ἃ δή, παρώσας καὶ δάμαρτα καὶ τέκνα
καὶ κτῆσιν ἄλλην ὀμπνίαν κειμηλίων,
σὺν τῷ γεραιῷ πατρὶ πρεσβειώσεται,   1265
πέπλοις περισχών, ἦμος αἰχμηταὶ κύνες,
τὰ πάντα πάτρας συλλαφύξαντες πάλῳ,
τούτῳ μόνῳ πόρωσιν αἵρεσιν, δόμων
λαβεῖν ὃ χρῄζει κἀπενέγκασθαι δάνος.
τῷ καὶ παρ' ἐχθροῖς εὐσεβέστατος κριθείς,   1270
τὴν πλεῖστον ὑμνηθεῖσαν ἐν χάρμαις πάτραν
ἐν ὀψιτέκνοις ὀλβίαν δωμήσεται,
τύρσιν μακεδνὰς ἀμφὶ Κιρκαίου νάπας
Ἀργοῦς τε κλεινὸν ὅρμον Αἰήτην μέγαν,
λίμνης τε Φόρκης Μαρσιωνίδος ποτὰ   1275

---

[a] The Aborigines (Strabo 228 ff.).
[b] Aeneas received from Helenus in Epirus a prophecy
that he would be guided in founding a city by a sow.
When he was sacrificing on the banks of the Tiber, a sow,
one of the intended victims, escaped and fled inland, finally
resting on a hill where it gave birth to thirty young. The
number thirty is variously interpreted in legend; here with
reference to the thirty Latin towns of which Lavinium was
the metropolis. According to the usual version the sow was
white, *e.g.* Verg. *A.* iii. 392 "Alba, solo recubans" Hence

places of the Boreigonoi [a] a settled land beyond the
Latins and Daunians—even thirty towers, when he
has numbered the offspring of the dark sow,[b] which
he shall carry in his ship from the hills of Ida and
places of Dardanus, which shall rear such number
of young at a birth. And in one city [c] he shall set
up an image of that sow and her suckling young,
figuring them in bronze. And he shall build a
shrine to Myndia Pallenis [d] and establish therein
the images of his fathers' gods.[e] He shall put
aside his wife and children and all his rich possessions and honour these first, together with his aged
sire,[f] wrapping them in his robes, what time the
spearmen hounds, having devoured all the goods
of his country together by casting of lots, to him
alone shall give the choice to take and carry away
what gift from his house he will. Wherefore being
adjudged even by his foes to be most pious, he
shall found a fatherland of highest renown in battle,
a tower blest in the children of after days, by the
tall glades of Circaeon [g] and the great Aeëtes haven,[h]
famous anchorage of the Argo, and the waters of

some suppose Lycophron in his riddling manner to mean
here horrid, terrible, "black" metaphorically.

  [c] Lavinium, founded where the sow came to rest.

  [d] Athena : Myndia, cult-name of Athena from Myndus in
Caria. A temple of Athena Pallenis lay between Athens
and Marathon.

  [e] Penates.

  [f] Anchises. Xenoph. *Cyn.* 1. 15 says : "Aeneias, by
saving his paternal and maternal gods and saving his father,
won such renown for piety that to him alone of all whom
they conquered in Troy the enemy granted that he should
not be robbed of his possessions." *Cf.* Aelian, *V.H.* iii. 22,
Serv. on *Aen.* ii. 636.

  [g] Circeji.   [h] Cajeta.

LYCOPHRON

Τιτώνιόν τε χεῦμα τοῦ κατὰ χθονὸς
δύνοντος εἰς ἄφαντα κευθμῶνος βάθη,
Ζωστηρίου τε κλιτύν, ἔνθα παρθένου
στυγνὸν Σιβύλλης ἐστὶν οἰκητήριον,
γρώνῳ βερέθρῳ συγκατηρεφὲς στέγης.   1280

Τοσαῦτα μὲν δύστλητα πείσονται κακὰ
οἱ τὴν ἐμὴν μέλλοντες αἰστώσειν πάτραν.

Τί γὰρ ταλαίνῃ μητρὶ τῇ Προμηθέως
ξυνὸν πέφυκε καὶ τροφῷ Σαρπηδόνος,
ἃς πόντος Ἕλλης καὶ πέτραι Συμπληγάδες   1285
καὶ Σαλμυδησὸς καὶ κακόξεινος κλύδων,
Σκύθαισι γείτων, καρτεροῖς εἴργει πάγοις,
λίμνην τε τέμνων Τάναϊς ἀκραιφνὴς μέσην
ῥείθροις ὁρίζει, προσφιλεστάτην βροτοῖς
χίμετλα Μαιώταισι θρηνοῦσιν ποδῶν.   1290

Ὄλοιντο ναῦται πρῶτα Καρνῖται κύνες,
οἳ τὴν βοῶπιν ταυροπάρθενον κόρην
Λέρνης ἀνηρείψαντο, φορτηγοὶ λύκοι,
πλᾶτιν πορεῦσαι κῆρα Μεμφίτῃ πρόμῳ,
ἔχθρας δὲ πυρσὸν ἦραν ἠπείροις διπλαῖς.   1295
αὖθις γὰρ ὕβριν τὴν βαρεῖαν ἁρπαγῆς
Κουρῆτες ἀντίποινον Ἰδαῖοι κάπροι

---

[a] Lacus Fucinus.
[b] The schol. says "Titon, a river of Italy near the river Circaeus, which does not flow into the sea but is swallowed up by the earth."
[c] Apollo.   [d] Cumae.
[e] Asia, mother of Prometheus by Iapetus (Apollod. i. 8).
[f] Europa, mother of the Cretan Sarpedon by Zeus.
[g] Hellespont.
[h] The Euxine, i.e. Hospitable, previously called Axine, i.e. Inhospitable.
[i] The river Don.
[j] The idea is that the water of the Don does not mingle with the water of the sea. So Arrian, Periplus

the Marsionid lake of Phorce [a] and the Titonian [b]
stream of the cleft that sinks to unseen depths
beneath the earth, and the hill of Zosterius,[c] where
is the grim dwelling [d] of the maiden Sibylla, roofed
by the cavernous pit that shelters her.

So many are the woes, hard to bear, which they
shall suffer who are to lay waste my fatherland.

For what has the unhappy mother [e] of Prometheus
in common with the nurse [f] of Sarpedon? Whom
the sea [g] of Helle and the Clashing Rocks and Salmy-
dessus and the inhospitable [h] wave, neighbour to the
Scythians, sunder with strong cliffs and Tanais [i]
divides with his streams—Tanais who, undefiled,[j]
cleaves the middle of the lake [k] which is most dear
to Maeotian men who mourn their chilblained feet.

My curse, first, upon the Carnite [l] sailor hounds!
the merchant wolves who carried off from Lerne
the ox-eyed girl, the bull-maiden, to bring to the
lord of Memphis a fatal bride, and raised the beacon
of hatred for the two continents. For afterwards
the Curetes,[m] Idaean boars, seeking to avenge the

Eux. Pont. 8 says of the Phasis that ἐπιπλεῖ τῇ θαλάσσῃ,
οὐχὶ δὲ συμμίγνυται.

    [k] Lake Maeotis or Sea of Azov.

    [l] The quarrel between Asia and Europe (Herod. i. 1 ff.)
began with the carrying off of Io, daughter of Inachus king
of Argos (Lerne), by the Phoenicians (Carna or Carnos is the
port of Arados, Strabo 753). Io was turned into a cow by
Zeus, hence "bull-maiden." She became wife of Telegonus,
king of Egypt (Apollod. ii. 9), who is here "lord of Memphis"; or, if Io is here equated with Isis, the lord of
Memphis will be Osiris.

    [m] The Cretans (Curetes) carried off Europa, daughter of
Phoenix, from Phoenicia (Sarapta or Sarepta, town on coast
of Phoenicia) to become wife of Asterus, king of Crete. The
"bull-formed vessel" rationalizes the myth that Zeus in
form of a bull carried Europa to Crete to become his bride.

LYCOPHRON

ζητοῦντες, αἰχμάλωτον ἤμπρευσαν πόριν
ἐν ταυρομόρφῳ τράμπιδος τυπώματι
Σαραπτίαν Δικταῖον εἰς ἀνάκτορον
δάμαρτα Κρήτης Ἀστέρῳ στρατηλάτῃ.
οὐδ' οἵ γ' ἀπηρκέσθησαν ἀντ' ἴσων ἴσα
λαβόντες, ἀλλὰ κλῶπα σὺν Τεύκρῳ στρατὸν
καὶ σὺν Σκαμάνδρῳ Δρανκίῳ φυτοσπόρῳ
εἰς Βεβρύκων ἔστειλαν οἰκητήριον,
σμίνθοισι δηρίσοντας, ὧν ἀπὸ σπορᾶς
ἐμοὺς γενάρχας ἐξέφυσε Δάρδανος,
γήμας Ἀρίσβαν Κρῆσσαν εὐγενῆ κόρην.

Καὶ δευτέρους ἔπεμψαν Ἄτρακας λύκους
ταγῷ μονοκρήπιδι κλέψοντας νάκην,
δρακοντοφρούροις ἐσκεπασμένην σκοπαῖς.
ὃς εἰς Κύταιαν τὴν Λιβυστικὴν μολών,
καὶ τὸν τετράπνην ὕδρον εὐνάσας θρόνοις,
καὶ γυρὰ ταύρων βαστάσας πυριπνόων
ἄροτρα, καὶ λέβητι δαιτρευθεὶς δέμας,
οὐκ ἀσμένως ἔμαρψεν ἐρράου σκύλος,
ἀλλ' αὐτόκλητον ἁρπάσας κεραΐδα,
τὴν γνωτοφόντιν καὶ τέκνων ἀλάστορα,
εἰς τὴν λάληθρον κίσσαν ἡρματίξατο,
φθογγὴν ἐδώλων Χαονιτικῶν ἄπο
βροτησίαν ἱεῖσαν, ἔμπαιον δρόμων.

1300

1305

1310

1315

132

---

^a The Cretans sent an army to the Troad under Teucer and Scamandrus, who received an oracle bidding them settle "wherever the earth-born (γηγενεῖς) should attack them." This happened at Hamaxitos, where the "earth-born" proved to be a plague of field-mice which devoured the leathern parts of their armour. So they abode there (Strabo 604). Arisba, daughter of Teucer, became wife of Dardanus, and thus ancestress of Cassandra.
^b Trojans.   ^c The voyage of the Argonauts.
^d Thessalian, from Atrax in Thessaly Hestiaeotis.

428

rape by their heavy deed of violence, carried off
captive in a bull-formed vessel the Saraptian heifer
to the Dictaean palace to be the bride of Asteros,
the lord of Crete. Nor were they contented when
they had taken like for like; but sent with Teucer [a]
and his Draucian father Scamandrus a raping army
to the dwelling-place of the Bebryces [b] to war with
mice; of the seed of those men Dardanus begat
the authors of my race, when he married the noble
Cretan maid Arisba.

And second [c] they sent the Atracian [d] wolves to
steal for their leader of the single sandal [e] the fleece [f]
that was protected by the watching dragon's ward.
He came to Libyan Cytaea [g] and put to sleep with
simples that four-nostrilled snake, and handled the
curved plough of the fire-breathing bulls,[h] and had
his own body cut to pieces in a caldron [i] and, not
joyfully, seized the hide of the ram. But the self-
invited crow [j] he carried off—her who slew her
brother [k] and destroyed her children [l]—and set her
as ballast in the chattering jay [m] which uttered a
mortal voice derived from Chaonian abode and well
knew how to speed.

[e] Jason (Pind. *P.* iv.).

[f] The Golden Fleece.

[g] In Colchis.

[h] Pind. *P.* iv. 224 ff. ; Apoll. Rh. iii. 1284 ff.

[i] Medea renewed the youth of Jason by boiling him in a
magic caldron.

[j] Medeia.

[k] Apsyrtus.

[l] When Jason married the daughter of Creon, king of
Corinth, Medea in revenge slew her own children by Jason.

[m] The ship Argo, in which, while it was being built,
Athena inserted a piece of the oak of Dodona (hence
Chaonian), which gave it the gift of human speech and of
prophecy.

LYCOPHRON

Πάλιν δ' ὁ πέτρας ἀσκέρας ἀνειρύσας
καὶ φασγάνου ζωστῆρα καὶ ξίφος πατρός,
ὁ Φημίου παῖς, Σκῦρος ᾧ λυγροὺς τάφους
κρημνῶν ἔνερθεν αἰγίλιψ ῥοιζουμένων   1325
πάλαι δοκεύει τὰς ἀταρχύτους ῥιφάς,
σὺν θηρὶ βλώξας τῷ σπάσαντι δηίας
Μύστῃ Τροπαίας μαστὸν εὔθηλον θεᾶς,
ζωστηροκλέπτης, νεῖκος ὤρινεν διπλοῦν,
στόρνην τ' ἀμέρσας καὶ Θεμισκύρας ἄπο   1330
τὴν τοξόδαμνον νοσφίσας Ὀρθωσίαν.
ἧς αἱ ξύναιμοι, παρθένοι Νεπτουνίδος,
Ἔριν λιποῦσαι, Λάγμον, ἠδὲ Τήλαμον,
καὶ χεῦμα Θερμώδοντος Ἀκταῖόν τ' ὄρος,
ποινὰς ἀθέλκτους θ' ἁρπαγὰς διζήμεναι,   1335
ὑπὲρ κελαινὸν Ἴστρον ἤλασαν Σκύθας
ἵππους, ὁμοκλήτειραν ἱεῖσαι βοὴν
Γραικοῖσιν ἀμνάμοις τε τοῖς Ἐρεχθέως.
καὶ πᾶσαν Ἀκτὴν ἐξεπόρθησαν δορί,
τοὺς Μοψοπείους αἰθαλώσασαι γύας.   1340
    Πάππος δὲ Θρῄκης οὑμὸς αἰστώσας πλάκα
χώραν τ' Ἐορδῶν καὶ Γαλαδραίων πέδον,
ὄρους ἔπηξεν ἀμφὶ Πηνειοῦ ποτοῖς,
στερρὰν τραχήλῳ ζεύγλαν ἀμφιθεὶς πέδαις,

---

^a Theseus. For the legend see Introduction to Calli-
machus, *Hecale.*

^b Aegeus.

^c Poseidon, who was said to be the real father of Theseus
(Bacchyl. 16).

^d Theseus either threw himself from a cliff in Scyrus or
was pushed over by Lycomedes, king of the island. His
bones were brought to Athens in 473 B.C. by Cimon (Plut.
Thes. 35-36).

^e Heracles, who was initiated in the Eleusinian mysteries
before he went to bring Cerberus from Hades.

430

ALEXANDRA

And again he[a] that took up from the rock his
father's[b] shoes and sword-belt and sword, the son
of Phemius,[c] on whose sad grave[d]—whereto he was
hurled without funeral rites — steep Scyrus long
keeps watch beneath its hissing precipices—he went
with the wild beast, the Initiate,[e] who drew the
milky breast of the hostile goddess Tropaea,[f] and
stole the belt[g] and roused a double feud, taking
away the girdle and from Themiscyra carrying off
the archer Orthosia[h]; and her sisters, the maidens
of Neptunis,[i] left Eris, Lagmus and Telamus and
the stream of Thermodon and the hill of Actaeum
to seek vengeance and relentless rape. Across the
dark Ister[j] they drove their Scythian mares, shouting
their battle-cry against the Greeks and the descendants of Erechtheus. And they sacked all Acte[k]
with the spear and laid waste with fire the fields
of Mopsopia.[k]

And my ancestor[l] laid waste the plain of Thrace
and the country of the Eordi and the land of the
Galadraei, and fixed his bounds beside the waters
of Peneius, fettering them with a stern yoke laid
upon their necks, in battle a young warrior, most

[f] Hera, who by a trick was induced to give the breast to
Heracles (Diod. iv. 9, Paus. ix. 25).
[g] Hippolyte's girdle.
[h] The Amazon Antiope, here called Orthosia, a cult-title
of Artemis (Pind. O. iii. 30).
[i] The scholiast says this was a name of Hippolyte. Holzinger takes it as a cult-name of Artemis from Nepete in
Etruria. The Amazons, in revenge for the expedition
against them of Heracles and Theseus, invade Attica.
[j] Danube.
[k] Attica.
[l] Ilus, great-grandfather of Cassandra, invaded Thrace
and Macedonia; cf. Herod. vii. 20 and 75.

431

ἀλκῇ νέανδρος, ἐκπρεπέστατος γένους.   1345
ἡ δ' ἀντὶ τούτων τάρροθον βοηλάτην
τὸν ἐξάπρυμνον, στέρφος ἐγχλαινούμενον,
στείλασα, λίστροις αἰπὺν ἤρειψεν πάγον,
τὸν ἡ παλίμφρων Γοργὰς ἐν κλήροις θεῶν
καθιερώσει, πημάτων ἀρχηγέτις.   1350

  Αὖθις δὲ κίρκοι, Τμῶλον ἐκλελοιπότες
Κίμψον τε καὶ χρυσεργὰ Πακτωλοῦ ποτά,
καὶ νᾶμα λίμνης, ἔνθα Τυφῶνος δάμαρ
κευθμῶνος αἰνόλεκτρον ἐνδαύει μυχόν,
Ἄγυλλαν Αὐσονῖτιν εἰσεκώμασαν,   1355
δεινὴν Λιγυστίνοισι τοῖς τ' ἀφ' αἵματος
ῥίζαν γιγάντων Σιθόνων κεκτημένοις
λόγχης ἐν ὑσμίναισι μίξαντες πάλην.
εἷλον δὲ Πῖσαν καὶ δορίκτητον χθόνα
πᾶσαν κατειργάσαντο τὴν Ὄμβρων πέλας   1360
καὶ Σαλπίων βεβῶσαν ὀχθηρῶν πάγων.

  Λοῖσθος δ' ἐγείρει γρυνὸς ἀρχαίαν ἔριν,
πῦρ εὗδον ἤδη τὸ πρὶν ἐξάπτων φλογί,
ἐπεὶ Πελασγοὺς εἶδε Ῥυνδακοῦ ποτῶν
κρωσσοῖσιν ὀθνείοισι βάψαντας γάνος.   1365
ἡ δ' αὖθις οἰστρήσασα τιμωρουμένη
τριπλᾶς τετραπλᾶς ἀντιτίσεται βλάβας,
πορθοῦσα χώρας ἀντίπορθμον ἠόνα.

---

  [a] Europe sends Heracles to sack Troy.
  [b] Reference to the oxen of Geryon.
  [c] Hom. *Il.* v. 640 ff. (Heracles) ὅς ποτε δεῦρ' ἐλθὼν ἔνεχ' ἵππων Λαομέδοντος | ἐξ οἵης σὺν νηυσὶ . . . | Ἰλίου ἐξαλάπαξε πόλιν.
  [d] The skin of the Nemean lion.
  [e] Hera.
  [f] Tyrrhenians from Lydia come to Etruria.
  [g] Echidna.
  [h] The Pelasgians.

eminent of his race. And she [a] in return for these things sent her champion, the driver of the oxen,[b] him of the six ships,[c] robed in a hide,[d] and laid in ruins with the spade their steep hill; and him shall Gorgas,[e] changing her mind, consecrate in the estate of the gods, even she that was the prime mover in his woes.

And in turn the falcons[f] set forth from Tmolus and Cimpsus and the gold-producing streams of Pactolus and the waters of the lake where the spouse[g] of Typhon couches in the hidden recess of her dread bed, and rioted into Ausonian Agylla and in battles of the spear joined terrible wrestling with the Ligurians and them[h] who drew the root of their race from the blood of the Sithonian[i] giants. And they took Pisa and subdued all the spear-won land that stands near the Umbrians and the high cliffs of the Salpians.[j]

And, last, the fire-brand[k] wakens the ancient strife, kindling anew with flame the ancient fire that already slept since she[l] saw the Pelasgians[m] dipping alien pitchers in the bright waters of Rhyndacus.[n] But the other[o] in turn in a frenzy of revenge shall repay the injury threefold and fourfold, laying waste the shore of the land across the sea.

[i] Sithonia and Pallene, the middle and southern spurs of Chalcidice, are the home of the giants; cf. 1406 f.

[j] Unknown. Some suppose the reference is to the Alps. Holzinger takes it as = the Σάλυες or Salvii in N.W. Etruria.

[k] Paris.

[l] Asia.

[m] Argonauts.

[n] River in Mysia.

[o] Europe sends the Greeks against Troy.

LYCOPHRON

Πρῶτος μὲν ἥξει Ζηνὶ τῷ Λαπερσίῳ
ὁμώνυμος Ζεύς, ὃς καταιβάτης μολὼν   1370
σκηπτῷ πυρώσει πάντα δυσμενῶν σταθμά.
σὺν ᾧ θανοῦμαι, κἂν νεκροῖς στρωφωμένη
τὰ λοίπ᾽ ἀκούσω ταῦθ᾽, ἃ νῦν μέλλω θροεῖν.

Ὁ δεύτερος δέ, τοῦ πεφασμένου κέλωρ
ἐν ἀμφιβλήστροις ἔλλοπος μυνδοῦ δίκην,   1375
καταιθαλώσει γαῖαν ὀθνείαν, μολὼν
χρησμοῖς Ἰατροῦ σὺν πολυγλώσσῳ στρατῷ.

Τρίτος δ᾽, ἄνακτος τοῦ δρυηκόπου γόνος,
τὴν τευχοπλάστιν παρθένον Βραγχησίαν
παραιολίξας βῶλον ἐμπεφυρμένην   1380
νασμοῖς ὀρέξαι τῷ κεχρημένῳ δάνος,
σφραγῖδα δέλτῳ δακτύλων ἐφαρμόσαι,
Φθειρῶν ὀρείαν νάσσεται μοναρχίαν,
τὸν πρωτόμισθον Κᾶρα δηώσας στρατόν,
ὅταν κόρη κασωρὶς εἰς ἐπείσιον   1385
χλεύην ὑλακτήσασα κηκάσῃ γάμους
νυμφεῖα πρὸς κηλωστὰ καρβάνων τελεῖν.

ª Agamemnon, in reference to cult of Zeus-Agamemnon in Sparta. Lapersios consequently is here transferred from the Dioscuri (see 511) to Zeus. The *real* meaning of this word is of course very obscure.

ᵇ Orestes, son of Agamemnon, occupies Aeolis.

ᶜ Apollo.

ᵈ Reference to popular derivation of Αἰολεῖς from αἰόλος, "varied."

ᵉ Neleus founds Miletus in Ionia.

ᶠ Codrus, the last king of Athens. The Peloponnesians, invading Attica, were told by the Delphic oracle that they would be successful if they did not kill the Athenian king. This becoming known to the Athenians, Codrus disguised himself and went out of the city gates to gather firewood. Picking a quarrel with two enemy scouts, he slew one and

First there shall come a Zeus [a] who bears the name of Zeus Lapersios; who shall come with swooping thunderbolt to burn all the habitations of the foe. With him shall I die, and when I flit among the dead I shall hear these further things which I am about to utter.

And, second,[b] the son of him that was slain in a net, like a dumb fish, shall lay waste with fire the alien land, coming, at the bidding of the oracles of the Physician,[c] with a host of many tongues.[d]

And third, the son[e] of the woodcutter king,[f] beguiling the potter maiden[g] of Branchidae to give him in his need earth mixed with water, wherewith to set on a tablet his finger-seal, shall found the mountain monarchy of the Phtheires,[h] when he has destroyed the host of the Carians—the first to fight for hire[i]—what time his wanton daughter[j] shall abuse her nakedness and say in mockery of marriage that she will conclude her nuptials in the brothels of barbarians.[k]

was himself slain by the other, thus saving his country. Lycurgus, *Contra Leocrat.* 84 ff.

[g] Neleus was told by an oracle to found his city where he should first receive " earth and water." At Branchidae near Miletus he asked a potter maid for some clay (the so-called *terra sigillata* or γῆ Λημνία) for a seal. She gave him the moist clay, thus giving him " earth and water."

[h] Φθειρῶν ὄρος (Homer, *Il.* ii. 868), near Miletus.

[i] *Cf.* Archiloch. fr. 30 (Hiller) καὶ δὴ 'πίκουρος ὥστε Κὰρ κεκλήσομαι.

[j] Neleus received at Delphi an oracle which bade him " go to the golden men " (*i.e.* the Carians, *cf. Il.* ii. 872) and that " his daughter would show him." Returning to Athens ἤκουσε τῆς θυγατρὸς γυμνῆς τυπτούσης τὸ ἐπείσιον καὶ λεγούσης· Δίξεο σεῦ μάλα ἐς θαλερὸν πόσιν ἢ ἐς Ἀθήνας ἢ ἐς Μίλητον· κατάξω πήματα Καρσί. *Cf. E.M. s.v. ἀσελγαίνειν.*

[k] Carians.

Οἱ δ' αὖ τέταρτοι τῆς Δυμαντείου σπορᾶς,
Λακμώνιοί τε καὶ Κυτιναῖοι Κόδροι,
οἳ Θίγρον οἰκήσουσι Σάτνιόν τ' ὄρος,   1390
καὶ χερσόνησον τοῦ πάλαι ληκτηρίαν
θεᾷ Κυρίτᾳ πάμπαν ἐστυγημένου,
τῆς παντομόρφου βασσάρας λαμπούριδος
τοκῆος, ἥτ' ἀλφαῖσι ταῖς καθ' ἡμέραν
βούπειναν ἀλθαίνεσκεν ἀκμαίαν πατρός,   1395
ὀθνεῖα γατομοῦντος Αἴθωνος πτερά.
Ὁ Φρὺξ δ', ἀδελφὸν αἷμα τιμωρούμενος,
πάλιν τιθηνὸν ἀντιπορθήσει χθόνα
τοῦ νεκροτάγου, τὰς ἀθωπεύτους δίκας
φθιτοῖσι ῥητρεύοντος ἀστεργεῖ τρόπῳ.   1400
ὃς δή ποτ' ἀμφώδοντος ἐξ ἄκρων λοβῶν
φθέρσας κύφελλα καλλυνεῖ παρωτίδας,
δαπταῖς τιτύσκων αἱμοπώταισιν φόβον.
τῷ πᾶσα Φλεγρὰς αἷα δουλωθήσεται
Θραμβουσία τε δειρὰς ἤ τ' ἐπάκτιος   1405
στόρθυγξ Τίτωνος αἵ τε Σιθόνων πλάκες
Παλλήνια τ' ἄρουρα, τὴν ὁ βούκερως
Βρύχων λιπαίνει, γηγενῶν ὑπηρέτης.
Πολλῶν δ' ἐναλλὰξ πημάτων ἀπάρξεται
Κανδαῖος ἢ Μάμερτος, ἢ τί χρὴ καλεῖν   1410
τὸν αἱμοφύρτοις ἑστιώμενον μάχαις;

ᵃ Lycophron now passes to Dorian settlements in Asia,
founded by Dorians from N. Greece.
ᵇ Dymas, Pamphylus, and Hyllus were the eponyms of
the three Dorian tribes—Dymanes, Pamphyli, and Hylleis.
ᶜ Codrus (cf. 1378 n.) here merely = " ancient."
ᵈ In N.W. Thessaly.   ᵉ In Doris.
ᶠ Unknown places in Caria.   ᵍ The Cnidian Chersonese.
ʰ Erysichthon, see Callim. H. vi. ; Ovid, M. viii. 738 n.
ⁱ Demeter.
ʲ Mestra, daughter of Erysichthon, got from Poseidon the

And then, again, the fourth,[a] of the seed of Dymas, [b] the Codrus-ancients[c] of Lacmon[d] and Cytina[e]—who shall dwell in Thigros[f] and the hill of Satnion[f] and the extremity of the peninsula[g] of him[h] who of old was utterly hated by the goddess Cyrita[i]: the father of the crafty vixen[j] who by daily traffic assuaged the raging hunger of her sire—even Aethon,[k] plougher of alien shires.

And the Phrygian,[l] avenging the blood of his brothers,[m] will sack again the land[n] that nursed the ruler[o] of the dead, who in loveless wise pronounces relentless judgement on the departed. He[p] shall spoil the ears of the ass, lobes and all, and deck his temples, fashioning a terror for the ravenous blood-suckers.[q] By him all the land of Phlegra shall be enslaved and the ridge of Thrambus and spur of Titon by the sea and the plains of the Sithonians and the fields of Pallene, which the ox-horned Brychon,[r] who served the giants, fattens with his waters.

And many woes, on this side and that alternately, shall be taken as an offering by Candaeus[s] or Mamertus[s]—or what name should be given to him who banquets in gory battles?

---

gift of assuming whatever form she pleased. When her father, in order to get the means of satisfying his hunger, sold her in one form, she returned in another to be sold again (Ovid, *M. l.c.*).   [k] = Erysichthon.

[l] Midas who, according to Lycophron, invades Thrace and Macedonia.

[m] Trojans.   [n] Europa.   [o] Minos.

[p] Midas, in a musical contest between Pan and Apollo, gave unasked his verdict against Apollo, who, in revenge, gave him the ears of an ass, to hide which Midas invented the tiara (Ovid, *M.* xi. 180 f. " Ille quidem celat turpique onerata pudore Tempora purpureis tentat velare tiaris ").

[q] *i.e.* flies.   [r] River in Pallene (Hesych.).   [s] Ares.

Οὐ μὰν ὑπείξει γ' ἡ 'πιμηθέως τοκάς,
ἀλλ' ἀντὶ πάντων Περσέως ἕνα σποράς
στελεῖ γίγαντα, τῷ θάλασσα μὲν βατὴ
πεζῷ ποτ' ἔσται, γῇ δὲ ναυσθλωθήσεται   1415
ῥήσσοντι πηδοῖς χέρσον. οἱ δὲ Λαφρίας
οἶκοι Μαμέρσας, ἠθαλωμένοι φλογὶ
σὺν καλίνοισι τειχέων προβλήμασι,
τὸν χρησμολέσχην αἰτιάσονται βλάβης.
ψαίνυνθα θεσπίζοντα Πλούτωνος λάτριν.   1420
στρατῷ δ' ἀμίκτῳ πᾶσα μὲν βρωθήσεται,
φλοιῶτιν ἐκδύνουσα δίπλακα σκέπην,
καρποτρόφος δρῦς ἀγριάς τ' ὀρειθαλής.
ἅπας δ' ἀναύρων νασμὸς αὐανθήσεται,
χανδὸν κελαινὴν δίψαν αἰνομένων.   1425
κύφελλα δ' ἰὼν τηλόθεν ῥοιζουμένων
ὑπὲρ κάρα στήσουσι, Κίμμερός θ' ὅπως,
σκιὰ καλύψει πέρραν, ἀμβλύνων σέλας.
Λοκρὸν δ' ὁποῖα παῦρον ἀνθήσας ῥόδον,
καὶ πάντα φλέξας, ὥστε κάγκανον στάχυν,   1430
αὖθις παλιμπλώτοιο γεύσεται φυγῆς,
μόσσυνα φηγότευκτον, ὡς λυκοψίαν
κόρη κνεφαίαν, ἄγχι παμφαλώμενος,
χαλκηλάτῳ κνώδοντι δειματουμένη.

  Πολλοὶ δ' ἀγῶνες καὶ φόνοι μεταίχμιοι   1435
λύσουσιν ἀνδρῶν οἱ μὲν ἐν γαίᾳ¹ πάλας
δειναῖσιν ἀρχαῖς ἀμφιδηριωμένων,
οἱ δ' ἐν μεταφρένοισι βουστρόφοις χθονός,
ἕως ἂν αἴθων εὐνάσῃ βαρὺν κλόνον,
ἀπ' Αἰακοῦ τε κἀπὸ Δαρδάνου γεγὼς   1440

¹ One expects " on the sea," but no satisfactory emenda-
tion has been proposed.

---

^a Asia.   ^b Xerxes.

ALEXANDRA

Yet the mother [a] of Epimetheus shall not yield, but in return for all shall send a single giant [b] of the seed of Perseus, who shall walk over the sea on foot and sail over the earth,[c] smiting the dry land with the oar. And the shrines of Laphria Mamerse [d] shall be consumed with fire together with their defence of wooden walls,[e] and shall blame for their hurt the prater of oracles, the false prophesying lackey [f] of Pluto. By his unapproachable host every fruit-bearing oak and wild tree flourishing on the mountain shall be devoured, stripping off its double covering of bark,[g] and every flowing torrent shall be dried up,[h] as they slake with open mouth their black thirst. And they shall raise overhead clouds of arrows hurtling from afar, whose shadow shall obscure the sun, like a Cimmerian darkness [i] dimming the sun. And blooming for a brief space, as a Locrian rose,[j] and burning all things like withered ear of corn, he shall in his turn taste of homeward flight, glancing fearfully towards the oaken bulwark hard at hand, even as a girl in the dusky twilight frightened by a brazen sword.

And many contests and slaughters in between shall solve the struggles of men, contending for dread empire, now on land, now on the plough-turned backs of earth, until a tawny lion [k]—sprung from Aeacus and from Dardanus, Thesprotian at

[c] Reference to the bridging of the Hellespont and the canal through Athos.

[d] Athena on the acropolis at Athens.   [e] Herod. viii. 51.

[f] Apollo is here the servant of Pluto because his oracle causes death to the defenders of the Acropolis.

[g] Herod. viii. 115.   [h] Herod. vii. 21.   [i] Od. xi. 14-19.

[j] Pollux v. 102 ῥόδον παρειαῖς φυτεύει, αὐθωρὸν ἀνθοῦν καὶ θᾶττον ἀπανθοῦν κατὰ τὸ Λοκρόν. It is the type of that which is fleeting.

[k] For this passage see Introduction, pp. 309 f.

439

Θεσπρωτὸς ἄμφω καὶ Χαλαστραῖος λέων,
πρηνῆ θ᾽ ὁμαίμων πάντα κυπώσας δόμον
ἀναγκάσῃ πτήξαντας Ἀργείων πρόμους
σῆναι Γαλάδρας τὸν στατηλάτην λύκον
καὶ σκῆπτρ᾽ ὀρέξαι τῆς πάλαι μοναρχίας.   1445
ᾧ δὴ μεθ᾽ ἕκτην γένναν αὐθαίμων ἐμὸς
εἷς τις παλαιστής, συμβαλὼν ἀλκὴν δορὸς
πόντου τε καὶ γῆς κεἰς διαλλαγὰς μολών,
πρέσβιστος ἐν φίλοισιν ὑμνηθήσεται,
σκύλων ἀπαρχὰς τὰς δορικτήτους λαβών.   1450

Τί μακρὰ τλήμων εἰς ἀνηκόους πέτρας,
εἰς κῦμα κωφόν, εἰς νάπας δασπλήτιδας
βαΰζω, κενὸν ψάλλουσα μάστακος κρότον;
πίστιν γὰρ ἡμῶν Λεψιεὺς ἐνόσφισε,
ψευδηγόροις φήμαισιν ἐγχρίσας ἔπη,   1455
καὶ θεσφάτων πρόμαντιν ἀψευδῆ φρόνιν,
λέκτρων στερηθεὶς ὧν ἐκάλχαινεν τυχεῖν.
θήσει δ᾽ ἀληθῆ. σὺν κακῷ δέ τις μαθών,
ὅτ᾽ οὐδὲν ἔσται μῆχος ὠφελεῖν πάτραν,
τὴν φοιβόληπτον αἰνέσει χελιδόνα.   1460

Τόσσ᾽ ἠγόρευε, καὶ παλίσσυτος ποσὶν
ἔβαινεν εἰρκτῆς ἐντός. ἐν δὲ καρδίᾳ
Σειρῆνος ἐστέναξε λοίσθιον μέλος,
Κλάρου Μιμαλλών, ἢ Μελαγκραίρας κόπις
Νησοῦς θυγατρός, ἤ τι Φίκιον τέρας,   1465
ἑλικτὰ κωτίλλουσα δυσφράστως ἔπη.
ἐγὼ δὲ λοξὸν ἦλθον ἀγγέλλων, ἄναξ,

    ᵃ Apollo, who gave to Cassandra the gift of prophecy,
but so that no one believed her prophecies.
    ᵇ Aesch. *Ag.* 1208 f.
    ᶜ Cassandra. The swallow is the type of unintelligible
speech (Aesch. *Ag.* 1050, Aristoph. *Ran.* 93).

once and Chalastraean — shall lull to rest the grievous tumult, and, overturning on its face all the house of his kindred, shall compel the chiefs of the Argives to cower and fawn upon the wolf-leader of Galadra, and to hand over the sceptre of the ancient monarchy. With him, after six generations, my kinsman, an unique wrestler, shall join battle by sea and land and come to terms, and shall be celebrated among his friends as most excellent, when he has received the first fruits of the spear-won spoils.

Why, unhappy, do I call to the unheeding rocks, to the deaf wave, and to the awful glades, twanging the idle noise of my lips? For Lepsieus [a] has taken credit from me, daubing with rumour of falsity my words and the true prophetic wisdom of my oracles, for that he was robbed of the bridal which he sought to win.[b] Yet will he make my oracles true. And in sorrow shall many a one know it, when there is no means any more to help my fatherland and shall praise the frenzied swallow.[c]

So [d] much she spake, and then sped back and went within her prison. But in her heart she wailed her latest Siren song—like some Mimallon of Claros [e] or babbler of Melancraera,[f] Neso's daughter, or Phician monster,[g] mouthing darkly her perplexed words. And I came, O King, to

[d] Here begins the Epilogue, spoken by the slave who watched Cassandra.

[e] Μιμαλλών is properly a Bacchant; here "Mimallon of Claros" (famous for cult of Apollo) means merely frenzied prophetess; cf. Eustath., Dion. Per. 445 καὶ παρὰ τῷ Λυκό-φρονι ἡ Κασσάνδρα Κλάρου Μιμαλὼν λέγεται, τουτέστι βάκχη καὶ μάντις Κλαρία.

[f] Sibyl (of Cumae), daughter of Dardanus and Neso.

[g] Sphinx; cf. Φῖκ' ὀλοήν, Hes. Th. 326.

LYCOPHRON

σοὶ τόνδε μῦθον παρθένου φοιβαστρίας,
ἐπεί μ᾽ ἔταξας φύλακα λαΐνου στέγης
καὶ πάντα φράζειν κἀναπεμπάζειν λόγον   1470
ἐτητύμως ἄψορρον ὤτρυνας τρόχιν.
δαίμων δὲ φήμας εἰς τὸ λῷον ἐκδραμεῖν
τεύξειεν, ὅσπερ σῶν προκήδεται θρόνων,
σώζων παλαιὰν Βεβρύκων παγκληρίαν.

announce to thee this the crooked speech of the maiden prophetess, since thou didst appoint me to be the warder of her stony dwelling and didst charge me to come as a messenger to report all to thee and truly recount her words. But may God turn her prophecies to fairer issue — even he that cares for thy throne, preserving the ancient inheritance of the Bebryces.[a]

[a] Trojans.

INDEX OF PROPER NAMES

A. = Aratus, *Phaenomena.*
C. = Callimachus, *Hymns.*
E. = Callimachus, *Epigrams.*
L. = Lycophron, *Alexandra.*

445

INDEX

INDEX

447

INDEX

Atarneus, t. in Mysia opposite Lesbos, E. i. 1

Ate Hill or Hill of Doom, L. 29

Athamas, s. of Aeolus, f. of Phrixus and Helle ; after Helle is named the Hellespont, L. 1285

Athena (Athenaea), C. v. 35, 51, 79, vi. 75, A. 529

Athos, mt. in Chalcidice, L. 1334 ; canal dug through it by Xerxes (Herod. vii. 22 ff.), L. 1415

Atintanes, tribe on the Aoüs in Epirus (Strabo vii. 326), L. 1044

Atlas, f. of Electra, L. 72, and Calypso, L. 744, g.f. of Dardanus, L. 72, g.g.f. of Prylis, L. 221

Atrax, t. in Thessaly (Strabo ix. 438, etc.), L. 1309

Attica (Acte), L. 111, 504, 1339 ; (Mopsopia), L. 1340

Auge, d. of Aleus and Neaera, to whom Mt. Parthenium in Arcadia was sacred, C. iv. 70

Aulis, in Boeotia on the Euripus, where the Greek fleet assembled on the way to Troy, and where Iphigeneia was sacrificed ; *cf.* L. 202 ff., 195 ff.

Auriga. See Heniochus

Ausigda, t. in Cyrenaica, L. 885

Ausonian = Italian, L. 44, 593, 615, 702, 922, 1047, 1355

Autonoë, d. of Cadmus, m. of Actaeon, C. v. 107

Avernus. See Aornos

Axeinos Pontus, *i.e.* the Euxine or Black Sea, L. 1286

Azania, district in N.-W. Arcadia and so Arcadia generally, C. iii. 235

Azilis (Aziris), in Libya, where the Greeks from Thera settled before founding Cyrene (Herod. iv. 157), C. ii. 89

Bacchus, E. ix. 2

Baius, L. 694

Balearides. See Gymnesiae

Basilo, E. xxii. 2

Battiadae = Cyrenaeans, C. ii. 96

Battus, s. of Polymnestus of Thera, founder of Cyrene, C. ii. 65

Bears, The. See Arcti

448

Bebryces, mythical people of Bithynia, then = Trojans, L. 516 1305, 1474

Bephyrus, r. in Macedonia, L. 274

Berecynthian = Phrygian, C. iii. 246

Berenice, d. of Lagos, w. of Ptolemy I., m. of Arsinoë, deified after her death, E. lii. 3

Bia = Athena, L. 520

Bisaltii, Thracian tribe, L. 417

Bistones, Thracian tribe, L. 418

Blame. See Momos

Boagidas = Heracles, L. 652

Boagrios, r. near Thronion in Locris, L. 1146

Boarmia = Athena, L. 520

Bocarus, r. in Salamis, L. 451

Boëdromios = Apollo, C. ii. 69

Bombyleia = Athena, L. 786

Boötes = Arctophylax, A. 92, 96, 136, 581, 608

Boreas, North wind, A. 25 and *passim*, C. iii. 114, iv. 26, 65, 281, 293, L. 898 ; cave of Boreas in Thrace, C. iv. 65

Boreigonoi, " a tribe in Italy " (schol.), as if Northmen, possibly with reference to Aborigines, L. 1253

Briares (Briareos), C. iv. 143

Brimo = Hecate, L. 1176

Bringer of Light, or Torch-bearer, epithet of Artemis, C. iii. 11 and 204

Britomartis, nymph of Gortyn in Crete, d. of Zeus and Carme, beloved by Artemis, C. iii. 190, also called by the Cretans Dictynna, C. iii. 198, who also called Artemis herself by the same names, C. iii. 205

Brontes, one of the Cyclopes, C. iii. 75

Brychon, r. in Pallene, L. 1407 f.

Budeia = Athene, L. 359

Bulaius = Zeus, L. 435

Bura, in Achaea, C. iv. 102, L. 586 ff.

Byblus, t. in Phoenicia, cult of Adonis there, visited by Menelaus, L. 828 ff.

Byne = Leucothea, L. 107, 757

Cabeiri, E. xli. 1

Cadmilus = Hermes, L. 162

INDEX

449

INDEX

Charmus, s. of Diophon, E. xvi. 2

Charybdis, L. 668, 743

Cheiras, or Choiras = Aphrodite, L. 1234

Cheiron, C. iv. 104

Chelae, or Claws, *i.e.* the Claws of the Scorpion, The Balance or Scales, 7th sign of Zodiac, A. 89, 232, 438, 521, 546, 607, 612, 619, 626

Chelys, or The Shell, *i.e.* the constellation Lyra, A. 268

Chersonesus, *i.e.* peninsula ; (1) Thracian, L. 331 ff., 533 ; (2) Cnidian, L. 1391 ; (3) Tauric, L. 197 ff.

Chesion, C. iii. 228

Chimaereus, L. 132

Chios, C. iv. 48, A. 638

Chitone, *i.e.* Artemis, C. i. 77, iii. 11, 225

Choiras. See Cheiras

Chonia, district on W. of gulf of Tarentum, L. 983

Chrysaor, L. 842

Cilla, L. 320

Cimmerians, dwell on Bosphorus, milk mares, under their King Lygdamis attack temple of Artemis at Ephesus, C. iii. 253 ; but the Cimmerians of Homer (*Od.* xi. 14 ff.) dwell in the extreme West and so in the region of darkness, L. 1427, localized near Cumae, L. 695

Cimon, E. lxi. 1

Cimpsos, r. in Lydia, L. 1352

Cinyphos or Cinyps, r. in N. Africa, L. 885

Circaeum (= Circeii), cape in Latium, L. 1273

Circe, L. 673, 808 ff.

Cissus, L. 1237

Cithaeron, C. iv. 97

Clarius, epithet of Apollo, C. ii. 70

Claws. See Chelae

Cleinias, E. vi. 11

Cleisithera, L. 1222 ff.

Cleombrotus, E. xxv. 1

Cleonicus, E. xxxii. 1

Clete, an Amazon, L. 995 ff.

Clytaemnestra, L. 1099 ff., 1114 ff., 1372

Cnacion, L. 550

Cnidus, C. vi. 25 ; *cf.* L. 1391

Cnossus, C. i. 42, 43, L. 1214

Cocytus, L. 705 f.

Codrus, the last king of Athens, L. 1389

Coetus = Apollo, L. 426

Coeüs, C. iv. 150

Colchians, L. 1022 ff. ; *cf.* L. 632, 887

Colotis = Aphrodite, L. 867

Comaetho, L. 934 f.

Comyrus = Zeus, L. 459

Concheia, L. 869

Conopion, E. lxiv. 1

Corax, Corvus, Crow, S. constellation, A. 449, 520

Core, the Maiden, (1) Persephone, L. 698 ; (2) Athena, L. 359, 985

Coriё, by-name of Artemis as Goddess of Maidens, C. iii. 234

Corinth, L. 1024

Coroneia, C. v. 61, 63

Corybantes. See Cyrbantes

Corythus, L. 58

Cos, C. iv. 160

Coscynthus, L. 1035

Couralius, r. in Boeotia, C. v. 64

Crab, The, Cancer, the 4th zodiacal sign, A. 147, 446, 491, 495, 500, 539, 545, 569, 893, 996

Cragus, mt. in Lycia, cult of Zeus ; hence by-name of Zeus, L. 542

Crannon, C. iv. 138, vi. 77 ; *cf.* E. 2

Crater, S. constellation, A. 448, 520, 603

Crathis, (1) E. xviii. 1 ; (2) r. in Achaea, C. i. 26 ; (3) r. near Sybaris, L. 919, 1079 ; (4) uncertain river in Illyria, L. 1021

Creion, hill at Argos, C. v. 40, 41

Creophylus, s. of Astycles, ancient poet of Chios or Samos, E. vii. 1

Crestone, district in Thrace where Munitus was fatally bitten by a snake, L. 499 ; cult of Ares (Candaon) there, L. 937

Cretan, C. i. 8, 9, 34, iii. 41, 205, E. xiii. 2, xxiv. 1, lxiii. 1 ; in L. 1297 Curetes = Cretans, who carry off Europa from Phoenicia in vengeance for the rape of Io

Crete, A. 31, C. iii. 191, iv. 272, 309, L. 1301

Cretheus, s. of Aeolus, f. of Aeson, g.f. of Jason, L. 872

Creusa, wife of Aeneas, left by him in Troy, L. 1263

INDEX

Crimisa, t. near Croton founded by Philoctetes, L. 913
Crimisus, L. 961
Crisa, t. in Phocis, L. 1070; Crisaean plains near Delphi, C. iv. 178
Crisus, L. 939 ff.
Critias, (1) E. xiv. 4; (2) E. lvi. 2
Cromna, t. in Paphlagonia with cult of Poseidon, L. 522
Cronian laws, C. v. 100
Cronides, *i.e.* son of Cronus, C. i. 61, 91
Cronion, hill at Olympia, L. 42
Cronus, C. i. 53, A. 35 (deceived by Curetes)
Croton, t. in Bruttium, L. 859 ff., 1002 ff., 1071
Crown, Stephanos, Corona Borealis, A. 71, 572, 574, 625, 660
Ctarus = Hermes, L. 679
Curetes, similar to and sometimes confused with the Corybantes: with beating of drums and war-dance they protect the infant Zeus from Cronus, C. i. 52, A. 35; in L. 1295 = Cretans; in L. 671, a tribal name for Acarnanian (Homer, *Il.* ix. 529 puts the Curetes in Pleuron)
Cychreus, prehistoric king of Salamis, L. 451
Cyclades, islands round Delos, C. iv. 3, 198
Cyclopes, C. iii. 9, 46, 67, 81, 85, E. xlvii. 2, L. 659 ff., 765
Cycnus, s. of Poseidon and Calyce, L. 232 ff.
Cydonia, t. in N.-W. Crete, C. i. 45, iii. 81, 197
Cylistarnus, r. in Italy near Lagaria, L. 946
Cyllene, mt. in Arcadia, A. 597, C. iv. 272
Cynaetha, t. in Arcadia with cult of Zeus; hence Cynaetheus = Zeus, L. 400
Cynossema. See Hecabe
Cynosura, (1) district in Arcadia, hence Cynosurian dogs, C. iv. 94; (2) The Lesser Bear, Ursa Minor, A. 36 ff., 52, 182, 227, 308
Cynthus, mt. in Delos, C. ii. 61, iv. 10, E. lxiii. 1
Cynus, t. in Locris, L. 1147

Cyon, Canis Major, The Dog, S. constellation, A. 327, 342, 352, 503, 595, 603, 676, 755. In A. 342, 676 called the " The Great Dog " in contrast to Procyon, Canis Minor. See further Sirius, Procyon
Cypeus = Apollo, L. 426
Cyphus, t. in Thessaly (Perrhaebia), L. 897
Cypris = Aphrodite, C. iv. 21, 308, v. 21, E. vi. 2, L. 112, 1143
Cyrbantes = Corybantes, L. 78
Cyre, C. ii. 88
Cyrene, (1) d. of Hypseus, C. iii. 208; (2) t. in N. of Africa, colony from Thera, named after Cyrene (1), C. ii. 73, 94, E. xv. 2, xxii. 5, xxiii. 2. Legend of the foundation of Cyrene (Herodot. iv. 145 ff.), L. 877 ff.; see Battus
Cyrita = Demeter, L. 1392
Cyrnus = Corsica, C. iii. 58, iv. 19
Cyta, t. in Colchis, home of Medeia, L. 174, 1312
Cytina = Cytinion (Thuc. i. 107), t. in Doris, L. 1389
Cyzicus, t. in the Propontis, E. xiv. 1

Daeira = Persephone, L. 710
Danaans, the people of Argos, C. v. 142
Danaus, s. of Belus, b. of Aegyptus, King of Argos, C. v. 48
Daphnis, E. xxiv. 3
Dardanus, (1) s. of Zeus and Electra, d. of Atlas, L. 72, married Arisba (d. of Teucer) also called Bateia, after whom was named the town in the Troad, L. 1308, ancestor of the " Lion at once Thresprotian and Chalastraean," L. 1440. He came from Arcadia or from Crete to Samothrace, and thence during the flood on a raft of skins to the Troad, L. 78 ff., where he founded Dardania. Buried in Troad, L. 72. His son, Ilus, was father of Laomedon, father of Priam; (2) unknown t. in Apulia, with cult of Cassandra, L. 1129 ff.
Daunia, S.-Eastern Italy (Apulia

INDEX

INDEX

INDEX

Graea, *i.e.* Tanagra in Boeotia, L. 645

Graeae, L. 846

Graeci, Greeks, L. 532, 891, 1195, 1338

Guneus, (1) an Arab, L. 128 ; (2) leader of the men of Cyphus (Perrhaebi), L. 877 ff., 897 f.

Gygaea = Athena, L. 1152

Gymnesiae, the Balearic islands. The inhabitants were famous slingers (popular derivation from βάλλω, hence Βαλιαρεῖς) carrying three slings, one on head, one round neck, the third round waist, L. 633 ff.

Gyrae Rocks, L. 390 ff.

Gyrapsius = Zeus in Chius, L. 537

Gytheion, L. 98

Hades, C. iv. 277

Haemus, mountain range in Thrace, C. iii. 114, iv. 63

Halcyone, a Pleiad, A. 262

Hales, r. near Colophon, L. 425

Haliartus, t. in Boeotia, C. v. 61

Halicarnassus, t. in Caria, E. ii. 4

Hamaxae, The Wains, A. 27, 93, *cf.* I. 1. 119 ; see Arcti

Harpe = Drepane, *i.e.* Corcyra, L. 762

Harpies, L. 167, 653

Harpina, L. 167

Havens, Watcher of (Limenoscopos), *i.e.* Artemis, C. iii. 259

Healing of All (Panaceia), C. ii. 40

Hebe, Youth, bride of Heracles, L. 1349

Hecabe, L. 1177

Hecaerge, d. of Boreas, C. iv. 292

Hecaergus, *i.e.* Apollo, C. ii. 11

Hecate, d. of Perses (Perseus) and Asteria, L. 1175

Hector, L. 260 ff., 280, 464 ff., 527 ff., 1204 ff.

Hegemone, *i.e.* Artemis, C. iii. 227

Helen, d. of Zeus (Tyndareus) and Leda, C. iii. 232

Helen's Isle = Cranaë off Attica, L. 110

Helice, (1) t. in Achaea, C. iv. 101 ; (2) Ursa Major, A. 37 ff., 51, 59, 91, 160

Helicon, A. 216, 218, C. iv. 82, v. 71, 90

Hellas, E. ix. 4

Helle, d. of Athamas, sister of Phrixus, L. 22, 1285

Hellen, L. 894, C. iv. 172

Hellespont, L. 22, 27, 1285, 1414

Helorus, r. in Sicily, L. 1033, 1184

Hemera, Gentle, by-name of Artemis, C. iii. 236

Heniochus, Auriga, N. constellation, A. 156, 167, 175, 177, 482, 679 ff., 716. On his left shoulder is The Goat (Aix, Capella, *a* Aurigae), and on his left wrist are The Kids (Eriphi, Haedi)

Hephaestus, C. i. 76, iii. 48, 74, iv. 144

Hera, C. iii. 30

Heracleia Hodos, Strabo 245. " The Lucrine Gulf extends in breadth as far as Baiae ; it is separated from the sea by an embankment eight stadia in length and the breadth of a carriage-way ; this they say that Heracles built (διαχῶσαι) when he was driving away the cattle of Geryones." This embankment is the Heracleia Hodos ; *cf.* Diodor. iv. 22, who confuses the Lucrine with the Lacus Avernus, L. 697

Heracleitus, elegiac poet of Halicarnassus, E. ii. 1

Heracles, (1) s. of Zeus and Alcmena, C. iii. 108, 159, v. 30 ; (2) s. of Alexander the Great and Barsine, slain by Polysperchon, L. 801 ff.

Hercynna, d. of Trophonius but = Demeter, L. 153

Hermes (Hermeias, Hermaon), A. 269, 674, E. xlvi. 3, C. iii. 69, 143, iv. 272

Hermione, d. of Menelaus and Helen, L. 103

Hermou Pterna, L. 835

Hesiod, E. xxix. 1

Hesione, d. of Laomedon, slave-wife of Telamon, m. of Teucer, aunt of Cassandra, L. 452 ff. She was exposed to a sea-monster which Heracles slew, L. 34 ff., 470 ff. Laomedon refused to pay Heracles his promised reward, L. 523. Hesione ransomed her brother Podarces from Heracles with

454

INDEX

her golden veil, and thenceforth he was called Priamus (πρίαμαι, buy), L. 337 ff. After the fall of Troy she was given by Heracles to Telamon, L. 469

Hesperides, L. 885

Hesperis=Berenice, t. in Cyrenaica, E. xxxviii. 6

Hesperus, the Evening-star, C. iv. 174, 280, 303, vi. 7, 8, E. lvi. 4

Hestia, C. vi. 109

Hïë Pheëon. See Paeëon

Hippacus, E. xiv. 1

Hippaeus,. E. lxi. 2

Hippegetes=Poseidon, L. 767

Hippo, an Amazon punished by Artemis, C. iii. 239, 266

Hippocrene, C. v. 71, A. 217 f.

Hippolyte, an Amazon whose girdle was carried off by Heracles and Theseus, L. 1329 ff.

Hipponion=Vibo Valentia in Bruttium, L. 1069

Hippos, Equus, later called Pegasus, The Horse, N. constellation, A. 205, 209, 215, 219, 223, 281, 283, 487, 524, 601, 627, 693

Hodoedocus, f. of Oileus (Ileus) and g.f. of Aias (2), L. 1150

Homer, E. vii. 3

Homolois=Athena, L. 520 ; cf. Zeus Homoloios as a cult-name, especially in Thessaly and Boeotia

Hoplosmia=Hera, L. 614, 858

Horites=Apollo, L. 352

Horse, The. See Hippos

Hyades, star group in Taurus, A. 173

Hydor, Aqua, Water, part of the constellation Hydrochoüs, Aquarius, A. 399

Hydra, Anguis, S. constellation, A. 414, 519, 594, 602, 611, 697

Hydrochoüs, Aquarius, the 11th sign of the Zodiac, A. 283, 389, 392, 398, 502, 548, 693

Hylaeus, a Centaur, C. iii. 221

Hylates=Apollo at Hyle in Cyprus, L. 448

Hyleus, L. 491 ff.

Hyperboreans, C. iv. 281 ff.

Hypsarnus, r. in Boeotia, L. 647

Hypseus, s. of Peneius, King of the Lapithae, and f. of Cyrene, C. ii. 92, iii. 208

Hyrrhadius, E. i. 2

Iaon, r. of Arcadia, C. i. 22

Iapyges, L. 852

Iasides, i.e. Cepheus, A. 179

Iasius, f. of Atalanta, C. iii. 216

Iason, s. of Aeson of Iolcus and leader of the Argonauts ; grandson of Cretheus, f. of Aeson, L. 892, 1310 ff.

Iatros=Apollo, L. 1207, 1377

Iberians, L. 643

Icarian Sea, i.e. the Aegean Sea S.W. of Asia Minor, C. iv. 14

Ichnaia, epithet of Themis from Ichnae in Thessalia Phthiotis or in Macedonia, L. 129

Ichthyes, Pisces, The Fishes, the 12th Zodiacal constellation, A. 240, 246, 282, 357, 362, 548, 700

Ichthys Notios, The Southern Fish, A. 387, 390, 572, 701

Ida, (1) mt. in Troad, C. v. 18, L. 496, 1256 ; (2) mt. in Crete, L. 1297, A. 33, C. i. 6, 47, 51

Idas, s. of Aphareus and b. of Lynceus, L. 553 ff.

Idomeneus, King of Crete, L. 431 ff., 1214 ff.

Ileus (Oileus), L. 1150

Ilios, L. 984

Ilus, s. of Tros and g.f. of Priam, so g.g.f. of Cassandra, L. 319, 1341, receives the Palladium from Zeus, L. 364, founds Ilios, L. 29, conquers Thrace and Macedonia, L. 1342 ff., grave in Troad, L. 319 ff.

Imbrasus, r. in Samos, hence Artemis Imbrasia, C. iii. 228

Inachus, s. of Oceanus and Tethys, founder and king of Argos, C. v. 140. His daughter Io was turned into a cow (Bous) which gave her name to the Cimmerian Bosporus, C. iii. 254, identified with Isis, E. lviii. 1. Inachus was also name of a river at Argos, C. iv. 74, v. 50

Ino, d. of Cadmus and Harmonia, becomes a sea-goddess under name of Leucothea, also called Byne, L. 107, 757

455

INDEX

INDEX

457

INDEX

Mopsops, L. 733

Mopsos, (1) s. of Apollo and Manto ; famous seer, L. 427 ; (2) Argonaut, from Titaron in Thessaly, L. 881

Morpho = Aphrodite, L. 449

Munippus, L. 224 ff., 319 ff.

Munitus, L. 495 ff.

Munychia, C. iii. 259

Muses, A. 16

Mycale, C. iv. 50

Myconos, L. 388, 401

Myleus = Zeus, L. 435

Myllaces = Illyrians, L. 1021

Myndia = Athena, L. 950, 1261

Myrina, L. 243

Myrrha, m. of Adonis, L. 829

Myrtilus, L. 162 ff.

Myrtusa, C. ii. 91

Mysian : Mysian Olympus, C. iii. 117

Mystes = Heracles, L. 1328

Mytilene, home of Pittacus, E. i. 2

Naryx, t. in Locris, L. 1148

Nauaethus (Neaethus), L. 921

Naubolus, L. 1067

Naucratis, E. xl. 1

Naumedon = Poseidon, L. 157

Nauplius, L. 384 ff., 1093 ff., 1217 ff.

Navel, Plain of the. See Omphalion

Naxos, E. xx. 1

Neapolis = Naples, L. 717

Neda, C. i. 33, 38

Nedon, L. 374

Neilos, C. iv. 185, 208

Neleus, s. of Codrus, founder of Miletus, C. iii. 226

Nemesis, C. iv. 56

Neoptolemus, L. 183, 323 ff.

Neptunis (v.l.), Nepunis = Artemis at Nepete in Etruria, L. 1332

Nereus, g.f. of Triton, L. 886 ;= sea, L. 164, C. i. 40

Neriton, mt. in Ithaca, L. 769, 794

Nesaia, a Nereid, L. 399

Neso, m. of Sibyl, L. 1465

Nessus, L. 50 f.

Nicippe, priestess of Demeter, C. vi. 43

Nicoteles, E. xxi. 2

Nile. See Neilos

Niobe, C. ii. 22 ff.

Nireus, L. 1011 ff.

Nomius, name of Apollo as god of herds, C. ii. 47 ; see Amphrysus

Nonacriates = Hermes, L. 680

Nyctimus, L. 481

Nyx, Night, A. 409 ff., L. 437

Obrimo = Persephone, L. 698

Ocinarus, r. near Tereina, L. 729, 1009

Odysseus, L. 344, 815, 1030

Odysseus, Cape of, the W. point of Cape Pachynus in Sicily, L. 1031 f., where Odysseus built a cenotaph for Hecabe, L. 1181 ff.

Oebalus, f. of Tyndareus, hence " children of O."= Spartans, L. 1125

Oeceus, f. of Dexamenus and Hipponous, C. iv. 102

Oedipus, L. 437, called Oedipodes C. ii. 74

Oekourous = Dionysus, L. 1246

Oeneus, s. of Porthaon, King of Calydon in Aetolia, f. of Tydeus, Meleager, Deianeira ; failed to honour Artemis who in revenge sent the Calydonian boar, C. iii. 260

Oeno. See Oenotropi

Oenomaus, L. 161 ff.

Oenone, (1) d. of Cebren and wife of Paris, dies with him, L. 57-68. See Corythus ; (2) old name of Aegina, L. 175

Oenopion, A. 640

Oenotria, L. 912

Oenotropi, dd. of Anius (so g.dd. of Apollo) and Rhoeo d. of Staphylus s. of Dionysus (and so g.g.dd. of Dionysus) who subsequently married Zarax, L. 570 ff. When the Greeks suffered from hunger before Troy, they brought the Oenotropi from Delos ; to help them to escape, Dionysus changed them into doves, L. 581 ff. ; see Anius

Oeta, L. 486

Ofenus = Oceanus, L. 231

Ogygus, L. 1206

Oileus, s. of Hodoedocus, f. of Locrian Aias, L. 1150

Oïstos, Sagitta, Eratosthenes' Τόξον, N. constellation, A. 311, 598, 691

INDEX

Olen, C. iv. 305

Olenos, t. in Achaia, L. 590

Olosson, t. in Thessaly, L. 906

Olympus, (1) mt. in Macedonia, home of the gods, C. i. 62, iv. 220, vi. 59, L. 564 ; (2) mt. in Mysia, C. iii. 117

Ombrius = Zeus as god of rain, L. 160

Ombroi = Umbrians, L. 1360

Omphalion Pedon, in Crete, C. i. 45

Oncaea = Demeter, L. 1225

Onchestus, t. on Lake Copais in Boeotia with temple of Poseidon, L. 646

Onoi, Asini, The Asses, constellations N. and S. of Phatne, q.v., A. 898, 906

Onou Gamphelae = Onou Gnathos L. 94

Opheltes, mt. in Euboea, L. 373

Ophion, L. 1192

Ophis, Anguis, Serpens, N. constellation, A. 82 ff., 578, 665

Ophiuchus, Serpentarius, N. constellation, A. 74 ff., 488, 521, 577, 665, 724

Ophrynion, t. in Troad with grave of Hector (Strabo 595), L. 1208

Orchieus = Apollo, L. 562

Orestes, E. lx. 1 ff.

Orion (Oarion), giant hunter of Boeotia, C. iii. 265. As S. constellation, A. 232, 310, 323, 361, 518, 588, 636, 639, 676, 730, 756

Ormenidae, ss. of Ormenus, i.e. men of Ormenion ; t. in Thessalian Magnesia, C. vi. 76

Ornis, The Bird = Latin Cygnus, The Swan, N. constellation, A. 272, 273, 274, 312, 487, 599, 628, 691

Orthanes = Paris, L. 538

Orthosia, properly cult-name of Artemis, Pind. Ol. iii. 30 ; in L. 1331 = an Amazon

Ortygia, old name of Delos, C. ii. 59 ; myth that Delos is a quail (ὄρτυξ) turned to stone, L. 401. In E. lxiii. 1 epithet of Artemis, who was worshipped at Ortygia in Syracuse (Pind. N. i. 2 f.)

Ossa, (1) mt. in Thessalian Magnesia, C. iii. 52, iv. 137 ; (2) mt. in Campania, L. 697

Othronos, island near Corcyra, L. 1034 ; in L. 1027 an island near Sicily (?)

Othrys, mt. in Thessalia Phthiotis, C. vi. 86

Otos, s. of Poseidon and Iphimedeia, b. of Ephialtes, slain by Apollo or Artemis, C. iii. 264

Otrera, an Amazon, m. of Penthesileia, L. 997

Pachynus, cape in Sicily, L. 1029, 1182

Pactolus, r. in Lydia, C. iv. 250, L. 272, 1352

Paeëon, Paeon, Paean, by-name of Apollo, C. ii. 21, 97, 103

Palaemon, (1) = Melicertes, s. of Ino Leucothea, children sacrificed to him at Tenedos, L. 229 ; (2) by-name of Heracles, L. 663

Palamedes, s. of Nauplius and Clymene, L. 1098

Palauthra, t. in Thessalia Magnesia, home of Prothoüs, L. 899

Palladium, the image of Pallas which was said to have fallen from heaven and which was the pledge of the safety of Ilios, L. 363 f. ; stolen by Odysseus, L. 658

Pallas = Athena, C. v. passim

Pallatides, rocks near Argos, C. v. 42

Pallene, peninsula on Thermaic gulf ; its former name Phlegra (-ai), and associated with the giants, L. 127, 1407

Pallenis = Athena, L. 1261

Pamphilus, E. l. 3

Pamphylus, L. 442

Pan, C. iii. 88, E. xlvi.

Panaceia. See Healing of All

Panacra, hill in Crete, C. i. 51 f.

Panemos, Macedonian name for month of July, E. xlvi. 1

Pangaeum, mt. with gold and silver mines in Thrace, C. iv. 134

Panope, a Nereid, A. 658

Panopeus, s. of Phocus, f. of Epeius, L. 932 ff.

Paris, L. 86, 91, 168, etc.

Parnassus, C. iv. 93

Parrhasia, t. in Arcadia (Hom. Il. ii. 608), hence Arcadia generally, C. i. 10, iii. 99

459

INDEX

Parthenia, old name of Samos, C. iv. 49

Parthenium, mt. in Arcadia sacred to Auge, C. iv. 71

Parthenope, L. 714 ff.

Parthenos, Virgo, The Maiden, the 6th sign of the Zodiac, A. 491, 546, 597, 606; the myth, A. 97 ff.

Pasiphaë, C. iv. 311

Patareus = Apollo, L. 920

Pausanias, E. xii. 4

Pegasus, the winged horse of Bellerophon, given by Zeus to Eos, L. 17; see also Hippos

Pelagones, C. i. 3

Pelasgian, C. iv. 284, v. 4, 51, vi. 26, E. xl. 1, L. 177, 245, 1083, 1364

Peleus, s. of Aeacus, f. of Achilles by Thetis, L. 175 ff., 901 f.

Pelion, mt. in Thessaly, C. iv. 118

Pellaios (?), E. xv. 6

Pellene: its colonists in Italy—Ausones Pellenii—kill Philoctetes, L. 922

Pelopeis = Peloponnesus, C. iv. 72

Pelops, L. 53 ff., 152 ff.

Peneius, r. in Thessaly, C. iv. 105, 112, 121, 128, 148, L. 1343

Penthesileia, L. 997 ff.

Pephnos, L. 87

Perge, (1) t. in Pamphylia with temple of Artemis, C. iii. 187; (2) a hill in Etruria, L. 805

Perrhaebi, L. 905

Persephone, L. 710

Perseus, (1) = Perses, f. of Hecate, L. 1175; (2) s. of Zeus and Danaë, L. 837; (3) Perseus (2) was set among the stars after his death as a N. constellation, A. 249, 484, 685, 687, 711

Peuceus = Heracles, L. 663

Phaeacians, L. 632

Phaedrus, (1) E. lvii. 4; (2) = Hermes, L. 680

Phalacra, L. 24, 1170

Phalanna, t. in N. Thessaly, L. 906; see Polypoetes

Phalerus, founder of Naples, L. 717

Phalorias, t. in Locris, L. 1147

Phatne, The Manger, A. 892, 898, 905, 996

Phausterius = Dionysus, L. 212

Phegion, mt. in Aethiopia, L. 16

Phemius, L. 1324

Pheneius, t. in Azania in Arcadia, C. iv. 71

Pherae, (1) t. in Thessalia Pelasgiotis, cult of Artemis-Hecate (on coins of Pherae represented seated with torch on horseback); hence Pheraean as epithet of Artemis-Hecate, C. iii. 259, L. 1180; (2) t. in Messenia, hence Pheraeans, L. 552

Phereclus, L. 97

Phician Monster, i.e. the Sphinx (Phix), in L. 1465 = Cassandra

Phigaleus = Dionysus, L. 212

Phileratis, E. xxxv. 1

Philippus, E. xxi. 1, xlvii. 3

Philoctetes, s. of Poeas, bitten by snake and left by the Greeks in Lemnos, L. 62, 912 ff.

Philoxenides, E. lvii. 4

Philyra, d. of Oceanus, m. of Cheiron by Cronus, C. i. 36, iv. 118

Phlegra, in Pallene, scene of the battle of the giants, L. 1404

Phocians: the Phocian = Pylades, E. lx. 3; Phocians found Temesa in Bruttium, L. 1067

Phocus, s. of Aeacus and Psamathe, f. of Crisus and Panopeus, slain by Peleus and Telamon, his half-brothers, who had in consequence to leave Aegina, L. 175

Phoenician Goddess = Athena in Corinth (schol.), L. 658

Phoenicians, A. 39, C. iv. 19, Phoenician Cyrnus (Corsica), as a Phoenician settlement

Phoenix, s. of Amyntor, tutor of Achilles (κουροτρόφον πάγουρον), L. 419 in ref. to his age (Hom. Il. ix. 446 and 487 ff.) and King of the Dolopes near Tymphrestus. Buried by Neoptolemus at Eion, L. 417-423

Phoenodomas, Trojan who had three daughters and who proposed that Laomedon's daughter Hesione should be exposed to the sea-monster, L. 470 ff., 952 ff.

Phorce, Lake = prob. Lacus Fucinus, L. 1275

Phorcides, dd. of Phorcus and Ceto, also called Graeae, cf. L. 846

INDEX

Phorcus, L. 376, 477

Phrygia, C. ii. 23, iii. 159, E. li.

Phrygian : the Phrygian, C. v. 18 = Paris

Phtheires, L. 1383

Phthia, (1) in Thessaly, C. iv. 112 ; (2) mistress of Amyntor, L. 421

Phthonus, C. ii. 105, 107, 113

Phylamus, r. in Daunia, L. 594

Physadeia, fountain at Argos, C. v. 47

Phyxius = Zeus, L. 288

Pilgrim Ship, The, θεωρίς (ναῦς), C. iv. 314

Pimpleia, mt. and fountain in Pieria, C. iv. 7, L. 275

Pindus, C. iv. 139, vi. 83

Pisa, t. in Etruria, L. 1241, 1359

Pitane, C. iii. 172

Pithecusa or Pithecusae, island or islands off coast of Campania, beneath which the giants are buried, L. 688

Pittacus, E. i. 1

Plato, E. xxv. 3

Pleiades, A. 255, 1066, 1085

Pleistus, r. in Phocis, C. iv. 92

Pluto, E. xv. 4

Plynos, L. 149

Podaleirius, s. of Asclepius, buried in Daunia, where he heals the sick who sleep on sheep-skins and are sprinkled with the water of the Althaenus, L. 1047 ff.

Podarces, earlier name of Priam, L. 339

Poimandria, L. 326

Pola or Polae, t. in Istria, L. 1022 (which, however, may refer to another Pola given by Steph. Byz. as in Illyricum)

Polyanthes, r. in Chaonia, L. 1046

Polydegmon, L. 700 = the Apennines, possibly in reference to the use of Polydegmon as a by-name of Hades in Hom. *Hymn Dem.* 31—thus Hades-hill in reference to volcanic action

Polydeuces (Pollux), one of the Dioscuri, L. 506, he being son of Zeus while Castor was son of Tyndareus (Pind. *N.* x. 80 ff.). In the fight with Idas and Lynceus Polydeuces killed Lynceus

and Idas with the help of Zeus' and voluntarily undertook to share his immortality with Castor, who had been mortally wounded by Idas, L. 553 ff.

Polygonus, L. 124

Polymestor, L. 331

Polyneices, L. 437

Polyphemus, Cyclops, E. xlvii. 1

Polypoetes, s. of Peirithous, leader at Troy of men from various Thessalian towns, *e.g.* Olosson and Phalanna (Hom. *Il.* ii. 738 ff., where ῎Ορθη = Φάλαννα), L. 906

Polysperchon (Polyperchon), one of the generals of Alexander the Great, who in 319 B.C. was nominated by Antipater as his successor in Macedonia (in preference to his own son Cassander). In 316 he was driven from his kingdom by Cassander. In 315 Antigonus appointed him commander of the Peloponnesus and Greece was declared free. A peace was concluded in 311 by which Greece fell to Cassander, while Polysperchon was confined to some towns in Peloponnesus. Later he was induced by Antigonus to support the claim to the throne of Macedonia of Heracles, s. of Alexander and Barsine. He accordingly invaded Macedonia but accepted the proposal of Cassander to divide the kingdom of Macedonia, with an independent army and dominion in Peloponnesus. Thereupon he assassinated Heracles (309 B.C.). He is the " Tymphaean dragon " of L. 801

Polyxena, d. of Priam and Hecabe, sister of Cassandra, L. 314 ; she was sacrificed by Neptolemus at the grave of Achilles, L. 323 ff., her throat being cut with a knife which Peleus had received from Hephaestus

Polyxo, mt. of Actorion, C. vi. 78

Pontus Euxeinos : the expression κακόξεινος κλυδών, L. 1286, refers to the old name of the Black

461

INDEX

Sea, πόντος ἄξεινος. The name is said to have been changed to εὔξεινος either after the voyage of the Argonauts, or after Heracles' expedition against the Amazons or after the foundation of the Milesian colonies. Pind. *P.* iv. 203, has ἐπ' Ἀξείνου στόμα (he is speaking of the Argonauts), but *N.* iv. 49 Εὐξείνῳ πελάγει

Porceus, one of the two snakes (Porceus and Chariboea) which came from Calydnae and killed Laocoön and one of his two sons. The story was told by Arctinus in his *Iliupersis*, L. 347

Poseidon, C. iii. 50, iv. 101, 271, vi. 98, helps Apollo to build walls of Troy, L. 522, 617; carries off Pelops, L. 157; destroys Locrian Aias, L. 390 ff.; f. of Proteus, L. 125; Cycnus, L. 237; Theseus, L. 1324; cultnames, Aegaeon, L. 135; Amoebeus, L. 617; Amphibaeus, L. 749; Enipeus, L. 722; Hippegetes, L. 767; Melanthus, L. 767; Naumedon, L. 157; Prophantus, L. 522; Phemius, L. 1324; Lord of Cromna, L. 522

Poseidon: Cape of Poseidon near Poseidonia (Paestum), L. 722

Poseidon, the stars of, A. 756. The scholiast's interpretation seems to be correct: "The stars of Poseidon are those which show forth storms and fair weather; the stars of Zeus are those which indicate weather suitable for agriculture." *Cf.* Avien. 1377 ff.: "Hic est fons, unde et deduxit tempora lunae Navita cum longum facili rate curreret aequor, Et cum ruris amans telluri farra parenti Crederet; ingenti petat haec indagine semper Seu qui vela salo, seu qui dat semina terrae"

Potamus, Flumen, The River, S. constellation, A. 358, 589, 600, 624, 728; also called Eridanus, A. 360. Cicero calls it Eridanus ("Eridanum cernes . . . funestum magnis cum viribus am-

nem") and adopts the legend that it represents the tears of Phaëthon's sisters; Germanicus, 361, calls it Amnis and follows the same legend; Avienus, 780, calls it Flumen, but refers to the Ausonians of old who call it Eridanus and to the Phaëthon legend

Practis, unknown place in Epirus. Some take it to mean Acroceraunium. Holzinger thinks Practis = avenger = Erinys and that Elephenor built a shrine to her, beside which he built his city

Praxandrus: leads Laconians of Therapnae from Troy to Cyprus, L. 586

Problastus = Dionysus, L. 577

Procris, d. of Erechtheus, w. of Cephalus, companion of Artemis, C. iii. 209

Procyon, Canis Minor or in particular α Canis Minoris. So called because it rises nearly a fortnight before Cyon, The Dog, Canis Major, A. 450, 595, 690

Proetus, King of Argos, s. of Abas; driven from Argos by his twinbrother Acrisius he went to Lycia and married Sthenoboea; returning to Peloponnesus he became king of Tiryns. Founds two shrines to Artemis when his daughters were healed of their madness, C. iii. 232

Promantheus = Zeus, L. 537

Prometheus, s. of Asia, L. 1283

Pronians, the suitors of Penelope, so called from t. in Cephallenia (Προνναῖοι, Thuc. ii. 30, Προνῆσος, Strabo 455), L. 791

Prophantus, by-name of Poseidon at Thurii, L. 522

Protesilaus, s. of Iphiclus, leader of Thessalians in Trojan War, first to leap ashore at Troy, killed by Hector; tomb at Mazusia, L. 530 ff. In answer to the prayers of his wife Laodameia (or Polydora) he was allowed to return for a short space to the upper world

Proteus, s. of Poseidon, comes from his home in Egypt to Pal-

INDEX

3 = the Cabiri (Samothraces di, Varro, *L.L.* v. 58 ; "magnaque Threicia sacra reperta Samo," Ov. *A.A.* ii. 602). See Saos

Saon, of Acanthus, s. of Dicon, E. xi. 1

Saos, old name of Samothrace, L. 78, where it is called the foundation of the Cyrbantes = Corybantes = Cabiri

Sarapis (Serapis), Egyptian deity, E. xxxviii. 3

Saraptia = Europa, d. of Phoenix, from Sarepta, t. in Phoenicia, L. 1300

Sardis, capital of Lydia, C. iii. 246

Sardo = Sardinia, C. iv. 21 ; in L. 796 Σαρδωνικῆς seems to be "Sardinian"

Saronic gulf, between Sunium and Scyllaeum on the Isthmus of Corinth, C. iv. 42

Sarpedon, s. of Zeus and Europa, L. 1284

Satnios, hill in Caria, L. 1390

Satrachus, r. in Cyprus, L. 448

Saunii = Σαυννῖται = Samnites, L. 1254

Saviour. See Soter

Scaean Gates, of Troy, L. 774

Scamander, f. of Teucer, g.f. of Arisba, L. 1304 ff.

Scandeia, haven of Cythera (Hom. *Il.* x. 268), L. 108

Scapaneus = Heracles, L. 652

Scarpheia, t. in Locris (Scarphe, Hom. *Il.* ii. 532), L. 1147

Schedius, b. of Epistrophus, s. of Iphitus and g.s. of Naubolus, L. 1067

Schoineis = Aphrodite, L. 832

Sciastes = Apollo, L. 562

Scolus, t. in Boeotia (Hom. *Il.* ii. 497), L. 646

Scorpius, Scorpio, The Scorpion, 8th sign of the Zodiac, A. 85, 304, 307, 403, 438, 506, 545, 635, 643, 667

Scyletria = Athena, L. 853

Scylla, L. 45, 669

Scyrus, L. 185, 277, 1324

Scythia, C. iii. 174, 256

Selenaea, E. vi. 2

Seriphos, one of the Cyclades, L. 844 f.

Setaea, Trojan captive who with her fellow captives set fire to some of the Greek ships on the way from Troy and was bound to a rock (Setaeum) near Crathis, where she was devoured by seabirds (other versions of the legend in Strabo 264, Plut. *Rom.* 1, *Aet. Rom.* 6), L. 1075 ff.

Sibyl, d. of Dardanus and Neso, d. of Teucer ; the Erythraean = Cumaean Sibyl, L. 1145 ; her cave at Cumae, L. 1278 ff. Another name for the Cumaean Sibyl is Melancraira (Arist. *De mir. ausc.* 95), L. 1464

Sicanian, properly of the Sicani in Sicily, but used for Sicilian in general (Lycophron has not Σικελοί nor Σικελία), L. 870, 951, 1029 (in all cases with first syllable long), C. iii. 57 (with first syllable short, Τρινακίη Σικανῶν ἕδος)

Sidonians, A. 44

Silarus. See Laris

Simois, r. in Troad, C. v. 19

Simone, E. xxxix. 2

Simus, E. xlix. 1

Sinis, L. 982

Sinon, s. of Aesimus (or Sisyphus), b. of Anticleia, m. of Odysseus by Laertes or Sisyphus, and hence cousin of Odysseus, L. 344 ff.

Sirens, L. 671, 712

Siris, L. 978

Sirius, α Canis Majoris, The Dog-star, A. 332, 340. It has been supposed that in Archiloch. fr. 61, Hesiod, *W.* 585, *S.* 397, by Sirius is meant the Sun and so ἀκτὶς Σειρία, L. 397 is interpreted of the rays of the Sun

Sisyphus, L. 344, 980, 1030

Sithon, King of Thrace, f. of Rhoeteia, L. 583, 1161, Pallene and Phyllis

Sithonia : Sithonian giants, L. 1357 = the Pelasgians who are said to have come from Thessaly to found Agylla (Strabo 220).

Smintheus, L. 1306

Smyrna, E. vi. 12

Soli, t. in Cilicia, native town of Aratus, who is hence called ὁ Σολεύς, E. xxix. 3

464

INDEX

INDEX

Thessaly, C. iv. 103, 109, 140, E. xxxii. 1

Thetis, d. of Nereus and Doris. L. 861, sister of Nesaia, L. 399 ; she helped Zeus when Poseidon and Athena wanted to bind him, L. 400. She married Peleus to whom she bore six sons whom she killed in infancy by putting them in fire to test their immortality ; the seventh, Achilles, was saved by Peleus, L. 179. Mourns the early death of Achilles, C. ii. 20 ; *cf.* L. 240, 274, 857. A mixing-bowl which she received from Bacchus serves as urn for the ashes of Achilles, L. 273. Buries the Locrian Aias, L. 398. Metonymy for " Sea," L. 22

Thigros, t. in Caria, L. 1390

Thoas of Aetolia, s. of Andraemon and Gorge. At the request of Odysseus, Thoas scourged Odysseus to enable him to enter Troy as a spy, L. 779 ff. After the fall of Troy he goes with Nireus to Libya, Epeirus, and Illyria, L. 1011 ff.

Thoraios = Apollo, L. 352

Thracian, C. iii. 114, iv. 63, A. 355 (Boreas)

Thrambus, t. in Pallene, L. 1405

Thrascias, N.N.W. wind, L. 925

Thraso = Athena, L. 936

Thronion, (1) t. in Epeius, L. 1045 ; (2) t. in Locris, L. 1148

Thuria = Demeter, L. 153

Thysai = Thystades = Thyiades, female Bacchants, L. 106

Thyterion, Ara, The Altar ; S. constellation, A. 404, 408, 434, 440, 692, 710

Tilphusius = Apollo, L. 562, from his sanctuary at Tilphossa near Haliartus in Boeotia

Timarchus, E. xii. 1

Timodemus, E. xl. 3

Timon, E. iii. 1, s. of Echecratides, Κολλυτεύς, famous misanthrope towards end of fifth century B.C.

Timonoë, E. xvii. 1

Timotheus, E. xvii. 2

Tiphys, s. of Agnius, from Tiphae (Siphae) near Thespia, was pilot of the Argo, L. 890

Tiryns, t. in Argolis, native town of Amphitryon, hence Heracles, C. iii. 146, is Τιρύνθιος ἄκμων

Titanis = Tethys, L. 231, C. iv. 17

Titans, C. iv. 174

Titaron, t. in Thessaly, home of Mopsus, L. 881

Titarus, mt. in Thessaly, L. 904

Tithonus, s. of Laomedon and Strymo or Rhoeo, and thus half-brother of Priam (s. of Laomedon and Leucippe). On account of his beauty he was carried off by Eos to Aethiopia, obtaining the gift of immortality but not eternal youth, L. 18 ff.

Tito = Eos, L. 941

Titon, mt. in Thrace, L. 1406

Titonian, L. 1276

Tityus, s. of Gaia, giant who insulted Leto (or Artemis herself), and was slain by Artemis, C. iii. 110

Tmarus (Tomarus), hill near Dodona in Thresprotia (Hesychius mentions a Tmarion hill in Arcadia), C. vi. 52

Tmolus, (1) mt. in Lydia, L. 1351 ; (2) s. of Proteus and Torone, L. 124

Torone, wife of Proteus, after whom is named Torone in Chalcidice, L. 115

Toxeuter or Toxotes, Sagittarius, The Archer, 9th zodiacal sign, A. 306, 400, 506, 547, 665, 673

Toxon, the bow of the preceding, A. 301, 305, 506, 621, 623, 664, 665, 965

Trachis, t. founded by Heracles at foot of Mt. Oeta, L. 905

Trambelus, s. of Telamon and Hesione (?) or another, and so brother or half-brother of Teucrus, L. 467

Trampya, t. in Epeirus with oracle of Odysseus, L. 800

Traron, L. 1158

Tricephalus = Hermes, L. 680

Trimorphus = Hecate, L. 1176

Trinacia or Trinacria, old name of Sicily from its three promontories (ἄκραι), C. iii. 57 ; also called τρίδειρος, L. 966

INDEX

Printed in Great Britain by R. & R. CLARK, LIMITED, *Edinburgh*

STAR-MAPS.

Definitions :

Circulus Arcticus (Polaris) : an imaginary circle 23½°
from the N. Pole. It should be noted that the Arctic Circle of
the ancients is not a fixed circle, but varies with the latitude
of the observer. Thus Geminus IV. : ἀρκτικὸς μὲν οὖν ἐστι
κύκλος ὁ μέγιστος τῶν ἀεὶ θεωρουμένων κύκλων, ὁ ἐφαπτόμενος
τοῦ ὁρίζοντος καθ᾽ ἓν σημεῖον καὶ ὅλος ὑπὲρ γῆν ἀπολαμ-
βανόμενος· ἐν ᾧ τὰ κείμενα τῶν ἄστρων οὔτε δύσιν οὔτε
ἀνατολὴν ποιεῖται, ἀλλὰ δι᾽ ὅλης τῆς νυκτὸς περὶ τὸν πόλον
στρεφόμενα θεωρεῖται. For Rhodes (ἐν τῇ καθ᾽ ἡμᾶς οἰκουμένῃ), adds Geminus, this circle is defined by the front
foot of the Great Bear. The corresponding circle 23½° from
S. Pole is called the Antarctic Circle.

Tropicus Cancri : an imaginary circle marking the
extreme Northern limit of the Sun's path, 23½° North
of the Equator: Cf. Gemin. IV. θερινὸς δὲ τροπικὸς κύκλος
ἐστὶν ὁ βορειότατος τῶν ὑπὸ τοῦ ἡλίου γραφομένων κύκλων κατὰ
τὴν τοῦ κόσμου γινομένην περιστροφήν· ἐφ᾽ οὗ γενόμενος ὁ
ἥλιος τὴν θερινὴν τροπὴν ποιεῖται, ἐν ᾗ μεγίστη μὲν πασῶν τῶν
ἐν τῷ ἐνιαυτῷ ἡμέρα, ἐλαχίστη δὲ ἡ νύξ γίνεται. μετὰ μέντοι
γε τὴν θερινὴν τροπὴν οὐκέτι πρὸς τὰς ἄρκτους προοδεύων ὁ
ἥλιος θεωρεῖται, ἀλλ᾽ ἐπὶ τὰ ἕτερα μέρη τρέπεται τοῦ κόσμου.
διὸ κέκληται τροπικός.

Note: *These maps are reproduced with certain simplifications from the edition of Aratus by Buhle, Leipzig 1801 who took
them from Schaubach's edition of the Catasterismi of Eratosthenes.*

Tropicus Capricorni : an imaginary circle marking the extreme Southern limit of the Sun's path, 23½° South of the Equator. Cf. Gemin. IV. χειμερινὸς δὲ τροπικὸς κύκλος ἐστιν ὁ νοτιώτατος τῶν ὑπὸ τοῦ ἡλίου γραφομένων κύκλων κατὰ τὴν τοῦ κόσμου γινομένην περιστροφήν· ἐφ' οὗ γενόμενος ὁ ἥλιος τὴν χειμερινὴν τροπὴν ποιεῖται, ἐν ᾗ ἡ μεγίστη μὲν πασῶν τῶν ἐν τῷ ἐνιαυτῷ νὺξ ἐπιτελεῖται, ἐλαχίστη δὲ ἡμέρα. μετὰ μέντοι γε τὴν χειμερινὴν τροπὴν οὐκέτι πρὸς μεσημβρίαν προοδεύων ὁ ἥλιος θεωρεῖται, ἀλλ' ἐπὶ τὰ ἕτερα μέρη τρέπεται τοῦ κόσμου. διὸ κέκληται καὶ οὗτος τροπικός.

Circulus Aequinoctialis : or Celestial Equator, a Great Circle, the plane of which passes through the centre of the earth, and is at right angles to the **axis** of rotation; all points on this circle are 90° from the Poles. Cf. Gemin. IV. ἰσημερινὸς δέ ἐστι κύκλος ὁ μέγιστος τῶν πέντε παραλλήλων κύκλων, ὁ διχοτομούμενος ὑπὸ τοῦ ὁρίζοντος, ὥστε ἡμικύκλιον μὲν ὑπὲρ γῆν ἀπολαμβάνεσθαι, ἡμικύκλιον δὲ ὑπὸ τὸν ὁρίζοντα· ἐφ' οὗ γενόμενος ὁ ἥλιος τὰς ἰσημερίας ποιεῖται, τήν τε ἐαρινὴν καὶ τὴν φθινοπωρινήν.

Circulus Eclipticus : a Great Circle, marking the apparent annual path of the Sun among the fixed stars. The belt of sky on either side of this is called the Zodiac. Cf. Gemin. IV. οὗτος δὲ ἐφάπτεται δύο κύκλων ἴσων τε καὶ παραλλήλων· τοῦ μὲν θερινοῦ τροπικοῦ κατὰ τὴν τοῦ Καρκίνου πρώτην μοῖραν, τοῦ δὲ χειμερινοῦ τροπικοῦ κατὰ τὴν τοῦ Αἰγόκερω πρώτην μοῖραν, τὸν δὲ ἰσημερινὸν δίχα τέμνει κατὰ τὴν τοῦ Κριοῦ πρώτην μοῖραν καὶ κατὰ τὴν τοῦ Ζυγοῦ πρώτην μοῖραν.

HEMISPHAERIUM AUSTRALE.

THE LOEB CLASSICAL LIBRARY

VOLUMES ALREADY PUBLISHED

LATIN AUTHORS

AMMIANUS MARCELLINUS. J. C. Rolfe. 3 Vols. (*2nd Imp. revised*.)

APULEIUS : THE GOLDEN ASS (METAMORPHOSES). W. Adlington (1566). Revised by S. Gaselee. (*7th Imp.*)

ST. AUGUSTINE, CONFESSIONS OF. W. Watts (1631). 2 Vols. (Vol. I *7th Imp.*, Vol. II *6th Imp.*)

ST. AUGUSTINE : SELECT LETTERS. J. H. Baxter. (*2nd Imp.*)

AUSONIUS. H. G. Evelyn White. 2 Vols. (*2nd Imp.*)

BEDE. J. E. King. 2 Vols. (*2nd Imp.*)

BOETHIUS : TRACTS AND DE CONSOLATIONE PHILOSOPHIAE. Rev. H. F. Stewart and E. K. Rand. (*6th Imp.*)

CAESAR : ALEXANDRINE, AFRICAN AND SPANISH WARS. A. S. Way.

CAESAR : CIVIL WARS. A. G. Peskett. (*5th Imp.*)

CAESAR : GALLIC WAR. H. J. Edwards. (*10th Imp.*)

CATO AND VARRO : DE RE RUSTICA. H. B. Ash and W. D. Hooper. (*3rd Imp.*)

CATULLUS. F. W. Cornish : TIBULLUS. J. B. Postgate ; and PERVIGILIUM VENERIS. J. W. Mackail. (*12th Imp.*)

CELSUS : DE MEDICINA. W. G. Spencer. 3 Vols. (Vol. I *3rd Imp. revised*, Vols. II and III *2nd Imp.*)

CICERO : BRUTUS AND ORATOR. G. L. Hendrickson and H. M. Hubbell. (*3rd Imp.*)

CICERO : DE FATO ; PARADOXA STOICORUM; DE PARTITIONE ORATORIA. H. Rackham. (With De Oratore, Vol. II.) (*2nd Imp.*)

1

CICERO : DE FINIBUS. H. Rackham. (*4th Imp. revised.*)

CICERO : DE INVENTIONE, etc. H. M. Hubbell.

CICERO : DE NATURA DEORUM AND ACADEMICA. H. Rackham. (*2nd Imp.*)

CICERO : DE OFFICIIS. Walter Miller. (*6th Imp.*)

CICERO : DE ORATORE. E. W. Sutton and H. Rackham. 2 Vols. (*2nd Imp.*)

CICERO : DE REPUBLICA AND DE LEGIBUS. Clinton W. Keyes. (*4th Imp.*)

CICERO : DE SENECTUTE, DE AMICITIA, DE DIVINATIONE. W. A. Falconer. (*6th Imp.*)

CICERO : IN CATILINAM, PRO MURENA, PRO SULLA, PRO FLACCO. Louis E. Lord. (*3rd Imp. revised.*)

CICERO : LETTERS TO ATTICUS. E. O. Winstedt. 3 Vols. (Vol. I *6th Imp.*, Vols. II and III *4th Imp.*)

CICERO : LETTERS TO HIS FRIENDS. W. Glynn Williams. 3 Vols. (Vols. I and II *3rd Imp.*, Vol. III *2nd Imp. revised and enlarged.*)

CICERO : PHILIPPICS. W. C. A. Ker. (*3rd Imp.*)

CICERO : PRO ARCHIA, POST REDITUM, DE DOMO, DE HARUSPICUM RESPONSIS, PRO PLANCIO. N. H. Watts. (*3rd Imp.*)

CICERO : PRO CAECINA, PRO LEGE MANILIA, PRO CLUENTIO, PRO RABIRIO. H. Grose Hodge. (*3rd Imp.*)

CICERO : PRO MILONE, IN PISONEM, PRO SCAURO, PRO FONTEIO, PRO RABIRIO POSTUMO, PRO MARCELLO, PRO LIGARIO, PRO REGE DEIOTARO. N. H. Watts. (*2nd Imp.*)

CICERO : PRO QUINCTIO, PRO ROSCIO AMERINO, PRO ROSCIO COMOEDO, CONTRA RULLUM. J. H. Freese. (*2nd Imp.*)

[CICERO] : RHETORICA AD HERENNIUM. H. Caplan.

CICERO : TUSCULAN DISPUTATIONS. J. E. King. (*4th Imp.*)

CICERO : VERRINE ORATIONS. L. H. G. Greenwood. 2 Vols. (Vol. I *3rd Imp.*, Vol. II *2nd Imp.*)

CLAUDIAN. M. Platnauer. 2 Vols.

COLUMELLA : DE RE RUSTICA ; DE ARBORIBUS. H. B. Ash, E. S. Forster, E. Heffner. 3 Vols. (Vol. I *2nd Imp.*)

CURTIUS, Q. : HISTORY OF ALEXANDER. J. C. Rolfe. 2 Vols.

FLORUS. E. S. Forster ; and CORNELIUS NEPOS. J. C. Rolfe. (*2nd Imp.*)

FRONTINUS : STRATAGEMS AND AQUEDUCTS. C. E. Bennett and M. B. McElwain. (*2nd Imp.*)

FRONTO : CORRESPONDENCE. C. R. Haines. 2 Vols. (Vol. I *3rd Imp.*, Vol. II *2nd Imp.*)

THE LOEB CLASSICAL LIBRARY

GELLIUS. J. C. Rolfe. 3 Vols. (*2nd Imp.*)

HORACE: ODES AND EPODES. C. E. Bennett. (*14th Imp. revised.*)

HORACE: SATIRES, EPISTLES, ARS POETICA. H. R. Fairclough. (*8th Imp. revised.*)

JEROME: SELECT LETTERS. F. A. Wright. (*2nd Imp.*)

JUVENAL AND PERSIUS. G. G. Ramsay. (*7th Imp.*)

LIVY. B. O. Foster, F. G. Moore, Evan T. Sage and A. C. Schlesinger. 14 Vols. I-XIII. (Vol. I *4th Imp.*, Vols. II, III, V and IX *3rd Imp.*, Vols. IV, VI-VIII, X-XII *2nd Imp. revised.*)

LUCAN. J. D. Duff. (*3rd Imp.*)

LUCRETIUS. W. H. D. Rouse. (*7th Imp. revised.*)

MARTIAL. W. C. A. Ker. 2 Vols. (Vol. I *5th Imp.*, Vol. II *4th Imp. revised.*)

MINOR LATIN POETS: from PUBLILIUS SYRUS to RUTILIUS NAMATIANUS, including GRATTIUS, CALPURNIUS SICULUS, NEMESIANUS, AVIANUS, with " Aetna," " Phoenix " and other poems. J. Wight Duff and Arnold M. Duff. (*3rd Imp.*)

OVID: THE ART OF LOVE AND OTHER POEMS. J. H. Mozley. (*3rd Imp.*)

OVID: FASTI. Sir James G. Frazer. (*2nd Imp.*)

OVID: HEROIDES AND AMORES. Grant Showerman. (*4th Imp.*)

OVID: METAMORPHOSES. F. J. Miller. 2 Vols. (Vol. I *10th Imp.*, Vol. II *8th Imp.*)

OVID: TRISTIA AND EX PONTO. A. L. Wheeler. (*3rd Imp.*)

PETRONIUS. M. Heseltine; SENECA: APOCOLOCYNTOSIS. W. H. D. Rouse. (*8th Imp. revised.*)

PLAUTUS. Paul Nixon. 5 Vols. (Vols. I and II *5th Imp.*, Vol. III *3rd Imp.*, Vols. IV-V *2nd Imp.*)

PLINY: LETTERS. Melmoth's translation revised by W. M. L. Hutchinson. 2 Vols. (*6th Imp.*)

PLINY: NATURAL HISTORY. H. Rackham and W. H. S. Jones. 10 Vols. Vols. I-VI and IX. (Vol. I *3rd Imp.*, Vols. II-IV *2nd Imp.*)

PROPERTIUS. H. E. Butler. (*6th Imp.*)

PRUDENTIUS. H. J. Thomson. 2 Vols.

QUINTILIAN. H. E. Butler. 4 Vols. (*3rd Imp.*)

REMAINS OF OLD LATIN. E. H. Warmington. 4 Vols. Vol. I (Ennius and Caecilius). Vol. II (Livius, Naevius, Pacuvius, Accius). Vol. III (Lucilius, Laws of the XII

THE LOEB CLASSICAL LIBRARY

Tables). Vol. IV (Archaic Inscriptions). (Vol. IV *2nd Imp.*)

SALLUST. J. C. Rolfe. (*3rd Imp. revised.*)

SCRIPTORES HISTORIAE AUGUSTAE. D. Magie. 3 Vols. (Vol. I *3rd Imp.*, Vols. II and III *2nd Imp. revised.*)

SENECA: APOCOLOCYNTOSIS. *Cf.* PETRONIUS.

SENECA: EPISTULAE MORALES. R. M. Gummere. 3 Vols. (Vol. I *4th Imp.*, Vols. II and III *3rd Imp. revised.*)

SENECA: MORAL ESSAYS. J. W. Basore. 3 Vols. (Vol. II *3rd Imp. revised,* Vols. I and III *2nd Imp. revised.*)

SENECA: TRAGEDIES. F. J. Miller. 2 Vols. (Vol. I *4th Imp.*, Vol. II *3rd Imp. revised.*)

SIDONIUS: POEMS AND LETTERS. W. B. Anderson. 2 Vols. Vol. I. (*2nd Imp.*)

SILIUS ITALICUS. J. D. Duff. 2 Vols. (Vol. I *2nd Imp.*, Vol. II *3rd Imp.*)

STATIUS. J. H. Mozley. 2 Vols. (*2nd Imp.*)

SUETONIUS. J. C. Rolfe. 2 Vols. (Vol. I *7th Imp.*, Vol. II *6th Imp.*)

TACITUS: DIALOGUS. Sir Wm. Peterson; and AGRICOLA AND GERMANIA. Maurice Hutton. (*6th Imp.*)

TACITUS: HISTORIES AND ANNALS. C. H. Moore and J. Jackson. 4 Vols. (Vols. I and II *3rd Imp.*, Vols. III and IV *2nd Imp.*)

TERENCE. John Sargeaunt. 2 Vols. (*7th Imp.*)

TERTULLIAN: APOLOGIA AND DE SPECTACULIS. T. R. Glover; MINUCIUS FELIX. G. H. Rendall. (*2nd Imp.*)

VALERIUS FLACCUS. J. H. Mozley. (*2nd Imp. revised.*)

VARRO: DE LINGUA LATINA. R. G. Kent. 2 Vols. (*2nd Imp. revised.*)

VELLEIUS PATERCULUS AND RES GESTAE DIVI AUGUSTI. F. W. Shipley. (*2nd Imp.*)

VIRGIL. H. R. Fairclough. 2 Vols. (Vol. I *18th Imp.*, Vol. II *14th Imp. revised.*)

VITRUVIUS: DE ARCHITECTURA. F. Granger. 2 Vols. (Vol. I *2nd Imp.*)

GREEK AUTHORS

ACHILLES TATIUS. S. Gaselee. (*2nd Imp.*)

AENEAS TACTICUS, ASCLEPIODOTUS AND ONASANDER. The Illinois Greek Club. (*2nd Imp.*)

4

THE LOEB CLASSICAL LIBRARY

AESCHINES. C. D. Adams. (*2nd Imp.*)

AESCHYLUS. H. Weir Smyth. 2 Vols. (Vol. I 6*th Imp.*, Vol. II 5*th Imp.*)

ALCIPHRON, AELIAN AND PHILOSTRATUS: LETTERS. A. R. Benner and F. H. Fobes.

APOLLODORUS. Sir James G. Frazer. 2 Vols. (Vol. I 3*rd Imp.*, Vol. II 2*nd Imp.*)

APOLLONIUS RHODIUS. R. C. Seaton. (4*th Imp.*)

THE APOSTOLIC FATHERS. Kirsopp Lake. 2 Vols. (Vol. I 8*th Imp.*, Vol. II 6*th Imp.*)

APPIAN'S ROMAN HISTORY. Horace White. 4 Vols. (Vol. I 3*rd Imp.*, Vols. II, III and IV 2*nd Imp.*)

ARATUS. *Cf.* CALLIMACHUS.

ARISTOPHANES. Benjamin Bickley Rogers. 3 Vols. (Vols. I and II 5*th Imp.*, Vol. III 4*th Imp.*) Verse trans.

ARISTOTLE: ART OF RHETORIC. J. H. Freese. (3*rd Imp.*)

ARISTOTLE: ATHENIAN CONSTITUTION, EUDEMIAN ETHICS, VIRTUES AND VICES. H. Rackham. (3*rd Imp.*)

ARISTOTLE: GENERATION OF ANIMALS. A. L. Peck. (2*nd Imp.*)

ARISTOTLE: METAPHYSICS. H. Tredennick. 2 Vols. (3*rd Imp.*)

ARISTOTLE: METEOROLOGICA. H. D. P. Lee.

ARISTOTLE: MINOR WORKS. W. S. Hett. "On Colours," "On Things Heard," "Physiognomics," "On Plants," "On Marvellous Things Heard," "Mechanical Problems," "On Indivisible Lines," "Situations and Names of Winds," "On Melissus, Xenophanes, and Gorgias." (2*nd Imp.*)

ARISTOTLE: NICOMACHEAN ETHICS. H. Rackham. (5*th Imp. revised.*)

ARISTOTLE: OECONOMICA AND MAGNA MORALIA. G. C. Armstrong. (With Metaphysics, Vol. II.) (3*rd Imp.*)

ARISTOTLE: ON THE HEAVENS. W. K. C. Guthrie. (3*rd Imp.*)

ARISTOTLE: ON THE SOUL, PARVA NATURALIA, ON BREATH. W. S. Hett. (2*nd Imp. revised.*)

ARISTOTLE: ORGANON. H. P. Cooke and H. Tredennick. 3 Vols. Vol. I. (2*nd Imp.*)

ARISTOTLE: PARTS OF ANIMALS. A. L. Peck; MOTION AND PROGRESSION OF ANIMALS. E. S. Forster. (3*rd Imp.*)

ARISTOTLE: PHYSICS. Rev. P. Wicksteed and F. M. Cornford. 2 Vols. (Vol. I 2*nd Imp.*, Vol. II 3*rd Imp.*)

ARISTOTLE: POETICS and LONGINUS. W. Hamilton Fyfe;

DEMETRIUS ON STYLE. W. Rhys Roberts. (*5th Imp. revised.*)

ARISTOTLE: POLITICS. H. Rackham. (*4th Imp.*)

ARISTOTLE: PROBLEMS. W. S. Hett. 2 Vols. (*2nd Imp. revised.*)

ARISTOTLE: RHETORICA AD ALEXANDRUM. H. Rackham. (With Problems, Vol. II.)

ARRIAN: HISTORY OF ALEXANDER AND INDICA. Rev. E. Iliffe Robson. 2 Vols. (Vol. I *3rd Imp.*, Vol. II *2nd Imp.*)

ATHENAEUS: DEIPNOSOPHISTAE. C. B. Gulick. 7 Vols. (Vols. I, V and VI *2nd Imp.*)

ST. BASIL: LETTERS. R. J. Deferrari. 4 Vols. (*2nd Imp.*)

CALLIMACHUS AND LYCOPHRON. A. W. Mair; ARATUS. G. R. Mair. (*2nd Imp.*)

CLEMENT OF ALEXANDRIA. Rev. G. W. Butterworth. (*3rd Imp.*)

COLLUTHUS. *Cf.* OPPIAN.

DAPHNIS AND CHLOE. *Cf.* LONGUS.

DEMOSTHENES I: OLYNTHIACS, PHILIPPICS AND MINOR ORATIONS: I-XVII AND XX. J. H. Vince. (*2nd Imp.*)

DEMOSTHENES II: DE CORONA AND DE FALSA LEGATIONE. C. A. Vince and J. H. Vince. (*3rd Imp. revised.*)

DEMOSTHENES III: MEIDIAS, ANDROTION, ARISTOCRATES, TIMOCRATES, ARISTOGEITON. J. H. Vince. (*2nd Imp.*)

DEMOSTHENES IV-VI: PRIVATE ORATIONS AND IN NEAERAM. A. T. Murray. (*2nd Imp.*)

DEMOSTHENES VII: FUNERAL SPEECH, EROTIC ESSAY, EXORDIA AND LETTERS. N. W. and N. J. DeWitt.

DIO CASSIUS: ROMAN HISTORY. E. Cary. 9 Vols. (Vols. I and II *3rd Imp.*, Vols. III and IV *2nd Imp.*)

DIO CHRYSOSTOM. 5 Vols. Vols. I and II. J. W. Cohoon. Vol. III. J. W. Cohoon and H. Lamar Crosby. Vols. IV and V. H. Lamar Crosby. (Vols. I-III *2nd Imp.*)

DIODORUS SICULUS. 12 Vols. Vols. I-VI. C. H. Oldfather. Vol. VII. C. L. Sherman. Vols. IX and X. Russel M. Geer. (Vols. I-III *2nd Imp.*)

DIOGENES LAERTIUS. R. D. Hicks. 2 Vols. (Vol. I *4th Imp.*, Vol. II *3rd Imp.*)

DIONYSIUS OF HALICARNASSUS: ROMAN ANTIQUITIES. Spelman's translation revised by E. Cary. 7 Vols. (Vols. I-IV *2nd Imp.*)

EPICTETUS. W. A. Oldfather. 2 Vols. (*2nd Imp.*)

EURIPIDES. A. S. Way. 4 Vols. (Vols. I and II *7th Imp.*, Vols. III and IV *6th Imp.*) Verse trans.

EUSEBIUS: ECCLESIASTICAL HISTORY. Kirsopp Lake and J. E. L. Oulton. 2 Vols. (Vol. I *3rd Imp.*, Vol. II *4th Imp.*)

GALEN: ON THE NATURAL FACULTIES. A. J. Brock. (*4th Imp.*)

THE GREEK ANTHOLOGY. W. R. Paton. 5 Vols. (Vols. I and II *5th Imp.*, Vol. III *4th Imp.*, Vols. IV and V *3rd Imp.*)

THE GREEK BUCOLIC POETS (THEOCRITUS, BION, MOSCHUS). J. M. Edmonds. (*7th Imp. revised.*)

GREEK ELEGY AND IAMBUS WITH THE ANACREONTEA. J. M. Edmonds. 2 Vols. (Vol. I *3rd Imp.*, Vol. II *2nd Imp.*)

GREEK MATHEMATICAL WORKS. Ivor Thomas. 2 Vols. (*2nd Imp.*)

HERODES. *Cf.* THEOPHRASTUS: CHARACTERS.

HERODOTUS. A. D. Godley. 4 Vols. (Vols. I-III *4th Imp.*, Vol. IV *3rd Imp.*)

HESIOD AND THE HOMERIC HYMNS. H. G. Evelyn White. (*7th Imp. revised and enlarged.*)

HIPPOCRATES AND THE FRAGMENTS OF HERACLEITUS. W. H. S. Jones and E. T. Withington. 4 Vols. (*3rd Imp.*)

HOMER: ILIAD. A. T. Murray. 2 Vols. (Vol. I *7th Imp.*, Vol. II *6th Imp.*)

HOMER: ODYSSEY. A. T. Murray. 2 Vols. (*8th Imp.*)

ISAEUS. E. S. Forster. (*2nd Imp.*)

ISOCRATES. George Norlin and LaRue Van Hook. 3 Vols. (Vols. I and III *2nd Imp.*)

ST. JOHN DAMASCENE: BARLAAM AND IOASAPH. Rev. G. R. Woodward and Harold Mattingly. (*3rd Imp. revised.*)

JOSEPHUS. H. St. J. Thackeray and Ralph Marcus. 9 Vols. Vols. I-VII. (Vol. V *3rd Imp.*, Vol. VI *2nd Imp.*)

JULIAN. Wilmer Cave Wright. 3 Vols. (Vols. I and II *3rd Imp.*, Vol. III *2nd Imp.*)

LONGUS: DAPHNIS AND CHLOE. Thornley's translation revised by J. M. Edmonds; and PARTHENIUS. S. Gaselee. (*3rd Imp.*)

LUCIAN. A. M. Harmon. 8 Vols. Vols. I-V. (Vols. I and III *3rd Imp.*, Vols. II, IV and V *2nd Imp.*)

LYCOPHRON. *Cf.* CALLIMACHUS.

LYRA GRAECA. J. M. Edmonds. 3 Vols. (Vol. I *4th Imp.*, Vols. II and III *3rd Imp.*)

THE LOEB CLASSICAL LIBRARY

LYSIAS. W. R. M. Lamb. (3rd *Imp.*)
MANETHO. W. G. Waddell; PTOLEMY: TETRABIBLOS. F. E.
    Robbins. (2nd *Imp.*)
MARCUS AURELIUS. C. R. Haines. (4th *Imp. revised.*)
MENANDER. F. G. Allinson. (3rd *Imp. revised.*)
MINOR ATTIC ORATORS. 2 Vols. K. J. Maidment and
    J. O. Burtt. (Vol. I 2nd *Imp.*)
NONNOS: DIONYSIACA. W. H. D. Rouse. 3 Vols. (Vol.
    III 2nd *Imp.*)
OPPIAN, COLLUTHUS, TRYPHIODORUS. A. W. Mair. (2nd
    Imp.)
PAPYRI. NON-LITERARY SELECTIONS. A. S. Hunt and C. C.
    Edgar. 2 Vols. (2nd *Imp.*) LITERARY SELECTIONS.
    (Poetry). D. L. Page. (3rd *Imp.*)
PARTHENIUS. *Cf.* LONGUS.
PAUSANIAS: DESCRIPTION OF GREECE. W. H. S. Jones. 5
    Vols. and Companion Vol. arranged by R. E. Wycherley.
    (Vols. I and III 3rd *Imp.*, Vols. II, IV and V 2nd *Imp.*)
PHILO. 10 Vols. Vols. I-V. F. H. Colson and Rev. G. H.
    Whitaker; Vols. VI-IX. F. H. Colson. (Vols. I-III,
    V-IX 2nd *Imp.*, Vol. IV 3rd *Imp.*)
    Two Supplementary Vols. Translation only from an
    Armenian Text. Ralph Marcus.
PHILOSTRATUS: THE LIFE OF APOLLONIUS OF TYANA. F. C.
    Conybeare. 2 Vols. (Vol. I 4th *Imp.*, Vol. II 3rd *Imp.*)
PHILOSTRATUS: IMAGINES; CALLISTRATUS: DESCRIPTIONS.
    A. Fairbanks. (2nd *Imp.*)
PHILOSTRATUS AND EUNAPIUS: LIVES OF THE SOPHISTS.
    Wilmer Cave Wright. (2nd *Imp.*)
PINDAR. Sir J. E. Sandys. (7th *Imp. revised.*)
PLATO I: EUTHYPHRO, APOLOGY, CRITO, PHAEDO, PHAEDRUS.
    H. N. Fowler. (11th *Imp.*)
PLATO II: THEAETETUS AND SOPHIST. H. N. Fowler. (4th
    Imp.)
PLATO III: STATESMAN, PHILEBUS. H. N. Fowler; ION.
    W. R. M. Lamb. (4th *Imp.*)
PLATO IV: LACHES, PROTAGORAS, MENO, EUTHYDEMUS.
    W. R. M. Lamb. (3rd *Imp. revised.*)
PLATO V: LYSIS, SYMPOSIUM, GORGIAS. W. R. M. Lamb.
    (5th *Imp. revised.*)
PLATO VI: CRATYLUS, PARMENIDES, GREATER HIPPIAS,
    LESSER HIPPIAS. H. N. Fowler. (4th *Imp.*)

8

THE LOEB CLASSICAL LIBRARY

PLATO VII : TIMAEUS, CRITIAS, CLITOPHO, MENEXENUS, EPI-
STULAE. Rev. R. G. Bury. (3rd *Imp.*)

PLATO VIII : CHARMIDES, ALCIBIADES, HIPPARCHUS, THE
LOVERS, THEAGES, MINOS AND EPINOMIS. W. R. M. Lamb.
(2nd *Imp.*)

PLATO : LAWS. Rev. R. G. Bury. 2 Vols. (3rd *Imp.*)

PLATO : REPUBLIC. Paul Shorey. 2 Vols. (Vol. I 5th *Imp.*,
Vol. II 3rd *Imp.*)

PLUTARCH : MORALIA. 14 Vols. Vols. I-V. F. C. Babbitt ;
Vol. VI. W. C. Helmbold ; Vol. X. H. N. Fowler. (Vols.
I, III and X 2nd *Imp.*)

PLUTARCH : THE PARALLEL LIVES. B. Perrin. 11 Vols.
(Vols. I, II, VI, VII and XI 3rd *Imp.*, Vols. III-V and
VIII-X 2nd *Imp.*)

POLYBIUS. W. R. Paton. 6 Vols. (2nd *Imp.*)

PROCOPIUS : HISTORY OF THE WARS. H. B. Dewing. 7 Vols.
(Vol. I 3rd *Imp.*, Vols. II-VII 2nd *Imp.*)

PTOLEMY : TETRABIBLOS. *Cf.* MANETHO.

QUINTUS SMYRNAEUS. A. S. Way. (2nd *Imp.*) Verse trans.

SEXTUS EMPIRICUS. Rev. R. G. Bury. 4 Vols. (Vols. I and
III 2nd *Imp.*)

SOPHOCLES. F. Storr. 2 Vols. (Vol. I 9th *Imp.*, Vol. II 6th
Imp.) Verse trans.

STRABO : GEOGRAPHY. Horace L. Jones. 8 Vols. (Vols. I,
V and VIII 3rd *Imp.*, Vols. II-IV, VI and VII 2nd *Imp.*)

THEOPHRASTUS : CHARACTERS. J. M. Edmonds ; HERODES,
etc. A. D. Knox. (3rd *Imp.*)

THEOPHRASTUS : ENQUIRY INTO PLANTS. Sir Arthur Hort.
2 Vols. (2nd *Imp.*)

THUCYDIDES. C. F. Smith. 4 Vols. (Vol. I 4th *Imp.*, Vols.
II-IV 3rd *Imp.*)

TRYPHIODORUS. *Cf.* OPPIAN.

XENOPHON : CYROPAEDIA. Walter Miller. 2 Vols. (Vol. I
4th *Imp.*, Vol. II 3rd *Imp.*)

XENOPHON : HELLENICA, ANABASIS, APOLOGY, AND SYMPO-
SIUM. C. L. Brownson and O. J. Todd. 3 Vols. (Vols. I
and III 3rd *Imp.*, Vol. II 4th *Imp.*)

XENOPHON : MEMORABILIA AND OECONOMICUS. E. C. Marchant. (3rd *Imp.*)

XENOPHON : SCRIPTA MINORA. E. C. Marchant. (2nd *Imp.*)

(*For Volumes in Preparation see next page.*)

THE LOEB CLASSICAL LIBRARY

VOLUMES IN PREPARATION

GREEK AUTHORS

ARISTOTLE: DE MUNDO, etc.   D. Furley and E. S. Forster.
ARISTOTLE: HISTORY OF ANIMALS.   A. L. Peck.
PLOTINUS.   A. H. Armstrong.

LATIN AUTHORS

ST. AUGUSTINE: CITY OF GOD.
CICERO: PRO SESTIO, IN VATINIUM, PRO CAELIO, DE PROVINCIIS CONSULARIBUS, PRO BALBO.   J. H. Freese and R. Gardner.
PHAEDRUS AND OTHER FABULISTS.   B. E. Perry.

DESCRIPTIVE PROSPECTUS ON APPLICATION

CAMBRIDGE, MASS.
HARVARD UNIV. PRESS
Cloth $2.50

LONDON
WILLIAM HEINEMANN LTD
Cloth 15s.